KU-752-549

Madagascar

THE BRADT TRAVEL GUIDE

Sixth Edition

Hilary Bradt

Bradt Publications, UK
The Globe Pequot Press Inc, USA

First published in 1988 by Bradt Publications,
This sixth edition published in 1999 by Bradt Publications
41 Nortoft Road, Chalfont St Peter, Bucks SL9 0LA, England
web: bradt-travelguides.com
Published in the USA by The Globe Pequot Press Inc, 6 Business Park Road,
PO Box 833, Old Saybrook, Connecticut 06475-0833

Text copyright © 1999 Hilary Bradt
Maps copyright © 1999 Bradt Publications

The author and publisher have made every effort to ensure the accuracy of the
information in this book at the time of going to press. However, they cannot accept any
responsibility for any loss, injury or inconvenience resulting from the use of information
contained in this guide.

All rights reserved. No part of this publication may be reproduced, stored in a retrieval
system, or transmitted in any form or by any means, electronic, mechanical, photocopying,
recording or otherwise without the prior consent of the publishers.
Requests for permission should be addressed to Bradt Publications,
41 Nortoft Road, Chalfont St Peter, Bucks SL9 0LA in the UK;
or to The Globe Pequot Press Inc,
6 Business Park Road, PO Box 833, Old Saybrook, Connecticut 06475-0833
in North and South America.

ISBN 1 898323 97 6

British Library Cataloguing in Publication Data
A catalogue record for this book is available from the British Library

Library of Congress Cataloging-in-Publication Data
Bradt Hilary
     Madagascar : the Bradt travel guide / Hilary Bradt. - 6th ed.
          p. cm.
     Rev. ed. of: Guide to Madagascar.
     Includes index.
     ISBN 1-898323-97-6
     1. Madagascar-Guidebooks. I. Title: Guide to Madagascar. II. Title
DT469.M25 B73 1999
916.9104'53—dc21   99-44249
                                                                      CIP

Cover photograph Ring-tailed lemur (Nick Garbutt)
Colour photographs Hilary Bradt (HB), Elisabeth Cox (EC), Nick Garbutt (NG), Mark
Hannaford (MH), Roland Hejdstrøm (RH), Bill Love (BL), Kay Thompson (KT)
Illustrations Nick Garbutt, Cherry-Anne Lavrih
Maps Alan Whitaker

Typeset from the author's disc by Wakewing
Printed and bound in Spain by Grafo SA, Bilbao

Author/Contributors

Hilary Bradt has visited Madagascar some 20 times since her first trip in 1976. She is a tour leader and lecturer for American, South African, Australian and British tour and cruise operators; and lectures, broadcasts and writes on the joys and perils of travelling in Madagascar and other countries. She is also proprietor of Bradt Publications.

CONTRIBUTORS

Ian Anderson (*The Music of Madagascar*) is the editor of the magazine Folk Roots and a regular broadcaster on the subject of folk music.

Anne Axel (information on the Andapa area) first went to Madagascar with her bicycle in 1994, became hooked on the country, and returned a couple of years later to study indri.

Janice Booth (*Malagasy without Tears*, etc) has visited Madagascar four times, particularly enjoying its people, languages and landscape – and weevils!

Marius Burger (*The Wild Trade in Reptiles*) is a research assistant at Eastern Cape Nature Conservation in South Africa, and leads herping trips to Madagascar.

Joanna Durbin (*The Environmental Action Plan*) works for the Durrell Wildlife Conservation Trust (DWCT) in Madagascar.

Nick Garbutt (photos and miscellaneous information) is a zoologist, photographer, tour leader and the author of the definitive guide to Madagascar's mammals.

Jonathan Hughes (*Natural History*) is an author and lecturer in ecology in London.

Frances Kerridge (*Getting a job in Conservation...* plus travel information) is a regular correspondent and post-doctoral researcher, currently studying carnivores in southeast Madagascar.

Bill Love (Photographs and *The Wild Trade in Reptiles*) is a private breeder of reptiles and amphibians in Florida and, through Blue Chameleon Ventures, runs tours to Madagascar. He has a photo library of herpetology subjects.

Derek Schuurman (*Birding in Madagascar* and much more...) runs the South African agency Unusual Destinations. He is the author of two books and countless articles on Madagascar.

Adela Stockton (*Childbirth in Madagascar* and travel information) is a midwife who worked as a volunteer in Madagascar in 1998.

Seraphine Tierney (*Famadihana Diary*) is the attaché at the Madagascar Consulate in London and runs the travel consultancy, Discover Madagascar.

Jane Wilson-Howarth (*Health*) is a medical doctor with a degree in biology. She has researched and practised medicine in several tropical countries, writes about travellers' health for *Wanderlust* magazine, and is the author of two travellers' health guides.

Contents

Introduction

Twenty-four years ago I attended a slide show in Cape Town given by a zoo collector who had just returned from a country called Madagascar. By the end of the evening I knew I had to go there. It wasn't just the lemurs, it was the utter otherness of this little-known island that entranced me. So I went, and I fell in love, and I've been returning ever since.

Last April I was back again, taking a group to visit a new national park in the south. The scenes in my memory could have been from 20 years ago. First there was the rural market. Groups of people in their best clothes were walking in from villages many miles away, smiling, chatting and laughing. This is their main social event of the week. Young men wore combs in their hair to show they were looking for a wife. While the women sold little pyramids of tomatoes, the men gambled the money away in games of roulette (the wheel borrowed from a bicycle) and cards. The atmosphere was resonant with happiness. A few hours later we were walking in the spiny forest, through groves of weird and wonderful didierea trees. There were no other tourists there. A nocturnal lemur peered warily from its resting place, a snake rustled the leaf litter, and a chameleon played at being invisible.

In the last two decades nothing has changed and everything has changed. This is what's so magical about Madagascar... in so large an island you can still find yourself among people who have rarely seen a white person, or you can join other tourists in a fail-safe wildlife experience in Périnet or Berenty, where the accommodation is excellent, the guides superb, and the animals so accustomed to humans that you know you will get a close view. Or you can retreat to one of the new luxury island lodges off Nosy Be where the marine wonders are the equal to those anywhere in the Indian Ocean, and the landscape and plants are unrivalled.

The choice is yours – lucky you!

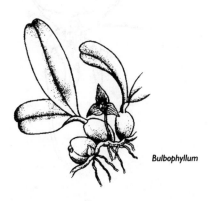

Bulbophyllum

Acknowledgements

This guide has evolved from readers' experiences and letters and I owe them a debt of gratitude that can never be repaid. So many people have spent time and effort compiling new information, writing about their experiences, and keeping me up to date with happenings in obscure parts of Madagascar. In each edition there are evocative and amusing descriptions from earlier contributors who I couldn't bear to lose, in addition to the wonderful new bits and pieces from numerous correspondents. I receive some astonishing letters – long, detailed, entertaining... wonderful. Some are only a few lines but equally useful. There is never a letter which does not add to my knowledge and understanding of the country.

Some of the names below are well-known experts on Madagascar, others are ordinary travellers – and just as valued. Heartfelt thanks to all of you: Josephine Andrews, Hery Andrianiantefana, Sir Mervyn Brown, Jeremy and Lindie Buirski, Philippa & Angus Crawford, Bjørn Donnis, Lee Durrell, Kimberly de Morgan, Ania Dudziec, Bronwen Eastman, Thomas Feichtinger, Ken & Lorna Gillespie, Jim & Carol Grevatt, Sharon Giarratana, Clare & Johan Hermans, Harriet & Mike Kendrick, Dick Macken, Liza & Pat McCarthy, Peter Meyer, Tim Pickles, Rupert Parker, Bryan & Eve Pinches, Elizabeth Pollock, Claude Rambeloson, Monique Rodriguez, Adela Stockton, Caroline Sylge, Pat Tillman, G D Twigger, Jerry Vive, and Michelle Zjhra. My apologies if I have missed anyone out.

To everyone: *Misaotra*!

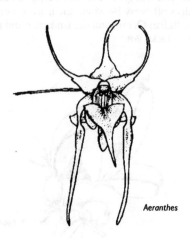

Aeranthes

Perspectives on Madagascar

'[Madagascar is] the chiefest paradise this day upon earth.'

Richard Boothby, 1630

'I could not but endeavour to dissuade others from undergoing the
miseries that will follow the persons of such as adventure themselves for
Madagascar ... from which place, God divert the residence and adventures
of all good men.'

Powle Waldegrave, 1649

As it was in the 17th century, so it is today. Some people love Madagascar, others
hate it. If this book helps to dissuade some from making an expensive trip that
could leave them bitter and disappointed, I will have done a good job. If I recruit
some more Madophiles I shall be happy.

My love affair with Madagascar has lasted 23 years and, like any lover, I tend to
be blind to its imperfections and too ready to leap to its defence. I am therefore
fortunate to receive so much feedback from travellers both new and experienced,
wide-eyed or blasé, to help me appreciate why Madagascar is not for everyone. In
recent years the infrastructure has improved enormously, but this is still not a
holiday island in the conventional sense, and as an exotic destination it lacks
tangible tourist sights and events. As one disappointed traveller put it: 'I need to be
hit in the face with garish temples, outrageous costumes, bizarre practices. I agree
toying with Grandad's bones is pretty bizarre but what chance has a tourist like me
of seeing a *famadihana*?'

Madagascar faces the dilemma of many developing countries: its government is
anxious to encourage tourism and there are a large number of potential visitors who
have seen television programmes about the island's natural history or are looking
for a new holiday destination. And yet this is one of the poorest countries in the
world, getting to grips with the concept of democracy and struggling to repair
decades of financial mismanagement. Change will continue to be slow.
Furthermore, the Malagasy culture is based on respect for the past rather than
anticipation of the future.

So why does Madagascar continue to work for me? Well, these are a few of my
favourite things:

The natural history I have seen spectacular wildlife in many parts of the world,
but nothing to equal the surprises of Madagascar's small-scale marvels, such as the
uroplatus, the spiny tenrec, the spiders with their golden webs, the weird and
wonderful beetles. Nor have I seen any mammals more endearing than lemurs.
For the anthropomorphic, gooey brigade they are winners!

The beauty of the Malagasy people I remember sitting in a bus and gazing at the faces around me as though I was in an art gallery. I never get tired of their infinite variety. That it is combined with smiles and courtesy is an added delight.

The scenery Always varied, often beautiful; from the air there's the tragic drama of the great red fissures in the overgrazed hillsides like terracotta fingers clawing the soft green landscape, and the emerald rectangles of rice paddies stacked like tiles up the mountain slopes. From the ground, the granite crags and domes that dominate the road to the south dramatically contrast with the small red-earth villages.

The food The tiniest village or the humblest hotely is capable of producing an astounding meal. Even travellers on rock-bottom budgets write to me misty-eyed about some of the meals they ate.

Serendipity Madagascar's size and former isolationist government have kept it free from many western influences. Wander away from the main tourist places in any town and you are likely to stumble across a market, a street fair, a group of musicians, or a gathering that brings home what we have lost in our culture: the ability to be joyful despite poverty, and a sense of wonder.

Now for the negative aspects, which irritate or depress all visitors, and are the last straw for some:

The towns Excluding some of those in the highlands, there are few attractive Malagasy towns. All are shabby and some are in an advanced state of decay.

The poverty Over 1,500 people in Antananarivo live exclusively off rubbish tips and there are many child beggars. Despite the ever-present laughter, seeing such deprivation is profoundly saddening to many visitors. Poverty has led to a rise in street crime against tourists.

Transport Flights are sometimes delayed or cancelled and other public transport is more crowded and less reliable than in comparable countries. However fast the roads are improved they deteriorate with equal speed, so the situation is unlikely to change in the short term.

Here are some final words extracted from letters I've received. Some travellers love it...

'The beauty of the land I had expected, but the gentle openheartedness and hospitality of the people took me by storm. I have lived and travelled extensively in South America, Europe and Eastern Africa but I have never encountered such lovely people as the Malagasy!' (Adela Stockton, UK)

'We had the most fabulous time. Being keen naturalists Madagascar was a dream come true although, much as we loved the lemurs, birds and scenery, it was in fact the people who made our trip so magical and memorable.' (H & M Kendrick, UK)

'I got back from a two-month solo trip around Madagascar a few months ago and haven't yet managed to get it out of my system... I can't read enough about all things Malagasy and need a daily fix of Malagasy music.' (Ania Dudziec, UK)

And some are not so keen:

'We spent five days in Madagascar. We had intended to stay longer but found the poverty much too depressing...The country is a disaster.'

'My advice is to see Madagascar before the Malagasy finish with it.'

Most independent travellers, however, reflect Stephen Cartledge, who wrote (back in 1994):

'We have travelled quite extensively in Africa and Asia but never quite encountered the problems we had in Madagascar... You sometimes want to pick up the country and shake it, demanding that it gets its act together! But for all that, we have found the charm and openness of the Malagasy people, the wonder of the scenery and national parks, the delights of the small towns in the south simply wonderful. When you leave Madagascar, you leave a country that has touched you with its many problems but one that has also left indelible and lasting memories. Go with an open mind, with plenty of patience and a strong sense of humour. Then you will appreciate Madagascar for what it really is: a remarkable country!'

And, take heart from a recent letter:

'We really feel you perhaps painted a rather too bleak picture of the country. Maybe we were just lucky but we were astonished at how "easy" Madagascar was compared to some of the nightmare scenarios painted in your book.'

Looking for comments for this section from my many correspondents was encouraging. Only one negative, quoted here, and numerous positive. The country really is getting its act together...

'Some day, when I am old and worn and there is nothing new to see, I shall go back to the palm-fringed lagoons, the sun-drenched, rolling moors, the pink villages, and the purple peaks of Madagascar.'

E A Powell, *Beyond the Utmost Purple Rim*, 1925

Experience
MADAGASCAR'S
incomparable diversity with the Experts

njoy discovering the wonders of the Lost World with us. Our
speciality is tailor-made (custom-made) itineraries suited to all
interests and special requirements.

Our extensive experience combined with the knowledge and
expertise of our Malagasy agents, guarantee the widest range
of itineraries for individuals and for groups.

- Natural history packages (general wildlife, birding, lemurs, reptiles, botany)
- Sightseeing, hiking and cultural trips
- Birding tours with Lyn Mair and Ian Davidson
- Discovery tours with Hilary Bradt and Marius Burger
- Beach, scuba diving and honeymoon packages
- Live-aboard yacht charter packages (Nosy Be archipelago)
- SPECIAL LOW COST AIRFARES FROM SOUTH AFRICA

Contact us NOW in Johannesburg at:

UNUSUAL DESTINATIONS
Tel: (27-11) 706 1991 or fax: 463 1469
E-mail: unusdest@global.co.za
Website: www.unusualdestinations.com

UNUSUAL
DESTINATIONS

Part One

General Information

Fanaloka

Fosa

The Country

FACTS AND FIGURES
Location

Madagascar, also known as the Malagasy Republic ('Malagasy' is the correct adjective, not 'Madagascan'), lies some 400 kilometres (250 miles) off the east coast of Africa, south of the equator. It is separated from Africa by the Mozambique channel and is crossed by the Tropic of Capricorn near the southern town of Toliara (Tuléar).

Size

The world's fourth largest island (after Greenland, New Guinea and Borneo), Madagascar is about 1,580 kilometres (1,000 miles) long by 570 kilometres (350 miles) at its widest point. Madagascar has an area of 590,000 square kilometres (227,760 square miles), 2½ times the size of Great Britain and a little smaller than Texas.

Topography

A chain of mountains runs like a spine down the east-centre of the island descending sharply to the Indian Ocean, leaving only a narrow coastal plain. These mountain slopes bear the remains of the dense rainforest which once covered all of the eastern section of the island. The western plain is wider and the climate drier, supporting forests of deciduous trees and acres of savannah grassland. Madagascar's highest mountain is Maromokotro (2,876m/9,450ft), part of the Massif of Tsaratanana, in the north of the island. In the south is the 'spiny forest' also known as the 'spiny desert'.

Climate

A tropical climate with rain falling in the hottest season – coinciding with the northern hemisphere winter. The amount of rainfall varies greatly by region: the wettest area in the east averages 355cm (140ins) annually; in the dry zone (southwest) the annual average is 30cm (12ins). It is hot and humid in low-lying areas. Temperatures can drop to freezing in Antananarivo (4,100ft/1,250m) and close to freezing in the extreme south during the coldest month of June.

Flora and fauna

A naturalist's paradise, most of the island's plants and animals are unique to Madagascar and new species and even new genera are being found by each scientific team that goes there. Of the native plants 80% are endemic. All of the mammals are endemic, excluding those introduced by man; and half of the birds and well over 90% of the reptiles are found nowhere else. The incredible number of unique species is due to the island's early separation from the mainland some 165 million years ago, and to the relatively recent arrival of man (around 2,000 years ago).

History

Madagascar was first sighted by Europeans (the Portuguese) in 1500, but there were Arab settlements from about the 9th century. Marco Polo named it (perhaps confusing it with Mogadishu in Somalia). It was mostly united under one monarch from the early 19th century, a time of British influence through the London Missionary Society. It became a French colony in 1896 and regained independence in 1960.

Ethnic groups

The people of Madagascar, the Malagasy, are of Afro-Indonesian origin, officially divided into 18 main 'tribes' or clans. Other races include Indian/Pakistani, Chinese and European.

Government

A period of 'Christian Marxism' from 1975 to 1991 under President Didier Ratsiraka was followed by an attempt at parliamentary democracy which collapsed mainly because of the unconstitutional behaviour of the next president, Albert Zafy. In 1997 Ratsiraka was re-elected as president and secured major amendments to the constitution which restored most of his previous dictatorial powers and deprived the multi-party National Assembly of any real power. The prime minister is Tantely Andrianarivo.

Population

The population numbers about 13 million, nearly half of whom are under the age of 15. Formerly it was thought that 85% of the population lived in rural areas, but a new report shows it to be only 57%. Since independence the population of Antananarivo has grown by 4% per annum and per capita consumption has dropped by 45%. A third of this decline has taken place since 1993. Some 75% of Madagascar's population lives below the poverty line and 85% of the children in Tana are undernourished; 15% of all children die before their first birthday. The average mother has 6.6 children. The 'doubling time' of the population is approximately 22 years.

Some statistics

Only 10% of all households have electricity, 10% have running water and only 2% have WCs. 35% have a radio, 6% a telephone but only 1% have a refrigerator.

RACIAL DISHARMONY

Astute travellers will notice that there is a degree of racial unease between the Merina people in the Highlands and the other clans. Probably no society is free of racism since no multi-ethnic society has evolved without wars or at least internal dissent. However, the Malagasy reserve their racial hatred for what they perceive to be a common enemy: the Indians and Pakistanis who own most of the businesses and are accused of exploiting the Malagasy and failing to integrate. In this respect Madagascar closely mirrors East Africa. In the south, resentment has spilled over into riots in both Toliara (Tuléar) and most recently (October 1998) in Taolagnaro (Fort Dauphin). In each case the shops of wealthy Pakistanis and Indians were pillaged then set on fire.

Relations with the large Chinese population appear easier, perhaps because the Chinese appear to integrate more readily into Malagasy society.

Religion
Christianity is the dominant organised religion, with the Catholic church slightly stronger than other denominations. Islam and Hinduism are also practised, mainly by the Asian community, but to the majority of Malagasy their own unique form of ancestor worship is the most important influence in their lives.

Economy
The economy suffered badly under Christian Marxism in the 1980s and declined further during the political upheavals from 1991 to 1997. There has been some improvement following economic reforms supported by international donors, and inflation has fallen from 60% to 6%. But Madagascar is still ranked as the eleventh poorest country in the world, with 75% of the population below the poverty line and over 60% classified as extremely poor. GNP growth averages only 0.5% per year. Hopes of recovery, based partly on expanding tourism, exports of shellfish and a more dynamic industrial sector, are threatened by a serious plague of locusts which could take many years to eradicate.

The World Bank considers that Madagascar is capable of growth superior to the average of 4.5% in subSaharan Africa.

Education
The reduction of public funding and shortage of teachers in rural areas have resulted in a fall in educational standards. A recent survey showed that of the school-age population only 66% reach the second primary year and only 28% finish primary school. Private schools meanwhile are flourishing, with one quarter of Madagascar's children being educated privately. Over one third of Madagascar's children receive no education at all. The literacy rate is approximately 45% .

Language
The first language is Malagasy, which belongs to the Malayo-Polynesian family of languages. French is widely spoken in towns and is the language of business. Some English is spoken in the capital and major tourist areas.

Place names
Since independence the colonial names of some towns have been changed. Many foreigners – and people who deal with foreigners – still use the easier-to-pronounce old names. However, I use the Malagasy names (apart from one or two cases where there is exceptional resistance to the change) but with the other name in parenthesis so as to avoid confusion: Taolagnaro (Fort Dauphin), Toliara (Tuléar), Andasibe (Périnet), Nosy Boraha (Ile Sainte Marie), Antsiranana (Diego Suarez), Mahajanga (Majunga). Antananarivo (Tananarive) is often shortened to Tana.

Time
Greenwich Mean Time plus three hours.

Voltage
220.

Currency
The Malagasy franc (Franc malgache, Fmg) floats against hard currencies so these rates (August 1999) are approximate only: £1 = 10,368Fmg, US$1 = 6,490Fmg, 1Ff = 1,034Fmg, 1DM = 938Fmg.

HISTORY
The first Europeans

The first Europeans to sight Madagascar were the Portuguese in 1500, although there is evidence of earlier Arab settlements on the coast. There were unsuccessful attempts to establish French and British settlements during the next couple of centuries; these failed due to disease and hostile local people. Hence a remarkably homogeneous and united country was able to develop under its own rulers.

By the early 1700s, the island had become a haven for pirates and slave-traders, who both traded with and fought the local kings who ruled the clans of the east and west coasts.

The rise of the Merina Kingdom

The powerful Merina kingdom was forged by Andrianampoinimerina (be thankful that this was a shortened version of his full name: Andrianampoinimerinandriantsimitoviaminandriampanjaka!). Succeeding to the tiny kingdom of Ambohimanga in 1787, by 1808 he had united the various Merina kingdoms and conquered the other highland tribes. In many ways the Merina kingdom at this time paralleled that of the Inca Empire in Peru: Andrianampoinimerina was

ROBERT DRURY

The most intriguing insight into 18th-century Madagascar was provided by Robert Drury, who was shipwrecked off the island in 1701 and spent over 16 years there, much of the time as a slave to the Antandroy or Sakalava chiefs.

Drury was only 15 when his boat foundered off the southern tip of Madagascar (he had been permitted by his father to go to India with trade goods). The shipwreck survivors were treated well by the local king but kept prisoner for reasons of status. After a few days they made a bid for freedom by seizing the king and some of his courtiers as hostages and marching east. They were followed by hundreds of warriors who watched for any relaxation in the guard; they were without water for three days as they crossed the burning hot desert, and just as they came in sight of the river Mandrare (having released the hostages) they were attacked and many were speared to death.

For ten years Drury was a slave of the Antandroy royal family. He worked with cattle and eventually was appointed royal butcher, the task of slaughtering a cow for ritual purposes being supposedly that of someone of royal blood – and lighter skin. Drury was a useful substitute. He also acquired a wife.

Wars with the neighbouring Mahafaly gave him the opportunity to escape north across the desert to St Augustine's Bay, some 400 kilometres away. Here he hoped to find a ship to England, but his luck turned and he again became a slave, this time to the Sakalava. When a ship did come in, his master refused to consider selling him to the captain, and Drury's desperate effort to get word to the ship through a message written on a leaf came to nothing when the messenger lost the leaf and substituted another less meaningful one. Two more years of relative freedom followed, and he finally got away in 1717, nearly 17 years after his shipwreck.

Ever quick to put his experience to good use, he later returned to Madagascar as a slave trader!

considered to have almost divine powers and his obedient subjects were well provided for; each was given enough land for his family's rice needs, with some left over to pay a rice tribute to the king, and community projects such as the building of irrigation canals were imposed through forced labour (though with bonuses for the most productive worker). The burning of forests was forbidden.

Conquest was always foremost in the monarch's mind, however, and it was his son, King Radama I, who fulfilled his father's command to 'Take the sea as frontier to your kingdom'. This king had a friendly relationship with Britain, which in 1817 and 1820 signed treaties under which Madagascar was recognised as an independent state. Britain supplied arms and advisers to help Radama conquer most of the rest of the island.

The London Missionary Society

To further strengthen ties between the two countries, the British Governor of Mauritius, which had recently been seized from the French, encouraged King Radama I to invite the London Missionary Society to send teachers. In 1818 a small group of Welsh missionaries arrived in Tamatave (now Toamasina). David Jones and Thomas Bevan brought their wives and children, but within a few weeks only Jones remained alive; the others had all died of fever. Jones retreated to Mauritius, but returned to Madagascar in 1820 to devote the rest of his life to its people, along with equally dedicated missionary teachers and artisans. The British influence was established and a written language introduced for the first time (apart from some ancient Arabic texts) using the Roman alphabet.

'The wicked queen' and her successors

Radama's widow and successor, Queen Ranavalona I, was determined to rid the land of Christianity and European influence, and reigned long enough (33 years) to largely achieve her aim. These were repressive times for Malagasy as well as foreigners. One way of dealing with people suspected of witchcraft or other evil practices was the 'Ordeal by Tangena' (see box on page 9).

It was during Queen Ranavalona's reign that an extraordinary Frenchman arrived in Madagascar: Jean Laborde, who, building on the work of the British missionaries, introduced the island to many aspects of Western technology. He remained in the queen's favour until 1857 – much longer than the other Europeans (see box on page 160–1).

The queen drove the missionaries out of Madagascar and many Malagasy Christians were martyred. However, the missionaries and European influence returned in greater strength after the queen's death and in 1869 Christianity became the official religion of the Merina kingdom.

After Queen Ranavalona I came King Radama II, a peace-loving and pro-European monarch, who was assassinated after a two-year reign in 1863. There is a widely held belief, however, that he survived strangulation with a silk cord (it was taboo to shed royal blood) and lived in hiding in the northwest for many years (see box on page 329). There is also a belief (less widely held) that he was assassinated because he was the illegitimate son of Queen Ranavalona I and Jean Laborde.

After the death of Radama II, Queen Rasoherina came to the throne, but the monarchy was now in decline and power shifted to the prime minister who shrewdly married the queen. He was overthrown by a brother, Rainilaiarivony, who continued the tradition by marrying three successive queens and exercising all the power. During this period, 1863–96, the monarchs (in title only) were Queen Rasoherina, Queen Ranavalona II and lastly Queen Ranavalona III.

The French conquest

Even during the period of British influence the French maintained a long-standing claim to Madagascar and in 1883 they attacked and occupied the main ports. The Franco-Malagasy War lasted 30 months, and was concluded by a harsh treaty making Madagascar a form of French protectorate. Prime Minister Rainilaiarivony, hoping for British support, managed to evade full acceptance of this status but the British government signed away its interest in the Convention of Zanzibar in 1890. The French finally imposed their rule by invasion in 1895. For a year the country was a full protectorate and in 1896 Madagascar became a French colony. A year later Queen Ranavalona III was exiled to Algeria and the monarchy abolished.

The first French Governor-General of Madagascar, Joseph Simon Gallieni, was an able and relatively benign administrator. He set out to break the power of the Merina aristocracy and remove the British influence by banning the teaching of English. French became the official language.

British military training and the two World Wars

Britain has played an important part in the military history of Madagascar. During the wars which preceded colonisation British mercenaries trained the Malagasy army to fight the French. During World War I, 46,000 Malagasy were recruited for the allies and over 2,000 killed. In 1942, when Madagascar was under the control of the Vichy French, the British invaded to forestall the possibility of the Japanese Navy making use of the great harbour of Diego Suarez (see box on page 288).

In 1943 Madagascar was handed back to France under a Free French Government. An uprising by the Malagasy against the French in 1947 was bloodily repressed (some 80,000 are said to have been killed) but the spirit of independence lived on and in 1960 the country achieved full independence.

The first 30 years of independence

The first president, Philibert Tsiranana, was pro-France but in 1972 he stepped down in the face of increasing unrest and student demonstrations against French neo-colonialism. An interim government headed by General Ramanantsoa ended France's special position and introduced a more nationalistic foreign and economic policy.

In 1975, after a period of turmoil, a military directorate handed power to a naval officer, Didier Ratsiraka, who had served as foreign minister under Ramanantsoa. Ratsiraka established the Second Republic, changing the country's name from The Malagasy Republic to The Democratic Republic of Madagascar. He introduced his own brand of 'Christian-Marxism' and his manifesto, set out in a 'little red book', was approved by referendum. Socialist policies such as the nationalisation of banks followed. Within a few years the economy had collapsed and has remained in severe difficulties ever since. Ratsiraka was nevertheless twice re-elected, though there were claims of ballot rigging and intimidation.

The 1990s

In 1991 a pro-democracy coalition called the Forces Vives, in which the churches played an important part, organised a remarkable series of strikes and daily demonstrations calling for Ratsiraka's resignation. In August an estimated 500,000 demonstrators marched on the president's palace. Though unarmed and orderly, they were fired on by the presidential guards and an estimated 100 demonstrators died. This episode further weakened Ratsiraka and at the end of the year he was compelled to relinquish executive power and agree to a referendum which approved a new constitution and fresh elections.

TANGENA

When James Hastie, royal tutor, arrived in Madagascar in 1817 he witnessed and described one of the more barbaric tortures that King Radama I was using on his subjects: the Ordeal by Tangena. *Tangena* is a Malagasy shrub with a poisonous kernel in its fruit. This poison was used to determine the guilt or innocence of a suspected criminal. A 'meal' consisting of three pieces of chicken skin, rice, and the crushed *tangena* kernel was prepared. The suspect was then forced to drink large quantities of water to make him – or her – vomit. If all three pieces of chicken skin reappeared the person was innocent (but often died anyway as a result of the poison). If the skin remained in the stomach the unfortunate suspect was killed, usually after limbs, or bits of limbs and other extremities, had been lopped off first.

One of the successes of Hastie's influence on the king was that the monarch agreed that, although the Ordeal by Tangena should continue, dogs could stand in for the accused. This decision was ignored by Queen Ranavalona who used it freely on the Christian martyrs she persecuted with such enthusiasm. Sir Mervyn Brown (from whose book *A History of Madagascar* this information is extracted) estimates that several thousand Malagasy met their deaths through the *tangena* shrub during Queen Ranavalona's long reign. Even during this period of xenophobia the queen was reluctant to subject the Europeans under arrest to the ordeal because of the inevitable political repercussions. Prudently, the poison was administered to chickens; all but one promptly died (the 'innocent' chicken/European was a bit too useful to condemn).

The Ordeal by Tangena was finally abolished by Queen Ranavalona's son, King Radama II, in 1861.

A transitional administration was formed with Professor Albert Zafy, who had led the Forces Vives opposition to Ratsiraka, at its head and a coalition government with Ratsiraka's nominee Guy Razanamasy as prime minister. Presidential elections took place in 1992/93 and were won by Albert Zafy. The Third Republic, born in 1993, soon ran into trouble. The new parliamentary constitution provided for a constitutional president with a prime minister elected by the National Assembly. But Albert Zafy refused to accept the limitations on his presidential role and in 1995 won a referendum which gave him, rather than the Assembly, the right to appoint the prime minister.

Zafy's continuing breaches of the constitution led to his impeachment by the National Assembly in 1996. When the impeachment was confirmed by the High Constitutional Court, Zafy resigned but immediately declared himself a presidential candidate, as did the other former president, Didier Ratsiraka. With 13 other candidates splitting the opposition vote, Ratsiraka and Zafy came in first and second and qualified for a run-off election early in 1997. Ratsiraka won and piloted through major amendments to the constitution which restored most of the dictatorial powers that he had enjoyed during his previous period in office. In subsequent National Assembly elections his party AREMA emerged as the largest, but had to rely on coalition partners for a majority.

With the opposition parties divided and no credible alternative leader in sight, there is at least the prospect of a period of political stability after years of upheaval. Whether Prime Minister Tantely Andrianarivo is able to halt and reverse Madagascar's economic decline remains to be seen.

CLIMATE

Madagascar has a tropical climate: November to March – summer (wet season), hot with variable rainfall; April to October – winter (dry season), mainly dry and mild.

Southwest trade winds drop their moisture on the eastern mountain slopes and blow hot and dry in the west. North and northwest 'monsoon' air currents bring heavy rain in summer, decreasing southward so that the rainfall in Tolagnaro is half that of Toamasina. There are also considerable variations of temperature dictated by altitude and latitude. On the summer solstice of December 22 the sun is directly over the Tropic of Capricorn, and the weather is very warm. Conversely, June is the coolest month.

Average midday temperatures in the dry season are 25°C (77°F) in the highlands and 30°C (86°F) on the coast. These statistics are misleading, however, since in June the night-time temperature can drop to near freezing in the highlands and it is cool in the south. The winter daytime temperatures are very pleasant, and the hot summer season is usually tempered by cool breezes on the coast.

The east of Madagascar frequently suffers from cyclones during February and March and these may brush other areas in the north or west.

The map on page 11 and chart below give easy reference to the driest and wettest months and regions but remember – nothing is as unpredictable as weather, and even in the rainiest months there will be sunny intervals. For advice on the best months to visit Madagascar see *When to Go*, page 77.

Climatic regions
West

Rainfall decreases from north to south. Variation in day/night winter temperatures increases from north to south. Average number of dry months: seven/eight. Highest average annual rainfall within zone: Majunga, 152cm. Lowest: Toliara, 36cm.

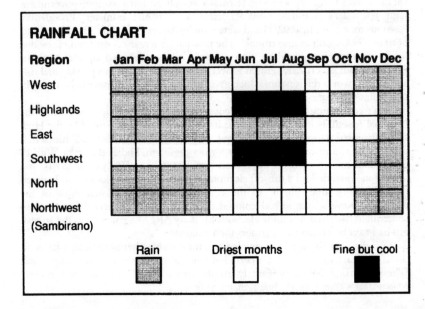

RAINFALL CHART

Region	Jan	Feb	Mar	Apr	May	Jun	Jul	Aug	Sep	Oct	Nov	Dec

Legend: Rain | Driest months | Fine but cool

Central

Temperature and rainfall influenced by altitude. Day/night temperatures in Antananarivo vary by 14°C. The major rainy season starts at the end of November. Highest average annual rainfall within zone: Antsirabe, 140cm.

East

In the northeast and central areas there are no months (or weeks) entirely without rain; but drier, more settled weather prevails in the southeast. Reasonably dry months: May, September, October, November. Possible months for travel: April, December, January (but cyclone danger in January). Difficult months for travel (torrential rain and cyclones) are February, March. Highest annual rainfall in zone: Maroantsetra 410cm. Lowest: Taolagnaro, 152cm.

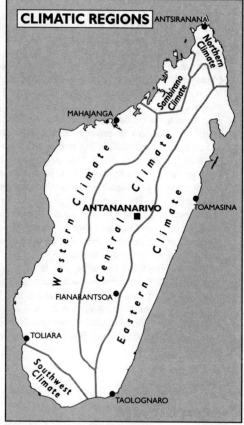

Southwest

The driest part of Madagascar. The extreme west may receive only 5cm of rain a year, increasing to around 34cm in the east.

North

This is similar to the east zone except for the dry climate of the Antsiranana region, which gets only 92cm of rain per year, with a long and fairly reliable dry season.

Northwest (Sambirano)

Dominated by the Massif of Tsaratanana, with Maromokotro the highest mountain, this region includes the island of Nosy Be and has a micro-climate with frequent heavy rain alternating with sunshine.

THOSE TIRESOME KIDS

Next time you feel hassled by crowds of children, reflect on their day-to-day existence compared with those at home. Life in cities and in the countryside is equally tough for the vast majority of children; 15% of Madagascar's children die before their first birthday.

Thousands of Malagasy children sleep rough in the tunnels of Tana -- if they are lucky. Many are rounded up by the police as suspected thieves and sent to prisons or detention centres. At both places the regime can be brutal, the warders ex-convicts, and punishments dire.

Family ties in rural areas are strong, but life, if anything, is even tougher. Here is an extract from the newsletter of the charity Feedback Madagascar, by Julia Spencer. 'Vola is a friend of mine and she is six. Her day consists of looking after her second youngest brother Gourda, who is 15 months old. She carries him all day on her back, watches him play, shows him good and bad and walks the two miles to their mother in the fields so she can feed him two or three times a day. She is just one of hundreds of thousands of little women who hold such a huge responsibility. She will cook the family's meagre meal of rice twice a day, finding wood and lighting the small fire under the family's prized pot. When the rice is finished she will soak the pot with hot water to make ranon'anpango tea from the burnt rice that sticks to the sides. When I look at Vola with Gourda wrapped sleeping on her back, I always wonder how her back does not nearly break under his weight. Although six years old she is the same height and weight as a British four-year-old.'

DID YOU KNOW?

- Earthquakes mean the whales are bathing their children.
- If a woman maintains a bending posture when arranging eggs in a nest, the chickens will have crooked necks.
- If the walls of a house incline towards the south, the wife will be the stronger one; if they incline towards the north it will be the husband.
- Burning a knot on a piece of string causes the knees to grow big.

The People

ORIGINS

Archaeologists believe that the first people arrived in Madagascar from Indonesia/Malaya about 2,000 years ago. A journey in a reconstructed boat of those times has proved that the direct crossing of the Indian Ocean – 6,400 kilometres – was possible, but most experts agree that it is much more likely that the immigrants came in their outrigger canoes via southern India and East Africa, where they established small Indonesian colonies. The strong African element in the coastal populations probably derived from later migrations from these colonies since their language is also essentially Malayo-Polynesian with only slightly more Bantu-Swahili words than elsewhere in the island. The Merina people of the highlands retain remarkably Indonesian characteristics and may have arrived as recently as 500–600 years ago.

Later arrivals, mainly on the east coast, from Arabia and elsewhere in the Indian Ocean were also absorbed into the Malagasy-speaking population while leaving their mark in certain local customs clearly derived from Islam. The two-continent origin of the Malagasy is easily observed, from the highland tribes who most resemble Indonesians, to the African type characterised by the Bara or Makoa in the south. In between are the elements of both races which make the Malagasy so varied and attractive in appearance. Thus there is racial diversity but cultural uniformity.

BELIEFS AND CUSTOMS

The Afro-Asian origin of the Malagasy has produced a people with complicated and fascinating beliefs and customs. Despite the various tribes or clans the country shares not only a common language but a belief in the power of dead ancestors (*razana*). This cult of the dead, far from being a morbid preoccupation, is a celebration of life since the dead ancestors are considered to be potent forces who continue to share in family life. If the *razana* are remembered by the living, the Malagasy believe, they thrive in the spirit world and can be relied on to look after their descendants in a host of different ways. These ancestors wield considerable power, their 'wishes' dictating the behaviour of the family or community. Their property is respected, so great-grandfather's field may not be sold or changed to a different crop. Calamities are usually blamed on the anger of *razana*, and a zebu bull may be sacrificed in appeasement. Large herds of zebu cattle are kept as a 'bank' of potential sacrificial offerings.

Belief in tradition, in the accumulated wisdom of the ancestors, has shaped the Malagasy culture. Respect for their elders and courtesy to all fellow humans is part of the tradition. But so is resistance to change.

Spiritual beliefs

At the beginning of time the Creator was Zanihari or Andriananahary. Now the Malagasy worship one god, Andriamanitra, who is neither male nor female. (Andriamanitra is also the word for silk, the fabric of burial shrouds.)

Many rural people believe in 'secondary gods' or nature spirits, which may be male or female and which inhabit certain trees or rocks (which are known as *ody*) or rivers. People seeking help from the spirit world may visit one of these sites for prayer. Spirits are also thought to possess humans who fall into a trance-like state, called *tromba* by the Sakalava and *bilo* by the Antandroy. Some clans or communities believe that spirits can also possess animals, particularly crocodiles.

The Malagasy equivalent of the soul is *ambiroa*. When a person is in a dream state it can temporarily separate from the body, and at death it becomes an immortal *razana*. Death, therefore, is merely a change and not an end. A special ceremony usually marks this rite of passage, with feasting and the sacrifice of zebu. The mood of the participants alternates between sorrow and joy.

Fady

The dictates of the *razana* are obeyed in a complicated network of *fady*. Although *fady* (the plural is also *fady*) is usually translated as 'taboo' this does not truly convey the meaning: these are beliefs related to actions, food, or days of the week when it is 'dangerous to...'. *Fady* vary from family to family and community to community, and even from person to person.

The following are some examples related to actions and food among the Merina: it may be *fady* to sing while you are eating (violators will develop elongated teeth); it is also *fady* to hand an egg directly to another person – it must first be put on the ground; for the people of Andranoro it is *fady* to ask for salt directly, so one has to request 'that which flavours the food'. Also, Merina do not usually eat pork or goat. A *fady* connected with objects is that the spade used to dig a grave should have a loose handle since it is dangerous to have too firm a connection between the living and the dead.

Social *fady*, like *vintana* (see below), often involve the days of the week. For example, among the Merina it is *fady* to hold a funeral on a Tuesday, or there will

FADY AND THEIR ORIGINS

The intruders and the geese During the rule of King Andrian-ampoinimerina, thieves once attempted a raid on the village of Ambohimanga. The residents, however, kept geese which caused a commotion when the intruders entered the compound, thus alerting the people who could take action. Geese are therefore not eaten in this part of Madagascar.

The baby and the drongo Centuries ago the communities of the east coast were persecuted by pirates who made incursions to the hills to pillage and take captives. At the warning that a pirate band was on its way the villagers would flee into the jungle. When pirates approached the village of Ambinanetelo the women with young children could not keep up with the others so hid in a thicket. Just as the pirates were passing them a baby wailed. The men turned to seek the source of the cry. It came again, but this time from the top of a tree: it was a drongo. Believing themselves duped by a bird the pirates gave up and returned to their boats. Ever since then it has been *fady* to kill a drongo in Ambinanetelo.

The tortoise and the pot A Tandroy man put a tortoise in a clay pot of boiling water to cook it, but the tortoise kicked so hard that the pot shattered to smithereens. The man declared that his descendants would never again eat tortoise because it broke his pot.

be another death. Among the Tsimihety, and some other groups, it is *fady* to work the land on Tuesdays; Thursday is also a *fady* day for some people, both for funerals and for farming.

A *fady* is not intended to restrict the freedom of the Malagasy but to ensure happiness and an improved quality of life. That said, however, there are some cruel *fady* which Christian missionaries have been trying, over the centuries, to eliminate. One is the taboo against twins among the Antaisaka people of Mananjary. Historically, twins were killed or abandoned in the forest after birth. Today this is against the law but still persists and twins may not be buried in a tomb. Catholic missionaries have established an orphanage in the area for the twins born to mothers torn between social tradition and maternal love. Many mothers who would otherwise have to suffer the murder or abandonment of their babies can give them to the care of the church.

Many *fady* benefit conservation. For instance the killing of certain animals is often prohibited, and the area around a tomb must be left undisturbed. Within these pockets of sacred forest, *ala masina*, it is strictly forbidden to cut trees or even to burn deadwood or leaf litter. In southeast Madagascar there are *alam-bevehivavy* (sacred women's forests) along a stretch of river where only women may bathe. Again, no vegetation may be cleared or damaged in such localities.

For an in-depth study of the subject try to get hold of a copy of *Taboo* by J Rund (see *Further Information*, page 361).

Vintana

Along with *fady* goes a complex sense of destiny called *vintana*. Broadly speaking, vintana is to do with time – hours of the day, days of the week, etc – and *fady* usually involves actions or behaviour. Each day has its own *vintana* which tends to make it good or bad for certain festivals or activities. Sunday is God's day; work undertaken will succeed. Monday is a hard day, not a good day for work though projects undertaken (such as building a house) will last; Tuesday is an easy day – too easy for death so no burials take place – but all right for *famadihana* (exhumation) and light work; Wednesday is usually the day for funerals or *famadihana*; Thursday is suitable for weddings and is generally a 'good' day; Friday, Zoma, is a 'fat' day, set aside for enjoyment, but is also the best day for funerals; Saturday, a 'noble' day, is suitable for weddings but also for purification.

As an added complication, each day has its own colour. For example, Monday is a black day. A black chicken may need to be sacrificed to avoid calamity, dark-coloured food should not be eaten, and people may avoid black objects. Other day-colours are: Tuesday multicoloured, Wednesday brown, Thursday black, Friday red, Saturday blue.

Tody and Tsiny

A third force shapes Malagasy morality. In addition to *fady* and *vintana*, there is *tody* and its partner *tsiny*. *Tody* is somewhat similar to the Hindu/Buddhist kharma. The word means 'return' or 'retribution' and indicates that for any action there is a reaction. *Tsiny* means 'fault', usually a breach of the rules laid down by the ancestors.

After death

Burial, second burial, and exhumation is the focus of Malagasy beliefs and culture. To the Malagasy, death is the most important part of life, when a person abandons his mortal form to become a much more powerful and significant ancestor. Since a tomb is for ever whilst a house is only a temporary dwelling, it follows that tombs should be more solidly constructed than houses.

Burial practices differ among the various tribes but all over Madagascar a ritual known as *sasa* is practised immediately after a death. The family of the deceased go to a fast-flowing river and wash all their clothes to remove the contamination of death.

Funeral practices vary from clan to clan. The Antankarana (in the north) and Antandroy (south) have 'happy' funerals during which they may run, with the coffin, into the sea. An unusual ritual, *tranondonaky*, is practised by the Antaisaka of the southeast. Here the corpse is first taken to a special house where, after a signal,

TOMB ARCHITECTURE AND FUNERARY ART

In Madagascar the style and structure of tombs define the different clans or tribes better than any other visible feature, and also indicate the wealth and status of the family concerned. Below is a description of the tombs.

Merina In early times burial sites were near valleys or in marshes. The body would be placed in a hollowed-out tree trunk and sunk into the mud at the bottom of a marsh. These *fasam-bazimba* marshes were sacred. Later the Merina began constructing rectangular wooden tombs, mostly under the ground but with a visible structure above ground. In the 19th century the arrival of the Frenchman Jean Laborde had a profound effect on tomb architecture. Tombs were built with bricks and stone, no longer just from wood. It was Laborde's influence which led to the elaborate structure of modern tombs, which are often painted with geometric designs. Sometimes the interior is lavishly decorated.

Sakalava During the Vazimba period, the Sakalava tombs were simple piles of stones. As with the Merina the change occurred with the introduction of cement and a step design was added. At a later stage, wooden stelae, *aloalo*, were placed on the tombs, positioned to face east. These were topped with carvings of a most erotic nature. Since Sakalava tombs are for individuals and not families, there is no attempt at maintaining the stelae as it is believed that only when the wood decays will the soul of the buried person be released. Not all the carvings, however, are erotic – they may just depict scenes from everyday life or geometric paintings.

Tomb construction commences only after the person's death and can take up to six weeks, the body meanwhile being kept in a house. While a tomb is under construction, many zebu are sacrificed to the ancestors. The Sakalava call their tombs *izarana*, 'the place where we are separated'.

Antandroy and Mahafaly The local name of these tombs is *fanesy* which means 'your eternal place'. Zebu horns are scattered on the tomb as a symbol of wealth (on Sakalava tombs, zebu horns are only a decoration, not an indication of status). The Antandroy and Mahafaly tombs have much the same architecture as those of the Sakalava, but are more artistically decorated. The Mahafaly *aloalo* bear figures depicting scenes from the person's life, and the entire length is often carved with intricate designs. These tombs are carefully maintained, and it is probably the Mahafaly tombs in the southern interior which are the most colourful and striking symbols of Malagasy culture. Antandroy tomb paintings tend to be merely decorative and do not represent scenes from the deceased person's life.

the women all start crying. Abruptly, after a second signal, they dance. While this is happening the men are gathered in the hut of the local chief from where, one by one, they go to the house where the corpse is lying and attach money to it with a special oil. The children dance through the night, to the beat of drums, and in the morning the adults wrap the corpse in a shroud and take it to the *kibory*. These tombs are concealed in a patch of forest known as *ala fady* which only men may enter, and where they deliver their last messages to the deceased. These messages can be surprisingly fierce: 'You are now at your place so don't disturb us any more' or 'You are now with the children of the dead, but we are the children of the living'.

More disturbing, however, is the procedure following the death of a noble of the Menabe Sakalava people. The body may be placed on a wooden bench in the hot sun until it begins to decompose. The bodily fluids which drip out are collected in receptacles and drunk by the relatives in the belief that they will then take on the qualities of the deceased.

It is *after* the first burial, however, that the Malagasy generally honour and communicate with their dead, not only to show respect but also to avoid the anger of the *razana* who dwell in the tombs. The best-known ceremony in Madagascar is the 'turning of the bones' by the Merina and Betsileo people: *famadihana* (pronounced 'famadeean'). This is a joyful occasion which occurs from four to seven years after the first burial, and provides the opportunity to communicate with and remember a loved one. The remains of the selected relative are taken from the tomb, rewrapped in a new burial shroud *(lamba mena)*, and carried around the tomb a few times before being replaced. Meantime the corpse is spoken to and informed of all the latest events in the family and village. The celebrants are not supposed to show any grief. Generous quantities of alcohol are consumed amid a festive atmosphere with much dancing and music. Women who are trying to conceive take small pieces of the old burial shroud and keep these under their mattresses to induce fertility.

By law a *famadihana* may take place only in the dry season, between June and September. It can last up to a week and involves the family in considerable expense, as befits the most important celebration for any family. In the Hauts Plateaux the practice of *famadihana* is embraced by rich and poor, urban and rural, and visitors fortunate enough to be invited to one will find it a strange but very moving occasion; it's an opportunity to examine our own beliefs and rituals associated with death. For an account of what *famadihana* means to a sophisticated London-based Merina woman, see pages 18–19.

Variations of *famadihana* are practised by other tribes. The Menabe Sakalava, for example, hold a *fitampoha* every ten years. This is a royal *famadihana* in which the remains of deceased monarchs are taken from their tomb and washed in a river. A similar ritual, the *fanampoambe*, is performed by the Boina Sakalava further north.

Healers, sorcerers and soothsayers

The 'Wise Men' in Malagasy society are the *ombiasy*; the name derives from *olona-be-hasina* meaning 'person of much virtue'. Traditionally they were from the Antaimoro clan and were the advisers of royalty: Antaimoro *ombiasy* came to Antananarivo to advise King Andrianampoinimerina and to teach him Arabic writing.

The astrologers, *mpanandro* ('those who make the day'), work on predictions of *vintana*. There is a Malagasy proverb, 'Man can do nothing to alter his destiny'; but the *mpanandro* will advise on the best day to build a house, or hold a wedding or

FAMADIHANA DIARY

Seraphine Tierney Ramanantsoa

I travelled across the seas to be here today. This day was long awaited, I would soon be in contact with my mother again. She had died seven years previously and I had not been able to be at her funeral. Tradition had always been so important to her so I knew she would be happy as I have come for her *famadihana*.

The meeting point is at 6am outside Cinema Soa in Antananarivo. My household woke up at about 4am to pack the food that had been prepared during the previous week. Drinks and cutlery are all piled into the car. A great number of people are expected as it is also the *famadihana* of the other members of my mother's family.

Fourteen cars and a big taxi-brousse carrying in all about 50 people, squashed one on top of the other, turn up. Everybody is excited. It is really great to see faces I haven't seen since my childhood. Everybody greets each other and exchanges news.

At 8am we all set off. We are heading towards Ifalimanjaka (meaning 'Joy Reigns Here'), in the *fivondronana* of Manjakandriana. Driving through villages with funny names like Ambohitrabiby (The Town of Animals) brings me back to the time when such names were familiar. We make one stop at Talatan'ny volon'ondry for a breakfast of rice cakes and sausages: another opportunity to re-acquaint myself with long lost cousins with whom I spent the long summer holidays as a child. We used to run around together playing games like catching grasshoppers and then finding carnivorous plants and dropping the insect in to see how long it took the plant to close its top to eat its prey.

10am. We arrive at the tombs. Faces are bright, full of expectancy. I ask what the day means to them. They all agree that it's a day for family togetherness, a day for joy, for remembrance.

We are in front of my mother's tomb. It is made out of stone and marble, very elegant. The family will have spent more money on keeping that tomb nice and well maintained than on their own house.

Everybody stands around in front of the tomb waiting for the main event to start: the opening of the tomb door. We have to wait for the president of the *fokon'tany* (local authority) to give permission to open the tomb. Although it had been arranged beforehand he cannot be found anywhere. This wait, after such anticipation, is taken patiently by all – just one of those things.

Mats are laid on the ground on one side of the tomb. The atmosphere of joy is so tangible! Music is blaring out. Permission is finally granted to enter the tomb. The *ray aman-dreny* (the elders) are the first to enter.

The inside of my mother's tomb looks very comfortable with bunk beds made out of stone. It is very clean. There are names on the side of the beds. The national flag is hoisted on top of the tomb as a sign of respect. The conversation goes on happily on the little veranda outside the tomb's door, people chatting about the event and what they have been doing in the last few days.

They start to take the bodies out. Voices could be heard above the happy murmur: 'Who is this one? This is your ma! This one your aunt! Here is your

famadihana. Though nowadays *mpanandro* do not have official recognition, they are present in all levels of society. A man (or woman) is considered to have the powers of a *mpanandro* when he has some grey hair – a sign that he is wise enough to interpret *vintana*. Antandroy soothsayers are known as *mpisoro*.

uncle! Just carry them around!' The closest relations carry the body but others could touch and say hello. When carrying them, they make sure that the feet go first and the head behind. Everybody carries their loved ones out of the tomb in a line, crying but happy.

When all the bodies are out, they are put on the ground on the front side of the tomb, the head facing east, with their immediate family seated around their loved one. This is a very important moment of the *famadihana*: the beginning of the wrapping of the body. The old shroud in which the body was buried is left on and the new silk shroud put on top of it, following the mummified shape and using baby safety pins to keep it in place. There are three new silk shrouds for my mother which have been donated in remembrance and gratitude. The belief is that she won't be cold and the top shroud befits her, being of top quality silk with beautiful, delicate embroidery. This is the time to touch her, give her something, talk to her. Her best friend is there, making sure that my mother is properly wrapped, as the ritual has to follow certain rules. Lots of touching as silent conversation goes on, giving her the latest news or family gossip, and asking for her blessing. Perfume is sprinkled on her and wishes made at the same time.

The music plays on, everyone happily sitting around the mummified bodies. Flowers are placed on the bodies. The feeling of togetherness and love is so strong. This occasion is not just for the immediate family, but for cousins, and cousins of cousins, uncles and aunts and everybody meeting, bonded by the same ties, belonging to one unique extended family.

Photographs of the dead person are now put on top of each body. There is a photograph of a couple on top of one body: they were husband and wife and are now together for ever in the same silk shroud.

Food is served in the forest area just next to the tombs. The huge feast and celebration begins.

Back to the bodies. We lift them, carrying them on our shoulders. We sing old rhymes and songs and dance in a line, circling the tomb seven times, moving the body on our shoulder and making it dance with us.

The last dance ends. The bodies have to be back inside the tombs by a precise time and the tomb is immediately closed after a last ritual cleaning. This moment of goodbye is very emotional. The next time the tomb will be opened will not be for happiness but grief because it will be for a burial. *Famadihana* only happens once every seven or ten years.

Everybody returns to the cars and drives to the next meeting place – my uncle's, where a huge party finishes the day. Everyone is happy at having done their duty, *Vita ny adidy*!

It has been a very special day for me. My mother was extremely traditional, spending endless energy and money during her lifetime to keep the traditions. It all makes sense now because this *famadihana* brought so much joy, a strong sense of belonging and identity, and giving a spiritual feeling that death is not an end but an extension into another life, linked somehow with this one.

Misaotra ry neny (thank you mum).

The Malagasy have a deep knowledge of herbal medicine and all markets display a variety of medicinal plants, amulets and talismans. The Malagasy names associated with these are *ody* and *fanafody*. Broadly speaking, *ody* refers to fetishes such as sacred objects in nature, and *fanafody* to herbal remedies – around 60% of the plants so far catalogued in Madagascar have healing properties. Travellers will sometimes come across conspicuous *ody* in the form of stones or trees which are sacred for a whole village, not just for an individual. Such trees are called *hazo manga*, 'good tree', and are presided over by the *mpisoro*, the senior man of the oldest family in the village. Another type of *ody* is the talisman, *aoly*, worn for protection if someone has transgressed a *fady* or broken a promise. *Aoly* are sometimes kept in the house or buried. *Ody fiti* are used to gain love (white magic) but sorcerers also sell other forms of *ody* for black magic and are paid by clients with either money, zebu or poultry (a red rooster being preferred).

Mpamonka are witch doctors with an intimate knowledge of poison and *mpisikidy* are sorcerers who use amulets, stones, and beads (known as *hasina*) for their cures. Sorcerers who use these in a destructive way are called *mpamosavy*.

On their death, sorcerers are not buried in tombs but are dumped to the west of their villages, barely covered with soil so that feral dogs and other creatures can eat their bodies. Their necks are twisted to face south.

Thanks to Nivo Ravelajaona who provided much of the above information.

The way it is...

Visitors from the West often find the beliefs and customs of the Malagasy merely bizarre. It takes time and effort to understand and respect the richness of tradition that underpins Malagasy society, but it is an effort well worth making.

Leonard Fox, author of *Hainteny*, sums it up perfectly: 'Whoever has witnessed the silent radiance of those who come to pray... at the house of Andrianampoinimerina in Ambohimanga and has experienced the nobility, modesty, unobsequious courtesy, and balanced wholeness of the poorest Merina who has remained faithful to his heritage can have no doubt as to the deep integrative value of the Malagasy spiritual tradition.'

MALAGASY SOCIETY
Marriage and children

The Malagasy have a strong sense of community which influences their way of life. Just as the ancestors are laid in a communal tomb, so their descendants share a communal way of life, and even children are almost considered common property within their extended family. Children are seldom disciplined but learn by example.

Marriage is a fairly relaxed union and divorce is common. There is no formal dowry arrangement or bride price, but a present of zebu cattle will often be made. In rural communities the man should bring his new wife home to his village (not vice versa) or he will lose face. You often see young men walking to market wearing a comb in their hair. They are advertising their quest for a wife.

Most Malagasy (and all Christians) have only one wife, but there are exceptions. There is, for example, a well-known man living in Antalaha, in the northeast, who has 11 wives and 120 children. This arrangement seems to work surprisingly well, with each wife working to support her own children, and a head wife to whom the others defer. The man is wealthy enough to provide housing for all his family.

The village community

Malagasy society is a structured hierarchy with two fundamental rules: respect for the other person and knowing one's place. Within a village, the community is based on the traditional *fokonolona*. This concept was introduced by King Andrianampoinimerina when these councils of village elders were given responsibility for, among other things, law and order and the collection of taxes. Day-to-day decisions are still made by the *fokonolona*.

Rural Malagasy houses are always aligned north/south and generally have only one room. Furniture is composed of mats, *tsihy*, often beautifully woven. These are used for sitting and sleeping, and sometimes food is served on them. There are often *fady* attached to *tsihy*. For example, you should not step over a mat, particularly one on which meals are eaten.

Part of the Malagasy culture is the art of oratory, *kabary*. Originally *kabary* were the huge meetings where King Andrianampoinimerina proclaimed his plans, but the word has now evolved to mean the elaborate form of speech used to inspire and control the crowds at such gatherings. Even rural leaders can speak for hours, using highly ornate language and many proverbs; a necessary skill in a society that reached a high degree of sophistication without a written language.

The market plays a central role in the life of rural people, who will often walk 15–20 kilometres to market with no intention of selling or buying, but simply to catch up on the gossip or continue the conversation broken off the previous week. You will see well-dressed groups of young people happily making their way to this social centre. Often there is a home-made tombola, and other outlets for gambling.

Festivals and ceremonies
Malagasy Christians celebrate the usual holy days, but most tribes or clans have their special festivals.

Ala volon-jaza
This is the occasion when a baby's hair is cut for the first time. With the Antambahoka people in the south the haircut is performed by the grandparents. The child is placed in a basin filled with water, and afterwards bathed. Among the Merina the ceremony is similar but only a man whose parents are still alive may cut a baby's hair. The family then have a meal of rice, zebu, milk and honey. Coins are placed in the bowl of rice and the older children compete to get as many as possible.

Circumcision
Boys are usually circumcised at the age of about two; a baby who dies before this operation has been performed may not be buried in the family tomb.

The operation itself is often done surgically, but in some rural areas it may still be performed with a sharpened piece of bamboo. The foreskin is not always simply discarded. In the region of the Antambahoka it may be eaten by the grandparents, and in Antandroy country it could be shot from the barrel of a gun!

Different clans have their own circumcision ceremonies. Among the Antandroy, uncles dance with their nephews on their shoulders. But the most famous ceremony is *Sambatra*, which takes place every seven years in Mananjary. See pages 278–9.

Tsangatsaine
This is a ceremony performed by the Antankarana. Two tall trees growing side by side near the house of a noble family are tied together to symbolise the unification of the tribe, as well as the tying together of the past and present, the living and the dead.

Fandroana
This was the royal bath ceremony which marked the Malagasy New Year. These celebrations used to take place in March, with much feasting. While the monarch was ritually bathed, the best zebu was slaughtered and the choicest rump steak

HAINTENY

References in this book to the Merina have hitherto been focused on their military abilities, but this tribe has a rich and complex spiritual life. Perhaps the shortest route to the soul of any society is through its poetry, and we are fortunate that there is now a book of the traditional Malagasy poetry, *Hainteny*. Broadly speaking, *hainteny* are poems about love: love between parent and child, between man and woman, the love of nature, the appreciation of good versus evil, the acceptance of death. Through the sensitive translations of Leonard Fox, the spiritual and emotional life of the Merina is made available to the reader who cannot fail to be impressed by these remarkable people. As Leonard Fox says: 'On the most basic level, *hainteny* give us an incomparable insight into a society characterised by exceptional refinement and subtlety, deep appreciation of beauty, delight in sensual enjoyment, and profound respect for the spiritual realities of life.'

There are two examples of *hainteny* below, and others are scattered throughout this book.

> What is the matter, Raivonjaza,
> That you remain silent?
> Have you been paid or hired and your mouth tied,
> That you do not speak with us, who are your parents?
> ~ I have not been paid or hired
> and my mouth has not been tied,
> but I am going home to my husband
> and am leaving my parents,
> my child, and my friends,
> so I am distressed,
> speaking little.
> Here is my child, dear Mother and Father.
> If he is stubborn, be strict, but do not beat him;
> and if you hit him, do not use a stick.
> And do not act as though you do not see him
> when he is under your eyes, saying:
> "Has this child eaten?"
> Do not give him too much,
> Do not give him the remains of a meal,
> and do not give him what is half-cooked,
> for I will be far and will long for him.
>
> Do not love me, Andriamatoa, as one loves
> the banana tree exposed to the wind,
> overcome and in danger from cold.
> Do not love me as one loves a door:
> It is loved, but constantly pushed.
> Love me as one loves a little crab:
> even its claws are eaten.

presented to the village nobles. The day was the equivalent of the Malagasy National Day, but the French moved this to July 14, the date of the establishment of the French Protectorate. This caused major resentment among the Malagasy as effectively their traditional New Year was taken from them. After independence the date was changed to June 26 to coincide with Independence Day. These days, because of the cost of zebu meat and the value attached to the animals, the traditional meat has been replaced by chicken, choice portions again being given to the respected members of the community. In the absence of royalty there is, of course, no royal bath ceremony.

Music
Music infuses the lives of the Malagasy people and, like *Hainteny*, it is the outward expression of their feelings towards nature and human relationships. Traditional musical instruments are often natural objects – dried reeds or gourds, rubbed together or shaken to the beat of the music – while the words reflect the spiritual essence of the culture. Pop music is encroaching on this tradition, of course, but the charity Valiha High (see page 130) is helping preserve the traditions.

ETHNIC GROUPS
This section was originally taken from A Glance at Madagascar *(written in 1973 and now reprinted) and has subsequently been added to from a variety of sources.*

The different clans of Madagascar are based more upon old kingdoms than upon ethnic grouping. Traditions are changing: the descriptions below reflect the tribes at the time of Independence, rather than in the more fluid society of today.

In the last few years there have been several anthropological books published in English about the people of Madagascar. See *Further information*, page 361.

The tribes may differ but a Malagasy proverb shows their feeling of unity: *Ny olombelona toy ny molo-bilany, ka iray mihodidina ihany*; 'Men are like the lip of the cooking pot which forms just one circle'.

Antaifasy (People-of-the-sands)
Living in the southeast around Farafangana they cultivate rice, and fish in the lakes and rivers. Divided into three clans each with its own 'king' they generally have stricter moral codes than the other tribes. They have large collective burial houses known as *kibory*, built of wood or stone and generally hidden in the forest away from the village.

Antaimoro (People-of-the-coast)
These are among the most recent arrivals and live in the southeast around Vohipeno and Manakara. They guard Islamic tradition and Arab influence and still use a form of Arab writing known as *sorabe*. They use verses of the Koran as amulets.

Antaisaka
Centred south of Farafangana on the southeast coast but now fairly widely spread throughout the island, they are an offshoot of the Sakalava tribe. They cultivate coffee, bananas and rice – but only the women harvest the rice. There are strong marriage taboos amongst them. Often the houses may have a second door on the east side which is used only for taking out a corpse. They use the *kibory*, communal burial house, the corpse usually being dried out for two or three years before finally being put there.

Antankarana (Those-of-the-rocks)
Living in the north around Antsiranana (Diego Suarez) they are fishers or cattleraisers whose rulers came from the Sakalava dynasty. Their houses are usually

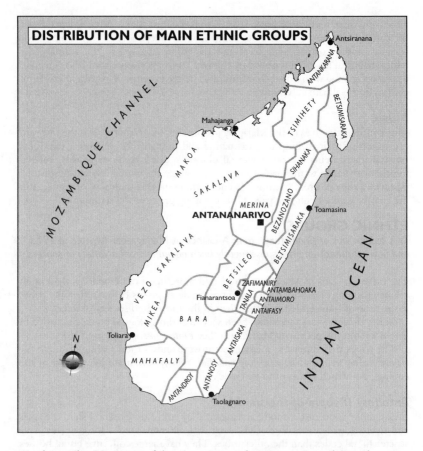

DISTRIBUTION OF MAIN ETHNIC GROUPS

raised on stilts. Numerous *fady* exist amongst them governing relations between the sexes in the family; for example a girl may not wash her brother's clothes. The legs of a fowl are the father's portion, whereas amongst the Merina, for instance, they are given to the children.

Antambahoaka (Those-of-the-people)
The smallest tribe, of the same origin as the Antaimoro and living around Mananjary on the southeast coast. They have some Arab traits and amulets are used. They bury in a *kibory*. Group circumcision ceremonies are carried out every seven years.

Antandroy (People-of-the-thorns)
Traditionally nomadic, they live in the arid south around Ambovombe. A dark-skinned people, they wear little clothing and are said to be frank and open, easily roused to either joy or anger. Their women occupy an inferior position, and it is *fady* for a woman to milk a cow. The villages are often surrounded by a hedge of cactus plants. Until recently they ate little rice, their staples being maize, cassava and sweet potatoes. They believe in the *kokolampo*, a spirit of either good or bad influence. Their tombs are similar to those of the Mahafaly tribe. Sometimes it is *fady* among them for a child to say his father's name, or to refer by name to parts

of his father's body. Thus he may say *ny fandiany* (the-what-he-moves-with) for his feet, and *ny amboniny* (the-top-of-him) for his head.

Antanosy (People-of-the-island)

The island is a small one in the Fanjahira river. They live in the southeast principally around Taolagnaro (Fort Dauphin). Their social structure is based on clans with a 'king' holding great authority over each clan. There are strict *fady* governing relationships in the family. For example, a brother may not sit on or step over his sister's mat. As with many other tribes there are numerous *fady* regarding pregnancy: a pregnant woman should not sit in the doorway of the house; she should not eat brains; she should not converse with men; people who have no children should not stay in her house overnight. Other *fady* are that relatives should not eat meat at a funeral and the diggers opening a tomb should not wear clothes. When digging holes for the corner posts of a new house it may be *fady* to stand up so the job must be performed sitting down.

Bara

Originally in the southwest near Toliara, these nomadic cattleraisers now live in the south-central area around Ihosy and Betroka. Their name has no special meaning but it is reputed to derive from an African (Bantu) word. They may be polygamous and women occupy an inferior position in their society. They attach importance to the *fatidra* or 'blood pact'. Cattle stealing is regarded as proof of manhood and courage, without which a man cannot expect to get a wife. They are dancers and sculptors, a unique feature of their carved wooden figures being eyelashes of real hair set into the wood. They believe in the *helo*, a spirit that manifests itself at the foot of trees. In the past a whole village would move after somebody died owing to the fear of ghosts. They use caves in the mountains for burial. It is the custom to shave the head on the death of a near relative.

Betsileo (The-many-invincibles)

They are centred in the south of the Hauts Plateaux around Fianarantsoa but about 150,000 of them also live in the Betsiboka region. They are energetic and expert rice producers, their irrigated, terraced ricefields being a feature of the landscape. Famadihana was introduced to their culture by the Merina at the time of Queen Ranavalona I. It is *fady* for the husband of a pregnant woman to wear a *lamba* thrown over his shoulder. It may be *fady* for the family to eat until the father is present or for anyone to pick up his fork until the most honourable person present has started to eat.

Betsimisaraka (The-many-inseparables)

They are the second largest tribe and live on the east coast in the region between Toamasina and Antalaha. Their culture has been influenced by Europeans, particularly pirates. They cultivate rice and work on vanilla plantations. Their clothes are sometimes made from locally woven raffia. Originally their society included numerous local chiefs. The *tangalamena* is the local official for religious rites and customs. The Betsimisaraka have many superstitious beliefs: *angatra* (ghosts), *zazavavy an-drano* (mermaids), and *kalamoro*, little wild men of the woods, about 63cm high with long flowing hair, who like to slip into houses and steal rice from the cooking pot. In the north coffins are generally placed under a shelter, in the south in tombs. It may be *fady* for a brother to shake hands with his sister, or for a young man to wear shoes while his father is still living.

Bezanozano (Many-small-plaits)

The name refers to the way in which they do their hair. They were probably one of the first tribes to become established in Madagascar, and live in an area between the Betsimisaraka lowlands and the Merina highlands. Like the Merina, they practise *famadihana*. As with most of the coastal tribes their funeral celebrations involve the consumption of considerable quantities of *toaka*, rum.

Mahafaly (Those-who-make-taboos or Those-who-make-happy)

The etymology of the word is sometimes disputed but the former meaning is generally regarded as being correct. They probably arrived around the 12th century, and live in the southwest desert area around Ampanihy and Ejeda. They are farmers, with maize, sorgho and sweet potatoes as their chief crops; cattle rearing occupies a secondary place. They kept their independence under their own local chiefs until the French occupation and still keep the bones of some of their old chiefs – this is the *jiny* cult. Their villages usually have a sacrificial post, the *hazo manga*, on the east of the village where sacrifices are made. Some of the blood is generally put on the foreheads of the people attending.

The tombs of the Mahafaly attract a great deal of interest. They are big rectangular constructions of uncut stone rising about a metre above the ground and decorated with *aloalo* and the horns of the cattle slain at the funeral feast. The tomb of the Mahafaly king, Tsiampody, has the horns of 700 zebu on it. The *aloalo* are sculpted wooden posts set upright on the tomb, often depicting scenes from the person's life. The burial customs include waiting for the decomposition of the body before it is placed in the tomb. It is the practice for a person to be given a new name after death – generally beginning with 'Andria'.

The divorce rate is very high and it is not at all uncommon for a man to divorce and remarry six or seven times. It is very often *fady* for children to sleep in the same house as their parents. Their *rombo* (very similar to the *tromba* of the Sakalava) is the practice of contacting various spirits for healing purposes. Amongst the spirits believed in are the *raza* who are not real ancestors and in some cases are even supposed to include *vazaha* (white foreigners), and the *vorom-be* which is the spirit of a big bird.

Mikea

The Mikea are an offshoot of the Sakalava. The name refers not so much to a tribe as to a lifestyle. They subsist by foraging in the dry forests of the west and southwest. Various groups of people up the west coast are called Mikea, although their main area is the Forêt des Mikea between Morombe and Toliara. The Mikea are Malagasy of various origins, having adopted their particular lifestyle (almost unique in Madagascar) for several reasons, including fleeing from oppression, taxation etc exerted on them by various powers: the Sakalava, the French, and the government of the 2nd Republic. (Information from Dr J Bond)

Makoa

Mainly of African origin, and generally lowly regarded by other Sakalava groups, the Makoa live in the northwest (Ambongo) region. They are probably descended from African slaves and are said to be the most primitive group in Madagascar.

Merina (People-of-the-Highlands)

They live on the Hauts Plateaux, the most developed area of the country, the capital being 95% Merina. They are of Malayo-Polynesian origin and vary in colour from ivory to very dark, with straight hair. They used to be divided into three castes: the Andriana (nobles), the Hova (freemen) and the Andevo (serfs);

but legally these divisions no longer exist. Most Merina houses are built of brick or mud; some are two-storey buildings with slender pillars, where the people live mainly upstairs. Most villages of any size have a church – probably two, Catholic and Protestant. There is much irrigated rice cultivation, and the Merina were the first tribe to have any skill in architecture and metallurgy. The *famadihana* is essentially a Merina custom.

Sakalava (People-of-the-long-valleys)
They live in the west between Toliara and Mahajanga and are dark skinned with Polynesian features and short curly hair. They were at one time the largest and most powerful tribe, though disunited, and were ruled by their own kings and queens. Certain royal relics remain – sometimes being kept in the northeast corner of a house. The Sakalava are cattleraisers, and riches are reckoned by the number of cattle owned. There is a record of human sacrifice amongst them up to the year 1850 at special occasions, such as the death of a king. The *tromba* (trance state) is quite common. It is *fady* for pregnant women to eat fish or to sit in a doorway. Women hold a more important place than in most other tribes.

Sihanaka (People-of-the-swamps)
Their home is the northeast of the old kingdom of Imerina around Lake Alaotra and they have much in common with the Merina. They are fishers, rice growers and poultry raisers. Swamps have been drained to make vast ricefields cultivated with modern machinery and methods. They have a special rotation of *fady* days.

Tanala (People-of-the-forest)
These are traditionally forest dwellers, living inland from Manakara, and are rice and coffee growers. Their houses are usually built on stilts. The Tanala are divided into two groups: the Ikongo in the south and the Menabe in the north. The Ikongo are an independent people and never submitted to Merina domination, in contrast to the Menabe. Burial customs include keeping the corpse for up to a month. Coffins are made from large trees to which sacrifices are sometimes made when they are cut down. The Ikongo usually bury their dead in the forest and may mark a tree to show the spot.

Some recent authorities dispute that the Tanala exist as a separate ethnic group.

Tsimihety (Those-who-do-not-cut-their-hair)
The refusal to cut their hair (to show mourning on the death of a Sakalava king) was to demonstrate their independence. They are an energetic and vigorous people

THE VAZIMBA
Vazimba is the name given to the earliest inhabitants of Madagascar, pastoralists of the central plateaux, who were displaced or absorbed by later immigrants. Once thought to be pre-Indonesian aboriginals from Africa, it is now generally accepted that they were survivors of the earliest Austronesian immigrants who were pushed to the west by later arrivals.

Vazimba come into both legends and history of the Malagasy. Vazimba tombs are now places of pilgrimage where sacrifices are made for favours and cures. It is *fady* to step over such a tomb. Vazimba are also thought to haunt certain springs and rocks, and offerings may be made here. They are the ancestral guardians of the soil.

MALAGASY WITHOUT (TOO MANY) TEARS
Janice Booth

Once you've thrown out the idea that you must speak a foreign language correctly or not at all, and that you must use complete sentences, you can have fun with only a few words of Malagasy. Basic French is understood almost everywhere, but the people – particularly in villages – warm instantly to any attempts to speak 'their own' language.

If you learn only three words, choose *misaotra* (thank you), pronounced misowtr; *veloma* (goodbye), pronounced veloom; and *manao ahoana* (pronounced roughly manna owner), which is an all-purpose word meaning hello, good morning or good day. If you can squeeze in another three, go for *tsara* (good); *aza fady* (please), pronounced azafad; and *be* (pronounced beh), which can be used – sometimes ungrammatically, but who cares! – to mean big, very or much. Thus *tsara be* means very good; and *misaotra be* means a big thank you. Finally, when talking to an older person, it's polite to add *tompoko* (pronounced toompk) after thank you or goodbye. This is equivalent to Madame or Monsieur in French. If your memory's poor, write the vocabulary on a postcard and carry it round with you.

In a forest one evening, at dusk, I was standing inside the trunk and intertwining roots of a huge banyan tree, looking up through the branches at the fading sky and a few early stars. It was very peaceful, very silent. Suddenly a small man appeared from the shadows, holding a rough wooden dish. Old and poorly dressed, probably a cattle herder, he stood uncertainly, not wanting to

in the north-central area and are spreading west. The oldest maternal uncle occupies an important position.

Vezo (Fishing people)
More usually referred to as Vezo-Sakalava, they are not generally recognised as a separate tribe but as a clan of the Sakalava. They live on the coast in the region of Morondava in the west to Faux Cap in the south. They use little canoes hollowed out from tree trunks and fitted with one outrigger pole and a small rectangular sail. In these frail but stable craft they go far out to sea. The Vezo are also noted for their tombs, which are graves dug into the ground surrounded by wooden palisades, the main posts of which are crowned by erotic wooden carved figures.

Zafimaniry
A clan of some 15,000 people distributed in about 100 villages in the forests between the Betsileo and Tanala areas, southeast of Ambositra. They are known for their wood carvings and sculpture, and are descended from people from the Hauts Plateaux who established themselves there early in the 19th century. The Zafimaniry are thus interesting to historians as they continue the forms of housing and decoration of past centuries. Their houses, which are made from vegetable fibres and wood with bamboo walls and roofs, have no nails and can be taken down and moved from one village to another.

Ste Marians
The population of Ile Ste Marie (Nosy Boraha) is mixed. Although Indonesian in origin there has been influence from both Arabs and European pirates.

disturb me. I said 'Manao ahoana,' and he replied. I touched the bark of the tree gently and said 'tsara'. 'Tsara,' he agreed, smiling. Then he said a sentence in which I recognised 'tantely' (honey). I pointed questioningly to a wild bees' nest high in the tree. 'Tantely,' he repeated quietly, pleased. I pointed to his dish – 'Tantely sakafo?' Yes, he was collecting wild honey for food. 'Tsara. Veloma, tompoko.' I moved off into the twilight. 'Veloma,' he called softly after me. So few words, so much said.

Another day, in Tana, a teenaged girl was pestering me for money. She didn't seem very deserving, but wouldn't give up. Then I asked her in Malagasy, 'What's your name?' She looked astonished, eyes suddenly meeting mine instead of sliding furtively. 'Noro.' So I asked, very politely, 'Please Noro, go away. Goodbye.' Nonplussed, she stared at me briefly before moving off, the cringing attitude quite gone. By using her name, I'd given her dignity. You can find that vocabulary – all seven words of it! – in the Language appendix on page 354.

'What's your name?' is probably the phrase I most enjoy using. Say it to a child and its eyes grow wider, as a timid little voice answers you. Then you can say 'Manao ahoana', using the name, and you've forged a link. Now find out from the Appendix how to say 'My name is...' – and you're into real conversation!

When I'm in Madagascar I still carry a copy of the Language Appendix in my bag. It's dog-eared now, and scribbled on. But it's my passport to a special kind of contact with friendly, gentle and fascinating people.

LANGUAGE

The Indonesian origin of the Malagasy people shows strongly in their language which is spoken, with regional variations of dialect, throughout the island. (Words for domestic animals, however, are derived from Kiswahili, indicating that the early settlers, sensibly enough, did not bring animals with them in their outrigger canoes.) Malagasy is a remarkably rich language, full of images, metaphors and proverbs. Literal translations of Malagasy words and phrases are often very poetic. 'Dusk' is *maizim-bava vilany*, 'darken the mouth of the cooking pot'; 'two or three in the morning' is *misafo helika ny kary*, 'when the wild cat washes itself'. The richness of the language means that there are few English words that can be translated to a single word in Malagasy, and vice versa. An example given by Leonard Fox in his book on the poetry of Madagascar, *Hainteny*, is *miala mandry*; *miala* means 'go out/go away' and *mandry* means 'lie down/go to sleep'. Together, however, they mean 'to spend the night away from home, and yet be back in the early morning as if never having been away'! No wonder there is no concise Malagasy/English dictionary for travellers!

There is, however, an excellent cassette and accompanying phrase book which will enable you to learn the rudiments of the language without becoming overwhelmed by its complexities: *Malagasy Basics* by Rasoanaivo Hanitrarivo. The author is better known as Hanitra Anderson, the leader of *Tarika*, the internationally known group of Malagasy musicians. *Malagasy Basics* is available from FMS in London; tel: 020 8340 9651, email: froots@cityscape.co.uk. Another very useful book is *Guide to Communication: Malagasy, Français, English* by James Yount. This is available in the Librairie de Madagascar in Antananarivo.

Learning, or even using, the Malagasy language may seem a challenging prospect to the first-time visitor. Place names may be 15 characters long (because they usually have a literal meaning, such as Ranomafana: hot water), with seemingly erratic syllable stress. With a reasonable grasp of French you can travel easily and communicate with educated Malagasy. In fact children now learn French in school from primary onwards, although this is a new development. However, particularly in rural areas, a smattering of Malagasy works wonders, and it's a courtesy to speak to the local people in their own – rather than an 'imported' – language. In the last edition Frankie Kerridge wrote: 'I attempted to learn some Malagasy using *Malagasy Basics*. I found the excellent book and cassette a tremendous help. Just being able to pronounce Malagasy names, and to use and recognise nouns, impressed my hosts and friends, and endeared me to strangers that I met who I felt were all too used to impatient tourists shouting English or French.' However, after a subsequent visit she added: 'While I would encourage people to learn as much Malagasy as they can, remember that in out of the way places Malagasy don't get a chance to practise the French that they have learned. So I don't think it is too much of an insult to use French greetings occasionally.'

See page 354 for some Malagasy vocabulary.

SOME MALAGASY PROVERBS

Tantely tapa-bata ka ny foko no entiko mameno azy.
This is only half a pot of honey but my heart fills it up.

Mahavoa roa toy ny dakam-boriky.
Hit two things at once like the kick of a donkey.

Tsy midera vady tsy herintaona.
Don't praise your wife before a year.

Ny omby singorana amin' ny tandrony, ary ny olona kosa amin' ny vavany.
Oxen are trapped by their horns and men by their words.

Tondro tokana tsy mahazo hao.
You can't catch a louse with one finger.

Ny alina mitondra fisainana.
The night brings wisdom.

Aza manao herim-boantay.
If you are just a dung beetle don't try to move mountains.

Aza midera harena, fa niter-day.
Do not boast about your wealth if you are a father.

Ny teny toy ny fonosana, ka izay mamono no mamaha.
Words are like a parcel: if you tie lots of knots you will have to undo them.

Natural History

3

This section, as far as Conservation, *is written by Jonathan Hughes with additional information by Nick Garbutt. Jonathan Hughes is a consultant for the British Ecological Society, a lecturer in ecology and author of numerous articles on ecology, evolution and biology in general. His involvement with Madagascar began while working at the Royal Botanic Gardens, Kew, mapping and classifying the conservation needs of the island's habitats.*

INTRODUCTION

Madagascar's natural history is its most striking single feature. There are over 200,000 species on the island, living in habitats ranging from rainforests to deserts and from mountain tops to mangrove swamps. The residents are as unique as they are diverse, so that a list of Malagasy species reads like a hurried appendix tagged on the end of a catalogue of the world's wildlife – 'The ones found nowhere else'. Six whole plant families exist only on Madagascar, as do 1,000 orchid species, many thousands of succulents, countless insects, over 300 species of frog, 270 kinds of reptile, five families of birds and more than 100 different mammals, including an entire group of primates, the order to which we belong. One thing is certain: whatever animal or plant you gaze upon during your visit, you are unlikely to see it anywhere else.

This magnificent menagerie is the product of a spectacular geological past. More than 165 million years ago, Madagascar was a land-locked plateau at the centre of the largest continent the Earth has ever seen, Gondwanaland. This was during the age of the reptiles at about the time when the flowering plants were beginning to blossom and primitive mammals and birds were finding a niche among their giant dinosaur cohabitants. With a combination of sea-level rises and plate movements Gondwanaland subsequently broke into the island continents of Australia, Antarctica, South America and Africa. As the Indian Ocean opened up between once neighbouring territories, Madagascar cast away from the African coast, setting itself adrift as one of the Earth's great experiments in evolution.

Some of the plants and animals present on the island today are the results of adaptation from the original, marooned Gondwanaland stock. Ancient groups such as the ferns, cycads, palms and pandans, and primitive reptiles such as the boas and iguanids, are descendants of this relic community. Yet, the magic of Madagascar is that a select band of species have enriched the community by arriving *since* the break-up. Flying, swimming, journeying as seeds or riding the floodwaters of the east African rivers in hollow trunks, wave after wave of more recent plants and animals came from over the horizon during a period of 100 million years, bringing with them the latest adaptations from the big world beyond. Colonisers, such as the lemurs and carnivores, may have had a helping hand from a partial land-bridge which is thought to have appeared from beneath the waves of the Mozambique Channel about 40 million years ago.

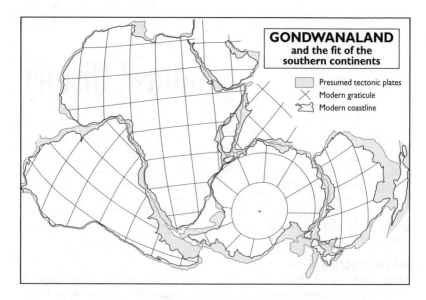

GONDWANALAND
and the fit of the
southern continents

Presumed tectonic plates
Modern graticule
Modern coastline

Yet, whatever their mode of transport, upon land-fall each species spread outwards in every direction, through the tremendous range of habitats on offer, changing subtly as they encountered new environments, sometimes to the extent that new species were formed. This evolutionary process is termed *adaptive radiation* and it results in the creation of an array of new species found nowhere else.

The patterns in the island's diversity tell us something of the timing of these colonisations. A large number of unique succulent plants indicates an early arrival from Africa in the dry west, followed by a radiation eastwards ending in the rainforests. On the contrary, the two Malagasy pitcher plants found on the east coast probably arrived at about the same time as the Malagasy, and from the same direction. The remoteness of Madagascar's rainforests, positioned as they are, across a stretch of dry plateaux and over a spine of high mountains, may have made these humid lands tantalisingly out of reach for African rainforest species. Certainly many of the Malagasy species seem to have closer associations with Asian and South American groups with whom they share Gondwanaland ancestors. As a result of these various evolutionary processes and chance events, the island is blessed with animals and plants of many descriptions, most unique to the island, and a fair proportion of which we have very little knowledge.

GEOLOGY

The main geological features of Madagascar are a Pre-Cambrian crystalline basement (eastern two-thirds of the island) overlaid with laterite, a sedimentary region in the south and west (Jurassic, Cretaceous and Tertiary) and volcanic outcrops. The Ankaratra mountains near Antananarivo are of volcanic origin. There are no active volcanoes but in the highlands there are many hot springs, craters and ash cones.

Millions of years of weathering have produced the smooth granite mountains of the southern highlands, the eroded sandstone shapes of Isalo in the southwest, and the extraordinary spikes of the *tsingy* or limestone karst.

A great variety of precious and semi-precious gemstones are found in Madagascar, including several types of tourmaline, amethyst, citrine, rhodonite, celestine, amazonite, Labradorite (moonstone), iolite, kornerupine, sphene, spinel, chrysoberyl, rose quartz, milky quartz, and grossular garnets (known as cinnamon stone in Madagascar). There is a rare, dark blue variety of aquamarine (beryl); and the finest Morganite in the world comes from Madagascar. The largest crystal ever found was in Madagascar: a beryl measuring 18 metres long and 3.5 metres in diameter; it weighed about 380 tons. There is currently a sapphire boom in the country (see box on page 19).

This enormous diversity of beautiful minerals may be found in the markets and shops of Madagascar in the form of colourful Solitaire sets and similar souvenirs. There are tours available specialising in minerals and gemstones; well worth considering if you are a rock-hound.

MADAGASCAR'S BIODIVERSITY

Madagascar is one of the 12 most important countries for biodiversity on the planet. It is home to so many species for two reasons: it is near to the equator and it contains an astonishing array of habitats. The tropical climate is a perfect host to the processes of life – far more living things survive within the tropics than in cooler regions, while the habitat variety provides more opportunity for animal and plant variation. It is in this evolutionary playground that every now and then a member of a mainland plant or animal group has found itself marooned. Little wonder then that Madagascar has such biodiversity – a feature that has served to fascinate centuries of travellers, but one that has also placed a tremendous responsibility upon a troubled nation.

Flora

Madagascar has one of the richest floras in the world. The upper estimates of its diversity, at 12,000 species, make the island the world's number one floral hotspot for an area of its size. The key to this richness is its *endemism* – 80% of Madagascar's plant species are not found anywhere else. The fortuitous break from Africa and Asia at a time when the flowering plants were just beginning to diversify, allowed many groups to develop their own lineage, supplemented occasionally by the later colonisations of more advanced forms.

Ferns and cycads

Ferns were in their heyday before even Gondwanaland was formed. Their best efforts were the impressive tree-ferns, which had large spreading fronds sprouting from a tall, scaly stem. These structures created vast forests in all warm, humid areas during the Carboniferous Period, 350 million years ago; forests that were later to persist only as coal seams in the rocks. Although they eventually lost ground to seed-bearing plants in the age of the dinosaurs, it is a credit to the fern design that they are still abundant and successful. Indeed the soft, symmetrical foliage of ferns very much symbolises the lushness of wet, hot places. It's true that they have been relegated to a life in the shade of more recently evolved plants, but at this they excel, out-competing all others.

Although some species are present in dry habitats, the vast majority of Madagascar's ferns decorate the branches and trunks of the eastern rainforest. One noticeable species is the huge **bird's nest fern** (*Asplenium nidus*), which adorns most of the large trunks with luxuriant balconies of leaves. The ancient **tree-ferns** (*Cyathea* spp), that once supplied the forest canopy, are still present on its floor, contributing to the prehistoric atmosphere of the forest. Many other species inhabit the shady world among the tree roots or swell the foliage at riverbanks. In all, the diversity and delicacy of the ferns much enhance the rainforest experience.

Often mistaken for a tree-fern, the **cycad** (*Cycas* spp), is significantly different.

THE EXTINCT MEGAFAUNA

Today, Madagascar's wildlife is as rich as anywhere on Earth. The tragedy is that it was once richer still. When, just 2,000 years ago, humans arrived they found a world covered with forests and populated by huge tortoises, dwarf hippos, lemurs the size of gorillas and the 'elephant bird' which, at three metres high, made an ostrich look like a goose. All are now extinct, possibly as a result of both direct hunting and indirect effects such as competition with humans for food, habitat or space. It is no accident that these animals represent what, at the time, would have been the 'biggest ones' on the island – the *megafauna*. Large animals are not only more worthwhile prey for humans, but they are also more impinged by human activities for they have higher demands on the environment.

The 16 or so species of lemur that became extinct were all larger than the present title-holders – the indri and diademed sifaka. Some species hung like a sloth from branches, while others browsed on the forest floor. The elephant bird, or *Aepyornis*, was not one species but several, one of which, *A. maximus*, weighing over 300kg, may have been the largest bird that has ever lived. Recent finds reveal that the birds only became extinct a few hundred years ago. Indeed tales of '*vorombe*', or big bird, are still fresh in Malagasy folklore. Such tales may have filtered through to Marco Polo who wrote of the giant *roc* able to lift an elephant, on the island south of Zanzibar.

The roc as visualised by an artist in 1598

It is one of the original seed-bearing plants which marked the end of the ferns' dominance on Earth. Its innovation, leading eventually to the evolution of the flowering plants which currently command all of the world's habitats. Ironically, cycads are much more unusual today than their fern predecessors. Resembling a tree-fern with palm-like leaves, the single Malagasy representative of the genus *Cycas* is found only in the eastern rainforest. If seen, it is worth a close look. The cone that it bears holds seeds which, 300 million years ago, became the most significant single plant adaptation in Earth's history.

Palms

Madagascar is home to one of the world's richest palm floras. There are around 170 species, three times more than in the rest of Africa put together, and of these

SCIENTIFIC CLASSIFICATION

Since many animals and plants in Madagascar have yet to be given English names, I have made much use of the Latin or scientific name. For those not familiar with these and the associated terminology, here is a brief guide:

Having been separated into broad **classes** like mammals (*mammalia*), angiosperms (*angiospermae*) – flowering plants – etc, animals and plants are narrowed down into an **order**, such as Primates or Monocotyledons. The next division is **family**: Lemur (*Lemuridae*) and Orchid (*Orchidaceae*) continue the examples above. These are the general names that everyone knows, and you are quite safe to say 'in the lemur family' or 'a type of orchid'. There are also subfamilies, such as the 'true lemurs' and 'the indri subfamily' which includes sifakas. Then come **genera** (**genus** in singular) followed by species, and the Latin names here will be less familiar-sounding. It is these two names that are combined in the scientific name precisely to identify the animal or plant. So *Lemur catta* and *Angraecum sesquipedale* will be recognisable whatever the nationality of the person you are talking to. We call them ring-tailed lemur and comet orchid; the French say *maki* and *orchidée comète*. With a scientific name up your sleeve there is no confusion.

165 are found nowhere else. Experts claim that this diversity is evidence that south Gondwanaland was rich in palms at about the time the island was created. The dominance of species with Asian relatives betrays the fact that Madagascar severed with India millions of years after it left Africa's shores.

The species present range from the famous to the recently discovered, from dwarf to giant, and almost all have intriguing characteristics. One palm has led to a Malagasy word entering our language – the **raffia palm** (*Raphia ruffia*). The fibres from its leaves are woven into the hats, baskets and mats that characterise the Malagasy. Of the 50 new palm species discovered in the last decade, one is worth particular attention – *Ravenea musicalis*, the world's only 'water palm'. It starts life actually underwater in only one of Madagascar's rivers. As it grows it surfaces, eventually bears fruit, and then seeds. Its discoverer named it *R. musicalis* after being charmed by the chimes of its seed pods as they hit the water below. There are other riverside palms in Madagascar adapted to tolerate the recurrent floods of the island's lowland rainforest, but none as perfectly as the musical water palm.

One other unusual group is named the **'litter-trapping palms'**. The crown of their leaves is arranged like an upturned shuttlecock, sprouting at first from the forest floor, and then gaining height as the stem grows from below. Its watertight crown catches leaves falling from the canopy, perhaps to obtain trace minerals, but no one really knows. A strange consequence of this growth is that the roots of other plants, which originally grew through the soil into the crown by mistake, later dangle down from its heights as alabaster-white zigzags.

Although the vast majority of palms live among the hardwoods of the lowland rainforest, there are species which brave the more arid environments, notably the **feather palms** (*Chrysalidocarpus* spp), which nestle in the canyons of Isalo National Park and stand alone amongst the secondary grasslands of the west. An extremely rare and unusual palm, *Ravenea xerophila*, is even to be found within the semidesert of the spiny forest.

A distinct lack of large herbivores in Madagascar has left its palms spineless and without poisons. Pollination is mostly by bees and flies, but some species have tiny flowers to entice unknown insect guests. For seed dispersal lemurs are often employed. The ring-tailed, black, red-ruffed and the browns all assist in scattering the seeds. The bright colours of some fruits serve to attract birds and forest pigs. While the few African palms, which normally use elephants as dispersers, presumably make do with zebu.

Looking like a messy cross between a palm and a pine tree, **pandan palms**, or screw pines (*Pandanus* spp), are different from those above, but equally fond of Madagascar. Their foliage consists of untidy grass-like mops which awkwardly adorn rough branches periodically emerging from their straight trunks. Common in both rain and dry forests, there are 75 species, only one of which is found elsewhere, placing the country alongside Borneo in the pandan diversity stakes.

Trees

Until the arrival of humans, Madagascar was almost entirely cloaked in forest. There remain examples of each of the original forests, but vast areas of Madagascar have become treeless as a result of *tavy* (slash and burn) agriculture and soil erosion. Most of the **evergreen trees** remaining form the superstructure of the rainforest. They are normally 30m high, with buttressed roots, solid hardwood trunks and vast canopies. There can be up to 250 species of trees per hectare in the lowland rainforest, but from the ground they all look very similar. To identify a species, botanists must often wait for flowering, an event that is not only extremely difficult to predict, but also one that takes place 30m above the ground. One obvious tree is the **strangler fig** (*Ficus* spp), which germinates up in the canopy on a branch of its victim, grows down to the floor to root, and then encircles and constricts its host leaving a hollow knotted trunk. The Malagasy prize the forest hardwoods; one canopy tree is called the 'kingswood' because its wood is so hard that, at one time, any specimens were automatically the property of the local king for use as a staff.

The only evergreen species to be found outside the rainforest are the **tapia tree** (*Uapaca bojei*), the nine species of **mangrove tree** and some of the **succulent trees** to be found in the extreme southwest where sea mists provide water year-round. In tolerating the conditions of west Madagascar, these evergreens have borne their own unusual communities.

The rest of Madagascar's trees are **deciduous**, that is they lose their leaves during the dry season. The largest dry forests of the west are dappled with the shadows of **leguminous trees** such as *Dalbergia* and *Cassia*, characterised by their long seed pods and symbiotic relationships with bacteria which provide fertilisers within their roots. Sprawling **banyan figs** (*Ficus* spp), and huge **tamarind trees** (*Tamarindus indica*), create gallery forest along the rivers of the west and south, yielding pungent fruit popular with lemurs. Where the soil is rich in lime, Madagascar's most celebrated trees, the **baobabs** (*Adansonia* spp), dominate. Madagascar is truly the home of baobabs. Of the eight species on Earth, seven are found here and six of these are found nowhere else. Characterised by their massive, swollen, succulent trunks, smooth reddish-grey bark and trunk-top frenzy of splayed branches, they help to form some of the most memorable landscapes in Madagascar. Largely immune to fires, and too huge to uproot, magnificent, ancient specimens dot the grasslands of the dry west and sometimes form dramatic avenues, such as those near Morondava. In the southwest, where it is drier still, they join the resident *Didierea* and other succulent trees (see below) to create one of the most unusual forests on earth.

The western Malagasy have many baobab legends, stemming from their close relationship with the trees. They use the bark fibre to make rope, cloth, waterproof hats and even strings for their musical instruments. They use the wood pulp to

TAVY
Jamie Spencer

Slash and burn farming, or in Malagasy *tavy*, is blamed for the permanent destruction of the rainforest. Those practising *tavy* agree with this. They also respect this forest and they can see that *tavy* greatly jeopardises the future for the next generations. So why destroy what you love and need?

One answer to a very complex question is the practical need. The poverty is extreme and there are few options. Life's priority is to feed your family and children. Rice, the food staple, is grown both on the flat ground in sustainable paddy fields, and on the steep slopes of slashed and burned forest. The last cyclone washed away much of the paddy rice crop and wiped out the earth dams and irrigation waterways built at great cost and effort. Some farmers had recently invested a lifetime's savings employing labour for their construction. So if floods strike, people rely on the hill rice. Fertility in these fields is not replenished as in paddies where nutrients are carried in the water. The soil quickly becomes unproductive so new slopes must be cut after a few years.

The cultural explanation for *tavy* is less obvious. The people of Sandrakely are Tanala, meaning 'people of the forest'. The forest is their world and to survive in this surprisingly harsh environment they clear the land with fire – the ancient agricultural technique brought by the original immigrants from Indonesia perhaps 2,000 years ago. In more recent history the Tanala were forced into the forest by warring neighbours and colonial occupants of more fertile areas.

As the traditional means of survival and provision *tavy* can be seen as central to society's make-up and culture. The calendar revolves around it, land ownership and hierarchies are determined by its practice, and politics is centred on it. It is the pivot and subject of rituals and ceremonies. The forest is the domain of the ancestors and site of tombs and religious standing stones. *Tavy* is an activity carried out between the living and the dead: the ancestors are consulted and permit its execution to provide for the living. The word *tavy* also means 'fatness', with all the associations of health, wealth and beauty.

If they have the choice, many people are happy to pursue the sustainable kind of agriculture so Feedback is ready to help them. But the practical and cultural context must always be respected. The new alternatives must be rock solid when people's lives are at stake and to be truly enduring they must be accommodated within the culture by the people themselves. It is they who understand the problems and know the solutions that are acceptable. They must not be forced.

Jamie Spencer runs the charity Feedback Madagascar; see pages 128–9

make paper. The fresh leaves provide medicines, and their seeds are a source of protein, oil and vitamin C. Perfect for food on long journeys because, harboured in an outer case, the pulp does not rot, baobab seeds were carried for centuries by ocean-going Arab traders who visited the island. Closer to home, many villages have a treasured baobab growing in the central square. A famous 700-year-old tree is rooted in the middle of Mahajanga.

One last species deserves a mention. The **traveller's tree** (*Ravenala madagascariensis*) is one of Madagascar's most spectacular plants. It earns its name from the relief it affords a thirsty traveller: water is stored in the base of its leaves and can be released with a swift blow. A relation of the banana, its elegant fronds are arranged in a dramatic vertical fan, which is decorative enough to have earned it a role as Air Madagascar's symbol. Its large, bulbous flowers sprout from the leaf axils and, during the 24 hours that they are receptive, are visited by unusual pollinators – ruffed lemurs. The lemurs locate flowers which have just opened, and literally pull them apart to get at the large nectary inside. Keeping a lemur fed is quite a demand on the tree, but it produces flowers day after day for several months, and during this time, the lemurs eat little else. The traveller's tree is perhaps the only native species to have benefited from *tavy* agriculture, for it dominates areas of secondary vegetation on the central plateau and east coast.

Orchids

Adaptive radiation is once again in evidence within the orchid family. There are over 1,000 species of orchids on the island, far more than in the whole of Africa. The vast majority live as epiphytes in the eastern rainforests. Perched high up on the substantial branches of the canopy trees, they reap the benefits of high sunlight intensities and the plethora of insect pollinators. Their variety is spectacular. Although the leathery green foliage is relatively constant between species, the flowers are unique. All colours, patterns, shapes and sizes, they display lavish cascades, distilling sweet, heady perfume into the forest air in order to entice eager insects, whose physiques and lifestyles are a perfect match for the structure and development of the flowers.

Dependent on each other, the flower-pollinator partnership becomes more exclusive with time. This way the pollen from a flower is more likely to end up on another flower of the same species, and the pollinator gets its own private food supply. Realising this, Darwin took little time, when presented with Madagascar's white comet orchid (*Angraecum sesquipedale*), with its staggering 30cm long nectary, in declaring that there must be a Malagasy moth with an equally long tongue to get at the syrup inside. Sure enough a well-endowed hawkmoth has since been discovered and named *X. m. praedicta* in honour of Darwin's foresight. When tied in to such a relationship, it is essential that the two species synchronise their life cycles as completely as they do their physiques. The flowering of each orchid species is timed to coincide with the adulthood of its pollinator. Species catering for nocturnal moths generally have white flowers, which catch the moonlight guaranteed to be in place by the rhythm of the moth's life cycle. Those that entice daytime insects are more liberal in their colours.

Not all the island's orchids are epiphytic. In montane rainforest, many orchids live terrestrial lives as underground tubers which bring forth deciduous leaves and flower stems. Those with what look like bulbs at their bases are **Bulbophyllum**; they often hide flowers within their foliage. Others grow on damp rocks or cliffs, largely missed unless in flower, and above the tree line on the highest peaks, hardy orchids share the rock faces with succulents. There is even one rainforest species which, cast into the dark world of the forest floor, has abandoned photosynthesis altogether and instead joins forces with a fungus to gain sustenance. However, the most specialised orchids in Madagascar, and possibly the world, are rare epiphytes that live upon succulent trees in the dry southwest. In order to save water, their leaves have vanished, and instead green roots have taken on the job of harvesting the sun's rays.

It is important to stress that orchids should not be collected from the wild or bought from street traders. Their export is tightly controlled, and in many cases prohibited.

XEROPHYTES AND SUCCULENTS – PLANTS IN DRY HABITATS

Unlike animals, plants cannot escape harsh environments. The plants of Madagascar's dry southwest have therefore adapted to tolerate strong sunlight, high temperatures and most restricting of all, desiccation. Here, as elsewhere in the world, these high demands have produced unusual-looking, but fascinating, plant species called xerophytes.

All xerophytes have deep root systems to acquire what little water there is available. Their leaves are usually small and covered in hairs, and much of the photosynthesis is done by the green stems. This design lowers the surface area of the plant and traps still air adjacent to the leaf, reducing water loss – the key aim. In addition to desiccation, overheating is as much a problem for plants as it is animals. Many xerophytes are therefore orientated to minimise heating, usually having their narrowest edge facing the sun, and they often add grey pigments to their leaves to deflect the intense light of midday.

The most extreme adaptations for a dry life are to be seen in the succulents. This general term describes all xerophytes which store water in their waxy leaves, roots or stems. Such water is a valuable commodity in a dry habitat, and one that must be protected from thirsty grazers. Succulents usually employ toxins, or spines, and this need for defence has given rise to the most spectacular plants on the island – the didierea 'trees' of the spiny forest.

Pitcher plants

There are only two species of pitcher plant (*Nepenthes* spp) on Madagascar, but they are spectacular enough to deserve a mention. In wetlands in the south, they poke out of the marsh beds like triffids planning an ambush. One of their leaves wraps upon itself to create a fly trap, which then serves up trace elements, from the flies' remains, unobtainable from the mud below. The rest of the family live thousands of miles away in Southeast Asia, and it is thought that the arrival of these two species stemmed from a fortuitous migration along the same path that originally brought the Malagasy – perhaps they inadvertently shared the boats!

Succulents

In Madagascar, wherever rainfall is below about 400mm a year, succulents reign. The entire southwest of the island is dominated by their swollen forms. Further north they decorate the natural rock gardens of Isalo, Itremo and the countless outcrops on the central plateau. They also appear within the sparse dry forests of the west, among the stone chaos of the *tsingy*, and even venture on to the grasslands and into the rainforests.

The **euphorbias** are the most widespread group. They have diversified into a thousand different forms, from bushes resembling strings of sausages, to trees sprouting smooth green branches, but few leaves, to spiny stalks emerging from an underground swollen tuber. Many species shed their leaves at the start of the dry season, but when present they are swollen with water, and shining with wax. To replace the leaves they often yield wonderful flowers and, in so doing, brighten up the landscape. Another succulent group, the **pachypodia**, is perhaps even more unusual. They are stem succulents with sometimes grotesquely swollen bodies, so that the tallest look like short, fat trees sprouting at their tips, whereas the smaller species resemble grey bottles sprouting either stubby leaves or flowers, depending on the season. **Aloes**, **kalanchoes** and **senecios** are leaf succulents, existing essentially as a collection of swollen leaves sprouting from the earth. The leaves are often ornamental, tinged with terracotta and bearing harsh spines, but also showy red flowers during the drought. Some species do have stems to raise their broad foliage above the ground. The largest aloes have stocky 3m stems covered in untidy dead scales which sport the huge succulent leaves and, in June and July, a large, red inflorescence. Other succulents in Madagascar include *Adenia*, which looks even more rock-like than the pachypodia, swollen, straggling milkweed and succulent relatives of the cucumber family with disc-shaped leaves.

ETHNOBOTANY IN MADAGASCAR

Ethnobotany is the study of the traditional knowledge and uses of plants by local peoples, for example for food, medicines, fibre.

Already mentioned in this book (page 36–7) are some of the many uses for various parts of the baobabs. The wealth of palm species on the island are equally valuable, providing wood and thatch for house construction, and leaf fibre for basketry, hat-making and raffia cloth. Some have edible palm-hearts and fruit, and other uses such as for medicine, irrigation pipes, brooms, blowpipes, etc.

Most Malagasy today still rely to some extent on wild-harvested plants for their medicines. However, with increasing deforestation, urbanisation and an aspiration to Western values, many are now turning to modern drugs which they can ill afford, and which are often inappropriately prescribed by street vendors. Meanwhile much of the traditional plant lore is in danger of being lost. Since ethnobotanists have a joint interest in both the people and the plants that they study, they are well-placed to apply their research to help meet the needs of local communities through education, healthcare and marketing in a way which promotes conservation of the plants and their habitats. Among the ethnobotanical projects now under way in Madagascar are:

The Manangarivo Project WWF-funded healthcare service, using a combination of traditional and Western medicine to treat disease, and to evaluate the efficiency of this treatment. Contact WWF, BP 8511, Antananarivo.

Masoala Project Ethnobotanical studies taking place in conjunction with the establishment of the new National Park. Contact Philip Gallery, Wildlife Conservation Society, BP 27, Antalaha 206.

Ankaranfantsika Project An ethnobotanical inventory of the Strict Nature Reserve, funded by Conservation International; BP 5178 Antananarivo.

Projet Renala Working, in association with the Royal Botanic Gardens (Kew), with the Mikea people of the southwest. Among the plans are a mobile, integrated healthcare service and various local conservation initiatives. Contact Jim Bond, Manguzi Hospital, P/Bag X301, KwaNgwanase, 3973 South Africa.

Didierea

To botanists the **Didiereaceae** of the arid southwest are the most intriguing plants in Madagascar, for they are an entire family of bizarre plants found nowhere else on Earth. The common name of one species, the octopus tree, gives some indication of their eccentricities. They look similar to some forms of cacti and they are often quoted as examples of *convergent evolution* – where two separate groups of organisms have adapted similar features to cope with a similar environment. However they do differ from typical cacti in that they do not have green swollen stems, but instead bear small, deciduous leaves, protected by immense thorns, on grey, wooded branches. A number of these spiny branches sprout from near the base of each plant and soar unsteadily into the sky, so that the entire structure has an unkempt and uninviting appearance from afar. In various guises, these magnificent didierea join the succulent trees to create the unworldly landscape of the spiny forest in the southwest.

At first sight the mass of thorns and branches confuses the eye, let alone identification, but if you want to name a species try to recognise individual silhouettes, and look for the following features:

- **Didierea madagascariensis**, the octopus tree – most abundant between Morondava and Toliara (Tuléar), the erratic branches of this tree, which sprout from close to the base, are covered with very long thorns and in the wet season long thin leaves, giving it a fuzzy appearance.
- **Didierea trolli** – when adult they are similar to *D. madagascariensis*, but are distinguished when younger by having lateral branches at the base of the stem, which creep over the ground keeping browsing animals at a distance.
- **Decaryia madagascariensis**, the zigzag plant – found between Ampanihy and Ambovombe, it has a complex crown of thorny, zigzagging branches and produces small, white flowers.
- **Alluaudiopsis fiherenensis** – found north of Toliara (Tuléar), it is bushy but short (up to 2m) and sprouts yellow-white flowers.
- **Alluaudia procera** – this is the most abundant of the trees in much of the spiny forest. When young it is little more than a mesh of wild, extremely thorny bush. However, when closer to its maximum height of 15m, it takes on a more regal appearance with a single trunk crowned by a series of substantial branches. Its leaves sprout in curious lines which spiral up the branches during the wet season to be shed at the start of the dry. Thorns patrol the leaves on each side and hence themselves form further spirals. Tiny flowers sometimes adorn tufts on the tips of the branches.
- **Alluaudia ascendens** – Up to 20m tall this tree shares the skies with *A. procera*. A solitary woody trunk divides into a series of long slim, skyward branches, hence the Latin name. Even when juvenile the single stem is present with its spiralling thorns.
- **Alluaudia montagnacii** – only found near Itampolo, it has few leaning branches, covered in spirals of thorns and finishing in bouquets of leaves and flowers. The fact that they look like a cross between *A. procera* and *A. ascendens* has led some to suggest that they are nothing more than hybrids.
- **Alluaudia comosa** – common along the road from Toliara (Tuléar) to Andranavory, these trees resemble very thorny, squat acacia, their dark crowns often formed into an anvil shape.
- **Alluaudia dumosa** – grows between Ampanihy and Fort Dauphin. It has a woody trunk with few leaves and even fewer spines. The diverging greyish-brown branches above the main trunk carry out most of the photosynthesis. The flowers are white with red stigmas.

Foreigners

In common with many islands around the globe, Madagascar has suffered from accidental or intended introductions of 'alien' species. Referred to as 'weedy' species, these are the botanical equivalents of cats and rats – species that should not really be there, but that cause havoc when they arrive. Out-competing native species, sharp tropical grasses from South America permanently deface the burnt woodlands of the west and, avoided by cattle, their populations explode. Where thick forest is cleared, fast-growing *Eucalyptus* and *Psidium* trees step in. They either suffocate competitors with their dense growth, or poison the soil with their toxins. In drier areas, superbly adapted and profoundly damaging cacti spread from the nearby sisal plantations and flourish where there was once spiny forest. Needless to say, the native animal populations, unable to adapt to these invaders, also suffer, and this, perhaps more than the endangerment of plant species, has prompted action from conservation bodies.

The value of the flora

Many Malagasy plants crop up in garden centres throughout Europe. Familiar to horticulturalists are the dragon tree (*Dracaena marginata*), the crown of thorns (*Euphorbia millii*), the *Areca* palm, the flamboyant tree (*Delonix regia*) and the Madagascar jasmine (*Stephanotis floribunda*) of bridal bouquet fame. Other natives are valued for their uses rather than their aesthetic qualities. Recent interest has grown in Madagascar's various wild coffees, *Rubiaceae*. Many are naturally decaffeinated and hybrids with tastier coffees are currently being produced. More seriously, the rosy periwinkle (*Catharanthus roseus*) is a champion of those who campaign to conserve natural habitats. It contains two alkaloid chemicals proven to assist treatment of leukaemia and other cancers in children. There may well be other plants in a position to offer equally useful products, but the rate of forest destruction may be extinguishing these before we have a chance to appreciate them. Slowly we are learning that there is great value in diversity alone.

Fauna

Compared with the breathtaking ecosystems of mainland Africa, Madagascar's fauna has far more subtle qualities. A combination of ancient Gondwanaland stock and the descendants of the last 165 million years' wayfarers, it is more intriguing than dynamic. Here are a seemingly random collection of animal groups that had the opportunity to prove themselves in the absence of big predators and herbivores. The resulting 180,000 species existing in habitats from rainforests to coral reefs bring human opportunity too, for dozens of truly unique safaris.

Invertebrates

There are well over 150,000 species of invertebrate on Madagascar, the majority in the eastern rainforests. To spot them turn over leaves and logs on the forest floor, peer very closely at the foliage or switch on a bright light after dark. Although creepy, let alone crawly, they do contribute substantially to the experience of wild areas on the island and, providing you can suppress the spine shivers, your mini-safaris will be well worthwhile.

It is a difficult task to pick out the most impressive invertebrates, but notable are the huge **Golden orb-web spiders** (*Nephila madagascariensis*), which gather on telephone lines in all the towns. Their silk is so strong that it was once used as a textile – Queen Victoria even had a pair of Nephila silk stockings! Equally

LEECHES
Hilary Bradt

Few classes of invertebrates elicit more disgust than leeches. Perhaps some facts about these extraordinarily well-adapted animals will give them more appeal.

Terrestrial leeches such as those found in Madagascar are small (1–2cm long) and find their warm-blooded prey by vibrations and odour. Suckers at each end enable the leech to move around in a series of loops and to attach itself to a leaf by its posterior while seeking its meal with the front end. It has sharp jaws and can quickly – and painlessly – bite through the skin and start feeding. When it has filled its digestive tract with blood the leech drops off and digests its meal. This process can take several months since leeches have pouches all along their gut to hold as much blood as possible – up to ten times their own weight. The salivary glands manufacture an anticoagulant which prevents the blood clotting during the meal or period of digestion. This is why leech wounds bleed so spectacularly. Leeches also inject an anaesthetic which is why you don't feel them biting.

Leeches are hermaphrodite but still have pretty exciting sex lives. To consummate their union they need to exchange packets of sperm. This is done either the conventional way via a leechy penis or by injection, allowing the sperm to make its way through the body tissues to find and fertilise the eggs.

Readers who are disappointed with the small size of Malagasy leeches will be interested to hear that an expedition to French Guiana in the 1970s discovered the world's largest leech: at full stretch 45cm long!

oversized are the **pill millipedes** (*Sphaerotherium* spp) which roll up when startled to resemble a striped, brown golf ball. Among the forest foliage are superbly camouflaged **praying mantis**, **net-throwing spiders**, which cast their silk nets at fliers-by, and nymphs and bugs of all shapes, colours and adornments. Among the leaf litter there are spectacular, striped **flatworms** and vast numbers of wonderful **weevils**.

The 300 species of **butterfly** are all descendants of African voyagers. The most visible are the heavily-patterned swallowtails, and the nymphalids with their dominant blue and orange liveries. Madagascar's **moths** are significantly older in origin and are probably descendants of the Gondwanaland insects marooned on the island. This explains the diversity in place – there are 4,000 species, and many groups are active in the daylight, filling niches that elsewhere are currently the realm of butterflies. Most dramatic is the huge, yellow comet moth (*Argema mittrei*), which has a wingspan of up to 25cm, and the elaborate urania moths (*Chrysiridia*), which look just like swallowtails decorated with emeralds. A very close relative is found in the Amazon rainforest.

Fish

The inhabitants of Madagascar's abundant lakes, marshes, estuaries, rivers and mountain brooks have been as much isolated by history as those of the land. The most interesting species are the **cichlids**, with their huge variety, colourful coats and endearing habits of childcare – they protect their young by offering their mouths as a retreat in times of danger. Other Malagasy species demonstrate the parental instinct, a feature rare in fish. Some of the island's **catfish** also mouth-brood and male **mudskippers** in the mangroves defend their nest burrows with the vigour of a proud father.

Another major group is the **killifish**, which resemble the gouramis to be found in pet shops. Specialised **eels** live high up in mountain brooks, and in the underground rivers of west Madagascar blind **cave fish** live, sometimes entirely on the rich pickings of bat guano. The one problem with the island's fish is that they are not big and tasty. Consequently many exotic species have been introduced into the rivers and are regularly on display in the nation's markets. These new species naturally put pressure on the native stock and, as is often the story, the less-vigorous Malagasy species seem to be on the retreat.

More robust are the marine species to be found swimming off the island's 4,000km of coastline. Madagascar is legendary for its **shark** populations and a quick dip off the east coast should be considered carefully, but on the west coast there are **coral reefs** bursting with life, outdoing even the Red Sea for fish diversity. The reefs are host to a typical Indo-Pacific community of clownfish, angelfish, butterflyfish, damselfish, tangs and surgeons, triggerfish, wrasse, groupers, batfish, blennies and gobies, boxfish, lionfish, moray eels, flutefish, porcupinefish, pufferfish, squirrelfish, sweetlips and the Moorish Idol.

CHAMELEONS
Hilary Bradt

Everybody thinks they know one thing about chameleons: that they change colour to match their background. Wrong! You have only to observe the striking *Calumma parsonii*, commonly seen at Périnet, staying stubbornly green while transferred from boy's hand to tree trunk to leafy branch, to see that in some species this is a myth. Most chameleons are cryptically coloured to match their preferred resting place (there are branch-coloured chameleons, for instance, and leaf-coloured ones) and some do respond to a change of background, but their abilities are mainly reserved for expressing emotion. An anxious chameleon will darken and grow stripes and an angry chameleon, faced with a territorial intruder, will change his colours dramatically. The most impressive displays, however, are reserved for sexual encounters. Chameleons say it with colours. Enthusiastic males explode into a riot of spots, stripes and contrasting colours, whilst the female usually responds by donning a black cloak of disapproval. Only on the rare occasions that she is feeling receptive will she present a brighter appearance.

Chameleons use body language more than colour to deter enemies. If you spot a chameleon on a branch you will note that his first reaction to being seen is to put the branch between you and him and flatten his body laterally so that he is barely visible. If you try to catch him, he will blow himself up, expand his throat, raise his helmet (if he has one) and hiss. His next action will be to either bite, jump, or try to run away. Fortunately they must be the slowest of all lizards, are easily caught, and pose for the camera with gloomy resignation (who can resist an animal that has a constantly down-turned mouth like a Victorian headmistress?). This slowness is another aspect of the chameleon's defence: when he walks, he moves like a leaf in the wind. This is fine when the danger is an animal predator, but less effective when it is a car. In a tree, his best protection is to keep completely still. He can do this by having feet shaped like pliers and a prehensile tail so he can effortlessly grasp a branch, and eyes shaped

Frogs

The only amphibians on Madagascar are frogs. Newts, salamanders and toads are absent, but the frog abundance more than makes up for these omissions. On average a new species of Malagasy frog is discovered every eight weeks. There are currently 170 catalogued species, but the actual number may be closer to 300 and all but two of these are endemic.

Most of the species, restricted by their permeable skins, spend their lives in the humid forests of the east. With their bulbous finger tips, which help them to grip on to the waxy forest leaves, large brightly-coloured eyes and loud whistles, the **tree frogs** are appealing to most visitors. They either return to small streams to breed, hang their egg batches from overhanging branches (a habit which demands high-dive routines from the tadpoles), or abandon the waterways altogether to raise their young in the miniature pools among pandan leaves or between the epiphytes of the canopy. Closer to the forest floor there are other, more brightly-coloured frogs, such as the large, blushing **tomato frog** (*Dyscophus antongili*) and the magnificent miniature *Mantella* species, which resemble the famed poison arrow frogs from the Amazon in that they display their toxic inners with lurid coats of black, gold and blue.

Away from the mature forest, frogs congregate around fast-flowing mountain streams littered with mossy rocks, alongside the sticky marshes that house pitcher

like gun-turrets which can swivel 180 degrees independently of each other, enabling him to view the world from front and back without moving his head. This is the chameleon's true camouflage.

The family *Chamaeleonidae* is represented by three genera, the 'true chameleons' *Calumma* and *Furcifer*, and the little stump-tailed chameleons, *Brookesia*. Unlike the true chameleons, the *Brookesia's* short tail is not prehensile.

In chameleons there is often a striking colour difference between males and females. Many males have horns (occasionally used for fighting) or other nasal protruberances. Where the two sexes look the same you can recognise the male by the bulge of the scrotal sac beneath the tail, and a spur on the hind feet.

It is interesting to know how the chameleon achieves its colour change. It has a transparent epidermis, then three layers of cells – the top ones are yellow and red, the middle layer reflects blue light and white light, and the bottom layer consists of black pigment cells with tentacles or fingers that can protrude up through the other layers. The cells are under control of the autonomic nervous system, expanding and contracting according to a range of stimuli. Change of colour occurs when one layer is more stimulated than others, and patterning when one group of cells receives maximum stimulation.

In the early 17th century there was the firm conviction that chameleons subsisted without food. A German author, describing Madagascar in 1609, mentions the chameleon living 'entirely on air and dew' and Shakespeare refers several times to the chameleon's supposed diet: 'The chameleon ... can feed on air' (*Two Gentlemen of Verona*) and 'of the chameleon's dish: I eat the air promise-crammed' (*Hamlet*). Possibly at that time no-one had witnessed the tongue flash out in a quarter of a second to trap an insect.

The name apparently comes from Greek: *chamai leon*, dwarf lion. I suppose a hissing, open-mouthed reptile *could* remind one of a lion, but to most visitors to Madagascar they are one of the most appealing and bizarre of the 'strange and marvellous forms' on show.

plants and even in the drier Hauts Plateaux and Isalo regions where they rumble through the floor litter defying dehydration.

Reptiles

The unique evolutionary history of Madagascar is particularly evidenced by the reptiles on the island. There are scattered species derived from ancient Gondwanaland stock, many of which are more closely related to South American or Asian reptiles than to African. There are also large groups of closely related species marking the radiations that stemmed from African immigrations in more recent times. The most dramatic example of the latter concerns chameleons. Madagascar is home to about half the world's chameleon species including the smallest and the largest. With impressive adaptive dexterity, they have dispersed throughout the habitats of the island to occupy every conceivable niche (see box, pages 44–5).

Similar in their success have been the **geckoes**. The 70-odd gecko species seem to be split between those that make every effort imaginable to camouflage themselves and those that are quite happy to stick out like a sore thumb. The spectacular **day gecko** (*Phelsuma madagascariensis*) and its relatives can be seen by passing motorists from some distance. Their dazzling emerald coats emblazoned with day-glo orange splashes are intended for the attentions of the opposite sex and competitors. Once in their sights they bob their heads and wave their tails as if an extra guarantee of visibility is needed. In contrast a magnificently-camouflaged **leaf-tailed gecko** (*Uroplatus* spp) could easily be next to your hand on a tree trunk without you noticing it. With its flattened body, splayed tail, speckled eyes, colour-change tactics and complete lack of shadow, you may remain ignorant until, nervous, it gapes a large, red tongue in your direction.

A quiet scuttle on the floor of a western forest may well be a **skink**, while louder ramblings could be due to one of the handsome **plated lizards**. However, the most significant disturbances, both in the forest and the academic world, are made by the **iguanids**. This group of large lizards is primarily found in the Americas, and never in Africa. Hence its presence on Madagascar is a sign that its ancestors were members of the original party that separated from Africa.

Madagascar's three **boas** are in the same boat. They only exist as fossils in Africa, supplanted by the more stealthy pythons, but they do have distant relatives in South America. Most often seen is the Madagascar tree boa (*Sanzinia madagascariensis*), which although decorated in the same marbled glaze, varies in colour from orange (when juvenile) to grey and black, brilliant green or brown and blue, depending on the location. Its larger relative the ground boa (*Acrantophis madagascariensis*) is also often spied at the edge of waterways in the humid east and north. Of the remaining species of snake, the one-metre long **hog-nosed snake** (*Leioheterodon madagascariensis*), in its dazzling checkerboard of black and yellow, is most frequently encountered, usually gliding across a carpet of leaves on the lookout for frogs.

Despite the fact that none of the island's snakes are a danger to humans, the Malagasy are particularly wary of some species. The blood-red tail of one harmless tree snake (*Ithycyphus perineti*), known to the Malagasy as the '*fandrefiala*', is believed to have powers of possession. It apparently hypnotises cattle from up high, then drops down tail-first to impale its victim. Similar paranormal attributes are bestowed on other Malagasy reptiles. The chameleons, for example, are generally feared by the Malagasy, and when fascinated *vazaha* go to pick one up, there is often a bout of surprised gasps from the locals. Another reptile deeply embedded in the folklore is the **Nile crocodile** (*Crocodilus niloticus*) which, although threatened throughout the island, takes on spiritual roles in some areas (see Lac Antanavo).

A number of Madagascar's **tortoises** are severely threatened with extinction. Captive breeding programmes at Ampijoroa are currently successfully rearing the ploughshare (*Geochelone yniphora*) and flat-tailed tortoises (*Pyxis planicauda*) and further south, the Beza-Mahafaly reserve is protecting the handsome radiated tortoise (*Geochelone radiata*). **Terrapins** are common in the western waterways, and beyond in the Mozambique Channel, there are several **turtles** which periodically risk the pot as they visit their nesting beaches.

Birds

Madagascar's score sheet of resident birds is surprisingly short. There are only about 270 species of birds on the island. However, of these, 110 species are endemic, there are five endemic families, and 36 endemic genera – rendering Madagascar the hot-spot for bird endemism in Africa.

The key endemics include the three extremely rare **mesites** – the brown mesite (*Mesitornis unicolor*) in the rainforests, the white-breasted mesite (*Mesitornis variegata*) in the western dry forests and the subdesert mesite (*Monias benschi*) in the south's spiny forest. A similar allocation of habitats is more generously employed by the nine species of **couas** which lighten up forests from Masoala to Toliara (Tuléar) with their blue-masked faces. Six species are ground-dwellers, occupying the roles filled elsewhere by pheasants and roadrunners. Much harder to see are the **ground-rollers**, which patrol the rainforest floors in their pretty uniforms. One rebellious member of the family, the long-tailed ground-roller (*Uratelornis chimaera*), has left the forest for the challenge of living among the didierea in the southwest. More restricted in range are the **sunbird asities** (*Neodrepanis* spp) which appear as flashes of blue and green in the canopies of montane rainforests, their down-turned beaks designed for the nectaries of canopy flowers.

Yet, beak variation is more the domain of Madagascar's most celebrated endemic family – the **vangas**. All 15 member species have perfected their own craft of insect capture, filling the niches of various absent African birds, so that, physically, they are very dissimilar. They often flock together, or with other Malagasy birds, presenting a formidable offensive for the local insects. The most prominent is the sickle-billed vanga (*Falculea pallinata*) which parallels the tree-probing habits of African woodhoopoes. The heavy carnivorous diet of the shrikes is adopted here by the hook-billed vanga (*Vanga curvirostris*), while the dramatic, blue-billed helmet vanga (*Euryceros prevostii*) resembles a small hornbill. Other species mimic nuthatches, treecreepers and tits. In short, if *The Beagle* had been caught by the West Wind Drift and Darwin had arrived in Madagascar instead of the Galapagos, the vangas would certainly have ensured that his train of thought went uninterrupted.

Malagasy representatives of families found elsewhere make up the bulk of the remaining birdlife. Herons, coots, grebes and ducks take up their usual positions in the wetlands alongside endemics such as the Madagascar teal (*Anas bernieri*) and the Madagascar malachite kingfisher (*Alcedo vintsioides*). In the forests and open scrub small game birds, the impressive crested ibis (*Lophotibis cristata*), doves and the drab but tuneful vasa parrots (*Coracopsis* spp) occupy the various strata of the vegetation. More colourful birds in the air include the grey-headed lovebird (*Agapornis cana*), the olive bee-eater (*Merops superciliosus*), the paradise flycatcher (*Terpsiphone mutata*) and the blushing pink hoopoe (*Upupa epops*) with bold black-and-white stripes and crest feathers. Unmistakable, and common, are the red fody (*Foudia madagascariensis*), which dance about the savannah landscape dressed in scarlet during the breeding season (November to April), and the crested drongo (*Dicrurus forticatus*), which has coal-black plumage and a strongly forked tail. The rock-thrushes (*Monticola* spp) of the drier south look just like European robins in morning suits. The real thing, the

BIRDING IN MADAGASCAR
Derek Schuurman

To see a fair spectrum of Madagascar's endemic birds, you'll need to visit at least one site in the island's three chief climatic/floristic zones: eastern rainforest, southern 'spiny forest', and western dry deciduous forests. Each holds its own complement of regional endemics. In addition a select band of birds is dependent on the dwindling wetlands, so include those in your itinerary. The transition forest of Zombitse should also be included if possible. During a stay of two or three weeks and armed with two helpful new field guides (see *Further Information*, page 362) you should be able to tick off most of the sought-after 'lifers'.

Below is a review of the sites on the standard birding route.

Eastern rainforest
Rainforest birding is best in spring and early summer (late August to January).

Ranomafana National Park
Above all known for its ground-rollers (pitta-like, short-legged and rufous-headed especially). Other 'megaticks' often seen include brown mesite, the three oxylabes (white-throated and yellow-browed oxylabes, and Crossley's babbler), grey-crowned greenbul, forest rock-thrush and Pollen's vanga. Velvet and common sunbird asitys are plentiful. On ridges, look for yellow-bellied sunbird asity, brown emutail and cryptic warbler. In the Vohiparara Marsh, you might find Madagascar rail, grey emutail and Madagascar flufftail.

Périnet Reserve, Mantadia National Park and surrounds
At Périnet (Analamazaotra), you'll easily find most of the generally distributed Malagasy endemics. 'Specials' include red-fronted coua, Rand's warbler, coral-billed nuthatch vanga and Tylas. With luck, you'll locate Madagascar wood-rail, Madagascar flufftail and collared nightjar.

In Mantadia National Park nearby, the pitta-like, scaly (rare), rufous-headed and short-legged ground-rollers occur, as do the three oxylabes, velvet asity, common and yellow-bellied sunbird asitys, Ward's flycatcher and brown emutail. Two wetlands nearby, the Torotorofotsy Marsh and more accessible Ampasipotsy Marsh, hold Madagascar rail, Madagascar snipe, Meller's duck, grey emutail, Madagascar swamp warbler and even the ultra-rare slender-billed flufftail.

Masoala National Park
Birding in this lowland rainforest is exceptional. Aside from nearly all the broadly distributed rainforest birds, the 'specials' here include brown mesite, red-fronted coua, scaly ground-roller and the helmet and Bernier's vangas. Two extremely rare species are protected here: the Madagascar serpent eagle and Madagascar red owl. But seeing them is not guaranteed as both are elusive.

endemic Madagascar magpie robin (*Copsychus albospecularis*), sports black-and-white attire and has the habit of flirting fearlessly with humans.

The Madagascar kestrel (*Falco newtoni*) is joined by other **birds of prey** such as the banded kestrel (*Falco zoniventris*), the Madagascar harrier-hawk (*Polyboroides radiatus*), Frances's sparrow-hawk (*Accipiter francesii*), the Madagascar buzzard (*Buteo brachypterus*), the Madagascar cuckoo-falcon (*Aviceda*

Tropical dry deciduous forests (western region)
Ampijora Forest Station
This is an outstanding birding locality year round and is included in all birding itineraries because there you'll get most of the birds local to western Madagascar. They include white-breasted mesite, Coquerel's coua, Schlegel's asity and Van Dam's vanga. Several other vangas (sicklebill, Chabert's, white-headed, blue and rufous) are commonly seen. Raptors abound, including Madagascar fish eagle, Madagascar gymnogene, Madagascar buzzard, Madagascar sparrow-hawk and Frances's sparrow-hawk. Broadly distributed endemics easily ticked off include Madagascar crested ibis, white-throated rail and Madagascar pygmy kingfisher. At nearby wetlands, the chances of seeing Humblot's heron, Madagascar white ibis and Madagascar jacana are excellent.

Transition Forest
Zombitse National Park
A serious 'OOE' (Orgasmic Ornithological Experience) and long included in all birding itineraries for its 'megatick', the Appert's greenbul, this forest also holds an impressive variety of other endemics, like giant and crested couas as well as the recently described olive-capped coua.

Vangas include blue, sicklebill, hook-billed, rufous, white-headed and Chabert's. Look out for Madagascar partridge, Madagascar buttonquail, Madagascar sandgrouse, greater and lesser vasa parrots, grey-headed lovebird, Madagascar green pigeon, Madagascar hoopoe, Thamnornis warbler, common newtonia, common jery, longbilled green sunbird and Sakalava weaver. Great birding all year.

Southern sub-arid thorn thicket ('spiny bush' or 'spiny forest')
Excellent birding year-round; start just before daybreak.

Ifaty
Ifaty's bizarre Euphorbia-didiereaceae bush holds some extremely localised 'megaticks': sub-desert mesite, long-tailed ground-roller, La Fresnaye's vanga and Archbold's newtonia. Look also for running coua and subdesert brush-warbler. This is a good place for banded kestrel and white-browed owl too.

St Augustine's Bay and the Arboretum d'Antsokay
The bush in St Augustine's Bay is lower and more scrubby than in Ifaty. The following endemics are best sought here: Verreaux's coua, littoral rockthrush and the recently described red-shouldered vanga. At puddles along the road, look for the rare Madagascar plover.

The Arboretum provides excellent and easy birding for those staying at the Auberge de la Table (see page 198).

---

madagascariensis) and six species of owl. The two eagles found on the island are both extremely rare. The Madagascar fish eagle (*Haliaeetus vociferoides*) is sparsely distributed on the west coast, fishing the freshwater lakes, mangroves and estuaries between Morondava and Antsiranana. The Madagascar serpent eagle (*Eutriorchis astur*) was recently rediscovered, after a period of 50 years, hunting on the Masoala peninsula.

Mammals

Madagascar's mammals are the prize exhibit in the island's incredible menagerie. They exist as an obscure assortment of primates, insectivores, carnivores, bats and rodents, representing the descendants of parties of individuals who, curled up in hollow trunks or skipping across temporary islands, accidentally completed the perilous journey from eastern Africa to the island beyond the horizon at different times over the last 100 million years. Once established, they gradually spread through the diverse habitats of their paradise island, all the time evolving and creating new species.

Biologists often refer to Madagascar as a 'museum', housing 'living fossils'. This is because almost all the mammals on the island today closely resemble groups that once shone on the mainland but have since been replaced by more advanced species. Although evolution has certainly occurred on the island, it seems to have had less momentum than it had back in Africa. Hence, while their cousins on the

A LAYMAN'S GUIDE TO LEMURS
Nick Garbutt

Unless you are a keen natural historian, sorting out Madagascar's 50 varieties (taxa) of lemur is challenging. The information below, together with the scientific classification (see box on page 35), should help you put names to faces: and if you know in which region/reserve the most common species are found you'll be better able to decide what that leaping animal high in the trees is likely to be.

Diurnal lemurs (active during the day)
The largest and the easiest to identify, these are usually found in groups of between three and twelve individuals.

Ring-tailed lemurs (Lemur catta) Recognisable by their banded tails, and more terrestrial than other lemurs, these are seen in troops of around 20 animals in the south and southwest, notably in Berenty reserve.

Ruffed lemurs These are large lemurs (genus Varecia) and commonly found in zoos but seldom seen in the wild. There are two species: black-and-white ruffed lemur and red ruffed lemur. Both live in the eastern rainforest, the black-and-white in Mantadia or Nosy Mangabe, and the red in Masoala.

True lemurs This family has only recently been grouped under a new generic name, Eulemur. They are all roughly cat-sized, have long noses, and live in trees. A confusing characteristic is that males and females of each species are coloured differently. The best-known Eulemur is the **black lemur**, E. macaco (called maki by the Malagasy), of northwest Madagascar, notably Nosy Komba and Lokobe. Only the males are black; females are chestnut brown. Visitors to Ranomafana usually see the **red-bellied lemur**; the male has white 'tear-drop' face markings. In the northern reserves you'll find the **crowned lemur**, Eulemur coronatus.

Brown lemurs (Eulemur fulvus) present the ultimate challenge. There are six subspecies and, since the males mostly look quite different from the females, you have 12 animals to sort out. Fortunately for you their ranges do not overlap. Two neighbouring brown lemurs have beautiful cream or white eartufts and side whiskers: **Sanford's brown lemur** (E. f. sanfordii) is found in the northern reserves; the **white-fronted brown lemur**, E. f. albifrons (the males have bushy white heads and side whiskers of almost Santa Claus proportions), in the northeast. Moving south you'll find the **common brown**

mainland were subjected to extreme competition with the species that were to develop subsequently, the Malagasy mammals were able to stick more rigidly to their original physiques and behaviours.

The word 'cousins' is especially poignant when applied to the lemurs, for back in Africa primate evolution was eventually to lead to the ascent of humankind. How opportune then for our understanding of our own natural history that one of our direct ancestors managed to end up on this island sanctuary and remain, sheltered from the pressures of life elsewhere, relatively true to its original form for us to appreciate 35 million years later.

The lemurs

Lemurs are to a biologist what the old masters are to an art critic: they may not be contemporary, but historically they are very important and they are still beautiful to look at. Lemurs belong to a group of primates called the *prosimians*, a word which

---

lemur (*E. f. fulvus*) in the east and also the west. The **red-fronted brown lemur** (*E. f. rufus*) lives in the southeast and southwest. Females all look pretty much the same – boring and brown.

Bamboo lemurs (genus *Hapalemur*) These are smaller than the 'true lemurs', with short muzzles and round faces. They occur in smaller groups (one to three animals), cling to vertical branches, and feed on bamboos. You may see these in the eastern reserves of Périnet and Ranomafana; the commonest species is the **grey bamboo lemur** (*Hapalemur griseus*), although in Ranomafana you could see the **golden bamboo lemur**, *H. aureus*.

Indri The largest of the lemurs, and the only one without a tail, this black-and-white 'teddy bear' lemur is unmistakable. It is seen in Périnet .

Sifakas (genus *Propithecus*) The sifakas (sometimes pronounced Shee-fahk) belong to the same family as the indri, sharing its characteristic of long back legs; sifakas are the 'dancing lemurs' that bound upright over the ground and leap spectacularly from tree to tree. The commonest sifakas are white or mainly white and so are unlike any other lemur. The **white sifaka** (*P. verreauxi verreauxi*) shares its southern habitat with the ring-tailed lemur, and its cousin the **Coquerel's sifaka** (*P. V. coquerel*), which has chestnut arms and legs, is seen in Ampijoroa, in the northwest. You may also see the dark-coloured **Milne-Edwards sifaka** (*P. diadem edwardsi*) in Ranomafana.

Nocturnal lemurs

Two genera of nocturnal lemur helpfully sleep or doze in the open so are regularly seen by tourists: **sportive lemurs** (lepilemurs) and **woolly lemurs** or **avahis** (guides may use both popular and generic names). Most species of lepilemur spend the day in a tree-hole from which they peer drowsily, and the woolly lemur sleeps in the fork of a tree or shrub.

During guided night walks you may see the eyes of **dwarf lemurs** – most likely the greater dwarf lemur at Périnet . The tiny **mouse lemurs** are quite common, and easiest to see at Ranomafana or Berenty.

You're very unlikely to see an unplanned **aye-aye**, but check the description on page 52 if you think you did...

See *Appendix 3* for a checklist of lemurs and where to find them.

means 'before monkeys'. Their basic body design evolved about 40 to 50 million years ago. With stereoscopic-colour vision, hands that could grasp branches, a brain capable of processing complex, learned information, extended parental care and an integrated social system incorporating a wide range of sound and scent signals, the lemurs were the latest model in evolution's comprehensive range of arboreal (tree-living) mammals. Their reign lasted until about 35 million years ago, when a new model, the monkey, evolved. Monkeys were superior in a number of ways: they were faster, could think more quickly, used their vision more effectively and were highly dextrous. Thus monkeys quickly replaced the lemurs who, destined for the fossil records, vanished from the forests of the world. That is, all but one forest, for on the island of Madagascar, a few stowaway lemurs had managed to take refuge. Today we see the results of 35 million years of their evolution. The single ancestral

THE AYE-AYE
Hilary Bradt

The strangest lemur is the aye-aye, *Daubentonia madagascariensis*. It took a while for scientists to decide that it was a lemur at all: for years it was thought to be a peculiar type of squirrel. Today it is classified in a family of its own, Daubentonidae. The aye-aye seems to have been assembled from the leftover parts of a variety of animals. It has the teeth of a rodent (they never stop growing), the ears of a bat, the tail of a fox, and the hands of no living creature since the middle finger is like that of a skeleton. It's this finger which so intrigues scientists as it shows the aye-aye's adaptation to its way of life. In Madagascar it seems to fill the ecological niche left empty by the absence of woodpeckers. The aye-aye evolved to use its skeletal finger to winkle grubs from under the bark of trees. It has added the skill (shown by the Chinese when using chopsticks to eat soup) of flicking coconut milk into its mouth; coconuts are now a favoured food. The aye-aye's fingers are unique among lemurs in another way – it has claws not fingernails (except on the big toe). When searching for grubs the aye-aye taps on the wood with its finger, its enormous ears pointing like radar dishes to detect a cavity. It can even tell whether this is occupied by a nice fat grub.

Another anatomical feature of the aye-aye that sets it apart from other primates is that it has inguinal mammary glands. In other words, its teats are between its back legs. This fascinating animal was long considered to be on the verge of extinction, but recently there have been encouraging signs that it is more widespread than previously supposed. Although destruction of habitat is the chief threat to its survival, it is also at risk because of its supposedly evil powers. Rural people believe the aye-aye to be the herald of death. If one is seen near a settlement it must be killed, and even then the only salvation may be to burn down the village. Nevertheless there are several places where you are likely to see wild aye-ayes: Mananara is the easiest, and Nosy Mangabe if you are fortunate. Being strictly nocturnal, aye-ayes can only be watched with the help of a torch (flashlight); so for a prolonged session with these amazing animals treat yourself to a visit to Jersey Zoo, Channel Islands, where the purpose-built 'night-into-day' aye-aye house allows you to watch their behaviour to your heart's content, or pay your fee for a night-time visit at Tana's zoo, Tsimbazaza (but there is no infra-red lighting).

species has adapted into 51 recognised varieties (see *Appendix 3*), and instead of gazing down at inanimate rocks, we have the luxury of being able to watch, hear and smell the genuine article.

Smell is an extremely important aspect of lemur lives. Through scents, lemurs communicate a wide range of information, such as who's in charge, who is fertile, who is related to whom and who lives where. They supplement this language with an audible one. Chirps, barks and cries reinforce hierarchies in lemur societies, help to defend territories against other groups and warn of danger. Socially the lemurs show a great variety of organisations and the strategy used by each species is largely dependent on the nature of their diet. The small, quick-moving, **insectivorous** lemurs such as the mouse lemurs and dwarf lemurs are nocturnal and largely solitary except during the mating season when they pair with a member of the opposite sex. Literally surrounded by their insect food, they only require small territories, hence they never cover large distances and spend their entire lives in the trees. A different way of life is led by the larger **leaf-eating** species such as the indri. In a rainforest there is no shortage of leaves, however as a food source leaves are fairly poor in nutrients, hence each lemur needs to consume a large amount. Leaf-eaters therefore tend to collect in small groups, together defending their territory of foliage with scents and often loud calls, which, in the dense forests, are the best forms of communication. Their sex lives vary, but most of these species have 'family' groups in which a single male dominates. The most social lemurs on the island are those with a more varied diet concentrating on **fruit**, but also including seeds, buds and some leaves. This group includes the ring-tailed lemur, the ruffed lemur and the 'true' lemurs (see box on page 50). The diet of these species requires active foraging over large areas during the day, so in order to defend their expansive territory, and to protect themselves in daylight, these lemurs form distinctive troops. The societies are run by matriarchs, who organise the troop's movement, courtship and defence, but there are also whole groups of males, which often separate for week-long excursions away from the home base. Usually operating in more open country these lemurs use a wide range of visual signals to accompany their scents and sounds. This makes them not only more colourful, but also particularly entertaining to watch.

Perhaps the most entertaining of all the lemurs is the **ring-tailed lemur** (*Lemur catta*). Among lemurs it forms the largest and liveliest troops. Each troop typically stirs at dawn, warms up with a period of sunning and then, guided by the matriarchs, heads off to forage, breaking at noon for a siesta. The troop moves along the ground, each individual using its distinctive tail to maintain visual contact with the others. If out of eyesight the troop members use the cat-like mews that prompted their scientific name. By dusk they return to the sleeping trees which they use for three or four days before the females move the group off to another part of the territory to harvest the food there. During the April breeding season, the males become less tolerant of each other and engage in 'stink-fights' where, after charging their tails with scent from glands on their wrists, they waft them antagonistically at opponents. Similar aggressive interactions occur when two ring-tailed troops meet, yet actual physical violence is rare.

The other mammals

Employing one of the most primitive mammalian body plans the **tenrecs** have been able to fill the vacancies created by an absence of shrews, moles and hedgehogs, and in doing so diversified into at least 24 different species. Five of the species are called the spiny tenrecs, most looking just like hedgehogs, some with yellow and black stripes. However, the largest of these, the tail-less common tenrec (*Tenrec ecaudatus*), has lost the majority of its spines. Not only is this species, at 1.5kg, the largest insectivore in the world, but it can also give birth to enormous litters, which the mother feeds with up to 24 nipples. The 19 species of furred tenrecs are mostly shrew-like in stature, although three species look and act more like moles, and one has become aquatic, capturing small fish and freshwater shrimps in the fast-flowing streams of the Hauts Plateaux.

Highly successful elsewhere, **rodents** have made little impression on Madagascar. There are 20 species, most of which are nocturnal. The easiest to see is the red forest rat (*Nesomys rufus*) which is active during the day. The most unusual are the rabbit-like giant jumping rat (*Hypogeomys antimena*) from the western forests and the two tree-dwelling *Brachytarsomys* species which have prehensile tails.

The island's eight **carnivores** belong to the civets and mongooses, *Viverridae*, which evolved 40 million years ago, at about the same time as the cats. The largest, known as the *fosa* (*Cryptoprocta ferox*), is very cat-like with an extremely long tail which assists balance during canopy-based lemur hunts. The size of a chubby cat, the striped civet (*Fossa fossana*) hunts in the eastern rainforests for rodents, and a third, very secretive animal, the *falanouc* (*Eupleres goudotii*) inhabits the northeastern rainforests where it lives almost entirely on earthworms. Each of Madagascar's forest types play host to mongooses. There are five species in all, the most obvious being the ring-tailed mongoose (*Galidia elegans*) which varies in colour, but is typically a handsome, rusty red.

Possessing, among mammals, the unique gift of flight, it is not surprising that most of Madagascar's **bats** are also found on mainland Africa or Asia. There are three species of fruit bat which are active during the day, very noisy, large (a wingspan of up to 1.5m) and unfortunately often on the Malagasy menu. If the fruit bats look like flying foxes (and they do), then the remaining 20 plus species are not unlike flying mice. These are nocturnal, prefer moths to figs and find them by echo-location, employing shell-like ears and distorted noses. It is known that some moths outdo the bats by chirping back at them in mid-flight, scrambling the echo and sending the aggressor off into the night.

The Bay of Antongil marks the northern extent of **humpback whale** migrations. The whales calve just beyond the coral reefs in July and August, and after this period migrate south as far as the Antarctic coast to feed. They share the bay with slow-moving **dugongs** or sea cows. The Vezo of the west coast share their fishing grounds with an abundance of **dolphins**, and regard them as kin. If a dolphin is discovered dead, they wrap it in shrouds and bury it with their ancestors.

MADAGASCAR'S WILDERNESS

For many of us it is the experience of wandering through the unique wilderness of Madagascar that draws us to the island. As evidenced by the previous section, Madagascar has some of the most unusual plants and animals on Earth, and alone each one is fascinating, but of course these species do not lead isolated lives. Each one contributes to the structure, function and diversity of an ecosystem. Ecologists have been aware for some time now that it is only when observing a species within its natural ecosystem that we can fully comprehend characteristics such as its behaviours, life cycle, physical structures and interactions with other species. An ecosystem is more than the sum of its parts. It is an abstract combination of all the species, the landforms, the soil types, the atmosphere and the waterways in an area. When walking into a rainforest or the spiny forest or the *tsingy* or swimming over

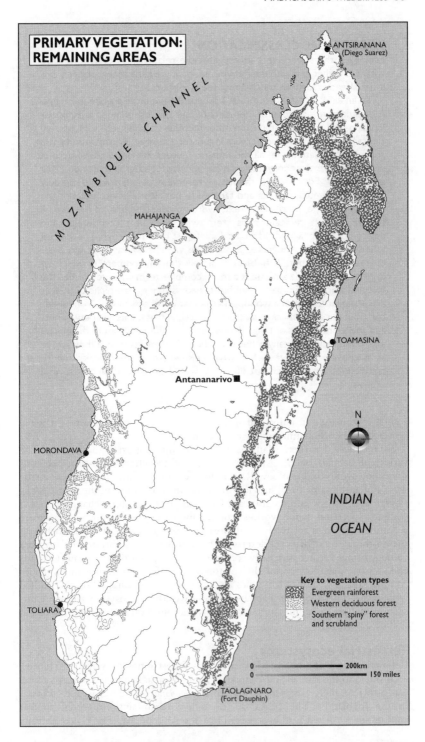

PRIMARY VEGETATION: REMAINING AREAS

ANTSIRANANA
(Diego Suarez)

MOZAMBIQUE CHANNEL

MAHAJANGA

TOAMASINA

Antananarivo

N

MORONDAVA

INDIAN

OCEAN

TOLIARA

Key to vegetation types
Evergreen rainforest
Western deciduous forest
Southern "spiny" forest
and scrubland

0 — 200km
0 — 150 miles

TAOLAGNARO
(Fort Dauphin)

ECOLOGICAL CLASSIFICATION

Ecology is the science that investigates the relationships organisms have with each other and with their environment. It is a fairly recent science, but it has already taught us much about the world.

To an ecologist some common-use words have quite precise meanings. A **population** is a group of members of one species, found in a particular location, and partly isolated from other members of the species. Hence we can talk of a population of lemurs in a nature reserve. A **community** is a group of populations, ie: all the lemurs, tenrecs, tamarind trees etc in a nature reserve. An **ecosystem** is a community together with its non-living environment. For example, the nature reserve ecosystem would not only include the lemurs, tenrecs and tamarinds, but also take into account the climate, soil type, nutrient content, hydrology and landform of the area. A **biome** is a large-scale ecosystem with a typical community and environment, eg: a lowland tropical rainforest or a mangrove. The species found in different mangroves around the world may vary but the basic ecosystem does not. A **habitat** is simply the environment in which an organism lives, while a **niche** is a more complex term which describes the role and place of an organism within its ecosystem, eg: the niche of an aye-aye is similar to that of a woodpecker in that it extracts insects from under bark, but it is also similar to that of a squirrel, in that it eats a variety of nuts and makes nests out of twigs. However, it is different from both squirrel and woodpecker in many other ways; hence ecologists regard the aye-aye as occupying a broad niche, which elsewhere in the world, where competition forces specialist lifestyles, would be divided among several organisms.

a coral reef, it isn't an individual species that takes your breath away – it is the spectacle of the whole functioning ecosystem.

As mentioned earlier, Madagascar has an amazing array of habitats. The variety of habitats on the island is a result of the effects of ocean currents, prevailing winds and geology. Rain is heaviest in the east, and lightest in the west; but at the same time, heaviest in the north and lightest in the south. Since rainfall is the single most significant factor in creating habitat characteristics, a complex spectrum of the world's tropical and subtropical habitats is therefore accommodated in a relatively small area of land – the wettest of rainforests in the northeast to the driest of deserts in the southwest. In addition, Madagascar's geology brings further variety by creating undulating coastlines, broad riverbeds and estuaries, shallow ocean shelves for coral reefs, high mountainous slopes and plateaux, a wealth of soil types and even bizarre limestone 'forests' riddled with caves. These various habitats house a wealth of ecosystems, and in this section each of the dominant ecosystem types found on and around the island will be described.

Terrestrial ecosystems

Before the arrival of humans, Madagascar was almost entirely covered with forests, each suited to the rainfall and altitude of the local area. In the east, where rainfall was sufficient, there was evergreen rainforest, *'lowland'* near the coast and *'montane'* in the highlands. The peaks of the tallest mountains supported thicket communities isolated as if on an island in a 'low-altitude sea'. The Hauts Plateaux

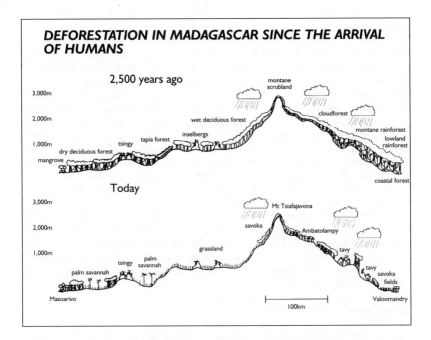

DEFORESTATION IN MADAGASCAR SINCE THE ARRIVAL OF HUMANS

were covered with deciduous wet forests interrupted occasionally by rocky outcrops, themselves infested with succulents. The western slopes of the Hauts Plateaux bore tapia trees adapted to the rain shadow of the highlands, and on the western coast vast belts of dry deciduous forest composed of baobabs and leguminous trees were a paradise for troops of lemurs. The southern arid region did not relent to desert, but instead kept the forest theme with the remarkable succulent trees and didierea, and along the west coast there were smatterings of mangrove swamps maintaining the coast margin and bringing a violent green trim to the reddish-brown of the interior.

Much of this once vast canopy which sheltered the soils of the entire island is now gone. In its place are poorer *secondary communities* of grasslands, forest mosaics and scrub, relying on impoverished soils which are constantly being washed into the sea. The communities are annually burnt in the practice of *tavy* (slash-and-burn) agriculture, and in the process foreign, virile species take the place of native plants. However, the original *primary communities* do exist in patches. There are still expanses of rainforest, spiny forest and mangroves. The great dry forest of the west is much reduced, but in evidence near to the coast. The remaining communities are particularly fragmented, harbouring amongst geological oddities such as the massif of Isalo and the *tsingy*, or depending on altitude or awkward slopes for their isolation. The one complete loss is the forest of the Hauts Plateaux which has been replaced by grasslands, ricefields and zebu.

Of these remnant communities, none is truly virgin. We know that there were many more lemurs, birds and plants on Madagascar before human settlement. These presumably became extinct as a result of the changes that occurred on the island after the advent of human colonisation. In removing such species communities are inevitably altered, but it is true to say that there are still good examples of natural communities on the island – and it is these primary communities that are of most interest to wildlife watchers.

Rainforests

The spine of mountains which border the central plateau force the wet air arriving from over the Indian Ocean to drop its moisture on the east coast of the island. Madagascar's rainforests therefore exist in a distinct band adjacent to the east coast where the continuous rainfall is high enough to sustain the evergreen canopy trees. Known as the *Madagascar Sylva*, this band of forest extends inland only as far as the mountain range, hence it is thickest in the northeast, even crossing to the west coast around Nosy Be, and becomes thinner as the mountain range approaches the coast towards Taolognaro. The end of the mountain range, just northwest of Taolognaro, forms a unique but fragile divide between the evergreen rainforest to the east and the arid spiny forest beyond. This region is particularly unusual in that it is actually *subtropical*, below the Tropic of Capricorn, and there are few areas in the world able to boast subtropical rainforests.

The *Sylva* is not one standard forest, but more a collection of local forest types. Variations occur due to latitude, underlying rock type, angle of slope, frequency of flooding and, towards Nosy Be, seasonality; but the most profound variation is due to altitude. In the tropics, temperature drops by up to 0.7°C for every 100m gained in altitude. As the climate changes so do the flora and fauna, hence rainforests are typically classified by their height above sea level.

Coastal rainforest (sea level)

Very little of Madagascar's unique coastal rainforest remains. Rooted in sand, washed with salty air, battered by cyclones and bordering lagoons and marshes the

RAINFOREST COMMUNITIES

If a plant could pick a place to live, it would choose one with constant high temperatures and an abundance of water. The hottest, wettest places on Earth occur near to the Equator and they are covered in the world's greatest conglomerations of plants – the tropical rainforests. The rainforests have thrived here for millennia, bathing in the planet's most powerful sunlight and heaviest, most dependable rainfall. In this evergreen habitat there is no autumn, though leaves are individually shed as they age and become inefficient. This constant shower of **leaf litter** builds up on the forest floor to become the fodder of fungi and soil bacteria, which work unceasingly to decompose the material. A quick turn around of nutrients is vital in a habitat that bears high rainfall, for with each torrent much of the soil surface is washed into the river systems. For the same reason rainforest soils are remarkably shallow, yet rainforest trees are remarkably tall, so throughout the world the trees employ **buttress** or **stilt roots** to give them some stability. Another common feature is the broad-leaf which comes to a point, known as a **drip-tip**, designed to shed the heavy rain as it lands.

The dominant trees block out the sun from below with a solid **canopy** many metres above the ground. Their broad branches inadvertently support tonnes of **epiphytic plants** such as orchids and ferns which, embedded in tiny patches of soil, sip water directly from the super-saturated air with bizarre 'air roots'. Trapped amongst their foliage are numerous **pools** of rainwater used by insects to raise larvae, which in turn serve as food for the tadpoles of tree frogs. On emerging, the vast numbers of insect species harvest the leaves, buds and shoots around them, each specialised to tolerate its host's defensive poisons. The insects themselves are food for birds, bats, tree frogs, lizards, spiders and

coastal forest harbours a very unusual community. The architecture of the forest is similar to the more widespread lowland forest, but the plants here are different: they are salt-tolerant and highly efficient at extracting water and nutrients from the shallow, porous sand beneath them. However, the very material that these plants flourish on, the sand, has recently become their downfall – titanium-rich sand in the most fragile of the coastal forests, that near Taolognaro, has attracted mining developments, which are likely to permanently disfigure the community.

Good examples: south of Antalaha and north of Sambava on the coast near Amboasary.

Lowland rainforest (0–800m)

Most of the rainforest in Madagascar can be described as lowland rainforest, that is the forest rising from sea level to around 800m. This type of forest is hot and sticky, with a saturated humidity of 100% and annual rainfall of up to 5,000mm. The forest canopy resides 30m above the ground, and there are few emerging trees beyond this height. As well as hardwoods, palms (including the litter-trappers) and pandans contribute to the canopy and under-storey. Most of Madagascar's orchid and fern species live epiphytically on the tree branches, providing rainwater pools for beautiful tree frogs and insects. Vast numbers of insect species hide amongst the foliage. Those that flaunt their bodies with bright colours are either dangerous, distasteful or pretending to be dangerous/distasteful. The most obvious insects are the flitting butterflies, monstrous beetles and the myriad ants and termites which patrol the forest floor. Ant colonies are extremely well organised and assign the infestation of every part

other insects, and to complete the food chain, there are predatory snakes within the canopy, birds of prey above, and mammalian carnivores below.

Rainforest animals have other roles. They are employed by plants to courier pollen about the forest. The plants advertise their nectar with magnificent, pungent flowers, each species timing the flowering event for a particular period in the month, year or even decade, so that its dispersed members can swap genes effectively. Once fertilised, the fruits and seeds of the plants are unwittingly dispersed by a different set of animal carriers, such as fruit bats, nut-cracking birds and the lemurs.

Many of the rainforest's residents never leave these hanging gardens, but below the canopy there is another world. An **under-storey** of smaller plants, such as palms and shrubs, lap up what light is allowed through from above. The huge trunks of the canopy trees are encumbered with lianas, creepers and ferns, and at their bases the **forest floor**, cloaked in darkness and largely devoid of plant growth, is the realm of fungi, ants and termites. Despite appearances, the floor is more dormant than dead, for its soil is riddled with baby trees, stunted by the darkness, but waiting patiently for their one chance to join the others above – a tree fall. If this occurs, the light comes streaming down from above, and opportunistic saplings take their chance by throwing their growth into top gear. In the years it takes for the saplings to climb and close up the canopy once more, a flourish of '*chablis*' plants and animals revel in this short-lived paradise, their entire lifecycles designed to support the precarious existence of jumping between tree fall events.

This, then, is the rainforest, the most complex, productive and dynamic community on Earth.

of the forest within their territory to predictable days in each month. Within the dark field layer of tree roots, tree-ferns and cycads, are leeches, spiders and occasionally chameleons. The abundance and diversity of chameleons is one of the characteristic features of Malagasy forests, and it is wise to spend some time looking for them.

The stars of the forest, the lemurs, nonchalantly skip among the forest branches and the liana climbers which serve as highways between the forest floor and the world above. Most common are the brown lemurs and wherever you find bamboo growing in clumps under the canopy, the grey bamboo lemur. The lemurs dominate the ecosystem, quite capable of eating virtually every plant food that it yields. Preying on the lemurs, fosa are at home among the canopy branches, and above the leaves, birds of prey and fruit bats patrol. An unusual sight from ground-level are what look like strange fungi blossoming from the bark of the canopy trees. These are in fact the trees' flowers and fruit sprouting directly from their trunks and branches. A habit known as *cauliflory*, it is intended to make life easier for their pollinators and seed-bearers. Below this vivid display, tenrecs and forest birds rummage through the litter on the floor, and the Madagascar striped civet and mongooses wait to pick off any unsuspecting prey.

Good examples: Lokobe (Nosy Be); Masoala (the most diverse area on the island); Nosy Mangabe and Marojejy.

Montane rainforest (800–1,300m)

As altitude increases and air temperature drops, the tree species of the lowland rainforest give way to those more able to tolerate the cooler conditions. These species have lower canopies, and are the foundation of a different type of rainforest known as *montane*. The change from lowland to montane forest is a gradual one, influenced by a number of factors. In southern Madagascar, due to the effects of higher latitudes montane forest occurs further down the mountains, and in the north where it is warmer, lowland forest continues from sea level up to about 900m. To accommodate this variation an arbitrary altitude of 800m is often used to define the boundary between the two types of forest in Madagascar.

WATCHING WILDLIFE IN THE FOREST

Although the forest is full of life, a stroll among its trunks can be disappointing. To see its characters you must be patient and quiet, and it doesn't hurt to maximise your chances of sightings by employing a local guide, or enhancing your vantage point. A good location is on the lip of a slope. This places the canopy below you at eye level, so that you are staring straight at the action among its branches. Another good position is on a riverbank, where light penetrates further and walls of palms, pandans and ferns exploit the illumination. Numerous rivers and streams dissect the forest and are the favourite spots of insects, particularly butterflies which 'puddle' on the damp earth of the riverbanks. If nothing else you may get to see some of the freshwater eels! An extremely good time to see wildlife is actually after dark when a totally different set of players appear to enact their lives. Caught in the torchlight you can often see the eyes of nocturnal species such as the mouse lemurs, carnivores and perhaps, if you are in the right place, the aye-aye. Set up a torch behind a mosquito net, and within a short time you will have species of moths and beetles unknown to science to inspect.

Once in true montane forest the landscape is very different from the lowland forest below. Not only is the canopy lower and the temperature very much cooler, but the under-storey is far more dense. Tree-ferns and bamboos litter the forest floor and the gallery above is festooned with epiphytes and mosses lazily hanging off its branches. There is a tight tangle of trunks, roots and woody lianas, all sporting furry lichens and lines of bright fungi. Some orchid species have abandoned the branches and have rooted on the forest floor, where they are joined by determined succulent species.

Montane reserves are excellent places to spot mammals and birds. At the three best sites there are many lemur species harbouring amongst the trunks and climbers, some only recently discovered. Bright forest birds, chameleons and boas are also at large.

Good examples: Ranomafana (with its newly discovered golden bamboo lemur and many other mammal species); Périnet (for indri and other lemurs); Montagne d'Ambre (with many easy trails and beautiful scenery).

Cloudforest (above 1,300m)

The forest beyond 1,300m has an even lower canopy and is characteristically thick with ferns and mosses. Its proper title is 'high-altitude montane', but because it is often cloaked in mists, the emotive label of 'cloud forest' is often applied. The low temperature of the cloud forest slows down decomposition, creating waterlogged peaty soils in valleys. Termites do not live this high up, so large earthworms and beetles take the role of detritivores. The canopy is as low as 10m above the ground and in places the under-storey gives way to a thicket of shrubs. Mosses, lichens and ferns inhabit every branch and stone, and cover the floor along with forest succulents and *Bulbophyllum* orchids. A variety of lemurs brave the low temperatures and thick vegetation.

Good examples: Marojejy; Andringitra; Ambohitantely.

Montane scrubland

On the peaks of Madagascar's tallest mountains there are extremely isolated and unusual communities, which have yet to be studied to satisfaction. In a climate that often provides snow, the canopy here is so low that it eventually reaches a habitat which is less like a forest and more like dense scrub. It is characterised by a single stratum of strange, evergreen heath-trees belonging to the daisy family and an unusual genus called *Philippia*. Among these, and on exposed rocks, are specialist euphorbia and orchids. With the nearest equivalent habitat thousands of kilometres away, these species have evolved isolated on 'high-altitude islands' as remote as any in the ocean. Even at these heights lemurs are found, such as bamboo lemurs and troops of ring-tails with specialised diets.

Good example: Andringitra (higher up).

Tapia woodland

Growing in fragmented clumps among the canyons of the rocky western slopes of the Hauts Plateaux are the wonderful tapia trees (*Uapaca bojeri*). Although deprived of rain by the highlands to their east and pounded by hot sunlight throughout the year, the tolerant tapias manage to maintain a canopy year round by feeding upon the little water that rolls down over the rocks into their canyon homes. Similar in appearance to the stunted cork oaks of the Mediterranean, they share the 10m high canopy with other evergreens, which, unable to withstand fires to the same degree, are becoming less of a feature. The canopy is not as closed as that of the rainforest, so an under-storey of shrubs is well developed, criss-crossed with lianas. Although *pandans* are common, in this drier habitat, tree ferns and most palms and epiphytes

THE BIODIVERSITY OF THE RAINFOREST

Scientists still don't really understand how the rainforests are so diverse. Their rates of photosynthesis are the highest on Earth, and this leads to an abundance of food unparalleled in other habitats, but it still doesn't account for the incredible diversity. We don't know how many species there are in the rainforest, but it is estimated that they hold 50% of the species on the planet, yet they take up only 7% of the land area. The vast majority of these species are **insects**. It seems that in any one rainforest the numbers of endemic insects are astronomical. One ecologist sprayed a single rainforest tree with poison and collected the insects that fell down from the tree in nets. Seventy-five per cent of them were new to science, and many of these would only ever be found on that one tree species. By working out what would happen if he sprayed all the tree species in the world's rainforests, he decided that there may be up to 15 million species in rainforests – far more than the 1.8 million recorded so far.

An important feature of rainforests is its **tree diversity**. When walking through a temperate forest you are unlikely to see more than three or four species of trees, and one almost always dominates. In rainforests it is common to find 250 species of tree per hectare, none dominating. Naturally this will increase the number of insect species, which are normally exclusive to one plant, and in turn the number of insect-eaters such as birds, lizards, spiders and bats. But why isn't one type of tree dominant in the rainforest? One suggestion is that the numerous seed-eaters on the forest floor have a strong influence. They tend to devour all the seeds that fall in a bunch around a parent tree, but perhaps leave those that have been dispersed further afield. This would create a mosaic of tree species, each widely dispersed throughout the forest – in fact, exactly what happens.

Other theories target the great **age** of the rainforests. Perhaps time alone can account for the development of so many intricate niches; after all in many places rainforests have remained undisturbed for millennia. Not everyone is convinced. Some of the most diverse forests are still relatively young. Perhaps the constant climate is important, for it brings **stability** to the forest. Further away from the equator, where conditions change from hot summers to cold winters, species must put up with a range of discomforts, and thus may not have the luxury of specialising to the same extent. A lack of specialisation certainly reduces diversity.

Whatever the answer, the rainforests exist as a biodiversity phenomenon. It is a great misfortune that the forest's complexity, as well as being its major contribution, may also be its downfall. Constructed of such specialist niches, rainforests are **fragile ecosystems**, and the escalating extent of human disturbance is having far-reaching and catastrophic results.

are absent. One exception is the beautiful feather palm (*Chrysalidocarpus isaloensis*), endemic to Isalo National Park.

The tapia forests are the sole home of Madagascar's endemic silkworm which lives off the leaves of the tapia trees. Mammals are uncommon, but troops of ring-tailed lemurs and Verreaux's sifaka are sometimes seen.

Good example: Isalo National Park.

Dry deciduous forest

The magnificent dry forests of the west once covered the vast lowland plain west of the Hauts Plateaux. Now, this kind of forest is only to be found in patches sharing the coast with the mangroves, bordering the largest rivers of the south and dotted about the plains near Isalo and inland from Mahajanga. The forest supports far fewer species than the eastern rainforests, but has higher rates of endemism, and so has attracted the attentions of conservationists. The trees of these dry forests are less densely arranged, and the canopy is lower, at 12–20m. It is too dry here for any epiphytes except some tolerant orchids in wetter areas, but the adventurous lianas are still to be found.

There are several distinct types of dry deciduous forest varying with soil conditions. Growing on the clayey and sandy soils near to the west coast are forests dominated by leguminous trees such as *Dalbergia* and *Cassia*. Where these forests meet the broad rivers of the west and south, enormous tamarind trees, *Tamarindus indica*, and sprawling banyan figs, *Ficus*, are common. The banyans, with typical fig audacity, can cover a significant area with their numerous stilt trunks, so that each individual creates its own miniature forest. On the limestone plateaux near the west coast, the alkalinity of the soil allows the baobabs (*Adansonia spp*) to take over. There are seven species of baobab in Madagascar and they are symbols of this vegetation, often forming impressive avenues about the forest tracks.

The title 'deciduous' refers to the shedding of the canopy during the seven or eight months of the dry season. A carpet of leaves begins to accumulate on the forest floor shortly after the rains stop in May, and through decomposition, they help to create a thick humus layer in the soil. During 'the dry' much of the animal life goes to ground, quite literally. Amphibians and insects bury themselves in the soil and await October when the rains return. Upon the advent of the first rainstorm the forest floor bubbles with emerging animal life and the canopy branches sprout leaves once again.

Foraging within this landscape are many bird and mammal species, each adapted to extract one element of the forest's bounty. Sifakas, sportive lemurs, brown lemurs and the ubiquitous mouse lemurs are particularly in evidence, but more obscure species also inhabit specialised niches within the forest ecosystem. The tamarind forests are the classic backdrop in pictures of ring-tail troops patrolling the floor with their tails in the air. Vangas and other birds form multi-species flocks within the canopy, and the tuneful vasa parrots make territories in the understorey. The deep litter layer is home to tenrecs, tortoises, boas and hog-nosed snakes. Fosas and mongooses regularly run along their patrol trails, and are prepared to pursue prey into the canopy if the need arrives.

Good examples: Kirindy (jumping rat, lemurs and birds); Ampijoroa; Berenty (ring-tailed lemurs).

Inselberg and tsingy communities

Where the island's underlying rocks break through the landscape in the west, localised communities develop, composed of specialised plants and animals. Rain simply rolls off the rock surfaces or passes through its porous body, so all the residents must be tolerant to desiccation. These communities, known in Africa as 'rupicolous shrubland', are particularly interesting in Madagascar, because they are the sole retreat for many of the island's more ornamental succulents. Magnificent euphorbias, aloes, kalanchoes and pachypodia tuck themselves into the tiny pockets of soil available among the crevices, bringing foliage and flowers to the smooth rock face. Insects, birds and lemurs rely on these structures for sustenance, only retreating, in the heat of the day, to the copses of trees in nearby canyons.

Such plants are also to be found harbouring among the knife-edge pinnacles of three spectacular limestone karst massifs known locally as the *tsingy*. A result of unimaginable periods of erosion, the jigsaw landscape of the *tsingy* enables a complex mosaic of communities to live side-by-side. For this reason, a trip to the *tsingy* can be an extremely rewarding wildlife event. The towering pinnacles which sport the succulents are in fact the ornate roofs of extensive cave systems below. The caves are inhabited by bats, rodents and tonnes of arthropods feeding on the bat guano. Blind cave fish swim in the broad, dark rivers, as do, it is rumoured, cave crocodiles. Where the cave roofs have collapsed sunny gullies are crowded with dense, dry forests, rich in baobabs.

This diversity of habitat naturally supports a diversity of birds and mammals, and the *tsingy* massifs are good places to see a wealth of lemur species. It has even been said that Ankarana has the highest density of primates on Earth. It is certainly famous for its 'blade-running' crowned lemurs, *Eulemur coronatus*, troops of Sanford's brown lemurs, *Eulemur fulvus sanfordi*, and even the aye-aye, *Daubentonia madagascariensis*, but for a dry habitat to boast that claim the Ankarana ecosystem must be very special indeed.

Good examples: Isalo National Park (for inselberg communities); the *tsingy* massifs of Ankarana, Bemaraha and Namoroka.

Spiny forest

Whenever photographers wish to startle people with the uniqueness of Madagascar, they head for the 'spiny forest'. Its mass of tangled, spiny branches and swollen succulent trunks creates a habitat variously described by naturalists as 'a nightmare' and 'the eighth wonder of the world'. Stretching in a band around the southwest coast from Morombe to Taolagnaro, the spiny forest is the only primary community able to resist the extreme arid environment of this region. All the plants here are beautifully adapted to sporadic rainfall, even surviving without water for more than a year. The unworldly landscape of this community is largely a result of the striking forms of didierea trees (see descriptions in *Flora* section), which also provide most of the spines in the forest. Side-by-side with the didierea, forming impenetrable thickets, are emergent baobabs, bloated 'bottle-tree' pachypodia and tree euphorbia. Of the latter group the most recognisable are the huge *E. enterophora*, with its umbrella-shaped crown of slender green branches atop a black trunk, the sausage tree, *E. oncoclada*, and the spiky grey-green *E. stenoclada* which is so designed to capture the condensing sea mist near the coast. Dramatic, tall aloes and broad-leaved grey kalanchoe 'trees' can be found amongst the spiny branches contributing to the peculiar visage, and endemic orchids and palms, extremely specialised to withstand the aridity, are additional oddities. Where bordering the coast, the community can benefit from condensing sea mists and is in places evergreen.

The most evident animal life, aside from reptiles and desert arthropods, are the groups of sifakas which somehow avoid the nasty spines of the didierea as they leap from one trunk to another. These leaps can be impressive, assisted by the frog-like back legs of this group of lemurs. However, if the forest is too sparse the sifaka is forced to skip along the hot sandy floor in a comic routine likened by John Cleese to a mad butler doing the tango.

Good examples: Berenty; Ifaty; along the Taolagnaro-Ambovombe road; Beza-Mahafaly.

Secondary communities

Plants are the foundation of any community. Wherever plants have been removed directly or indirectly by human activities the entire community collapses. It

SUCCESSION

Natural communities do not instantly appear, they are built up over long periods of time in a process known as **succession**. It is succession that, with time, transforms a derelict area of land, or a badly-kept lawn, into a patch of scrub or a full-blown forest. In general, as time goes on, it is natural for soils to become deeper, for taller plants to arrive and for animals to become more abundant. In mowing the lawn we prevent all this from happening.

When cutting down or setting fire to natural communities we are in effect knocking back succession, so that the process has to start again from an earlier point. With time the original community should return, but more often than not, its succession is interfered with by human activities. New plants are grown, new animals imported, the soil is exploited for nutrients and waterways are redirected or overused. The result is that the land cannot support the original **primary community**, and instead a new, poorer community tends to develop on the site, full of fast-growing, 'weedy' species. Often where there were forests, there are now grasslands, and where there were grasslands there are semideserts. Ecologists call these artificial wildernesses **secondary communities**, and they are sadly common in today's world.

sometimes returns later but in a poorer form called a secondary community. Madagascar is particularly prone to this degrading process as a result of its frightening rate of soil erosion. The resulting communities are typically infested with competitive foreign plants and are poor in animal life. There are several widespread secondary communities on the island, but as with primary communities there are limitless gradations of these where two meet.

Savoka

This is the local name for the secondary rainforest that tends to grow back after *tavy*. It is sadly dominated by foreign tree species which will eventually infest all returning forest, changing Madagascar's rainforest communities for ever. Some native plants have managed to compete with these exotics. The traveller's tree (*Ravenala madagascariensis*), really comes into its own in *savoka*, dominating vast tracts. Malagasy bamboos and pandans also line the remaining primary forest, but there are few animals living in this vegetation. *Tavy* has reduced the rainforest to *savoka* along much of the east coast, particularly inland of the Pangalanes Canal where slash-and-burn has been particularly ruthless.

Hauts Plateaux grassland

Over a thousand years of *tavy* has destroyed the wet forests that existed on the central highlands. At first the forest must have battled to return, but eventually it failed, smothered by vigorous grass species which provided grazing for the introduced zebu cattle. All that remains now is a barren, sterile grassland dominated by uninviting species such as the knife-sharp *Heteropogon*.

Once dependent upon zebu the Malagasy continued burning the high country in order to bring fresh 'green bite' grass shoots for their cattle. This has, over hundreds of years, left the landscape scarred with deep cuts in the topsoil, called *lavaka*. The soil from these unsightly scars is washed into Madagascar's rivers, turning them iron red in the process. Eventually the sediment flows out into the sea clogging up mangroves and coral reefs. The net loss of soil from the surface of Madagascar as a result of *tavy* is the country's most pressing problem.

Parts of the plateaux support plantations of imported *Eucalyptus* and pine trees. Quick-growing, they are used for firewood by the highlanders. The establishment of these trees is at least proof that in parts of the plateaux, the soils are still rich enough to support the forest that once covered the area.

Palm savannah

Further west where dry forests have suffered the same fate as those of the highland, a dramatic 'palm savannah' exists. Again, the majority of the ground is covered by tall grasses, but there are also scattered palm and baobab trees which can withstand the annual burning. Unfortunately this is likely to be a temporary landscape. The saplings of the trees are less resistant to the flames, so no new trees will be replacing the few remaining ones.

Southern cactus scrub

The harsh environment of the south prevented serious agriculture in this region until recently, hence the spiny forest has remained relatively protected. New sisal plantations have, however, led to colonisation by Mexico's *Agave* cactus creating a secondary cactus scrub in some areas. The current practice of producing charcoal from the spiny forest may well increase the spread of the *Agave* in the future.

CORAL REEF COMMUNITIES

Coral reefs earn their glamorous title, the 'rainforests of the sea', for they are easily as diverse as rainforests, and for similar reasons. The foundation species, the **reef-building corals**, are miniature relatives of the jellyfish, who have taken to living in vast colonies, surrounding themselves with a protective skeleton of calcium carbonate and grabbing plankton out of the water with their stinging tentacles. Together, these colonies can, over many years, create massive solid structures, full of nooks and crevices, in and on which a myriad of fish and invertebrates live.

There are two basic types of corals – the slow-growing **massive corals**, which add 1cm each year to their bulk; and the more delicate **branching corals**, which grow ten times faster, but fracture easily during storms. The resulting architecture of a reef is similar to that of a rainforest for one very good reason – corals, like trees, grow towards the light. They do this in order to sustain the most intimate of symbiotic relationships, for, living within the tentacles of each coral individual, or **polyp**, are millions of single-celled **algae**. The algae, bathed in the tropical light, provide the polyp with food, while the polyp returns the favour by protecting the algae from predators. This in-house harvesting system works most efficiently in clear, tropical waters, where nutrient levels are poor enough to deter smothering seaweeds and temperatures high enough to permit active reef-building. It is therefore a very fruitful relationship for it creates a prosperity of life in waters that are essentially the subaqua equivalent of a desert.

Competition between corals for a place in the sun is remarkably heated. If two colonies of the same species grow close to each other they tend to fuse, but if different species are neighbours warfare begins. The corals launch filaments which digest the skeleton of the enemy, and this explains the

Aquatic ecosystems

Madagascar's aquatic ecosystems are under-rated as sites of ecological interest. On the coast there are excellent stands of mangrove swamp, numerous lagoons and estuaries and, fringing the shore and forming barriers out at sea, magnificent coral reefs. Inland, the island's high lakes provide isolated havens for unusual bird species and even rare lemurs. Aquatic ecosystems are less restricted by the terrestrial climate and tend to offer more stable habitats for a rich diversity of species.

Wetlands

Wetlands everywhere are regarded as important habitats. Where water accumulates there is an abundance of plants and insects. The plants are terrestrial species adapted to tolerate waterlogging and periodic dry spells, and the insects depend on the water for reproduction, for many species have underwater larval stages. Lakes, swamps and marshes all over the island are therefore popular with birds, attracted by the shelter and materials of the reeds and rushes, and the sustenance to be gained from the insect life. On open water and lagoons near the coast, flamingos group in large flocks, accompanied in their feeding by a variety of waders. The rare Madagascar fish eagle can be seen in some locations, and among the marshes that border the inland lakes are white-throated rails, cuckoo-rollers and the Madagascar pygmy kingfisher.

However, in Madagascar it is not only birds that make their homes among the reeds. In the reed beds of Lake Alaotra, a rare subspecies of the grey bamboo lemur, *Hapalemur griseus alaotrensis*, has given up bamboo for papyrus to become

significant gaps between colonies on a reef. Their sex life is equally dramatic. It was only recently that divers swimming at night, just after the full moon, stumbled upon corals engaging in mass spawning events, where the water is filled with sperm and eggs, all desperately trying to locate an ideal partner. Fish time their migrations to coincide with this phenomenon, which may take place only once a year, and feed in a frenzy on the abundant platter.

More permanent residents light up the habitat with their colours and behaviours. Unlike their oceangoing relatives, **reef fish** have an interest in defending their favourite location – a protective crevice or a bountiful patch of sponge. They do this with a combination of poisons, startling territorial displays and plain aggression. For human voyeurs the effect is one of constant theatre, each fish and invertebrate playing its role with finesse. Parrot fish have strong enough 'beaks' to chip away at the coral and extract polyps. Clown-fish harbour among stinging anemones, free from harm due to an oily secretion on their scales. Cleaner wrasse run 'cleaning stations', which fish periodically visit to have their parasites removed, while a mimic of the wrasse exploits this chance for deception, and instead of removing unwanted hangers-on, removes chunks of flesh. The goby and the bulldozer shrimp team up to build burrows. The shrimp does the digging and the more vigilant goby watches for danger. All are kept on edge by small sharks patrolling the reef edges and trapped lagoons for stray prey.

Such a wondrous play is enacted daily on the stage of the coral reef, and has been for millions of years. The only threat to its continued run is, in effect, its audience. Soil erosion, pollution, the direct removal of fish and shells, and insensitive tourist activities add to the natural disturbances of storms and pest plagues to take their toll on the health of reefs all over the world.

the world's only reed-dwelling primate. Currently under surveillance by primatologists, this subspecies is known to be critically endangered due to the draining of the lake for agriculture. In southern Madagascar another marsh character hides among the foliage, although this time it's a fellow plant. The insectivorous pitcher plant, *Nepenthes madagascariensis*, overcomes the low nutrient levels of the boggy soil beneath by enticing unwitting flies into its smelly pitcher. Once inside they are slowly digested to relinquish their valuable trace elements. An equivalent fate is sometimes faced by the Malagasy themselves in the lakes and waterways that play host to healthy and even sacred populations of crocodiles.

Good examples: Lake Alaotra; Lake Ampitabe; Lake Ravelobe, Ampijoroa (fish eagle); Lake Antanavo (crocodiles).

Mangroves

Where trees dominate the wetlands instead of grasses, there are swamps. By far the most important swamps on the island are the mangroves. Madagascar possesses the largest area of mangroves in the western Indian Ocean. About 330,000ha of the land/water margin are dominated by their characteristic salt tolerant trees, which straddle the water at low tide with weight-bearing roots, their tips sticking upwards, unable to gain oxygen in the thick estuarine mud. Some of the trees get a headstart in life by germinating their seeds whilst still on the parent tree. Sporting a shoot and leaves, the seed then drops at low tide into the mud below to attempt a planting.

Mangroves are important and rich ecosystems. They support a wealth of bird species, which arrive to feast on the swarms of swamp insects above the water and shoals of fish below. Many marine fish and crustacean populations treat the underwater architecture of the mangroves as a nursery, coming in from the sea to mate, breed and rear their young in relative safety. Consequently, as mangroves are being uprooted to make way for hotels elsewhere around the Indian Ocean, the local fishermen are finding their livelihood disappearing. So far, no such problems face the Malagasy; Malagasy mangroves are inaccessible enough to serve as their own protection.

Good examples: All the important mangrove sites are on the west coast, with some of the best areas a short trip from Mahajanga: Katsepy; Marovoay.

Coral reefs

Madagascar has 1,000km of coral reef, and some of the best dive sites in the western Indian Ocean. As with other coral reef areas about the world, most of the species are from a community of globetrotting fish, corals and invertebrates, which crop up wherever the environment is just right. However, Madagascar's reefs are less polluted than those of India and East Africa, and hence in comparison they are diverse and healthy.

There are 63 genera of reef-building corals working to manufacture the island's numerous fringing and barrier reefs. The 1,600km of latitude that Madagascar has to offer creates a gradual cooling of the waters towards the south of the island enabling different corals, and therefore different communities, to predominate. The continental shelf surrounding Madagascar also contributes to diversity. A speedy drop-off on the east coast into deep waters allows only limited fringing reef growth stretching in patches from Fenoarivo to the Masoala peninsula. Off the west coast, the vast and shallow shelf spreading out under the Mozambique Channel, warmed by the Agulhas current coming down from the equator, creates far more reef opportunities.

Along this coast there are fringing and barrier reefs sporting remote cays and a wealth of fish and invertebrates. Loggerhead, green and hawksbill turtles cruise the underwater meadows between corals and nest on the beaches. International travellers such as boobies, terns and tropic birds feed on reef residents such as lobsters, oysters and the enormous prawns that Madagascar is now famed for in Western restaurants. Dugongs, one of the bizarre sea cows, can occasionally be seen floating nonchalantly along in the Bay of Antongil, near Nosy Mangabe, and in July–August they are joined by migrating humpback whales who use the warm waters for breeding, before heading to Antarctica for a plankton feast.

Overall Madagascar's coral reefs offer some excellent opportunities to see prosperous communities at work. Their only threats are those of overfishing, insensitive tourists and, most significantly, the increasing tonnage of sediment flowing out of Madagascar's river mouths.

Good examples: Sainte Marie; Nosy Be; Nosy Ve; Nosy Santana.

CONSERVATION
An age-old problem

When people first settled in Madagascar, the culture they brought with them depended on rice and zebu cattle. Rice was the staple diet and zebu the spiritual staple, the link with the ancestors. Rice and zebu cannot be raised in dense forest, so the trees were felled and the undergrowth burned.

Two hundred or so years ago King Andrianampoinimerina punished those of his subjects who wilfully deforested areas. The practice continued, however. In 1883, 100 years later, the missionary James Sibree commented:

CONSERVATION IN ACTION: KEW'S MADAGASCAR PROJECTS

The Royal Botanic Gardens at Kew, London, is responsible for a number of conservation projects in Madagascar. Of primary importance is the construction of an accurate catalogue of the flora and the collection of specimens for inclusion in their growing seedbank. A different project combines ex- and in-situ conservation to save orchid species. A team in Madagascar fertilise orchid seeds and send them in the post to Kew. Here, scientists use carefully controlled propagation units to conduct the notoriously difficult germination of the orchids and then return the plants to Madagascar for planting in reserves.

In order to ascertain the conservation needs of the different plant communities, staff at Kew's Herbarium use Geographical Information Systems (GIS), which, using satellite images, are able to build up accurate maps of the remaining primary vegetation in Madagascar. By overlaying these with other maps indicating geology and the location of protected areas, they have become better placed to maximise conservation in Madagascar, for the work has highlighted the relatively poor protection of its mangroves, coastal rainforests, spiny forest and clay areas of the western dry forests. In addition, by adding to the map the known locations of rare plant species, it's possible to accurately predict just how widespread each species is. In this way many more plants have been highlighted as threatened, and placed on the endangered list, which previously held few Malagasy plants.

THE DURRELL WILDLIFE CONSERVATION TRUST
Lee Durrell

The Durrell Wildlife Conservation Trust (formerly the Jersey Wildlife Preservation Trust) was founded by Gerald Durrell in 1963. Our headquarters is at Jersey Zoo on the English Channel Island of Jersey. We began working in Madagascar in the early 1980s. Our current efforts concern nine threatened species, all inhabiting western forests or wetlands – fragile and poorly studied ecosystems only now beginning to receive attention from conservationists.

Our most advanced programme is for the endangered ploughshare tortoise, or *angonoka*. This animal is found only in the remote bamboo scrub of the northwest and probably numbers no more than a thousand. Our work on the *angonoka* began in 1986 with the establishment of a breeding centre at the Ampijoroa Forestry Station. An adult herd of 20 tortoises has produced more than 200 young. These and future offspring will be used to bolster the remaining wild populations as needed. We have also undertaken field research, both on the wild tortoises and on the way of life of the people who live near them, and have offered training opportunities for young Malagasy conservationists. With the results to date we are optimistic that the *angonoka* will eventually recover its numbers and become viable as a species once again. This programme has become the model on which our work with other threatened species in Madagascar is based.

Lake Alaotra is the largest freshwater wetland in Madagascar. Loss of forest in the watershed, transformation of the marshes into ricefields, use of pesticides and introduction of non-native fish have turned what was once a biologically rich and productive region of Madagascar into an ecological disaster. Pockets of intact marsh and clean water still exist, supporting fishing, reed-gathering and, potentially, recreation, but native wildlife has suffered. We maintain breeding groups of the endangered Alaotran grey bamboo lemur, Madagascar pochard and Meller's duck at Jersey Zoo, and at Lake Alaotra we have catalysed a strong community initiative to protect the remaining marshes.

'Again we noticed the destruction of the forest and the wanton waste of trees.' The first efforts at legal protection came as long ago as 1927 when ten reserves were set aside by the French colonial government, which also tried to put a stop to the burning. Successive governments have tried – and failed – to halt this devastation.

Since independence in 1960, Madagascar's population has more than doubled (to about 13 million) and the remaining forest has been reduced by half. Only about 10% of the original cover remains and an estimated 2,000 square kilometres is destroyed annually – not by timber companies (although there have been some culprits) but by impoverished peasants clearing the land by the traditional method of *tavy*, slash and burn, and cutting trees for fuel or to make charcoal. However, Madagascar is not overpopulated: the population density averages only 21 people per square kilometre, while in Great Britain it is 228. The pressure on the forests is because so much of the country is sterile grassland. Unlike in neighbouring Africa, this savannah is lifeless because Malagasy animals evolved to live in forests; they are not adapted to this new environment.

Change in Madagascar's vegetation is by no means recent. Scientists have identified that the climate became much drier about 5,000 years ago. Humans have just speeded up the process.

The Madagascar giant jumping rat, flat-tailed tortoise and narrow-striped mongoose are all confined to a small area of western deciduous woodlands. Their severely restricted distribution renders these species extremely vulnerable. Jersey Zoo coordinates the breeding of the jumping rat in Europe, and the breeding centre at Ampijoroa has had good success with the little tortoise. Research on the three species in the wild is ongoing. Also severely endangered are the Madagascar teal and the Madagascar side-necked turtle in the west. The teal probably number less than a thousand. First breeding of the teal occurred in Jersey in 1998, and a breeding nucleus of the turtle has recently been established at Ampijoroa. Biological field research and community work related to these species and their habitat are intensifying.

In addition to the focus on species, our other efforts include technical and financial aid to two zoos and conservation education centres in Madagascar. Also, we offer off-site training in endangered species management for Malagasy students at the International Training Centre based at Jersey Zoo. Fifteen Malagasy had graduated from the Centre by the end of 1998.

The Durrell Wildlife Conservation Trust carries out recovery programmes for threatened species all over the world, in partnership with governments and non-governmental organisations, both international and local. Each programme is tailored to address the particular conservation opportunities and constraints as defined by human (and other) impacts on the species in question both on-site and off-site. The programmes are usually long-term, in recognition of the fact that there are no quick fixes to the problems most endangered species face today. The strategic use of partnerships and grassroots-led action make the Trust's programmes more effective at less cost than those of many larger conservation organisations. Donations are welcome at the following address: Durrell Wildife Conservation Trust, Les Augrès Manor, Trinity, Jersey JE3 5BP, Channel Islands, British Isles; tel: +44 (0)1534 860000; fax: +44 (0)1534 860001; email: jerseyzoo@durrell.org.

The race against time

Madagascar has more endangered species of mammal than any other country in the world. The authorities are not unaware of this environmental crisis: as long ago as 1970 the Director of Scientific Research made this comment in a speech during an international symposium on conservation: 'The people in this room know that Malagasy nature is a world heritage. We are not sure that others realise that it is *our* heritage.' Resentment at having outsiders make decisions on the future of their heritage without proper consultation with the Malagasy was one of the reasons there was little effective conservation in the 1970s and early 1980s. This was a time when Madagascar was demonstrating its independence from Western influences.

Things changed in 1985, when Madagascar hosted a major international conference on conservation for development. The Ministry of Animal Production, Waters and Forests, which administered the protected areas, went into partnership with the World Wide Fund for Nature (WWF). Their plan was to evaluate all protected areas in the country, then numbering 37 (2% of the country), and in their strategy for the future to provide people living near the reserves with economically viable alternatives. They have largely achieved their aims. All the protected areas have been evaluated and recommendations for their management made. They are now the responsibility of the National Association for

HOW TO GET A JOB IN CONSERVATION
Frances Kerridge

Not easy. Basically the jobs are few and far between and tend to be short-term contracts. Built into nearly all projects is a strong training and educational component so that the inhabitants can conserve their own environment and encourage their fellow country people to do the same. Far more effective than *vazaha* telling people what to do! Of course this means that you don't have a job for long! It's very important to get as much experience as possible and make as many contacts as you can. This may mean working as a volunteer for a conservation project. I think the route that most people take these days is to do a broad-based biology/life sciences degree and then take an MSc in Conservation Biology which often has fieldwork possibilities attached to it. Most organisations are interested in volunteers only. If they need new personnel they would advertise somewhere like *New Scientist*.

If working in Madagascar the volunteer must be able to communicate in French. MICET is in the process of putting together a programme for volunteers (ie: indivduals who want to work for one month or more on any of their specialist areas). Here's their mission statement:

> 'MICET is a Malagasy non-profit organisation founded in 1997 and is one of the first self-funding NGOs in Madagascar. Its main intervention areas are the Ranomafana National Park and its peripheral zone and the Moramanga region. MICET maintains a good reputation in Madagascar for its expertise in the field of biodiversity conservation and its personnel's diverse experience. MICET conducts several environment-related programmes such as environmental education and health programmes as well as providing research facilitation services. Besides its field projects, MICET also provides administrative and legal support to a wide range of environmental programmes in Madagascar, collaborating closely with both international and national institutions.'

I would definitely recommend MICET to anyone doing research in Madagascar for the first time. Contact: Dr Benjamin Andriamihaja, MICET, Lot IIIL-102 Tsimbazaza (BP 3715), Antananarivo 101; tel: 22 653 74; email: micet@dts.mg.

Before you get too excited about working in Madagascar, read Frankie's report from the field on page 94. HB.

Management of Protected Areas (Association Nationale pour la Gestion des Aires Protegées, ANGAP) which was established under the auspices of the Environmental Action Plan (EAP), sponsored by the World Bank. Among their successes has been a three-year 'Debt for Nature' swap negotiated by the WWF with the Central Bank of Madagascar.

The WWF funds a number of projects in Madagascar. Other outside agencies involved in conservation are the Durrell Wildlife Conservation Trust (formerly the Jersey Wildlife Preservation Trust), Conservation International, Missouri Botanical Gardens, Duke University Primate Center, and the Peregrine Fund; also USAID (US Agency for International Development), La Coopération Suisse, UNDP (United Nations Development Programme) and UNESCO.

The stated aims of the WWF and other conservation agencies working in Madagascar are to: 'Ensure the conservation of Malagasy biodiversity and ecological processes by stopping, and eventually reversing, the accelerating environmental degradation, and by helping to build a future in which humans live in harmony with nature'.

How you can help
- Support the organisations listed in *Chapter 7*.
- Do not interrupt the work of scientists in the reserves.
- Do not buy products made from endangered species, including shells. (Crocodiles are farmed for their skins and butterflies bred for the trade in mounted specimens, so buying these does not endanger the species' survival).
- Do not encourage the illegal domestication of protected species by admiring or paying to photograph pet animals.
- Pay the full park/reserve fees with good grace. The money is used for conservation.
- Do not berate the Malagasy for destroying their forests, nor impose your own cultural values in respect to their treatment of animals. Try to learn about the people whose country you are visiting.

NATIONAL PARKS AND RESERVES
Categories
There are six categories of protected area, of which the first three have been established to protect natural ecosystems or threatened species:

1. Réserves Naturelles Intégrales (strict nature reserves)
2. Parcs Nationaux (national parks)
3. Réserves Spéciales (special reserves)
4. Réserves de Chasse (hunting reserves)
5. Forêts Classées (classified forests)
6. Périmètres de Reboisement et de Restauration (reafforestation zones).

1. Three of the reserves in this category are mentioned in this book, although only areas outside the park or in the 'buffer zone' may currently be visited: Tsingy de Bemaraha, Andringitra and Lokobe. Andohahela was formerly in this category and has been made into a national park. The others may follow.

These reserves protect representative ecosystems, and are open only to authorised scientific research.

2. As in other countries, national parks protect ecosystems and areas of natural beauty, and are open to the public (with permits). There are now eight national parks: Ranomafana, Montagne d'Ambre and Isalo are the long-established ones, with Périnet-Analamazaotra and Mantadia joining the ranks as Andasibe National Park. Recent arrivals are Zombitse, Andohahela, Masoala and Marojejy and more will be added in the next few years.

3. There are 20 or so special reserves, of which Ankarana, Cap Sainte Marie, Beza-Mahafaly, Andranomena, Anjanaharibe-Sud and Nosy Mangabe are described.

THE ENVIRONMENTAL ACTION PLAN: PAST RESULTS AND FUTURE PLANS
Joanna Durbin

The integrated conservation and development projects in Madagascar (for example, Ranomafana National Park) were always intended to be experimental, and it is only to be expected that some development initiatives would be successful and others would be less so. They were funded during the first phase of the National Environmental Action Plan (1990–96) in order to test the hypothesis that providing alternatives and improvements to the standards of living of local people would take pressure off protected areas and promote sustainable management of natural resources.

After periods of three to five years these projects were evaluated, and although there were some promising results, there was a general feeling that they had not been as successful as originally anticipated. This is probably partly due to the fact that changes in attitudes and resource use cannot be expected within such short time frames. A justified criticism of such projects is that they were generally very expensive in relation to their achievements. It has been recognised that some smaller projects such as the MEF/ANGAP/WWF Zombitse/Vohibasia project and the MEF/Durrell Wildlife Angonoka project have had relatively good success. Their small size and budget have worked in their favour as they do not create big self-sufficient technical development departments, but must work closely with partners, including government services and other local NGOs, and must rely on motivation from the villagers themselves. The emphasis is on finding locally appropriate, non-technological solutions, and negotiating agreements about resource use between different interest groups. The small project teams have to build up good communication and good relations with all their various partners. This good communication is an important prerequisite for learning about the resource issues relevant to the region and developing, together with the partners, more sustainable forms of management. One could also argue that such projects are more likely to have long-lasting impacts and to be sustainable in the long term as they have not become reliant on large-scale external inputs (such as money, materials and technical expertise).

There is a move towards this smaller-scale type of project in the proposals for the second phase of the Environmental Action Plan (1997–2002). In addition, it was recognised that it did not always make sense to concentrate efforts and resources around existing protected areas, and a more regional approach to conservation and development has been adopted. It must still be recognised that conservation and development problems in Madagascar will not be solved within a few years.

We should hope to improve the chances of maintaining the extraordinary and magnificent Malagasy biodiversity in some areas, while also trying to help improve productivity of natural resources upon which the vast majority of the Malagasy population rely for their livelihoods.

These reserves are for the protection of ecosystems or threatened species. Not all are supervised. Access may be limited to authorised scientific research.

4. Four lakes (including Kinkony and Ihotry) are duck-hunting reserves.

5 and 6. The 158 classified forests and 77 reafforestation zones conserve forests and watersheds using accepted forestry principles. Ampijoroa and Manjakatompo classified forests are described in this book.

There are also some private reserves, the most famous of which is Berenty, with the Swiss-administered Kirindy in second place.

Ecotourism

Ecotourism, or 'discovery tourism' (as opposed to mass tourism), was part of the National Environmental Action Plan set up in 1990. The aim was that tourism should generate about a third of the funding for 'protected area' maintenance by the end of the century. Now we have reached the end of the century and, although the target has not been met, the statistics are encouraging. Tourism to Madagascar is rising (23% in one year) and encouragingly, there was an eightfold increase in visitors to protected areas between 1992 and 1997. In 1995 only 20% of visitors to Madagascar went to a national park or reserve; now it is 50%. At present only four national parks – Isalo, Montagne d'Ambre, Ranomafana and Andasibe/Périnet – are easy to visit, and these generate 60% of the total revenue from entrance fees.

There are two main reasons that the protected areas are not yet self supporting. One is that half the revenue from entrance fees goes (thank goodness!) to local community development projects, and the other is that of the entire network of national parks and reserves, many are not open to tourists at all, and those that are may be difficult to reach or have no facilities (not that that stops my readers getting there and enjoying the solitude!).

Permits

Permits to visit the reserves and national parks cost foreigners 50,000Fmg per person per reserve. Half this entrance fee goes to ANGAP and half to local communities, so each visitor is playing his or her part. Permits are mostly available at the park/reserve entrance (be sure to get a receipt) but you may wish to visit the ANGAP office in Antananarivo for the latest information.

Hiring guides

After years of confusion and consequent resentment, fees for guides are more or less standardised and posted by the entrance to the popular parks and reserves: currently 20,000Fmg (about £2/US$3.20) for a two-hour day walk or 40,000Fmg for a night walk. This is for a maximum of three people – larger groups pay more. Some expert guides in places like Périnet charge a higher rate to take specialist groups such as birders: 250Ff per day.

Always check and confirm the fee before you set out. If the guide has been exceptional, by all means add a tip or present, but do not feel that it is obligatory. Bear in mind the enormous earnings of these people compared with, say, the 160,000Fmg (£60/US$25) per month earned by a labourer in the sisal plantations.

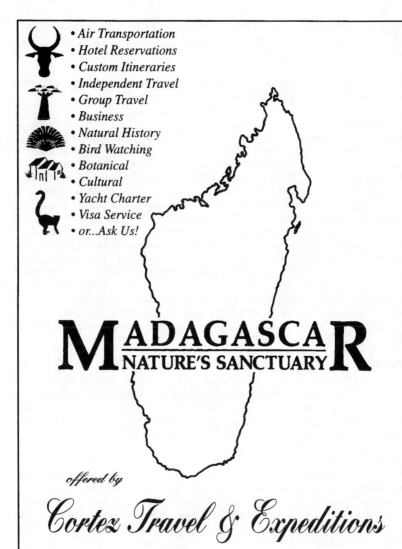

76

- Air Transportation
- Hotel Reservations
- Custom Itineraries
- Independent Travel
- Group Travel
- Business
- Natural History
- Bird Watching
- Botanical
- Cultural
- Yacht Charter
- Visa Service
- or...Ask Us!

MADAGASCAR
NATURE'S SANCTUARY

offered by

Cortez Travel & Expeditions

Since 1987

In the U.S.

Cortez Travel Inc.
124 Lomas Santa Fe Drive
Solana Beach, CA 92075
Tel: 800-854-1029
Fax: 858-481-7474
susan@cortez-usa.com

In Madagascar

Cortez Expeditions
25 Rue Ny' Zafindriandiky
Antanimena, Antananarivo
Tel: 261-2022-219-74
Fax: 261-2022-213-40
cortezmd@bow.dts.mg

Relais du Masoala
Maroantsetra
Tel: 15
Fax: 261-2022-349-93
relais@simicro.mg

visit our website: www.madagascar–marketplace.com

Planning and Preparations

WHEN TO GO

Read the section on climate (page 10) before deciding when to travel. Broadly speaking, the dry months are in the winter between April and September, but rainfall varies enormously in different areas. The months you may want to avoid are August and during the Christmas holidays, when popular places are crowded, and February and March (the cyclone season) when it will rain. However, the off-peak season can be rewarding, with cheaper international airfares and accommodation and fewer other tourists. September is nice, but often windy in the south. April and May often have lovely weather, and the countryside is green after the rainy season.

Keen naturalists have their own requirements: botanists will want to go in February when many of the orchids are in flower, and herpetologists will also prefer the spring/summer because reptiles are more active – and brightly coloured – during those months. Bear in mind that giant jumping rats, dwarf lemurs, tenrecs and some reptiles are less active so harder to see during the cold dry months of June, July and August.

My favourite months to visit Madagascar are October and November, when the weather is fine but not too hot, the jacarandas are in flower, the lemurs have babies, and lychees are sold from roadside stalls.

RED TAPE
Visas

A visa is required by everyone (except citizens of Malawi and Lesotho) and is normally issued for a stay of 30 days. Visas, costing 170Ff or the equivalent in other hard currencies (about £16/US$26), are now issued at the airport in Antananarivo on arrival – at present a much easier and cheaper option than applying through your local embassy or consulate. The situation could change, however, and if you require more than 30 days or are travelling on business you should obtain your visa before leaving home.

Long-term visas are usually available for stays of more than 90 days, but need authorisation from Antananarivo so can take about two months to process. Travellers who apply for a visa extension during their stay are usually successful.

Embassy and consulate addresses

Australia Consulate; Floor 7, 19–31 Pitt St, Sydney, NSW 2000; tel: 02 9252 3770; fax: 02 9247 8406. Hours 09.00–13.00. Visas are issued within 24 hours and cost AUS$38. The consul-general, Anthony Knox, is very enthusiastic and helpful. He is also the agent for Air Madagascar.

Austria Consulate; Pötzleindorferstr 94, A-1184 Wien; tel: 47 91 273; fax: 47 91 2734.

Belgium Embassy; 276 Av de Tervueren, 1150 Bruxelles; tel: 770 1726 & 770 1774; fax: 722 3731; email: ambassade.madagascar@skynet.be.

Canada Embassy; 649 Blair Rd, Gloucester, Ontario K1J 7M4; tel: (613) 744 7995; fax: (613) 744 2530; email: ambmgnet@inexpres.net.
Honorary Consulate; 8530 Rue Saguenay, Brossard, Québec, J4X IM6; tel/fax: (450) 672 0353.
Honorary Consulate; 8944 Bayridge Drive SW, Calgary, Alberta T2V 3M8; tel: (403) 262 5576; fax: (403) 262 3556.
France Embassy; 4 Av Raphael, 75016 Paris; tel: 1 45 04 62 11; fax: 1 45 03 31 75. Visas take up to three days and cost 170Ff (single) or 200Ff (multiple).
Consulate; 234 Bd Perrier, 13008 Marseille; tel: 4 91 15 16 91; fax: 4 91 53 79 58.
Germany Consulate; Rolandstrasse 48 (Postfach 1200251), 53179 Bonn; tel: 0228 95 35 90; fax: 0228 33 46 28; email: 320044351112-0001@t-online.de.
Italy Embassy; Via Riccardo Zandonai 84/A, Roma; tel: 36307797; fax: 06 329 43 06.
Kenya Honorary Consulate; First floor, Hilton Hotel (PO Box 41723), Nairobi; tel: 225 286; fax: 252 347. Allow 24 hours.
Mauritius Embassy; Av Queen Mary, Port Louis; tel: 686 3956; fax: 686 7040.
Réunion Consulate; 73 Rue Juliette Dodu, 97461 Saint-Denis; tel: 21 05 21/21 65 58. Visas cost the same as in France.
South Africa Consulate; No 13 6th St, Houghton Estate, Johannesburg; tel: 442 3322; fax: 442 6660; email: consul@infodoor.co.za; 30-day visa, single entry R120, multiple entry $140; 90-day visa, single entry R180, multiple entry R200.
Consulate; Hon Consul: David Fox; 201 Percy Osborne Rd, Morningside, Durban; tel/fax: 312 9704; email: mdconsul@icon.co.za. Visas issued for 90 days only, single entry R120, multiple entry R140.
Spain Honorary Consulate; Balmes 202–2a, 08006 Barcelona; tel: 415 1006; fax: 415 2953.
Switzerland Honorary Consulate; 2 Theaterplatz, 3011 Bern; tel: 311 3111; fax: 311 0871; email: Hocomad@Datacomm.ch.
UK Honorary Consulate; 16 Lanark Mansions, Pennard Rd, London W12 8DT; tel: 020 8746 0133; fax: 020 8746 0134. Hours 09.30–13.00. Visas supplied immediately or by post; very helpful. £40 (single entry) or £50 (double entry). Business visas cost £55. Note: a visa can be easily bought at the airport in Antananarivo for £16.
United States Embassy; 2374 Massachusetts Av NW, Washington DC 20008; tel: 202 265 5525.
Permanent Mission of Madagascar at the UN; 801 Second Street, New York NY 10017; tel: 212 744 3816; fax: 212 986 6271; email: mission.madagascar@itu.ch. For some reason visas from here cost double the normal rate!
Honorary Consulate; It's convenient that the Hon Consul in California is Monique Rodrigues, who runs the specialist tour operator, Cortez Travel; 124, Lomas Santa Fe Drive, No 208, Solana Beach, CA 92075; tel: 619 792 6999. Visas in the US usually cost US$33.45 for a single-entry visa.

Extending your visa

A visa extension is usually easy to obtain. As early in your trip as possible go to the Ministry of the Interior, five minutes from the Hilton Hotel in Antananarivo. For your *prolongation* you will need three photos, a photocopy of your currency declaration, a typewritten declaration (best done at home) of why you want to stay longer, a *Certificat d'Hébergement* from your hotel, your passport, your return ticket and 180,000Fmg (£30/US$45). Every provincial town has an immigration office, or at least a Commissariat de Police, so in theory you can extend your visa anywhere.

Currency restrictions and taxes

You are no longer required to fill in currency forms, and there are no restrictions on changing or using foreign money in Madagascar.

There is an international and a domestic airport tax (see page 137). Tourists staying in upmarket hotels are required to pay a small tourist tax.

The international airport tax is payable in hard currency or Malagasy francs (Fmg): Ff80 (or equivalent) to Indian Ocean destinations (including South Africa), Ff100 for other places. There is a domestic 'security tax' of 11,000Fmg.

Note: only change as much money into Fmg as you are likely to need. You cannot change it back into hard currency on departure.

Film-makers

Making a wildlife film in Madagascar is expensive. Even amateurs must declare their camcorder when they pass through Customs on arrival, and will be asked to pay a high charge if filming in Tsimbazaza Zoo. Professionals filming in nature reserves are charged a high fee and must request a permit before they arrive in Madagascar. All equipment they are bringing in must be declared; any item that is not on the permit may be confiscated (note: amateurs do not need a permit – this applies to professionals only). Your local Madagascar consulate should be able to give you more details.

GETTING THERE
By air

If you are planning to take several domestic flights during your stay, Air Madagascar should be the international carrier since they offer a discount called 'Decomad' which gives a 33% discount on flights between the most popular destinations in Madagascar, providing visitors also book their international flight on Air Madagascar. This pass is only valid for visitors staying one to four weeks; those on an extended visit pay the full rate.

TAM, which flies between Réunion and Nosy Be and covers some domestic airports, offers a similar discount (30%).

From Europe

As with any long-haul flight it is often cheaper to book through an agency such as Trailfinders (tel: 020 7938 3366), WEXAS (tel: 020 7581 8768) or STA (tel: 020 7361 6262) rather than phoning the airline direct. At the time of writing only Air Madagascar and Air France fly to Madagascar.

Air Madagascar The country's national airline is due to be privatised. Contact Air Madagascar, Première House, Betts Way, Crawley, West Sussex RH10 2GB; tel: 01293 596 666; fax: 01293 512 229.

There are, as yet, no Air Madagascar flights from London – it is necessary to fly to Paris and connect with the Air Mad flight from CDG Airport (section 2a). 1999 airfares from Paris range from £640 (low season) to £850 (high season) but there are often special promotions with lower fares.

Flight schedules are reviewed half-yearly. At the time of writing (June 1999) they leave Paris on Tuesdays (direct), Wednesdays (direct), Thursday (via Munich and Nairobi), Saturdays (via Rome and Nairobi) and Sundays (direct). These flights are overnight, taking approximately 14 hours.

Travellers from mainland Europe will want to contact the nearest Air Madagascar office: the address of the head office in Paris is 29, Rue des Boulets, Paris 75011; tel: 53 27 21 10 or 43 79 42 10; fax: 43 79 30 33. There are also Air Madagascar offices in Brussels (tel: 02 712 6420); Rotterdam (tel: 010 437 9911); Munich (tel: 089 2900 3940) Vienna (tel: 01 5853 63088); Geneva (tel: 022 732 42 30, fax: 022 731 16 90), Zürich (tel: 01 816 40 51). In Italy there are offices in Rome (tel: 47 47 368), Verona (tel: 04 5670 0802), Palermo (tel: 09 1611 3366/7), and Florence (tel: 05 5496 663).

Air France Flights depart from Heathrow via Paris on Mondays, Wednesdays and Fridays, returning from Tana the following day. The fares are the same as Air Madagascar – currently from 5150Ff to 8900Ff, depending on the season.

CORSAIR This is the cheapest option, 4,535Ff in 1999, but tickets can only be purchased in Paris through Nouvelles Frontières, 3 Boulevard Saint-Martin, 75003 Paris; tel: 01 4027 0208; fax: 01 4027 0019; website: www.nouvelles-frontieres.fr.

On most airlines serving Madagascar there are low-season and high-season rates. Low season is from January to the end of June, and mid-September to mid-December. High season is July and August, and the Christmas holiday.

From other Indian Ocean islands
Réunion
The following airlines fly from Paris to Réunion: Air France, AOM French Airlines, Air Liberté, and British Airways. From Réunion there are almost daily Air Madagascar flights to Antananarivo, and also to Nosy Be and Mahajanga. TAM and Austral both operate between Réunion and Nosy Be. TAM also flies to Antsiranana (Diego Suarez). A return flight between Réunion and Nosy Be costs around £175/US$280.

Mauritius
Air Mauritius and Air Madagascar fly between Mauritius and Antananarivo.

Comoro Islands
Air Austral and Air Madagascar fly from Mayotte and Air Mauritius from Moroni. Both go to Nosy Be.

From Africa
Kenya
There are several flights per week (Air Madagascar, Air Mauritius and Air France) from Nairobi. With so many cheap flights from London to Nairobi, this may be a good option – if you can stand the departure time of 02.50 Thursday morning and 06.00 Sunday morning, and the danger of the planes being overbooked since they are coming from Europe. Current (1999) fares for a 30-day excursion are US$460, but for over 30 days it goes up to US$760.

South Africa
Flights go twice a week from South Africa. Air Madagascar (tel: 011 784 7724) flies from Johannesburg on Sundays at 08.30, returning on Saturdays at 17.05; and Inter Air (tel: 011 397 1445) flies on Tuesdays at 08.30, returning on Wednesdays. The flight takes four hours and, at a discounted rate through a tour operator, costs about R1,600.

From the USA
Madagascar is about as far from California as it is possible to be. Indeed, San Francisco and the southern town of Toliara *are* as far apart as it is possible to be. Understandably, therefore, fares from the USA are expensive, but are coming down. Currently the best deal from New York is US$1300 (November and February) or US$2200 (July and August); from California you can travel west via Singapore for about US$1800. Phone Air Madagascar on 800 821 3388, fax: 619 792 5280.

An agency providing cheap flights to Africa, including Madagascar, is Africa Air Center; tel: 800 727 7207.

From Australia
Air Madagascar has an office in the same building as the Sydney Consulate. Flights are usually routed via Singapore, from where there is an Air Madagascar flight to Antananarivo on Fridays. Alternatively you can go from Melbourne or Perth to Mauritius (Air Mauritius) connecting with an Air Madagascar flight to Antananarivo, or flying from Perth via Johannesburg.

By sea
From South Africa
There is no longer a passenger-carrying cargo boat running from Durban, but many people sail their own yacht to Madagascar.

Yacht clubs
Royal Natal Yacht Club PO Box 2946, Durban 4000; tel: 031 301 5425; fax: 031 307 2590.
Point Yacht Club PO Box 2224, Durban 4000; tel: 031 301 4787; fax: 031 305 1234.
Richards Bay Yacht Club PO Box 10387, Meer'en'see 3901; tel: 0351 788 0256; fax: 0351 788 0254.
Royal Cape Yacht Club PO Box 777, Cape Town 8000; tel: 021 4211 354; fax: 0214216 028.

Many yachts sail from Natal to Madagascar and the Durban consulate was set up to cope with their visas. It takes six to seven days to sail to Anakao, the most popular port (south of Toliara). Most stop en route at Europa island, where a French garrison will advise on the next stage. Experienced sailors and divers will want to reach the atoll of Bassas da India which offers superb diving but has been responsible for the shipwreck of numerous vessels.

Because of the increasing number of yachts visiting the northwest of Madagascar, I give information for 'yachties' in the Nosy Be chapter.

Boat charters (South Africa)
Andrew Wright Tel/fax: 031 708 5664.
SA Cruising Association Dennis Wiggins; tel: 031 305 2125.

WHAT TO TAKE
Luggage
A sturdy duffel bag or backpack is more practical than a suitcase (and you may not be allowed to take a suitcase on a Twin Otter plane). Backpackers should consider buying a rucksack with a zipped compartment to enclose the straps when using them on airlines. Or – a cheaper option – roll up the straps and bind them out of the way with insulating tape. Bring a light folding nylon bag for taking purchases home, and the largest permissible bag to take as hand baggage on the plane. Pack this with everything you need for the first four or so days. Lost or delayed luggage is then less of a catastrophe.

Clothes
Before deciding what clothes to pack, take a look at the Climate section on page 10. There is quite a difference between summer and winter temperatures, particularly in the highlands and the south where it is distinctly cold at night between May and September. A fibre-pile jacket or a body-warmer (down vest) is useful in addition to a light sweater. At any time of the year it will be hot during the day in low-lying areas, and very hot between October and March. Layers of clothing – T-shirt, sweatshirt, light sweater – are warm and versatile, and take less room than a heavy

sweater. Don't bring jeans, they are too heavy and too hot. Lightweight cotton or cotton mix trousers such as Rohan Bags are much more suitable. The Bags have a useful inside zipped pocket for security. At any time of year you will need a light showerproof jacket, and during the wet season, or if spending time in the rainforest, appropriate raingear and perhaps a small umbrella. A light cotton jacket is always useful for breezy evenings by the coast. Don't forget a hat.

For footwear, trainers (running shoes) and sandals are usually all you need. 'Sports sandals' which strap securely to the feet are better than flip-flops. Hiking boots may be required in places like Ankarana and Isalo but are not necessary for the main tourist circuits.

Give some thought to beachwear if you enjoy snorkelling. You may need an old pair of sneakers (or similar) to protect your feet from coral and sea urchins, and a T-shirt and shorts to wear while in the water to prevent sunburn.

Toiletries

You can buy most things in Madagascar now, but it's still sensible to bring everything you need. You should also bring a roll of toilet paper, though you can usually buy adequately soft toilet paper in supermarkets. Don't rely on the local WCs supplying any sort of paper.

A correspondent notes with satisfaction that condoms are very cheap and reliable. Certainly Madagascar is addressing the problem of AIDS with enthusiasm: in the drawer of my posh Tana hotel was Gideon's Bible and a condom!

Bring as many baby-wipes or – better – moist toilet tissues as you can. Apart from the pleasure of being able to freshen up during a long trip, these are essential for washing hands when there is no water and will help you avoid traveller's diarrhoea.

Some toilet articles have several uses: dental floss is excellent for repairs as well as for teeth, and a nail brush gets clothes clean too.

Don't take up valuable space with a bath towel – a hand towel is perfectly adequate.

Protection against mosquitoes
Repellents

With malaria on the increase, it is vital to be properly protected. For maximum protection use repellent containing at least 50% DEET. Other nicer-smelling but less effective repellents based on eucalyptus or citronella are OK if you are unlikely to be outside at dawn or dusk. Buzz-Bands (made by Traveller International Products) which slip over the wrists and ankles are recommended as easy to use and effective.

For hotel rooms, pyrethrum coils which burn slowly through the night and repel insects with their smoke are available all over Madagascar. The brand name is Big-Tox. They really do work.

Mosquito nets

Most Category A and B hotels either have effective screening or provide mosquito nets, but if you are staying in C hotels or travelling by overnight taxi-brousses (which may stop or break down) you should bring a mosquito net. Because most hotels do not have anything to hang a net from, a self-standing net is more practical (though a lot more expensive). In Britain the best are probably those made by Bedouin (tel: 01752 609104) and in the USA by Long Road (tel: 800 359 6040; website: www.longroad.com). They have a built-in groundsheet giving protection from bed bugs and fleas as well as mosquitoes. This means, however, that you must use your own sleeping bag inside it. You should also treat these nets with Permethrin, which kills bugs on contact.

If you decide to go for a conventional hanging net, and can be creative with drawing pins (thumb tacks) or Blu-tack, nets sold in Britain by SafariQuip (tel: 01433 620320) or Nomad Medical (tel: 020 8889 7014) are recommended.

Rough travel equipment

Basic camping gear gives you the freedom to travel adventurously and can add a considerable degree of comfort to overland journeys.

The most important item is your backpack: this should have an internal frame and plenty of pockets. Protect it from oil, dirt and the effluent of young or furry/feathered passengers with a canvas sack or similar adapted covering. The plastic woven rice sacks sold outside the Marché Artisanal in Tana are ideal for this purpose (bring a large needle and dental floss to do the final custom-fitting in Tana).

In winter (June to August) a lightweight sleeping bag will keep you warm in cheap hotels with inadequate bedding, and on night stops on – or off – 'buses'. A sheet sleeping bag plus a light blanket or space blanket are ideal for the summer months (October to May) and when the hotel linen may be missing or dirty.

An air-mattress or pillow pads your bum on hard seats as well as your hips when sleeping out. One of those horseshoe-shaped travel pillows lets you sleep sitting up (which you'll need to do on taxi-brousses).

A lightweight tent allows you to strike out on your own and stay in nature reserves, on deserted beaches and so forth. It will need to have a separate rain-fly and be well-ventilated. A bivi-sac, or a Long Road or Bedouin mosquito net tent (treated with Permethrin), is sufficient for the occasional night out.

Most people forgo a stove in order to cut down on weight, but if you will be camping extensively bring a stove that burns petrol (gasoline) or paraffin (kerosene). Meths (*alcohol à bruler*) is usually available as well. There are always fresh vegetables for sale in the smallest village so bring some stock cubes to make vegetable stew.

Take your own mug and spoon (and carry them with you always). That way you can enjoy roadside coffee without the risk of a cup rinsed in filthy water, and market yoghurt without someone else's germs on the spoon. Milk powder tastes (to most people) better in tea or coffee than condensed milk. You can buy it locally, or bring it from home. Don't forget a water-bottle. The sort that has a belt attached – or that can be attached to a belt – is ideal.

Give some thought to ways of interacting with the locals (see *Show and tell* items below). Bring the Malagasy phrase-book and cassette (see page 29) and practise your language skills on fellow passengers. Take along some playing cards or dominoes.

A good book allows you to retreat from interaction for a while (but you won't be able to read on a taxi-brousse). Bring enough reading matter with you – English-language books are not easy to find in Madagascar. If you want to read at night, buy a 100-watt bulb (bayonet type) to substitute for the 40-watt one supplied by Category C hotels.

Photographic equipment

Ordinary print film is available in Madagascar, but it is safer to bring plenty. It can be competently developed in Tana, Fianar and Nosy Be. Slide film is harder to find. Bring twice as much film as you think you'll need.

You will not need a telephoto lens for the lemurs of Berenty and Nosy Komba (wide-angle is more useful for these bold animals) but you'll want a long lens plus very fast film (400 ASA) and a flash for most forest creatures. For landscapes 64 or 100 ASA is ideal. A macro lens is wonderful for all the weird insects and reptiles. Don't overburden yourself with camera equipment – there's no substitute for the eye/brain combination!

Photocopies

Pay a visit to a photocopy shop before you leave home and take copies of the information page of your passport, Madagascar visa (if you have bought it in advance) and air tickets. Then, if the worst happens and you lose all your most precious possessions you can at least replace these items easily.

Miscellaneous

Bring a roll of insulating tape or – also known as gaffer tape – which can be used for all manner of things. Blu-Tack is equally versatile; bring enough to make a plug for your sink, to stop doors banging or to hold them open. A Swiss Army knife (or similar) is essential. A rubber wedge will secure your hotel door at night, and a combination lock is useful in a variety of ways (see the section on safety, page 105). Many readers report (and I agree) that a small tape recorder/Walkman is a great asset during lone evenings in dingy hotel rooms or on an all-night taxi-brousse. Earplugs are just about essential, to block out not only the sounds of the towns but those of enthusiastic nocturnal animals when camping in reserves! (Personally I think it's worth being kept awake by these, but it can pall after several nights.) A large handkerchief or bandana has many uses and protects your hair and lungs from dust, and the uses for a *lamba* (Malagasy sarong) are too numerous to list.

If you are a keen snorkeller it would be best to bring your own mask and snorkel; they are not always available for hire at the resorts, even in Nosy Be.

Checklist

Small torch (flashlight) with spare batteries and bulb, or headlamp (for nocturnal animal hunts), travel alarm clock (or alarm wristwatch), penknife, sewing kit, scissors, tweezers, safety pins, insulating tape or Sellotape (Scotchtape), string, felt-tipped pen, ballpoint pens, a small notebook, a large notebook for diary and letters home, envelopes, plastic bags (all sizes, sturdy; Zip-loc are particularly useful), universal plug for baths and sinks (though Blu-Tack does the job just as well), elastic clothes line or cord and pegs, concentrated detergent, ear plugs, insect repellent, sunscreen, lipsalve, spare glasses or contact lenses, sunglasses, medical and dental kit (see *Chapter 5*), dental floss, a water bottle, water purifying tablets or other sterilising agent. Compact binoculars, camera and film, books, miniature playing cards, Scrabble/pocket chess set, French dictionary and Malagasy phrasebook.

Goods for presents, sale or trade

This is a difficult area. In the past tourists have handed out presents to children and created the tiresome little beggars you will encounter in the popular areas (if you don't now know the French for pen or sweets, you soon will). They have also handed T-shirts to adults with similar consequences. There are, however, plenty of occasions when a gift is appropriate, although as Will Pepper points out 'On a number of occasions people said this souvenir of Ireland is all well and good but I would prefer cash'. Giving money in return for services is entirely acceptable so in rural areas it's best to pay cash and refrain from introducing a new consumer awareness.

In urban areas or with the more sophisticated Malagasy people, presents are a very good way of showing your appreciation for kindness or extra good service.

Music cassettes often go down well with taxi-brousse drivers, but only pop music. It's worth bringing some duty-free cigarettes, however much you disapprove of the habit. It is probably the present most gratefully received.

If you want to contribute something a little more intellectually satisfying, here is a suggestion from Dr Philip Jones, who travels in Madagascar on behalf of the charity Money for Madagascar. 'I was asked several times for an English Grammar, so any such books would be valued gifts. If visitors take a French–English dictionary, why not leave it in Madagascar?' Frances Kerridge suggests English-language tapes as an alternative to books: 'Almost everyone seems to want to learn English.'

Show and tell items

In previous editions I wrote: 'Better than presents are the things you can bring which allow you to interact with the locals: postcards of your country, picture books, paper and a knowledge of origami, string and a knowledge of cat's cradles. Simple conjuring tricks go down a treat. Photos of your family will be pored over gratifyingly or, if you haven't got a family, the Royal Family will do. If you're unfortunate enough to come from a country that doesn't have a Royal Family, film stars are a good substitute – particularly the male muscle-bound type, preferably scowling. Any colour picture is an attraction; I've been told that the photos in this book drew about 50 viewers at one time! Frisbees and balls all add to the fun. However, to call yourself a real traveller you should be capable of being entertaining without the use of props.'

This last sentence drew the following response from a reader: 'Let me take you to task over a sentence which seemed not to fit with the rest of the book... I've travelled for a few years in a few countries; and I've never felt that I needed to be entertaining in order to interact. How about learning from the people? Finding out what they can contribute? By all means suggest that we have some interactive "props" to use with the relatively sophisticated people we may meet on public transport or in the cities; but please please don't ask us to insult the more remote villagers by assuming that we should lead them in the interaction. I have so often been made aware of – and humbled by – how much they have to teach us, in terms of human qualities and courtesies.' I agree.

MONEY

How much money to take, and how to get emergency funds, is covered in *Chapter 6*, but give some thought to how to take it.

It is far easier to change cash (any hard currency) so this is the best option if you are on a prepaid group tour. Do not bring US$100 bills – these are not being accepted because of the large number of counterfeit ones doing the rounds. The same problem may occur with 500Ff. Otherwise bring travellers' cheques: US dollar or (for Europeans) French franc cheques are the best.

Some of the large hotels accept credit cards, but there are some notable exceptions, such as the Dauphin in Taolagnaro. However, credit cards may be used to draw cash, but with restrictions. The Banque Malgache de l'Océan Indien accepts Visa cards only, and Madagascar Air Tours is the agent for American Express. The French for Visa card is Carte Bleue.

WAYS AND MEANS

I used to think (and write) that Madagascar was not for everyone; this is the point in the book where I wrote 'Are you sure you want to go?'. Now I've come to believe that everyone *can* enjoy Madagascar but not everyone does because they do not take sufficient care in matching the trip to their personality. When planning a holiday most people only consider their interests and how much they are prepared to spend. I feel that a vital component has been missed out.

What sort of person are you?

The Catch 22 of tourism in Madagascar is that the type of person who can afford the trip is often the type least suited to cope with the Malagasy way of life. In our culture assertiveness, a strong sense of right and wrong, and organisational skills are the personality traits which lead to success in business, and thus the income to finance exotic travel. But these 'A' type personalities often find Madagascar unbearably 'inefficient' and frustrating. By having control over their itinerary through a tailor-made tour, or by renting a vehicle and driver, such people are more likely to get the most out of their trip. A group tour, where they must 'go with the flow', may be the least successful option.

Conversely, the happiest travellers are often either those who choose to travel on a low budget (providing they're not obsessed with being ripped off) or those who can adopt the attitude of one elderly woman on a group tour who said 'I'm going to give up thinking; it doesn't work in Madagascar'. It doesn't, and she had a great time!

These days there is a trip to suit everyone in this extraordinary country. It won't be a cheap holiday, but it will be one you never forget so choose wisely. Below are the main options, in descending order of price and comfort.

Expedition cruising

This is the softest choice in that you know that you will sleep in a comfortable bed each night and eat familiar food. It is thus ideal for the adventurous at heart who are no longer able to take the rigours of land travel. It is also sometimes the only way of getting to remote offshore islands and for snorkelling over some of the best reefs in the world. Since I accepted (without too much delay) an offer to lecture on the ships chartered by Noble Caledonia (UK) and Special Expeditions (US) I have become a convert – indeed, I've had some of my best Madagascar experiences ever from the *Caledonian Star* and the *Professor Khromov*. Contact Noble Caledonia Ltd, 11 Charles St, London W1X 7HB (tel: 020 7491 4752) or Quark Expeditions, 980 Post Rd, Darien, CT 06820, USA (tel: 800 356 5699) or Lindblad Special Expeditions (tel: 800 397 3348). In South Africa try Starlight Cruises (tel: 011 884 7680 (Alan Foggitt)), and in Australia Adventure Associates (tel: 02 9389 7466).

Tailor-made tours

This is the ideal option for a couple or small group who are not restricted financially. It is also the best choice for people with special interests or who like things to run as smoothly as possible. You will be the decision-maker and will choose where you want to go and your preferred level of comfort, but the logistics will be taken care of. Tour operators which specialise in tailor-made tours in Madagascar are listed below. Alternatively use the travel consultant Seraphine Tierney, who runs Discover Madagascar. This Malagasy woman (and contributor to this book) has the advantage that she straddles two cultures so understands better than anyone in Britain what is, and is not, possible in Madagascar. She is particularly interested in advising on cultural trips; tel: 020 8995 3529; email: dismad@globalnet.co.uk.

Special interests

It is easy for groups with a shared interest to have a tour organised for them with an expert leader and local guide. Some sample tours to consider are: fishing, diving, trekking, river journeys, sailing, mineralogy, speleology, birdwatching, herpetology, botany (which can be further split into orchids and succulents), and entomology. Specialist tour operators are included in the list below.

Group travel

Group travel is usually a lot of fun, ideal for single people who do not wish to travel alone, and if you choose the tour company and itinerary carefully you will see a great deal of the country, gain an understanding of its complicated culture and unique wildlife, and generally have a great time without the need to make decisions (but you need to be able to relinquish the decision-making; not everyone can do this).

TRAVEL IN YOUR OWN OR A HIRED VEHICLE
In your own vehicle
Derek Schuurman

More and more adventure travellers are taking on challenging overland trips in the most remote parts of Madagascar. Some ship their 4WD vehicles to Tamatave harbour and start (and end) there. Here are a couple of things to bear in mind while planning:

1) Vehicle insurance: This can be arranged in Tamatave; must include Third Party insurance. Optional cover includes theft, fire, etc. The cover cost per vehicle depends on the type of 4WD (value, number of seats, etc)

2) Petrol/gasoline costs 2,290Fmg/litre (1999); diesel is 1,770Fmg/litre.

It is recommended you use diesel rather than petrol while in Madagascar. Be sure to find out from a reliable source where on your route there are filling stations. (You'd be surprised at how many remote places actually have a filling station, but not all of them do.) Check on the best maps for road conditions/possible routes and then check again in Antananarivo as to which routes are feasible. The best time for these overland adventure trips is, of course, the dry season.

In a hired vehicle
Ken and Lorna Gillespie

Following advice from other travellers we hired a private guide with extensive botanical knowledge (that being our main interest) and, through Trans-Continents, a driver and 4WD vehicle. Very expensive ($115 per day excluding the guide), but it eased us into Malagasy travel ensuring everything was relatively drama-free. Such an arrangement suits our limited time and, most importantly, allows the flexibility to pursue our botanical interests, whilst maintaining comfort. Our accommodation choice was always local and unpretentious, and produced many cherished memories. The Malagasy Basics tape and book were a wonderful introduction to the language.

We averaged 15km/h for three days in perfect weather, but frustration with travel evaporates along roads flanked by adasonias. The Malagasy desire to be traders provides ample opportunity to purchase food even if it isn't market day, but we were unable to locate methylated spirits for our stove. The most sought-after item we carried was our plastic bucket.

Many of the listed tour operators in the UK and the USA do set departures (ie: group tours rather than tailor-made trips) to Madagascar.

Working holidays

There is a growing interest in paying to be a volunteer in a scientific project in Madagascar. The pioneer here is Earthwatch. Among other things in Madagascar you can work with Dr Alison Jolly or Josephine Andrews on lemur research. Addresses: Belsyne Court, 57 Woodstock Rd, Oxford OX2 6HU, England, tel: 01865 311600; and PO Box 9104, Watertown, MA 02272-9104, USA, tel (800) 776 0188; email: info@earthwatch.org. A similar organisation for students is World Challenge Expeditions, Black Arrow House, 2 Chandos Rd, London NW10 6NF, tel: 020 8961 1122; fax: 020 8961 1551; email: welcome@world-challenge.co.uk.

Semi-independent travel

If you have a fax machine or email and are willing to persevere with Madagascar's erratic telecommunications (which are rapidly improving), you can save money by dealing directly with a tour operator in Madagascar. The best ones are listed later in this chapter. The level of satisfaction in arranging a tour this way is very high. Now tourism is established in Madagascar, local operators have a clear understanding of tourists' needs and are impressively efficient. Of course things go wrong (and if they do there is no point in suing) but the cause is usually poor infrastructure rather than incompetence.

Perhaps the ideal do-it-yourself trip is to hire a local driver/guide and vehicle. This way you are wonderfully free to stop when you please and stay where you wish. This is best done through a tour operator in Tana, but I can recommend Claude Rambeloson who is personable, fun and has his own 4WD vehicle. Claude speaks excellent English and German, is knowledgeable on a wide range of subjects, and an expert on orchids. He can be contacted on BP 1223, Antananarivo 101; tel/fax: (261 20) 22 472 35; mobile phone: (261) 32 07 052 01.

Independent travel

Truly independent travellers usually have a rough idea of where they want to go and how they will travel, but are open to changes of plan dictated by local conditions, whim and serendipity. Independent travellers are not necessarily budget travellers: those who can afford to fly to major towns, then rent a vehicle and driver, can eliminate a large amount of hassle and see everything they set out to see – providing they set a realistic programme for themselves. What they miss out on is contact with the local people, and some of the smells, sounds and otherness of Madagascar.

The majority of independent travellers (and users of this book) go by public transport and stay in B or C Category hotels. They are exposed to all Madagascar's joys and frustrations and most seem to love it, even if they agree that they have never travelled in a country that is so difficult to get around in (though this is changing – the popular circuits are usually pretty trouble-free). The key here is not to try too much. *Chapter 6* tells you about the trials and tribulations of travelling by taxi-brousse: no problem providing you allow time for delays.

The seriously adventurous

Madagascar must be one of the very few countries left in the world where large areas are not yet detailed in a guidebook. A study of the standard 1:2,000,000 map of Madagascar reveals some mouth-watering possibilities, and a look at the more detailed 1:500,000 maps confirms the opportunities for people who are willing to walk or cycle. In my very thick Readers' Letters file I have some wonderful accounts from travellers who did just that. Not everyone is courageous enough to step or pedal into the unknown like this, but in fact it's one of the safest ways to travel: the Malagasy that you meet will, once they have got over the shock of seeing you, invariably be welcoming and hospitable. The risk of crime is very low.

It's how I first saw Madagascar and why I fell in love with the place.

Tour operators
UK
Abercrombie and Kent Travel Tel: 020 7559 8600; fax: 020 7730 9376; email: info@abercrombiekent.co.uk. Escorted wildlife tours.

Africa Exclusive Tel: 01604 628979; fax: 01604 639879; email: africa@africaexclusive.co.uk. Tailor-made trips. (See inside back cover.)

ACE Study Tours Tel: 01223 835055; fax: 01223 837394; email: ace@study-tours.org. Occasional Madagascar trips.

Animal Watch Tel: 01732 811838; fax: 01732 455441; email: mail@animalwatch.co.uk. Regular wildlife trips to Madagascar.

Arc Journeys Tel: 020 7681 3175 (24hr phone and fax line); mobile: 0370 986653; email: arc@travelarc.com. Tailor-made cultural and nature tours.

Crusader Travel Tel: 020 8744 0474; fax: 020 87440574; email: info@crusadertravel.com. Includes diving trips. (See page 132.)

David Sayers Travel Tel: 01572 821330; fax: 01572 821072; email: ABROCK3650@aol.com. Regular trips to Madagascar with a botanical angle. All tours are escorted by David Sayers.

Discover the World Ltd Tel: 01737 218800; fax: 01737 362341; email: sales@arctic-discover.co.uk. Regular trips to Madagascar; no special focus. (See page 132.)

Earthwatch Tel: 01865 311600; fax: 01865 311383; email: info@uk.earthwatch.org. Several trips focus on Madagascar (wildlife). See *Working holidays*, page 000.

Explore Worldwide Ltd Tel: 01252 319448; fax: 01252 319100; email: res@explore.co.uk. Regular Madagascar trips; no special focus.

Naturetrek Tel: 01962 733051; fax: 01962 736426; email: info@naturetrek.co.uk. Special focus: birds and mammals.

Okavango Tours & Safaris Tel: 020 8343 3283; fax: 020 8343 3287; email: info@okavango.com. No special focus. (See page 226.)

Ornitholidays 29 Straight Mile, Romsey, Hampshire SO51 9BB; tel/fax: 01794 519445; email: ornitholidays@compuserve.com. Birdwatching.

Papyrus Tours Tel: 01302 371321. Small group wildlife tours.

Partnership Travel Tel: 020 8343 3446; fax: 020 8349 3439; email: info@partnershiptravel.co.uk. (See page 264.)

Reef & Rainforest Tours Tel: 01803 866965; fax: 01803 865916; email: reefrain@btinternet.com. Specialists in Madagascar with a wide variety of tours. (See page 94.)

Southern Africa Travel Tel: 01483 419133; fax: 01483 860180; email: sat.london@btinternet.com.

Sunbird Tel: 01767 682969; fax: 01767 692481; email: sunbird@sunbird.demon.co.uk. Regular Madagascar birding trips.

Tim Best Travel Tel: 020 7591 0300; fax: 020 7591 0301; email: t.besttravel@easynet.co.uk. Tailor-made tours (especially wildlife and birds).

Worldwide Adventures Abroad Tel: 0114 247 3400; fax: 0114 251 3210; email: abroad@globalnet.co.uk; website: www.adventures-abroad.com.

Worldwide Journeys & Expeditions Tel: 020 7381 8638; fax: 020 7381 0836; email: wwj@wjournex.demon.co.uk. Tailor-made trips to Madagascar. (See page 132.)

USA

Cortez Travel Services 124 Lomas Santa Fe Dr, Solano Beach, CA 92075; tel: (619) 755 5136 or (800) 854 1029; fax: (619) 481 7474; email: cortez-usa@mcimail.com. Cortez is the specialist Madagascar operator in the US; Monique Rodriguez has been running trips there for nearly two decades and knows the practicalities better than anyone else in the travel business. She is agent for Air Madagascar and Honorary Consul.

Australia

Adventure Associates Pty Ltd 197 Oxford St Mall, Bondi Junction, Sydney, NSW 2022 (PO Box 612, Bondi Junction, NSW 1355); tel: 02 9389 7466; fax: 02 9369 1853; email: mail@adventureassociates.com; website: www.adventureassociates.com. They are the only tour operator in Australia with regular Madagascar departures.

South Africa

The specialists here are Unusual Destinations, PO Box 97508, Petervale 2151 Gauteng, SA; tel: 011 706 1991; fax 011 463 1469; email: unusdest@global.co.za; website: www.unusualdestination.com. Operations manager Derek Schuurman is the author of a couple of books and numerous articles on Madagascar. His particular interest is in birding and natural history. Regular group departures and specialist natural history trips.

Madagascar

There are many tour operators in Madagascar. This is by no means a complete list, just a selection of those that I can recommend. For a complete list of accredited tour operators (member of TOP – Tours Opérateurs Professionnels) contact TOP: tel/fax: (261 20) 22 788 59; email: topmad@dts.mg.

The full telephone code for Tana is (261 20) 22 followed by the number.

Boogie Pilgrim Villa Michelet, Lot A11, Faravohitra, Antananarivo; tel: 258 78; fax: 625 56; email: bopi@bow.dts.mg. Organise tours of every sort, including some by light aircraft. Owners of Bush House (Pangalanes). Recommended.

Cortez Expeditions 25 Rue Ny Zafindraindiky, Antanimena, Antananarivo; tel: 219 74; fax: 247 87; email: cortez@dts.mg. Probably the most experienced tour operator in Madagascar and owner of the Relais du Masoala in Maroantsetra.

Mad Caméléon Lot II K6, Ankadivato, Antananarivo; BP 4336; tel: 630 86; fax: 344 20; email: madcam@dts.mg. Specialise in river trips and are the only operator to offer the Manambolo river.

Madagascar Airtours 33 Av de l'Indépendance, Antananarivo; BP 3874; tel: 241 92; fax: 641 90. Also at the Hilton Hotel. The most experienced agency, with offices in most major towns, they can organise a wide variety of specialist tours including natural history, ornithology, speleology, trekking, mineralogy, river trips, sailing, etc.

Malagasy Tours Lot VX29, Avaradrova, Antananarivo; tel/fax: 356 07. The owner, Olivier Toboul, runs specialised itineraries for ethnobotany (amongst other things) using local people who can explain the complexities of the Malagasy culture. Good for off-the-beaten-track exploration, too.

Roots Rhythms Madagascar BP 235, Nosy Be 207; tel: Nosy Be (86) 611 30 (office hours); email: @simicro.mg. Traditional music in and wildlife in Nosy Be.

Rova Travel Tours 35 Rue Refotaka, Analakely; tel: 276 67; fax: 276 89; email: rtt@bow.dts.mg.

SETAM Rue du 26 Juin 1960, Antananarivo; tel: 359 14/324 33; fax: 324 35; email: setam@bow.dts.mg. Very helpful and efficient. Recommended.

Transcontinents 10 Av de l'Indépendance, Antananarivo; BP 551; tel: 223 98; fax: 283 65; email: transco@dts.mg. Efficiently run. Recommended.

Tropika Touring 41 Rue Ratsimilaho; BP 465; tel: 222 30 or 276 80; fax: 349 01; email: tropica@dts.mg.
Tropic Tours and Travel 30, Rue de Russie, Isoraka, Antananarivo; BP 8019; tel: 645 16/634 99; fax: 645 17; email: tropic@bow.dts.mg.
Voyages Bourdon 15 Rue P Lumumba, Antananarivo; BP 8196; tel: 296 96; fax: 285 64; email: bourdon@dts.mg.
Za Tour Lot ID 33 Bis, Ambohitsorohitra, Antananarivo 101; tel: 656 48; fax: 656 47; email: za.tour@dts.mg.

HIGHLIGHTS AND ITINERARIES

Having sorted out the 'hows' of travelling in Madagascar you must turn your attention to the all-important subject of 'where'. One of the hardest decisions facing the first-time visitor to a country as large and diverse as Madagascar is where to go. Even a month is not long enough to see everything so itineraries must be planned according to interests and the degree of comfort wanted. First, the highlights, according to interests.

Highlights
Wildlife
The best reserves: Périnet, Montagne d'Ambre, Nosy Mangabe, Ranomafana, Berenty, Kirindy, Ampijoroa, Ankarana.

Scenery
The central highlands between Fianarantsoa and Ambalavao, Isalo National Park, Andohahela National Park (Tsimehely), Avenue of the Baobabs (Morondava), Ankarana, Montagne d'Ambre.

Beaches and watersports
Madagascar's best beaches are on the west coast, but disappoint many people because of the shallow water (it is often impossible to swim at low tide). The beautiful beaches of the east coast are for sunbathing only –sharks are a danger to swimmers. The very best beaches are found at Nosy Be and – better – its outlying islands, Ile Sainte Marie, and south of Toliara, but there are plenty of other lovely ones.

The best diving and snorkelling is on Nosy Mitsio and other small islands off Nosy Be, on Ile Sainte Marie (where you can swim with the whales!) and Ifaty and Nosy Ve near Toliara.

Sport fishing can be organised from Nosy Be.

Fun times
The people of southern Madagascar are the most outgoing on the island, with two good discos in Taolagnaro and Toliara, but Nosy Be is undoubtedly where the action is.

Museums
Madagascar has only a few good museums so it is worth listing them here. The best by far – really super! – is the Museum of the Antandroy in Berenty Reserve. Toliara has a good ethnological museum (and you can see a coelacanth at its marine museum). The Museum of Art and Archaeology in Antananarivo is nicely laid out and interesting, as is the Museum Akiba in Mahajanga. The only natural history museum that I am aware of is in Tsimbazaza in Tana.

People and tombs

Your tour operator may be able to organise a visit to a *famadihana* (only in the Highlands and only between June and September). An unforgettable experience. Merina tombs can easily be seen between Antananarivo and Antsirabe, but the most intriguing and interesting tombs are those of the Mahafaly in the Toliara region.

Itineraries

Luxurious Madagascar

The opening of several top-class hotels in recent years means that it is now possible to see some of the highlights of Madagascar in style. Here are the top-class options: Relais de la Reine (Isalo National Park), Vakona Lodge (Périnet and Mantadia), Relais de Masoala (Maroantsetra), Cocoterie Robert (Ile Ste Marie), Marlin Club Annex or l'Hotel Tsarabajina (Nosy Mitsio, Nosy Be); Anjajavy (northwest coast).

Reliability and comfort

An itinerary which includes the following will provide a good overview of the country and its wildlife, and have hotels of international standard: Antananarivo, Périnet Reserve, Antsirabe, Toliara, Taolagnaro (Fort Dauphin) and Berenty, and Nosy Be or Ile Sainte Marie. The stretches between Antananarivo and Antsirabe should be done by taxi or private car, and the rest by plane.

Nature reserves in moderate comfort

These are accessible by good road and have good-to-moderate accommodation: Ranomafana, Ampijoroa (as a day trip from Mahajanga), Montagne d'Ambre (as a day trip from Antsiranana), Lokobe (Nosy Be) and Berenty.

Camping only reserves

Some of the following can be visited as a day trip, but you will miss the best animal viewing times of dawn and dusk: Kirindy, Tsingy de Bemaraha, Ampijoroa, Ankarana, Marojejy, Masoala, Nosy Mangabe, Andohahela and Beza Mahafaly.

CAVING

Madagascar has some fabulous caves, and several expeditions have been mounted to explore them. Caving is not a popular Malagasy pursuit , however, so cavers should take particular care to explain what they are doing and get the necessary permits for exploring protected areas. An experienced local tour operator will help with the red tape.

The best karst area are in the north and west, as follows.

Ankarana Known for its *tsingy*, this is the best explored and mapped of all karst areas.

Narinda The longest cave, Anjohibe, is 5,330m.

Namoroka Access difficult and safety a problem in this area.

Bemaraha Excellent possibilities for exploration now this tsingy area is being opened up to tourism.

Toliara region Mickoboka Plateau to the north has pits to a depth of 165m, and the Mahafaly Plateau to the south contains numerous small caves.

Birding
See page 48 for full details on the best birding places, but these cover all the different habitats: Ampijoroa (and along the road from Mahajanga), Ranomafana, Marojejy, Masoala, Forest of Ambohetantely, Andohahela or Ifaty (spiny forest), and Zombitse.

Here's a special place for birders: a new restaurant in Tana, the Tonga Soa (see page 147), is planning to become a birding centre. Nick Garbutt reports: 'Brian Finch, the owner's brother, is a well-known birding tour leader (what else could he do with a name like his?) in Madagascar and both he and Patrick are keen to establish Tonga Soa as a place for the exchange of up-to-date information about wildlife. Their intention is to establish a small reference library relating to Malagasy natural history and have a visitor's book that anyone can contribute too as they pass through Tana and say what's been seen where and when. Others looking in may then be able to take advantage of such recent news.'

Landscape, people and tombs
For those whose interest lies more in the people and the countryside, a journey overland is recommended. RN7 from Antananarivo to Toliara gives a wonderful overview from rice-paddies in the highlands to the lovely town of Ambalavao and its magnificent granite mountains, and the small villages between Ihosy and Toliara. It also gives you a chance to see Isalo National Park. The journey is best done in a private vehicle so you can stop and look; there are good hotels in the main towns.

A more adventurous alternative (but still on a good road) is by plane or bus to Toamasina then north by public transport to Soanierana-Ivongo and by boat to Ile Sainte Marie.

Mountain biking and hiking
Madagascar is becoming increasingly popular for travelling using your own muscle-power. The advantages are obvious: bad roads and broken down vehicles do not delay you, con-men will not overcharge you and – most important – by passing slowly through Madagascar's small villages and communities you will experience the Malagasy culture in an unforced way. These advantages far outweigh the inevitable security risks of being totally at the mercy of local people. You are far more likely to be overwhelmed by hospitality than robbed.

Mountain biking is covered in detail under *Transport,* pages 110 and 112.

As yet no organised trekking is being offered on a regular basis in Madagascar. A pity, the grassy, rolling hills of the Ambalavao area of the Highlands beg to be explored on foot. Flying south from Tana you look down on tantalising tracks and paths connecting small villages.

Working in Madagascar
Many tourists, having fallen in love with Madagascar, want to return to work. A few achieve it, but only after much perseverance. Madagascar does not have enough jobs for its own citizens, so only welcomes outsiders who have specialised skills. This also applies to volunteers. Adela Stockton, who worked in Madagascar as a midwife, gives this advice: 'White people are rarely seen outside the main cities. Many Malagasy are actively afraid of them and in some areas there are people who have never seen a white person.

'In the light of this the role of the Western volunteer worker is a sensitive one. If you are professionally skilled in your field of expertise and have a good working knowledge of French, your pair of hands may be useful in certain circumstances. I would suggest you approach specific organisations appropriate to the skills you offer, either in your own country or when in Madagascar. Be prepared to prove your qualifications and expertise and to adapt your skills to local practice rather than imagine that you know best. Remember, the Malagasy may prefer to place their trust in their own people.'

Many people fondly visualise a job working in conservation. (See box on page 72.) This account from one of my regular correspondents Frances Kerridge (Frankie Be) who is studying carnivores in the southeast shows the realities of such work. 'It took nearly two weeks to get from Tana to Vevembe. The vehicle broke down and we were stuck for two days in torrential rain. My fruit and veg started rotting, all the cardboard boxes full of food dissolved, rice and coffee went mouldy, and beans and peanuts started sprouting... Then the river we had to ford was too high for the (mended) car so I had to pay porters to carry everything – traps and other research equipment, tents, tarps, all the kitchen stuff, three months' supply of food etc – the rest of the way. Cost a bloody fortune but we're there. Rosette gets on with her mapping and the student and I get down to the radio-tracking. Then the student breaks his antenna, gets water in his receiver and tells me he really can't do the work, it's too hard and he will be ill. Back to Tana while I search for another student. Another highlight was my guide getting a leech on his eyeball. Mega shouting and screaming, and I thought the student was going to faint. Got it off by killing it (slowly) with a tobacco leaf.'

Reef and Rainforest Tours

OFF-THE-BEATEN-TRACK ANNUAL GROUP TOURS LED BY:

- HILARY BRADT – The author and publisher
- QUENTIN BLOXAM – Jersey Zoo Programme Director, biologist and veteran Madagascar expert
- NICK GARBUTT – Well-known biologist, photographer, and Madagascar tour leader
- 2001: ECLIPSE TOUR See a total eclipse of the sun on 21 June 2001

BROCHURE AVAILABLE

Competitive Fares Offered with AIR MADAGASCAR and AIR FRANCE

TAILOR-MADE/ BESPOKE ITINERARIES FOR ONE OR MORE PERSONS:

- Flexible Dates & Departures.
- Fully Guided (Specialist Birding Guides available).
- All Private Transfers, Flights and Accommodation Arranged.
- Superb Diving Available.
- Camping Specially Organised (All Equipment and Meals Provided).
- Full Consultation and Advice.
- Enjoy this remarkable island on a tour which suits your interests perfectly.

VISIT: PERINET, MAROMIZAHA, MANTADY, HAUTS PLATEAUX, NOSY VE, ANAKAO, IFATY, ISALO, BERENTY, KIRINDY, AMPIJOROA, NOSY BE, ANKARANA, MONTAIGNE D'AMBRE, MASOALA, NOSY MANGABE, RANOMAFANA, ILE STE MARIE.

CONTACT THE MADAGASCAR SPECIALISTS

DURRELL WILDLIFE CONSERVATION TRUST
SAVING SPECIES WORLDWIDE

Reef and Rainforest Tours Ltd.
1 The Plains · Totnes · Devon TQ9 5DR
Tel: 01803-866 965 Fax: 01803-865 916
Email: reefrain@btinternet.com

ATOL
4088

Health and Safety

HEALTH

The health section is written by Dr Jane Wilson-Howarth, who led two expeditions to Ankarana and has travelled the length and breadth of the country. She studied bilharzia near Morondava and has worked as a health adviser in Asia for the last 11 years. She is the author of Bugs, Bites and Bowels *(Cadogan),* Your Child's Health Abroad *(Bradt) and* Lemurs of the Lost World *(Impact).*

Before you go
Malaria prevention

Malaria (including cerebral malaria) is a risk in Madagascar and it is important to protect yourself by avoiding bites between dusk and dawn and also by taking tablets. There is some chloroquine resistance so Mefloquine (Lariam) taken weekly is probably the best prophylactic. However, many people have experienced unpleasant side effects from this drug, so take it for two and a half weeks (three doses) before departure and if it makes you feel weird or gives you nightmares stop it and take another regime. Two chloroquine (Nivaquine) weekly and two proguanil (Paludrine) daily will probably be suggested instead but take advice from a travel clinic or from the Malaria Reference Laboratory in London; phone 0891 600 350 for recorded information (it costs 49p a minute).

Chloroquine and proguanil cause nausea if taken on an empty stomach so take with or soon after food (or milk or biscuits). If pregnant or planning a pregnancy take medical advice before travelling. Some travellers like to carry tablets for the emergency treatment of malaria; if you choose to do this make sure you understand when and how to take them.

Take plenty of insect repellent (DEET-based are best), long-sleeved shirts, long trousers, and consider carrying a mosquito net (see page 82). Nets are most effective if treated with Permethrin or a similar contact insecticide. Kits are sold at many travel clinics.

Immunisations

Seek advice about immunisations a couple of months before travel; in the UK you can see your GP or visit a travel clinic such as those operated by British Airways (phone 01276 685040 for the nearest of the 30 BA clinics); they offer constantly updated health briefs as well as immunisations. It's important that your immunisations for tetanus, polio and typhoid are up to date. A highly effective vaccine against Hepatitis A, Havrix, is recommended for those travelling for several months. Two shots provide protection for ten years.

An 'ordinary' intramuscular shot against rabies is now available and may be worth arranging if you are travelling in remote areas. The disease is a problem in Madagascar because of the half-wild dogs found in many parts of the island. Remember that 'live' vaccines cannot be given within a fortnight of each other, so plan well ahead. There is a list of vaccination centres at the end of this section.

Teeth
Have a dental check-up before you go and if you have a lot of fillings and crowns carry a Dental Emergency Kit (from some pharmacies or ask your dentist).

Insurance
Make sure you have insurance covering the cost of an air ambulance and treatment in Réunion or Nairobi, which offer more sophisticated medical facilities than are available in Madagascar. Europ Assistance International, which has an office in Antananarivo, gives cover for scuba-diving.

Water sterilisation
Bringing water to the boil kills all the microbes that are likely to make you ill on your travels so tea, coffee or *ranovola* (the water rice is boiled in) bought in hotelys are probably the most convenient safe drinks. If travelling with small children you can take a thermos flask; almost-boiling water kept in this for 15 minutes will be thoroughly sterilised. Mineral water is not always available and can be quite expensive, and studies in other countries suggest it may be contaminated. Chemical sterilisation methods do not render water as safe as by boiling, but it is good enough for most purposes. Silver-based sterilising tablets (sold in Britain under the trade name Micropur) are tasteless so recommended. A cheaper and more effective sterilising agent is iodine (preferable to chlorine because it kills amoebic cysts), which is available in liquid or tablet form. To make treated water more palatable, add vitamin C after the sterilisation time is complete or bring packets of powdered drink. An alternative is a water filter such as the Pur system, or Aqua-pure Traveller, which provide safe water with no unpleasant flavour; they are expensive, however. Cheaper, and more versatile, is a plug-in immersion heater, so that you can have a nice hot cuppa (if you bring teabags).

Note that most travellers acquire diarrhoea from inadequately cooked, or reheated, contaminated food – salads, ice, ice-cream, etc – rather than from disobeying the 'don't drink the water' rule.

Some travellers' diseases
Malaria and insect-borne diseases
Tablets do not give complete protection from malaria, though they should make it less serious if it does break through; it's important to protect yourself from being bitten. The mosquitoes which give you malaria usually bite in the evening (from about 17.00) and throughout the night, so it's wise to dress in long trousers and long-sleeved shirts, and to cover exposed skin with insect repellent. *Anopheles* mosquitoes generally hunt at ankle level, and tend to bite the first piece of exposed flesh they encounter, so DEET-impregnated ankle bands are fairly effective in reducing bites. In most countries, malaria transmission is rare in urban environments, but it does occur around Antananarivo because ricefields are so close to the city. Most hotels have screened windows or provide mosquito nets. Bring your own net if staying in cheap hotels. Burning mosquito coils reduces but does not eliminate the risk of bites.

Be sure to take your malaria tablets meticulously until a month after you get home. Even if you have been taking your malaria prophylaxis carefully, there is still a slight chance of contracting malaria. The symptoms are fevers, chills, joint pain, headache and sometimes diarrhoea – in other words the symptoms of many

DO NOT GET SICK IN ANDAPA!

Anne Axel

I consulted three different doctors for an illness with recurrent fever, diarrhoea, vomiting and stomach pain. The first doctor made a house call. He said I had typhoid fever and to take Bactrium. The second doctor said I had eaten too many lychees and the third doctor said perhaps I had malaria. These doctors were incredibly nice, seeing me on a Sunday evening in their home, for no charge. They suggested I come back the next day for a malaria test. Which I did. They then remembered that there are no malaria tests on Mondays. It was Monday. Then I ran into the first doctor who took me to a public hospital. I was glad I'd brought my own needle – all they had was a box of used razor blades. The test was negative.

Note: You take pot luck if you get sick in Madagascar. Some rural clinics are excellent, many are dreadful.

illnesses including flu. Bear in mind that malaria can take as little as seven days to develop. Consult a doctor (mentioning that you have been abroad) if you develop a flu-like illness within a year of leaving a malarious region. The life-threatening cerebral malaria will become apparent within three months and can kill within 24 hours of the first symptoms.

Mosquitoes pass on not only malaria but also elephantiasis, dengue fever and a variety of other unpleasant viral fevers. By avoiding mosquito bites you also avoid these serious diseases, as well as those itching lumps which so easily become infected. Once you've been bitten, tiger balm, calamine lotion or calamine-based creams help stop the itching.

Travellers' diarrhoea

Diarrhoea is very common in visitors to Madagascar, and you are more likely to suffer from this if you are new to tropical travel. Tourists tend to be obsessed with water sterilisation but, contrary to popular belief, travellers' diarrhoea usually comes from contaminated food not contaminated water. Ice-cream, sadly, is particularly risky: a survey in Antananarivo some years ago showed that 100% of home-made and 60% of factory-made ice-creams contained the faecal bacteria which cause diarrhoea. So if you want to stay healthy avoid ice-cream, and also ice, salads, fruit with lots of crevices such as strawberries, uncooked foods and cooked food that has been hanging around or has been inadequately reheated. Sizzling hot street food is likely to be far safer than the food offered in buffets in expensive hotels, however gourmet the latter may look. Yoghurt is usually safe, as are sorbets. Remember **peel it, boil it, cook it or forget it!**

The way to the quickest recovery from travellers' diarrhoea is to reduce your normal meals to a few light or high carbohydrate items, avoid milk and alcohol and drink lots of clear fluids. You need to replace the fluids lost down the toilet, and drinks containing salt and sugar are most easily absorbed. Add a little sugar to a salty drink, such as Marmite or Oxo, or salt to a sugary drink like Coca-Cola. Sachets of rehydration mixtures are available commercially, but you can make your own by mixing a rounded dessertspoon (or four teaspoons) of sugar with a quarter-teaspoon of salt and adding it to a glass of boiled and cooled water. Drink two glasses of this every time you open your bowels – more often if you are thirsty. Substituting glucose for sugar will make you feel even better. If you are in a rural area drink young coconut water or *ranovola* (water boiled in the pot that rice is cooked in).

Hot drinks and iced drinks cause a reflex emptying of the bowel, so avoid these while the diarrhoea is at its worst; they will make the belly-ache worse, too. Once the bowel has ejected the toxic material causing the diarrhoea, the symptoms will settle quite quickly and you should begin to feel better again after 24–36 hours. Should the diarrhoea be associated with passing blood or slime, it would be sensible to have a stool check at some stage, but provided you continue to drink clear fluids, no harm will come from waiting for a few days.

Holiday schedules often make it impossible to follow the 'sit it out' advice. When a long bus journey or flight is anticipated you may wish to take a blocker such as Imodium. Just remember that such drugs slow up the action of the bowel so you tend to feel ill for a longer period of time and they are dangerous if you have dysentery. Safer and far more effective is the antibiotic Ciprofloxacin taken as a three-day course (500mg twice daily). Discuss this with your doctor or travel clinic. Drink lots whatever treatment you are taking and if you are worried or feel very ill, seek local medical advice. As long as you keep well hydrated the symptoms will usually settle without further treatment. Even bacillary dysentery and cholera will usually resolve within a week without treatment, as long as you drink plenty of clear fluids.

Other bowel beasties

There is a high prevalence of tapeworm in Malagasy cattle, so eat your steaks well done. If you do pass a worm, this is alarming but treatment can wait, and indeed travellers often carry only one and so need no treatment.

CHILDBIRTH IN MADAGASCAR
Adela Stockton

I am a qualified midwife, and in 1998 I took three months' unpaid leave to work in Madagascar as a volunteer alongside midwives on a local maternal and child health care programme and at a public maternity unit in Tana.

There is an average of seven live children per family, with some women totalling up to 35 pregnancies during their childbearing years. Forty per cent of women have had their first baby by the age of 19.

For families who can afford to pay, there are private maternity units with good facilities, but for the majority the choice lies between the state hospital and home. The public maternity unit was filthy, the rooms infested with mosquitoes and fleas, with mattresses soiled and windows broken. There is limited funding even for basic plumbing and electricity.

Malagasy women have no pain relief during childbirth. They labour in silence as it is culturally unacceptable to make a noise when in pain. Their attendants (partner/mother/sister/friend) look after them, cleaning up the blood and supporting them, and sleep on the floor.

Malagasy midwives hold equal professional status to doctors. Those I worked alongside were highly skilled and diligent in their practice, although overworked and underpaid.

In some rural areas no maternity services exist at all except for a woman in the village who 'knows something about childbirth'. The women with problems may have to travel 200km to the nearest medical centre over rough dirt roads which, during the raining season, are impassable.

CHOLERA IN MADAGASCAR

During 1999 there was an outbreak of cholera in Madagascar. The authorities appear to have overreacted and set up road blocks where travellers were forced 'at gunpoint' to take three tetracycline pills unless they could prove that they had been immunised against cholera. Jane Wilson-Howarth writes: 'Although it has a fearsome reputation, cholera doesn't usually make ordinary healthy people ill. It takes the debilitated, poor and half-starved of famine and conflict zones, or it is present along with other severe gastro-intestinal infections: it might be seen as a "marker" of faecal contamination. Cholera is avoided in the same way as other filth-to-mouth diseases (peel it, boil it, cook it or forget it) and – if there are symptoms – it can be treated with the usual oral rehydration fluids that all wise travellers know as treatment for simple travellers' diarrhoea.

'Taking two or three antibiotic capsules or tablets is unhelpful, usually, in curing infections and encourages bacterial resistance to antibiotics; this means that when a proper course of treatment is prescribed it is less likely to cure. In addition there are specific contra-indications for taking tetracycline: it should be avoided in pregnancy and in children. It can also cause rashes provoked by sun exposure – though this is unlikely if just taking a couple of pills. The strongest argument against this "treatment" is that it helps no-one and Madagascar could better use its scarce medical resources.'

Bilharzia

This is a nasty, debilitating disease which is a problem in much of lowland Madagascar. The parasite is also carried by pond snails and is caught by people who swim or paddle in clean, still or slow-moving water (not fast-flowing rivers) where an infected person has defecated or urinated. The parasite causes 'swimmer's itch' when it penetrates the skin. Since it takes at least ten minutes for the tiny worm to work its way through your skin, a quick wade across a river, preferably followed by vigorous towelling off, should not put you at risk. Bilharzia is cured with a single dose of Praziquantel. If you think you may have been exposed to the disease, ask your doctor to arrange a blood test when you get home. This should be done more than six weeks after but ideally within 12 weeks of the last exposure.

Sexually transmitted infections

These are common in Madagascar and AIDS is on the increase. If you enjoy nightlife, male or female condoms will make encounters less risky.

Rabies and animal bites

Bites from pet lemurs and habituated animals are on the increase in Madagascar and even the smallest danger of the animal being rabid has to be taken seriously. Do not try to stroke wild or captive animals. Should you be unfortunate enough to be bitten by any mammal, wild or domesticated, you are at risk from both rabies and tetanus. If you're not immunised against tetanus, you must seek medical help speedily. The risk of rabies should also be taken seriously if you haven't been immunised, particularly if you have been bitten by a dog. Whether immunised or not, you should immediately scrub the wound under running water for five minutes, then flood it with alcohol or iodine. Once the rabies virus enters the body, it migrates slowly along the nerves until the virus reaches the brain and causes an agonising death. Once symptoms have appeared, rabies is untreatable and invariably fatal. Before the onset of symptoms, the disease can be prevented by a simple course of injections into the arm (the painful ones in the abdomen have long been superseded). Although it's wise to seek medical help as soon as possible after you are bitten (and bites to the face must be attended to within days) it may not be too late to do so after you get home. If the bite was on the leg you probably have weeks or even months, but seek help as soon as you can. Even if you have been immunised, it is advisable to seek medical attention if the bite is severe, or if the wound is dirty or deep. Two rabies boosters are recommended after any suspect bite.

Infection and trivial breaks in the skin
The skin is very prone to infection in hot, moist climates, so anything that makes even the slightest break to its surface is likely to allow bacteria to enter and so cause problems. Mosquito bites – especially if you scratch them – are a common route of infection, so apply a cream to reduce the itching. Toothpaste helps if you are stuck for anything better. Cover any wounds, especially oozing ones, so that flies don't snack on them. Fairly major infections can arise through even a small nick in the skin. Antiseptic creams are not advised, since they keep the wounds moist and this encourages further infection. A powerful antiseptic which also dries the skin is potassium permanganate crystals dissolved in water. Another alternative is diluted tincture of iodine (which you may be carrying anyway as a water steriliser). Bathe the wound twice a day, more often if you can, by dabbing with cotton wool dipped in dilute potassium permanganate or iodine solution. Bathing in sulphur springs cures mild skin infections.

Sunburn
Light-skinned people burn remarkably quickly near the equator, especially when snorkelling. Wearing a shirt, preferably one with a collar, protects the neck and back, and long shorts can also be worn. Use a sunscreen with a high protection factor (up to 25) on the back of the neck, calves and other exposed parts.

Prickly heat
A fine pimply rash on the trunk is likely to be heat rash; cool showers, dabbing (not rubbing) dry, and talc will help relieve it. Treat the problem by slowing down to a relaxed schedule, wearing only loose, baggy 100% cotton clothes and sleeping naked under a fan; if it's bad you may need to check into an air-conditioned hotel room for a while.

Foot protection
Wear old trainers (running shoes) by or in the sea to avoid getting coral or urchin spines in the soles of your feet, and for some protection against venomous fish spines. If you tread on a venomous fish or are charged by a lion-fish soak the foot (or affected part) in hot (but not scalding) water until some time after the pain subsides; this may mean 20–30 minutes' submersion in all. If the pain returns re-immerse. Once the venom has been heat-inactivated, get a doctor to check and remove any bits of fish spines in the wound.

The nasty side of nature
Animals
Malagasy **land-snakes** are back-fanged, and so are effectively non-venomous. Sea-snakes, although venomous, are easy to see and are rarely aggressive.

It's wise to be wary of **scorpions** and **centipedes**, particularly when in the dry forest. Neither is fatal, but their sting is very unpleasant. Scorpions often come out after rain. They are nocturnal, but they like hiding in small crevices during the day. If you are camping in the desert or the dry forest, it's not unusual to find they have crept into the pocket of a rucksack – even if you have taken the sensible precaution of suspending it from a tree. Scorpion stings are very painful for about 24 hours. After a sting on the finger, I had an excruciatingly painful hand and arm for several days. The pain was only eased with morphine. My finger had no feeling for a month, and over ten years later it still has an abnormal nerve supply.

Large **spiders** can be dangerous – the black widow is found in Madagascar, as well as an aggressive hairy spider with a nasty bite. Navy digger **wasps** have an unpleasant sting, but it's only the scorpions that commonly cause problems because they favour hiding places where one might plunge a hand without looking. If you sleep on the ground, isolate yourself from these creatures with a mat, a hammock or a tent with a sewn-in ground sheet.

Leeches can be a nuisance in the rainforest, but are only revolting, not dangerous (AIDS cannot be spread via leeches). They are best avoided by covering up, tucking trousers into socks and applying insect repellent (even under the socks and shoes – but beware, DEET dissolves plastics). Once leeches have become attached they should not be forcibly removed or some mouth parts may remain causing the bite to itch for a long time. Either wait until they have finished feeding (when they will fall off) or encourage them to let go by applying a lit cigarette, a bit of tobacco, chilli or salt. A film canister is a convenient salt container. The wound left by a leech bleeds a great deal, and may become infected if not kept clean. For more on leeches see box on page 43.

Beware of strolling barefoot on damp, sandy riverbeds. This is the way to pick up jiggers (and geography worms). **Jiggers** are female sand fleas, which resemble maggots and burrow into your toes to feed on your blood while incubating their eggs. Remove them, using a sterilised needle, by picking the top off the boil they make and teasing them out (this requires some skill, so it's best to ask a local person to help). Disinfect the wound thoroughly to prevent infection.

Plants

Madagascar has quite a few plants which cause skin irritation. The worst one I have encountered is a climbing legume which has pea-pod-like fruits that look furry. This 'fur' penetrates the skin as thousands of tiny needles, which must be painstakingly extracted with tweezers. Prickly pear fruits have the same defence. Relief from the secretions of other irritating plants is obtained by bathing. Sometimes it's best to wash your clothes as well, and immersion fully clothed may be the last resort!

Medical kit

Apart from personal medication taken on a regular basis, it's unnecessary to weigh yourself down with a comprehensive medical kit, as many of your requirements will be met by the Malagasy pharmacies.

Expeditions or very adventurous travellers should contact MASTA (see *Useful addresses*, below). The absolute maximum an ordinary traveller needs to carry (I always carry less) is: malaria tablets; lots of plasters (Band-Aid/Elastoplast) to cover broken skin, infected insect bites, etc; antiseptic (potassium permanganate crystals to dissolve in water are best); small pieces of sterile gauze (Melonin dressing) and adhesive plaster; soluble aspirin or paracetamol (Tylenol) – good for fevers, aches and for gargling when you have a sore throat. Lanosil or Sudocrem or some kind of soothing cream for sore anus (after diarrhoea); also useful in cases of severe diarrhoea where a cough or sneeze can be disastrous are panti-liners or sanitary pads; Canesten for thrush and athlete's foot; foot powder; Vaseline or Heel Balm for cracked heels. A course of Amoxycillin (or Erythromycin if you're penicillin-allergic) which is good for chest infections, skin infections and cystitis; Cicatrin antibiotic powder for infected bites, etc; antibiotic eye drops; anti-histamine tablets; travel sickness pills (for those winding roads); tiger balm or calamine lotion for itchy bites; pointed tweezers for extracting splinters, sea-urchin spines, small thorns and coral.

Useful addresses
UK
British Airways Travel Clinic and Immunisation Service 156 Regent St W1, tel: 020 7439 9584. This place also sells travellers' supplies and has a branch of Stanford's travel book and map shop. There are now BA clinics all around Britain and three in South Africa. To find your nearest one, phone 01276 685040.

Nomad Travel Pharmacy and Vaccination Centre 3–4, Wellington Terrace, Turnpike Lane, London N8 0PX; tel: 020 8889 7014.

Thames Medical 157 Waterloo Rd, London SE1 8US; tel: 020 7902 9000. Competitively priced, one-stop travel health service. All profits go to their affiliated company InterHealth which provides health care for overseas workers on Christian projects.

CLOSE ENCOUNTERS OF THE TURD KIND

The surf sparkled in the early morning sun and the sand was firm underfoot as the tourist strode along the beach, revelling in the freedom of miles and miles of eastern coastline. As he approached the picturesque fishing village of bamboo and reed huts he saw people on the beach: the villagers, wrapped in their *lambas*, were squatting near the water. He approached, curious to see every aspect of their daily lives, and the men greeted him politely. Then he saw what they were doing. Turning away in acute embarrassment and disgust, he headed quickly back to the hotel. His morning's walk was spoiled.

Even the most basic pit toilets are unknown to most rural Malagasy. This lack of concern over one of the West's most taboo bodily functions is rightly disturbing. No rationalisation can diminish the disgust we feel when confronted by a neat pile of human faeces in a rural beauty spot. And disgust turns to anxiety when we consider the role that flies play in spreading disease.

The tourist involved in the beach experience asked a Malagasy why they do not bury their faeces. He was told that this would be *fady* because the dead (ie: ancestors) are interred in the earth. Dr Jane Wilson-Howarth, who studied schistosomiasis and intestinal parasites in western Madagascar, made the following observations in *Journal of Tropical Medicine and Hygiene*. 'It is common to find human faeces within 10 metres of houses. It is *fady* for Sakalavas to use latrines, or to defaecate in the same place as siblings of the opposite sex. There are several well-defined areas for defaecation, and also places where it is *fady* – but usually out of respect for the ancestors rather than for reasons of public health.'

Much as I support the adherence to local customs and traditions, this is one that I hope disappears soon.

Trailfinders Immunisation Centre 194 Kensington High St, London W8 7RG; tel: 020 7938 3999. Also 254–284 Sauchiehall St, Glasgow G2 3EH; tel: 0141 353 0066.
MASTA (Medical Advisory Service for Travellers Abroad) Keppel St, London WC1 7HT; tel: 09068 224100. This is a premium-line number, charged at 50p per minute.

USA
Centers for Disease Control The Atlanta-based organisation is the central source of travel information in the USA with a touch-tone phone line and fax service: Traveler's Hot Line, (404) 332 4559. Each summer they publish the invaluable Health Information for International Travel which is available from Center for Prevention Services, Division of Quarantine, Atlanta, GA 30333.
Connaught Laboratories PO Box 187, Swiftwater, PA 18370; tel: 800 822 2463. They will send a free list of specialist tropical-medicine physicians in your state.
IAMAT (International Association for Medical Assistance to Travelers) 736 Center St, Lewiston, NY 14092. A non-profit organisation which provides lists of English-speaking doctors abroad.

Australia
TMVC Tel: 1300 65 88 44; website: www.tmvc.com.au. TMVC has 20 clinics in Australia, New Zealand and Thailand, including:
Brisbane Dr Deborah Mills, Qantas Domestic Building, 6th floor, 247 Adelaide St, Brisbane, QLD 4000; tel: 7 3221 9066; fax: 7 3321 7076
Melbourne Dr Sonny Lau, 393 Little Bourke St, 2nd floor, Melbourne, VIC 3000; tel: 3 9602 5788; fax: 3 9670 8394.
Sydney Dr Mandy Hu, Dymocks Building, 7th floor, 428 George St, Sydney, NSW 2000; tel: 2 221 7133; fax: 2 221 8401.

South Africa
There are four **British Airways travel clinics** in South Africa: *Johannesburg*, tel: (011) 807 3132; *Cape Town*, tel: (021) 419 3172; *Knysna*, tel: (044) 382 6366; *East London*, tel: (0431) 43 2359.

As a postscript, Dr Jane comments on a study she did in Indonesia. Village mothers were given soap and an explanation of the need for handwashing after using the toilet and before eating, to protect their children from faecal-oral diarrhoea. The reduction in diarrhoea during the study was 89%, and two years later it was still down 75%! Travellers too should be careful about handwashing; other people's microbes on door handles are dangerous. Consider, also, the filthy hands that have brought the distinctive appearance to the bank notes you handle every day.

SAFETY
Sadly, the widening gap between rich and poor in Madagascar has produced a sharp rise in crime against tourists. Robbery is now a danger in all large towns, especially Antananarivo. There it pays to be paranoid, but remember that the vast majority of Malagasy are touchingly honest; often you will have people call you back because you have overpaid them (while still unfamiliar with the money) and every traveller can think of a time when his innocence could have been exploited – and wasn't. In my experience, too, hotel employees are, by and large, trustworthy. So try to keep a sense of proportion. Like health, safety is often a question of commonsense. Keep your valuables hidden, keep alert in potentially dangerous situations, and you will be OK. Remember, thieves have to learn their profession so theft is common only where there are plenty of

MADAGASCAR: ISLAND OF EXCITEMENT!

Henk Beentje

We spent three days in Farafangana, collecting palms in the Manombo Forest [Henk is employed by Kew Gardens]. On leaving we were mobbed by about 200 irate locals who accused my Malagasy companion and me of being *voleurs de sang* and of abducting young maidens. On the advice of my companion we reported to the police, who thought this was quite funny but advised us to leave town all the same. We were escorted out of town by the Chief of Police himself, who was careful to use the side streets. Two days later we were back at Ranomafana. As we got into our Landcruiser we were stopped by three gendarmes, one of whom was toting a submachine gun. We were arrested and taken to the Gendarmerie. There had been an 'all points bulletin' to arrest two *vazaha* (one Merina, one white) in a red Landcruiser. We were accused of having abducted no fewer than three girls from Farafangana, and to have put them in sacks at the back of the vehicle (this clearly referred to my palm collection, indeed ensconced in large sacks). It took us four hours to regain our freedom and I was very glad we had reported to the Farafangana police, because after a request from us they were contacted and could confirm our story. Who said you cannot have adventures any more in this streamlined world of ours?

tourists to prey on. In little-visited areas you can relax and enjoy the genuine friendliness of the people.

Crime prevention

Violent crime is still relatively rare in Madagascar, and even in Antananarivo you are probably safer than in a large American city. The response to a potentially violent attack is the same in Madagascar as anywhere: if you are outnumbered or the thief is armed, it is sensible to hand over what they want.

You are far more likely to be robbed by subterfuge. Razor-slashing is very popular (with the thieves) and is particularly irritating since your clothes or bag are ruined, maybe just for the sake of the used tissue that caused the tempting-looking bulge in your pocket. When visiting crowded places avoid bringing a bag (even a daypack carried in front of your body is vulnerable); bring your money in a moneybelt under your clothes, or in a neck pouch. Women have advantages here: the neck pouch can be hooked over their bra so no cord shows at the neck and a moneybelt beneath a skirt is safe since it needs an unusually brazen thief to reach for it! If you must have a bag, make sure it is difficult to cut.

Your backpack is vulnerable to nimble fingers or razor slashers. An effective lockable mesh backpack cover, the Pacsafe, is now available in the UK; tel: 0116 234 0800.

Passengers in taxis may be the victims of robbery: the thief reaches through the open window and grabs your bag. Keep it on the floor by your feet.

Having escorted dozens of first-timers through Madagascar, I've learned the mistakes the unprepared can make. The most common is wearing jewellery ('But I always wear this gold chain'), carelessness with money, etc ('I just put my bag down while I tried on that blouse'), and underestimating the value of clothes ('It's not as though it was an expensive T-shirt...').

Tips for avoiding robbery

- Remember that most theft occurs in the street not in hotels; leave your valuables hidden in a locked bag in your room or in the hotel safe.
- If staying in C Category hotels bring a rubber wedge (or Blu-Tack) to keep your door closed at night. If you can't secure the window put something on the sill which will fall with a clatter if someone tries to enter.
- Lock your bag when travelling by plane or taxi-brousse; combination locks are more secure than small padlocks. Make or buy a lockable cover for your backpack.
- Leave your valuable-looking jewellery at home. You do not need it in Madagascar. Likewise your fancy watch; buy a cheap one.
- Carry your cash in a moneybelt, neck pouch or deep pocket. Make these yourself by cutting the bottom off existing pockets and adding an extra bit. Fasten the 'secret' pocket with velcro. Wear loose trousers that have zipped pockets. Keep emergency cash (eg: a 100 dollar bill) in a Very Safe Place.
- Divide up travellers' cheques so they are not all in one place. Keep a note of the numbers of your travellers' cheques, passport, credit cards, plane ticket, insurance, etc in your moneybelt. Keep photocopies of the above in your luggage.
- Remember, what the thief would most like to get hold of is money. Do not leave it around (in coat pockets hanging in your room, in your hand while you concentrate on something else, in an accessible pocket while strolling in the street). If travelling as a couple or small group have one person stand aside to keep watch while the other makes a purchase in the street.
- Avoid carrying a handbag or daypack in cities where it is an obvious target for thieves. In a restaurant never hang it on the back of a chair or lay it by your feet (unless you put your chair leg over the strap).
- For thieves, the next best thing after money is clothes. Avoid leaving them on the beach while you go swimming (in tourist areas) and never leave swimsuits or washing to dry outside your room near a public area.
- Bear in mind that it's impossible to run carrying a large piece of luggage. Items hidden at the bottom of your heaviest bag will be safe from a grab and run thief. Couples or small groups can pass a piece of cord through the handles of all their bags to make them one unstealable unit when waiting at an airport or taxi-brousse station.
- Avoid misunderstandings – genuine or contrived – by agreeing on the price of a service before you set out.
- Enjoy yourself. It's preferable to lose a few unimportant things and see the best of Madagascar than to mistrust everyone and ruin your trip.

...and what to do if you are robbed

Have a little cry and then go to the police. They will write down all the details then send you to the chief of police for a signature. It takes the best part of a day, but you will need the certificate for your insurance. If you are in a rural area, the local authorities will do a declaration of loss.

Women travellers

Things have changed a lot in Madagascar. During my independent travels in the 1980s my only experience of sexual harassment (if it could be called that) was when a small man sidled up to me in Nosy Be and asked: 'Have you ever tasted Malagasy man?'.

Sadly, with the increase of tourism comes the increase of men who think they may be on to a good thing. A firm 'no' is usually sufficient; try not to be too offended: think of the image of Western women that the average Malagasy male is shown via the cinema or TV.

Anne Axel, who travelled solo safely and happily in 1996, has noticed a significant change in male attitudes: 'The sexual harassment we experienced was so prevalent and so pervasive that we were forced to be more distant. We didn't freely engage in conversation and were wary of all men who tried to stop us in the street to talk.'

A woman Peace Corps volunteer gave me the following advice for women travelling alone on taxi-brousses: 'Try to sit in the cab, but not next to the driver; if possible sit with another woman; if in the main body of the vehicle, establish contact with an older person, man or woman, who will then tend to look after you.' All women readers agree that you should say you are married, whether or not you wear a ring to back it up.

Men travellers

To the Malagasy, a man travelling alone is in need of one thing: a woman. Lone male travellers will be pursued relentlessly, particularly in beach resorts. Prostitutes are ubiquitous and very beautiful. And successful. Venereal disease is common.

John Kupiec reports: 'I was constantly fighting off women wherever I went. One night in Fort Dauphin I actually had to run away!' He was also offered the mother of the Président du Fokontany in one village. Saying you're married is considered irrelevant...

Are you *suffering* from

Wanderlust ?

then subscribe to the only
magazine that guarantees NO CURE !

Wanderlust is the magazine for people with a *passion* for travel, covering destinations near and far, plus a host of features covering all aspects of independent and special-interest travel!

Available on subscription worldwide, with a money-back guarantee – for details phone **(01753) 620426**, or fax (01753) 620474 or write to
Wanderlust(BP), PO Box 1832, Windsor, Berks. SL4 6YP, U.K.

In Madagascar

MONEY
Cost of travel

By most people's standards Madagascar is not expensive, and if you are prepared for a certain amount of hardship it is cheap. For those travelling mainly by bus or taxi-brousse and staying in Category C hotels, £18/US$30 per day for a couple is about average, and allows for an occasional splurge. Note that couples can travel almost as cheaply as singles, since most hotels charge by the room (with double bed). Sleep cheap and eat well is a good recipe for happy travels.

Costs mount up if you are visiting many national parks or reserves, which cost 50,000Fmg (about £10/$US16) along with another US$10 or so for the guide.

The easiest way to save money on a day-to-day basis is to cut down on bottled water: a bottle of Eau Vive costs over £1/US$1.65 in most hotels. Bring a water container and sterilising agent. If you are a beer drinker, be careful where you buy it: from a supermarket it costs 2,500Fmg (about 30p/50c); in a cheap restaurant you could pay 5,000Fmg, and in the best hotels it could be 13,000Fmg.

Malagasy francs

Madagascar's currency has always been difficult to cope with. Here is an extract from an account written over a hundred years ago:

> 'The French five-franc piece is now the standard of coinage in Madagascar; for small change it is cut up into bits of all sizes. The traveller has to carry a pair of scales about with him, and whenever he makes a purchase the specified quantity of this most inconvenient money is weighed out with the greatest exactness, first on his own scales, and then on those of the suspicious native of whom he is buying.'

Ariary confusion

Madagascar's unit of currency is the franc malgache (Fmg). With recent inflation one rarely sees the small lower-denomination brass coins of 5, 10 and 20 francs (which are practically worthless), but there are silver coins which look, at face value, to be for 10 and 20 francs. Closer inspection reveals that they are *ariary*; one ariary is five francs, so they are worth 50 and 100 francs respectively. For a while the banknotes perpetrated the same deceit on unsuspecting foreigners but now, mercifully, they have mostly returned to the old system of writing the ariary value in words and the francs in figures. Watch out, however, for 2,500Fmg notes, boldly written as 500 (ariary) and the 25,000Fmg one which likewise can be confused with 5,000Fmg.

The colour of money

Keep the following in mind: big green = 5,000 ariary/25,000Fmg; pink and green = 500 ariary/2,500Fmg; brown = 10,000Fmg; purple = 5,000Fmg; blue = 1,000Fmg. Filthy brown = once green = 500Fmg.

Learn too the approximate value of each colour. At the 1999 exchange rate it was convenient to think of 25,000Fmg (big green) as £2.50/$5 and 10,000Fmg (brown) as the equivalent of a pound, and 5,000Fmg (purple) a bit under a dollar. This is near enough when making quick calculations while bargaining.

Exchange rate

The Malagasy franc floats against hard currencies, but has remained pretty stable during the last couple of years. Even so, the August 1999 exchange rates given below should be used as a rough guide only. More useful is the exchange rate of your currency to the French franc (Ff) since that is the hard currency quoted by the Malagasy.

£1 = 10,368Fmg
US$1 = 6,490Fmg
Ffr = 1,034Fmg
DM1 = 938Fmg

Changing money

There are no restrictions these days, and you are permitted to make purchases using American dollars – indeed, the tourist-aware vendors in places visited by cruise ships are quite unhappy if offered Malagasy francs.

The best place to change money is at the airport on arrival. After that it's simplest to use a hotel, though banks will give a slightly better rate.

Transferring funds

Now that you can draw cash from many BTM banks using your credit card you are less likely to need money transferred from home. If you are staying a long time in Madagascar, however, it's best to make the transfer arrangement beforehand. The best bank for this is Banque Malgache de l'Océan Indien, Place de l'Indépendance, Antananarivo. Its corresponding bank in the UK is Banque Nationale de Paris, 8–13 King William St, London EC4P 4HS; tel 020 7895 7070.

If you need cash in a hurry there are now Western Union offices in Madagascar to which money can be transfered from home in a few hours, or in minutes if your nearest and dearest are willing to go to a Western Union office with cash. The fee (in the UK) is £32 if done with a credit card but, for the obliging mum, partner or whatever in your home country, it is a simple procedure which can be done over the phone saving the journey to a Western Union office. They need to phone Western Union on 0800 833 833 (in the USA: 800 325 6000) and know the town from where you wish to pick up the money. There are Western Union offices in Antananarivo, Mahajanga, Toamasina, Fianarantsoa and Nosy Be. Phone (Tana) 22 313 07 for addresses or further information or check their website: www.westernunion.com.

TRANSPORT

You can get around Madagascar by road, air and water and – with luck – by rail. Whatever your transport, you'd better learn the meaning of *en panne*; it is engine trouble/breakdown. During these *en panne* sessions one can't help feeling a certain nostalgia for the pre-mechanised days when Europeans travelled by *filanzana* or palanquin. These litters were carried by four cheerful porters who, by all accounts, were so busy swapping gossip and telling stories that they sometimes dropped their unfortunate *vazaha* in a river. The average distance travelled per day was 30 miles – not much slower than a taxi-brousse today! The *filanzana* was used for high officials as recently as the 1940s. To get around town the locals depended on an earlier version of the current rickshaw, or *pousse-pousse*. The *mono-pousse* was a chair slung over a bicycle wheel. One man pulled and another pushed. The more affluent Malagasy possessed a *boeuf-cheval*: a zebu trained to be ridden. (I've seen a photo; the animal looks rather smug in its saddle and bridle.)

By road

'If I make roads, the white man will only come and take my country. I have two allies – *hazo* [forest] and *tazo* [fever]...' King Radama I

Coping with the 'roads' is one of the great travel challenges in Madagascar. It's not that the royal decree has lasted 180 years but there's a third ally that the king didn't mention – the weather: torrential rain and cyclones destroy roads as fast as they are constructed. But they are being repaired and reconstructed, mostly with foreign aid. At the time of writing many of the most important roads (the *Routes Nationales*) are either paved or in the process of being paved. The others are dreadful, but then...that's Madagascar. Here's a comment from a Belgian traveller: 'A good example of how the Malagasy maintain their roads comes before Rantabe [east coast]. A huge tree fell over the road. Instead of cutting the log in two they made a big hole under the tree in the road!'

Taxi-brousse is the generic name for public transport in Madagascar. Car-brousse and taxi-be are also used, but they all refer to the 'bush taxis' which run along every road in the country. These have improved a lot in recent years, especially along tourist routes. Even so, stories like those on page 111 are still not unusual.

Taxi-brousse
Vehicles
Taxi-brousses are generally minibuses or Renault vans with seats facing each other so there is no good view out of the window (a *baché* is a small van with a canvas top). More comfortable are the Peugeot 404s or 504s, sometimes known as taxi-be (although some people call the 25-seater buses taxi-be) designed to take nine people, but often packed with 14 or more. A car-brousse is usually a 'Tata' sturdy enough to cope with bad roads.

Practicalities
Vehicles leave from a *gare routière* on the side of town closest to their destination. You should try to go there a day or two ahead of your planned departure to check times and prices, and for long journeys you should buy a ticket in advance (from the kiosk – don't give your money to a ticket tout). 'Don't be embarrassed to ask to see the vehicle, the Malagasy do. Reserve your seat – they will write your name on a hand-drawn plan in an exercise book – and get them to write your place on the ticket. Once you have anything written on a piece of paper it is regarded as law and once it is typed it must be gospel! The best seats in a car are in the front, either next to the driver if you have short legs (you'll be sitting where the hand brake should be) or next to the window if you have long legs – but beware of the sun cooking your right arm. In the front you have the added advantage that you can turn down the volume of the stereo when the driver is not looking.'

'Never be late for a taxi-brousse. Some of them do leave on time, especially on popular journeys or if the departure time is horrendous, eg: 2am. Get there early to claim your seat, then read your book, write your diary or whatever. Be ready with soap and towel for a bath stop. Follow the women and children to get some degree of privacy.' (Frances Kerridge)

On short journeys and in remote areas, vehicles simply leave as soon as they fill up. Or if they have a schedule expect them to leave hours late, and always be prepared (with warm clothing, fruit, water, etc) for a night trip, even if you thought it was leaving in the morning.

There is no set rate per kilometre; fares are calculated on the quality of the vehicle, the roughness of the road and the time the journey takes. They are set by the government and *vazahas* are only occasionally overcharged. Ask other passengers what they are paying. Taxi-brousses are very cheap. It will not cost you more than US$10 for an all-day journey. Faster routes (tarred roads) may be a bit more expensive. Passengers are occasionally charged for luggage that is strapped on to the roof.

Drivers stop to eat, but usually drive all night. If they do stop during the night most passengers stay in the vehicle or sleep on the road outside.

There is much that a committed overland traveller can do to soften his/her experiences on taxi-brousses – see *What to take* on page 83. If you're prepared for the realities, an overland journey can be very enjoyable and gives you a chance to get to know the Malagasy.

Car hire

More and more visitors have been renting cars or 4WD vehicles in recent years. You would need to be a competent mechanic to hire a self-drive car in Madagascar, and generally cars come with chauffeurs (providing a local person with a job and you with a guide/interpreter). A few days on Madagascar's roads will cure you of any regret that you are not driving yourself. Night-time driving is particularly challenging: headlights often don't work, or are not switched on. Your driver will know that the single light bearing down on you is more likely to be a wide truck than a narrow motorbike and react accordingly. The Merina Highway Code (informal version) decrees that drivers must honk their horns after crossing a bridge to ensure that the spirits are out of the way.

There are car-hire firms in most large towns. The Maison du Tourisme in Antananarivo has a comprehensive list, and I have included them in town information.

Prices currently work out at about £50/US$75 per day, including fuel and driver, for a small saloon car driving around Antananarivo. For a week's hire of a 4WD you should expect to pay about £750/US$1,125.

Mountain bicycle

An increasingly popular means of touring Madagascar is by the most reliable transport: mountain bike. Bikes can be hired in Antananarivo, Antsirabe, Taolagnaro (Fort Dauphin), Antsiranana (Diego Suarez) and Nosy Be. Or you can bring your own. You can do a combination of bike and taxi-brousse or bike and plane, or you can set out to cycle the whole way. Don't be overambitious; dirt roads are so rutted you will make slow progress, and tarred roads can be dangerous from erratic drivers.

People worry, understandably, about the safety aspect. So far I have not heard of anyone being harmed while on a bike, but of course you are vulnerable. You must make your own decisions. All I can recommend is to cycle off the beaten track. Here you will meet only hospitality and curiosity, and will be in no danger – intentional or unintentional – from other road-users. But what I really want to say is 'Go for it – and damn the risk!'.

By air

Air Madagascar started its life in 1962 as Madair but understandably changed its name after a few years of jokes. Most people now call it Air Mad. It serves 59

VIVE LE TAXI-BROUSSE!

Taxi-brousses are improving, especially on the main tourist routes, but I couldn't resist repeating – and adding to – these entertaining stories!

'At about 10 o'clock we (two people) went to the taxi-brousse station. "Yes, yes, there is a car. It is here, ready to go." We paid our money. "When will it go?" "When it has nine passengers." "How many has it got now?" "Wait a minute." A long look at notebooks, then a detailed calculation. "Two." "As well as us?" "No, no including you." It finally left at about 7 o'clock.'
Chris Ballance

'After several hours we picked up four more people. We couldn't believe it – the driver had to sit on someone's lap!'
Stephen Cartledge

'The taxi-brousse from Tana to Majunga was supposed to leave in the early afternoon. At 4pm we left (all ten of us) and went to a furniture stall to buy pineapples – well it makes sense. At 6pm we had the first of seven punctures. The driver pushed his tyre two kilometres down the road to get it mended... We drove all night (four punctures) and as the light rose over the countryside we – well, you guessed – had a puncture. Now we had no spare and no airpump. A lorry eventually passed and helped to repair the tyre. At 11am we had another puncture... I took my rucksack off the car roof and hitchhiked into Majunga.'
Jonathan Miller

'At last we were under way. I had my knees jammed up against the iron bar at the back of the rows in front where sat a very sick soldier, who spent most of the journey with his head out of the window spewing lurid green bile at passers-by like something from a horror-movie... After about 20 minutes we had to stop at a roadside stall to buy mangoes. Since I was now on the sunny side of the vehicle the temperature of my shirt rose to what, had it been made of polyester, would have been melting point. Our next stop was Antsirabe where we were surrounded by about 50 apple vendors and all and sundry went absolutely beserk. I hadn't seen so many apples since...since we left Ambositra. At about 5pm the radio was turned on so we could listen to two men shouting at each other at a volume which would have caused bleeding of the eardrums in Wembley Stadium. When one passenger complained our driver managed to find a few extra decibels. At about 6pm it started to get decidedly brisk, and since the ailing squaddie in front of me showed no sign of having rid himself of toxic enzymes I now had to endure an icy blast in my face. Our next stop was for grapes. We now had enough fruit on board to start a wholesale business in Covent Garden, and I was a bit tetchy.'
Robert Stewart

'We eventually made it after an eventful four-hour taxi-brousse journey which entailed the obligatory trawl around town for more passengers, selling the spare tyre shortly after setting off, a 30-minute wait outside the doctor's as the driver wasn't feeling very well, and all of us having to bump-start the vehicle every time we stopped to pick anyone up.'
H & M Kendrick, 1998

THROUGH MADAGASCAR BY MOUNTAIN BIKE
Bishop Brock and Anne Axel

Madagascar is an excellent country for cycle touring, definitely one of my favourite places in the world, and I've taken my holidays by bicycle for the last 13 years. Route 7 now has a good-to-excellent surface most of the way and there are lots of opportunities for interesting side trips. Having a bike gave me access to places that otherwise can only be reached on foot. If I had to advise a prospective cyclist with limited time I would say that Fianar to Manakara and Fianar to Sakaraha were the favourite parts of my trip. I should add that it's not a problem to put the bike on a train or taxi-brousse after payment of a small fee.

Preparation, equipment and spares: bring a spare tyre, tubes, spokes, spanners and tools, puncture kit, and – very important – a Teflon-based lubricant that does not attract dust. The sandy, dusty roads play havoc with the gear system. It is advisable to install sealed hubs and headset to cut down the amount of maintenance. Carry extra cables and spokes and, for a long trip, store some extra tools and spare parts in Tana. And don't forget your repair manual. Carry a compass and a cyclometer as the roads often take a different course to those shown on the map; locking cleats are dangerous on sandy roads – use toe clips or dual purpose pedals. Finally, stay at the Tana hotel Relais des Pistards since the owner, M Colney, is an avid cyclist and can offer advice.

Don't take your bike as unaccompanied luggage! Travel with your bike whatever the excess baggage charge.

destinations, making it the most efficient way – and for some people the only way – of seeing the country. You are no longer required to pay your fare in hard currency. Here are some sample one-way fares (1999) from Antananarivo: Mahajanga US$74, Nosy Be US$86, Antsiranana (Diego Suarez) US$86, Toliara (Tuléar) US$63, Toamasina (Tamatave) US$74, Nosy Boraha (Ile Sainte Marie) $67. Remember that you can get a 33% discount on domestic flights providing you chose Air Mad as your international carrier.

Air Madagascar has the following planes: Boeing 747 (jumbo) on the Paris to Antananarivo route, Boeing 737 to the larger cities and Nosy Be, the smaller Hawker Siddeley 748 and the very small and erratic Twin Otter and Piper to the smaller towns.

The recent rise in tourism in Madagascar has brought more passengers than Air Mad can cope with, particularly at peak holiday times. Try to book in advance through one of their agents (see page 79) or through an Antananarivo tour operator. If you are doing your bookings once you arrive, avoid the crush by getting to the Air Mad office when it opens in the morning. Often flights which are said to be fully booked in Antananarivo are found to have seats when you reapply at the town of departure. In any case, you should reconfirm your next flight as soon as you arrive at your destination (at the Air Mad office in town). Rupert Parker, a frequent traveller to Madagascar, reveals his secret: 'Because you are still allowed to make a reservation without payment, flights always appear full, but the trick is to go to the airport two hours in advance and put your ticket on the counter. The *liste d'attente* works on a first come first served basis and half an hour before the flight is due to leave they start filling the empty seats, taking the tickets in order of arrival. We have never, in ten years, been disappointed – it just increases the stress level but we have always got on the plane.' Conversely, passengers with booked seats who check in late will find their seats sold to waiting-list passengers. Always arrive at least an hour before the scheduled departure.

There are no numbered seats or refreshments on internal flights, although on longer flights you'll be given a drink and a sweetie. Domestic flights are now non-smoking. It is useful to know that *Enregistrement Bagages* is the check-in counter and *Livraison Bagages* is luggage arrival.

Frances Kerridge gives this advice for flying by Twin Otter: 'The check-in is hilarious – they weigh you as well as your luggage, so a bit of dieting between flights will cover those extra souvenirs you've bought! I recommend getting there early – about an hour before they say – to check in as there will be lots of Malagasy, each trying to cart a market-stall equivalent of whatever goods are a speciality of that region. The smaller your bag, the more popular you will be as other passengers eagerly claim your unused luggage allowance.' She goes on to emphasise that luggage should be locked, but that airport thieves know how to pick locks so keep your luggage in sight for as long as possible.

Air Madagascar schedules are reviewed twice-yearly, at the end of March and the end of October (maddening: in the peak travel month), but are subject to change at any time and without notice. Air Mad has a website: www.air-mad.com.

With a shortage of aircraft and pilots, planes are sometimes delayed or cancelled. Almost always there is a perfectly good reason: mechanical problems, bad weather. Air Mad is improving and on the whole they provide as reliable a service as one can expect in a poor country. In the last edition I wrote: 'I confess to nicking one of their marvellous Safety Instructions cards which tell you to "Sit on the thrush and skid feet first". I have a nasty feeling that those thrushes may soon be extinct!' They are. Shame!

Air Mad does not have a monopoly on domestic flights. TAM covers many destinations. Their prices are usually more expensive than Air Mad but this could easily change.

There is an airport tax on domestic and international flights. See page 137.

Private charters

For a small group this is a viable option and not as expensive as you may think. TAM (Travaux Aériens de Madagascar) offer light aircraft for one to seven passengers. Prices range from about US$150 per flying hour for a two-seater to US$700 per flying hour for a seven-seater. The cost of fuel must be added: US$40 to US$170 per flying hour. Bigger planes fly faster, so they may not end up being more expensive. Some flying-time examples for a six-seater Piper: Antananarivo–Sainte Marie–Antananarivo, 1 hr 46 mins; Antananarivo–Fort Dauphin–Antananarivo, 5hrs 20 mins. Remember there is no such thing as a one-way flight – you still have to pay for the pilot to return to Antananarivo. It's more sensible to pay him to spend the night.

TAM's address is 31 Avenue de l'Indépendance, Antananarivo; tel: 222 22. They also have an operations office at Ivato airport.

There are, however, other companies so shop around. Madagascar Air Services is one that has been recommended.

Some tour operators, such as Boogie Pilgrim (see page 90) and Baobab (see page 345), have small planes and can organise special trips such as flights over the *tsingy*.

By boat

The Malagasy are traditionally a seafaring people (remember that 6,000km journey from Indonesia) and in the absence of roads, their stable outrigger canoes are used to cover quite long sea distances. *Pirogues* without outriggers are used extensively on the rivers and canals of the watery east. Quite a few adventurous travellers use *pirogues* for sections of their journeys. Romantic though it may be to sail in an outrigger canoe, it can be both uncomfortable and, at times, dangerous.

Ferries and cargo boats travel to the larger islands. These provide a different version of discomfort.

River rafting is becoming increasingly popular as a different way of seeing the country. This is not the hair-raising white-water variety, but a gentle float down the wide, lazy rivers of the west. For more information see page 349.

Transport within cities
Buses
Most cities have cheap buses but few travellers use these because of the difficulty of understanding the route system. No reason not to give it a try, however.

Taxis
Taxi rates are reasonable – usually a fixed price for the centre of town – and they will sometimes pick up other passengers. They have no meters, so you must agree on the price before you get in.

Rickshaws (Pousse-pousses)
Pousse-pousses were introduced into Madagascar by British missionaries who wanted to replace the traditional palanquin with its association with slavery. The name is said to originate from the time they operated in the capital and needed an additional man behind to push up the steep hills. They are now a Madagascar speciality (unlike the pedal rickshaws in other parts of the world, these are pulled by a running man). Most towns have *pousse-pousses* – the exceptions are the hilly towns of the Highlands.

Many Western visitors are reluctant to sit in comfort behind a running, ragged, sweating man and no-one with a heart can fail to feel compassion for the *pousse-pousse* pullers. However, this is a case of needing to abandon our own cultural hang-ups. These men want work. Most rickshaws are owned by Indians to whom the 'drivers' must pay a daily fee. If they take no passengers they will be out of pocket – and there's precious little in their pockets. Bargain hard (before you get in) and make sure you have the exact money. It would be optimistic to expect change. For most medium-length journeys 2,000Fmg is generous payment. *Pousse-pousse* pullers love carrying soft-hearted tourists and have become quite cunning – and tiresome – in their dealings with *vazahas*. However, remember how desperately these men need a little luck – and an innocent tourist could make their day!

Rail
Rail services in Madagascar have deteriorated dramatically in the last few years. The lines have been damaged by cyclones, and the locomotives and rolling-stock allowed to decay. Derailments are common, and some lines have been closed to passenger transport.

The services currently operating (sometimes) are Anatananarivo to Antsirabe, Antananarivo to Moramanga (this no longer continues to Toamasina), Moramanga to Ambatondrazaka and Fianarantsoa to Manakara.

Keep an eye out for the *Micheline*. This luxury, white 'rail-bus' runs on and off between Antananarivo and Toamasina. Enquire at the railway station in Tana, tel: 22 205 21.

Previous page Gastrorchis humbiotii, a widespread ground orchid endemic to Madagascar, found in humid evergreen forest (JH)

Above The white sifaka, *Propithecus verreauxi verreauxi*, also known as Verreaux's sifaka, is common in Berenty and other southern reserves. (BL)

Left Male crowned lemur, *Eulemur coronatus*. This attractive lemur is restricted to a small area of the north, but is common in Ankarana. (NG)

Above Female snub-nosed chameleon, *Furcifer labordi*, in aggressive posture (NG)

Above right Leaf-tailed gecko, *Uroplatus ebenaui* (NG)

Right Hedgehog tenrec, *Echinops telfairi* (BL)

Below right Painted burrowing frog, *Scaphiophryne gottlebei* (NG)

Below left Giraffe-necked weevil, *Trachelophorus giraffa*, one of the extraordinary animals found in Ranomafana and Périnet (KT)

Left Fosa, *Cryptoprocta ferax*. Madagascar's largest carnivore is neither dog nor cat, but is distantly related to the African civet. Fosas are nocturnal and secretive, but are sometimes seen in Kirindy. (NG)

Above Long-tailed ground roller, *Uratelornis chimaera*, a bird of the spiny forest (NG)

Right Helmet vanga, *Euryceros prevostii*, the most spectacular of the endemic vanga family, occasionally seen in Masoala National Park (NG)

Below Pitta-like ground roller, *Atelornis pittoides*, one of Madagascar's more colourful birds found in montane forest such as Périnet (NG)

ACCOMMODATION

Hotels in Madagascar are classified by a national star system – five star being the highest – but in my experience this indicates price, not quality. In this book I have used three categories: A, B and C. Until recently hotels in the upper range required payment in hard currency. Fortunately this no longer applies, although most still print their prices in French francs. There is a tourist tax, *vignette touristique*, of 3,000Fmg per person per night – about £0.30/$0.50 so no hardship.

Outside the towns, hotels in the form of a single building are something of a rarity. Accommodation is usually in bungalows which are often constructed of local materials and are quiet, atmospheric and comfortable.

A word about bolsters. Visitors who are not accustomed to the ways of France are disconcerted to find a firm, sheet-covered sausage anchored to the top of the bed. In the better hotels you can usually find a pillow hidden away in a cupboard. Failing that, I make my own pillow with a sweater stuffed into a T-shirt.

Breakfast is rarely included in the room price.

What you get for your money
Category A
Up to international standard in the large towns and tourist areas, but sometimes large and impersonal and usually foreign-owned. There has been a boom in hotel building during the last few years, and there are now some very good Malagasy-owned hotels in this category, so the difference between A and B has become somewhat blurred. Top prices are around 150Ff (£20/US$35) to 1,000Ff (£125/US$188) double.

Category B
These are often just as clean and comfortable, and have en-suite bathrooms. There will be no TV beaming CNN into your bedroom, but you should have comfortable beds though bolsters are the norm. The hotels are often family-run and very friendly. The average price is £10/US$15.

Category C
In early editions I described these as 'Exhilaratingly dreadful at times' until a reader wrote: 'We were rather disappointed by the quality of the Category C hotels... We found almost all the beds comfortable, generally acceptably clean, and not one rat. We felt luxuriously cheated!' Take heart: the following description from Rupert Parker of a hotel in Brickaville should gladden the masochistic heart, '...a conglomeration of shacks directly beneath the road bridge. The rooms are partitioned-off spaces, just large enough to hold a bed, in a larger wooden building – the partitions don't reach to the ceiling and there is only one light bulb for all the rooms – the hotel manageress controls the switch. Not only can you hear everyone's conversation and what they're up to, but when there is a new arrival, at whatever time of the night, the light comes on and wakes everyone up – that is if you've managed to ignore the rumbling and revving of trucks as they cross the bridge above you, or the banging on the gate which announces a new arrival. Suffice to say the toilet and washing facilities are non-existent.'

Such hotels certainly give the flavour of how Madagascar used to be, and in remote areas you will still find the occasional sagging double bed and stinking hole toilet. Usually you can find the toilet by the smell, but ask for the WC ('doble vay say'), not *toilette* which means shower or bathroom. In these hotels (and some B ones too) used toilet paper should not be thrown into the pan but into the box provided for it. Not very nice, but preferable to a clogged loo.

Most of the C hotels in this book are clean and excellent value, only earning the C because of their price. Almost always they are run by friendly Malagasy who will rustle up a fantastic meal. In an out-of-the-way place you will pay as little as £1/US$2.50 for the most basic room, though £3/US$4.50 or £4/US$6 would be more usual.

Hotely usually means a restaurant/snack bar rather than accommodation, but it's always worth asking if they have rooms.

Many B and C hotels will do your washing for you at a very reasonable price. In A hotels laundry is expensive.

Hotel prices in this book

Category A hotels are usually given in French francs (Ff) because that's the hard currency quoted by the hotels. With fluctuating exchange rates it's probably easiest for you to do your own conversion to pounds, dollars or whatever.

Local prices are given only when the information is reasonably current: mid 1998–1999. In cases where the information is over a year old I say 'about' before the price, and prices are omitted when I have no information since the last edition.

I often use readers' reports to update hotels and restaurants. 'Recommended' means that more than one reader has praised the place or that I know it personally.

FOOD AND DRINK
Food

Eating well is one of the delights of Madagascar, and even the fussiest tourists are usually happy with the food. International hotels serve international food, usually with a French bias, and often do special Malagasy dishes. Lodges and smaller hotels serve local food which is almost always excellent, particularly on the coast where lobster (crayfish), shellfish and other seafood predominates. Meat lovers will enjoy the zebu steaks, although they are usually tougher than we are used to. Outside the capital, most hotels offer a set menu (*table d'hôte* or *menu*) to their guests. This can cost as little as 30,000Fmg (£3/US$5). At the upper end you can expect to pay 125,000Fmg (£13/US$22).

Where the menu is à la carte it is a help to have a French dictionary or phrasebook.

The national dish in Madagascar is *romazava* (pronounced 'roomazahv'), a meat and vegetable stew, spiced with ginger and containing *brèdes* (pronounced 'bread'), tasty, tongue-tingling greens. Another good local dish is *ravitoto*, shredded manioc leaves with fried pork.

Independent travellers will find Chinese restaurants in every town; these are almost always good and reasonably priced. *Soupe Chinoise* is available almost everywhere, and is filling and tasty. The Malagasy eat a lot of rice, but most restaurants cater to foreign tastes by providing chips (French fries). But away from the tourist routes most dishes are accompanied by a sticky mound of rice.

For a real Malagasy meal, eat in a *hotely*. These are often open-sided shacks where the menu is chalked up on a blackboard:

Henan-omby (or *Hen'omby*)	beef
Henan-borona (or *Hen'akoho*)	chicken
Henan-kisoa	pork
Henan-drano (or *Hazan-drano*)	fish

It may end with *Mazotoa homana*. This is not a dish, it means *Bon appétit*!

Along with the meat or fish and inevitable mound of rice (*vary*) comes a bowl of stock. This is spooned over the rice, or drunk as a soup.

Thirst is quenched with *ranovola* (pronounced 'ranoov<u>oo</u>l) obtained by boiling water in the pan in which the rice was cooked. It has a slight flavour of burnt rice, and since it has been boiled for several minutes it is safe to drink.

If you don't feel like a full meal, *hotelys* are a great source of snacks. Here are some of the options: *tsaramasy* (rice with beans and pork), *vary sosoa* (rice pudding), *mofo boule* (slightly sweet bread rolls), and *koba* (rice and banana, wrapped in a leaf and served in slices).

For do-it-yourself meals there is a great variety of fruit and vegetables, even in the smallest market. A selection of fruit is served in most restaurants, along with raw vegetables or crudités. From June to August the fruit is mostly limited to citrus and bananas, but from September there are also strawberries, mangoes, lychees, pineapples and loquats. Slices of coconut are sold everywhere, but especially on the coast where coconut milk is a popular and safe drink, and toffee-coconut nibbles are sold on the street, often wrapped in paper from school exercise books.

Madagascar's dairy industry is growing. There are some good, locally produced cheeses and Malagasy yoghurt is excellent and available in the smallest shops. Try the drinking yoghurt, *yaourt à boire*.

Vegetarian food

Madagascar is becoming more accustomed to *vazaha* vegetarians and with patience you can usually order meatless dishes even at small *hotelys*. 'Tsy misy hena' means 'without meat'. Frances Kerridge reports: 'In more remote places it is actually easier to be accepted as a vegetarian as people are more accepting of *fady* than in the towns.'

Drink

The most popular drink, Three Horses Beer (THB), is wonderful on a hot day. I think it's wonderful on a cold day, too. The price goes up according to the surroundings: twice as much in the Hilton as in a *hotely* and there is always a hefty deposit payable on the bottle. A newish beer is Queens, which is slightly weaker, and there is also Gold. Why does the Star brewery give its beer English names that the Malagasy can't pronounce? And why horses and queens when the country has few of either (and not much gold)? I don't know.

Madagascar produces its own wine in the Fianarantsoa region, and some is excellent. L'azani Betsileo (*blanc* or *gris*, *reservé*) is recommended.

A pleasant aperitif is Maromby (the name means 'many zebu') and I have been told that Litchel, made from lychees, is good. Rum, *toaka gasy*, is very cheap and plentiful, especially in sugar-growing areas such as Nosy Be; and fermented sugar-cane juice, *betsabetsa* (east coast), or fermented coconut milk, *trembo* (north), make a change. The best cocktail is *punch au coco*, with a coconut-milk base, which is a speciality of the coastal areas. Yummy!

The most popular mineral water is called Eau Vive, but other brands are now available: Olympiko and La Source. Fresh is an agreeable shandy, and Tonic is – you guessed it – tonic water. And, of course, there is Coca-Cola and other popular soft drinks such as Sprite and Fanta. The locally produced *limonady* sadly bears no resemblance to lemons, and Bon Bon Anglais is revolting (although I do know one anglaise who rather likes it!). Cartons of Tiko fruit juice are recommended.

Caffeine-addicts have a problem. The coffee is OK if drunk black, but usually only condensed milk is available. I find that one quickly regresses to childhood and surreptitiously spoons the condensed milk not into the coffee but into the mouth. If you prefer unsweetened white coffee it's best to bring your own powdered milk.

The locally grown tea is very weak, the best quality being reserved for export. A nice alternative is *citronelle*, lemon-grass tea, which is widely available.

HANDICRAFTS AND WHAT TO BUY

You can buy just about everything in the handicrafts line in Madagascar. Most typical of the country are wood carvings, raffia work (in amazing variety), crocheted and embroidered table-cloths and clothes, leather goods, carved zebu horn, Antaimoro paper (with embedded dried flowers), and so on. The choice is almost limitless, and it can all be seen in the artisans' market (Marché Artisanal) and other handicrafts markets and shops in Antananarivo and throughout the country.

In the south you can buy attractive heavy silver bracelets that are traditionally worn by men. In Tana, and the east and north (Nosy Be), you will be offered vanilla pods, peppercorns, cloves and other spices, and honey.

Do not buy products from endangered species. That includes tortoiseshell (turtle shell), snake skins (now crocodiles are farmed commercially, their skins may be sold legally), shells and coral and, of course, live animals. Butterflies are farmed commercially so buying mounted specimens is permitted. Also prohibited are endemic plants, fossils and any genuine article of funerary art. To tell turtle shell from zebu horn, hold it up to the light: turtleshell is semi-transparent.

To help stamp out the sale of endangered animal products, tourists should make their feelings – and the law – known. If, for instance, you are offered tortoise or turtle shell, tell the vendor it is *interdit*; and to push the point home you can say it is *fady* for you to buy such a thing.

The luggage weight-limit when leaving Madagascar is normally 20kg – bear this in mind when doing your shopping.

If you want to buy Malagasy craft items after your return home (to Britain) ask for a copy of Discover Madgascar's catalogue (tel: 020 8995 3529; email: dismad@globalnet.co.uk).

Semi-precious stones

Madagascar is a rewarding place for gem hunters, with citrin, tourmaline, and beryl inexpensive and easy to find. The solitaire sets using these stones are typical and most attractive. Precious stones are also available: emeralds and sapphires, but the quality is poor by Western standards (they are opaque). The centre for gems is Antsirabe but they are for sale in many Highland towns. Ranohira is now the centre of the sapphire trade. If you buy uncut stones bear in mind the cost of having them cut at home, and the additional expense of having them made into jewellery.

Permits

Some purchases need, in theory, an export permit, but the rule is seldom enforced with tourists. If you are buying a large quantity of goods check the latest regulations with your tour operator or the Maison du Tourisme in Tana.

MUSIC

In recent years Malagasy music has become well known, with several Malagasy groups such as Tarika now touring internationally (see box on page 148); Paddy Bush and the *valiha* player Justin Vali have formed a collaboration which has brought Malagasy music to a wider audience through Kate Bush's recording *The Red Shoes* and a new CD *The Sunshine Within*. See their website: www.madagascan. net/music/justinvali.

If you have a particular interest in Malagasy music, consider signing up for a specific music tour. Jules, who lives in Nosy Be with his naturalist wife Josephine Andrews, has put together an itinerary which combines the local music and natural history. See page 317 for contact details.

BLUE GOLD

A few years ago I bought two black stones from a nervous-looking man near Antsirabe. He had found them in a river and swore they were sapphires and that there were plenty more. I paid the equivalent of £1 for them. A year later I had them authenticated by a jeweller ('yes, they are sapphires but poor quality'), cut and made into a pair of earrings. The final cost was well over £100 so it wasn't a particularly good buy.

Now sapphires of superb quality have been discovered in the south: 'Sapphires of a quality and colour rarely seen on jewellery markets are being crunched underfoot' reported *The Sunday Times*. The first inkling of what was to come was in 1995 when a football-sized sapphire was found. It weighed 17kg, but this was thought at the time to be a one-off discovery. Not so. Now in 1999 the world's gem buyers are descending on Ilakaka, on the edge of Isalo National Park. And an unsavoury lot they appear to be, swaggering around like cowboys with wide-brimmed hats and guns at their hips. Some of the happiest prospectors are said to be policemen who were dispatched to Ilakaka to keep order and promptly deserted the force to try their luck. Politicians have also cashed in on the find and secured the best concessions.

The local people, as always, are unlikely to benefit much, although everyone is having a go. The government sells prospecting licences and allows prospectors to keep what they find. One lucky lad found and sold a sapphire for the equivalent of £8,000. He was killed that night in a car crash after celebrating with his friends. He was just one of 40 or so who have lost their lives in the six months since the mine opened. The holes are up to 3m deep with horizontal galleries vulnerable to earth collapses: suffocation is the cause of most deaths.

You may run into Malagasy music anywhere, but Antananarivo is probably your best bet; see page 148 for the best places.

MISCELLANEOUS
Tipping

A service charge is added to most restaurant meals so tipping is not strictly necessary, but waiters in tourist hotels now expect it. About 5–10% is ample. Taxi drivers should not expect a tip, though you may want to add something for exceptional service. Before you give a dollar to the doorman for carrying your bag from the taxi to the hotel lobby, bear in mind the average earnings of a Malagasy labourer. A reader points out that 'we tourists sometimes hand out tips that are the equivalent of a week's wages. I have seen a man tipped by a Malagasy 500Fmg (10 pence) and be happy with it. It must be remembered that not many Malagasy earn more than 25,000Fmg per week. A good brick carrier in Tana can manage 18 a time on his head and is paid 5Fmg per brick – so they have to carry 500 bricks before they earn 10 pence.' (G D Twigger)

Frances Kerridge adds a plea: 'If you are over generous it makes life much harder for those *vazaha* who live here on local wages as all foreigners are then seen to be wealthy.'

Electrical equipment

The voltage in Madagascar is 220. Outlets (where they exist) take 2-pin round plugs. If you use a 3-pin fused plug plus adapter, bring a spare fuse for the plug.

Business hours
Most businesses open 08.00–12.00 and 14.00–18.00. Banks are open 08.00–16.00, and are closed weekends and the afternoon before a holiday.

Communications: keeping in touch
Telephone
The phone service has improved enormously in the past two years, with cellphones very popular. You can now buy phonecards for 25, 50 and 100 units, costing from 10,000Fmg to 60,000Fmg and use them for overseas calls from a public phone box (Publiphone). Phonecards are available from hotels or large post offices. Rates are much cheaper in the evenings after 22.00 and on Sundays.

Below are the current cheap-rate prices for calls per minute made from Telecom Malagasy offices:

France and Italy	8,750Fmg (12,500Fmg peak rate)
Other European countries	12,820Fmg
North America	13,125Fmg
Between zones in Madagascar	5,375Fmg.

The telephone code for Madagascar is 261 20 (+ town code + the number). Below are the phone codes for all of Madagascar (this information is repeated under relevant town information).

Antananarivo (Tana)	22	Morondava	95
Antsirabe	44	Moramanga	56
Antsiranana (Diego Suarez)	82	Nosy Be	86
Fianarantsoa	75	Sambava	88
Ile Sainte Marie	57	Taolagnaro (Fort Dauphin)	92
Maintirano	69	Toamasina (Tamatave)	53
Mahajanga (Majunga)	62	Toliara (Tuléar)	94
Manankara	73		

Mail
The mail service is reasonably efficient and letters generally take about two weeks to reach Europe and a little longer to North America. Postcards to Europe currently cost 1,950Fmg; letters are 3,200Fmg. The smaller post offices often run out of stamps, but some hotels sell them. Clare Hermans adds: 'Malagasy stamps are a meal in themselves! Bring a sponge or dunk in the nearest puddle.'

If you want to receive mail, have your correspondent address the envelope with your initial only and your surname in capitals, and send it to you c/o Poste Restante in whichever town you will be in. It will be held at the main post office. If you are an Amex member the Amex Client Mail Service allows you to have letters sent to their office in the Hilton Hotel. They keep mail for a month.

BP in an address is Bôite Postale – the same as PO Box...

Courier service
Colis Express hooks up with DHL. There is an office in Tana (see page 154) and in all the large towns.

Internet
Cybercafés are now opening in the capital (see page 154) and other major towns will no doubt follow suit.

PUBLIC HOLIDAYS

The Malagasy take their holidays seriously. In every town and village there will be a parade with speeches and an air of festivity. 'New Year was celebrated throughout the night, and on New Year's Day everyone paraded their new clothes through the streets in a Malagasy version of an Easter Parade. New Year parties were held by every conceivable organisation during the next two months.' (Bryan and Eve Pinches)

Official holidays

January 1	New Year's Day
March 29	Commemoration of 1947 rebellion
Easter Monday (movable)	
May 1	Labour Day
Ascension Day (movable)	
Whit Monday (movable)	
June 26	Independence Day
August 15	Feast of the Assumption
November 1	All Saints' Day
December 25	Christmas Day
December 30	Republic Day

When these holidays fall on a Thursday, Friday will be tacked on to the weekend. Banks and other businesses often take a half day holiday before the official holiday.

ART·OF·TRAVEL

Tailormade Safaris, using small personal camps and lodges in the remote wilderness areas of Eastern and Southern Africa together with luxury Resorts on the coast and in The Indian Ocean Islands of the Seychelles and Mauritius

21 The Bakehouse, 119 Altenburg Gardens, London, SW11 1JQ
Tel: 0171 738 2038   Fax: 0171 738 1893   ATOL: 2914
e-mail: safari@artoftravel.co.uk   web site: http://www.artoftravel.co.uk

Discover Madagascar with Za Tour.
We'll take care of all your travel arrangements!

Our services include:
* Airport meet & greet and assistance with formalities * Cultural and shopping excursions
* Flight reconfirmations and reservations * Organised camping expeditions
* Guided excursions to all nature reserves and national parks * Hotel reservations
* Escorted overland tours with experienced drivers & guides * Trekking / hiking trips
* Experienced, English speaking Malagasy guides * Natural history itineraries

Za Tour, Lot ID 33 Bis Ambohitsorohitra, Antananarivo 101, Madagascar
Tel : (+261-20) 22 - 656 48 Fax : 22 - 656 47 Email: za.tour@dts.mg

HAINTENY

The dingadingana has borne fruit without coming into leaf,
the hazotokana has borne fruit without coming into flower,
and the fishing has been uncertain this year.
Why have these changes occurred, my elder brother?
– Have you forgotten, perhaps, the sayings of our ancestors?
Consider, children, the conditions here on earth:
the trees grow, but not unceasingly,
for if they grew unceasingly, they would reach the sky.
Not only this,
but there is a time for their growing,
a time for their becoming old,
and a time for their breaking.
So it is, too, for man: there is a time for youth,
a time for old age,
a time for good,
a time for evil,
and a time for death.

Madagascar and You

Tsihy be lambanana ny ambanilantra
'All who live under the sky are woven together like one big mat.'
Malagasy saying

RESPONSIBLE TOURISM

In recent years there has been a welcome shift of attitude among visitors to developing countries from 'What can I get out of this trip?' to 'How can I give something back?' This chapter addresses those issues, and suggests ways in which you can help this marvellous, but often tragic country.

They do things differently there

I once caught our Malagasy guide scowling at himself in the mirror. When I teased him he said: 'As a Malagasy man I smile a lot. I can see that if I want to work with tourists I must learn to frown.' He knew that the group considered him insufficiently assertive. Tolerance and the fear of causing offence is an integral part of Malagasy social relationships. So if a tourist expresses anger in a way that is entirely appropriate in his or her own culture, it is counter-productive in Madagascar. It is deeply unsettling to the person at the receiving end who often giggles in response, thus exacerbating the situation. If you are patient, pleasant and keep your temper, your problem will be solved more quickly.

Avoid being too dogmatic in conversation (you do not have exclusivity of the truth). Make use of 'perhaps' and 'maybe'. Be excessive in your thanks. The Malagasy are very polite; we miss the nuances by not understanding the language. Body language, however, is easier to learn. For instance, 'excuse me, may I come through?' is indicated by a stooping posture and an arm extended forward. Note how often it is used.

Part of responsible tourism is relinquishing some of our normal comforts. Consider this statistic: fuelwood demand in Madagascar has far outstripped supply. Wood and charcoal are the main sources of energy, and the chief users are city dwellers. In rural areas, tourist establishments will be the main consumers. Do you still feel that hot water is essential in your hotel?

One of the keys to responsible tourism is ensuring that as much as possible of the money you spend on your holiday remains in Madagascar. Independent travellers should try, whenever possible, to stay at small hotels run by Malagasy; tourists on an organised tour will probably find themselves in a foreign-owned hotel, but can do their bit by buying handicrafts and donating to local charities.

Madagascar's shortcomings can be maddening. Sometimes a little reflection reveals the reasons behind the failure to produce the expected service, but sometimes you just have to tell yourself 'Well, that's the way it is'. After all, you are not going to be able to change Madagascar, but Madagascar may change you.

Photography

Lack of consideration when taking photos is probably the most common example of irresponsible tourist behaviour – one that each of us has probably been guilty of at some time. It is so easy to take a sneak photo without first establishing contact with the person, so easy to say we'll send a print of the picture and then not get round to it, so easy to stroll into a market or village thinking what a wonderful photo it will make and forgetting that you are there to experience it.

'PLEASE SEND ME A PHOTO'

It is not always easy to keep a promise. Of course we intend to send a print after someone posed cheerfully for the photo, but after we get home there are so many other things to do, so many addresses on torn-out pages of exercise books. I now honour my promises. Here's why.

I was checking my group in to a Nosy Be hotel when the bellboy asked if he could speak to me. He looked nervous, so suspecting a problem with the bookings I asked him to wait until everyone was in their rooms.

When we were alone he cleared his throat and recited what was obviously a carefully prepared speech: 'You are Mrs Hilary Bradt. Ten years ago you gave your business card to the lady at Sambava Voyages and she gave it to a schoolboy who wrote to you. But you were away so your mother answered the letter. She wrote many letters. My name is Murille and I am that boy. And now I want to talk to you about Janet Cross and Brian Cross and Andrew and...' There followed a list of every member of my family. As I listened, incredulous, I remembered the original letter. 'We love England strongly,' he wrote, 'especially London, Buckingham, Grantham, Dover...' I remembered passing it to my mother saying I was too busy for such a correspondence but maybe she'd like to write. She kept it up for several years, answering questions such as 'How often does Mrs Hilary go to Grantham and Dover?' and she sent a photo of the family gathering at Christmas, naming every member on the back of the photo.

This brought an indignant letter from a cousin. 'I have seen your photo. It is a very nice one. I asked Murille if he would lend it for one day only because we all study English so we must have photo of English people more to improve this language, but he refused me strongly because they are only his friends not mine...'

Murille brought out the treasured photo. It had suffered from the constant handling and tropical heat and was peeling at the edges. He wanted to trim it, he explained, 'but if I do I will have to cut off a bit of your mother's beautiful chair and I can't do that.'

Later that year I sent Murille a photo album filled with family photos. I never heard from him again – that's the way it is in Madagascar – but the story has a twist to its tail.

I recently went back to Sambava, 12 years after the original visit, and found myself addressing a classroom of eager adult students of English and their local teacher. Searching for something interesting to say, I told them about the time I was last in Sambava and the series of letters between Murille and my mother. And I told them about the cousin who also wrote to her. 'I think his name was Patrice,' I said. The teacher looked up. 'I'm Patrice. Yes, I remember writing to Janet Cross...'

The rules are not to take people's photos without permission, and to respect an answer of 'no'. Give consideration to the offence caused by photographing the destitute. Be cautious about paying your way to a good photo; often a smile or a joke will work as well, without setting a precedent. People love to receive pictures of themselves. If you are travelling on an organised tour your guide is sure to visit that area again so can deliver the prints that you send to him. If you are travelling independently write down the addresses and honour your promise (see page 131).

Philip Thomas writes: 'A Malagasy, for whom a photograph will be a highly treasured souvenir, will remember the taking of the photograph and your promise to send them a copy, a lot longer than you might. Their disappointment in those who say one thing and do another is great, so if you think you might not get it together to send the photograph then do not say that you will.'

A responsible attitude to photography is so much more fun! And it results in better pictures. It involves taking some time getting to know the subject of your proposed photo: making a purchase, perhaps, or practising your Malagasy greetings (if that doesn't draw hoots of laughter nothing will!).

Beggars

Whether or not to give to professional beggars is up to you. I believe that it is wrong to give to the little ragamuffin children who follow you around because it is better to give to the charities (see *How you can help*, page 128) that work with them. Actually, the same applies to all age-groups. My policy is to give to the elderly and I also single out 'beggar days' when I fill my pockets with small change and give to every beggar who looks needy and over school age. And if I make some trickster's day, so be it.

It is important to make up your mind about beggars before you hit the streets so you can avoid standing there looking through a conspicuously fat wallet for a low-denomination bill.

The effects of tourism on local people

The impact of foreigners on the Malagasy was noted as long ago as 1669 when a visitor commented that formerly the natives were deeply respectful of white men but were changed 'by the bad examples which the Europeans have had, who glory in the sin of luxury in this country...'.

In developing countries tourism has had profound effects on the inhabitants, some good, some bad. Madagascar seems to me to be a special case – more than any other country I've visited it inspires a particular devotion and an awareness of its fragility, both environmental and cultural. Wildlife is definitely profiting from the attention given it and from the emphasis on ecotourism. For the people, however, the blessings may be very mixed: some able Malagasy have found jobs in the tourist industry, but for others the impact of tourism has meant that their cultural identity has been eroded, along with some of their dignity and integrity. Village antagonisms are heightened when one or two people gain the lion's share of tourist revenue and gifts, leading in one case to murder, and hitherto honest folk have lapsed into corruption or thievery.

Giving presents

This is a subject often discussed among experienced travellers who cannot agree on when, if ever, a present is appropriate. Most feel that giving presents is appropriate only when it is in exchange for a service. Many tourists to the developing world, however, pack sweets and trinkets 'for the children' as automatically as their sunglasses and insect repellent.

My repeat visits to Madagascar over the course of 23 years have shaped my own view: that giving is usually done for self-gratification rather than generosity, and that one thoughtless act can change a village irreparably. I have seen the shyly inquisitive children of small communities turn into tiresome beggars; I have seen the warm interaction between visitor and local turn into mutual hostility; I have seen intelligent, ambitious young men turn into scoundrels. What I haven't sorted out in my mind is how much this matters. Thieves and scoundrels make a good living and are probably happier than they were in their earlier state of dire poverty. Should we be imposing our cultural views on the Malagasy? I don't know.

But giving does not have to be in the form of material gifts. 'Giving something back' has a far broader meaning. We should never underestimate our value as sheer entertainment in an otherwise routine life. We can give a smile, or a greeting in Malagasy. And we can learn from people who in so many ways are richer than us. See pages 28–9 and 312 for more thoughts on the subject.

My views over present-giving are backed up by Laura Benson, who spent several weeks researching government, church and private programmes to help the poor. She wrote: 'I am convinced now that giving to children directly is only hurting the situation, and that if you really want to help then a donation to an organisation is the best way. Giving pens, etc can have an even worse effect, especially if you only have one to give. I saw many fights started among children over who got the pen or the empty Coke bottle.'

More and more...

Visitors who have spent some time in Madagascar and have befriended a particular family often find themselves in the 'more and more and more' trap. The foreigner begins by expressing appreciation of the friendship and hospitality he or she received by sending a gift to the family. A request for a more expensive gift follows. And another one, until the luckless *vazaha* (white foreigner) feels that she is seen as a bottomless cornucopia of goodies. The reaction is a mixture of guilt and resentment.

Understanding the Malagasy viewpoint may help you to come to terms with these requests. You may be considered as part of the extended family, and family members often help support those who are less well-off. You will almost certainly be thought of as fabulously wealthy, so it is worth dispelling this myth by giving some prices for familiar foodstuffs at home – a kilo of rice, for instance, or a mango. Explain that you don't have servants, that you pay so much for rent, and that you have a family of your own that needs your help. Don't be afraid to say 'no' firmly.

Do's and don'ts when travelling off the beaten path

Travellers venturing well off the beaten path will want to do their utmost to avoid offending the local people, who are usually extremely warm and hospitable. Unfortunately, with the many *fady* prohibitions and beliefs varying from area to area and village to village, it is impossible to know exactly how to behave, although *vazahas* and other outsiders are exempt from the consequences of infringing a local *fady*.

Sometimes, in very remote areas, Malagasy will react in sheer terror at the sight of a white person. This probably stems from their belief in *mpakafo* (pronounced 'mpakafoo'), the 'stealer of hearts'. These pale-faced beings are said to wander around at night ripping out people's hearts. So it is understandable that rural Malagasy often do not like going out after dark – and a problem if you are looking for a guide. The arrival of a pale-faced being in their village is understandably upsetting. In the southeast it is the *mpangalak'aty*, the 'taker of the liver', who is feared.

Villages are governed by the *Fokonolona*, or People's Assembly. On arrival at a village you should ask for the *Président du Fokontany*. Although traditionally this was the village elder, these days it is more likely to be someone who speaks French – perhaps the schoolteacher. He will show you where you can sleep (sometimes a hut is kept free for guests, sometimes someone will be moved out for you). You will usually be provided with a meal. Now travellers have penetrated most rural areas, you will be expected to pay. If the *Président* is not available, ask for *Ray amandreny*, an elder.

Philip Thomas, a social anthropologist who has conducted research in the rural southeast, points out several ways that tourists may unwittingly cause offence. 'People should adopt the common courtesy of greeting the Malagasy in their own language. *Salama*, *manahoana* and *veloma* are no more difficult to say than their French equivalents, and to insist on using French displays an ignorance of Madagascar's colonial past.

'*Vazaha* sometimes refuse food and hospitality, putting up tents and cooking their own food. But in offering you a place to sleep and food to eat the Malagasy are showing you the kindness they extend to any visitor or stranger, and to refuse is a rejection of their hospitality and sense of humanity. You may think you are inconveniencing them, and this is true, but they would prefer that than if you keep to yourselves as though you were not people (in the widest sense) like them. It may annoy you that it is virtually impossible to get a moment away from the gaze of the Malagasy, but you are there to look at them and their activities anyway, so why should there not be a mutual exchange? Besides, you are far more fascinating to them than they are to you, for their view of the world is not one shaped by mass education and access to international images supplied by television.

SNAKES ALIVE!
Bill Love

The last trip was great! This time I wrote ahead to the two-room school in Ankify, c/o of Le Baobab Hotel nearby, to arrange a cultural visit for my group on a Monday morning. The visit was a huge success! Besides exchanging questions and answers about life in the USA and Madagascar, everyone with me brought a mountain of school supplies to donate, which went a long way even among the 140 kids ranging from 6 to 15 years old.

We also brought in a harmless native snake we found the previous day for a live 'biology lesson' that turned out to be the most memorable part of all! The kids were verging on terror when they first saw the snake. I arranged for Angelin Razafimanantsoa, our local guide, to be the first one seen holding the snake so the kids would see a Malagasy unafraid. This worked perfectly, as we had most students coming forward to touch it within minutes, including most of the girls. The students' reactions and curiosity were unforgettable!

I'll be making this an annual event since I always return to this area. I have approached my hometown elementary school here in Florida to introduce an ongoing cultural exchange relationship with them, kind of like a 'sister' school abroad.

Bill Love is a herpetologist and tour operator who regularly runs 'herping' trips to Madagascar. The northwest around Ambanja is his favourite stopover area. This is how he is 'giving something back' to the region.

'It is perfectly acceptable to give a gift of money in return for help. Gifts of cash are not seen by the Malagasy as purchases and they themselves frequently give them. Rather, you give as a sign of your appreciation and respect. But beware of those who may try to take advantage of your position as a foreigner (and you may find these in even the remotest spot), those who play on your lack of knowledge of language and custom, and their perception of you as extremely wealthy (as of course you are by their standards).

'You may well see memorial sites by the side of the road or tombs marked on maps, especially in the southeast. Do not think it is OK to visit these or photograph them if no-one is around to ask. Seek out someone, a male elder being best, and ask if you can be allowed to visit the site and under what terms. More often than not your request will be accepted. But what annoys people here is that *vazaha* see something beside the road then trample all over it, photographing it, then carry on with their journey as if they cared nothing for the feelings of those that own the site. To do so shows little respect, as the Malagasy understand it, neither to themselves nor to the dead commemorated there.'

Both Henk Beentje and Philip Thomas recommend presenting yourself and your passport to the *Gendarmerie* if you are staying in a small village. Apart from being good manners, this could avoid problems for both you and your Malagasy hosts (see box page 104).

HOW YOU CAN HELP

There are ways in which you can make a positive contribution. By making a donation to a local project you can help the people – and the wildlife – without creating new problems. Charities based in Tana are described on page 140. All of these welcome visitors and donations.

My favourite (because I've visited many times) is the Streetkids Project, which was started by a couple of English teachers, Jill and Charlie Hadfield. Visiting a charity run by the Sisters of the Good Shepherd in Tana, they could see where a little money could go a long way. The nuns run – amongst other things – a preparatory school for the very poor. When the children are ready to go on to state school, however, the parents can't afford the £15 a year they must pay for registration, uniform and books, so the children were condemned to return to the streets as beggars. The Streetkids Project raises money to continue their education and is administered in Britain through Money For Madagascar.

The organisations and charities listed below are all working with the people of Madagascar, and, by extension, habitat conservation. Most of them are very small, run by dedicated volunteers, who would welcome even small donations. Other charities work specifically for wildlife. What better way to channel your empathy for Madagascar and its problems?

Charities assisting Madagascar
People

Money for Madagascar 7 Pinetree Close, Burry Port, SA16 0TF, UK. This long-established and well-run small charity funds rural health and agricultural projects, and supports street children and other deprived groups in urban areas.

Feedback Madagascar Westering, Crinan, Argyll PA31 8SR, UK; tel/fax: 01546 830240. A small but highly effective Scottish charity which bases its activities on feedback from the local Malagasy who identify and agree on development and conservation projects (see box opposite). These have included irrigation dams, the rebuilding of a school, and a 'school reserve' near Ranomafana. Other schemes are a women's market-gardening cooperative, an agricultural training centre and the silk project near Ambalavao.

FROM LITTLE ACORNS...

Jamie Spencer is an anthropologist who first visited Madagascar at 22 to write his university dissertation. Moved by the poverty and the incredible dignity and strength of the Tanala people, he promised to return to try and help. That was ten years ago. Funding for the first trip was raised by a sponsored cycle ride. He took with him a microscope donated by a local distillery and a sack full of medicines begged from hospitals and chemists, and headed for the eastern rainforest. Thus **Feedback Madagascar** was born. The local people themselves are the driving force behind the development and conservation projects. It is they who identify and realise them with Feedback's support. So far Sandrakely has irrigation dams for 40 hectares (100 acres) of sustainable ricefields and a new school where attendance has rocketed from 24 to 96 children. The children have helped create their very own school reserve, the first of its kind in Madagascar: ten hectares (25 acres) of rainforest donated by Lentaka, the late chief of the region. Though small, it is the home of four species of lemur and also provides a vital reservoir of water for Sandrakely. The only people allowed access to the forest are the government foresters and the schoolchildren themselves, who are being aided in their environmental studies by the WWF. See also boxes on pages 37 and 185.

Josephine Andrews also studied anthropology (and geography). She fulfilled her dream of visiting Madagascar when she won a Winston Churchill Scholarship to do a survey of Madagascar's environmental problems. Like Jamie she fell in love with the island and its people, and determined to go back. The **Black Lemur Forest Project** was established in Nosy Be, using funds begged from a variety of businesses. The aim was to conserve the remaining untouched forests of Lokobe, the black lemurs' dwindling habitat, by working with the local people to find alternative means of support, particularly through Nosy Be's thriving tourist industry. After several years working on a shoestring budget, Josephine and her Malagasy husband were awarded the Whitely Award for Conservation. Most recent developments include a community centre in the village of Ambanoro on the western edge of Lokobe Reserve, which encompasses a Visitor Centre for tourists and a shop for locally made handicrafts.

Liz Caldicott is a very ordinary tourist who briefly visited Madagascar off a cruise ship. Going ashore in Nosy Komba she was disappointed to find that the handicrafts did not truly reflect the island's main attraction: lemurs and chameleons. She wanted to see soft toys for sale and wondered why the local women did not make such saleable items. 'They don't know how to' came the answer. So she enlisted the help of Josephine. Back in England, Liz worked 'like a factory' producing a series of sample toys – a lepilemur, black lemurs of both sexes, and a panther chameleon – from locally available materials. These are now in production in Ambanoro, giving the islanders a reliable income from their sales, and tourists a delightful souvenir to take home with them. The same soft toys are also in production at the Centre Fihavanana in Tana (see page 140).

Three ordinary people with extraordinary perseverance, united by their love for Madagascar.

MOSS Boscawen Cottage, Back Lane, East Clandon, Nr Guildford, Surrey GU4 7SD, UK. The Madagascan Organisation for Saving Sight (MOSS) was set up in 1993 to help develop ophthalmic and general health services in Madagascar, where 300,000 people suffer blindness from treatable and preventable causes. MOSS is a small, but very active charity with a considerable number of achievements to their credit. Recent projects include the creation of a 'Madagascar eye game' to promote preventative measures. The charity has provided one operating microscope for use in opthalmic fieldwork and is seeking funds for a second one.

The Dodwell Trust Christina Dodwell, c/o Madagascar Consulate, 16 Lanark Mansions, Pennard Rd, London W12 8DT; tel: 020 8746 0133; fax: 020 8746 0134. A British registered charity running a radio project designed to help rural villagers, through the production and broadcast of a radio drama series for family health, family planning and welfare. The programmes are in Malagasy, by Malagasy, and based in Malagasy tradition. To enhance this programme The Dodwell Trust also runs a solar radio conversion project, and a clockwork or wind-up radio project which aims to put these radios into rural and rainforest villages. The listeners provide valuable feedback to the programme producers. The Trust is also helping with technical assistance throughout the field of radio production.

Andrew Lees Memorial Trust 31b Bassett St, London NW5 4PG; tel: 020 8748 0980. Set up in memory of the Friends Of The Earth campaigns director who died while researching the possible impact of a mining project on the forests of the southeast, the Trust helps fund environmental, research and educational programmes in that area. The Libanona Ecology Centre is one of their successes (see box on page 215). They are also funding 'Project Radio', to help spread vital information to rural people via wind-up or solar-powered radios.

Valiha High FMS, PO Box 337, London N4 1TW. This is not a registered charity but a project to maintain the musical traditions of Madagascar, instigated by the leader of the world-acclaimed Malagasy group, Tarika. Hanitrarivo Rasoanaivo was depressed at the influence of foreign cultures on the young people of Madagascar and the violent or pornographic videos which are now their preferred entertainment. The project, set up in 1997, has been very successful. Students are forming their own *valiha* groups, but their enthusiasm for the instrument is creating its own problem – they are wearing out and need to be replaced! A small donation goes a long way towards the cost of buying the instruments, training teachers, and for prizes for competitions.

STARFISH PO Box 18556, Cleveland, OH 44118, USA; tel: (216) 382 4297; fax: (216) 382 0385; email: JFSellers@stratos.net. The acronym is for Society Taking Active Responsibility for International Self-help; the aim is to provide the tools and training for local people to do their jobs. The emphasis is on medical help. Projects have included surgery training for student doctors and nurses, village health projects (working in conjunction with the WWF in villages adjoining reserves), the establishment of pharmacies, and the provision of bicycles to allow doctors and nurses to reach remote villages. Jim Sellers, who runs the Madagascar projects for STARFISH, sells Antaimoro paper, greetings cards, etc as a means of fundraising. Contact him at the above address.

Zaza Faly (Mission Aid for Children) Elke Driese, Oberonstr 8a, 13129 Berlin, Germany; local address: Lot 233-B bis, Amparatanana, Fenoarivo-Est 509. A non-religious charity that works with local people to help the street children of Fenoarivo, on the east coast.

Wildlife

World Wide Fund for Nature Av du Mont-blanc, 1196 Gland, Switzerland (International Office); Panda House, Weyside Park, Godalming, Surrey GU7 1XR, UK; 1250 24th St NW, Washington DC 20037-1175, USA; Aires Protégées, BP 738, Antananarivo 101, Madagascar.

Durrell Wildife Conservation Trust Les Augres Manor, Trinity, Jersey JE3 5BP, Channel Islands, British Isles; tel: 01534 860000; fax 01534 860001; email: jerseyzoo@durrell.org. For full details of this non-profit organisation see box on page 70.
Conservation International (USA) 1015 18th St NW, Washington DC, 20003, USA. Very active in Madagascar. Among other projects they help fund Ampijoroa Forest Reserve.
Black Lemur Forest Project c/o 53 Priory Way, North Harrow, Middx HA2 6DQ, UK. A small but effective project in Nosy Be, helping to protect the habitat and survival of one of Madagascar's most popular lemur species. See pages 129 and 316.

Organisations promoting responsible tourism
Tourism Concern Stapleton House, 277–281 Holloway Rd, London N7 8HN, UK. With the slogan 'putting people back in the picture', Tourism Concern 'promotes tourism that takes account of the rights and interests of those living in the world's tourist areas'. They put pressure on governments or companies which promote harmful tourism, run meetings and conferences, and publish an informative and interesting newsletter.
Center for Responsible Tourism PO Box 827, San Anselmo, CA 94979, USA. Full title: The North America Coordinating Center for Responsible Tourism (NACCRT). 'Exists to change attitudes and practices of North American travelers, to involve North Americans in the struggle for justice in tourism and to work for tourism practices that are compatible with a sustainable global society.'

Finally, if on your return to Britain you want to keep connections with Madagascar, how about joining the Anglo-Malagasy Society? The London consulate has information.

PHOTOGRAPHING PEOPLE
Janice Booth
In 1997, in Andapa, I took a photo of a woman selling vegetables on the pavement. I asked for her name and address – which she laboriously wrote as 'in front of the post office' – so that I could send her a print.

In August 1999, a letter arrived from a 19-year-old, writing in good French. 'You remember Mrs Florette Razananao who was selling vegetables (tomatoes) in front of the Andapa post office when you were in Madagascar in 1997. She is my godmother. Now we have left Andapa. We thank you for your fidelity in sending us her photo. We are happy that we have a friend abroad and are very sorry that it has taken us so long to send you our greetings. Now I will tell you the story of my life...'

And indeed he does, at great length!

The moral of the story? If people have been friendly and helpful about having their photos taken, *do* get their addresses and send them prints. (But don't ask for addresses unless you really intend to send the photos.) You may well never get an acknowledgement, but you'll give a huge amount of pleasure; and if you don't want to risk getting involved in correspondence then just omit your address.

Worldwide Journeys & Expeditions specialise in tailor-making itineraries throughout Africa and the Indian Ocean including the island of Madagascar. We pride ourselves in our first hand knowledge of each area and our prompt, friendly and efficient service.

8 Comeragh Road, London W14 9HP
Tel: 0207 381 8638 Fax: 0207 381 0836 E-mail: wwj@wjournex.demon.co.uk

See MADAGASCAR with DISCOVER THE WORLD

Join us on our specially designed tours and experience at close range the unique wildlife and matchless beauty of this vast tropical island. The trips may only last 17 days but the amazing sights, scents and sounds will stay with you for a lifetime. Limited to small groups and guided by experts, we explore some of the best Reserves and penetrate deep into the forests for some unforgettable encounters!

For details of these and other wildlife, whale watching and adventure holidays around the world, call our 24 hour brochure line or visit our website...

29 Nork Way, Banstead, Surrey SM7 1PB, UK
Fax: 01737 362341

01737 218801
www.arctic-discover.co.uk

ATOL 2896   AITO   ABTA V2823   DISCOVER the WORLD

THE NATURAL WORLD

Malagasy tours, African safaris and wildlife journeys throughout the world.

CRUSADER TRAVEL
57 Church Street, Twickenham, Middlesex TW1 3NR, England
Tel: **020 8892 7606** Fax: **020 8744 0574**
Email: naturalworld@crusadertravel.com   www.crusadertravel.com

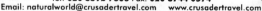

Part Two

The Highlands

Golden bamboo lemur

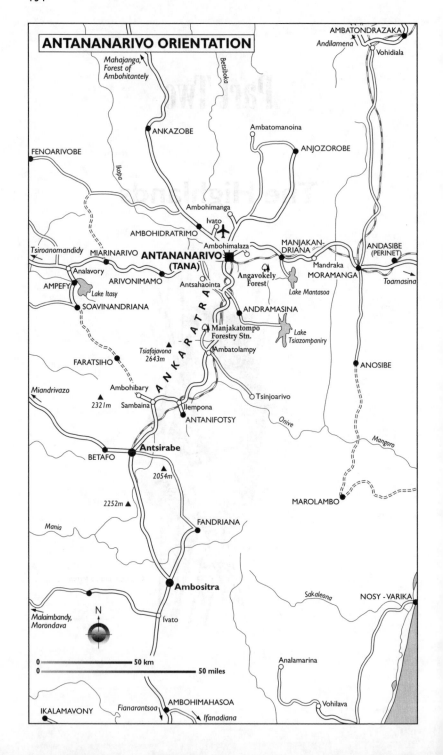

ANTANANARIVO ORIENTATION

Antananarivo and Area

OVERVIEW

Looking down from the plane window as you approach Antananarivo (Tana) you can see how excitingly different this country is from any of its near neighbours. Clusters of red-clay houses and steepled churches stand isolated on the hilltops overlooking a mosaic of green and brown paddy fields. Old defence ditches, *tamboho*, form circles around villages or estates, and dotted in the empty countryside are the white concrete Merina tombs from where the dead will be exhumed in the *famadihana* ceremony.

Most people stay only a day or so in Tana, but there is plenty to see in the city and the surrounding Hauts Plateaux. A week would not be too long to experience the cultural, historical and natural sites which lie within a day's excursion of the capital. The Kingdom of Imerina thrived for over a century before French colonisation, so it is here that the rich and fascinating history and culture of the Merina people are best appreciated.

History

The recorded history of the Merina people (who are characterised by their Indonesian features) begins in the 1400s with a chief called Andriandraviravina. He is widely thought to have started the Merina dynasty that became the most powerful in Madagascar, eventually conquering much of the country.

Key monarchs in the rise of the Merina include Andrianjaka, who conquered a Vazimba town called Analamanga built on a great rock thrusting above the surrounding plains. He renamed it Antananarivo and ordered his palace to be built on its highest point. With its surrounding marshland, ideal for rice production, and the security afforded by its high position, this was the perfect site for a Merina capital city.

In the 18th century there were two centres for the Merina kingdom, Antananarivo and Ambohimanga. The latter became the more important and around 1787 Ramboasalama was proclaimed king of Ambohimanga and took the name of Andrianampoinimerina. The name means 'the prince in the heart of Imerina' which was more than an idle boast: this king was the Malagasy counterpart of the great Peruvian Inca Tupac Yupanqui, expanding his empire as much by skilful organisation as by force, and doing it without the benefit of a written language (history seems to demonstrate that orders in triplicate are not essential to efficiency). By his death in 1810 the central plateau was firmly in control of the Merina and ably administered through a mixture of old customs and new. Each conquered territory was governed by local princes, answerable to the king, and the system of *fokonolona* (village communities) was established. From this firm foundation the new king, Radama I, was able to conquer most of the rest of the island.

Antananarivo means 'City of the Thousand', supposedly because a thousand warriors protected it. By the end of the 18th century, Andrianampoinimerina had taken Antananarivo from his rebellious kinsman and moved his base there from Ambohimanga. From that time until the French conquest in 1895 Madagascar's history centred around the royal palace or *rova*, the modest houses built for Andrianjaka and Andrianampoinimerina giving way to a splendid palace designed for Queen Ranavalona I by Jean Laborde and James Cameron. The rock cliffs near the palace became known as Ampamarinana, 'the place of the hurling', as Christian martyrs met their fate there at the command of the queen.

There was no reason for the French to move the capital elsewhere: its pleasant climate made it an agreeable place to live, and plenty of French money and planning went into the city we see today.

IVATO AIRPORT
Arriving
In the Good Old Days Ivato was like the cottage of a wicked witch, seducing innocent visitors through its beguiling doors. Once inside, only the good and the brave emerged unscathed. During the rebuilding and enlarging of the airport it became, if anything, more chaotic. Now (sigh) it is much the same as other international airports in the developing world. On arrival the procedure is as follows:

1. Fill in the Embarkation form. This should be handed to you on the plane, but more often than not you need to retrieve one from an official by the Immigration desk. The questions are straightforward, but be prepared to say where you'll be staying in Tana.
2. If you do not have a visa, fill in the appropriate form and have the required amount (see page 77) ready.
3. Join one of the 'queues' for passport and visa check. (Look at the signs above each desk to make sure you are in the correct queue.)
4. Pick up your luggage. There are now a good supply of trolleys to take your bags through customs. If you are carrying a video camera or something of value such as jewellery or a laptop computer you should pass through the red channel and declare it. Failure to do this may cause problems on departure. Still cameras need not be declared (note that in French *camera* means a video camera; a still camera is *appareil*). If queuing for the green 'Nothing to Declare' channel, try to stay with other tourists who are usually waved through without needing to open their bags. Luggage belonging to Malagasy arrivals is usually thoroughly searched.
5. If you can fight off the porters and taxi touts for a while longer, change money at the airport. The banks are always open for international flight arrivals.

Leaving
This is no longer a two-hour nightmare, but is still a little stressful for those used to more conventional airports. Remember that you *must* reconfirm your flight at least 72 hours before your flight departs. At this point you may be able to ask for a seat allocation.

1. Arrive at the airport at least two hours before the flight, with all or most of your Malagasy money spent. **Remember that you cannot change your Fmg back into hard currency.** The check-in counter is after you leave the main airport area (with shops), so once you have checked in there is nowhere to spend your Fmg.

2. Pay your departure tax at the kiosk marked *Adema*. These days you can pay in Fmg although the authorities prefer hard currency: 120Ff, DM36 or US$24 for flights to Europe, 95Ff, DM36 or US$24 for 'regional' destinations in the Indian Ocean, which include South Africa. Give the correct amount, otherwise you may receive change in another (unwanted) currency. The receipt will be stapled on to your air ticket.

3. Join the queue for the departure gate (with your luggage); prepare for a certain amount of jostling. You may be given a departure form to fill in.

4. When you reach the doorway show your ticket and passport, and pass through baggage security. If the X-ray machine is working you're unlikely to be asked to open your bags but have the keys ready. If you're carrying only a small amount of baggage, officials may 'encourage' you to take additional packages on behalf of their friends. Don't.

5. Proceed to the check-in counter. Any orderly queue will have disintegrated by now as people compete for priority. If the computer is working your seat will be assigned here.

6. Passport control. Hand in your departure form.

7. Departure tax check.

8. Final passport check, hand-luggage X-ray, and you're through into the departure lounge! There are souvenir shops here (hard currency only) and a bar. It is sometimes possible to change the Malagasy money you've belatedly found in your pocket into hard currency with the ladies who supervise the toilets.

Internal flights

The domestic building is separated from the main (international) airport by a long corridor. These flights are no-frills: there are no seat assignments – and no concept of queueing – and no meals (but drinks and sweeties). All domestic flights are now no-smoking. The domestic airport tax is 5,000Fmg.

Lost luggage

Sometimes your luggage doesn't arrive. Most people are on a tight schedule and cannot hang around waiting for the next flight. If you are on an organised tour your guide will handle it, but if on your own it can be a bit of a challenge. For someone else to pick up your luggage you will need to get a proxy form with a signature that is legalised in the town hall. The only alternative is to meet every international flight (assuming it was lost on the way to Madagascar) in the hope that your bag is on it. Unclaimed bags are put under lock and key, and finding *le responsable* may not be easy.

Transport to the city centre (12km)

In the past there was an airport bus service, Air Routes Service, but at the time of writing this is not running. Some of the larger hotels provide courtesy buses. Otherwise official taxis cost from 35,000Fmg to 50,000Fmg (about US$8), but if you walk purposefully across the car park you will find some unofficial ones for around 40,000Fmg. Experienced travellers can go for the local bus which stops at the road junction about 100m from the airport. It only costs about 25 cents, and you can pay for an extra seat for your luggage. This bus takes you to the Vasakosy area behind the train station.

ANTANANARIVO (TANA) TODAY

From the right place, in the right light, Tana is one of the most attractive capitals in the developing world. In the evening sunshine it has the quality of a child's

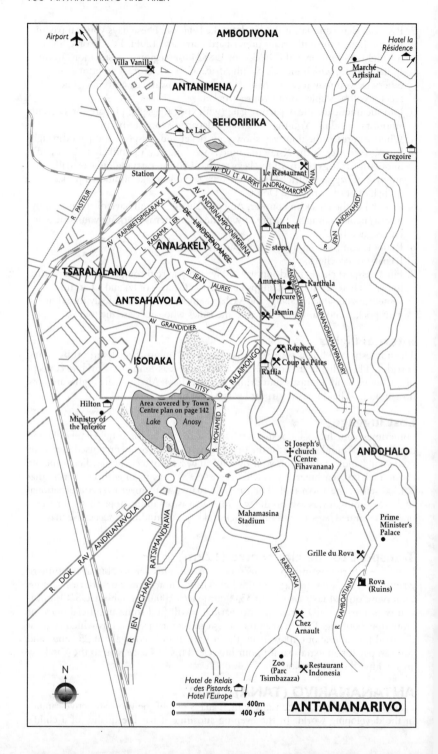

ANTANANARIVO

picture book, with brightly coloured houses stacked up the hillsides, and mauve jacarandas and purple bougainvillea against the dark blue of the winter sky. Red crown-of-thorn euphorbias stand in rows against red-clay walls, rice paddies are tended right up to the edge of the city, clothes are laid out on the canal bank to dry, and zebu-carts rumble along the roads on the outskirts of town. It's all deliciously foreign, and can hardly fail to impress the first-time visitor as he or she drives in from the airport. Indeed, this drive is one of the most varied and interesting in the Highlands. The good impression is helped by the climate – during the dry season the sun is hot but the air pleasantly cool (the altitude is between 1,245m and 1,469m).

Sadly, for many people, this wonderful first impression does not survive a closer acquaintance. Tana can seem squalid and dangerous, with conspicuous poverty, persistent beggars and a rising crime rate. The population of Tana is over two million and growing fast.

The geography of the city is both simple and confusing. It is built on two ridges which combine in a 'V'. On the highest hill, dominating all the viewpoints, is the ruined Queen's Palace. Down the central valley runs a broad boulevard, Avenue de l'Indépendance (sometimes called by its Malagasy name Fahaleovantena), which terminates at the station. It narrows at the other end to become Rue du 26 Juin. To escape from this valley means climbing steps, if you are on foot, or driving through a tunnel if you are in a vehicle.

It is convenient to divide Tana into the two main areas most often wandered by visitors: Avenue de l'Indépendance and the side streets to its southwest (district Analakely, or the Lower Town) and the smarter area at the top of the steps leading up from Rue du 26 Juin (district Isoraka, or the Upper Town). Of course there are lots of other districts but most tourists will take taxis rather than going on foot. This can be a challenging city to explore: streets are often unnamed, or change name several times within a few hundred metres, or go by two different names. (When reading street names it's worth knowing that *Lalana* means street, *Arabe* is avenue, and *Kianja* is a square.)

The telephone area code in Tana is 22.

Analakely and Tsaralalana (Lower Town)

Analakely (which means 'little forest') used to be famous for its large forest of white umbrellas, under which every product imaginable (and many unimaginable) used to be sold. Tana's *zoma* market was famous worldwide. Now it has all gone (well, not quite... see box). In the late 1990s the city authorities, tired of the ever-increasing crime, rubbish, beggars and traffic chaos, called in the Japanese to clean it up. In 1999 I was shocked by the transformation. Instead of smiling ladies trying to sell me a goose or a herbal remedy there were bustling young men with mobile phones pressed to their ears; instead of parasols obstructing the pavement there are parked cars; instead of claustrophobia in the press of humanity, there is agoraphobia in the wide open spaces. Nevertheless, the residents love it and traffic now flows so smoothly they have introduced (gasp!) Tana's first set of traffic lights.

Avenue de l'Indépendance is a broad boulevard (grassed in the centre) with shops, snackbars, restaurants and hotels up each side. If you start at the station and walk up the right-hand side you will pass the upmarket Tana Plaza and Palace hotels, the city's best bookshop (Librairie de Madagascar), and the Hotel de France. Continuing south you reach one of Tana's liveliest bars (Glacier) and then you're at the steps up to Isoraka.

This is not a street for strolling – there are too many persistent beggars and souvenir vendors. And thieves. So walk briskly. Shopwise, the north side of the

POVERTY IN ANTANANARIVO – WHAT'S BEING DONE?
Janice Booth

The very poor of Tana are known in French as 'les quatre mi' or 'the four mis'. This comes from the Malagasy words *miloka* (gambling), *mifoka* (drugs), *misotro* (drinking) and *mijangajanga* (prostitution). Some 10% of Madagascar's population of about 13 million are estimated to live in and around the capital, over half of them below poverty level. And it can be grim. However, encouragingly, more and more local organisations are targeting specific sectors.

The Sisters of the Good Shepherd, Centre Fihavanana (Soeurs du Bon Pasteur, 58 Lalana Stephani, Amparibe, 101 Antananarivo) aim their well-run activities mainly at women and children. There are six sisters: Sri Lankan, French, Lebanese and Malagasy. About 180 children aged 3–12 are taught in four classes and many do well enough to get into State primary school. Undernourished babies (about 70) are fed and their mothers given training. Teenagers come to the centre to learn basic skills and handicrafts. Elderly people (about 150) come twice a month for a little food, company and care. Food is taken weekly to over 300 women, teenagers and children in prison. Finally 72 women do beautiful embroidery at home, while caring for their families, which provides an income both for them and for the centre. Visitors can help with cash, by buying handicrafts, or by donating any unwanted clothes or medicines at the end of their holiday.

Akamasoa (Les Amis du Père Pedro, BP 640, 77103 MEAUX CEDEX) aims to provide Tana's poor and homeless with decent housing, paid work and schooling. In less than ten years, almost 45,000 people have been put back on their feet. The community works a quarry which produces stones, paving slabs and gravel; and homes (including plumbing, carpentry etc) are built by the families themselves. Kitchen gardens provide food. There are training centres, as well as medical and sports facilities. This project receives some international support, but individual donations are always welcome. Visitors can also buy handicrafts.

avenue is less interesting, but it does have several excellent snackbars, and the Air Madagascar office is here.

Tsaralalana is a more relaxing area of side streets to the south of Avenue de l'Indépendance (though maps do not indicate the steep climbs involved if you go too far). Walk down Rue Indira Gandhi (Rue Nice), past the bookshop Tout pour l'Ecole and the Mellis Hotel to the cumbersomely named Place du 19 Mai 1946. Beyond it are two mid-range hotels, the Taj and Imerina, and the very popular Sakamanga hotel/restaurant. To avoid a steep (rather dull) climb to Isoraka you can double back on one of the parallel streets to Avenue de l'Indépendance.

Antaninarenina and Isoraka (Upper Town)
This is the Islington of Tana; or the Greenwich Village. Here are the art shops, the craft boutiques, the atmospheric hotels, the inexpensive guest houses, and a terrific but almost unknown museum. There is also a rose garden where, in October, the jacaranda trees drip their nectar on to the heads below. I love Isoraka. There is no feeling of menace here (which is not to say crime doesn't exist) so this is the district for gentle strolling.

Accueil des Sans-abri (Lot II-Y-43G Ampasanimalo, BP 3763, 101 Antananarivo) helps street-dwellers to return to the land. (Many will have drifted in from the country many years before in search of work, and been trapped by poverty.) The process spreads over three years. First, 10–20 families are taken into a Centre for the Homeless in Tana, where they have access to food, clothing, medical care, schooling and training. The aim is to reawaken their sense of dignity and responsibility. In the second year, participants move to a farming centre close to Tana, where they have a practical introduction to farming. Monitors check for, and encourage, any special skills. In the third year, those who have proved well motivated are settled, with their families, on small (5-hectare) farm plots, and helped to get cultivation (and livestock) under way. The aim is eventual self-sufficiency. The project, which is proving successful, needs money for its Tana Centre and infrastructures elsewhere.

Akany Avoko (BP 29, Ambohidratrimo 105, Madagascar; Stephen & Happy Wilkinson; tel: 441 58) is a remand home for girls, run by the Protestant Federation of Madagascar. Its work began in 1959 when the Church asked the State to allow young girls accused of petty crime to be re-educated rather than sent to prison. The home is designed for up to 75 girls but at present has about 100; two-thirds of them placed there by the Juvenile Court in Tana, mostly for minor offences. The remaining one-third are either abandoned children or else girls placed by their families because of problems. Many of the court referrals are country girls who were sent to the city by their parents to work, but earned pitifully little and were tempted to steal. It may take up to two years for their cases to be heard. Many had little or no schooling so are taught literacy as well as handicrafts and gardening. Others may go to local schools. Girls who had felt rejected regain self-respect.

The State pays about 30c a day for those sent by the courts. Families who place girls in the home are expected to contribute something, but not all can. The World Food Programme provides some rice, cooking oil and beans, and other organisations have helped with specific projects (repairs, construction etc). Individual donations are welcome.

Start at the bottom of the steps, by the Select Hotel on Avenue de l'Indépendance and as you climb up, marvel that so many men can make a living selling rubber stamps. At the top is Place de l'Indépendance, and Jardin Antaninarenina with its jacarandas and rose bushes. And benches. Nearby is Le Buffet du Jardin where you can sip a fruit juice in the sun, and opposite is La Maison du Tourisme de Madagascar. Other landmarks are the new Ibis Hotel and the Champion supermarket. Turn left at the Maison and you come to the post office where, if you go through a side door to the philatelic counter, you can buy special issue Malagasy stamps. If you feel like a coffee cross the road to the Colbert. The streetside bar/café is where conservationists and other expats meet to discuss their latest challenges.

Now it's time to explore Isoraka. A 30-minute walk will show you the main sights. Start up Rue Rabehevitra, past the Radama Hotel and the good-value Isoraka Hotel. Turn left and you'll pass first the very nice little restaurant, Chez Sucette, then a cobbler's shop with a group of men sitting outside chatting and stitching. If you have anything that needs repairing, this is the place. On a corner is the small and friendly Résidence Lapasoa. At this point look out for a bronze

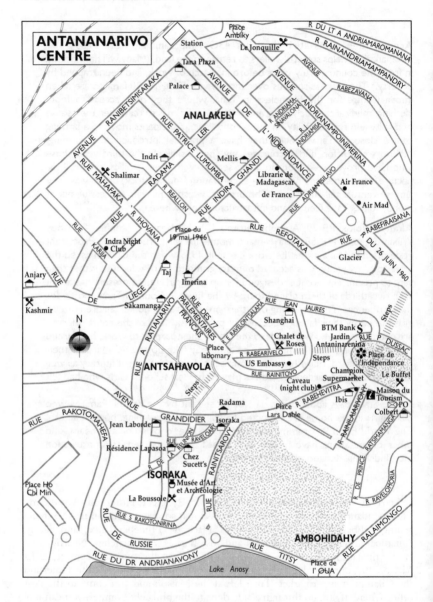

'tree' hung with clay pots. This marks the Musée d'Art et Archéologie, which is a super little museum. In 1999 it was housing a private collection of traditional musical instruments, beautifully displayed and carefully labelled. One of the attendants was gently playing a *valiha*. Exhibitions change, so the next one may not be as good, but it's worth taking the chance. Entrance is free but a donation is appreciated – and deserved.

On the way back, drop in at one of Tana's best craft shops, Galerie Yerden on Rue Dr Villette, then pick whatever street you fancy to get you back to Place de l'Indépendance.

THE SECRET ZOMA

If you stay at the Tana Plaza hotel, have a room overlooking the street at right angles to Avenue de l'Indépendance, and happen to glance out of the window at about 3am, an extraordinary sight will meet your eyes. In the small hours of each morning Rue Rainibetsimisaraka is thronged with rural Malagasy laying out their wares under the street lights amid whispered conversations. Pyramids of polished tomatoes, rows of huge cabbages, ranks of onions, their white bulbs glistening, heaps of rice, piles of pulses. For a few busy hours the people trade and sell, chat and argue, passing the time in the traditional Malagasy way. Soon after dawn they sweep up the remaining grains of rice, return unsold vegetables into their sacks, string the chickens' legs together, and trot off towards their smallholdings.

By the time the authorities arrive, the street is clear.

Getting around

Get to know the city on foot during the day (but carry nothing of value); use taxis for long distances, unknown destinations and always at night. Traffic jams and the resulting pollution are a serious problem in Tana. There are jams at all times of the day but it's worst at rush hours: morning, noon and evening. Often it's quicker to walk. Taxis should cost 5,000Fmg for a short trip within the city centre and 7,500Fmg for longer distances. They do not have meters so agree on the price before you get in. Expect to pay more than the locals, but avoid the exorbitant *vazaha* price charged by the taxis serving the big hotels. Battered old vehicles which wouldn't dare go near a hotel will be cheaper and you have the extra bonus of watching the street go by through the hole in the floor, or being pushed by helpful locals when the vehicle breaks down or runs out of petrol.

The great advantage of not having meters is that if the driver gets lost (which frequently happens) you will not pay any more for the extra journey. In my experience, Tana taxi drivers are honest and helpful and can be trusted to get you to your destination – eventually.

Buses are much cheaper, but sorting out the destinations and districts can be difficult. Good maps of Tana are now available which makes this task much easier.

Safety

Sadly, violent robbery has become quite common in Tana. Leave your valuables in the hotel (preferably in a safe deposit or locked in your bag) and carry as little as possible. Avenue de l'Indépendance seems particularly risky. The current scam is the 'Ballet of the Hats'. Kids carrying wide-brimmed straw hats encircle you and, using the hats to obscure your view, work through your pockets, money-belt, neck pouch or whatever. If you can manage to carry nothing at all – no watch, no camera, no money... not even a paper tissue in your pocket, you will bring back the best souvenirs: memories.

Do not risk taking the path over Lake Anosy to the World War I memorial, and if possible avoid wandering around the area near the Gare du Nord which has the highest incidence of muggings in the city.

Be careful when taking a taxi to keep your bag on the floor by your feet. Thieves sometimes grab handbags through the open window.

Always keep in mind that thieves are looking for valuables, and are rarely out to harm you physically. If you are not carrying anything they want, and have no bulging pockets to attract them, they will leave you alone.

Where to stay

New hotels and restaurants are opening all the time in Tana. This selection is by no means complete – be adventurous and find your own! If you are looking for family-style B&B accommodation (varying prices) look under the heading *Bed and Breakfast*.

Category A

Hilton Hotel On the western side of Lake Anosy; tel: 260 60; fax: 260 51; email sales_madagascar@hilton.com. One of Tana's skyscrapers (as you'd expect), very comfortable with good meals. Its advantages are the offices and shops in the building, including a cybercafé, and the swimming pool. In the pleasantly hot sun of the dry season this is a real bonus. It is some way from the centre of town (though the walk in is enjoyable). 1,098Ff double, 948Ff single. Most credit cards accepted. Free airport transfers.

Hotel Mercure Palissandre 13 Rue Andriandahifotsy; tel 203 00 and 326 19; fax 605 62; email: HotelMercure@simico.mg. A brand new luxury hotel, with all comforts but its location is not ideal – quite far from the centre of town and next to the Amnesia night club. Rooms: 490Ff; breakfast 49Ff.

Palace Hotel BP 607; tel: 256 63; fax: 339 43. Owned by Hotel de France, this is a smart hotel at the lower end of the Av de l'Indépendance. No restaurant, but a short walk to the Tana Plaza (same ownership). Rooms vary in size, the largest being studio apartments. 400–600Ff. Breakfast 35Ff.

Tana Plaza Av de l'Indépendance, near the station; tel: 662 60 and 218 65; fax: 642 19. An upmarket hotel with small but good rooms (the ones facing the street are noisy but some have a special view – see box on page 143). 300Ff.

Hotel de France 24 Av de l'Indépendance; tel: 202 93; fax: 201 18. Newly reburbished. About 250Ff.

Hotel Colbert Rue Printsy Ratsimamanga, Antaninarenina; tel: 202 02; fax: 340 12; email: COLBERT@bow.dts.mg. Very French, often full, my choice of the posh Tana hotels for its good location, nice atmosphere and excellent food. 450–1,500Ff per room (small double to studio apartment). Breakfast 40Ff. Most credit cards accepted.

Hotel Ibis 4 Pl de l'Indépendance; tel: 629 29; fax: 640 40; email: ibistana@simicro.mg. A new international hotel. Convenient, safe location, comfortable, well-run. 380–540Ff.

Radama Hotel 22 Av Grandidier, Isoraka; tel: 319 27; fax: 353 23; email: radama@hotels.online.mg; website: www.madonline.com/voyages/radama. A very nice small (18 room) hotel in a great location. Its restaurant, Tatao, is one of the best in Tana. Impractical for groups because there is no parking for tour buses, but ideal for business people (there is a conference room) or independent travellers. No lift (elevator). 350–560Ff (double room to studio apartment). Most credit cards accepted.

Hotel Gregoire Mahavoky, Besarety, near the Marché Artisanal; tel: 222 66; fax: 292 71. Used mainly by groups. 250,000Fmg double. Quiet, comfortable, friendly and efficient, with two very good restaurants, L'Aquarium and La Rotonde.

Category B

Karib Hotel Av de l'Indépendance; tel: 629 31. Two blocks down from Tana Plaza. Clean, safe, comfortable. Credit cards accepted. 130–180Ff.

White Palace Hotel 101 Rue de Liège, Tsaralalana; tel: 664 59; fax 602 89. A good-value new mid-range hotel conveniently located in the lower town. Studio rooms with cooking facilities 138,000Fmg; double/twin room with bath 113,000Fmg; with shower 93,000Fmg. All comforts including TV in rooms.

Indri Hotel 15 Rue Radama, Tsaralalana (1½ blocks from Av de l'Indépendance); tel/fax: 209 22. Comfortable, medium-sized hotel in a convenient location and with a cocktail bar and live entertainment.

Hotel Mellis Rue Indira Gandhi; tel: 234 25. A perennial favourite in a convenient location; 122,600Fmg for a room with a bath.

Taj Hotel 69 Rue Dr Razafindranovona (near Place du 19 Mai 1946); tel: 305 40; fax: 245 57. Comfortable rooms with hot water; 132,000Fmg single/double.

Imerina (formerly Central) Hotel 7 Rue Rajohnson (continuation of Indira Gandhi); tel: 227 94; fax: 357 04. Good value; single room and shared bathroom for 150,000Fmg.

Sakamanga Rue A Ratianarivo; tel: 35 809. (10 rooms) 80,000–120,000Fmg. French run, very pleasant (though noisy) but almost always full. There is an excellent, lively French restaurant, also heavily booked. For room reservations write to: Lot IBK 7B1S, Ampasamadinika, Antananarivo 101.

Hotel Anjary Rue Razafimahandry and Dr Ranaivo, Tsaralalana; tel: 244 09. Clean, large, secure, friendly. Hot water. 115,000Fmg double. Recommended.

Karthala Hotel 48 Rue Andriandahifotsy, BP 912; tel: 248 45 or 298 30. Not as conveniently located as some, but the chance to be at home with a Malagasy family. Madame Rafalimanana speaks good English. 'I have vivid memories of an old aunt gleefully taking control of Independence Day fireworks, flourishing Catherine Wheels and directing rockets over the rooftops.' (Ken and Lorna Gillespie). About 85,000 to 100,000Fmg, including breakfast.

Hotel Shanghai 4 Rue Rainitovo (near the US Embassy); tel: 314 72. Room rates are highly competitive, with a double room at 112,000Fmg. A good breakfast costs 13,000Fmg.

Jean Laborde Hotel 3 Rue de Russie, Isoraka; tel: 330 45; fax: 327 94. Once an excellent hotel, in a quiet, safe area, but reportedly becoming rather shabby. Nicknamed by one reader as Labordelle because of the group exodus of prostitutes in the early morning. But the staff are friendly, and there's an excellent French restaurant. 100,000–150,000Fmg. Frequently booked up, so make room or restaurant reservations in advance.

Résidence Lapasoa 15 Rue de la Réunion, Isoraka; tel/fax: 611 40. (7 rooms) A friendly little B&B in a nice part of town, ideal for nervous lone travellers. 150,000Fmg single, 158,000Fmg double including breakfast.

Hotel Raffia Rue Ranavalona III (Upper Town). A nice hotel with seven rooms and lovely views over Lake Anosy. About 50,000–65,000Fmg.

The White Palace Tsaralanana, near the Anjary hotel; tel: 664 59. New; good value.

Le Relais des Pistards BP 3550, Rue Fernand Kasanga (same road as Tsimbazaza), about 1km beyond the zoo; tel: 291 34. A friendly, family-style hotel run by Florent and Jocelyn Colney. .Pleasant communal dining room, and excellent cooking. Florent Colney is an avid mountain biker, so a stay here is a must for those planning to cycle in Madagascar. His advice will be invaluable. All prices include breakfast. From 55,000 (single, shared bathroom) to 105,000Fmg (double, en suite).

The following hotels are near the airport so handy for a late arrival or early departure.

Auberge du Cheval Blanc BP 23, Ivato; tel: 446 46. Rooms are 80,000Fmg single/double. Breakfast 9,000Fmg, meals (mediocre) 15,000–25,000Fmg. MasterCard and Visa accepted.

Le Manoir Rouge Tel: 441 04 Recommended by Jim Bond as 'definitely the best value I've come across around Ivato'. Good food.

Hotel Ivato Friendly, clean, hot showers. Reasonable restaurant. 50,000–60,000Fmg.

Résidence Tanikely BP31 Ivato Aeroport 105; tel: 453 96; fax: 453 97. (Two bungalows, four rooms.) French-owned, comfortable self-contained units set in a pleasant garden. 300,000Fmg double.

Auberge du Jardin Down a side road on the left as you approach Ivato (about 10 minutes from the airport). 'A very nice small place with a good restaurant'. 40,000–90,000Fmg. Airport transfers 12,000Fmg.

Other hotels on the road from the airport, which I've not checked out, include **Hotel Sitara** (tel: 450 64) and, side by side, **Hotel Emeraude** and **Hotel Saphir**. The latter two are likely to be the least expensive. Staying near Ivato saves the taxi fare into town if you are arriving on a late flight or leaving early in the morning.

Category C

Hotel Isoraka 11, Av Grandidier, Isoraka; tel: 355 81; fax: 658 54. One of the few budget hotels in the Upper Town. Clean, with hot water. Communal bathroom. Good value at 43,000–59,000Fmg. Offers airport transfers, snack bar and laundry service.

Hotel Lambert Up the opposite flight of stairs to those that lead to Place de l'Indépendance. Basic, clean, convenient. Good value and popular, but be prepared to climb a lot of stairs! 25,000–30,000Fmg.

Hotel Glacier Av de l'Indépendance. One of the oldest – and shabbiest – hotels in Tana, but it is conveniently located, has a lively bar (full of prostitutes) and excellent music with *salegy* bands from all over Madagascar. The rather dreadful rooms are 80,000Fmg.

Hotel Le Lac Behoririka (near a small lake, opposite Landis garage). Some rooms have en-suite shower. Quite primitive but adequate. 35,000–52,000Fmg.

Bed and breakfast

Villa Soamahatony BP 4313 Antananarivo 101; tel: +261 33 110 33 37; email: soamahatony@online.mg. (4 rooms) Stay en famille with Sahondra and Daniel, a very knowledgable French-Malagasy couple who have been helping visitors enjoy Madagascar for many years. Their villa, set in 2ha of grounds, is in Ankadivory, ten minutes by car from Ivato airport. Rooms 100,000Fmg; breakfast 10,000Fmg; evening meal 25,000Fmg.

Soamiandry Sarl BP 11035, Antananarivo; tel: 22 444 54; fax; 623 45. (16 rooms) Family run (so book ahead). 'Joshua and Fara try to do everything for you; it's one of those places you remember and want to go back.' Garden, swimming pool. 100FF double, with breakfast.

Where to eat

Hotel restaurants

Most of the better hotels serve good food. Expats and Malagasy professionals favour the **Colbert**. The 'all you can eat' Sunday buffet is good value (but beware of the health risks of eating cold buffets). There are two restaurants at the Colbert; the Taverne is the smartest and imposes a dress code on its diners. Phone 202 02 for reservations. Bring your French dictionary – menus are not translated.

The **Hilton** does a whole series of buffets – each lunch-time there is a 'businessman's buffet' with a 'gourmet buffet' on Sundays. Dishes from around the world are served in the evenings – a different nationality each night.

The restaurant at the **Radama** (Tatao) is very good, with excellent French and Malagasy cooking, and reasonably priced.

The **O! Poivre Vert** at the Hotel de France is trendy but very expensive.

The **Sakamanga** restaurant is crowded and lively, with good food.

Upper and middle range restaurants

Le Restaurant 65, Rue Emile Ranarivelo, Behoririka; tel: 282 67. A lovely colonial house with a terrace overlooking superb gardens. Excellent food, attentive service. Highly recommended.

Villa Vanille Pl Antanimena; tel: 205 15. A fine old Tana house five minutes by taxi from Tana Plaza, specialising in Creole food. Traditional music every evening.

Au Grille du Rova About 100 metres down from the ruins of the Queen's Palace; tel: 627 24; fax: 622 13. Wonderful food, eaten indoors or outside, with a view over the city. Traditional Malagasy music every Sunday, from midday to sunset. Closed Sunday evening. Good English spoken. Highly recommended.

Le Regency 15, Rue Ramelina, Ambatonakanga; tel: 210 13. French owned, and run with flair and elegance. Lovely atmosphere and super food.

Le Coupe de Pâtes Rue Ranavalona III. A small, friendly Italian restaurant offering a variety of à la carte dishes, plus two reasonably priced set menus.

La Pradelle Ambatoroka (southeast of the city); tel: 326 51. English spoken, Malagasy and European food, highly recommended by readers and residents.

La Boussole Rue de Dr Villette, Isoraka. A stylish French restaurant with excellent food, a cosy bar and a charming patio for outdoor dining. Especially lively on Friday nights.

La Jonquille 7 Rue Rabezavana, Soarano; tel 206 37. Good, imaginative menu, mainly Chinese. Especially good for seafood. Reasonable prices. Recommended.

Restaurant Jasmin 8 Rue Paul-Dussac; tel: 342 96. Good Chinese food.

Chez Arnault Rue Rabozaka (the road leading from Mahamasina stadium to the zoo). 'Without doubt the best pizza in town!' Also a good French menu and pasta dishes. Quite pricey, however.

Tonga Soa Mandrosoa (about 2km from Ivato airport); tel: 442 88. A small, intimate restaurant run by Mme Nina and husband (and chef) Patrick. 'This is the most pleasant little restaurant I know in Tana and a wonderful place to go for a quiet evening meal or on the way to the airport. The menu is not as extensive as some (because Patrick will only use fresh ingredients) but the food is the best in Tana' (Nick Garbutt). There is another reason to visit: 'The lush gardens are well planted with trees, shrubs and flowers that attract a wide variety of birdlife and there are also upwards of 50 Jewel chameleons here. They lay their eggs at the edges of the car park!'

Budget restaurants

Restaurant Chez Sucett's Isoraka; tel: 261 00. A pleasant small restaurant in a safe area.

Restaurant Pati Down the road from Tsimbazaza. Very good and economically priced meals. Large portions. Try the Chinese soup.

Restaurant Indonesia Directly across from the zoo entrance. Surprisingly, this is the only Indonesian restaurant in Madagascar. Recommended.

Chalet des Roses 13 Rue de l'Auximad (in the centre of town, opposite the American Embassy); tel: 642 33. 'A fabulous and cheap Italian restaurant.'

Kashmir 5–7 Rue Dr Ranaivo (opposite Anjary Hotel). Muslim, very good and reasonably priced food.

Shalimar 5 Rue Mahafaka, Tsaralalana; tel: 260 70. Good curries and a selection of vegetarian dishes.

For a cheap meal, local style, try the smaller restaurants (*hotely gasy*) down Avenue Andrianampoinimerina. Meals usually include Chinese soup which is filling and tasty. There are also plenty of good, cheap eateries on Avenue Rabezavana.

Snack bars

Le Buffet du Jardin Pl de l'Indépendance. This fast-food restaurant is the place for lunch, a beer or coffee, with pleasant outdoor tables. Ideal for people-watching and meeting other travellers or foreigners living in Madagascar. One tip: if you dislike being pestered by beggars and pedlars, choose a seat well away from the fence.

Croissant d'Or Rue Indira Gandhi. Serves great breakfasts and is open at 07.30 all week and 08.00 on Sundays.

THE MUSIC OF MADAGASCAR: A BRIEF INTRODUCTION
Ian A Anderson

The music of Madagascar is like the island itself – owing many things to other parts of the world, but unique.

The Malagasy are very fond of harmony singing, varying from Polynesian style (the Merina) to almost East African on the west coast. Traditional musical instruments include the celebrated *valiha*, a member of the zither family with 21 strings stretched lengthways all around the circumference of a hollow bamboo tube (there's also a box variety called the *marovany*); the *sodina*, an end-blown flute that can work magic in the hands of a master like Rakotofra (find his picture on the old 1,000Fmg note); the *kabosy*, a small guitar with paired strings and partial frets; the *jejy voatavo* with a gourd resonator and two sets of strings on adjacent sides of the neck; the *lokanga bara*, a three-string fiddle; and a great variety of percussion instruments.

You'll also find most Western instruments, successfully adapted to local music. Visit Ambohimanga, for example, to hear one of several generations of blind accordion players. Catch one of the *hiragasy* troupes and they'll be using ancient brass instruments and clarinets. Visit a nightclub or a larger concert and a modern band such as Jaojoby, Mily Clement or Tianjama will have electric guitars, synthesisers, and kit drums and might play one of the wild Malagasy dance styles such as *salegy*, *balesa*, *watsa watsa* or *sega*. Malagasy

Avenue de l'Indépendance has a growing number of eateries: **Tropique** (good pastries and ice-cream), **Honey** (very good for breakfast and ice-cream, but closed at weekends), **Solimar** for tamarind juice, and **Le Croissanterie** for fresh fruit juice. Also **Bouffe Rapide** and **La Potinerie** (near Air Mad). The **Glacier Hotel bar** is the best for people-watching.

In the Upper Town both the **Patisserie Suisse** (Rue Rabehevitra) and the **Patisserie Colbert** do good pastries and teas. Patisserie Suisse serves a delicious range of cakes and tarts, but closes at midday for up to 3½ hours.

Do-it-yourself meals can be purchased anywhere. Yoghurt is a particularly good buy and is available even in small towns. Carry your own spoon. Even more convenient – and delicious – is the drinking yoghurt, '*Yaourt à boire*'.

Nightlife
Papillon at the Hilton is a popular nightclub. Also **Le Caveau** (4, Rue Jeneraly Rabehevitra, Antaninarenina; tel: 343 93) which has the **Kaleidoscope** disco on the same premises. Another disco is **L'Amnesia** (8 Rue Andriandafotsy, Ambondrono; tel: 273 41). The **Indra** nightclub in Tsaralalana is also recommended. Located in Faravohitra (Rue Andrianahifotsy) on the slope above the market, is **Cocktails et Rêves**, which has a darts board for homesick Brits.

The most popular nightspot is **Piano Bar Acapulco**, near Place de l'Indépendance (14, Rue Ratsimilaho; tel: 232 25), which features local bands, jazz and solo piano.

A new favourite is the **Groove Box**, near Tsimbazaza. A live band plays jazz on Thursday, international music on Fridays, and dance music on Saturdays.

Traditional music
Traditional Malagasy music has become internationally famous in the last few years and many visitors would like to find the real thing in Tana. The following

music has also enjoyed a big explosion of outside interest in recent years. The artists who have gained the most success touring abroad in the mid '90s have been Tarika, the Justin Vali Trio, Jaojoby, Njava and guitarist D'Gary.

The local cassette market has greatly expanded in recent years, though tapes are of variable quality. There are now even a few locally marketed CDs, but Malagasy music on record is still best purchased in Europe or North America where there is now a huge CD selection. A regularly updated Madagascar CD-ography can be found on the Internet at: http://www.froots.demon.co.uk/madaged.html.

The following small sample is a good starting point:

Tarika: *Son Egal* (Xenophile XENO 4042) (USA)
The Justin Vali Trio: *Ny Marinal/The Truth* (Real World CDRW51) (UK)
Justin Vali: *The Sunshine Within* (Bush Telegraph Records) (UK)
Jaojoby: *Salegy!* (Xenophile XENO 4040) (USA)
Various: *Big Rd* (Nascente) (UK)
Various: *The Marovany of Madagascar* (Silex Y 225224) (France)
Various: *Madagasikara 2 - Current Popular Music* (GlobeStyle CDORBD 013) (UK)
Various: *Madagaskar 3 - Sounding Bamboo* (Feuer & Els FUEC 712) (Germany)
Various: *Les Grands Maitres Du Salegy* (Sonodisc) (France)

A good source for these Malagasy CDs in London is Stern's African Record Shop, 293 Euston Road, London W1P 5PA.

information is from Ian Anderson, taken from *The Rough Guide to World Music*.

'In Tana, a good bar venue for *salegy* bands is the funky Hotel Glacier in the Avenue de l'Indépendance, run by Charles Mourin Poty. More formal concerts take place at the Roxy Cinema, Centre Culturel Albert Camus in Analakely, the Cercle Germano-Malagas, also in Analakely (at the foot of the steps leading to Antaninarenina) and at the newly built Alliance Française (Ampefiloha Andavamamba). Restaurants and hotels such as La Résidence (Ankadindramano Ankerana), Le Palmier (Ankadilalana Tsimbazaza), Misty (Antsakarivo), Le Chapiteau (Ankorondrano), Le Damier (Ankadimbahoaka Androndra), Hotel Rubis (Ankorahotra Ampasanimalo) and Caf' Art (Ambatonakanga) are worth keeping an eye on. The Hilton Hotel's weekend basement discos are a bizarre experience, where you can encounter the Malagasy rich and beautiful getting down to unequal doses of international pop and local sounds – Spice Girls, Boyz II Men and Bon Jovi with brief interludes of Jaojoby. Oddly enough, the best bets for a good selection of original (ie: non-pirate) cassettes and increasingly now CDs of local music are the growing number of huge supermarkets that have opened up for the better-off – and you compensate for their higher prices by the diminished likelihood of having your pockets picked, as may well happen in the street markets.

You can find a good range at Magri, Géant Score, Conquette and Champion (near the central Post Office in Antaninarenina), and stock up on other fine Malagasy produce at the same time.'

Entertainment

If you are in Tana for a while, buy a local paper to see what's on or keep an eye out for posters advertising special shows or events. For a truly Malagasy experience try to find a performance of *hira gasy* (see box on page 150). Any entertainment that allows you to join a Malagasy audience will be worth the entrance fee (see box on page 380).

Films are dubbed into French.

HIRA GASY

For a taste of genuine Malagasy folklore, try to attend the traditional entertainment of *hira gasy* which takes place every Sunday in Tana. Taxi drivers may know where: ask for 'hira gasy' (pronounced 'heera gash') and see what happens.

In the British magazine *Folk Roots* Jo Shinner describes *hira gasy*: 'It is a very strange, very exciting affair: a mixture of opera, dance and Speaker's Corner bound together with a sense of competition.

'The performance takes place between two competing troupes of singers and musicians on a central square stage. It's an all-day event so the audience packs in early, tea and peanut vendors picking their way through the throng. Audience participation is an integral part – the best troupe is gauged by the crowd's response. Throughout the day performers come into the crowd to receive small coins offered in appreciation.

'The most immediate surprise is the costumes. The men enter wearing 19th-century French, red, military frock coats and the women are clad in evening dress from the same period. Traditional *lamba* are carefully arranged around their shoulders, and the men wear straw Malagasy hats. The musicians play French military drums, fanfare trumpets, flutes, violins and clarinets. The effect is bizarre rather than beautiful.'

'The *hira gasy* is in four parts. First there are the introductory speeches or *kabary*. Each troupe elects a speaker who is usually a respected elder. His skill is paramount to a troupe. He begins with a long, ferociously fast, convoluted speech excusing himself and his inadequacy, before the audience, ancestors, his troupe, his mother, God, his oxen, his ricefields and so on – and on! Then follows another speech glorifying God, and then a greeting largely made up of proverbs.

'The *hira gasy* pivots around a tale of everyday life, such as the dire consequences of laziness or excessive drinking, is packed with wit, morals and proverbs and offers advice, criticism and possible solutions. The performers align themselves along two sides of the square at a time to address different parts of the audience. They sing in harsh harmony, illustrating their words with fluttering hand movements and expressive gestures, egged on by the uproarious crowd's appreciation. Then it is the dancers' turn. The tempo increases and becomes more rhythmic as two young boys take to the floor with a synchronised display of acrobatic dancing that nowadays often takes its influence from karate.'

WHAT TO SEE/DO

As if to emphasise how different it is to other capitals, Tana has relatively little in the way of conventional sightseeing, and even less since the Queen's Palace (*Rova*) burned down. However, there's quite enough to keep you occupied for a few days.

La Maison du Tourisme de Madagascar Place de l'Indépendance; tel: 325 29. Produces printed lists of hotels, tour operators, car-hire companies, etc, and sells good quality T-shirts, handicrafts and postcards. They may have maps, but better quality ones can be bought in bookshops. Open 09.30–11.30, 15.30–17.30; closed on Sunday, and other times if they feel like it.

Rova

For over a century the Queen's Palace, or *Rova*, the spiritual centre of the Merina people, dominated the skyline of Tana. In November 1995 it was destroyed by fire – an act of arson unprecedented in Madagascar's history.

Work has now begun on the reconstruction of the *Rova*; it is estimated to cost US$66 million and the prime minister has appealed for further aid to cover the cost.

It is worth the walk up to the palace for the view and to imagine its former grandeur.

Prime Minister's Palace (Musée d'Andafiavaratra)

This former residence of Rainilaiarivony (he who married three queens) has been painstakingly restored and now houses the few precious items that were saved from the *Rova* fire. It was built in 1872 by the British architect William Pool. After independence it became in turn army barracks, law courts, a school of fine arts, the presidential palace and (again) the prime minister's palace. It was burned in 1975. The museum is open from 10.00 to 17.00. Closed Mondays. Entry fee 3,000Fmg.

Tsimbazaza

This comprises a museum (natural history and ethnology), botanical garden and zoo exhibiting – with a few exceptions – only Malagasy species.

The zoo and botanical garden

Until 1999 Tsimbazaza (pronounced Tsimbazaz, and meaning 'where children are forbidden', dating from when it was a sacred site) was the centre for the Madagascar Fauna Group, an international consortium of zoos and universities working together to help conserve Madagascar's wildlife. Sadly, the group has withdrawn its financial support, tired of the interminable struggle to bring the zoo up to Western standards. This is disheartening, but gives us a chance to step back and consider the importance of Tsimbazaza to the local people. They *love* coming here, and put on their best clothes for the occasion. As Joanna Durbin, of the Durrell Wildlife Conservation Trust (one of the former supporters), comments: 'It is full to overflowing on Sundays and Bank Holidays. I expect that many of those people save up to be able to take their entire family there. You also see lots of school groups during the week'. The chief attraction is the ostrich! And why not? An ostrich is a far more extraordinary animal to a Malagasy child than a lemur.

So, come to Tsimbazaza to see the lemurs and other animals, to look at fish eagles at close quarters, and to enjoy the Malagasy enjoying their zoo. Avoid tipping the 'guides' who should be looking after the animals not trailing after tourists, and hope that the authorities find a compromise between what we in the West expect a good zoo to be, and how the locals want it.

A neat example of the difference between the American and the Malagasy view of animal management and life in general is the argument over a project to have a free-ranging group of lemurs in the park. There was no problem agreeing on the desirability and visitor appeal of this, the conflict was about the components of the group. The American coordinator insisted on single-sex lemurs ('One thing we do *not* want are babies when we have a surplus of lemurs') whilst the Malagasy were holding out for a proper family unit: mother, father and children, because that's what happiness is all about.

Among the animals on display in the zoo are four aye-ayes. Arrangements may be made to visit them after dark when they are active, for a fee of 25,000Fmg per person.

The botanical garden is spacious and well laid out, and its selection of Malagasy endemics is being improved with the help of advisers from Kew (UK) and the Missouri Botanical Garden (USA). It provides a sanctuary for numerous birds including a huge colony of egrets. There are also some reproduction Sakalava graves.

The museum (Musée Académie Malgache)
This is an excellent museum for gaining an understanding of Madagascar's prehistoric natural history and the traditions and way of life of its inhabitants. Skeletons of now extinct animals, including several species of giant lemur and the famous 'elephant bird', provide a fascinating glimpse of the Madagascar fauna which the first humans helped to extinction (explanations in French only). There are also displays of stuffed animals, but the efforts of the taxidermist have left little to likeness and a lot to the imagination. It's worth taking a close look at the aye-aye, however, to study its remarkable hands.

The room housing the ethnological exhibits has recently been modernised, with clear explanations of the customs and handicrafts of the different ethnic groups.

Practicalities
Tsimbazaza is about 4km from the city centre. There are buses from Avenue de l'Indépendance (number 15), but it is easier to take a taxi there and bus back. It is open every day from 09.00 to 17.00. For tourists the entrance fee is 20,000Fmg (5,000Fmg for children aged 6 to 12). This fee goes towards the upkeep of the park, so watch out that a used ticket is not reissued. Sundays are always very busy, so don't anticipate peace and quiet then.

There is a souvenir shop with a good selection of high-quality T-shirts and postcards, but no restaurant or snack bar. And the toilets are difficult to find (ask at the shop).

Museum of Art and Archaeology
This lovely little museum is described under *Isoraka* (page 142). The hours are 09.00–17.00. Closed on Mondays

SHOPPING
The handicrafts markets
The Marché Artisanal, which is best reached by taxi, shows the enormous range and quality of Malagasy handicrafts. Most noteworthy is the embroidery and basketry, wood-carving, minerals, leatherwork (stiff cowhide, not soft leather) and the unique Antaimoro paper embedded with pressed flowers. The market is held in the Andravoahangy region of town. This is to the right of the station (as you face it) northeast on Rue Albertini. Open 10.00–17.00, except Sunday.

As an alternative to this somewhat risky market (plenty of pickpockets) try a quieter version, the new Marché Artisanal on the road to the airport. Tim Pickles reports: 'It's quite obvious at a road intersection on the left at the end of that stretch of road by the big canal. Around 150 stalls sell a variety of handicrafts. It felt completely safe and we were able to chat with stall-holders.' Bjørn Donnis adds: 'You can bargain the price down to about half the asking price, but... why bargain? Whoever you are, they need the money more than you do'. I agree.

Serious shopping
The best quality goods are sold in specialist shops. One of the best is **Galerie Le Bivouac**, Antsofinondry – on the road to Ambohimanga – which sells beautiful

painted silk items, wood carvings and other handicrafts of a high quality; tel: 429 50. Nearby is the **Atelier Jacaranda** which specialises in batik. The quality here is excellent and the prices low. The Jacaranda workshop is next to Le Bivouac (worth visiting if you have time), but sales are made from the gallery 1km down the road, on the other side of the canal.

Nearer the centre of town, though still a taxi ride away, is **Lisy Art Gallery** on the Route de Mausolée opposite the Cercle Mess de la Police, and near the Hotel Panorama; tel: 277 33. One of the cheapest shops in Tana is **Galerie Yerden** in Isoraka (see page 142). Although the prices are slightly higher than in the market, the peace and quiet, and wide range of arts and crafts, make a visit well worthwhile.

There's a good new art gallery, **La Flamant Rose**, at 45–47 Avenue de l'Indépendance; the **Galerie Aquelle** (past the zoo on Route Circulaire opposite Epicerie Tojo) has 'by far the nicest watercolours I found in Tana – really captured the flavour of Madagascar'.

Alan Hickling (tel: 400 79) sells hand-painted T-shirts of Malagasy wildlife and other good-quality handicrafts.

For exquisite (and consequently expensive) **weavings** based on traditional *lamba* designs contact British resident Simon Peers; tel: 295 02; fax: 319 56.

The best place in Tana to buy **Antaimoro paper** is at a small 'factory' on the way to the airport (it's a green building on the right) where an enterprising Malagasy, M Mahatsinjo, has a workforce which uses the traditional method of pressing the flowers into the paper pulp. This craft originated in Ambalavao (see page 183 for a detailed description of the paper and how it is made), but you can see all the stages just as easily here. The prices for the finished products are very reasonable, too.

For something a bit different, try the herbal **beauty products** made from Malagasy plants sold under the brand name Phytoline; they seem only to be available from the Hilton shop or in the airport departure lounge.

Finally, you can shop at the **Centre Fihavanana** (see page 140) in Mahamasina, near the stadium, which is run by the Sisters of the Good Shepherd. The centre is in a building set back from the road to the right of an orange-painted church. Ask the taxi driver to take you to the Eglise St Joseph. The women here work to a very high standard, producing beautiful embroidery, greetings cards and soft toys of Malagasy wildlife. The centre is always in need of funds to continue their admirable work with the very poor, and a visit will warm the most resilient of hearts. For an appointment phone Sister Lucy on 299 81.

Supermarkets

If you don't want handicrafts try some other locally-produced goodies such as chocolate (Chocolat Robert is excellent!) and wine. Both are available from the **Champion** supermarket, beneath the Ibis Hotel in the Upper Town. A cheaper supermarket is **Magri**, which is on the way to the airport.

Maps

A large selection of maps (and also old photo prints) can be bought at the Institut National de Géodésie et Cartographie (its long Malagasy name is shortened to FTM), Rue Dama-Ntsoha RJB, Ambanidia (tel: 229 35). Hours 08.30–12.00, 14.00–18.00. They produce a series of 12 maps, scale 1:500,000, covering each region of Madagascar. These are most inviting, but sadly not always completely accurate, and some are now out of print. There are also excellent maps of Nosy Be and Ile Sainte Marie. The staff are pleasant and helpful.

FTM maps of the more popular tourist areas can usually be bought in bookshops in the town centre – where you can also buy good maps of Tana.

Bookshops

The best bookshop is Librairie de Madagascar, near the Hotel de France on Avenue de l'Indépendance. Another, Tout pour l'Ecole, opposite the Hotel Mellis, has a good selection of maps and town plans. Also recommended is Librairie Md Paoly, a small Catholic bookshop on the other side of Avenue de l'Indépendance, opposite Sicam and the Banky Fampadrosoana. 'They've got the most amazingly beautiful hand-painted greetings cards. The same cards are sold at the airport for almost double the price.'

MEDIA AND COMMUNICATION
Couriers
Colis Express 11, Rue Randrianary Ratianarivo, Ampasamandinika; tel: 272 42.

Cybercafés
The most convenient is at the Hilton Hotel, but there is also Simicro, opposite the Kodak shop in Antaninarenina and Compro, next to Hyundai, in Behoririka.

Newspapers and magazines
The main daily newspapers are the *Madagascar Tribune* (in French) which tends to follow the government line and is relatively up-market, and *Midi Madagasikara* (in French and Malagasy), the paper with the highest circulation but little international news. Both these newspapers are given out free on domestic flights. *Dans les Média Demain* is an independent weekly magazine, and *Revue de l'Océan Indien – Madagascar* appears monthly.

Post office
The main post office is opposite the Hotel Colbert. There is a separate philately section where you can buy attractive stamps. The post office is open 24 hours a day for outgoing phone calls – useful in an emergency, and much cheaper than phoning from a hotel.

MISCELLANEOUS
Fixers
A local guide/fixer can take a lot of hassle out of planning an independent trip, but bear in mind that anyone recommended here will charge more than newcomers who you have found yourself!

Pierre (S Pierrot Patrick), Lot VT 62E, Ambohibato, Ambohipo, Antananarivo 101; tel: 295 52.
Henri Serge Razafison, Logt 1384, Cité des 67Ha, Antananarivo 101; tel: 34190.

Taxi drivers
Charles Razafintsialonina, tel: 238 61. ' Friendly and punctual.'
Joseph Rakotondratsoavina, tel: 782 90. Recommended by Anne Axel.
Christophe Andriamamoinona, tel: 445 08. 'Very knowledgeable.'

Information and permits for nature reserves
Association Nationale pour la Gestion des Aires Protégées (ANGAP) is the organisation responsible for the administration of almost all the protected areas of Madagascar. Permits for the national parks and reserves may be purchased here, though they are now usually available at the town serving the reserve. It is worth visiting the Tana office, however, for the latest information on the reserves that tourists are allowed to visit. It is in Antanimena – tell the taxi-driver 'en face de Promodim'. Hours 08.00–12.00, 14.00–16.00; tel: 319 94.

MALAGASY STAMPS

Like most things Malagasy, the choice of stamp design ranges from the sublime to the ridiculous. In the first category are the beautiful series on the fauna and flora: lemurs, birds, butterflies, orchids. However, their 1991 selection of competitive winter sports such as ski jumping (not a sport in which Madagascar has achieved international standing) was more surprising and there were pedigree dogs. Again surprising since most dogs one sees in Madagascar seem to be made out of discarded bits of string. And mushrooms from temperate climates. Never mind, the stamps are mostly very attractive and can be purchased from the philately department of the main post office, and from street vendors outside the Colbert Hotel.

The Forestry Station of Ampijoroa is still administered by the Direction des Eaux et Forêts in Nanisana; although the permit is available in Mahajanga, it can be a complicated process so you may prefer to buy it in Tana. Bus number 3 from Avenue de l'Indépendance stops outside the door. The hours are the same as ANGAP's.

The address for the World Wide Fund for Nature in Tana is BP 4373; tel: 255 41.

Visa extension

A two-month extension can be obtained overnight from the Ministry of the Interior near the Hilton Hotel (see page 77).

Airline offices

Air Madagascar Av de l'Indépendance. Hours: 07.30–11.00; 14.30–17.00. Be there when it opens to avoid the crush.
TAM Behind the Hilton hotel (tel: 296 91) and at the airport.

Bank and emergency funds

The BTM bank next to the Champion supermarket will let you draw up to US$200 a day on American Express or MasterCard. Banking hours: 08.00–15.00. Closed on Saturdays. The American Express office is in the Hilton Hotel.

Medical clinics (private)

MM 24 X 24 Mpitsabo Mikambana, Route de l'Université, tel: 235 55. Inexpensive and very good. Of the government hospitals, the military hospital is better equipped than the civilian one.
Laboratoire d'analyses médicales Pharmacie Hanitra, 172 Route Circulaire, Ankorahotra; tel: 312 81. Blood test for malaria or other nasties: 18,000Fmg.

Church services

Anglican (contact tel: 262 68): Cathedral St Laurent, Ambohimanoro; 09.00 service each Sunday. Roman Catholic (tel: 278 30): three churches have services in Malagasy, and three in French. Phone for details.

Golf course

There is a good golf course, the Club de Golf de Rova at Ambohidratrimo, 20km from town on the road to Mahajanga. It is open to visitors except at the weekend. Good meals are served at the clubhouse and the Wednesday buffet is particularly recommended.

THE MARTYR MEMORIAL CHURCHES
Dr G W Milledge

My grandfather, James Sibree, a civil engineer from Hull, was appointed by the London Missionary Society in 1863 to build four memorial churches to commemorate the Malagasy Christians put to death by order of Queen Ranavalona I during the period 1837 to her death in 1861. The sites, mainly within easy walking distance of the palace, were associated with the execution or imprisonment of the martyrs. Mr William Ellis of the London Mission had noted that the sites were suitable for church building, thought of the memorial churches and petitioned King Radama II for the sites to be reserved. This was granted. He also petitioned the mission board who agreed to raise funds in England.

Mention should be made of the difficulties and delays in starting to build large stone churches; quarry men, masons, carpenters all had to be trained. Stone was readily available but other materials were difficult to obtain. Workmen often departed for family functions, government work or military service, and work was held up for weeks. As the spire of Ambatonakangar rose to heights unknown in Malagasy buildings wives of his workmen pleaded with James Sibree not to ask their husbands to go up to such dangerous heights.

Ambatonakanga is situated at the meeting of five roads in an area given on the map as Ambohidahy. The first church in Madagascar was on this site: a low, dark, mud brick building in which Christians were imprisoned, often in chains, before, in many cases, being led out to execution. The first printing press was

Embassies

British Embassy Immeuble Ny Havana, Cité des 67Ha, Antananarivo (BP 167); tel: 277 49/273 70 (Ambassador Charles Mochan).

American Embassy Antsahavola (BP 620); tel: 200 89/212 57. For visa/passport business it is open Mondays, Wednesdays and Fridays.

South African Embassy Lot IIJ 169 Ivandry (BP 4417); tel: 424 94.

Italian Embassy Rue Pasteur Rabary, Ankadivato (BP 16); tel: 212 17.

French Embassy Rue Jean Jaurès (BP 204); tel: 237 00/200 08.

German Embassy Route Circulaire (BP 516); tel: 238 02.

TRANSPORT OUT OF TANA
Trains and buses

Trains run east to Moramanga from the station at the end of Avenue de l'Indépendance. Most people, however, will travel by bus or taxi-brousse. The *gares routières* for these vehicles are on the outskirts of the city at the appropriate road junctions. Fasan'ny karana is a new taxi-brousse station on the road to the airport which now serves the south and east of the country. Gare de l'Ouest, Anosibe (Rue Pastora Rahajason on the far side of Lac Anosy), serves the west and Gare du Nord (at Andravoahangy, behind the Artisans' market) serves the north.

Vehicle hire

Full details on hiring a car are given on page 110. If you are dealing with a Tana travel agent they will also be able to arrange car hire. Some car-hire firms are Europcar (tel: 336 47, fax: 311 65); Hertz (tel: 229 61, fax: 336 73); Locaut (tel: 219 81); Rasseta (tel: 257 70); Aventour (tel: 317 61/217 78) and Eurorent (tel: 297 66). A full list is available from the Maison du Tourisme.

also on this site and the first Malagasy bibles were printed here. The present church, opened in 1867, follows the Early English style, with 'Norman' arches. It was the first stone building in Madagascar.

Ambohipotsy is on a commanding site at the southern end of the ridge beyond the Queen's Palace. Its slender spire can be seen for miles around the surrounding plain. On this site the first martyr, a young woman called Rasalama, was speared to death in 1837. Later 11 other Christians suffered the same fate.

Faravohitra church is on the northern side of the city ridge, built where four Christians of the nobility were burnt to death on March 28, 1849. Though not as fine a site as Ambohipotsy, it also commands good views.

Ampamarinana church is a short way below the Palace on the west side of the ridge on the summit of 'The Place of the Hurling' from where prisoners were thrown to their deaths. Fourteen Christians were killed here on the same day in 1849.

So the four churches stand on historic sites as a memorial to those brave martyrs for their faith, and witness to the interest and concern of Christians in Britain for their fellows in Madagascar.

The late Dr Milledge travelled to Madagascar at the age of 88 to visit the place where he was born. Throughout the trip he was honoured as a descendent of James Sibree, one of Madagascar's major benefactors and perhaps the greatest writer the island has inspired.

Motorbikes
Holiday Bikes Auberge du Jardin, Ivato; tel/fax: 441 74. From mopeds to motorbikes, rates range from 100,000Fmg per day to 250,000Fmg, depending on the power. Credit cards accepted.

Bicycles
Bikes used to be available for hire in Tana, as in some other cities. Check with the Maison du Tourisme whether there are still bike-hire places. If you are a keen cyclist, however, you should bring your own bike (see page 112).

EXCURSIONS
East of Antananarivo
Ambohimanga
Lying 21km northeast of Antananarivo, Ambohimanga (pronounced Ambooimanga), meaning the 'blue hill', was for a long time forbidden to Europeans. From here began the line of kings and queens who were to unite Madagascar into one country, and it was here that they returned for rest and relaxation among the tree-covered slopes of this hilltop village. These days tourists find the same tranquillity and spirit of reverence and it is highly recommended as an easy day's trip, especially now its counterpart in Tana has been destroyed.

Ambohimanga has seven gates, though some are all but lost among the thick vegetation. One of the most spectacular gates, through which you enter the village, has an enormous stone disc which was formerly rolled in front of the gateway each night. Above the gateway is a thatched-roof sentry post and to the right is a bizarre Chinese pagoda (don't ask me what or why...). The entrance area has recently been 'developed' – for no obvious reason. There are some useful small shops here selling bread, drinks and the delicious drinking yoghurt.

Climbing up the stairs towards the compound you pass some handicrafts stalls with a variety of unique and appealing souvenirs, and in the courtyard are two huge fig trees providing shade for a picnic. Here you will probably be greeted by Noor, the very good local guide.

Ambohimanga still retains its spiritual significance for the Malagasy people. On the slope to the left of the door to the compound (where you must pay your 10,000Fmg fee) is a sacrificial stone. Melted candlewax and traces of blood show that it is still used for offerings, particularly in cases of infertility. Rituals involving the placing of seven small stones in the 'male' or 'female' hole will ensure the birth of a baby boy or girl.

The hours are 09.00–11.00, 14.00–17.00 (closed Mondays).

Inside the compound

The centrepiece here is the wooden house of the great King Andrianampoinimerina (1787–1810). The simple one-roomed building is interesting for the insight it gives into everyday (royal) life of that era. There is a display of cooking utensils (and the stones that surrounded the cooking fire), and weapons, and the two beds – the top one for the king and the lower for one of his 12 wives. The roof is supported by a ten-metre rosewood pole. A visit here can be full of surprises: 'Remember this is not a museum, it is the King's palace: he is there. On all my visits there were always several people asking the King for favours. On one memorable occasion I entered his hut to find what seemed like a party in full flow. A man had been possessed by the spirit of a king from the south, and he had come to the palace to greet, and be greeted by, King Andrianampoinimerina. The man had gone into a trance and a group of mediums were assisting him. They had found an accordion player and the man was dancing to get the king's attention. We were spellbound by all this, but the Malagasy visitors totally ignored what was going on and continued to look round the hut as though nothing was happening!' (Alistair Marshall)

Andrianampoinimerina's son, Radama, with British help, went a long way to achieving his father's ambition to expand his kingdom to the sea. His wife succeeded him as Queen Ranavalona. Three more queens followed and, although the capital had, by that time, been moved to Antananarivo, they built themselves elegant summer houses next to Andrianampoinimerina's simple royal home. These have now been renovated, and provide a fascinating glimpse of the strong influence of the British during those times, with very European decor and several gifts sent to the monarchs by Queen Victoria. French influence is evident too: there are two cannons forged in Jean Laborde's Mantasoa iron foundry. Here also is the small summer house belonging to Prime Minister Rainilaiarivony. Understandably cautious about being overheard (he wielded more power than the queens he married) he chose an open design with glazed windows so that spies could be spied first.

Also within the compound is a mundane-looking concrete pool (the concrete is a recent addition) which was used by the queens for ritual bathing and had to be filled, so they say, by 70 virgins, and a corral where zebu were sacrificed. An enclosing wall built in 1787, and faced with a rock-hard mixture of sand and egg, completes the tour.

From a high point above the bath you can get a superb view of the Haut Plateaux and Tana in the distance, and on an adjacent hill the white mausoleum of the king's *ombiasy*.

Getting there

Ambohimanga is reached on a good road by private taxi or bus/taxi-brousse from the Gare du Nord. The latter takes about 30 minutes and is cheap. To return to

Tana, go to the square below the stone-disc entrance where the taxi-brousses wait for passengers.

Where to eat
Ambohimanga is an ideal place for a picnic, and there is a nice restaurant (tables in the garden) off the palace courtyard. Meals are reasonably priced and there is live music at weekends.

If you take a taxi-brousse back to Tana, Jeremy Buirski and Lindie Meyer recommend the following: 'Show "Sabotsy Namehana, tsena" to a taxi-driver and he will drop you off in front of the Hotel au Bon Coin, 10km outside the city. Next door is the Resto Romazava, a clean restaurant with ridiculously low prices. Just try their papaya juice. To continue your journey to Tana, wait on the veranda for the taxis that pass every few minutes, or walk to the taxi-brousse station about 100m towards Tana.'

Ambohimalaza (La Nécropole Royale)
Off RN2 which leads to Toamasina is a remarkable cemetery. Ambohimalaza was one of the 12 sacred hills of King Andrianpoinimerina, and only the Merina aristocracy are buried here. Their tombs are topped by a *tranomanara* or 'cold house' resembling a little chalet, which indicates that the deceased was of royal blood, as does the red colour of some of the tombs. Nearby are the tiny graves of uncircumcised children who are not allowed to be buried in the family tombs. Around the perimeter you can see the remains of the deep moat and traces of a retaining wall. There is even one of those huge circular stones for closing off the entrance.

The whole area is resonant with atmosphere. Rupert Parker writes: 'It's difficult not to feel the presence of the ancestors of the royal family. My camera certainly felt them and gave up the ghost in the middle of the film – back in the UK they said it couldn't be fixed and my Malagasy friends gleefully pointed out that the ancestors had had their revenge. They also stole a shoe from one of my young nephews – that was his excuse anyway!'

Getting there
The easiest way is by private taxi, but taxi brousses run every day except Sunday from Ambasapito, on the east of Tana, to the village of Ambohmalaza then it's a 2km walk to the site.

Lake Mantasoa
Some 70km east of Antananarivo is Mantasoa (pronounced Mantas<u>oo</u>) where in the 19th century Madagascar had its first taste of industrialisation. Indeed, historians now claim that industrial output was greater then than it ever was during the colonial period. It was thanks to Jean Laborde that a whole range of industries was started including an iron foundry which enabled Madagascar to become more or less self-sufficient in swords, guns and gunpowder, thereby increasing the power of the central government. Jean Laborde was soon highly influential at court and he built a country residence for the queen at Mantasoa.

Many of the buildings remain, however, and a day's visit to Mantasoa is most rewarding. A stay of a few days would be even better, to give you a chance to walk the quiet, leafy tracks and enjoy the unspoilt small village.

Getting there
Mantasoa can be reached by taxi-brousse from Tana. The village and its attractions are quite spread out... a hired motorbike might be useful here.

THE TWO-MAN INDUSTRIAL REVOLUTION

Technology was largely introduced to Madagascar by two remarkable Europeans: James Cameron, a Scot, and Jean Laborde, a Frenchman.

James Cameron arrived in Madagascar in 1826 during the country's 'British' phase when the London Missionary Society (LMS) had attempted to set up local craftsmen to produce goods in wood, metal, leather and cotton. Cameron was only 26 when he went to Madagascar, but was already skilled as a carpenter and weaver, with a wide knowledge of other subjects which he was later to put to use in his adopted land: physics, chemistry, mathematics, architecture and astronomy. Cameron seemed able to turn his hand to almost anything mechanical. Among his achievements were the successful installation and running of Madagascar's first printing press (by studying the manual – the printer sent out with the press had died with unseemly haste), a reservoir (now Lac Anosy) and aqueduct, and the production of bricks.

Cameron's success in making soap from local materials ensured his royal favour after King Radama died and the xenophobic Queen Ranavalona came to power. But when Christian practice and teaching were forbidden in 1835 Cameron left with the other missionaries and went to work in South Africa.

He returned in 1863 when the missionaries were once more welcome in Madagascar, to oversee the building of stone churches, a hospital, and the stone exterior to the *Rova* or Queen's palace in Antananarivo.

Jean Laborde was even more of a 'renaissance man'. The son of a blacksmith, and with limited schooling, Laborde was shipwrecked off the east coast of Madagascar in 1831. He was befriended by a well-connected Frenchman, Napoléon de Lastelle, who spotted the young man's potential and arranged an introduction to the queen. Meanwhile Laborde had married a local girl, Emilie, and as a wedding present de Lastelle gave him a set of the best technical manuals of the time – which were soon to prove his 'bible'. Queen Ranavalona, no doubt

What to see

Beside the school playing field is a chimney, once part of the china factory. The cannon factory still stands and part of it is lived in, and the large furnace of the foundry remains. All are signposted and fascinating to see; you can just imagine the effort that was required to get them built.

Jean Laborde is buried in the cemetery outside the village, along with 12 French soldiers; an imposing mausoleum with a strikingly phallic monument. The very active *Les Amis de Jean Laborde* have started developing the area for tourism. If you have a special interest in this fascinating man you can phone them on tel: 402 97 or email: topoi@dts.mg.

The first project has been to restore Laborde's house which is now a very interesting museum set in a lovely garden. All the labels are in French but a guide may be available to translate. It is worth making the effort to follow Laborde's remarkable story and achievements (see box).

Where to stay/eat

Domaine de l'Ermitage BP 16, Mantasoa; cell phone: 030 23 836 09. The rooms are so-so but the meals and old-fashioned atmosphere make it well worth a stay. Rooms cost from 150,000Fmg to 250,000Fmg. Meals (very slow service) are 55,000Fmg, 65,000Fmg on Saturday nights. The Sunday buffet is excellent value for 60,000Fmg with

pleased to find a less godly European than Cameron, asked him to manufacture muskets and gunpowder, and he soon filled the gap left by the departure of Cameron and the other artisan-missionaries. Laborde's initiative and inventiveness were amazing: in a huge industrial complex built by forced labour, he produced munitions and arms, bricks and tiles, pottery, glass and porcelain, silk, soap, candles, cement, dyes, sugar, rum ... in fact just about everything a thriving country in the 19th century needed. At its peak, the complex involved some 10,000 workers. Ricefields were planted to provide them with food, and homes were built. Laborde directed the activities by day and pored over his manuals by night. He ran a farm which experimented with suitable crops and animals, and a country estate for the Merina royalty and aristocracy to enjoy such novelties as firework displays. And he built the original Queen's palace in wood (in 1839), which was later enclosed in stone by Cameron. The massive timbers used in its construction were so numerous that it was said the workers grew prematurely bald through carrying them on their heads!

By 1844 Laborde had completed a vast furnace and started to produce heavy cannons – for whose transport a good road was needed, so one was built. In all, 150 cannons were made, the largest of them nicknamed 'Besakafo' (be = big, sakafo = food) because of the amount of powder needed to charge it.

So successful was Laborde in making Madagascar self-sufficient, that foreign trade was discontinued and foreigners - with the exception of Laborde – expelled. He remained in the Queen's favour until 1857 when he was expelled because of involvement in a plot to replace the Queen by her son. The 1,200 workmen who had laboured without pay in the foundries of Mantasoa rose up and destroyed everything – tools, machinery and buildings. The factories were never rebuilt, and Madagascar's Industrial Revolution came to an abrupt end.

He returned in 1861 and became French consul, dying in 1878. A dispute over his inheritance was one of the pretexts used by the French to justify the 1883–85 war.

a small band playing songs from the 1950s. The Ermitage is set up as a country club and offers all sorts of recreational activities such as riding, tennis, boating on the lake, country walks, etc.

Motel le Chalet BP 12, Mantasoa; tel: 42 66 005. The Swiss owner, Mme Verpillot, seems to have been around since Jean Laborde's day, and has now handed over the running of the place to her son Adrian. There are five bungalows costing between 50,000Fmg and 70,000Fmg, and a restaurant serving excellent food.

Angavokely Station Forestière

Clare and Johann Herman recommend this day trip from Tana. 'At Carion, 30km from Tana on the RN2, you follow the track to Angavokely which takes about 30 minutes down a rutted track that has once been cobbled. It ends at an extraordinary turreted barrier which will be opened after you have applied at the offices a ten-minute walk away. They are located in a large set of buildings amongst a defunct sawmill. A permit costs 20,000Fmg. Faded direction signs and a map indicate the way to the Arboretum with picnic tables and parasols, and you can camp. Mt Angavokely is a fair climb up past the eucalyptus plantation and takes about 30 minutes. Thoughtfully, steps with railings are built in the rock face so you can enjoy the views from the top. A wide track leads back down through the Arboretum to the offices.'

Mandraka (Madagascar Exotic)

This is usually visited en route to Périnet, but can also be done as a day trip from Tana. If you take RN2 towards Toamasina (Tamatave) the 'Nature Farm' is situated opposite the hydro-electric power plant, just west of Anjiro. It is owned by one of Madagascar's most prominent naturalists, André Peyrieras.

The centre provides the opportunity to see and photograph some of Madagascar's most extraordinary reptiles and invertebrates, but at a price: the animals are kept in crowded and sometimes stressful conditions (though I'm

THE WILD TRADE IN REPTILES AND AMPHIBIANS IN MADAGASCAR: TWO POINTS OF VIEW

Marius Burger

The trade in live amphibians and reptiles ('Herps') for the exotic pet markets has become a lucrative business worth millions of dollars.

Malagasy herpetofauna were poorly represented in the exotic pet market until the mid-1980s. But consider the recent export figures for day geckos (*Phelsuma* spp): nearly 145,000 specimens of 17 different species between 1986 and 1991. Another popular group is the chameleons: 38,325 specimens comprising 21 species (CITES figures). In one year the legal export of Mantella frogs rose from 230 specimens to 11,058. These figures are an underestimation since they do not include illegal trading nor mortalities prior to exportation.

Herp dealers often try to justify their business by claiming that they are in actual fact saving species which would otherwise have become extinct due to habitat destruction. There is a fraction of truth in this statement, ie: a few species have benefited from captive propagation, but the overwhelming majority of herp keepers have contributed nothing to the conservation of the species in their collections. In fact, by purchasing these animals, they have created a demand which in some cases may lead to the over-exploitation of particular species.

Comparing a relatively lesser threat (collecting of live specimens) with a worse one (habitat destruction) in no way justifies the former. The exotic pet trade represents an additional threat for some species. And as for the so-called 'saving' of species by breeding them in captivity, this is mostly futile if not done in conjunction with a specific Species Survival Programme which incorporates genetic and pathological considerations. That does not necessarily mean that the trade in wild herps for the exotic pet market is an absolute no-no. Most species could probably sustain a reasonable measure of harvest. However, the current uncontrolled trade is increasing at an alarming rate and, coupled with a paucity of essential biological and distributional data, it is of conservation concern.

Very often the extreme rarity of a specific species causes it to be in particularly great demand, and thus fetch high prices. This leads to greed and unscrupulous dealings. A case in point is the theft of 75 specimens of the world's rarest tortoise, the *Anganoka*, from the breeding centre in Ampijoroa in 1996.

The unacceptable levels of discomfort and mortality often incurred during the capture, transport and subsequent housing of specimens are distressing. Chameleons, in particular, suffer great losses when collected from the wild. In short, the exotic pet trade generally has a bad name within conservation circles and it needs to clean up its act. But the trade is a reality and, in fact, it is also an opportunity. A reversal in conservation priorities from protection to utilisation can work if the profits of sustainable harvesting are equitably distributed to the people whose survival currently depends on cutting and burning the forest.

pleased to see that the attendants no longer handle them roughly, and the cages are mostly roomy and well designed). The main purpose of the centre is the breeding (for export) of various butterflies and moths, but the demand for reptiles for the pet trade is also satisfied.

The export of frogs and reptiles for the pet trade is a controversial subject which I have left to experts on both sides of the argument (see box).

Cold drinks are available here, along with handicrafts, postcards... and a clean toilet.

Visitors pay 10,000Fmg to tour the collection with a guide. Make sure you bring

Bill Love

The number of herps exported from Madagascar is merely a drop in the bucket compared to those permanently lost to habitat destruction. Animals are renewable resources that can replenish themselves if their environment is not severely disturbed or cleared. The ability to be naturally prolific has evolved as part of their survival strategy to counter wildfire, disease, predation, etc.

Local people collecting small animals typically take them from places where populations are dense to ensure profitable catches. As numbers dwindle, the effort becomes unprofitable and is quickly abandoned. Most animals such as lizards and frogs bounce back in numbers quickly.

Not all exported animals end up simply as pets. Some go to experienced modern breeders who dedicate vast amounts of time and effort in studying them to unravel their reproductive biologies. This, in turn, leads to self-sustaining captive colonies of less-stressed, parasite-free, healthy animals that will eventually nullify the need for continued large-scale importation of wild-origin stock.

Breeding farms are also under development in Madagascar. While there is no excuse for overcrowding, malnutrition, poor transportation methods, etc, these problems are being corrected, and can be viewed as regrettable consequences of a learning process to discover the 'recipes' for captive reproduction.

People don't care about things for which they feel no familiarity or passion. People purchasing live animals, and learning from the experience, gain a broader love and appreciation of wildlife generally. This leads to concern for nature later when their vote or donation could benefit conservation causes.

Attacking the live animal trade is a substitute for dealing with the seemingly intractable mega-problem of saving whole environments, or slowing the human population growth that is putting the intense pressure on the land and resources. If the same zeal focused against the pet trade was redirected there, accelerated progress would occur in protecting *all* species.

The demand for exotic pets will continue as surely as the Malagasy people's need to utilise their natural resources. The relatively new sustainable harvest concept may be the best solution since it recognises both factors. Human nature will surely find ways to fill its needs even if total 'hands-off' style legislation is enacted. The opportunity now exists to create new laws to take this predictable factor into account, and instead create a mutually beneficial system that recognises the interwoven relationship between commercialism and conservation, allowing both to coexist and work hand in hand toward a common goal.

fast film and a close-up lens to make the most of this unique opportunity to get pictures of species seldom seen in the wild.

Pizza Nino is a good, clean pizza restaurant on the left as you drive on RN2 towards Mandraka, near the village of Manjaka: a popular stop for resident *vazahas*.

West of Antananarivo
Antsahaointa
John Kupiec recommends a visit to this hilltop village which is a bus ride southwest of Tana. 'There are many royal tombs, a museum (small fee), wonderful views and a small house for visitors to sleep in. The guide speaks English.'

Lake Itasy
Off the road to Tsiroanomandidy (access town Analavory) this lake and its surrounding area are particularly beautiful and easily reached by taxi-brousse or private car. 'We could have walked for days through the hamlets which offered an insight into the day-to-day life of these exceptionally welcoming people' (P Crawford). The nearby village of **Ampefy** is full of once splendid French colonial mansions. There is a choice of accommodation: the Kavitaha, with very good food, and the humble Bungalows Administratifs. A better bet is the Village Touristique between the lakes: spacious but basic bungalows.

It is an 8km walk from Ampefy to Ilot de la Vièrge on Lac Itasy. 'From the Ilot there are fantastic views over the lake and surrounding hills. One of my abiding memories is descending the hill and hearing the beautiful singing at the Sunday service in the church at the bottom.' (PC). West of the road are the Chutes de la Lily (waterfalls) and about 45 minutes' drive northwest of Ampefy are some hot springs with spectacular mineral deposits.

Tsiroanomandidy
Lying about 200km to the west of Tana, on a surfaced road (four hours), this town is worth visiting for its huge cattle market, held on Wednesdays and Thursdays. The tribe to the south, the Bara, drive huge herds of cattle through the Bongolava plateau to sell at the market.

There are two hotels. Bishop Brock recommends Chez Marcelline: 'Marcelline is a good hostess and a pretty good cook. The hotel is north of the market, near the airport. Tsiroanomandidy is also a nice place to hang out: when viewed from a distance, with its twin-towered church against a backdrop of mountains, it reminded me of a town in Mexico!'

Tsiroanomandidy is linked to Maintirano and Majunga by Twin Otter, and also to Morondava. You can also travel west on river trips as far as the Manambolo gorges (see page 342).

Northwest of Antananarivo
The forest of Ambohitantely
The name means 'Where honey is found' and is pronounced 'Ambweetontel'. This is the last remnant of natural forest in the province of Ankazobe and there are hopes that it will shortly become a protected area. This report is by Dr Graham Noble and Sandra Baron of South Africa. 'It takes about 2½ hours to get to the forest which lies 150km northwest of Tana off the road to Mahajanga. The access village is Ararazana. The forest is 10km from the road and you do not see a tree until you reach the site. Estimates of its size vary from 1,400 to 3,000 hectares. It is surrounded by a barrier of burnt trees, but as you go two metres into the forest the

leaf-litter is already 10–15cm deep. There is a network of paths through the forest. The University of Antananarivo has a right to a part of it as a study site and refers to that section as the Botanical Garden. The forestry director is very keen to receive tourists into the area for day walks and will also organise provisions for overnight stays. Good birding and lots of orchids.'

Derek Schuurman adds: 'This is actually a very beautiful little rainforest, with rufous mouse lemurs and common brown lemurs as well as common tenrecs. Birds found there include the Madagascar blue pigeon, long-billed greenbul, forest rock thrush, blue vanga and, en route, the Réunion harrier.'

Check with ANGAP on the current status of the forest (and to buy a permit), and make a further visit to the Direction des Eaux et Forêts in Ankazobe, 106km from Tana. Because of a problem with bandits in the area, you are advised to check with the Eaux et Forêts people about where to stay/camp, and always travel with a reliable guide.

Aerangis

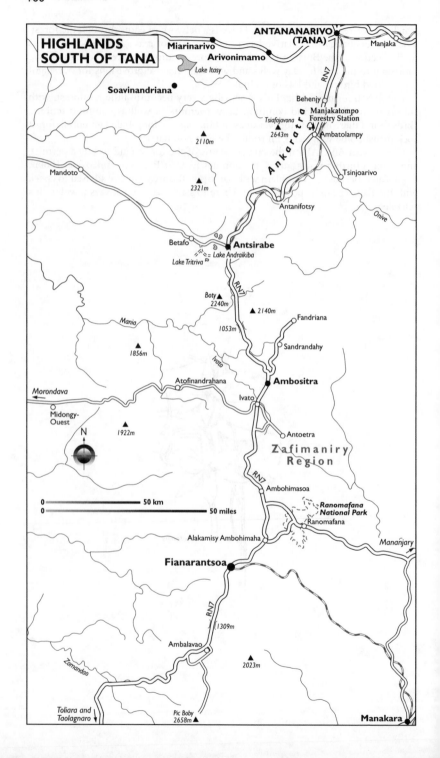

166

HIGHLANDS
SOUTH OF TANA

The Highlands South of Tana

OVERVIEW
Now that Route Nationale 7 (RN7) has been improved, many visitors drive its full length to Toliara, either by hired car or by public transport. It is a delightful journey, providing an excellent overview of the Hauts Plateaux and Merina and Betsileo culture, as well as spectacular scenery, especially around Fianarantsoa.

FROM TANA TO ANTSIRABE
All along this stretch of road you will see Merina tombs, and can watch the labour-intensive cultivation of rice paddies.

About 15km from Tana look out for a huge, white replica of the *rova* across the paddy fields on the right. This is President Ratsiraka's palace, funded by North Korea. When he briefly became ex-president and fled to France he stripped it bare. Now he is back in power and presumably the furnishings are back too.

Ambatolampy and region
Ambatolampy lies some two hours/68km from Tana and has a colourful market as well as a very good hotel/restaurant. It is also the starting point for two interesting excursions to Tsinjoarivo, with its summer *rova*, and the forestry station of Manjakatompo.

South of the town, near the Manja Ranch, is a newly-established insectarium set up by a Frenchman, Jean-Baptiste Cornet (admission 15,000Fmg). He is hoping to use the revenue to provide financial support to entomology students.

The area telephone area code for Ambatolampy is 42.

Where to stay/eat
Hotel au Rendezvous des Pecheurs Tel: 492 04 (nine rooms). Albanian-owned and renowned for its excellent, and reasonably priced, food (meals are 30,000Fmg). The rooms are simple but comfortable, with shared bathrooms (with a big bathtub) and hot water; 40,000–50,000Fmg.
Manja Ranch BP 36, Ambatolampy 104; tel: 492 34; email: ManjaRanch@hotmail.com. About 2km south of Ambatolampy and owned by Doug Cook, an American, and his Malagasy wife Bijou. This is a great place to relax for a few days. The area is beautiful and peaceful, there are horses and bikes for hire, or you can just potter round and breathe the fresh air. Rooms (shared bathrooms, unreliable water) are 30,000Fmg, but bungalows are being built with en-suite bathrooms; these will be 65,000Fmg. Meals (set menu) are 30,000Fmg; Sunday buffet with music 40,000Fmg.

Tsinjoarivo
From Ambatolampy a road leads southeast to Tsinjoarivo. Johan and Clare Hermans write: 'Check conditions before setting out; although only about 50km

it takes a good three to four hours by car and is not an all-weather road (there is an alternative road on higher ground which bypasses some of the boggiest stretches of the main road). The journey is worthwhile for the series of waterfalls and the *rova* of Queen Rasoherina; in her time it took three days to get there from Tana by palanquin. There is a guardian who will show you round the buildings, one for the queen with the remains of some fine wooden carving from her bed, and others for the prime minister, the chancellor and the guard. Situated on a promontory overlooking the falls, the site has spectacular views and an incredible atmosphere. There are stone steps down from the *Rova* to the viewpoint at the falls, complete with spray.'

Manjakatompo Forestry Station
A road leads west, and then north from Ambatolampy to Manjakatompo, an hour's drive (17km). 'The road passes through aluminium smelting villages – worth a stop to watch them making cutlery and cooking pots. Permits for the Manjakatompo Forest are obtainable at the gate, cost 20,000Fmg. Guides not obligatory (ours was not worth the money). Well signposted walks, sights include a small waterfall, Lac Froid, site of a village which is still used for folk medicine.' (Johan and Clare Hermans)

Merina tombs
About 15 minutes beyond Ambatolampy are some fine painted Merina tombs. These are on both sides of the road, but the most accessible are on the right.

Antanifotsy
This small town some 40km south of Antsirabe has a wonderful market on Mondays.

ANTSIRABE
Antsirabe lies 169km south of Antananarivo at 1,500m. It was founded in 1872 by Norwegian missionaries attracted by the cool climate and the healing properties of the thermal springs. The name means 'the place of much salt'.

This is an elegant city, and with its top-class hotels and interesting excursions merits a stay of a few days. A broad avenue links the handsome station with the amazing Hotel des Thermes; at the station end is a monolith depicting Madagascar's 18 main tribes.

Antsirabe is the agricultural and industrial centre of Madagascar, best known as the centre for beer. You can smell the Star Brewery as you enter the town.

This is the *pousse-pousse* capital of Madagascar. There are hundreds, perhaps thousands of them. The drivers are insistent that you avail yourself of a ride, and why not? But be very firm about the price. Now that tourists come to Antsirabe in some numbers, the drivers have found they can make a dollar just by posing for pictures. To actually have to run somewhere, towing a large *vazaha*, for the same price must seem very unfair.

On a promontory overlooking the baths stands the Hotel des Thermes: an amazing building in both size and architectural style. There is nothing else like it in Madagascar – it would not be out of place along the French Riviera and is set in equally elegant gardens (see *Where to stay*).

If you are travelling between May and September you will need a sweater in the evening. It gets quite cold.

The telephone area code in Antsirabe is 44.

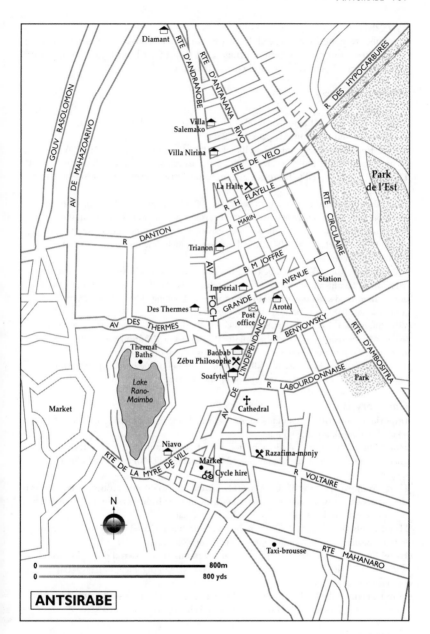

ANTSIRABE

Getting there and away
By rail
The train now only runs spasmodically, the journey from Tana taking from four to ten (!) hours. In theory there are trains three times a week, leaving both Tana and Antsirabe at 06.30. Check at the railway station in Tana or Antsirabe for the latest information.

By road

Antsirabe is generously served by buses and taxi-brousses. These leave from Anosizato station in Tana. The journey takes about four hours. Continuing south to Ambositra takes two hours and costs 7,000Fmg.

Where to stay
Category A

Aida A new hotel on the northern side of town, near the taxi-brousse station; tel: 492 98. Comfortable, and competitively priced at 225Ff.

Arotel Rue Ralaimongo, Antsirabe 110; tel: 481 20/485 73/485 74; fax: 491 49. A well-situated, comfortable and expensive hotel. Luxurious full-sized bathtubs. Unexciting food. 420–460Ff, breakfast 25Ff. There is a swimming pool that is open to non-residents, at 4,000Fmg.

Hotel des Thermes BP 72; tel: 487 61/2; fax 492 02. An amazing place from the outside, disappointing inside. There is a cosy bar and reasonably good food is served in the restaurant. In the warmer months the large garden and swimming pool make this a very pleasant place to relax. 190,000–325,000Fmg double, including breakfast. Visa and MasterCard accepted.

Villa Nirina Route d'Andranobe (BP 245), Antsirabe; tel: 485 97 or 486 69. Owned by Mrs Zanoa Rasanjison, who speaks fluent English as well as French and German, this is a private home and sometimes hard to get an advance booking. The rooms are very comfortable; 70,000Fmg double including breakfast.

Villa Salemako BP 14, Antsirabe; tel: 495 88. Another extraordinary private home with five rooms for visitors, run by Julia-Brigitte Rakotonarivo. Beautiful garden, furniture and ambience. To find the house look for the Malagasy motif on the chimney. 45,000–60,000Fmg; breakfast 10,000Fmg. 'Surely the best value in Madagascar' (K & L Gillespie). Often fully booked so write or phone before you arrive.

Category B

Imperial Hotel BP 74 (Grande Av), Antsirabe; tel: 483 33. Chinese run. Comfortable. 93,000Fmg; breakfast 10,000Fmg.

Hotel Diamant Route d'Andranobe; tel: 488 40. A medium-sized hotel offering a good selection of rooms at prices ranging from 34,000Fmg to 229,000Fmg. Good Chinese restaurant.

Hotel Manoro Tel: 480 77. Conveniently located next to the taxi-brousse station towards the south of the city. Rooms are good value with en-suite bathrooms for 45,000Fmg. The better ones are on the second floor. Food unexceptional.

Hotel Baobab Tel: 483 93. Seems to be on the decline but used to be clean and friendly, with hot water in some rooms. 35,000–45,000Fmg. Restaurant.

Hotel Soafytel Tel: 480 55. Four categories of rooms, now very run down, but with hot water and en-suite bathrooms. From about 55,000–85,000Fmg, including breakfast. Bicycles for hire.

Hotel Trianon Av Foch; tel: 488 81. This once popular hotel has seen better days. 'Very dirty; hideous.' However, the French restaurant is highly recommended.

Category C

Hotel Coin d'Or Just off Av de l'Indépendance in the centre of town. Clean but basic rooms.

Hotel Niavo (The full name is Hotel/Restaurant Fitsangantsanganana Niavo!) Rue Rakotondrainibe Daniel; tel: 484 67. A family-run hotel with a garden on the far side of the lake. A great setting and view, so popular, but very run down. 45,000Fmg. Good food, friendly staff.

Hotel Rubis Large bright rooms with shower and basin on a noisy street. 55,000Fmg.
Residence Camelia Small rooms, shared bathroom, but set in lovely gardens in the French part of town. 60,000Fmg to 80,000Fmg for shared facilities, 120,000Fmg en suite.
Eton'n Hotel A new basic hotel near the station. Very clean.

Where to eat
Le Zébu Philosophe Av Jean Ralaimongo; tel: 498 09. A new, buzzing coffee bar. Worth the visit for its extraordinary and appealing decor.
Restaurant la Halte Tel: 489 94. Once the best restaurant in Antsirabe this has recently disappointed several readers. However, it's friendly and not expensive so worth checking out.
Bar-Restaurant Razafimamonjy Antsenankely; tel: 483 53. 'The best restaurant in Madagascar! Super service from elderly waiters, a nice mix of Malagasy and tourists, and Saturday night entertainment.' Mainly Chinese; reasonable prices.
Restaurant Manambina Malagasy dishes.
Auberge Danielle Roughly opposite the Hotel Diamant. This little *hotely* serves good, cheap meals. Try also the *hotelys* on the left of the petrol station as you enter town from Tana.
Salon de Thé Moderne A pleasant snack bar opposite the Pharmacie Mahosa.
Helena Patisserie Near the Zébu Philosophe. Good for breakfast and take-away meals. 'Pizza, quiche, and the first apple turnovers I've tasted in Madagascar; OK, so they were made from strawberries but one can't be too fussy when travelling!' (F Kerridge)

Wheels and hoofs
In the first street (south) behind the daily market is a **bicycle hire** shop. Good mountain bikes for about 50,000Fmg per day. Bikes can also be hired from Soafitel and probably from other hotels. **Horses** may be hired near the Hotel des Thermes, the stables being near Parc d'Est.

What to see and do
Saturday is **market** day in Antsirabe, an echo of Tana before they abolished the *zoma* but with an even greater cross-section of activities. It's also much better organised, and is enclosed in a walled area of the city on the hill before the road to Lake Tritriva. 'The entire back wall of the market is a row of open barber stalls. Each has a small mirror, a chair and a little peg for one's hat. There are a few local gambling places nearby, too. They're hard to find, and the stakes can get pretty high.' (Maggie Rush). If you are self-catering note that: 'In the old covered section of the market is the best vegetable stall in Madagascar. The owner said she could have sold her produce several times over, it was so popular.' (K & L Gillespie)

It is worth paying a visit to the **thermal baths** (*thermes*). There is a wonderfully hot swimming pool full of laughing brown faces that laugh even harder at the sight of a foreigner. But it's friendly laughter. You can also take a private bath here (but there's a 20-minute limit) and have a massage.

If you are in a group, an interesting organised excursion is to the homes of various **craft workers**, using a horse-drawn *calèche* (Malagasy stagecoach). Touristy, but fascinating, and the chance to see craft workers in their homes – and to buy direct from them. My favourite was 'Miniature Mamy', where a soft-spoken man makes exquisite models of bicycles, *pousse-pousses*, cars etc, from scrap materials. His knowledge of engineering and painstaking eye for detail is admirable.

The tour ends with a traditional Malagasy meal, carefully served and accompanied by musicians. Contact Les Hautes Terres at 30, Rue Maréchal Lyautes, Antsirabe; tel: 480 97.

Excursions from Antsirabe
Lake Andraikiba
This large lake 7km west of Antsirabe is often overlooked in favour of the more spectacular Lake Tritriva. 'We found it scenic, soothing, and a very pleasant place for a picnic'. This is a good place to buy semi-precious stones.

Taxi-brousses heading for Betafo pass close to the lake.

Lake Tritriva
The name comes from *tritry* – the Malagasy word for the ridge on the back of a chameleon (!) – and *iva*, deep. And this emerald-green crater lake is indeed deep – 80 metres, some say. It is reached by continuing past Lake Andraikiba for 12km on a rough, steep road past small villages of waving kids. You will notice that these villages are relatively prosperous-looking for Madagascar – they grow the barley for the Star Brewery.

Apart from the sheer beauty of Lake Tritriva (the best light for photography is in the morning), there are all sorts of interesting features. The water level rises in the dry season and debris thrown into the lake has reappeared down in the valley, supporting the theory of underground water channels.

Look across the lake and you'll see two thorn trees growing on a ledge above the water with intertwined branches. Legend says that these are two lovers, forbidden to marry by their parents, who drowned themselves in Tritriva. When the branches are cut, so they say, blood, not sap, oozes out. You can walk right round the lake for impressive views of it and the surrounding countryside.

The local people have not been slow to realise the financial potential of groups of *vazahas* corralled at the top of a hill. There is an 'entrance charge' of 10,000Fmg, and once through the gate don't think you will be alone at the lake.

You can get to Tritriva by taxi (45 mins each way, about 60,000Fmg) or by bus to Lake Andraikiba and then walk. The most enjoyable way is to rent a bike and make it a day trip. If you are self-sufficient you can stay in the village of Belazao, midway between the two lakes (no hotel), or camp at the lake.

Betafo
About 22km west of Antsirabe, off the tarred road that goes as far as Morondava, lies Betafo, a town with typical highlands red-brick churches and houses. Dotted among the houses are *vatolahy*, standing stones erected to commemorate warrior chieftains. A visit here is recommended. It is not on the normal tourist circuit, and gives you an excellent insight into Merina small-town activities. Monday is market day. There is no hotel in Betafo, but you should be able to find a room by asking around.

At one end of the town is the crater lake Tatamarina. From there it is a walk of about 3km to the Antafofo waterfalls among beautiful views of ricefields and volcanic hills. You will need to find someone to show you the way. 'It's very inviting for a swim but they told me there are ghosts in the pool under the falls. If you go swimming they will pull at your legs and pull you to the bottom.' (Luc Selleslagh)

On the outskirts of Betafo there are hot springs, where for a few francs you can have a hot bath with no time limit.

Continuing south on RN7
Leaving Antsirabe you continue to pass through typical highland scenery of rice paddies and low hills. About 45 minutes beyond the town you'll cross a river and pass one of the nicest rural markets I've seen. There are strange fruit and

vegetables, lots of peanuts, and fascinating grey balls that turn out to be soap made from the fat from zebu humps. At the back of the market is a makeshift barbershop, and behind the men with the scissors are rolling green hills.

Bjørn Donnis describes another curiosity along the route: 'You will pass the region where Tapia fruits are grown. Was told that it was the only place in the world – well, the world hasn't missed so much.'

About 2½ hours after leaving Antsirabe you reach Ambositra.

AMBOSITRA

Ambositra (pronounced 'Amboostr') is the centre of Madagascar's wood carving industry. Even the houses have ornately carved wooden balconies and shutters. There is an abundant choice of carved figures and marquetry, in several shops, and the quality is improving although there are occasional lapses into pseudo-Africana. In an earlier edition I complained that I've yet to see a carved lemur. I've now seen some but sadly the carver obviously has yet to see a lemur... For carvings of people, however, one artist stands out. 'Jean' carves exquisite scenes from Malagasy life, many in a fine-grained, creamy wood known locally as *fanazava*. Jean has now opened a shop on one of the minor roads that joins the RN7 just south of the town. Look for the signs 'Société Jean et Frère'.

The best woodcarving shop (and workshop) is Chez Victor, opposite the Grand Hotel. It has a huge selection at very reasonable prices.

The telephone area code in Amboistra is 47, but note: there are no pay phones except at the post office.

Where to stay

Le Tropical French-Malagasy owned and provides – at last!– reasonable accommodation in Ambositra. Simple, clean rooms (shared facilities) from 43,000Fmg to 80,000Fmg.

Prestige Andrefan' i Vinani, Ambositra; tel: 711 35. Another contender for the best hotel in Ambositra: 'A beautiful, charming auberge. The owner, Francis Rakotonisa, couldn't have been more thoughtful and helpful. When I mentioned I had an interest in crafts he took me all around town, into narrow houses, stores and we spoke to all sorts of people. His establishment currently has three rooms, one with en-suite facilities. Prices 49,000–77,000Fmg. They are building bungalows and a pool.' (Sharon Giarratana)

Grand Hotel This non-grand hotel has been around a long time and has a loyal clientele among frequent Mad travellers. 'A beautiful old place, very woody'. Rooms have basin, bidet and screen, and not all have bed bugs. Good value at 55,000Fmg (twin).

Hotel Violette There are two hotels, the original Violette and its annexe. The old (and atmospheric) Violette is up the hill and to the left. 30,000Fmg and up. The Annexe is on the south side of town about 200m past the Grand Hotel, and is a little more expensive. Friendly, good restaurant.

Hotely ny Tanamasoandro (see below) has a few 'horrid rooms: big, grotty shacks', but only 25,000Fmg.

Where to eat

Hotely ny Tanamasoandro Good and cheap.

Hotely Gasy 'The best restaurant on our entire trip'. Amazing Scottish decor, huge portions, low prices.

Places of interest near Ambositra
Zafimaniry villages

The Zafimaniry people follow a traditional way of life in the forests southeast of Ambositra. This is not an area to attempt without an experienced guide, however.

The danger is not so much in getting lost, but in the detrimental effects uncontrolled tourism has already had on the villagers nearest the road.

If you decide to go it alone, you should at least know that taxi-brousses only make the journey to Antoetra, the nearest Zafimaniry village to the road, on market days, Saturdays and Tuesdays. On other days, if you can't afford a taxi, you are stuck with a 23km hike from Ivato on RN7.

If you want to see the results of catastrophic deforestation this is as good an area as any. The impact is heightened by the beauty of the untouched forest and the simple way of life practised by the inhabitants of the more remote villages, where the picturesque houses show that wood carving is still the main industry. Sharon Giarratana reports: 'We walked many hours through beautiful, rolling hills and deep valleys, pretty challenging in some places. In the remote Zafimaniry villages, you'll find small wooden dwellings, dark and smoky inside with corn hung from low ceilings to dry. Catholic village so tons of kids hanging around. The Zafimaniry tombs look like large square heaps of tightly-packed stones, topped with obelisks. I haven't seen anything like it elsewhere in Madagascar.'

Guided tours of the Zafimaniry countryside are advertised in hotels in Ambositra or Fianar (the Tsara Guest House, for instance). Dany and Sahondra, a

RICE

The Malagasy have an almost mystical attachment to rice. King Andrianampoinimerina declared: 'Rice and I are one,' and loyalty to the Merina king was symbolised by industry in the rice paddies.

Today the Betsileo are masters of rice cultivation (they manage three harvests a year, not the normal two) and their neat terraces are a distinctive part of the scenery of the central highlands. However, rice is grown throughout the island, either in irrigated paddies or as 'hill rice' watered by the rain. Rice production is labour-intensive. First the ground must be prepared for the seeds. Often this is done by chasing zebu cattle round and round to break and soften the clods – a muddy, sticky job, but evidently great fun for the boys who do it. Seeds are germinated in a small plot and replanted in the irrigated paddies when half grown. In October and November you will see groups of women bent over in knee-deep water, performing this back-breaking work.

The Malagasy eat rice three times a day, the annual consumption being 135kg per person (about a pound of rice per day!) although this is declining because of the availability of other foods and reduced productivity. Rice marketing was nationalised in 1976, but this resulted in such a dramatic drop in the amount of rice reaching the open market that restrictions were lifted in 1984. By that time it was too late to reverse the decline in productivity, which was mainly due to the decay of irrigation works. Despite a steady increase in acreage at the expense of the precious forest, production is continuing to fall: from 150kg per head of population in 1973 to an estimated 113kg in 1998.

Small farmers grow rice only for their own consumption but are forced to sell part of their crop for instant cash. Richer families in the community store this grain and sell it back at a profit later. To solve this small-scale exploitation, village co-operatives have been set up to buy rice and sell it back to the farmer at an agreed price, or at a profit to outsiders if any is left over.

French-Malagasy couple running a B&B in Tana (see page 146), do trekking trips and are extremely knowledgeable. Write to them at BP 4313, Antananarivo.

Sandrandahy and Fandriana
A rough road northeast of Ambositra leads to Fandriana, well known for its raffia work, hats and so on. It takes about three hours or so to reach here. Roughly half way is Sandrandahy which holds a huge Wednesday market. This is also a silk weaving centre, where exquisite *lambas* are made.

South from Ambositra on RN7
From Ambositra, the scenery becomes increasingly spectacular. You now pass remnants of the western limit of the rainforest (being systematically destroyed). The road runs up and down steep hills, past neat Betsileo rice paddies interspersed with eucalyptus and pine groves. The steepest climb comes about two hours after Ambositra, when the vehicle labours up an endlessly curving road, through thick forests of introduced pine, and reaches the top where stalls selling oranges or baskets provide an excuse for a break. Then it's down through more forest, on a very poor stretch of road, to **Ambohimahasoa**. Hotel Nirina serves good snacks. If heading for Ranomafana, enquire here about the short cut, bypassing Fianarantsoa.

Leaving Ambohimahasoa you pass more forests, then open country, rice paddies and houses as you begin the approach to Fianarantsoa.

FIANARANTSOA
The name means 'Place of good learning'. Fianarantsoa (Fianar for short) was founded in 1830 as the administrative capital of Betsileo. It is one of the more attractive Malagasy towns, built on a hill like a small-scale Antananarivo.

There is a dramatic contrast between the charming Upper Town and the unutterably dreary Lower Town. Travellers making only a brief stop tend to see only the Lower Town, dominated by a huge concrete stadium and the stink of urine, and are not impressed. The Upper Town, with its narrow winding streets and plethora of churches, should be visited for the wonderful views, especially in the early morning when the mist is curling up from the valley. It's quite a way up: take bus number 3 or a taxi, and walk back.

The telephone area code is 75.

Getting there and away
By road
For a tranquil journey the company KOFIAM, which operates buses between Fianar and Tana with a lunch stop in Ambositra, has been recommended. There is also the Jumbobus which runs between Tana and Toliara. See page 197.

For the onward journey to Toliara, a taxi-brousse (40,000Fmg) takes around 14 hours.

By air
The 1999 Air Mad schedule shows Twin Otter flights on Tuesdays and Sundays. I wouldn't bank on it.

Where to stay
Category A
Hotel Soafia BP 1479; tel/fax: 503 53. This large hotel (74 rooms) has all sorts of unusual features. 'Looks like a cross between Disneyworld, a Chinese temple and a

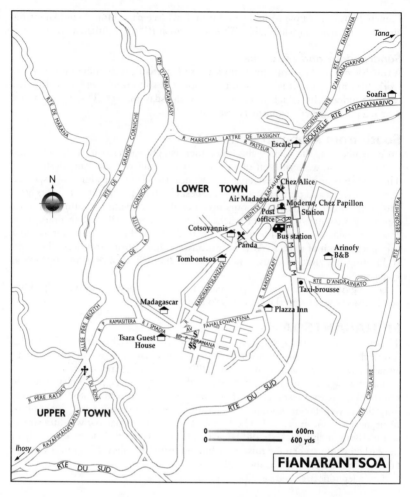

gigantic doll's house!' (J Hadfield). 'A veritable rabbit warren...walking around the spartan corridors made me feel I was going to round a corner and meet Jack Nicholson wielding an axe! A bizarre place.' (Jerry Vive). However, its patisserie sells wonderful bread, croissants and pastries, and there are all sorts of useful goodies for sale in the shop, such as phone cards and stamps, and the photo shop next door sells very high quality postcards. Double room 180Ff.

Radama Hotel Tel: 507 97; fax: 513 76; email: radama@hotels.online.mg. 32 rooms (14 rooms plus 18 studios) all with TVs, and en-suite facilities. Very good value at 50,000–90,000Fmg.

Hotel Moderne du Betsileo BP 1161; tel: 500 03. Part of the Papillon restaurant, located near the station. Comfortable, hot water 47,000Fmg. Only 12 rooms, so is often full.

Hotel Plazza Inn BP 1161; tel: 515 72; fax: 510 86. A newish hotel with 30 rooms. Worth checking out as an alternative to the flamboyant Soafia.

Tombontsoa Hotel Overlooks the football stadium near the Panda restaurant. Swimming pool and tennis court. Double room with hot shower and WC, about 50,000Fmg. Friendly and clean. Good Malagasy meals.

Category B

Tsara Guest House BP 1373, Fianarantsoa 301 (Ambatolahikosoa, New Town); tel: 502 06. For many years the Tsara has been the most popular *vazaha* place in Madagascar, universally praised by readers. It is located in an old house that began its life as a church, with a terrace from which you have a wonderful view of the town. The owners, Jim Heritsialonina and his Swiss wife Natalie, deserve their success – they have worked unstintingly to provide all the comforts and atmosphere that travellers desire. The Tsara hallmark is the good meals eaten communally around a large table, and the treks and excursions organised for their guests, making them feel part of a large family. 55,000–120,000Fmg. The more expensive rooms have en-suite bathroom. For others you will have to queue, and hot water tends to run out. The profits from this place go to support a small school at the edge of the rainforest.

Hotel Cotsoyannis Tel: 514 86. This long-established hotel has had its ups and downs. Improved by a recent extension: pleasant rooms, good views. 66,000Fmg per room. Old rooms may be available at a cheaper price.

Category C

Arinofy B&B BP 1426, Fianarantsoa 301. A clean and friendly place, a few hundred metres up the hill from the taxi-brousse depot. The best of the cheaper hotels. A twin-bedded room is about 50,000Fmg, and a four-bunk considerably less. You can eat in a communal dining room, and there is a laundry service.

Hotel Madagascar Tel: 511 32. Large double rooms with uncomfortable beds and shared facilities, but economically priced.

Hotel Escale Near the station. 'Malagasy and chiggers, but cheap at 35,000Fmg. They provide a buck of hot water.' (L & K Gillespie)

There are other cheap places in Fianar, especially around the station.

Where to eat

Chez Papillon Tel: 500 03. Many people feel its reputation as the best restaurant in Madagascar is overrated, but the majority still praise the quality and wide choice of dishes, and the service, though snooty, is second to none. The fixed menu is 45,000Fmg. Breakfast (8,000Fmg) is highly recommended.

Le Panda Across the street from the Hotel Cotsoyannis. Chinese. Inexpensive. Good.

Resto Blue Very good, inexpensive food. Friendly.

Chez Alice Pizzeria A block away from the Papillon. Clean, pleasant, inexpensive.

Tiki dairy shop Across from the train station. Great yoghurt and cheese.

MiniCroq A small restaurant with a shop in the front selling all sorts of goodies including ice-cream. Behind the main street in the lower town.

Nightlife

Moulin Rouge 'A fantastic nightclub on the outskirts of town. The place to be at the weekend. Varied music: Malagasy, African, Reggae, funny Euro-pop disco.'

What to see and do

This is a good town for strolling around. Take your time to explore the Upper Town and then check out the market. 'There is a wonderful market, close to the Rue Verdun, which features a great variety of herbal medicines and dried fish brought up by train from Manakara. There is a path leading to the market from the Arinofy B&B. If you like wine, there's the Domremy store, across the street from Le Panda. The store stocks a good selection of wines and aperitifs, and the French proprietors are very helpful.' (Maggie Rush)

Escorted tours

There are many places of interest within a day's excursion from Fianar. Jim, at the Tsara Guest House, can organise these, as can the owners of the Anofy B&B. Also recommended by (most) travellers is Stella Ravelomanantsoa. He (sic) can be found at the 'Regional Tourist Office', near the Papillon, opposite Lombardo; tel: 506 67 20.

Ania Dudziec recommends a visit (arranged by the Arinofy) with Narcisse to see the manufacture of Antaimoro paper. 'He takes you to his family and explains every stage of the paper-making process. Fascinating, and not far from the centre of town.'

Wine tasting

The Famoriana estate (Domaine Côtes de Famoriana) is one of the largest and best-known wine producers in Madagascar. Smaller ones, such as Maromby, also flourish. The vineyards are open to visitors. Famoriana is about 35km northwest of Fianar, beyond the small town of Isorana.

Tea estate

The Sahambavy Tea Estate is situated on one side of a very pretty valley beside Lake Sahambavy, 25km by road from Fianar, or by rail to the Sahambavy station on the way to Manakara. Although tea-growing was encouraged in Madagascar in precolonial times, this is a relatively new estate and is now managed by a Dutch company, HVA, and run by a Scot. The company employs 700 people and 75% of the tea produced must by law be exported.

Visitors are welcome at the estate which is a beautiful place for picnics. Camping is not encouraged because of the danger from cattle rustlers. The place is closed at weekends.

Train to Manakara

If it's running, the train usually leaves for Manakara on Saturdays and Wednesdays. The schedule seems to be endlessly flexible, so you will need to check current whims at the station. It generally leaves at 07.00 and takes six to eight hours. The ticket office opens at 06.00.

This can be quite an eventful trip. Ania Dudziec describes her journey in 1998. 'Amazing views, relatively comfortable seats for the first three hours. The complete journey took 24 hours. We stopped at the village of Tolongoina for 12 hours which, in retrospect, was fantastic. Spent the entire hot, hot, hot day trying to cool off by the river, picking coffee beans, wandering around the village, meeting 100% of the under-20 population, and just generally waiting. And waiting. The remainder of the journey got a bit much, really, with the basket on the shelf above (filled with vegetables and raw meat) dripping vinegar and blood on my head. I had to keep reminding myself that I'd chosen to take this train journey for fun, but for the other passengers it was a necessity.'

There is talk of this railway being privatised; probably good news for tourists.

RANOMAFANA

The name Ranomafana means 'hot water' and it was the waters, not the lemurs, which drew visitors in the colonial days and financed the building of the elegant-looking Hotel Station Thermale de Ranomafana.

These days the baths (which are wonderful – and cheap) are often ignored by visitors anxious to visit the Ranomafana National Park which was created in 1991. This hitherto unprotected fragment of mid-altitude rainforest first came to world

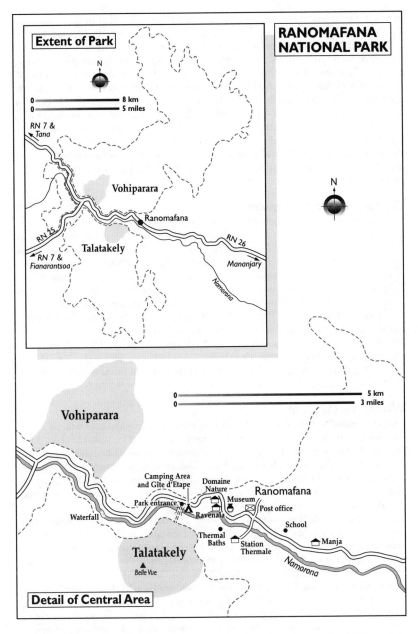

attention with the discovery of the golden bamboo lemur in 1986 and is particularly rich in wildlife.

Ranomafana is not universally popular but I love it! First you have the marvellous drive down, with the dry highland vegetation giving way to greenery and flowers. Then there are the views of the tumbling waters of the Namorona river, and the relief when the hillsides become that lovely unbroken, knobbly green of virgin forest and you know you are near the reserve. Hidden in these trees are 12 species of lemur: diademed (Milne-Edwards) sifaka, red-bellied brown lemur, red-fronted lemur, black-and-white ruffed lemur and three species of bamboo lemur. At night you can add mouse lemur, avahi, lepilemur, greater dwarf lemur, and even aye-aye. Then there are the birds: more than 100 species with 36 endemic. And the reptiles. And the butterflies and other insects. Even if you saw no wildlife, there is enough variety in the vegetation and scenery, and enough pleasure in walking the well-constructed trails, to make a visit worthwhile. And – I nearly forgot – in the warm summer months you can swim in the cold, clear water of the Namorona while a malachite kingfisher darts overhead. Some negative things: the trails are steep and arduous, accommodation is (so far) fairly basic and often full, and few of the guides have reached the Périnet standard. It often rains, and there are leeches.

Getting there and away

In your own transport the journey is about three hours from Fianar or four hours from Ambositra. There are two roads leading there from RN7: a little-known short cut from Ambohimasoa (via Vohiparara) which is often closed, and an all-weather but potholed one which starts at Alakamisy Ambohimaha, about 26km north of Fianar.

In the past, public transport has been a problem since it is so often full. Desperate *vazahas* often ended up paying nearly twice the going rate for a taxi-brousse from Fianar. Now there is a twice-daily minibus from Fianar to Ranomafana, leaving at 04.30 and 07.30. It costs only 2,500Fmg for the three-to-four-hour journey. A similar service runs from Ambositra (at the PNR Garage). Minibuses leave for Ranomafana at 07.20, 16.50 and 19.35. They return from Ranomafana at about the same times.

Coming from Manakara or Mananjary you should be at the taxi-brousse station as early as possible in the morning.

Where to stay/eat

Hotel Domaine Nature A very well-managed, friendly and popular hotel with six bungalows overlooking the river, halfway between the village and the park. However, the price has doubled in a year, and is now a hefty 154,000Fmg per bungalow with shared facilities (though they do have hot water). Good food, including vegetarian, for 25,000Fmg. The location is beautiful but difficult for those without their own transport: 30 minutes' walk from Ranomafana village and an hour's walk (at least) to the park entrance. Bookings (Tana) through Destinations Mada; tel: 02 31072, fax: 31067.

Station Thermale de Ranomafana (10 rooms) This once elegant hotel has deteriorated steadily over the years. At least the prices have stayed the same: 37,500Fmg for a mouldy-smelling room with stinking shared toilets. But the restaurant is very good, with the crayfish recommended (15,000–20,000Fmg). Beer by the fire in the cold season or drinks on the patio can bring back images of its former glory.

Hotely Manja (10 bungalows) On the road to Ifanadiana (RN 26), five minutes' walk east along the river. Excellent value at 35,000Fmg per bungalow with shared facilities (flush toilets and cold showers but they'll bring you a bucket of hot water on request). 'One of those places that made me consider tearing up my return airline ticket and staying forever!' says reader Bradley Rink. The very good restaurant burnt to the ground early in 1999, but the resourceful owners are sure to have rebuilt it by the time you read this. From the hotel it's quite a long walk to the park entrance.

Le Gîte D'Etape du Parc (8 beds in two dormitories with a shared kitchen) Situated right by the park entrance, this new log cabin, run by the National Park Service, is the most convenient and best value of all. 25,000Fmg pp.

Hotely Ravenala Up the road from the Thermale towards the park entrance. Basic, funky, very friendly, beautiful views, good food.

Resto Bamboo Between the post office and the museum. Good food, convenient location.

Hery's Bar In the centre of town opposite the market. Cold beer, good atmosphere.

Camping

Camping is no longer permitted in the park, but there is a campsite at the park entrance: 5,000Fmg with your own tent, or you can rent a large one for 10,000Fmg a night and pay an additional 10,000Fmg per person. There are six covered tent sites, with open-sided A-frame thatched shelters giving shade as well as protection from the rain, and one centrally located covered picnic table. A tap provides drinking water and there is a bungalow with kitchen facilities.

This campsite was built by the villagers and the money goes directly to the community after being collected by village elders.

Ranomafana and conservation

The national park is one of the country's flagship conservation projects, with the involvement of the local communities playing an important role. The Peace Corps is very active here and Cornell University has an office here. They are establishing a tree nursery project and developing an intensive system of rice culture. Feedback Madagascar are also involved: this British charity has recently helped to rebuild the hospital in Ranomafana.

The Ranomafana National Park Project, set up by Dr Patricia Wright, is involved in a large range of activities, from education and health care for the villagers on the periphery of the park, and an ecological monitoring team which works at several sites within the park. The museum is also administered by the project.

Much scientific research takes place in the park and there have been some clashes between researchers and tourists. Tourists have been known to push researchers aside in order to get a better photo, and to encourage guides to shake or bang on trees to pursuade a lemur to move. It goes without saying that this is irresponsible behaviour and is counter-productive since some researchers withhold information on the whereabouts of the rarer lemurs for fear of being disturbed in their work.

Visiting the national park
Getting there from your hotel

The entrance to the park is some 6km west of the hotel Station Thermale, on the main road. A *navette* (minibus) leaves the museum at 07.00 and 16.30 to take visitors and guides up to the park entrance.

Permits and guides

Permits (50,000Fmg) are obtainable from the National Park Office. You are not allowed into the park without a guide. Most only speak French, but they usually know the animals' names in English. More work needs to be done to ensure that the guides do not try to get extra money out of tourists and that they are skilled at their job – the best ones, such as Loret and his wife Eliane, tend to work for researchers. Some guides are very good – and honest; others are good but manipulative. Recommended guides for independent travellers are Edmond (Edmond le petit) and Roland. Loret is an expert on birds and their calls. Fidi and his brother, Jean-Chry, are very knowledgeable, but work more effectively with groups.

There have been problems in the past with guides trying to persuade visitors to part with extra money. The official fees are now posted at the park entrance. Groups of more than six must have two guides. There is an additional charge for nocturnal visits. Try to check the posted rate before hiring a guide, and confirm your intentions with him or her before you set out. You may always add a small tip on top of the standard fee if you feel your guide has been exceptional (and please write to me with his/her name for recommendation in the next edition).

In the forest

There are standard routes in the forest, most taking a few hours. The paths are moderate to steep, and sometimes slippery. Your guide will assume that it is lemurs you have come to see; so, unless you stress that you are interested in other aspects such as botany, he will tend to concentrate on mammals and birds. You are most likely to see red-fronted brown lemurs and perhaps the rarer red-bellied lemur. The golden bamboo lemur is less easily seen. The most memorable of the easily found lemurs is a subspecies of the diademed sifaka, Milne-Edward's sifaka. Unlike the more familiar Verreaux's sifaka which is largely white, this is dark brown with cream-coloured sides. They wear snazzy coloured identification collars, much to the annoyance of tourists who want to take photos.

A delightful, if strenuous, walk is along the river to Cascade Riana. This has now been made a circular walk, and shouldn't be missed. Allow at least two hours for the round trip plus time to swim in the pool at the base of the falls.

Another trail system has been built on flatter ground at Vohiparara, near the boundary of the park 12km west of Ranomafana on the main road. It only takes about three hours to do all the trails here with a guide. 'Vohiparara is especially good for birders. Among many others you'll find the brown emutail, Madagascar snipe, Meller's duck and the extremely rare slender-billed flufftail. The song of the cryptic warbler was first recorded here in 1987.' (Derek Schuurman). According to Nick Garbutt this is also the best place for the rufous-headed ground-roller and yellow-bellied sunbird-asity.

A nocturnal visit to Belle Vue, a popular viewpoint, is recommended for the habituated mouse lemurs which come for bananas, along with greater dwarf lemurs and the civet or fanaloka which is attracted by meat. 'There is now one fat, female red-bellied lemur who hangs around Belle Vue for the tourist bananas instead of finding a group to integrate into. She gets beaten up by another pair of *rubiventer* regularly.' (F Kerridge). Nick Garbutt reports that an equally rotund male has now joined her. There are good photo opportunities, and the steep paths have recently been made safer, but even so negotiating them by torchlight can be tricky. There are other reasons to do the night walk. Sharon Giarratana writes: 'The best part of the night walk was the beautiful starry sky, the orchestral night sounds, and the rush of the river.'

Museum/gift shop

This is part of the Ranomafana National Park Project to improve visitor understanding of the area. The museum is still being added to, but there is now quite a comprehensive collection labelled in English and Malagasy.

Thermal baths

These are close to the Station Thermale hotel: turn left out of the door, down the steps and follow the path. It costs only 5,000Fmg for a wonderful warm swim in the pool or 2,500Fmg for a private bath ('in a grotty little room where the door doesn't close all the way'). You can even have a massage! Hours are normally

07.00–12.00, 14.00–17.00 but a recent (1999) traveller reported the pool only open on Friday and Saturday night. I hope this is a temporary measure. It is closed on Wednesdays for cleaning.

On Thursday to Saturday nights you can have a nocturnal swim with poolside beers and barbecue.

THE ROAD TO MANAKARA

The journey by car takes about five hours, passing several interesting small towns all of which have shops and *hotelys*. This road would repay a more leisurely journey on foot or by bike. Bjørn Donnis points out that after Irondo, as you near the coast, the landscape become bone-dry – quite unexpected in the 'eastern rainforest'. This is due (you guessed it) to deforestation and overgrazing.

Manakara and other eastern towns are covered in *Chapter 13*.

Continuing south on RN7

Coming from Fianar the landscape is a fine blend of vineyards and terraced rice paddies (the Betsileo are acknowledged masters of rice cultivation), then after 20km a giant rock formation seems almost to hold the road in its grasp. Its name is, appropriately, *Tanan'Andriamanitra*, or Hand of God. From here to Ihosy is arguably the finest mountain scenery in Madagascar. Reader Bishop Brock who cycled the route writes: 'Those three days were the most rewarding of my career as a bicycle tourist. I pity people who only pass through that magnificent landscape jammed inside a taxi-brousse.'

It is worth noting that taxi-brousses from the north continue south in the afternoon. This may be the best time to get a place if you're pushed for time.

AMBALAVAO

Some 56km southwest of Fianarantsoa is my favourite town, Ambalavao. RN7 does not pass through the attractive part of town, and I strongly urge people to stop here for a few hours. 'Nowhere in Madagascar have I seen a town so resembling a medieval European village as here. Although the main street was not narrow, the wooden balconies with their handsomely carved railings leaned into the street, giving them that look of a fairytale book tilt. The roofs were tiled, and, lending that final touch of authenticity, pails of water were emptied on to people passing too near the gutter.' (Tim Cross)

Another attraction is the market which is held on Wednesdays. Or maybe Thursdays. Jill and Charlie Hadfield visited the cattle market (which is reached by walking off the road to the right of the taxi-brousse stop).

Getting there and away

Although Ambalavao is on RN7, southward-bound travellers may prefer to make it an excursion from Fianarantsoa, since vehicles heading to Ihosy and beyond will have filled up with passengers in Fianar.

Where to stay

Hotel Snackbar Aux Bougainvillées BP 14, Ambalavao 308; tel 01 (!). Next to the Antaimoro paper shop. The only upmarket place in town. New. Reasonably priced at 55,000Fmg for rooms with shared facilities, and 76,000Fmg for bungalows. Good breakfasts.
Stop Hotel Five double rooms with communal WC and washing facilities. Basic but adequate. They expect you to eat at least one meal a day in the restaurant and to order it in advance.
La Notre Similar in price and quality to Stop Hotel. Cockroaches an added bonus.

Frances Kerridge adds: 'NB: in both these hotels the beds are small so you need to be good friends or Malagasy sized.'

Antaimoro paper

Ambalavao is the original home of the famous Malagasy 'Antaimoro' paper. This papyrus-type paper impregnated with dried flowers is sold throughout the island as wall-hangings and lampshades. The people in this area are Betsileo, but paper-making in the area copies the coastal Antaimoro tradition which goes back to the Muslim immigrants who wrote verses from the Koran on this paper. This Arabic script was the only form of writing known in Madagascar before the LMS developed a written Malagasy language nearly 500 years later using the Roman alphabet.

Antaimoro paper is traditionally made from the bark of the *avoha* tree from the eastern forests, but sisal paste is now sometimes used. After the bark is pounded and softened in water it is smoothed on to linen trays to dry in the sun. While still tacky, dried flowers are pressed into it and brushed over with a thin solution of the liquid bark to hold the flowers in place. The open-air 'factory' (more flowerbeds than buildings) where all this happens is to the left of the town (signposted) and is well worth a visit. It is fascinating to see the step-by-step process, and you get a good tour (in French with a smattering of English) from the manager. A shop sells the finished product at reasonable prices.

Beyond Ambalavao

The scenery beyond Ambalavao is marvellous. Huge granite domes of rock dominate the grassy plains. The most striking one, with twin rock towers, is called *Varavarana Ny Atsimo*, the 'Door to the South' by the pass of the same name. Beyond is the 'Bonnet de l'Evêque' (Bishop's Hat), and a huge lump of granite shaped like an upturned boat, with its side gouged out into an amphitheatre; streams run into the lush vegetation at its base. This dramatic landscape begs to be explored on foot, but keep away from the Bishop's Hat. It is a current and ancient burial site which the local people do not want disturbed; visitors would not be welcome.

THE CATTLE MARKET, AMBALAVAO
Jill and Charlie Hadfield
This area of Madagascar is notorious for cattle-rustling: from Ambositra down to Tuléar is bandit country and for the Bara tribe cattle rustling is a test of manhood... What seems to have started out as a sporting activity is now a very dangerous pastime. From time to time the government makes a half-hearted attempt to put a stop to *dahalo* but it's doomed to failure. Most of the gendarmerie are in the pay of the bandits...

So we were very interested in the goings on at the Ambalavao cattle market which takes place Wednesdays on top of a hill with a circular view for miles and miles of bare, rolling countryside, with flame trees and the granite-topped mountains in the distance. We got there early and for the next hour or so could see herds of zebu being driven in from all directions – some come from as far as Tuléar, two days' drive away. Betsileo farmers, wearing straw hats and with their blankets draped like ponchos, stood and chatted or strolled round eyeing up the cattle, and leather-jacketed smoothies strutted round importantly, prodding zebu with their sticks or pulling their tails. Calculations were done on pocket calculators.

A REVIVAL OF MADAGASCAR'S SILK INDUSTRY

Madagascar has a tradition of silk production going back, one could say, to the beginning of time: Andriamanitra is the name for both silk and God the creator. Before the introduction of the European silkworm and its mulberry tree food, the Malagasy used an endemic 'silkworm', *Antherina swaka*, which flourishes in the south where it feeds on tapia trees. The rather coarse silk was spun and woven into shrouds for the dead.

In 1996 a group of impoverished single mothers in Ambalavao approached the charity Feedback Madagascar to help them revive the silk industry. They had to start from scratch, breeding the silkworms and planting mulberry trees, and building the spinning wheels and looms to create the final product. With the help of Feedback, the town's mayor and the British Embassy, the project is now flourishing, employing a growing number of women each year. Each year 100 women are being trained.

Feedback Madagascar plan to open the silk weaving centre, which is about 3km south of Ambalavao, to visitors. Look out for the sign 'Ankazondandy'. At the time of writing they can only receive guests who are able to make a donation to the project, and if the very busy staff have time to receive them. Contact CCD Namana (Feedback's partner in the project) in Fianar, tel: 75 501.

You will notice that not only the scenery but the villages are different. These Bara houses are solidly constructed out of red earth (no elegant Merina pillars here) with small windows. Bunches of maize are often suspended from the roof to dry in the sun.

Shortly after Ambalavao you start to see your first tombs – some painted with scenes from the life of the deceased.

The next town of importance is Ihosy, described in *Chapter 10*.

Andringitra and Pic Boby

South of Ambalavao lies the Andringitra massif, crowned by Madagascar's second highest mountain, Pic Boby (2,658m). The area constitutes the Réserve Naturelle Intégrale de l'Andringitra, which is one of the WWF's 'priority pilot zones'. Concerned as much with the communities surrounding the reserve as the protected area itself, the aim is to look at sustainable development which will include ecotourism. Although formerly a Strict Nature Reserve, visitors are now allowed here; contact ANGAP for the latest details.

Olivier Langrand, who made several research expeditions to the area in the mid 1990s, reports many exciting discoveries: all three species of bamboo lemur are found there, and an isolated population of ring-tailed lemurs live high up on the mountain. These have adopted a completely different lifestyle and diet to their compatriots in the far south. A new warbler species has been discovered there... and so it goes on. A chilly place (it quite often snows) but fascinating to the serious naturalist.

ANDROY: LAND OF THORNS

Pays où l'on a soif
où souvent l'on a faim
où les hommes sont forts et fiers.

A land where one goes thirsty
Where one often goes hungry
Where the people are strong and proud

Part Three

The South

Sifaka

THE SOUTH

TOTAL ECLIPSE, JUNE 21 2001

In the late afternoon of June 21 2001, Madagascar, along with parts of southern Africa, will experience the first total eclipse of the new millennium. The path of totality runs through southern Madagascar between Toliara and Morondava, but neither of these towns will experience the total eclipse.

The best places to view this awesome spectacle will be Isalo National Park and Morombe. Adventurous travellers will watch the eclipse from a boat on the River Mangoky or in the little village of Betroka, south of Ihosy.

Writing this a few days after seeing the 1999 eclipse in Cornwall, I can't *wait* to see another under the cloudless skies of Madagascar's mid-winter day!

The South

10

OVERVIEW

This is the most exotic and the most famous part of Madagascar, the region of 'spiny desert' where weird cactus-like trees wave their thorny fingers in the sky, where pieces of 'elephant bird' shell may still be found, and where the Mahafaly tribe erect their intriguing and often entertaining *aloalo* stelae above the graves. Here also is the country's most popular nature reserve (Berenty), and one of the country's loveliest accessible beaches (Libanona). No wonder Taolagnaro (Fort Dauphin) features on almost all tour itineraries.

History

Europeans have been coming to this area for a long time. Perhaps the earliest were a group of 600 shipwrecked Portuguese sailors in 1527. Later, when sailors were deliberately landing in Madagascar during the days of the spice trade in the 16th and 17th centuries, St Augustine's Bay, south of the modern town of Toliara (Tuléar), became a favoured destination. They came for reprovisioning – Dutch and British – trading silver and beads for meat and fruit. One Englishman, Walter Hamond, was so overcome with the delights of Madagascar and the Malagasy, 'the happiest people in the world', that fired by his enthusiasm the British attempted to establish a colony at St Augustine's Bay. It was not a success. The original 140 settlers were soon whittled down to 60 through disease and murder by the local tribesmen who became less happy when they found their favourite beads were not available for trade and that these *vazahas* showed no sign of going away. The colonists left in 1646. Fifty years later St Augustine was a haven for pirates.

The people today

Several ethnic groups live in the south: the Vezo (fishermen) and Masikoro (pastoralists) are subclans of the Sakalava. The Mahafaly, Antanosy, Antandroy and Bara all have their regions in the interior. These southern Malagasy are tough, dark-skinned people, with African features, accustomed to the hardship of living in a region where rain seldom falls and finding water and grazing for their large herds of zebu is a constant challenge. The **Bara** are particularly known for their association with cattle – this warlike tribe resisted Merina rule and were never really subdued until French colonial times. Cattle rustling is a time-honoured custom – a Bara does not achieve manhood until he has stolen a few of his neighbour's cows (see also page 25).

In contrast to the highland people, who go in for second burial and whose tombs are the collective homes of ancestors, those in the south (with the exception of the Bara) commemorate the recently dead. There is more opportunity to be remembered as an individual here, and a **Mahafaly** or

Masikoro man who has lived eventfully, and died rich, will have the highlights of his life perpetuated in the form of wooden carvings (*aloalo*) and colourful paintings adorning his tomb. Formerly the *aloalo* were of more spiritual significance; but just as we, in our culture, have tended to bring an element of humour and realism into religion, so have the Malagasy. As John Mack says (in *Island of Ancestors*), 'Aloalo have become obituary announcements when formerly they were notices of rebirth'.

Antandroy tombs may be equally colourful. They are large and rectangular (the more important the person the bigger his tomb) and, like those of the Mahafaly, topped with zebu skulls left over from the funeral feast. A very rich man may have over 100 skulls on his grave. They usually have 'male and female' standing stones (or, in modern tombs, cement towers) at each side. Modern tombs may be brightly painted with geometric patterns or imaginative paintings (unlike those of the Mahafaly these do not represent scenes from the life of the deceased).

In Antandroy country, burial sometimes takes place several months after the day of death, which will be commemorated by the sacrifice of cattle and ritual mourning or wailing. A few days later the body is placed in the coffin – and more zebu are sacrificed. Meanwhile finishing touches will be made to the tomb, before the internment ceremony which takes place over two days or more. The tomb is finally filled in with stones, and topped with the horns of the sacrificed zebu. Then the house of the deceased is burnt to the ground. The burial ceremonies over, the family will not go near the tomb again.

The **Antanosy** have upright stones, cement obelisks, or beautifully carved wooden memorials. These, however, are not over the graves themselves but in a sacred and secret place elsewhere.

Getting around

Road travel in the south can be a challenging affair, but the roads are being improved, and RN7 to Toliara (Tuléar) is now paved. Apart from this and the road between Taolagnaro (Fort Dauphin) and Ambovombe, the 'roads' that link other important towns are terrible, so most people prefer to fly. In addition to the regular flights to the main towns of Taolagnaro and Toliara there are occasional small planes to Ampanihy, Bekily and Betioky as well as Ihosy. Check the current schedule with Air Mad.

IHOSY

Pronounced 'Ee-oosh', this small town is the capital of the Bara tribe. It is a medium-sized town which has, among other things, a BTM bank.

Ihosy is about five hours from Fianar by taxi-brousse and lies at the junction for Toliara and Taolagnaro. The road to the former is good; to the latter, bad. A road also runs from Ihosy to Farafangana, on the east coast. This is still notorious for bandits, although it has become a popular route for overlanders. Drivers expecting to refuel at Ihosy, though, should be warned that they may be disappointed.

Where to stay/eat

Zaha Motel BP 67; tel: 740 83. Pleasant, comfortable bungalows, cold water (hot if you ask them to turn on the gas heater). Bungalows 62,000Fmg, breakfast 10,000Fmg, dinner approximately 25,000Fmg.

There is also the poor-value **Hotel Relais-Bara**; no hot water but a pleasant atmosphere. A better bet may be the **Hotel Ravaka**. For meals there is a nice little square of open-sided *hotelys* serving good Malagasy food. The **Hotely Dasimo** is recommended for its excellent *tsaramasy* (rice with beans and pork).

FROM IHOSY TO TAOLAGNARO (FORT DAUPHIN)

RN13 is in very poor condition. Adventurous travellers will enjoy the consequent lack of tourist development but don't underestimate the time it takes to travel even short distances.

The first town is **Betroka**, a friendly little place with a basic hotel and restaurant, Des Bons Amis, with a loo-shed outside. If you don't want to eat in the hotel there are plenty of *hotelys*. Next comes **Beraketa** which has the even more down-to-earth Herilaza Hotel. This seems to be the last accommodation (except in private houses) before Ambovombe and the paved road to Taolagnaro.

FROM IHOSY TO TOLIARA (TULEAR)

After leaving Ihosy, RN7 takes you for two hours across the Horombe Plateau, grasslands dotted with termite hills.

As you approach Ranohira, *Medemia* palms enliven the monotonous scenery. Henk Beentje of Kew Gardens writes: 'The palms are properly called *Bismarckia*, but the French didn't like the most common palm in one of their colonies to be called after a German so changed the name, quite illegally according to the Code of Botanical Nomenclature!'

RANOHIRA AND ISALO NATIONAL PARK

The small town of Ranohira lies 97km south of Ihosy and has sprung into prominence as the base for visiting the now popular Isalo National Park. However, the whole area, including the wonderful national park, is threatened by the 1998 discovery of sapphires in the area. 'It has the feel of the Wild West as sapphires have been discovered close by, and the place is now full of buyers from the Far East who go around with briefcases stacked with money, and the prospectors who dress like small-time gangsters with their wide-brimmed hats, dark glasses and money belts.' (Rupert Parker). Most accommodation in the town is basic and overpriced, and the shanty town which has sprung up along RN7 is an eyesore. 'There are huts selling food, spades, haircuts, and car repairs. There are even three night clubs, but no water, electricity or sanitation – a cholera outbreak is waiting to happen.' (Carol Grevatt). Apart from inflating prices in the area, it would be naive to think that such intense commercial activity will not affect the national park. We can only hope for the best.

Getting there and away

Getting to Ranohira is usually no problem: about two hours from Ihosy by taxi-brousse. If leaving from Toliara note that the taxi-brousses and buses depart early in the morning; it is best to book your seat the night before. Leaving Ranohira has been a problem in the past but there seems to be far more transport these days.

If time is short it's worth considering hiring a car and driver in Toliara.

Where to stay
Category A

Relais de la Reine This lovely French-run hotel is not in Ranohira but at Soarano, 9km further south, on the edge of the park. It has been thoughtfully designed to blend as much as possible into the surrounding landscape. There are blocks of six rooms grouped round a courtyard, and solar panels provide hot water. The water is drawn from their own stream. Fans cool the rooms in the hot season and the Golombier family are reported to be superb hosts. A twin-bedded room with bathroom costs 360Ff; breakfast 15Ff; dinner: 58,000Fmg. Bookings must be made through agencies in Tana, but the hotel will do meals (including breakfast) for non-residents anxious to take a look at what is probably Madagascar's best hotel (but you do need your own transport).

Hotel Orchidée d'Isalo The once good rooms have deteriorated and the place is overrun with sapphire dealers. However, it does have hot water and an extension is being built. Ensuite double: 60,000–80,000Fmg. Good restaurant.

Category C

Hotel les Joyeux Lémuriens The most popular backpacker hotel in Ranohira, but the rooms are small and noisy and the toilets have seen better days. Well run and friendly, however. 35,000–50,000Fmg; set menu 15,000Fmg.

Hotel Berny In the centre of town, next to the ANGAP office. An assortment of rooms round a courtyard. Basic; 25,000–38,000Fmg.

Isalo Ranch BP 3 313. A new group of eight bungalows 5km south of Ranohira. Basic facilities with communal (cold) showers, no electricity, but clean and comfortable, German-owned, and very good value at 30,000Fmg per bungalow. The meals are good too (18,000Fmg).

Hotel Kanto A nice *hotely* on the road south, serving good omelettes, *vary sosoa* (rice pudding), and *mofo boule* (slightly sweet bread rolls).

Camping

There appear to be two campsites: the Oasis, administered by Hotel Berny, and an area by the new Interpretation Centre. There is a guardian taking care of the latter (no facilities). A woman reader warns: 'Shut tent firmly against guardian who tends to leer and beware usual demands for money, clothes, gifts etc.' Follow the path for a couple of hundred metres along the river to find a small, but deep pool for bathing.

Isalo National Park

The combination of sandstone rocks (cut by deep canyons and eroded into weird shapes), rare endemic plants and dry weather (between June and August rain is almost unknown), makes this park particularly rewarding. For botanists there is *Pachypodium rosulatum* or elephant's foot – a bulbous rock-clinging plant – and a native species of aloe, *Aloe isaloensis*; and for lemur-lovers there may be sifakas, brown lemurs and ringtails. 'Isalo is fantastic! It is not just the abstract sculpturing and colours of the eroded terrain or the sweeping panoramas which so impressed, but also the absolute and enveloping silence. No birds, insects or other animals, no wind, no rumbling of distant traffic and no other people,' wrote a reader some years ago. These days you have to get off the beaten track to escape from other visitors but... it's a big area.

Isalo is also sacred to the Bara tribe. For hundreds of years the Bara have used caves in the canyon walls as burial sites. There is one for a king in Canyon des Singes, high up in the cliff wall, but there are others scattered everywhere. Ask your guide about this but it is wise not to push the issue. Their beliefs and traditions need to be preserved. 'On several occasions our guide said it was *fady* to go to such a place. Insisting on going will only lead to a breakdown between the tourist and the local person.' (Maggie Rush)

Tourists who do not wish to hike (and this should not be undertaken lightly – it can be very hot) or to pay the park fee have various options. Simply driving past the sandstone formations which can be seen from the road is exciting enough, and you can visit the Oasis, an idyllic palm-shaded grotto. The track leading here is about 10km south of Ranohira, on the left just before a 'milestone' ('Tulear 230 km'). There are *Pachypodium rosulatum* nearby, a waterfall and a pool.

Another popular visit – perhaps too popular at times – is to the Fenêtre, a natural rock formation providing a window to the setting sun. Walk behind the rocks for the proper Isalo feeling of space and tranquillity.

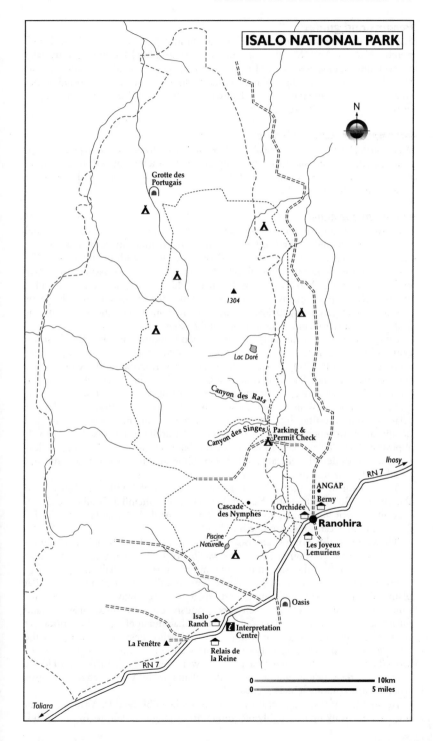

Permits and guides

For an excursion in the park you will need a permit (50,000Fmg) which must be purchased at the ANGAP office in Ranohira, next to Hotel Berny. You must take an accredited guide with you (Justin is strongly recommended by one reader, though he speaks no English). Charges (standard for most parks) are posted on the wall of the office: 40,000Fmg for a half day, 60,000Fmg full day. Schematic maps of the park are available from ANGAP.

Isalo Interpretation Centre

Well worth a visit to learn more about the people who live around the park, as well as the wildlife in national park itself. Apparently, to reach manhood the Bara have not only to steal some cattle, but also to pass a test in epizooty, or the study of parasites and disease in zebu!

Hiking in the park

The two most popular hiking excursions are to the Piscine Naturelle, a natural swimming pool; and to the Canyon des Singes (sometimes more correctly called Canyon des Makis) and its neighbour, Canyon des Rats. With the help of a 4WD vehicle you can do both of these in one day, but a circular tour lasting three days is more rewarding. Another canyon has been added: Namaza. Frances Kerridge warns: 'At one point it involves a choice of inching along a narrow ledge or swimming along a channel below and being hauled out at the other end.' But this is also one of its attractions: there are few other tourists.

Budget travellers with only a day in hand should opt for the **Piscine Naturelle**. It is a shorter distance to walk (6km/2hrs each way); and it provides the best viewpoints, *Pachypodium rosalatum* and *Aloe isaloensis*, and a wonderfully cool swim at the end. The increasing popularity of Isalo, however, means that you are unlikely to be alone in this idyllic spot. Starting from Ranohira (a guide is mandatory) it takes about two hours to walk to the pool. The first part is flat and relatively uninteresting, but once you reach the massif the views, colours and botany are pure enchantment. 'The Piscine Naturelle is the essential Isalo. It appears to have been taken right out of the book of Genesis. The crystal clear water is a wonderful sight after all that walking and the swim makes the toil worthwhile.' (Will Pepper)

Those with a 4WD vehicle can drive along a track (with one ford) from Ranohira for 30 minutes to the base of the rocks where the hiking trail starts. From there it is about 90 minutes to the pool. The Relais de la Reine has vehicles for guests, and they can sometimes be hired in Ranohira.

The **Canyon des Singes** can also be reached directly from Ranohira, either on foot (9km/3hrs each way) or part of the way by 4WD. In the dry season a vehicle can take you most of the way; in the rainy months it is more challenging.

Hikers make the trek direct from the Ranohira church, striding across a flat plain with the Canyons des Singes and des Rats tantalisingly in view the whole time. The hot sun should be taken very seriously: carry two litres of water (and purifying tablets for the canyon water), wear a hat and apply liberal quantities of sunscreen. The contrast between the space and yellowness of the plain and the ferny green of the canyon makes the effort well worthwhile; though when we arrived, sweat-soaked, at the first pool we were taken aback to find an elderly couple and their grandchild sitting in deckchairs at the water's edge. That was when I learned about vehicle access.

At the time of writing (1999) the canyon has been blocked by a landslide, but normally the walk up it is highly recommended, though the lemurs from which it gets its name are understandably shy (they are still hunted, despite the national park). A path goes over rocks and along the edge of the tumbling river; and there are pools into which you can fling yourself at intervals, and, at the top, a small waterfall under which to have a shower. The sheer rocks hung with luxuriant ferns broaden out to provide views of the bare mountain behind, and trees and palms provide shade for a picnic.

For the real Isalo experience you should trek for a few days. The combined Piscine/Canyon des Singes circuit is the most popular and usually done in three days. The first day to the campsite at the swimming pool is only two or three hours, then five or six rugged hours the next day to the canyon. It is then a three-hour walk back to Ranohira.

The less visited parts of the park are even more rewarding. Bishop Brock took a five-day hike. 'The forest of Sakamolia... is one of the most beautiful places I have ever camped in, perhaps not in absolute beauty but in contrasts. In the middle of the dry, grassy plain, surrounded on two sides by massive rock walls, a small crystal-clear river runs over a clean, sandy bottom supporting a 20-metre-wide luxuriant green-belt. Paradise!'

Warnings

Hiking Isalo is very hot work; bring a minimum of equipment (but remember it gets very cold at night between May and August) or hire porters. Bring plenty of drinking water, even in the rainy season. There have been reports of robberies from tents. This is a serious problem since it is impossible to protect yourself or your possessions. Discuss the matter with your guide and suggest he/she stays to guard the tent if camping in well-frequented places.

The popularity of the park is bringing its own problems. Under every stone lurks a piece of toilet paper. Bring matches and burn yours.

CONTINUING SOUTH

The drive from Isalo to Toliara takes a minimum of four hours. After you pass the landscape scars and shanty town of the sapphire mine, the rugged mountains give way to grasslands, and following the rains there are many flowers – the large white *Crinum firmifolium* and the Madagascar periwinkle – but in the dry season it's quite monotonous. It is the people aspect that makes this final stretch so rewarding. First there are some charming villages – Bara, Mahafaly and Antandroy – and, once you pass Sakaraha, there are some wonderful tombs with *aloalo* near the road. As you get closer to Toliara you'll see your first baobabs and pass through a cotton-growing region. Look out for the enormous nests of hammerkop birds in roadside trees.

Twenty-five kilometres northeast of Sakaraha is Zombitse National Park which is popular with birders. See *Excursions*, page 200. About half an hour beyond **Sakaraha** (Hotel Eden – basic) you will pass the first Mahafaly tombs on your right. There are groups of tombs all the way into Toliara, and they merit several stops (the group nearest Toliara are described under *Excursions*).

About two hours beyond Sakaraha is the small village of **Andranovory** which has a colourful Sunday market. Another hour and Toliara's table mountain, La Table, comes into view on the right; half an hour later you pass the airport and head for the town.

TOLIARA (TULEAR)

The pronunciation of the French, Tuléar, and the Malagasy names is the same: 'Toolee-ar'. Toliara's history is centred on St Augustine's Bay, described at the

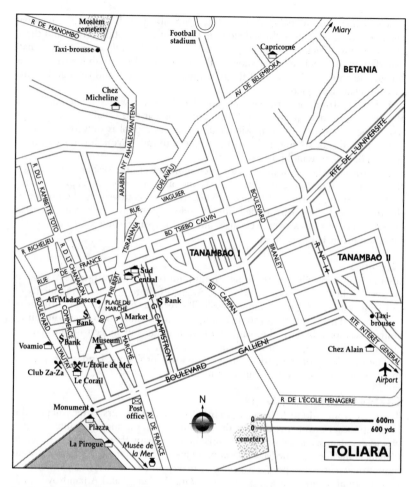

beginning of this chapter, although the name of the town is thought to derive from an encounter with one of those early sailors who asked a local inhabitant where he might moor his boat. The Malagasy replied: *Toly eroa*, 'Mooring down there'. The town itself is relatively modern – 1895 – and was designed by an uninspired French architect. His tree planting was more successfully aesthetic, and the shady tamarind trees, *kily*, give welcome respite from the blazing sun.

There are three good reasons to visit Toliara: the rich marine life with excellent snorkelling and diving, the Mahafaly and Masikoro tombs and a museum which puts it all in context, and the remarkable spiny bush in places north and south of the town.

The beaches north and south of the town have fine white sand, and this whole area is gradually opening up to tourism (fortunately the poor or non-existent roads are an effective deterrent to overdevelopment). Beyond the sandy beaches is an extensive coral reef but this is too far from shore to swim out to – a pirogue (for hire at the beach hotels) is necessary. Toliara itself, regrettably, has no beach, just mangroves and mud flats.

The telephone area code for Toliara is 94.

Warnings
In the cool season (May to October) the nights in Toliara are very cold. The cheaper hotels rarely supply enough blankets. And in the hot season (November to April) everything closes for siesta between 13.00 and 15.00.

Getting there and away
By road
Route Nationale 7 (RN7) is now a well-used road served by a variety of quite comfortable vehicles. There are two special tourist buses. One, operated by Mad Voyages (tel: 94 42 729), leaves Tana on Tuesdays, returning from Toliara on Thursdays at 07.00. The fare 200,000Fmg. The other is the Jumbobus, operated by Montana Voyage in Tana (tel: 25 861). The bus leaves Muraille de Chine (near the station) every Tuesday at 07.30, and makes several stops so you don't have to go all the way to Toliara. Tana to Toliara costs 150,000Fmg, to Isalo 110,000Fmg, and to Fianar 75,000Fmg.

By air
There are daily flights from Tana and Taolagnaro, but in the high season these tend to be fully booked. However, it's always worth going to the airport whatever they say in the office.

A taxi from the airport into town costs 10,000Fmg.

Vehicle hire
Car hire
Joshua Calixte Tel: 427 47
New Horizon Tel/fax: 427 73

Motorbike hire
Trajectoire BP 283, Toliara 601; tel/fax: 433 00.

Where to stay in town
Most visitors spending any time in the Toliara area stay at the beach resorts (see pages 201 to 203) but there are some good-value hotels in or near the town.

Category A
Hotel Capricorne BP 158; tel: 431 12/426 20; fax: 413 20. About 2km from the town centre (Betania) on RN7. Considered the best of the Toliara hotels. It has a lovely garden and is well run with excellent food and air-conditioning. 250Ff for a double room.

Hotel Plazza BP 486; tel: 419 00–2; fax: 419 03. Central, facing the ocean – or, to be more accurate, the mud flats where local people come to relieve themselves ('when they promised us a *vue de la mer* it should have been a *vue de la merde*'). Well run by the French owners, with hot water, all facilities and a nice garden. English spoken. 100,000Fmg single/double room, 120,000Fmg with air conditioning. Good restaurant: breakfast 15,000Fmg, dinner 40,000Fmg. Visa credit cards accepted.

Category B
Chez Alain BP 89; tel: 415 27; fax: 423 79. One of the most popular *vazaha* hotels (bungalows) in Madagascar. Well run, friendly, good food. 70,000Fmg with hot water (cheaper rooms available with cold water); 10,000Fmg for breakfast. Mountain bikes available for hire.

Chez Sol A nice Belgian-owned hotel near Chez Alain. Large quiet rooms with en-suite facilities. 55,000–70,000Fmg. Restaurant.

L'Hotel Analamanga Tel/fax: 415 47. Located on the outskirts of Toliara as you arrive on RN7. Five neat, small bungalows on stilts; clean communal bathrooms. 'Very friendly family business, father and daughters speak good French, and some English. Good food. Nice quiet setting out of town, cool under trees, but within easy walking distance. (Jim Bond)

Hotel Sud Place de la République; tel: 415 89. Reasonably priced and centrally located; double rooms with a basin, shower, WC and hot water.

Category C

Hotel Central Tel: 428 80 Bang in the centre of town, so convenient for the market and museum. Large, but noisy rooms. Good value at about 60,000Fmg.

Hotel Tropical Near the Hotel Central, with similar prices and facilities.

Chez Micheline Rue 18, Anketa; tel: 415 86. Micheline is a warm, friendly woman (and a good cook) beloved by the *vazahas* who have written recommending her hotel. It is located five minutes' walk (north) from the centre of town, near the *gare routière* for Ifaty. About 30,000Fmg. Micheline has opened a second hotel in Ifaty.

Le Corail Bungalows near the restaurant L'Etoile de Mer. Clean but very hot during the day (or cold at night, depending on the season) because of the tin roofs. 45,000Fmg. 'A funky, friendly place, very Malagasy, with a lovely terrace restaurant from which to have a beer and watch the sunset.' (S Giarratana)

La Pirogue Tel: 415 37. A two-person bungalow costs 38,000–50,000Fmg depending on the state of dilapidation. Clean, with en-suite WC and (cold) shower. Some have hot water. Noisy.

Hotel Voamio Primitive bungalows next door to the Za Za nightclub. 22,500–32,500Fmg. Fine if you are broke and also deaf.

Relais Mireille Opposite the taxi-brousse station; OK if you're desperate: 'Serves as a useful brothel and bred the biggest cockroaches we've ever seen!'

Auberge de la Table Though well away from the centre of town this is by far the best place to stay if you are a birder or botanist. Or if you just want a couple of days' rest. Part of the Arboretum d'Antsakay (see page 200), the five simple bungalows cost 45,000Fmg (with showers). The food is marvellous and the chance to wander in the arboretum in the cool, early morning hours makes this a must for plant or bird fanatics.

Where to eat

An excellent meal (seafood) can be had in an unpretentious wooden building on the seafront, L'Etoile de Mer, between the Plazza Hotel and the Voamio. Nearby is the Club Za Za (good fish) and Corail (excellent pizza and other dishes, and a pleasant bar), both recommended. According to most people the best food in town is at Chez Alain, located on the road to the airport, and Chez Micheline, but L'Etoile de Mer has maintained its high standards since I first visited Toliara in 1982, hence its success.

Good places for snacks are the three rival Salons de Thé, situated in a row next to each other, opposite the Hotel Central. They are Le Gourmet, Glace d'As (popularly known as 'frozen arse') and Le Maharaja.

Nightlife

'The Za Za Club has a following across the world. You have not been to Tuléar unless you have been to Za Za!' So wrote a reader a decade ago, and the Za Za still has many fans plus a few doubters: '*What* a disappointment! Full of old *vazaha* men buying cokes for their beautiful, scantily-dressed Malagasy "girl friends". And the music was poor.' (F Kerridge)

Watersports
Diving and snorkelling
For many people the main reason to visit Toliara is for the coral reefs, and the WWF recognises the importance of these in developing ecotourism in the area and a conservation programme is under way, centred at the University of Toliara. The goal of the project is 'to ensure that the coral reefs and coastal zone are effectively conserved through the establishment of a multiple-use marine park and sustainable economic development'. Certainly there is potential for marine ecotourism, although dead or dying coral is disturbingly evident on the reefs.

Serious underwater buffs should head for Nosy Ve and Nosy Satrana for snorkelling and Ifaty for scuba-diving. The main diving centres (all attached to hotels) are: Bamboo Club, Ifaty; Dunes Hotel, Ifaty; Deep Sea Club, Hotel Capricorne; Club Nautique, Hotel Lakana Vezo, Ifaty; La Mangrove, St Augustine; Safari Vezo, Anakao.

Sailing
Location Catamaran (tel: 433 17) organise catamaran trips to the Barren Islands, Belo Sur Mer, Andavadoka, Ifaty, Anakao and Itampolo.

Medical clinic
The Clinique Saint-Luc (tel: 421 76) is run by Dr Noel Rakotomavo who speaks excellent English. The profits from his paying beds go towards providing free treatment for the poor.

Shopping
L'Artisan Galerie d'Art   Tel/fax: 414 42. Run by Françoise and Philippe Schroeder; a good selection of high quality handicrafts.

SIGHTSEEING AND EXCURSIONS
Transport
For short trips there's a fixed taxi tariff in town of 3,000Fmg and *pousse-pousses* are available everywhere (bargain hard and have the agreed money ready. Change will not be given). For an efficient day's sightseeing it's probably worth hiring a taxi at a cost of around 75,000Fmg per person.

In town
Toliara has more 'official' sightseeing than most Malagasy towns. Some places are worth the trip, others are not. In town the most interesting place to visit is the small **museum** on Bd Philbert Tsiranana, run by the University of Toliara. The entry fee is 5,000Fmg. There are some remarkable exhibits, including a Mikea mask (genuine masks are rare in Madagascar) with real human teeth. These are well-displayed and labelled in Malagasy and French, and include some Sakalava erotic tomb sculptures. Marine enthusiasts should visit the **Musée de la Mer**, also run by the university, on Route de la Porte (tel: 41 612). The main attraction here is a coelacanth – the only one now on view in Madagascar. The **market** is lively and interesting.This is one of the best places in all of Madagascar for *lambas*. You can also find the mohair rugs that are made in Ampanihy, a terrific selection of herbal remedies (*fanafody*), and a wide range of fruit.

Tombs
The most spectacular tombs within easy reach of the town are those of the Masikoro, a sub-division of the Sakalava. This small tribe is probably of African

origin, and there is speculation that the name comes from *mashokora* which, in parts of Tanzania, means scrub forest. There are also Mahafaly tombs in the area.

The tombs are off RN7 a little over an hour from Toliara, and are clearly visible on the right. There are several large, rectangular tombs, flamboyantly painted with scenes from the distinguished military life of the deceased, with a few mermaids and Rambos thrown in for good measure.

Another tomb, on the outskirts of town beyond the university, is **King Baba's Tomb**. This is set in a grove of Didierea trees and is interesting more for the somewhat bizarre funerary objects (an urn and a huge, cracked bell) displayed there and its spiritual significance to the local people (you may only approach barefoot) than for any aesthetic value. This King Baba, who seems to have died about 100 years ago, was presumably a descendant of one of the Masikoro kings of Baba mentioned in British naval accounts of the 18th century. These kings used to trade with English ships calling at St Augustine's Bay and gave their family and courtiers English names such as the Prince of Wales and the Duke of Cumberland. On the way to King Baba's Tomb you may visit a little fenced-off park of banyan trees, all descending from one 'parent'. This is known as 'the sacred grove' and in theory would be a place for peaceful contemplation, but the hordes of tourist-aware children are a deterrent.

Day excursions from Toliara
Tour operators
Most excursions can be made by taxi but for something more ambitious where a guide is advisable the following tour operators are recommended.

Madagascar Airtours Office in the grounds of the Plazza Hotel.
Air Fort Services BP 1029; tel/fax: 426 84.
Hotel Capricorne Many excellent tours are run by this hotel.

Arboretum d'Antsakay
This botanical garden of rare southwestern flora makes an excellent day trip from Toliara. It costs 25,000Fmg for a day visit with the option of a delicious lunch based on the goat's cheese made there. Simple accommodation is available at the Auberge de la Table (see page 198) and there is a small shop selling erotic (or downright pornographic) wood carvings. The owners, Hermann and Simone Pétignat, are very hospitable. He is a Swiss-born botanist and passionate about conserving the area's rare plant species.

The turn-off to the hotel/arboretum is on the right, just north of the track to La Mangrove hotel and St Augustine on RN7. It is clearly signposted. A taxi here costs about 18,000Fmg. A trained guide takes you on a two-hour tour of the 'improved' area (7ha) of the 50ha arboretum. Here you will see the rare plants nurtured by M Pétignat, including 100 species of euphorbia and 60 species of kalenchoe. You will also see an abundance of birds and reptiles: 'We followed a running coua about for 15 minutes while it noshed on locusts, and saw a button quail nest on one of the flowerbeds. And we watched a large snake catch a frog.' (Derek Schuurman)

Try to arrive as early as possible in the morning to miss the heat of the day. Better still, stay overnight. There is no phone but messages can be sent by email: arbo.mada@usa.net.

Zombitse National Park
This pocket of forest (21,500ha) straddling RN7 some 25km northeast of Sakaraha is of major importance to birdwatchers. Zombitse and the neighbouring forest of Vohibasia are now protected areas under Madagascar's Environmental Action Plan with a low-involvement programme based on community participation. The

forests are an important example of a boundary zone between the western and southern domains of vegetation and so have a high level of biodiversity. Zombitse offers the chance to glimpse one of Madagascar's rarest endemics, Appert's greenbul, which is confined to this forest. Many other species may be seen. There are no official paths, only zebu trails, and tree felling in this vulnerable area is sadly evident. Nevertheless, a visit here is most rewarding. We were there at the worst possible time of day, noon, yet the forest was alive with birds and had we had more time I am sure we would have seen many species. This is also a wonderful place for invertebrates, particularly butterflies.

It takes two to three hours to reach Zombitse from Toliara, so serious birdwatchers should leave as early as possible in the morning. You should call in at the WWF office in Sakaraha to ask about permits and guides, or buy a permit in Tana.

BEACH RESORTS NORTH OF TOLIARA

Ifaty has long been established as Toliara's main beach resort, but hotels are now being built on beach areas further north.

Ifaty

Ifaty offers sand, sea and snorkelling, and has several sets of beach bungalows. The village lies only 27km north of Toliara, but the road is terrible so it can take as much as three hours by taxi-brousse. 'The villagers sometimes add to the difficulty by putting extra sand on the road, then "rescue" you and expect a tip' (Clare Hermans). In 1999 a bridge was washed away in flash floods and the only access to Ifaty was by sea.

Ifaty is a popular place for birdwatchers, having a good intact area of spiny forest where some of the southern endemics can be seen. The best bird-finders for the area, Masindraka and his son Mosa, can be contacted at the Hotel Mora Mora. There are other so-called guides: 'We paid 10,000Fmg for a "guide" who knew nothing except the way there. Numerous piles of wood, felled baobabs and new pirogues. Visit while there's still some forest left!' (F Kerridge)

Note: there are no money changing facilities in Ifaty.

Where to stay/eat
Category A
Ambala Beach Hotel A new hotel (being completed in 1999) south of Luakana Vezo, which promises to be the best hotel in Ifaty and one of the most luxurious in Madagascar. No further details at the time of writing.

Hotel Lakana Vezo c/o Capricorne, Ifaty, BP 158; tel: 462 20. One of the best hotels in Ifaty; one hour's walk south of the Dunes hotel. Ten bungalows; 310Ff per bungalow. The Club Nautique is run very professionally by Denis and Natalie Guillamot, with a wide variety of activities available, though snorkelling and scuba-diving are favourites. The hotel also offers powerboat excursions to Nosy Ve and Anakao.

Category B
Mora Mora BP 41; tel: 410 16. The longest-established of Ifaty's beach resorts. On the plus side are the two bird experts, Masindraka and his son Mosa, who will locate all the area's 'specials'. On the minus side are the two ringtailed lemurs confined in a small cage. If you are not a birder there are better places. 140,000Fmg per bungalow; meals 30,000Fmg.

Hotel/Club Bamboo BP 47; tel: 427 17. Five minutes' walk north of Mora Mora, so convenient for the spiny forest. French run, with swimming pool (much appreciated at low tide when it is impractical to swim in the sea) and table tennis; 160Ff/140,000Fmg per bungalow – good value, but very hot in summer. There's a good diving club: 40,000Fmg

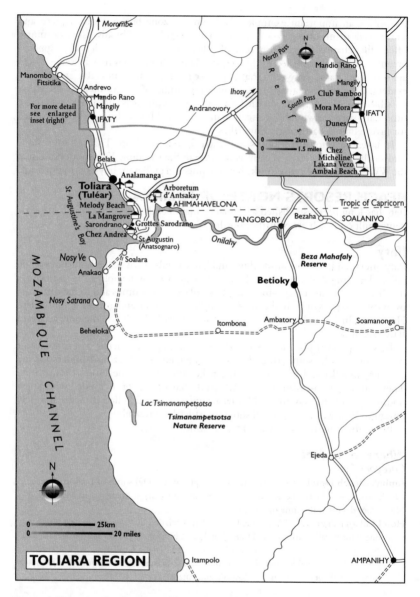

for snorkelling trips. For bookings enquire at the Bamboo shop opposite the Hotel Central in town. There are varying levels of enthusiasm from readers for the meals and service. It seems that if you are French you will get a warm welcome, but English-speaking vazahas may be ignored. A couple who loved it are Harriet and Mike Kendrick: 'Worth staying there just to travel in their courtesy bus – which resembled an old Mr Whippy van, circa 1950, complete with three-tone horn and one-eyed driver who cooked his sweet potatotoes on the engine! He was a star!'

Vovotely Tel: 429 14. A new set of 12 bungalows between Mora Mora and the Dunes Hotel which is receiving rave reviews from independent travellers (it does not take groups). 'We thought this place had the best food in Ifaty – great steaks and wonderful pizzas' (FK). 'A super little establishment; it's about time Ifaty had something like this.' (JM)

Dunes Hotel BP 285; tel: 428 85. A few kilometres south of Mora Mora, this is a set of concrete bungalows with two adjoining bedrooms: 62 rooms in all. Recent reports suggest that this once good hotel is becoming rather run-down, and the meals are poor. However, it is recommended for water sports. 340Ff/150,000Fmg per bungalow; breakfast 18,000Fmg. Transport from Toliara arranged.

Category C

Chez Micheline About 20 minutes' walk north of the Bamboo, this is the most popular backpacker place in Ifaty. Mme Micheline is well-known for her cooking and local knowledge. A few basic bungalows (shared cold shower and WC, no electricity). About 45,000Fmg full board per person. Excellent vegetarian meals served on request. Hair-plaiting and massage available from local villagers, snorkelling trips 15,000Fmg.

Deck's Down the beach from the Bamboo Club. 'Reggae atmosphere for 10,000Fmg per room (1996 price) with mozzies.' (Jim Bond)

Mangily

Recommended as being cheaper and more friendly than Ifaty, this small village to its north is easily reached by taxi-brousse from Toliara (6,000Fmg). There are a few basic beach hotels, a couple of bars and a shop (Les Arbres) near the beach.

Where to stay/eat

Chez Deka Good, basic and right on the beach; 15,000Fmg.

Chez Thomas 'Another cheap, basic, friendly place. Relaxed atmosphere, there is nothing Thomas and family would not do to make you feel welcome; tasty food (caters for vegetarians). Very basic facilities, exposed washing/toilet area, pigs wandering around, but perfectly comfortable. 15,000Fmg. Most taxi-brousse drivers will drop you right at the gate if you ask.' (Anna Dudziec)

Chez Alex The only place to go in the evening, apart from the smaller, darker, quieter and emptier Rambo. 'Lots of drinking and music in the evening; usually taped music but occasionally live *tsapiky* with everyone getting very drunk and dancing shamelessly!' (A D)

Mandio Rano

Jim Bond recommends **Chez Bernard** at this village 35km north of Toliara. 'Ideal for the discerning independent traveller – no tour groups. Five peaceful, comfortable bungalows near a quiet stretch of beach. Not far to walk to PK32 (the road). Excellent food, huge portions. Rustic douche facilities. No phone, so pot luck off the taxi-brousse. Bernard Forgeau is a very pleasant and interesting Breton bush-hand and explorer. BP 283, Toliara 601.'

CONTINUING NORTH TO MOROMBE AND MORONDAVA

A sandy track runs from the Mora Mora (Ifaty) roadhead (inland) to Morombe. This road is used mostly by cotton trucks; the only time it may be impassable is after rain in February. A taxi-brousse to Morombe leaves Toliara or Ifaty twice a week and takes about 22 hours. If you want to continue to Morondava, there is a choice of sea (by pirogue, risky) or road. A vehicle known as the 'Bon Bon Caramel' leaves Toliara at 06.00 on Thursdays, spending the night at Manja (good food and bungalows) and arriving in Morondava Friday evening. For a full description of this glorious Mercedes truck and its crew, see the Morondava section on page 347.

An easier overland option is to take the transport offered by Lakana Vezo to service their new bungalow complex in Morombe. More information – on the bungalows as well as the transport – from the Lakana Vezo in Ifaty.

As an easy alternative to travelling overland there are flights between Toliara and Morondava via Morombe.

BEACH RESORTS SOUTH OF TOLIARA
New beach hotels are opening up in the very attractive region south of Toliara, and it seems likely that these will soon become more popular than Ifaty.

St Augustine's Bay (Baie St Augustin)
St Augustine is full of natural wonders and history. This was the site of an ill-fated British colony, abandoned in 1646, and later frequented by pirates. St Augustine's Bay was mentioned by Daniel Defoe in *The King of Pirates*.

The natural wonders include dramatic sand dunes, a remarkable cave swimming pool, bloated moringa trees, and some good birdwatching.

The hotels in the region will arrange transfers from Toliara, but there is a regular taxi-brousse to Sarodrano.

Grottes Sarodrano and Sarodrano village
Don't miss this superb swimming hole. Under a rocky overhang is a deep pool of clear blue water. Swimmers will find the top layer of water warm and only mildly salty, while the cooler lower layer is saline. Fresh water flows from the mountain into the pool, on top of the warmer, heavier layer of salt water from the sea. In the area of the pool are some sureasitic bottle trees, known as bloated moringas.

Grottes Sarodrano is a 4km walk south from La Mangrove hotel (along an easy road). Kids with pirogues hang around there to take you back for 30,000Fmg. Well worth it!

Further south is the village of Sarodrano where there are impressive sand-dunes and spectacular cliffs. For naturalists a track leads up through spiny forest where you can find wild ring-tailed lemurs and southern endemic birds.

Where to stay
Hotel Melody Beach A new hotel (four bungalows) under the same management as Auberge de la Table and serving the same delicious food; 50,000Fmg per bungalow. Overlooking a sandy beach with good swimming, it is just 5km from the main road so is more easily accessible by public transport than St Augustine's Bay itself or Anakao. The Indian co-owner runs a shop in the market called Bon Marché and may be able to provide transport, but it is easy enough to walk in providing you have good footwear for the rough, rocky road.
La Mangrove 8km from RN7 (the turn-off is signposted). A nice French-run hotel under the same ownership as Chez Alain. Ten bungalows for 70,000–90,000Fmg, depending on whether they have en-suite WC or shared. Excellent meals at 35,000Fmg. There's no beach, but a rocky access to the sea for swimming. This is a diving centre, and boat excursions to Nosy Ve and Anakao can be arranged. Transfers from Chez Alain in town cost 30,000Fmg. If you want to hike it, avoid the heat of the day and keep to the road; the whole area is laced with confusing tracks.
Chez Andrea A new, Italian-owned hotel near Sarodrano. Thoughtfully designed, very friendly, excellent food and service.

Anakao
Anakao is a pretty little Vezo fishing village, with colourful boats drawn up on to the sands, and little to do except potter and swim. And that is one of its problems:

the local people – especially children – have become overfocused on tourists as a source of income, and you will be pestered mercilessly. Another problem is the dirty beach, used by the locals as a latrine.

Anakao is accessible from Toliara only from the sea so you really need to take the package offered by Safari Vezo (see below) or another motorised boat. Attractive though a pirogue trip may seem when you bargain with the fishermen, bear in mind that there is almost always a very strong head wind. The 'three-hour trip' can take up to nine hours. Even motorised pirogues are unreliable, breaking down with regularity.

Where to stay/eat

Safari Vezo BP 427, Toliara 601; tel: 413 81 This popular hotel, an unpretentious set of beach bungalows, is now run by Monique Vachoud, the Swiss lady previously at La Mangrove. Bungalows are 120Ff per night; meals 45Ff. Monique organises diving excursions, and the restaurant overlooking the sea is excellent. This hotel is a great favourite of visiting yachties from South Africa. The diving/snorkelling excursions from here are reportedly outstanding. Boat transfers from Toliara cost 170Ff per person.

Chez Clovis and **Chez Emile** are alternatives to Safari Vezo, if you can get to Anakao under your own steam. Both are very basic: 'toilette forêt' or hole in the ground, but they cost only 15,000Fmg.

Nosy Ve and Nosy Satrana

Nosy Ve (the name means 'Is there an island?'!) lies 3km west of Anakao, and is a sacred site for the Vezo people who annually sacrifice zebu at its northern point. It has a long history of European domination: the first landing was by a Dutchman in 1595, and Nosy Ve was officially taken over by the French in 1888 before their conquest of the mainland although it is hard to see why: it is a flat, scrub-covered little island.

What makes Nosy Ve special to modern-day invaders is the excellent snorkelling on its fringing reefs and the breeding colony of red-tailed tropic birds which are gradually increasing in number. During the first few months of the year you will see them at their nest sites under bushes at the southern tip of the island, as well as flying overhead: a thrilling sight.

Camping is no longer allowed on the island, and visits are dependent for their success on wind and tide (strong wind makes snorkelling difficult). With no natural shade on the island, make sure your boatman erects a sail on the beach to provide respite from the burning sun. And at low tide be prepared to push the boat through the shallow water!

If you are not a snorkeller there is endless pleasure to be had searching for shells and poking around in rock pools on the exposed part of the reef. Take care – a member of our party found a poisonous stone fish.

Nearby Nosy Satrana offers equally good snorkelling but no tropic birds.

A day's excursion to Nosy Ve, with snorkelling equipment provided, will cost around 150,000Fmg.

Lake Tsimanampetsotsa

This large, shallow soda lake, about 40km south of Anakao, is a haven for waterfowl and other rare endemic birds. It is a Strict Nature Reserve and as such is not accessible to tourists. Birding groups camp at the perimeter of the reserve (excursions can be organised by Safari Vezo amongst others) but independent travellers without their own 4WD will have great difficulty reaching it.

Beheloka

Further down the coast, this isolated village is developing into a low-key resort. A new palm-thatched hotel, Relaise la Canne à Sucre, has been built by the owner of Chez Alain. Four rooms for 60,000Fmg. Book through Chez Alain in Toliara (tel: 415 27).

A taxi-brousse from Toliara will cost around 25,000Fmg.

Itampolo

This small town, about 150km south of Toliara, is also developing as a resort. It has a beautiful white beach and the best surfing in Madagascar. The hotel here, also a Chez Alain establishment, is called Sud Sud.

Expect to pay about 40,000Fmg for a taxi-brousse from Toliara.

BEZA-MAHAFALY SPECIAL RESERVE

This reserve is the model for the WWF's integrated conservation and development efforts. It was established at the request of local people who volunteered to give up using part of the forest. In return they have been helped with a variety of social and agricultural projects; for example by the provision of a school and the building of irrigation channels.

The government has designated the reserve as its number one priority from ten sites in the Environmental Action Plan. Agroforestry is being developed under the guidance of Tana's School of Agronomy and the Direction des Eaux et Forêts, and many research projects take place there. The goal has always been to integrate conservation and rural development projects around the reserve, and to support the sustainable use of natural resources.

The reserve protects two distinct types of forest: spiny forest and gallery (riverine) forest. In this it mirrors Berenty, but there the comparison ends. Tourism is not discouraged, but at present the Malagasy locals and researchers come first. This is an enormously rewarding place for the serious naturalist, however. In addition to lemurs, the forest has four species of tenrec including the rare large-eared one, *Echinops telfairi*, three species of carnivores including the fosa, and lots of reptiles. About 90 species of birds have been recorded.

Practical information

Beza-Mahafaly is 35km north of Betioky along a very rough road. To get there you need a 4WD vehicle, a zebu cart, a bicycle, or a strong pair of legs.

Like other protected areas in Madagascar, permits can be obtained at the site or in Tana through ANGAP. Since the reserve is a research centre, permission to visit should be requested through the University in Antananarivo (tel: 323 19) or by writing to Beza Mahafaly Project, BP 10, Betioky Sud (612).

A programme to improve the facilities for visitors is under way. At present you should be self-sufficient and well prepared with camping gear, food and cooking equipment. The fee for camping and using the facilities (such as water and electricity) is 10,000Fmg per night. There is a cook who can prepare meals for you; 10,000Fmg per day. It is usually possible to rent tents for 10,000Fmg per person per night. Note that half of these fees are given to the local people surrounding the reserve for their own development projects. A local guide is available at 15,000Fmg per tour.

Beza Mahafaly Reserve is reached within 45 minutes with a 4WD from Betioky during the dry season. The access is quite difficult and sometimes impossible during the rainy season, so it is wise to check at the Beza Mahafaly Project office in Betioky, located near the Département des Eaux et Forêts. Whether driving or walking (ten hours), you should take a guide from Betioky to the reserve since the road there has many branches.

THE ROAD TO TAOLAGNARO (FORT DAUPHIN)

A taxi-brousse from Toliara to Taolagnaro takes two to three days. The fastest public vehicle is the Besalara truck, a Mercedes; the slowest is the Bienvenue. It's a shame to pass straight through such an exciting area, however. Much more interesting is to rent a vehicle and driver, or to do the trip by taxi-brousse in stages, staying at Betioky, Ampanihy and Beloha or Ambovombe, or – most interesting of all – by a combination of walking and whatever transport comes along, taking pot luck on where you'll spend the night.

Air Mad has withdrawn the Twin Otter service to these small towns.

Bezaha

A side trip to this town, which lies east of the road to Betioky, is worth it if you have your own vehicle; there are some lovely Mahafaly tombs along the road. The best hotel is the Hotel Teheza.

Betioky to Ampanihy

Betioky is a day's taxi-brousse ride from Toliara. The first 70km are on paved road, then it's a very dusty 70km or so, but worth it for the Mahafaly tombs alongside the road. In Betioky the best hotel (but still very basic) is the Mamyrano Annexe. There is also the popular Hotel Mahafaly.

Some 20km south of Betioky is the small village of **Ambatry**, with good Mahafaly tombs. Next comes **Ejeda**, about 2½ hours from Betioky on a reasonable dirt road. In the dry season you can watch the activity on the dry riverbed. Holes are dug to reach the water: upstream for drinking, midstream for washing, and downstream for clothes. The hotel here is 'good value for money: almost no value but also almost no money'. About 10km south of Ejeda are a few big Mahafaly tombs, one with over 50 zebu horns. Look for them on the right, on a hill.

Ejeda to Ampanihy takes about five hours by truck on a very bad, rocky road.

Ampanihy

The name means 'the place of bats', but now it is set to become the place of the goats (see box). It's worth a couple of days' stay. There is a WWF nursery for endemic plants, near the Protestant church. Walk 2km south to some good Mahafaly tombs.

LIGHT AND HEAVY INDUSTRY IN AMPANIHY

In the late 1990s, Ampanihy has been the recipient of a Japanese water aid programme which has dug 100 wells in the area. A South African company has started to mine graphite, which will bring some jobs to this formerly impoverished region and, more interestingly for tourists, the mohair carpet industry is being revived. This was a thriving business in the 1970s and 80s but the careless cross-breeding of the Angora goats reduced the quality of the wool until the industry collapsed. In 1994 a Frenchman, Eric Mallet, built a new carpet factory and trained local women to work the looms. The wool, however, was imported from France and New Zealand.

Thanks to EU funding, 1999 saw the first pure-bred angora goats born in Ampanihy for decades, and the industry seems set for a good future.

Where to stay/eat

Motel Relais d'Ampanihy A touch of luxury in the desert! No hot water. Excellent food. The owner, Luc Vital, can organise excursions to the forest adjoining the river Menarandra (lemurs), and to see baobabs and Mahafaly tombs.

Hotel Tahio About 300m from the big market. Very friendly, economically priced. Good meals. Showers.

Ampanihy to Ambovombe

After Ampanihy you enter Antandroy country and will understand why they are called 'people of the thorns' (Androy means 'the land of thorns'). The road deteriorates (if you thought that possible) as you make your way to **Tranaroa** (the name means two houses) in about five hours. There's an interesting Antandroy tomb here crowned by an aeroplane which moves in the wind. Another five hours and you approach Beloha on an improving road (much favoured by tortoises, which thrive in the area since it is *fady* to eat them) and with tombs all around.

Beloha is probably the best place to spend the night on this leg of the journey. It has a basic hotel, Mon Plaisir, with a restaurant, and elsewhere there is a bar, Les Trois Frères, which serves ice-cold drinks. Take a look at the new Catholic church with its beautiful stained glass, made by a local craftsman.

Between Beloha and Tsiombe is the most interesting stretch of the entire journey. There are baobabs, tortoises (sadly it is not *fady* for the local Antanosoy to eat them) and some wonderful tombs. 'On one occasion it was like arriving at a journey-fair. A tomb with a life-size taxi-brousse, one with a big aeroplane, and another with an ocean steamer! There are also people to ask for money to see these attractions.' These tombs are about 33km before **Tsiombe**.

'If "be" means "big" then "Tsiom" must mean "cockroach"!' Luc Selleslagh had reservations about his hotel, but there *is* a choice of simple *hotelys*. If you decide to push on to Ambovombe, where there is better accommodation, the road starts to improve.

THE FAR SOUTH

If you are in a 4WD vehicle or are a strong hiker, you should consider taking a side trip to the southernmost point of Madagascar. From Tsihombe a road runs south (30km) to Faux Cap and southwest to Cap Sainte Marie. Road conditions are very poor, but in the dry season an ordinary saloon car can make it in about six hours.

Some of the hotels and tour operators in Taolagnaro are offering this trip. Try the Petit Bonheur hotel on Libanona Beach or Air Fort Services. The latter charges 500,000Fmg per person.

Faux Cap

I made my first visit to this dramatic, lonely place in 1997, and predict that it will not be long before it is developed for tourism. Visit soon!

Faux Cap is a small community, isolated from the outside world by wild seas and a treacherous coral reef and by poor access roads. The huge, shifting sand-dunes are littered with fragments of *aepyornis* shell. It is an extraordinary place which is worth making considerable effort to visit (see box).

Getting there and away

The starting point for a trip to Faux Cap is Tsihombe. Stay at one of the *hotelys* and ask around for ongoing transport. Faux Cap is 30km from here and there is no water en route. If you decide to hike, be prepared to carry all that you need. There is a good chance that you will catch a lift, however. The village at Faux Cap is called Betanty.

LANDFALL AT FAUX CAP

Janice Booth

On an 'expedition cruise', coast-hopping round Madagascar on MV *Professor Khromov*, we were due to sail overnight from Fort Dauphin (southeast) to Tuléar (southwest). The captain agreed to pause en route so we could try to visit Faux Cap, at the island's remote southernmost tip. A sand-dune there contains fragmented fossil eggs of the *aepyornis* (elephant bird), extinct for around 800 years.

We didn't know whether tide, currents and the surrounding reef would allow us to land. *Khromov* dropped anchor far offshore at 1am. At dawn, the recce zodiac was launched, carrying expedition staff – and me, because I speak French and some Malagasy. As we bounced across oily swell the white girdle of waves on the reef appeared unbroken. Our zodiac veered sideways, searching for a gap.

Then we saw a wooden outrigger from the beach put to sea and steer for the reef. Suddenly there were two black heads in the water, sleek as seals, and two boys scythed through the waves towards us. We waved a welcome. They slithered wetly aboard the zodiac and, grinning proudly, piloted us ashore.

People were streaming down the cliff on to the beach. The village holds about 500 and it seemed few were absent! They stood on the sand, waiting. The zodiac scraped to a standstill and we clambered out; then it roared back to *Khromov* – boys determinedly still aboard – to collect the other passengers.

The villagers were tense and uncertain. I gave the traditional Malagasy greeting: '*Inona no vaovao?*' (What news?). There was a ripple of relief. At least the strangers knew how to behave correctly! Faces relaxed into smiles.

Some chatted in French. They'd seen the *Khromov* anchor but hadn't known why. 'As you can imagine, we didn't get much sleep last night,' one man admitted. Apparently we were the first visitors ever to arrive from the sea. A rumpled policeman introduced himself and politely requested passports, then waived his request as long as we didn't go inland.

The zodiac returned and was quickly surrounded by fascinated children. Stefan, our expedition leader, gestured 'OK' and they hurtled aboard, in a tangle of arms, legs and grinning faces. He zoomed them off on a quick loop of the lagoon (to the dismay of some parents!), their squeals of delight and excitement almost drowning the engine.

Meanwhile I asked carefully about the *aepyornis* eggs. Might we perhaps go to see them? A guide was found for the longish walk to the dune – which probably had been some huge midden, the fragments of fossilised shell lay so thickly on the ground. We could stroll and photograph (and, guiltily, collect) to our hearts' content. Two boys brought 'reconstructed' eggs for sale: diverse fragments stuck together to make unconvincingly lopsided wholes.

As we returned along the beach, children pattered beside us. A girl aged about eight touched my blouse curiously. In Malagasy I asked her name and told her mine. She stretched out her sandy little brown hand and shook my much larger white one, smiling shyly.

The midday sun poured gold on the sea as the zodiacs bounced us back to *Khromov*, wet, burnt, windswept – and happy, feeling like pioneers. It was an 'expedition' cruise indeed!

Where to stay/eat
Hotel Cactus Eighteen basic bungalows for 30,000Fmg. No running water or electricity but beautifully located and run by the very friendly Marie Zela. Good food with huge portions. A great place to relax for a few days.

Cap Sainte Marie
Cap Sainte Marie is as spectacular as its neighbour, with high sandstone cliffs and dwarf plants resembling a rock garden. It is also possible to get here without a vehicle. Andrew Cooke wrote: 'I suppose the highlight for me was taking a taxi-brousse to Beloha and then taking a chavette to Lavanono (on the coast) and then walking to Cap Sainte Marie (the distance is 30km which took us two days). All the way we met great hospitality. Water is in very short supply.' Note that since Cap Sainte Marie is a reserve, a permit must be purchased, and this should be arranged in Tana. Visitors arriving without a permit have been turned away.

This is a good area to see humpback whales; between September and November they can be observed quite close to shore with their calves.

Ambovombe to Amboasary and Taolagnaro
With the end in sight, most travellers prefer to push on to Taolagnaro, but there are several hotels in Ambovombe: the Relais des Androy (no running water; good food), the Oasis (running water), and the Fanantenana (very basic, but cheap). Ambovombe has a good Monday market. This town is interesting as a centre for sustainable development projects overseen by the Peace Corps, involving the local people. At their request, for example, the town now has 20 new wells.

About 30km from Ambovombe is Ambosoary, the village that marks the turn-off to Berenty. If you decide to drop in to Berenty, thus saving the very high transfer fee from Taolagnaro (Fort Dauphin), think again. Transport from Taolagnaro is part of the package and you may not be admitted on your own (although with your own car this is less of a problem). Budget travellers should visit the reserve of Amboasary Sud instead (see page 222).

From Amboasary to Taolagnaro is less than two hours on a paved road.

Amboasary
This thriving town with a bustling market makes a worthwhile stop if you are visiting Lake Anony or Amboasary Sud. Don't stay too long, though; 'without charm, like a Mexican border town and full of street kids.'

Where to stay/eat
Hotel-Restaurant Mandrare A complex of small bungalows constructed from *Alluaudia procera* [ouch!]. 'A bargain at 18,000Fmg. The price is excluding breakfast, but this is available; dinner is 10,000Fmg. Mary, the owner, has taught herself English and efficiently manages both the hotel and adjacent store. We arrived late at night and her welcoming smile and friendly manner were priceless. We appreciated the bucket of hot water and other homely touches.' Ken and Lorna Gillespie were in a hired vehicle, so welcomed the secure parking here.

TAOLAGNARO (FORT DAUPHIN)
History
The remains of two forts can still be seen in or near this town on the extreme southeast tip of Madagascar: Fort Flacourt built in 1643; and one that dates from 1504, thus the oldest building in the country, which was erected by shipwrecked Portuguese sailors. This ill-fated group of 80 reluctant colonists stayed about 15

Previous page Typical houses and landscape of Imerina (HB)

Top Children of Madagascar: Merina girl (EC) and girl from Mahajanga (RH)

Below Weary days in the market, Antananarivo (HB)

Above After a death, the deceased person's clothing is ritually washed in the nearest river – although this scene may just show the family laundry! (HB)

Below left Erotic Sakalava tomb carving (BL)

Below right Mahafaly *aloalo* ('wrestlers') (TC)

Next page The stonecutter and his child, Maromizaha (HB)

years before falling foul of the local tribes. The survivors of the massacre fled to the surrounding countryside where disease and hostile natives finished them off.

A French expedition, organised in 1642 by the Société Française de l'Orient and led by Sieur Pronis, had instructions to 'found colonies and commerce in Madagascar and to take possession of it in the name of His Most Christian Majesty'. An early settlement at the Bay of Sainte Luce was soon abandoned in favour of a healthier peninsula to the south, and a fort was built and named after the Dauphin (later Louis XIV) in 1643. At first the Antanosy were quite keen on the commerce part of the deal but were less enthusiastic about losing their land. The heavily defended fort only survived by use of force and with many casualties from both sides. The French finally abandoned the place in 1674, but their 30-year occupation formed one of the foundations of the later claim to the island as a French colony. During this period the first published work on Madagascar was written by Pronis's successor, Etienne de Flacourt. His *Histoire de la Grande île de Madagascar* brought the island's amazing flora and fauna to the attention of European naturalists, and is still used as a valuable historical source book.

Taolagnaro/Fort Dauphin today
The town itself is unattractive, but it is the most beautifully located of all popular destinations in Madagascar. Built on a small peninsula, the town is bordered on three sides by beaches and breakers and backed by high green mountains which dwindle into spiny forest to the west. More geared to tourism than any other Malagasy mainland town, Taolagnaro is a lively town offering a variety of exceptionally interesting excursions and some fine beaches. One eye-catching feature of the bay are the shipwrecks. A romantic imagination associates these with pirates or wreckers of a bygone era. In fact they are 'all unfortunate insurance scams with boats that should have been out of use years ago'. Pity!

Most people (myself included) still use the French name, Fort Dauphin, but to be consistent with the rest of the book I shall stick to Taolagnaro in the text.

The telephone area code for Taolagnaro is 92.

Warnings
Taolagnaro is buffeted by almost continuous strong winds in September and much of October. Muggings and sexual assaults have been reported on the beach below the Hotel Dauphin and Libanona beach.

Getting there and away
By road
The overland route from Tana (bypassing Toliara) is reportedly best done with the companies Sonatra or Tata which operate three times a week from the taxi-brousse station on the far side of Lake Anosy. These buses go via Ihosy, Betroka and Ambovombe. You should book your seat as far in advance as possible.

By air
There are flights to Taolagnaro from Tana and Toliara every day except Tuesday and Wednesday (but check the latest Air Mad schedule). Sit on the right for the best views of Taolagnaro's mountains and bays. Flights are usually heavily booked. Airport transfers from the de Heaulme hotels (see below) are expensive. Take a taxi (fixed rate) for the 4km ride into town.

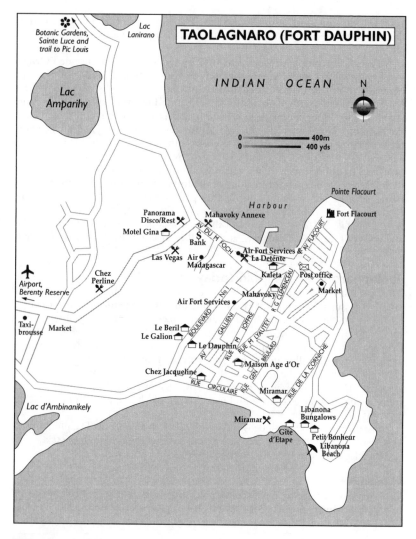

TAOLAGNARO (FORT DAUPHIN)

Botanic Gardens, Sainte Luce and trail to Pic Louis

Lac Lanirano

INDIAN OCEAN

N

Lac Amparihy

0 ——————— 400m
0 ——————— 400 yds

Pointe Flacourt

Harbour

Panorama Disco/Rest ✗ Mahavoky Annexe
Motel Gina 🏠
$ Bank
Las Vegas ✗ Air Madagascar ●
Chez Perline ✗
✈ Airport, Berenty Reserve

Fort Flacourt

Air Fort Services & La Détente ✗
Kaleta ● Post office 📮
Mahavoky Market

Air Fort Services ●

Taxi-brousse Market
Le Beril 🏠
Le Galion 🏠
Le Dauphin 🏠
Maison Age d'Or 🏠
Chez Jacqueline
RUE CIRCULAIRE
Miramar

Lac d'Ambinanikely

Miramar ✗
Gîte d'Etape
Petit Bonheur
Libanona Bungalows 🏠
Libanona Beach

AV DU M FOCH · BOULEVARD No. 1 · AV GALLIEN · RUE M JOFFRE · RUE M LYAUTEY · AV GEN BRULARD · R G CLEMENCEAU · AV FLACOURT · RUE DE LA CORNICHE

Where to stay

Most of Taolagnaro belongs to M Jean de Heaulme, the owner of Berenty Reserve. His hotels are the Dauphin, the Galion, and the Miramar. You are expected to stay in one of these if you want to visit Berenty.

Category A

Hotels Le Dauphin and Le Galion PO Box 54; tel: 212 38. The Dauphin is the main hotel and Galion its annexe. Meals are taken in the Dauphin which has a lovely garden. Prices are 390Ff single and 470Ff double, plus breakfast: 30Ff.

Le Beril Hotel Next to Le Galion; rooms for 100,000Fmg.

Hotel Miramar Nicely situated on the cliff road overlooking Libanona Beach. There is a limited number of rooms costing the same as the Dauphin, through which bookings must be made. About 50m down the road is its restaurant, one of the best in Taolagnaro, superbly located on a promontory with wonderful views over two beaches; a rough walk in the dark (bring a torch).

Category B

Libanona Bungalows BP 70; tel: 213 78; fax: 213 84. Its location vies with the Miramar as the best in Taolagnaro, but the bungalows vary in quality. About 55,000Fmg. Breakfast 10,000Fmg, dinner 25,000Fmg.

Petit Bonheur BP 210; tel: 211 56/212 74. Another very friendly hotel on Libanona beach. Single/double rooms with a shared shower, and bungalows. The hotel runs tours in 4WD vehicles, including Le Grand Sud (Cap Ste Marie and Faux Cap). They also operate boat trips to Lokaro (see Excursions).

Hotel Kaleta BP 70; tel: 212 87; fax: 213 84. Under the same management as Libanona Bungalows (both are government-owned). A 32-room hotel in the centre of town offering a good alternative for those looking for comfort and lemurs (they operate Amboasary Sud Reserve) but unable to afford the de Heaulme/Berenty prices. Rooms 250Ff, breakfast 30Ff.

Motel Gina BP 107; tel/fax: 212 66. Pleasant thatched or brick bungalows located on the outskirts of town, ranging from 85,000–120,000Fmg. There's an excellent – though quite expensive – restaurant. Unlike other hotels, the Gina accepts Visa credit cards. An annexe has opened across the road.

Hotel Casino A little further out of town but similar in quality to the Gina.

Category C

Hotel Relaxe The first hotel you come to when driving in from the airport.

Hotel Mahavoky Annexe Most rooms have a balcony with dramatic views of the shipwrecks in the bay. Nice friendly manager and staff, and centrally located; 50,000 Fmg a night for a double room with shower room (no single rooms available).

Hotel Mahavoky Tel: 213 32. Situated in the town centre opposite the Catholic cathedral. Inexpensive rooms with communal (outside) shower and WC. Occupies an old missionary school which gives added interest. There's a helpful, English-speaking manager and a good restaurant.

Maison Age d'Or Readers' praise has been heaped on this establishment, not for its comfort but for its hugely hospitable owner, Krishna Hasimboto. 'He endeavours to answer all your questions and make your stay memorable. He is incredibly proud of his home and has embellished the exterior with quoted recommendations and his guests' country of origin, plus some local architectural touches. Our stay here is one of our cherished memories'. (K & L Gillespie) There are six rooms (four large, two small) from 15,500–22,000Fmg, all but one with shared bathroom. Bring your own mosquito net. The Age d'Or is best reached via the Kaleta Hotel bus from the airport.

Chez Anita 50m from the Age d'Or and similarly priced and recommended. Good food for 12,000Fmg.

Gîte d'Etape BP 125, Libanona The unpretentious and inexpensive place is warmly recommended by Ania Dudziec. 'The best place to stay if you're after a bit of peace and want to be by the sea. Run by the very friendly Rehitrifa family . I was the only *vazaha*. No food, and quite a walk into town'. 15,000Fmg.

Libanona Ecology Centre bungalows Mark Fenn writes: 'We also have several guest bungalows complete with kitchen facilities. These bungalows are especially handy for people with small children or school groups (for which we can organise meals). We are not in the tourism business but it helps us to pay bills and upkeep on the buildings. The bungalows are simple, yet are older and have character. They are also situated on a penisula with breathtaking ocean views (and whale watching from July to November). People should contact us in advance via email: cel@dts.mg.

Hotel Chez Jacqueline Tel: 211 26. A new, family-run hotel on the cliff road in a nice location beyond the Miramar restaurant (Ampasimasay). Four clean rooms with en-suite bathroom for 50,000Fmg.

Where to eat
In Taolagnaro eating is taken seriously. All the Category A hotels serve very good food with an emphasis on 'fruits de la mer'. If you are dining away from your hotel, the following are recommended:

Miramar One of the best restaurants in Madagascar. Go for lunch, so you can enjoy the marvellous view. Not cheap, but worth every penny.

Gina's restaurant (Motel Gina) Again, not cheap but excellent food.

Mahavoky Annexe (in Hotel Mahavoky Annexe) Recommended by several readers and expats. 'An excellent little restaurant. The name means "to make satisfied with food!"'

Chez Perline 'A great small resto near the markets. Wonderful food but expect to wait at least an hour to get it!'. To avoid the long wait it's best to order your meals in advance.

La Détente 'An unassuming restaurant above the Air Fort Services office – nice food and excellent service.'

Restaurant Las Vegas Opposite Motel Gina. A lively and deservedly popular place run by Gabriella. 'The only place to eat, drink and meet people. Happy, friendly atmosphere, cheap tasty food. A brilliant place – I miss it and everyone there!' (Ania Dudziec)

Mahavoky Escale Buvette Near the Panorama disco. 'Claude and his wife Mamanina always are hospitable and friendly for those who want to get to know the locals better.' (Mark Fenn)

Chez Anita Serves delicious Sambos and zebu brochettes, while providing entertainment with a television that alternates between French-dubbed action movies and Malagasy pop-stars singing favourite tunes. The sound and picture quality is so bad it's impossible to know what's going on, but everyone sits glued to the tube anyway!

There are other small restaurants in the market area, some of which serve great food. Making your own discoveries is part of the fun.

Nightlife
'The **Panorama** disco is an institution for locals. On the road to the airport, not far from Motel Gina, it is open every night except Mondays and is considered by many as Madagascar's best disco. Much of its appeal is in its location, perched on the edge of the bay. When you get too hot and sweaty from dancing you can take a stroll outside to cool off in the ocean breeze and watch the waves roll in.' (R Mulder)

Shopping
Taolagnaro has some distinctive local crafts. Most typical are the heavy (and expensive) silver bracelets worn traditionally by men. These are often offered for sale outside the main hotels. The best souvenir shop in town is **Au Bout du Monde** boutique, on the left-hand side of the road to the airport.

If you go to Libanona Beach you will be offered shells or necklaces for sale by charming local girls who have expertly sussed out the guilt factor prevalent in most *vazaha* dealings. When you refuse to buy their goods they insist on giving you a simple shell necklace as a gift. There are no strings attached – they know that the next day you will be prepared to buy anything!

Vehicle hire/tour operators
Air Fort Services Located on Avenue Gallieni. Postal address: BP 159; tel/fax: 212 24; email: air.fort@dts.mg. The main tour operator in the region. They hire out bicycles,

THE LIBANONA ECOLOGY CENTRE

Madagascar suffers from a great shortage of trained Malagasy conservationists. The Libanona Ecology Centre was set up in Taolagnaro (Fort Dauphin) in August 1995, to help address this problem. It is currently managed by Mark Fenn of the WWF. The administrator is Jean Mananga, who works with a team of Malagasy professors. Classrooms and a library were built using funds from the Andrew Lees Memorial Trust, and with further help from the charity Azafady.

Various research and teaching programmes are being developed which cover a broad range of biological disciplines and also sociology and resource economics. Malagasy conservationists trained at the Centre teach in the surrounding villages and work with local people to find more sustainable ways of farming, timber-cropping, and fishing. The Centre also trains local tourist guides and runs various training programmes and summer schools for visiting scientists and students from abroad.

For further information, contact Mark Fenn on cel@dts.mg (Taolagnaro) or The Andrew Lees Memorial Trust in London: 020 8748 0980 or email yorengo@aol.com.

vehicles (from cars to buses) and even small planes, as well as offering a variety of tours including Andohahela National Park.

Safari Laka Tel: 212 66. Situated in the Hotel Gina, and offering adventure trips ranging from mountain biking to trekking and canoeing.

SIGHTSEEING AND EXCURSIONS
In and around town

Apart from its lively market, Taolagnaro offers a choice of beach and mountain.

The best beach is **Libanona**, with excellent swimming (but beware the strong current) and superb tide-pools. Admirers of the weird and wonderful can spend many hours poking around at low tide. The pools to the right of the beach (as you face the sea) seem the best. Look out for a bizarre, frilly nudibranch or sea-hare, anemones and other extraordinary invertebrates. Local hotels recommend that you visit in groups because of the danger of muggings. There is another beach below the Hotel Dauphin, but this is dirty (turdy) and there have also been muggings there.

Pic Louis, the mountain that dominates the town, is a straightforward though strenuous (and hot) climb up a good path and offers nice views. The trail starts opposite SIFOR, the sisal factory about 3km along the road to Lanirano. Alternatively you can take a taxi to the RC mission near the airport; the trail goes up past the statue of the Virgin Mary. Allow at least a half day to get up there and back – or better still take a picnic. Apart from birds there is not much wildlife to be seen, though Nick Garbutt reports: 'I was once up there with a group when someone called out "Oh look, a monkey!" A grey bamboo lemur leapt over the rocks and into the nearby bushes.'

Another arm of the de Heaulme empire is the **Saidia Botanical Gardens** situated about 16km out of town towards Sainte Luce.

Further afield

Apart from the reserves, which are described later, there are numerous places to visit in this beautiful part of Madagascar. If you haven't a car you will probably need to join an organised trip, though the energetic could reach most places by hired bike.

ZEBU

The hump-backed cattle, zebu, which nearly outnumber the country's human population, produce a relatively low yield in milk and meat. These animals are near-sacred and generally are not eaten by the Malagasy, other than at ceremonies of social or religious significance. Zebu are said to have originated from northeast India, eventually spreading as far as Egypt and then down to Ethiopia and other parts of East Africa. It is not known how they were introduced to Madagascar but they are a symbol of wealth and status as well as being used for burden.

Zebu come in a variety of colours, the most sought-after being the *omby volavita*, which is chestnut with a white spot on the head. There are 80 words in the Malagasy language to describe the physical attributes of zebu, in particular the colour, horns and hump.

In the south, zebu meat is always served at funerals, and among certain southern tribes the cattle are used as marriage settlements, as is done in Africa. Whenever there is a traditional ritual or ceremony, zebu are sacrificed, the heads being given to the highest ranking members of the community. Blood is smeared on participants as it is believed to have purification properties, and the fat from the hump of the cattle is used as an ingredient for incense. Zebu milk is an important part of the diet among the Antandroy; it is *fady* for women to milk the cows but it is they who sell the curdled milk in the market.

While zebu theft in the past was considered an act of bravery, it is now confined mainly to the Bara. The traditional penalty for cattle-rustling was the *dina* whereby the culprit and his family were reduced to slavery. Among the Antandroy and Mahafaly a fine of ten zebu would have to be paid by the thief: five for the family from whom the cattle were stolen and five for the king.

To the rural Malagasy a herd of zebu is as symbolic of prosperity as is a new car or a large house in our culture. Government aid programmes must take this into account; for instance improved rice yields will indirectly lead to more environmental degradation by providing more money to buy more zebu.

The French colonial government thought they had an answer: they introduced a tax on each animal. However, local politicians were quick to point out that since Malagasy women had always been exempt from taxation, the same rule should apply to cows!

Portuguese Fort (Ile aux Portuguais)

The tour to the old fort, built in 1504, involves a pirogue ride up the river Vinanibe, about 6km from Taolagnaro, and then a short walk to the sturdy-looking stone fortress (the walls are one metre thick) set in zebu-grazed parkland. This is the oldest building in Madagascar, and worth a visit for the beautiful surroundings though organised tours are expensive.

Baie Sainte Luce (Manafiafy)

About 65km northeast of Taolagnaro is the beautiful and historically interesting bay where the French colonists of 1638 first landed. There is a superb beach and a protected area of humid coastal forest here, owned by M de Heaulme, and also some bungalows (usual de Heaulme price). It is possible to reach Manafiafy by taxi-brousse but most people will opt for the organised tour run by Air Fort Services, among others: 640,000Fmg for a 4WD vehicle.

Lokaro
Another popular excursion which begins at Lake Lanirano, just north of Taolagnaro, then passes through various waterways and villages. The first leg is by a pirogue to Evatra, where lunch is served, after which you are taken on a 1½-hour walk round the peninsula before returning to the pirogues. The cost, 450,000Fmg (one or two people) or 150,000Fmg for a group of three or more, includes meals. Recommended.

THE WILDLIFE RESERVES
The southwest of Madagascar gives the best opportunity for wildlife viewing to suit all budgets and all levels of energy. Whilst Berenty is rightly world famous, adventurous visitors should give equal consideration to Andohahela, whilst those on a tight budget can consider Ambosoary Sud, and the new private reserve of Nahampoana. Don't think, however, that you can do them all. M Jean de Heaulme, the owner of Berenty, has quite unreasonably put restrictions on tourists visiting his reserve if they have also been to – or are planning to go to – the new national park of Andohahela. This ridiculous situation may change, but you would do well to make local enquiries.

Berenty Private Reserve
This is the key destination of most package tours and I've never known a visitor who hasn't loved Berenty (well, there was one...). The combination of tame lemurs, comfortable accommodation and the tranquillity of the forest trails makes this *the* Madagascar memory for many people. The danger is that Berenty is already becoming overcrowded, and too many groups bring problems. Fortunately there is only a limited amount of accommodation, so if you can arrange to spend a night or two you can still have the reserve to yourself in the magic hours of dawn and dusk.

Visits to the reserve must be organised through the Hotel Dauphin (or the Capricorne in Toliara). Accommodation is full board only, and the same price as the de Heaulme hotels: 310Ff per room (double occupancy) with meals an additional 130Ff. Transport from Taolagnaro (three or more people) costs 378Ff, so one night in Berenty will set you back about US$130.

The road to Berenty
The reserve lies some 80km to the west of Taolagnaro, amid a vast sisal plantation, and the drive there is part of the experience. For the first half of the journey the skyline is rugged green mountains often backed by menacing grey

LOCUSTS
In 1998 Madagascar was hit by a plague of locusts of Biblical proportions. In the southern region around Fort Dauphin the clouds of insects were dense enough to stop Air Madagascar's planes from landing. Near Manakara the swarms were estimated to be over 80km long; another swarm further south was estimated to be made up of 20 billion insects. It has been calculated that each insect devours one gram per day; 20 billion will therefore eat 20,000 tons of vegetation a day. It is hard to conceive of the impact this can have in a country already beset by natural disasters.

THE LEGEND OF THE SIFAKA

The name 'sifaka' comes from the animals' alarm call which sounds like: 'She-fahk!'. Or, to some ears, 'Froo-trahk!'. Here's why the sifaka swears at humans.

Once upon a time the sifaka was human (you can tell that by looking at its hands and feet). Then a wicked woman hit her stepdaughter in the face with a sooty cooking spoon and sent her flying into the trees where she stayed, with a black face. Now, when the sifaka's descendents see humans they threaten them with the cry 'Aforotrako!' – 'I'm going to get you!'

clouds or obscured by rain. Traveller's trees (*ravenala*) dot the landscape, and near Ranopiso is a grove of the very rare triangular palm, *Neodypsis decary*. (To see an example close up, wait until you arrive in Berenty where there is one near the entrance gate.)

Your first stop is to visit some **pitcher plants** – *Nepenthes madagascariensis* – whose nearest relatives are in Asia. The yellow 'flowers' (actually modified leaves) lure insects into their sticky depths where they are digested, probably for their nitrogen content.

The next (optional) stop before reaching the spiny forest is at an **Antanosy 'tomb'** (actually the dead are buried elsewhere) known as the tomb of Ranonda. It was carved by the renowned sculptor Fiasia. The artistry of this unpainted wooden memorial is of a very high standard though the carvings are deteriorating in the frequently wet weather. There's a girl carrying the Christian emblems of bible and cross; someone losing a leg to a crocodile; and the most famous piece, a boatload of people who are said to have died in a pirogue accident. On the far side there used to be a charming herd of zebu, portrayed with unusual liveliness (a cow turns her head to lick her suckling calf). In 1990 the cow and her calf were ripped away by thieves. To add to the poignancy, a row of cattle skulls indicate the zebu that had to be sacrificed to counteract this sacrilege. One hopes the revenge of the Ancestors was terrible.

The very reasonable response by the villagers to this desecration has been to fence off the tombs, which can now be viewed only through binoculars.

In the area are other memorials, but without carvings. These cenotaphs commemorate those buried in a communal tomb or where the body could not be recovered, and look like clusters of missiles lurking in the forest.

Shortly after **Ranopiso**, and the turn-off to Andohahela National Park, there is a dramatic change in the scenery: within a few kilometres the hills flatten and disappear, the clouds clear, and the bizarre fingers of *Didierea* and *Alluaudia* appear on the skyline interspersed with the bulky trunks of baobabs. You are entering the spiny forest, making the transition from the Eastern Domain to the Southern Domain. If you are on a Berenty tour your guide will identify some of the flora. If on your own turn to page 41.

The exhilaration of driving through the spiny forest is dampened by the sight of all the **charcoal sellers** waiting by their sacks of ex-Alluaudia. These marvellous trees are being cut down at an alarming rate by people who have no other means of support. While condemning the practice give uneasy thought to the fact that your sumptuous meals in Berenty will be cooked on stoves fuelled with locally-produced charcoal. And that it is city-dwellers who consume the most charcoal in Madagascar: on average two sacks a month.

One enterprising community is now selling **wood carvings** of subjects that hitherto have been hard to find in Madagascar: the local fauna. For a dollar or so you can buy delightful lemurs, tortoises and chameleons – a world better than the pseudo-African carvings found elsewhere.

If you pass through the village of Ankaraneno (25km from Taolagnaro) on a Thursday, do stop for the zebu market. Fascinating.

Amboasary (for accommodation see page 210), which also has a terrific market, is the last town before the bridge across the river Mandrare and the turn-off to Berenty. The rutted red road takes you past acres of sisal and some lonely-looking baobabs, to the entrance of the reserve.

The reserve

The name means 'big eel' but Berenty is famous for its population of ring-tailed lemurs and sifakas. Henri de Heaulme and now his son Jean have made this one of the best-studied 260 hectares of forest in Madagascar. Although in the arid south, its location along the river Mandrare ensures a well-watered habitat (gallery or riverine forest) for the large variety of animals that live there. The forest is

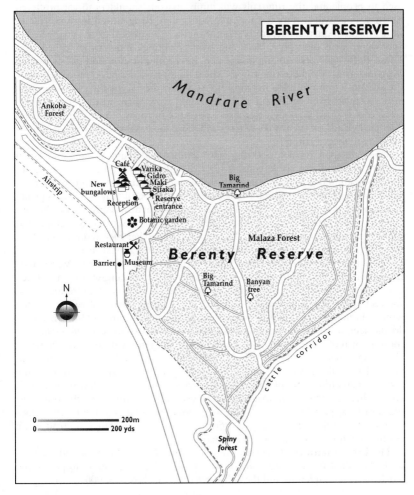

divided into two sections, Malaza (the section near the tourist bungalows) and Ankoba to its northwest.

The joy of Berenty is the selection of broad forest trails that allow safe wandering on your own, including nocturnal jaunts. Remember, many creatures are only active at night and are easy to spot with a torch/flashight; also the eyes of moths and spiders shine red, and all sorts of other arthropods and reptiles can be seen easily. A dusk visit (with a guide) to the reserve's area of spiny forest is a must: you'll observe mouse lemurs, but just seeing those weird, giant trees in silhouette and hearing the silence is a magical experience.

Next day get up at dawn; you can do your best birdwatching, see the sifakas opening their arms to the sun, and enjoy the coolness of the forest before going in to breakfast.

Berenty wildlife: an overview

Lemurs are what most people come here for, and seeing the following species is guaranteed: brown lemur, ring-tailed lemur and sifaka. The lemurs here are well-used to people and the ring-tails will jump on your shoulders to eat proffered bananas. They will also try to sneak into your cabin. **Ring-tailed lemurs** have an air of swaggering arrogance, are as at home on the ground as in trees, and are highly photogenic with their grey, black and white markings and waving striped tails. These fluffy tails play an important part in communication and act as benign weapons against neighbouring troops which might have designs on their territory. Ring-tailed lemurs indulge in 'stink fights' when they scent their tails with the musk secreted from wrist and anal glands and wave them in their neighbours' faces; that is usually enough to make a potential intruder retreat. They also rub their anal glands on the trunks of trees and score the bark with their wrist-spur to scent-mark their territory.

There are approximately 350 ring-tailed lemurs in Berenty, and the population has stayed remarkably stable considering that only about a quarter of the babies survive to adulthood. The females, which like most lemurs are dominant over the males, are receptive to mating for only a week or so in April/May, so there is plenty of competition amongst the males for this once-a-year treat (April is also the best time to observe 'stink-fighting' among males). The young are born in September and at first cling to their mother's belly, later climbing on to her back and riding jockey-style. Ring-tails eat flowers, fruit and insects – and the occasional chameleon.

Attractive though the ring-tails are, no lemur can compete with the **Verreaux's sifaka** for soft-toy cuddliness, with its creamy white fur, brown cap, and black face. Sifaka belong to the same family of lemur as the indri (seen in Périnet). The species here is *Propithecus verreauxi verreauxi* and there are about 300 of them in the reserve. Unlike the ring-tails, they rarely come down to the ground but when they do the length of their legs in comparison with their short arms necessitates a comical form of locomotion: they stand upright and jump with their feet together like competitors in a sack race. The best places to see them do this are on the trail to the left at the river and across the road by the aeroplane hangar near the restaurant and museum. Sifaka troop boundaries do not change, so your guide will know where to find the animals. The young are born in July. Like the ring-tails, sifaka make a speciality of sunbathing – spreading their arms to the morning rays from the top of their trees. They feed primarily on leaves and tamarind fruit so are not interested in tourist-proffered bananas.

The **brown lemurs** of Berenty were introduced from the West and are now well established and almost as tame as the ring-tails. There are two subspecies, the red-fronted brown lemur and the collared lemur. See box page 000.

There are other lemurs which, being nocturnal, are harder to spot although the **lepilemur** (white-footed sportive lemur) can be seen peering out of its hollow tree nest during the day. **Mouse lemurs** may be glimpsed in the beam of a flashlight, especially in the area of spiny forest near the reserve, a popular destination for night walks.

Apart from lemurs there are other striking mammals. **Fruit bats** or flying foxes live in noisy groups on 'bat trees' in one part of the forest which at present has been closed off to visitors because of undue disturbance. You will hear them and sometimes see them flying overhead.

Birdwatching is rewarding in Berenty, and even better in Bealoka ('Place of much shade') beyond the sisal factory. Nearly 100 species have been recorded. You are likely to see several families unique to Madagascar, including the hook-billed vanga, and two handsome species of couas – the crested coua and the giant coua which have dramatic blue face-markings. The cuckoo-like coucal is common, as are grey-headed lovebirds and the beautiful paradise flycatcher with its long tail feathers (a subspecies of the genus that occurs in East Africa). These birds come in two colour phases: chestnut brown, and black and white. Two-thirds of the Berenty paradise flycatchers are black and white. Look out for the nest which is built one metre from the ground. If you visit from mid-October to May you will see a variety of migrant birds from southeast Africa: broad-billed roller, Malagasy lesser cuckoo and lots of waders (sanderlings, greenshank, sandpiper, white-throated plover).

Then there are the **reptiles**. Although Berenty's chameleons are somewhat drab-coloured (two species are found here, *Furcifer verrucosus*, or warty chameleon, and *Furcifer lateralis*, often called jewel chameleon but in Berenty most un-gem like)

BROWN LEMURS AT BERENTY
John Buchan

Two subspecies of brown lemur, *Eulemur fulvus*, have been introduced to Berenty from other parts of the island.

The most numerous are the red-fronted lemurs, *Eulemur fulvus rufus*. There are two races in Madagascar, one of which comes from the southwest, near Toliara, and the other from the northeast. Colours are similar in both races: males are grey to grey-brown, with a black muzzle, pale patches above the eyes, and a fluffy orange cap; females lack the orange cap, have light grey cheeks as well as patches above the eyes, and are more of a rufous brown colour.

Note how these lemurs carry their young. Whereas a ring-tail baby clings to the mother's belly for the first couple of weeks and then transfers to her back, the red-fronted lemurs carry their young ventrally.

The other brown lemur is *E. f. collaris* which was introduced from the rainforest near Taolagnaro where it is endangered. The males have black faces, ears and crown of head, set off by bushy orange cheeks which extend to the neck forming a collar, hence the name. The females have greyish faces but the same orange cheeks/neck, although not as prominently as the male's. Both sexes are darkish brown to grey, with a stripe down the spine.

The two subspecies are interbreeding, so you may see hybrids in Berenty. This would not happen in their normal habitat where the ranges do not overlap.

they are plentiful. There is also a good chance of seeing huge ground boas. In captivity are sulky-looking crocodiles and some happy radiated tortoises.

Berenty has been welcoming tourists longer than any other place in Madagascar, and all who fall in love with it will want to do what they can to preserve it and its inhabitants. Cutting down on lemur feeding is one way, so please respect the notice restricting you to one banana per person. Voluntary restraints of this sort will avoid a 'Galapagisation' of Berenty, where strict rules will have to be imposed on tourists to protect the wildlife. Although you are free to explore the reserve on your own, a tour with the excellent English-speaking guides will greatly increase your knowledge and understanding. Their fee is paid by the reserve but a tip is appropriate.

Where to stay/eat

There are 12 new bungalows (sleep two, comfortable, fairly reliable hot water) and four older buildings with pairs of twin rooms. Accommodation is also available in Ankoba. Generators are switched off at 22.00, after which there is no electricity. Without the electric fans it can get very hot. Rooms are screened, but in the older bungalows you should burn a mosquito coil (provided).

There is a snack bar near the bungalows where breakfast is served, and the bar/restaurant (near the museum) offers good fixed-menu meals, and cool outdoor seats for your predinner drink. Near the restaurant is quite a good souvenir shop.

There are no telephones at Berenty. An efficient and reasonable laundry service is available – ask at Reception.

Excursions

Tourists staying more than a day should take the two excursions offered. The area of **spiny forest** here is superb (though hot) and may be your only chance to see mature *Alluaudia* trees. Some tower over 15m – an extraordinary sight. A visit to the **sisal factory** may sound boring but is, in fact, fascinating – and, for some, disturbing. On the natural history front, this is one of the best places in Madagascar to see and photograph the enormous *Nephila* spiders on their golden webs.

Museum of the Androy

This is undoubtedly the best ethnological museum in Madagascar, and if your interest in the region extends beyond the wildlife, you should allow at least an hour here. Several of the rooms are given over to an explanation (in English and French) of the traditional practices of the Antandroy people, illustrated by excellent photos. There are some beautiful examples of handicrafts and a small but interesting natural history section including a complete aepyornis egg. This museum should be seen in conjunction with the replica Antandroy 'village' near the botanical garden, where you can step inside a small house, very similar to those you pass on the road to Berenty.

All credit to M de Heaulme for celebrating the lives of the human inhabitants of the region in this way. Don't miss this opportunity to learn more about the People of the Thorns.

Amboasary Sud (Kaleta Park)

The private reserve, set up in competition with Berenty, is adjacent to that reserve and a good option for those who cannot afford the de Heaulme prices. The forest here is degraded (ie: not in its natural state) and has been browsed by domestic animals. That said, most visitors find the wildlife viewing as satisfying as at Berenty.

SISAL

This crop was introduced to Madagascar in the inter-war years, with the first exports taking place in 1922 when 42 tons were sent to France. By 1938, 2,537 tons were exported and 3,500 hectares of sisal were planted in the Tuléar and Fort Dauphin region. By 1950 production reached 3,080 tons. In 1952 a synthetic substitute was developed in the US and the market dropped. The French government stepped in with subsidies and bought 10,000 tons.

The Tuléar plantations were closed in 1958 leaving only the de Heaulme plantations in Fort Dauphin. In 1960 these covered 16,000 hectares, and by the mid 1990s 30,000 hectares of endemic spiny forest (that's about 100 square miles!) had been cleared to make way for the crop, with plantations under the ownership of six different companies. Workers earn 160,000Fmg per month. There is no sick pay or pension provision. The de Heaulme plantation alone employs 15,000 people.

And here's something to think about: in the late 1990s there has been a resurgence of demand for sisal, with exports predicted to reach 5,000 tons by the year 2005, putting more spiny forest at risk. Why? Because we 'green' consumers in the EU are demanding biodegradable packaging. What is the best biodegradable substance? Sisal!

The reserve is run by Rolande Laha, who for many years worked in Berenty, and is geared to independent travellers rather than groups. Hitherto most people came just for the day, but three new bungalows have been built (as yet with no water supply) and camping is allowed so overnight stays will soon become the norm.

One of the attractions here is the sifakas which are more approachable than in Berenty and even accept food from visitors. Whether this is a good thing for the sifakas, I'm not sure.

The usual Berenty extras along the road to Ambovombe – tombs and pitcher plants – are also visited.

The entrance fee is 50,000Fmg. If you also need transport it goes up to 500,000Fmg per person or 150,000Fmg for a group of three or more. Arrangements are best made through the Kaleta Hotel (tel: 212 87).

Réserve de Nahampoana

This is a new, readily accessible zoo cum reserve owned by Air Fort Services. The 67ha park is just 7km from Taolagnaro, on the way to Ste Luce, so easily visited in a day and provides the usual tame lemurs (both local species and introduced), reptiles (again, some chameleon species do not really belong here) and regional vegetation. The price, which includes transport, a pirogue trip on the lake, and a picnic lunch, is 100,000Fmg, or 50,000Fmg for a permit alone: the ideal lemur-fix for those on a tight budget. Bungalows, a restaurant and camping will be available soon.

Lac Anony

About 12km south of Amboasary is a brackish lagoon, Lac Anony. There are flamingoes here and a large number of other wading birds in a lunar landscape. There is a village, Antsovelo, and accommodation and food are available. Nearer the main road is the Hotel Bon Coin, which also has a restaurant.

Andohahela National Park

This new national park (pronounced Andoowah<u>e</u>la) which opened to tourists in September 1998, is a model of its kind. Much thought and sensitivity has gone into the blend of low-key tourist facilities and the involvement of local people, and all who are interested in how Madagascar is starting to solve its environmental problems should try to pay it a visit.

The reserve spans rainforest and spiny forest, and thus is of major importance and interest. A third component is the east/west transition forest which is the last place the triangulated palm (*Neodypsis decaryi*) can be found. These three distinct zones, or 'parcels' (from the French *parcelle*, meaning plot or area of land), make Andohahela unique in its biodiversity.

Andohahela Interpretation Centre (Centre d'Interpretation Andohahela)

Even if you are not able to visit Andohahela itself, do spend some time in this beautifully organised centre. It is a green building on the left-hand side of the road as you leave Taolagnaro.

The centre was set up with the help of the Peace Corps and the WWF, for both tourists and – more importantly – the local people. Through clear exhibits, labelled in English, French and Malagasy, it emphasises the importance of the forest and water to future generations of Malagasy, and explains the use of various medicinal plants. Local initiatives, overseen by the two energetic Peace Corps volunteers, Nancy Boriack and Mark Hillebrand, include the introduction of fuel-efficient cooking stoves that burn sisal leaves. Wind power is also being investigated. Schools are being built in the area, with educating the next generation on the importance of preserving the environment one of the priorities.

Visiting Andohahela

At the time of writing a visit to the National Park really requires the use of a 4WD vehicle and full camping gear. Fit and properly equipped hikers or cyclists can make it independently to the rainforest and transitional forest. All three sections are being developed for tourism, however, so find out the latest situation at the Interpretation Centre. The only tour operator currently offering packages to Andohahela is Air Fort Services (see page 214). Contact them for the latest details and prices.

The national park

The three 'parcels' of the national park are the spiny forest (Ihazofotsy village), the transition forest (Tsimalahy), and rainforest (Malio).

Ihazofotsy Visitors should remember that spiny forest is very hot, so camping/walking here can be quite arduous. That said, for the committed adventurer this is a wonderful area for wildlife, birding and botany. Even if you were to see no animals, the chance to walk through untouched spiny forest – the real Madagascar – gives you a glimpse of how extraordinary this land must have seemed to the first Europeans.

Apart from the fascinating trees and plants unique to this region, you should see sifaka (this is one of the areas where you can observe them leaping on to the spiny trunks of didierea trees without apparent harm), small mammals such as tenrecs (if you're lucky) and plenty of birds endemic to the south, such as running coua and sickle-billed vanga; also many reptiles. Equally you may see nothing! Remember that this is not Berenty; the wildlife tends to be shy, and is inactive during the heat of the day. Be patient.

MINING IN THE SOUTH: AN ENVIRONMENTAL AND SOCIOLOGICAL DILEMMA

The dry south of Madagascar has large deposits of titanium dioxide. Among other things this mineral is used as a base for paint. The Canadian company, Qit-Fer et Titane Inc (owned by Rio Tinto), in partnership with the Malagasy government, want to start mining for this mineral. Their plan is for the mine to be active for 40 or 50 years. It would be the largest such venture in Madagascar and would involve the building of a US$260-million factory, with a further US$90 million required to create a new harbour.

The project could bring 500 new jobs to a severely depressed area of the country. Jobs would create prosperity which would reduce the pressure on the environment caused by *tavy* and the felling of trees for charcoal. The project would involve clearing parts of the coastal littoral forest which has endemic flora and fauna.

A Rio Tinto representative writes: 'QIT and our Malagasy partner are well aware of the unique natural environment of Madagascar and the worldwide concern that it should be preserved and protected. That is why, in 1987, a comprehensive environmental study program which covered the range of physical, biological and community environments was initiated. An international team of specialists, each recognised in their respective fields, was drawn from Madagascar, Canada, the United States, Britain, Australia and France. A key issue identified by the report is the special botanical interest of the littoral forest that occupies some of the area to be mined.

'However, studies by QIT and others conclude that if the current rate of deforestation continues, most of the remaining littoral forest remnants would disappear within the next 25–40 years. The dilemma is how to meet the needs of villagers as well as conserve or restore key elements of the environment. QIT considers that social, conservation and rehabilitation programmes in association with the mining project could potentially be more beneficial than the "no mining" scenario.

'Additional environmental studies are required prior to an environmental review process by the government of Madagascar. After that, feasibility studies must be completed along with financing before an investment decision can be considered.'

In 1998 an estimated 30,000ha of forest was destroyed for agriculture; the mining programme will affect 4,000ha of forest.

At the time of writing there are no tourist facilities apart from a rudimentary trail system and trained guides, but campsites and possibly tourist bungalows are planned.

Tsimelahy I *loved* this place! Apart from reptiles (lizards and snakes), we saw little wildlife but the scenery and plants are utterly wonderful! This region is the only area in which the triangular palm is found; it says something for the rest of the botany that seeing this was not the highlight of our stay. The campsite for Tsimelahy is within a stone's throw of a large deep pool, fed by a waterfall, and fringed with elephant-ear plants. You can slip into the cool water from the smooth rocks and swim to your heart's content. The walk to this idyllic spot is equally enchanting: good trails run along both shores of the river Taratantsa, affording super views of white flowered *pachypodium lamerii*, and green forest. My favourite plant was the 'celebrity tree' (Lazar in Malagasy or *Cyphostema vitaceae*). It seems to start as a tree, then change its mind and become a true liana (it belongs to this family), draping its droopy top over neighbouring plants. Young Malagasy seeking popularity or success will ask the *mpanandro* (soothsayer) to ask the tree for help.

Another highlight for us was the visit to the little village of Tsimelahy. This is an inspiring example of how a newly-established protected area can involve and benefit the local people. There are well-made handicrafts for sale and you will be treated to a rousing song about the forest and its animals from the children in the tiny school room.

Tsimelahy is accessible for independent travellers who are prepared to hike the 12km trail (or 15km road) from Ranopiso. A permit and directions are obtainable from the Interpretive Centre.

Malio The rainforest area has a trail system and campsites. It has lagged behind the other two 'parcels' because most tourists have visited a rainforest reserve (Périnet or Ranomafana) by the time they reach Taolagnaro. This is part of its appeal... there will be no crowds. The area has all the rainforest requisites: waterfalls, orchids and lemurs (*Lemur fulvus*). To get there you take the paved road out of Taolagnaro for approximately 15km, turn north on a dirt road before the town of Manambaro and go 6km to the nice little village of Malio. Independent travellers can buy a permit at the ANGAP office in Taolagnaro and reach the trail head by taxi.

OKAVANGO TOURS & SAFARIS

Simply the best for tailored holidays
on
Madagascar
& the Indian Ocean Islands

We also specialise in
Botswana, Zambia, Malawi, Namibia
Zimbabwe, Tanzania, Uganda and Kenya

Tel 0181 343 3283   Fax 0181 343 3287

Marlborough House
298 Regents Park Road
London
N3 2TJ

info@okavango.com
www.okavango.com

Part Four

The East

Indri

Toamasina (Tamatave) and the Northeast

OVERVIEW

Punished by its weather (rain, cyclones), eastern Madagascar is notoriously challenging to travellers. In July 1817 James Hastie wrote in his diary: 'If this is the good season for travelling this country, I assert it is impossible to proceed in the bad.' With this in mind you should avoid the wettest months of February and March, and remember that June to August can be very damp as well. The driest months are September to November, with December and January worth the risk. April and May are fairly safe apart from the possibility of cyclones. The east coast has another problem: sharks (see box, page 233) and dangerous currents. So although there are beautiful beaches, swimming is safe only in protected areas.

Despite – or perhaps because of – these drawbacks, the northeast is perhaps Madagascar's most rewarding region for independent travellers. It is not yet on the itinerary for many groups, yet has a few beautifully situated upmarket hotels for that once-in-a-lifetime holiday, or wonderful exploratory possibilities for the intrepid backpacker. Much of Madagascar's unique flora and fauna is concentrated in the eastern rainforests and any serious naturalist will want to pay a visit. Other attractions are the rugged mountain scenery with rivers tumbling down to the Indian Ocean, the friendly people, abundant fruit and seafood, and access to the lovely island of Nosy Boraha (Ile Sainte Marie).

The chief products of the east are coffee, vanilla, bananas, coconuts, cloves and lychees.

History

This region has an interesting history dominated by European pirates and slave traders. While powerful kingdoms were being forged in other parts of the country, the east coast remained divided among numerous small clans. It was not until the 18th century that one ruler, Ratsimilaho, unified the region. The half-caste son of Thomas White, an English pirate, and briefly educated in Britain, Ratsimilaho responded to the attempt by Chief Ramanano to take over all the east coast ports. His successful revolt was furthered by his judiciously marrying an important princess; by his death in 1754 he ruled an area stretching from the Masoala Peninsula to Mananjary.

The result of this liaison of various tribes was the Betsimisaraka, now the second largest ethnic group in Madagascar. Some (in the area of Maroantsetra) practise second burial, although with less ritual than the Merina and Betsileo.

Getting around

Although the map shows roads of some sort running almost the full length of the east coast, this is deceptive. Rain and cyclones regularly destroy bridges so it is impossible to know in advance whether a selected route will be usable, even in the 'dry' season. The rain-saturated forests drain into the Indian Ocean in numerous rivers, many of which can only be crossed by ferry. And there is not enough traffic to ensure a regular service. For those with limited time, therefore, the only practical way to get to the less accessible towns is by air: there are regular planes to Nosy Boraha (Ile Sainte Marie), and flights between Toamasina (Tamatave) and Antsiranana (Diego Suarez). Planes go several days a week from Toamasina to Maroantsetra, Antalaha and Mananara, and to Sambava.

For the truly adventurous it is possible to work your way down (or up) the coast providing you have plenty of time and are prepared to walk.

TOAMASINA (TAMATAVE)
History
As in all the east coast ports, Toamasina (pronounced 'Tourmasin') began as a pirate community. In the late 18th century its harbour attracted the French, who already had a foothold in Ile Sainte Marie, and Napoleon I sent his agent Sylvain Roux to establish a trading post there. In 1811, Sir Robert Farquhar, governor of the newly British island of Mauritius, sent a small naval squadron to take the port of Toamasina. This was not simply an extension of the usual British/French antagonism, but an effort to stamp out slavery at its source, Madagascar being the main supplier to the Indian Ocean. The slave trade had been abolished by the British parliament in 1807. The attack was successful, and Sylvain Roux was exiled. During subsequent years, trade between Mauritius and Madagascar built Toamasina into a major port. In 1845, after a royal edict subjecting European traders to the harsh Malagasy laws, French and British warships bombarded Toamasina, but a landing was repelled leaving 20 dead. During the 1883–85 war the French occupied Toamasina but Malagasy troops successfully defended the fort of Farafaty just outside the town.

Theories on the origin of the name Toamasina vary, but one is that King Radama I tasted the seawater here and remarked 'Toa masina' – 'It's salty'.

Toamasina today
Toamasina has always had an air of shabby elegance with some fine palm-lined boulevards and once-impressive colonial houses. Since Cyclone Geralda, which struck with exceptional ferocity in 1994, it's a bit shabbier, but still bustling, with a good variety of bars, snack bars and restaurants.

The telephone area code is 53.

Getting there and away
By road
Route Nationale 2 (RN2) is arguably the country's best road, and thus attracts dangerous drivers. Nevertheless, this is the fastest and cheapest way of reaching Toamasina from Tana. Vehicles run only twice a day, morning or night, and take from six to 12 hours. There is a wide choice of vehicle: bus (auto-car), minibus, and Peugeot station wagon. The large buses are the most comfortable (MAMI is a popular bus company); a night bus may seem like a good option but it is impossible to sleep because of the radio turned up to top volume; 25,000Fmg. Minibuses and Peugeots are faster, and a little more expensive (35,000Fmg).

Book your seat at least a day in advance at the taxi-brousse departure point, Fasan'ny karana, on the road to the airport.

Warning: Even if you've never suffered from motion sickness, take precautions on this trip. The macho drivers and winding road are a challenge to any stomach.

The road north to Soanierana-Ivongo is paved; a taxi-brousse to this departure point for Ile Sainte Marie costs 15,000Fmg.

By air
There are daily flights between Tana and Toamasina.

By rail
The once-famous train from Tana to Toamasina sadly no longer runs to the coast. Or probably not. 'There are supposedly trains two or three days a week to/from Moramanga but it's uncertain whether they ever work. If they are working, the journey takes about 20 hours and that's on a good day.' (Rupert Parker)

By sea and river
Toamasina's harbour is also its Port Fluvial where you can look for boats to take you down the Pangalanes (see page 265). Serious masochists can book the infamous Rapiko here for a trip-from-hell to Sainte Marie (see page 258).

Where to stay
Category A
Hotel Miramar Tel: 328 70. Comfortable chalets in a good location. The pool is open to the public, and the hotel is very convenient for the airport. Excellent food, too, but an irritating recent requirement is that all guests eat breakfast (17,000Fmg). Chalets cost 185,000Fmg. MasterCard accepted.

Neptune 35 Bd Ratsimilaho (on the seafront); tel: 336 30; fax: 324 26. The poshest hotel in town. 425Ff double. Swimming pool, excellent food, good bar. Credit cards accepted.

Noor Hotel At intersection of Bd Mal Foch and Rue du Mal de Lattre de Tassigny (north side); tel: 338 45. 112,950Fmg (air conditioned), 92,500Fmg (with fan). No restaurant. Credit cards accepted.

Hotel Joffre 30 Bd Joffre; tel: 323 90. An atmospheric old hotel with all facilities; recently refurbished rooms 118,500Fmg. Credit cards accepted.

Hotel les Flamboyants Bd de la Libération; tel: 323 50. Air-conditioned room with WC and shower; 78,000Fmg; with fan 71,000Fmg. 'Best value in town.' Credit cards accepted.

Hotel Le Toamasina Rue Reine Betty; tel: 335 49; fax: 336 12. Round the corner from the Beau Rivage. Comfortable and efficient. 149,000–165,000Fmg. Reasonable food. Visa cards accepted.

Hotel Generation 129, Bd Joffre; tel: 321 05/328 34. A newish hotel serving excellent food. Their English-language menu offers, 'Swellfish' and 'crunched big shrimp'.

Category B
Capricorn Large rooms, some with balconies, and en-suite bathrooms; 60,000–78,000Fmg.

Hotel Etoile-Rouge 13 Rue du Mal de Lattre de Tassigny; tel: 322 90. A popular, friendly hotel. Most rooms are cell-like, but have fans or barred windows which can be left open. 30,000–35,000Fmg for rooms with shower or en-suite WC. No restaurant.

Hotel Beau Rivage (Better known by the name of its very good Italian restaurant, La Paillotte); tel: 330 35; Rue G Clémenceau. Twelve clean rooms, some with fan and balcony. 30,000–36,000Fmg.

Hotel Eden Appropriately situated near the Adam & Eve Snack Bar on Bd Joffre. No fans. Hot water.

Darafify Near the Hotel Miramar; tel: 326 18. Basic bungalows with cold showers and en-suite WC; 62,000Fmg.

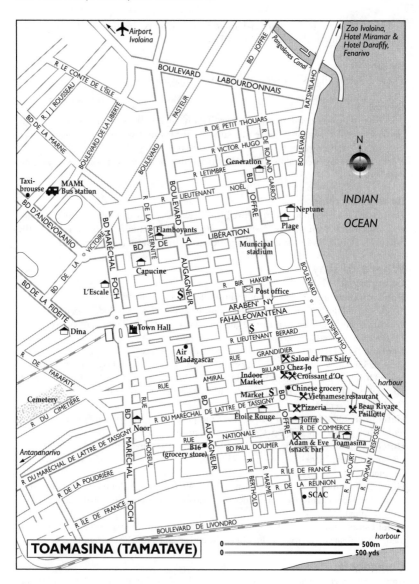

TOAMASINA (TAMATAVE)

Category C

Hotel Plage Bd de la Libération (round the corner from the Neptune); tel: 320 90. Quite clean and comfortable, but the disco is murder and appears to go on seven nights a week.

Hotel Capucine Near the railway station (off Bd Poincaré, opposite the Hotel de Ville). Clean, friendly, but very hot; 31,000Fmg.

Hotel Capucine Annexe Near taxi-brousse station so convenient for late arrival or early departure, but hot; 26,000Fmg.

Hotel Dina Basic, with cold water and smelly loos. 'Stand facing the railway station, go down the road to the right past some snack shops, before the road bends to the right there is a forked left turn which runs alongside the tracks. Go down this road, take the first road to the right, and the building on the corner is the Hotel Dina.'

Where to eat
The **Hotel Neptune** has the best restaurant; especially recommended is its all-you-can-eat Sunday buffet (lunch). The **Joffre** and **Flamboyants** are almost as good.

Jade Next door to the Noor Hotel. This is an upmarket Chinese restaurant with good food but quite expensive.

Vietnamese Restaurant Rue du Mal de Lattre de Tassigny. Recommended for vegetarians; 'excellent, inexpensive meatless curry'.

Restaurant Fortuna A very good Chinese restaurant.

La Pacifique Rue de la Batterie. A popular and good-value Chinese restaurant.

La Récrea 'A trendy place on the beach, north side. A bit pricey but a beautiful view' or 'the most lousy place we've been to'. Two opinions – you decide!

La Paillotte Rue de Commerce 'A great selection of Italian food, including pizzas, and good desserts.'

Queens Club (Round the corner from the Hotel Plage). Recommended.

Adam & Eve Snack Bar 13 Rue Nationale; tel: 334 56 (near Hotel Joffre). 'Best cuppa in Madagascar.' Other star features are good prices, strong, hot coffee and delicious samosas (sambos). Always busy, slow service.

Croissant d'Or Recommended for breakfast. Operates a small grocery with hard-to-find *vazaha* items.

Restaurant Tsarahaza Pizzeria Italian/French run, good food, nice atmosphere.

Shopping
B16 Supermarket, Bd Augagneur, in the south part of town has an excellent selection of goods.

The *Librairie* near the market is very good and sells CDs of Malagasy music as well as books and nice postcards.

Car hire
Aventour has an office here: Rue Bir Hakeim; tel: 322 43.

SAFETY UNDER WATER
South African diver and spearfisher Jeremy Buirski says that his first view of the east coast at Toamasina was a revelation. It confirmed his belief that the reason the area is notorious for shark attacks is the dirty water. All the way up the coast as far as Pointe Larée the water had been turned a muddy brown by the run-off from numerous rivers – he wasn't at all surprised that people got bitten there. At Sainte Marie, where the water varied from clear to moderately dirty (three metres' visibility), he never saw a shark.

Before venturing into the ocean in Madagascar ask local opinion about safety. The French word for shark is *requin* and in Malagasy it's *antsantsa*. Bear in mind, however, that drowning, not shark attacks, is responsible for most sea deaths, and that there is often a formidable undertow on the east coast.

In addition to keeping a wary eye on sharks, Jeremy warns prospective snorkellers to avoid coming into bodily contact with underwater plants, as there are several types that sting. He also saw at least one stonefish, and urges caution when peering into holes, because lionfish are common and spend most of the daylight hours hidden away.

Day excursion from Toamasina
Zoo Ivoloina

This began life in 1898 as a rather grand Botanical Garden, but is now an animal rehabilitation centre funded by the Durrell Wildlife Conservation Trust and Duke University (North Carolina, USA) and restored with great dedication by Charles Welch and Andrea Katz. Radiated tortoises live in ample enclosures, as well as a troop of white-fronted brown lemurs. The black-and-white ruffed lemurs are unique in Madagascar in that they were brought here from a zoo in the USA to form the nucleus of a population that will eventually be returned to the wild. There are plans to breed other highly endangered lemur species such as diademed sifaka. There is also a trio of grey bamboo lemurs, living in a small patch of bamboo out in the open – great for close-up photographs.

Various other lemurs at Ivoloina are being carefully prepared for rehabilitation; many of them were confiscated at the airport or rescued from being kept as pets. This is why some of the animals appear in poor condition.

Visitors who are keen to see what aid organisations are doing to help Madagascar with its appalling environmental problems should pay a visit to Ivoloina. There is an excellent new education centre with some beautiful displays, and a Peace Corps volunteer has been working with the local schoolchildren, who have a tree-planting scheme. Another project works with local people to provide alternative sources of food and income – chickens and bees – so they don't need to exploit the forest.

Ivoloina is 12km north of town, and is open daily from 09.00 to 17.00; the entrance fee is 15,000Fmg. Drinks (no food) are available at a kiosk next to the lake.

THE ROUTE NORTH

The road is tarred and in good condition as far as Soanierana-Ivongo. Beyond that it is usually passable as far as Maroantsetra. Then you have to take to the air or journey on foot across the neck of the road-free Masoala Peninsula.

Mahavelona (Foulpointe)

The town of Mahavelona is unremarkable, but nearby is an interesting old circular fortress with mighty walls faced with an iron-hard mixture of sand, shells and eggs. There are some old British cannons marked GR. This fortress was built in the early 19th century by the Merina governor of the town, Rafaralahy, shortly after the Merina conquest of the east coast. There may now be a charge to visit the fortress.

Where to stay/eat

Before reaching the town you pass the once very smart Manda Beach hotel and the smaller Au Gentil Pêcheur next door. Both offer bungalows and safe swimming, and the Gentil Pêcheur is known for its excellent food. Manda Beach may be booked in Tana (tel: 22 317 61) as well as locally (322 43). It accepts credit cards but adds a 6.5% fee.

Mahambo

A beach resort with safe swimming (but nasty sandfleas) and some beach chalets.

Where to stay/eat

Le Gîte The most comfortable of the two main hotels. Two-storey bungalows with hot showers and en-suite WC. Your stay will be enlivened by the four free-ranging lemurs (three black-and-white ruffed, and one crowned) and by the herds of zebu on the beach. About 250,000Fmg per bungalow. Set menu for 25,000Fmg.

Le Dola Spanish owned, dilapidated (cyclone damage), but with good food and mosquito nets. 137,000Fmg per bungalow (sleeps up to five people) with cold shower and en-suite WC. Alternatives are **Le Récif** or **Zanatany** (bungalows).

Heading west

Between Mahambo and Fenoarivo Atsinanana is a road leading inland to **Vavatenina**, where there is basic accommodation in bungalows, and on to **Anjahambe**. This town marks the beginning (or end) of the Smugglers' Path to Lake Alaotra (see page 276).

Fenoarivo Atsinanana (Fénérive)

Beyond Mahambo is the former capital of the Betsimisaraka empire. There is a clove factory in town which distils the essence of cloves, cinnamon and green peppers for the perfume industry. They are not geared up for tourist visits but will show you round if you ask.

There are several basic hotels, including **Belle Rose** bungalows on the road leading to the hospital. Dolphins can be seen swimming offshore.

West to Vohilengo

From Fenoarivo a road leads west to Vohilengo. This makes a pleasant diversion for those with their own transport, especially during the lychee season. 'We arrived at the start of a six-week lychee bonanza... Along the road to Vohilengo were prearranged pickup points where the pickers would bring their two ten-kilo panniers. Vohilengo is a small village, perfumed with the scent of cloves laid out to dry; the local *hotely* sells coffee at 80Fmg.' (Clare Hermans)

Soanierana-Ivongo

Known more familiarly as 'Sierra Ivongo', this little town is one of the starting-points for the boat ride to Sainte Marie. It is also the end of the tarred road.

Where to stay/eat

Hotel Zanatany (if still open) is a friendly, family-owned place. The **Bon Hotel** is, reportedly, not very *bon*. This lack of accommodation is certain to be rectified as S-Ivongo establishes itself as the gateway town to Sainte Marie.

Tour operator

Look out for Nord-Est Nature, run by Pascal Bonneton, a Frenchman, who is planning to develop tourism in the area. Contact details: BP 9; tel/fax: 53 333 80.

Ongoing transport

If you are continuing north, try to find 'Monsieur Cocos'. Go to the Bureau of Forestry at the S-Ivongo barge jetty (opposite the police station). The Chef de Forêt usually knows when M Cocos is expected. 'If Cocos is not due for a day or two ignore the Sainte Marie touts and ask for Ben and his pirogue. Ben will take you 16km along the inland waterways: a truly enchanting experience – birds, flowers, forest. A hidden corner of Madagascar.' (Paul and Sarah McBride)

CONTINUING NORTH (IF YOU DARE!)

From Soanierana-Ivongo the road is unreliable, to say the least. As fast as bridges are repaired they wash away again. You may have a fairly smooth taxi-brousse ride with ferries taking you across the rivers, or you may end up walking for hours and wading rivers or finding a pirogue to take you across. You should get local advice before setting out, especially if you have a lot of luggage to carry or are on a tight schedule.

Rupert Parker, who drove from Mananara to Toamasina in 1998, reports on the conditions: 'There are many ferries and bridges to cross. The last but one ferry (ie: the second one if driving north from S-Ivongo) is also dependent on high tide to work so you can have to wait up to six hours. The other problem is that ferries are only supposed to work in the hours of daylight, so you have to bribe the ferry men if you are travelling outside these hours, as well as having to send a boy in a pirogue to find them, as they're always on the opposite side of the river to you. The fare from Antanambe to Tamatave is 25,000Fmg and the trip took us 16 hours in a good Japanese 4WD, although it was raining constantly and we wasted time waiting for ferries. We also got stuck once but fortunately it was near a village and the population turned out to get us out, but that took a good hour. We also spent time attempting to extricate a taxi-brousse pickup truck which had sunk up to its chassis in the middle of a river and that added another hour to our journey.'

Andrangazaha

There is just one reason to stop at this little place midway between S-Ivongo and Manompana: Madame Zakia. 'Madame runs the best place north of Tamatave. All vehicles going north stop there to eat. Why? Because Madame feeds the drivers for free, passengers pay. Her food is excellent, bungalows clean with mozzie nets, away from the noise and bustle of town in the bush where you can wait for a lift in quiet comfort.' (Paul and Sarah McBride)

Manompana

For many years this village, pronounced 'Manompe', was *the* departure point for Nosy Boraha/Sainte Marie. Despite the competition from Soanierana-Ivongo, there are still boats to the island; see page 258.

Much of the information in this section was supplied by Paul and Sarah McBride, who live in Manompana. Paul and Sarah will welcome any tourist who wants to drop in at their boatshed on RN5 for up-to-date advice and an English 'cuppa'.

Around Manompana there is good surfing and swimming, 'the occasional shark, but by southern hemisphere standards no problem. Diving on the reefs is safe. There are three cascades in the rainforest nearby, all magnificent. A day's walk there and back but not overly tiring.'

Where to stay/eat

Chez Lou Lou Central; six beachfront A-frame bungalows, very clean, good toilets, good seafood.
Chez Vankies Far end of town; five beachfront bungalows. Secluded, no mozzie nets.
Mahle Hotel On Mahle Point, 1km from the village. French owned. It usually takes only prearranged package bookings from Réunion. 'Very beautiful place, oceanfront, good diving on 4km of reef, untouched forest, will allow campers, price varies depending on day and mood.'

Medical clinic

Manompana has a French-built first-aid post with eight beds and two resident doctors as well as an ample supply of medicines, but it's closed on weekends and holidays.

MANOMPANA TO MAROANTSETRA

Hotel Chez Lou Lou may be able to arrange for a 4WD taxi-brousse to take visitors from the town to Mananara-Nord 'sort of weekly' at 15,000Fmg per head.

Antanambe

Some 35km north of Manompana, on the edge of the UNESCO biosphere project, is this pretty little town and a French-owned hotel (four bungalows) which has everything: gas cooking, filtered running water, pressure showers and flushing toilets with soft paper, comfortable beds with mozzie nets; all this plus a superb restaurant with Creole and French cooking and fresh fish daily! Not surprisingly, it's already very popular, and being expanded. Alain and Céline Grandin arrange tours in the Mananara biosphere reserve, and diving and fishing excursions to a vast reef 1km from the hotel. The 1998 price was 60,000Fmg per bungalow and 25,000Fmg for a three-course meal. There is no way to contact Alain and Céline in advance, but it's worth taking pot luck and simply turning up.

There is just one problem with this otherwise idyllic place: 'When we were there we were attacked by tiny black sandflies which leave nasty red spots which take weeks to go away – they can cover your body in these in a matter of minutes and it's wise to be careful (we weren't...!) Apparently it is a seasonal problem so you might be lucky.' (Rupert Parker)

Permits to visit the reserve can be bought for 50,000Fmg in the ANGAP office adjacent to the hotel and it takes about two hours to walk to the entrance. It's possible to stay overnight in the park in huts but you will need a guide from the town. A nice day excursion is to walk to the edge of the park and skirt round it to a spectacular waterfall which has cold clear pools for swimming.

Mananara-Nord

Mananara, 185km north of Soanierana-Ivongo at the entrance to the Bay of Antongil, is the only place in Madagascar where one can be pretty much assured of seeing an aye-aye in the wild, on Aye-Aye Island. The hotel of choice is Hotel Aye-Aye on the beachfront opposite the airport. Bungalows with shower but shared WC cost 60,000Fmg. Good meals (must be ordered in advance) 25,000Fmg. The Malagasy owner, Oliver, offers island tours and other excursions.

Other hotels include the once recommended Chez Roger, which is poor value at 30,000Fmg. A better bet is the Ton-ton Galet, a friendly, modest set of bungalows located near the hospital.

Transport is usually advertised in the big Chinese shop in the square.

What to do in and around town

There is more to do in Mananara than Aye-Aye Island and a visit to the Biosphere reserve. There's a lively market, a good disco at weekends, and the ocean for relaxation. Three kilometres south of the town is a beautiful bay protected by a reef, with shallow, safe swimming.

Aye-Aye Island

Visitors who imagine Aye-Aye Island to be a chunk of pristine forest are in for a shock: 'Sharing the island with the aye-ayes are the warden and his family, dogs, chickens, pigs and a pet lemur. But seeing an aye-aye is almost guaranteed. On the night we visited we saw a mother and her baby. The warden was very entertaining and obviously very fond of, and proud of, his aye-ayes. It was a wonderful Experience.' (R Harris and G Jackson)

Visits to the island are best organised by the Aye-Aye Hotel. The cost is around 40,000Fmg.

Mananara National Park and Biosphere Reserve

This example of eastern rainforest has been described by John Dransfield of Kew Gardens as 'The Biosphere's Botanical Paradise'. To visit it you need a permit from the Biosphere office in Mananara-Nord or from ANGAP in the access town of Antanambe.

It is quite challenging to do the park on your own. The most interesting part of the park is inland. You drive to **Sandrakatsy** by taxi-brousse (the first one leaves at 08.00 and the journey takes about two hours) and then walk for 1¹/₂ hours to **Ivavary** where there is accommodation for park (Biosphere) visitors. From here to the park is a further 1¹/₂ hours.

If all this sounds too much like hard work, you can arrange an organised visit to the park through the Hotel Aye-Aye in Mananara or the hotel in Antanambe.

Mananara to Maroantsetra

To continue the journey north is an adventure, but that's part of the attraction.

The intrepid Luc Selleslagh set out in a small boat: 'On the way the sea got rougher and rougher, the waves twice as high as the boat... I thought we were going to end between the sharks. The five other passengers were all sick. I was too afraid to be sick. Finally the captain decided to return!' After that Luc set out on foot. The bridges across the rivers sounded almost as dangerous as the sea but at least he was master of his fate. After two days and one lift he reached **Rantabe** from where there is at least a vehicle a day heading for Maroantsetra. Luc warns that even in ideal conditions it takes at least eight hours to go the 110km.

More recently (1998) Rupert Parker did the trip by 4WD vehicle. 'The road is the worst I've ever experienced but also the most spectacular. It hugs the coast climbing up and down through virgin forest right down to the sea, affording stunning glimpses of cliffs and deserted bays if you can divert your attention from holding on for dear life. It took us four hours to do the 40km. There are ferries, broken-down bridges and some sections of the route which are like giant's staircases – huge boulders haphazardly scattered over steep inclines. Definitely mission impossible, but because of that the forest is largely uncleared and it's one of the most beautiful areas in Madagascar.

MAROANTSETRA AND THE MASOALA PENINSULA

Despite difficulty of access and dodgy weather, this has long been a sought-after destination for intrepid wildlife enthusiasts because of the nearby island reserve of Nosy Mangabe (aye-ayes, ruffed lemurs, plus uroplatus and other exciting fauna) and the Masoala Peninsula with its primary rainforest. Now that there is a first-class hotel, Maroantsetra seems likely to become a regular stop on the ecotourist circuit.

Maroantsetra

Nestled at the far end of the Bay of Antongil, Maroantsetra is Madagascar at its most authentic. Well away from the usual tourist circuits, it is a prosperous, friendly, and sleepy little town, just starting to accept its role as gateway to the best of the eastern rainforest.

Getting there and away
By air

Most people fly. Consequently flights tend to be booked well in advance. The 1999 schedule shows only one jet (737) flying on Saturdays; otherwise you must take your chance on the Twin Otter. Check latest schedules/availability with Air Mad. The airport is 8km from town.

By land and sea

There are two spectacular approaches to Maroantsetra on foot. The most beautiful, and easiest, is to walk from Mananara (see above). The tougher option is to hike from Antalaha (see page 243). Alternatively you can make your way here by sea.

MAROANTSETRA

Where to stay

Relais du Masoala Ten spacious, palm-thatched bungalows are set in 7ha of gardens and coconut groves overlooking the Bay of Antongil. Described proudly as 'Malagasy huts with American bathrooms', the rooms contain beds which are extra long to accommodate large *vazahas*, the showers work, and the covered verandas overlook the bay. There is a swimming pool and the food is excellent. US$50 per bungalow per day, or equivalent in Fmg. Bookings through Cortez Travel – email: cortez@dts.mg. The Relais runs tours to Nosy Mangabe (with optional camping overnight), birdwatching in the Masoala Peninsula, pirogue excursions up river, whale-watching, and many other trips. Near the hotel is a small forest where aye-aye are occasionally seen. The guide Julien (brother of Maurice and Patrice of Périnet) takes guests on night walks here. Mind you, you may not need to leave the hotel: 'An aye-aye was recently spotted on the roof of the Relais by Christophe who was working on the books, late at night'. (Monique Rodriguez)

Motel Coco Beach BP 1; tel: 18. Bungalows on the outskirts of town. 90,000Fmg. Meals in the spacious dining room are usually good, with an extensive menu. The owner is Patrice and his wife 'Madame Patrice'. One attraction of Coco Beach is the striped tenrecs running about in the garden at night. Tours to Nosy Mangabe or Masoala.

Hotel Vatsy New bungalows and older rooms at a reasonable price. Small restaurant. Recommended.

Hotel du Centre Across from the market offering rooms and bungalows for about 35,000Fmg. 'I rather like this place. The bungalows are modest but well-kept and in a tidy garden. The location is excellent and I would recommend it without hesitation to travellers on a tight budget' (MR)

Tropical Bungalows, cold water but hot water is brought to you in a bucket for washing. 'The toilet is a privy in the yard and consists of a raised shed with a seat on it. On the ground below is an oil drum so you need to aim carefully!' (Frances Kerridge)

Hotel Maroa Nice new bungalows with showers, etc. Excellent food, but slow service. Good value at 65,000Fmg per room.

Eating and making merry

John Kupiec recommends the following restaurant: 'Le Pagode de Chine across from the gas station serves wonderful seafood. Once I discovered it I ate nowhere else.'

'There's a brilliant disco called the Calypso. Very friendly. Should be 2,500Fmg entrance but *vazahas* get charged 5,000Fmg. Great atmosphere. The people still do a couple of the traditional dances as well as jive.' (Katie Bloxam)

Excursions

Andranofotsy and Navana

This very worthwhile tour is a pirogue trip up the Andranofotsy river to the village of the same name. The vegetation and riverlife viewed on the way are fascinating, and the unspoilt (so far) village, with its inquisitive inhabitants, is peaceful and endearing.

Equally worthwhile is a visit to **Navana**. Follow the coast east along a beach backed by thickets, through waterways clogged with flowering water-hyacinth and past plenty of forest. You need to cross a lot of water on a pirogue, a regular local service. It takes an hour through little canals and costs very little. There is a hotel in Navana and you can also get there by boat from Maroantsetra.

Nosy Mangabe

In fine weather the island of Nosy Mangabe is superb. It has beautiful sandy coves, marvellous trees with huge buttress roots and also strangler figs. And it's bursting with wildlife including, of course, its famous aye-ayes which were released here in the 1960s to prevent what was then thought to be their imminent extinction. If aye-ayes are what you're after, there's little point in coming here just for the day (they are nocturnal) but there is plenty to see on a day visit, including the weird and wonderful leaf-tailed gecko, *uroplatus fimbriatus*.

Relais du Masoala and Motel Coco Beach both run trips here.

Getting there and away

To visit the island you must have a permit. They are available from the Projet Masoala office near the market in Maroantsetra. A guide is mandatory. Information on boat hire can be had from the Motel Coco Beach. However, there is also the option (risky) of going by pirogue. All boats leave early in the morning when the Bay of Antongil is calm. It takes 45 minutes (by motorised launch) to Nosy Mangabe.

Don't forget to bring sunscreen and drinking water. If you're camping bring biodegradable soap to avoid polluting the brook at the site. There is a camping place on the island with erratic loos and a wonderful cold shower – a waterfall has been piped into a cubicle.

Exploring the island

Not everyone sees aye-ayes; the best time to view them is between June and September, when they come right down to the trees by the shore to feed. But there is a wealth of other creatures: white-fronted brown lemurs, black-and-white ruffed lemurs – these are quite difficult to see, but you will hear them – bright red frogs, and reptiles such as the marvellous uroplatus, chameleons, and snakes. The trails have recently been upgraded and walking, though strenuous, is not difficult.

To complete your experience of Nosy Mangabe climb the hill to the lighthouse. The views here are superb and en route you will have the chance to see all sorts of reptiles, invertebrates, as well as other sights, sounds and smells. It's a magical island. In rain, though, the paths are slippery and it's pretty unpleasant. And it rains often.

As you leave Nosy Mangabe the boatman will often take you to see some old (15th-century) inscriptions carved on some rocks on the shore. Fascinating! And there is also a recent shipwreck.

The Masoala Peninsula

The peninsula (pronounced 'Mashwahl') is one of the largest and most diverse areas of virgin rainforest in Madagascar, and probably harbours the greatest number of unclassified species. Any scientific expedition here hits the jackpot – for example a Harvard biologist identified 100 species of ant in Masoala alone, many of them new to science.

The peninsula's importance was recognised by the French back in 1927 when they gave it reserve status, but independent Madagascar was swift to degazette it in 1964. However, in 1996, 210,000ha of the Masoala Peninsula were declared a National Park. This, however, was only one-fifth of the area recommended for protection; now the park covers 410,000ha. A lot of thought has gone into getting it right this time. The US-based agency, CARE International, which is in charge of the project, has been involving the local people in all stages of the development of the plan, trying to find sustainable sources of income through tourism or other schemes which are not alien to the local traditions.

How to visit Masoala National Park

As always, the easiest way is to join a tour. Both the Motel Coco Beach and Relais du Masoala run comprehensive trips here with all arrangements taken care of. Independent travellers have a more exciting time, starting with the knowledge that one of the local boat owners hires the town dwarf to sit in the boat with his foot plugging the hole at the bottom to prevent the water coming in.

The area of the park currently visited by ecotourists is the part being studied by naturalists from the Missouri Botanical Gardens and the Peregrine Fund. The access village is **Ambanizana** (pronounced Ambani<u>zan</u>) which can only be reached by boat (2½ hours from Maroantsetra). Talk to the manager of the Coco Beach for details of boat availability and price. Pack your gear in plastic bags to protect it from rain, and bring sunscreen to protect yourself from sunburn.

At the Ambanizana landing point is a warden, George Modeste, and some palm-thatched shelters operated by Motel Coco Beach. These comprise a cooking/eating shelter, a long-drop toilet, and two simple shelters which provide extra protection from the frequent torrential rain. There is room to pitch tents under these. There are beds, and providing you have a good mozzie net you won't need a tent. But there are *lots* of mosquitoes!

A trail leads up into the forest. Local agriculture has impinged on this, and you will have to walk for half an hour or so before you reach true primary forest. Your goal will probably be red-ruffed lemurs, which have been hunted, so are shy, and the wealth of birds for which the peninsula is famous. One of the most significant recent finds at Masoala is the red owl. In 1995 the Peregrine Fund located some owls and radio-tagged the adult female and one of her young. Someone from the Peregrine Fund can take birders to see the owls at roost. In return, the visitor is asked for a donation which goes towards buying equipment for the village primary school. 'The pupils and their parents know that the gifts come from tourists wishing to see the special birds which are dependent on the local forest. The forest's existence depends on the parents...a neat and very simple ecotourism project.' (Gavin and Val Thomson)

Most visitors will content themselves with hiking the trails and examining the wonderful natural world around them. You need to be quite fit to do these hikes – the lower semi-cultivated slopes are very hot, and where it is cooler and wetter there are leeches – but the rewards are limitless, especially for birders. Species recorded here include helmet and Bernier's vanga, red-breasted coua and scaly ground-roller.

For the real Masoala experience, however, take a pirogue to **Andranobe**, about

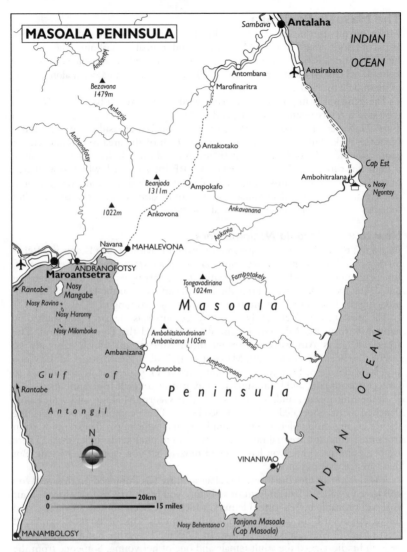

MASOALA PENINSULA

an hour's journey round the coast, and the research centre for the Peregrine Fund. 'This area is just fantastic! Pristine, primary forest comes right down to the ocean...' (Nick Garbutt). You are more likely to see rare species here than along the trails of Ambanizana. To return you can either walk the 7km back or take the pirogue (though afternoon seas tend to be choppy).

There is not just the forest to delight you. The village of Ambanizana is a peaceful collection of bamboo and palm-thatched huts and shyly curious people. There are no cars, no discarded rubbish (because there is nothing to discard) and no hassle. If visitors follow the principles of 'minimum impact' (which is what ecotourism should be all about) and do nothing that will alter this (and remember, one sweet or pen given to one child will cause immediate and irreversible change) then Masoala will have registered a significant success.

There are snorkelling possibilities around the coral reefs off Masoala but never go into the water without checking on safe areas with your guide; the Bay of Antongil is notorious for sharks. It is safe to swim off the beach at Ambanizana (but there is no coral).

Walking from Maroantsetra to Antalaha

I have heard mixed reports of this five-day hike. The distance is 152km, and in the heat it is very strenuous. Considering that you are mainly passing through secondary forest and cultivated areas, it doesn't attract me as much, say, as hiking the scenically marvellous road from Mananara to Maroantsetra. However, many people want to do it, and will be faced with the choice of going it alone or hiring a guide and porters.

Luc Selleslagh walked alone. He says the path is well used by local Malagasy and if you become confused you should just wait for someone to come. Abandon any idea of keeping your feet dry. A tent is useful in emergencies (and a mosquito net, or at least mosquito coils, essential) but there are houses you can stay in and meals will be cooked for you for a reasonable charge. The villagers may expect presents. They may also expect medicines. Be cautious of introducing – or perpetuating – expectations here. Independent walkers should buy the relevant FTM map, *Antalaha*. If you failed to buy it in Tana there is one in the Motel Coco Beach which you can trace.

Angus and Philippa Crawford, who did the trip in 1999, point out good reasons for taking a guide and porters: 'If you take neither guide nor porters you lay yourself open to hustlers who insist on accompanying you, and you also deprive local people of work. And the route is by no means obvious...'

Day 1 Maroantsetra to Mahalevona, the village beyond Navana, which is described under *Excursions*. A pleasant 5km walk.
Day 2 Mahalevona to Ankovona. The track climbs into the mountains and there are rivers to cross.
Day 3 Ankovona to Ampokafo. A long trek to Ampokafo which marks the halfway point. Very hilly and very beautiful, with lots of streams and orchids. The village has a small shop.
Day 4 Ampokafo to Analampontsy. Less wild, but still orchids along the way. Most villages en route have shops.
Day 5 Analampontsy to Antalaha. You emerge on to the road at the village of Marofinaritra, about 30km from Antalaha. From here you can get a taxi-brousse to Antalaha.

ANTALAHA AND BEYOND
Antalaha

A prosperous, vanilla-financed town with large houses and broad boulevards. There are excellent beaches nearby, making this a very pleasant place to spend a day or so.

The road to Sambava is rough in places, with one ferry crossing. It takes about three hours by taxi-brousse.

Where to stay/eat
Hotel Florida Tel: 813 30. The best hotel, with air conditioning and hot water.
Hotel du Centre Tel: 811 67. In the centre of town, European run, comfortable with good meals.
Hotel Ocean Plage Tel: 812 05.
Hotel Le Cocotier Tel: 811 77.

Cap Est

South of Antalaha and north of Masoala, the coastline bulges to Madagascar's most easterly point, Cap Est. An upmarket hotel, **La Résidence du Cap**, consisting of seven thatched bungalows, has received much praise from readers. Run by George, a South African, and his wife Magali, it provides everything you could wish for in Madagascar: rainforest, beach and wonderful food.

'A delightful spot... George organises fishing and snorkelling trips in his boat and it's safe to swim because it's protected by a reef.'

The hotel costs 240Ff per person per night (full board) single, or 200Ff double. Boat transfers from Antalaha are 900Ff round trip'.

The postal address is BP 206, Cap Est, Antalaha. Reservations can be made in Antalaha at the hotel's office, tel: 813 27. In Tana book through Eco-Tour; tel/fax: 22 262 81; or Silver Wings; tel/fax: 22 210 79 or tel: 22 200 92.

Getting there the hard way

Rupert Parker stayed at Cap Est in December 1998 and reports: 'There is a boat to Ambohitralanana (the nearest village to Cap Est) once a week which takes the locals – a sort of marine taxi-brousse – with all the same risks and this costs 20,000Fmg per person. Enquire in Antalaha. There is also a Project Masoala research boat which makes the trip – enquire at their office in town. The other alternative is to walk from Antsirabata, south of Antalaha – it takes around 12 hours – or hire bikes. We did the bike trip and the track is very rough; we ended up pushing the bikes most of the way, but you pass through many villages where you can get basic supplies – even beer. We left Antalaha around midday and it took about six hours – it was very hot and I would not recommend anyone else to do it at this time of day. We came back with the local boat which was piled high with people, cases, supplies and our bikes on the top. The boat journey takes about four hours and can be rough. Because the boat is piled so high, it is a potentially dangerous situation – George from the hotel provided us with life jackets, just in case.'

SAMBAVA

The centre of the vanilla and coconut growing region, and an important area for cloves and coffee production, Sambava merits a stay of a few days. The town has a definite charm, the people are friendly and easy-going, and there is plenty to see and do.

The telephone area code is 88.

Getting there and away

Sambava has quite good air connections with Toamasina and Antsiranana, and is accessible by road from Iharana (Vohemar), taking approximately seven hours. The airport is not far from town: you can even walk it if you are a backpacker. Be warned, however, that Sambava is a sprawling town with long distances between most places. The taxi-brousse station is on the northern outskirts, 30 minutes from the centre (shops, post office) and beach hotels are 10–15 minutes beyond that.

Where to stay/eat
Category A

Hotel Carrefour BP 53; tel: 60. Situated near the beach, with all mod cons (hot water, air conditioning). From 160–200Ff. Good food.

Le Club Plage (bungalows) BP 33; tel: 44. A posh hotel overlooking the sea with a swimming pool. Two-person bungalows for 120–140Ff. Also **Hotel Le Club** with conventional rooms at 50,000Fmg. Hotel Le Club offers a choice of several tours, including trekking; and transfer to and from the airport, 4WD vehicles with driver, and mountain bikes.

Las Palmas BP 120; tel: 87. Nicely situated by the beach, well run with conscientious and friendly staff. Hot water but poor water pressure. Good food. Air-conditioned rooms 125Ff/75,000Fmg, bungalows 70,000Fmg (1996). The hotel offers a variety of excursions, such as the Bemarivo river.

Category B

Hotel Esmeralda BP 113; tel: 128. This is the backpackers' favourite Sambava hotel, pleasantly located with rooms and bungalows overlooking the ocean. Cold water only; en-suite WC. The downside is the tethered lemurs and staff who have developed apathy into an art form. From 35,000Fmg.

Hotel Cantonnais Tel: 124. A hotel rather than beach bungalows, but in a quiet part of town and most rooms have balconies. There are five rooms with toilets; hot water (with good pressure). Good value. The Chinese owner also sells precious stones.

Nouvel Hotel Good value and recommended for its food.

Category C

Chez M Jaoravo Six rooms on the left side of the cemetery, on the main road. Rooms very hot but clean. Cold water, cold staff. 20,000Fmg.

Hotel Pacifique Tel: 124. Three rooms, also bungalows.

Hotel Calypso BP 40; tel: 108. An unassuming, reasonably priced hotel in town.

La Romance North of the taxi-brousse station. Basic romance costs about 20,000Fmg.

All the restaurants at the above hotels serve good meals. Specialist restaurants include **Cantonnais** and **Mandarin** (Chinese) and the **Etoile Rouge** and **Etoile Rouge Annexe**. The latter is said to serve the better food.

For do-it-yourself meals head for the *épicerie* to the right of the cemetery. Prices and staff are more user-friendly than in the supermarket.

Things to do
In and around town

Sambava itself is one long main street with parallel dirt roads, so you won't get lost. There is a good **market** which is known as **Bazaar Kely**, not because it's small or *kely* (it isn't – and certainly not on Tuesdays, market day) but because there used to be two markets and no-one thought of changing the name when they amalgamated them.

As this is one of the main vanilla-producing areas in Madagascar, a tour of the **vanilla factory**, Lopat, is interesting and teaches you a lot about the laborious process of preparing one of Madagascar's main exports. Likewise a visit to the **coconut plantation** (*germoir pépinière*), some 3km south of the airport, is more rewarding than it sounds. You need a permit and a guide so it's easiest to go on an organised tour arranged by one of the hotels.

The highlight for us, however, was a visit to CLUE, the Center for Learning and Understanding English. This lively place was set up by the Peace Corps and welcomes visits from tourists to help the (adult) students practise their spoken English and understanding of a variety of accents. For the visitors it's an excellent chance to learn from the people of the east coast. CLUE is on the main street (you can't miss it) and you should look for Patrice, the Malagasy English teacher. Don't miss this opportunity to do something for cross-cultural understanding. 'A wonderful experience.' (Anne Axel)

North of Sambava is a beautiful beach with safe swimming, and marvellous *Nephila* spiders on their golden webs between the branches of the shady trees.

VANILLA IN MADAGASCAR
Clare and Johan Hermans

Vanilla is the major foreign currency earner for Madagascar, which together with Réunion and the Comoros grows 80% of the world's crop. Its cultivation in Madagascar is centred along the eastern coastal region, the main production centres being Andapa, Antalaha and Sambava.

The climbing plants are normally grown supported on 1.5m high moisture-retaining trunks and under ideal conditions take three years to mature. When the plants bloom, during the drier months, the vines are checked on alternate days for open flowers to hand-pollinate. The pod then takes nine months to develop; each 15–20cm pod will contain tens of thousands of tiny seeds.

The pods are taken to a vanilla processing plant to begin the long process of preparing them for the commercial market. First they are plunged into a cauldron of hot water (70°C) for two minutes, and are then kept hot for two days. During this time the pods change colour from green to chestnut brown. At this stage they are exposed to the sun (mornings only to avoid over-cooking) for three to four weeks.

After maturing, the pods are sorted by size; the workers sit in front of a large rack with 'pigeonholes' for the different lengths. The bundles of sorted pods, approximately 30 to a bunch, are tied with raffia. They are checked for quality by sniffing and bending before being packed into wooden crates with 90% of the product going to the USA for use in the ice-cream industry.

The vanilla used in cultivation in Madagascar is *Vanilla planifolia* which originates from Mexico. It was brought to Madagascar by the French once the secret of hand pollination had been discovered – the flower has no natural pollinator in its foreign home. The culinary and pharmaceutical use of vanilla dates back to pre-Aztec times when it was used as a drink or as an ingredient of a lotion against fatigue for those holding public office. Similarly a native Malagasy vanilla stem can be found for sale in the *zoma* in Tana as a male invigorator.

Four different species of vanilla orchid occur naturally in Madagascar, most of them totally leafless. One species can be seen on the roadside between Sambava and Antahala resembling lengths of red-green tubing festooned over the scrub, another is to be found in the spiny forest near Berenty in the south. Most of the native species contain sap that burns the skin and their fruits contain too little vanillin to make cultivation economic.

Uses for vanilla pods

Although conventionally used for cooking, vanilla is also an insect repellent or the wonderful-smelling pods can be put in drawers instead of the traditional pomander to scent clothing or linen.

When cooking with vanilla you can reuse the pods for as long as you remember to retrieve them – wash and dry them after each use. Vanilla does wonders to tea or coffee (just add a pod to the teapot or coffee filter, or grind a dried pod with the coffee beans) and can be boiled with milk to make a yummy hot drink (add a dash of brandy!) or custard. If you take sugar in tea or coffee put some beans in your sugar tin and the flavour will be absorbed. Vanilla adds a subtle flavour to chicken or duck, rice or... whatever you fancy.

Excursions further afield

The tour operator Sambava-Voyages (BP 28a; tel: 110) offers a variety of excursions including the trek from Sambava to Doany. The manageress, Mme Seramila, speaks some English.

River Bemarivo

A pleasant do-it-yourself excursion is up the Bemarivo, though this won't be possible at the end of the dry season – the river is very shallow. Take a taxi-brousse to Nosiarina, on the road north, and look for a pirogue to take you the five-hour journey up-river to Amboahangibe. Anne Axel paid 25,000Fmg for five people plus gear. 'It's a beautiful river trip. The river is wide and there are some small villages that you pass periodically. However, the land by the river has been deforested.'

It is also possible to find a cargo boat to Amboahangibe. This is quite a large village with several grocery stores and some houses with rooms. Look for the sign 'Misy Chambres'. These fill up with vanilla-pickers during the harvest. Anne Axel found the last room in town, at the **Hotel Fandrosoana**. 'It had a captive crocodile in the yard next to the WC.' As an alternative to taking a boat back, it is a pleasant hike along the river, with some interesting above-ground coffins and groves of shady giant bamboos.

CONTINUING NORTH

The road to the next town of importance, Iharana (Vohemar), is excellent and transport is no problem (about six hours). For a description of this pleasant town see *Chapter 14*, page 301.

ANDAPA AND AREA

Andapa lies in a fertile and beautiful region, 108km west of Sambava, where much of Madagascar's rice is grown. This is also a major coffee-producing area and it was to facilitate the export of coffee that the EEC provided funding for the building of an all-weather road in the 1960s (see box). This remains one of the best roads in Madagascar. The journey to Andapa is most beautiful, with the jagged peaks of the massif of Marojejy (now a thrilling new national park) to the right, and bamboo and palm-thatch villages by the roadside. The journey takes about three hours by taxi-brousse.

Anne Axel spent six weeks in the region in 1998 and provided this comprehensive update.

Where to stay

Hotel Vatasoa (pronounced 'Vats') BP 46; Andapa 205; tel: 39 Comfortable (but sometimes noisy) rooms with hot water cost 42,000–60,000Fmg. The food is amazing (but a set meal and not good for vegetarians) and the hotel has all sorts of pluses. There is a large detailed map on the wall of the lounge which shows footpaths and tracks in the area (actually, a reproduction of the FTM 1:100,000 which can be purchased in Tana). For hikers this is invaluable for planning (see *Excursions*). The Chinese owner, Mr Tam Hyok, is 'Mr Andapa'. This dynamic man likes to take a personal interest in his guests and their plans, and will accompany those whom he feels will most benefit from his attentions.

Chez Tam Hyok About 15 minutes' drive towards Sambava is Mr Tam Hyok's pièce de résistance: his own house and some bungalows under construction overlooking arguably the most beautiful mountain view in Madagascar. Free-range lemurs (white-fronted and crowned lemurs) leap around the trees, and flowering shrubs blaze against the dark green of the Marojejy massif. Bureaucratic problems have slowed down the work on these bungalows. For information enquire at the Hotel Vatasoa in town.

Hotel du Centre Basic clean rooms, but a 'less than pleasing WC. Wear sturdy shoes; not for the weak of heart or poor of bowels'. No shower, but acceptable overall; 10,000Fmg.

Where to eat

Mini-Restaurant On the opposite side of the street to the Vatasoa, about a block down the road. Popular with locals and WWF employees, but 'unwilling to cook vegetarian meals and unable to follow instructions.' 5,000–7,500Fmg per plate.

Restaurant au Bon Plaisir One block away from the taxi-brousse station, on the same street as Hotel du Centre. 'Our favourite *hotely*. We would place an order for a vegetarian meal several hours in advance and they would have it ready at the appointed hour. They never baulked at our requests although they became more bizarre as the weeks went by.' 3,000–5,000Fmg per plate.

Sweet-tooth orgy

'Local peanut brittle is excellent. Initially there was only one source, the Brittle-Man at the taxi-brousse station. Other vendors then started to appear; we worried that we had started a Brittle Boom which would become a Brittle Bust after our departure. Our favourite is the Brittle Girls located on the corner of the main street near the bank.'

Services

There is a good **pharmacy** with a reliable supply of antibiotics. The **post office** cannot really cope with *vazaha* mail. 'It helps if you know the basic cost of mailing letters and postcards home. Buy the biggest envelope you can to accommodate the numerous, small-denomination stamps – and don't forget the glue stick.' The two **banks** won't change travellers' cheques, only cash. There's an **airport**, but no planes; and there's an Air Mad office.

Excursions

This is a wonderful area for wandering. At every step you see something interesting from the people or wildlife perspective (in the latter category butterflies, snakes and chameleons) and the scenery is consistently beautiful.

Mr Tam Hyok will have suggestions for more organised sightseeing, including the local **cemetery** where the dead are interred in coffins above the ground or in the trees.

Hiking

By using the map in the Hotel Vatasoa you can plan a variety of day hikes. Almost any dirt road through villages would bring you the pleasures we experienced on our 1996 hike. Here are some of the highlights: chameleons in the bushes, coffee laid out to dry on the ground, an entire school of shrieking kids surging up the hill towards us, a village elder matching his stride with ours in order to converse in French, little girls fishing with basket-nets in the irrigation channels, home-made musical instruments, smiles, laughter and stares. It helped that we had our local guide with us who could interpret the village activities. In one place we experienced the power of Malagasy oratory (*kabary*) at full throttle. The theme was communal work. The 20 or so men of the village listened respectfully as the Président du Fokontany exhorted them to contribute their labour towards the building of a new fence. Some young men demurred: they would rather pay the let-out fee of 2,500Fmg. The Président discussed the issue with them, explaining the importance of the community working together. By the end of the discussion the young men had started stripping the leaves of a raffia palm to bind up the bamboo poles and begin fence-making.

If you explore off the beaten path, just remember the enormous power you have to change things irreversibly. Your gift or payment will certainly be received with delight and will make you feel warm inside; but will it benefit the village in the long run?

PROTECTED AREAS
In the last few years the area around Andapa has opened two of its most exciting reserves to visitors. The newly gazetted Marojejy National Park and Anjanaharibe-Sud Special Reserve are at the heart of one of WWF's main Integrated Conservation and Development Projects and for the first five years these areas will be administered by the WWF regional office in Andapa. After this period ANGAP will take over the reins. WWF are very keen to develop ecotourism in this infrequently visited part of the country. Both places lack the well-made paths and tourist infrastructure found in the popular parks and reserves: the few paths are narrow and often very steep – these are some of the most remote and pristine rainforests remaining on the island – and visitors need to be fit and willing to put up with a fair degree of discomfort.

Anjanaharibe-Sud Reserve
The Anjanaharabe-Sud Special Reserve/Befingitra Forest region, some 20km southwest of Andapa, is an easier option than the magnificent but challenging new

FOREIGN AID IN ANDAPA
Before 1963, Andapa's only link with the rest of the island was through Air Madagascar's flights to Sambava and Antalaha. This made the export of its cash crops, vanilla and Robusta coffee, prohibitively expensive. The newly-independent government, under President Tsiranana whose tribal roots (Tsimihety) were the same as those of the people of Andapa, applied to the EEC for funding to build a road to the coast. Also at the request of the government, a European team carried out a thorough agronomic survey and census of the region in the early 1960s, which led to 20 years of agricultural development overseen by a Belgian agency.

The initial achievements were considerable. Traditional hill rice (dependent on rain so with low productivity) gave way to irrigated rice paddies, served by a pumping station and irrigation channels. Thus 3,000ha of land were brought under cultivation. The hand-plough was replaced by more efficient zebu-hauled ploughs, and fertilisers and improved seeds were introduced. The same expertise was put into improving coffee production, and after ten years the previous yield of 300–450kg per hectare had risen to over 2,000kg/hectare for some farmers.

In the mid 1990s Andapa has retained some of this prosperity, but the high yields have fallen victim of Madagascar's malaise: deforestation. The once-verdant forests that encircled the Andapa Basin have been depleted and smoke rises from the new areas of *tavy* hacked out by land-hungry peasants. Topsoil has poured into the rivers which feed the pumping station, clogging the machinery and causing the closure of the station. Less rice means more poverty which means more deforestation. The story of Madagascar.

MAROJEJY – A WALK IN THE PARK, 1976
Hilary Bradt

Marojejy was to be the highlight of my first visit to Madagascar. I had fallen deeply in love with the country, and here was a reserve that looked so wonderful on the map – all brown swirling contours and green forest, with no roads for miles and miles. The map showed a path running across it which, we reckoned, would take two days to walk.

As we flew into Sambava we could see the green peaks of Marojejy poking up through a covering of cloud. But there was something strange: it looked as though a box of matches had been strewn over the soft crumpled landscape. There had been a cyclone the previous week which had felled numerous huge trees as well as destroying much of Sambava. Unperturbed, we hitched towards Marojejy. A shopkeeper offered us his floor for the night and an introduction to a representative from the Département des Eaux et Forêts. To our relief we now had the required permit but we had mixed feelings when he said he was coming with us. He didn't really seem dressed for a two-day backpacking trip: he had no luggage apart from a briefcase carrying his official papers, a clean shirt, and three hats. He was wearing plastic sandals.

We would never have found the way ourselves. The narrow trail climbed steeply up the mountain to a large stone which marked the edge of the reserve. Our Man then told us that he had never actually walked in the reserve. Never mind, the trail was clear and we made good progress, until the first fallen tree blocked our way. For the rest of the day we scrambled over or crawled under trees. Our heavy packs unbalanced us, the heat debilitated us, and sweat ran into our eyes. That night we cooked a sumptuous supper. It had been a strenuous day so we deserved a treat.

Next morning we followed the path to the river, which we crossed. There was no path the other side. We boulder-hopped after Our Man as he followed the river upstream. With a heavy pack this was very tiring, and we asked plaintively where the trail was. He didn't know. Should we turn back? No, if we followed the river we would soon find another path. We didn't.

The river entered a canyon, impossible to boulder-hop or even to wade. We climbed the steep, slippery clay sides, hanging on to lianas and hauling ourselves up to the overhanging jungle. I learned later that the high-altitude rainforest in Madagascar is the densest in the world. I believe it. Without a machete to slice away the vegetation we could only move very slowly. The forest floor – what we could see of it – was composed of moss-covered logs and spongy leaves. Each step was a false step, the rotting matter giving way and plunging us into hidden holes. When we grabbed at plants or branches they hit back. There were plants that stung, plants that stabbed and plants that sliced. Blood soon mixed with the sweat that ran down our bodies. Huge trees, toppled by the cyclone, blocked our passage. Their overhanging branches harboured fire-ants which dropped down our necks when we crawled underneath. I started to cry.

Back at the river, we sat down to consider our situation. We were lost. The map didn't make sense, Our Man was silent. We turned our attention to our blotched and blood-streaked arms and legs. Fat leeches were fastened to our ankles and between our fingers. Since I refused to turn back and repeat the cliff and jungle trek, the only course was to follow the river. The map showed it winding towards Ambatobe, our destination. We no longer cared about wet boots nor safety when we crossed the river on moss-slippery tree trunks. Your sense of balance seems much better when you don't much care whether you live or die.

After 12 hours of unmitigated effort we stopped for the night. Wordlessly we set up the tent and cooked the last of our food: soup followed by tea and raisins. We were up at dawn. Knowing the rigours ahead, we drank our tea and ate our three raisins in even deeper gloom. The first six hours were the same as the previous day: slither, trip, sweat and push our way through water and jungle with no lunch to give us renewed energy. Then, in the early afternoon, Our Man shouted in delight. He was pointing to a human footprint in the damp sand by the river. Robinson Crusoe's heart cannot have lifted as did ours at this sign that our ordeal could be coming to an end. A few hours later we saw the sight we had long dreamed of – a solitary hut on the mountain side above the river.

The climb up was one of the hardest yet and we were bitterly disappointed to find the hut had long been abandoned. Still, there were some edible plants growing in the garden and Our Man was thrilled to find tobacco. He also found some other tasty food, collecting a bag full of large weevils. They were delicious roasted, he said. Supper was an almost cheerful occasion. We ate boiled leaves, Our Man coughed happily over his home-made cigars, and we found one last teabag at the bottom of my pack. We didn't roast the weevils.

Our mood was shattered again the following morning when we topped the hill above the hut and saw, not a village, but miles and miles of unbroken jungle. Six hours later we reached a trail but felt none of the anticipated elation. We were too tired. We just trudged onward until a voice greeted us from behind. We sat down and let Our Man and the woman chatter away. 'She knows my family' he told us excitedly. 'My wife is wondering where I am!'

The woman led us to her hut and we lay down on the palm-leaf mats while the family regarded us with gratifying respect and sympathy as Our Man told our story. Each newcomer was entertained with an ever lengthier version. Then a huge bowl of rice was brought in, along with several kinds of vegetables. Feeling almost human we set off along the path to Ambatobe. With Civilisation at hand we realised the appearance we presented: our clothes had been wringing wet with rain and sweat for four days, we were covered in dried blood from scratches and leech bites, and we stank. When we came to a stream we motioned to Our Man to go ahead. With clean bodies and fresh clothes we approached the village. The inhabitants were all lined up on each side of the path, hands outstretched, shouting 'Salama! Salama!'. 'Salama!' we grinned, shaking the outstretched hands. It seemed a huge population for such a small village. Then we realised that the people at the the back of the line were running to the front for a second go.

Reverently we were guided to the biggest hut where we found Our Man already enthroned and talking. The room filled with people and we smiled and nodded as the epic journey was described. It had the audience enthralled. Our Man was evidently a master of the art of storytelling. Then supper arrived. They had killed a chicken in our honour, so we had not only rice and greens, but chicken stew. Then came a plate of what looked like large peanuts. The weevils! They had a pleasant nutty flavour. The next day two youths were enlisted to carry our packs and we almost floated along the trail to the road. We arrived in under two hours, having covered about the same distance that we'd achieved in the previous three days.

national park of Marojejy. Anjanaharabe-Sud can be equally rewarding for naturalists with sufficient time to seek out the shy wildlife. This is the most northerly range of the indri which here occurs in a very dark form – almost black. The silky sifaka is also found here, but you are more likely to see the troops of white-fronted brown lemurs. Birders will be on the lookout for four species of ground-roller.

Even without seeing any mammals it is a most rewarding visit, with an easy-to-follow (though rugged) trail through primary forest to some hot springs. The reserve is also a vital element in the prosperity of the area. The Lokoho River, which rises in Anjanaharibe-Sud, is the *only* source of water for the largest irrigated rice producer in the country.

Befingotra and Andasibe

If you are making your own way to the reserve you will spend some time in these two gateway towns looking for ongoing transport. Befingotra has a couple of *épiceries* with basic supplies (rice, beans, etc) and there is a small restaurant. Andasibe is the larger town with several *épiceries* and *hotelys* offering a reasonable range of food. Anne camped in the centre of each village – OK, but not exactly private.

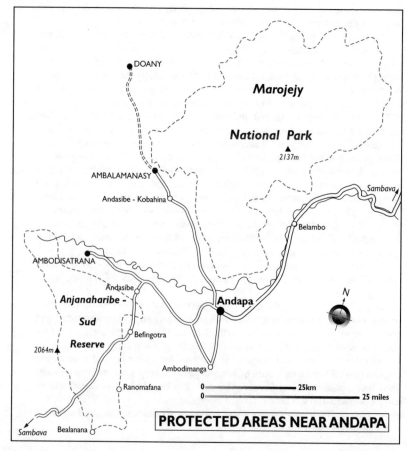

PROTECTED AREAS NEAR ANDAPA

MAROJEJY – A WALK IN THE PARK, 1998
Nick Garbutt

Since first visiting Madagascar I'd always wanted to go there. The first problem was its pronunciation – 'marrow-jay-gee' just seemed plain wrong and was too difficult to get my tongue around (but then everywhere in Madagascar is like that). I was informed 'marro-jayj' was close enough. Now I could say it, surely I could visit it? Again it wasn't that simple. Marojejy was a Strict Reserve and off limits to all but official scientists – I applied three times for permission and was denied three times. Acute frustration.

However, in November 1998 Marojejy became a national park and accessible for those with determination to visit. As luck would have it, I got to the head of the queue. I was escorting a small group of keen-spirited and adventurous British naturalists from Reef & Rainforest Tours and the seven of us were the first non-scientists ever to officially get into Marojejy.

Excited apprehension perhaps best summed up the mood as we set off from Andapa – we knew there was a six-hour walk from the road to the campsite and by all accounts it was tough going, damn tough at times – but adrenaline works wonders. After wading two sizeable rivers in the first half hour, all attempts to keep feet dry were abandoned. At the park boundary rice paddies gave way to native trees and we were soon enveloped in lush pristine lowland rainforest. I faced a constant dilemma: do I concentrate on my feet – one in front of the other – and staying on the path? Or do I look up into the canopy to see what's going on – and risk going arse over apex? I plumped for the latter and caught a glimpse of a helmet vanga – but went arse over apex several times to boot!

Later, the paths got more treacherous, a couple of raging torrents had to be negotiated, the hills got steeper – and more slippery – and we wondered if a campsite existed at all. Six hours after leaving the road, we arrived: for 'Campsite' read 'Slight clearing in the forest next to a stream'. But what a view! Down and across the valley, with imposing mountainous cliffs cloaked in forest rising like citadels on the other side – nothing but awesome natural splendour. Tents were pitched, a fire was made and the rain came down in bucketfuls – but hell this was a rainforest!

Next morning we set off early up the path that wends its way eventually to the summit of Marojejy – although we had no intention of reaching it. Our objective was to see the silky sifaka – one of the few lemurs I'd never seen. We'd been told the higher we went, the better the chances would be. So we climbed, and climbed and climbed some more – no sign of the sifaka anywhere. Five hours later, at around 1500m, with limbs like jelly, we decided to call a halt and head back down. But the view alone was worth it – above the cloud, with waves of rainforest rippling away into the distance. Then when almost back – in fact within spitting distance of camp – the guide, who had gone ahead, came running back up the path to beckon us, quick, quick, quick. Down the path we tumbled and then I heard the characteristic sneeze-like 'tzisk, tzisk, tzisk'. Through small gaps in the trees we could see them – silky sifakas, a group of four, no five, watching us warily. They continued to alarm call – starring at us then tossing and shaking their heads indignantly. As quickly as they'd appeared, they disappeared, but they left behind a contented warmth and seven very happy people. I can't wait to get back to Marojejy!

Visiting the reserve

A permit to visit the reserve can be obtained from the Hotel Vatasoa.

Mr Tam Hyok can arrange a day visit to Anjanaharabe-Sud, or you can look for another private vehicle for hire in Andapa (expect to pay around 300,000Fmg) but it is possible and rewarding to visit it on your own. Camping is permitted and allows you to get the most out of your stay. Anne Axel, who made four lengthy visits to the reserve in 1998, recommends two tough, but inexpensive ways of getting there: 'one is to take a taxi-brousse to Andasibe, the last town on the decent road, from where it's a steep two-to-three-hour hike to Befingotra, then another two to three hours to the trailhead; or from Andapa or Andasibe wait for a truck heading for Bealanana and have them drop you off at the reserve'. A guide is not mandatory, but these days the trailhead is very hard to find, so you will probably need to be shown where to enter the forest, and where to find water near the campsite.

If you merely need to be shown the way, and get help carrying gear, look for a guide and/or porters in Andasibe or Befingotra. Be warned, however, that they are unlikely to speak French. Serious naturalists should seek out Gaston, who works for the WWF and is being trained by them as a tourist guide. The Hotel Vatasoa should know where to find him. Anne recommends him as very knowledgable, with good English. He does not come cheap: 50,000Fmg per day for guiding and 25,000Fmg for carrying luggage. Gaston will also arrange for transport to the trailhead.

When I was there in 1997 the trailhead was indicated with a nice WWF board: 'Piste Touristique de Ranomafana Source Thermal à 4260m' giving the time needed for the return trip as being five hours which is roughly right, although it does not allow much time for examining, watching and listening. Or photography.

The path is clearly marked – the trees are tagged with coloured tape: orange indicates the route to the hot springs, and other colours, with metres written on them, show the distance to the campsite – it takes about an hour of brisk walking. The hot springs are an hour beyond the campsite. From the road the trail follows an up-and-down route, slippery at times, but full of interest. On our rather fast day trip we saw no mammals, but campers should see brown lemurs and perhaps indri. John Kupiec reports: 'When you get to the river area it is hard to find the springs without someone to show you. There are three: one is too hot to keep your feet in; another is shallow but it meets a stream which makes it easier to take; the third is a pool to swim in which also merged with stream water.'

Marojejy National Park

This is another former Réserve Naturelle Intégrale that has recently (November 1998) been regazetted as a national park. This park is not for the faint-hearted, but the rewards are high – there are few other areas in Madagascar to compare with Marojejy for awesome splendour and the feeling of ultimate wilderness. Imposing mountains and craggy cliffs are surrounded by lush rainforests that bristle with life. However, wildlife watching can be tough and often frustrating – encounter rates with lemurs are low, as most groups are still very shy, and birdwatching is also difficult as the forest is so dense.

Visiting the park

At present access is via the village of Manantenina on the Sambava to Andapa road. Self-sufficient camping is currently the only option for visitors and WWF can provide knowledgable local guides that know the way. Porters can be arranged in Manantenina, from where it takes about two hours to walk to the park boundary through rice paddies and cultivated areas. You must also wade across two large rivers. Campsite 1 (there are no facilities at these camps) is a two-hour walk from the perimeter of the park and is situated in the heart of superb lowland rainforest. Here you stand a good chance of seeing helmet vanga and various ground-rollers. You may also see white-fronted brown lemurs. Campsite 2 is a further two-hour walk and lies at the transition between lowland and mid-altitude rainforest (at around 800m). Above this campsite the trails become very steep and continue right through all the altitudinal zones to the peak of the Marojejy Massif at 2,137m. The areas above Campsite 2 are best for silky sifaka and also red-bellied lemurs.

Cymbidiella

'The breast-leaper... It is a small animal which attaches itself to the bark of trees and being of a greenish hue is not easily perceived; there it remains with its throat open to receive the flies, spiders and other insects that approach it, which it devours. This animal is described as having attached to the back, tail, legs, neck, and the extremity of the chin, little paws or hooks like those at the end of a bat's wing with which it adheres to whatever it attaches itself in such a manner as if it were really glued. If a native happens to approach the tree where it hangs, it instantly leaps upon his naked breast, and sticks so firmly that in order to remove it, they are obliged, with a razor, to cut away the skin also.'

Samuel Copland, *History of the Island of Madagascar*, 1822

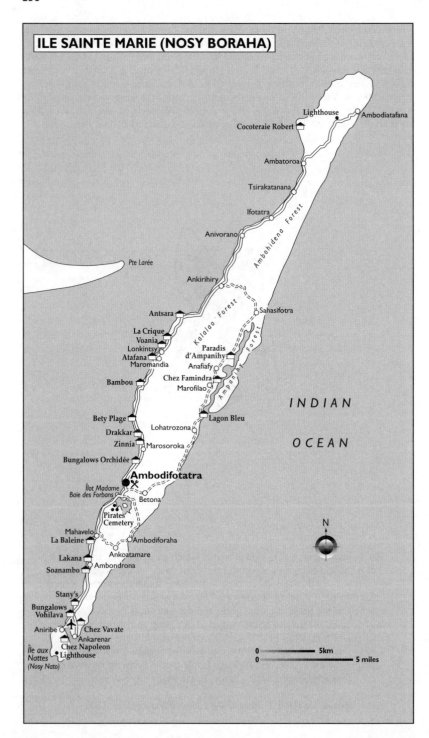

ILE SAINTE MARIE (NOSY BORAHA)

Lighthouse
Ambodiatafana
Cocoteraie Robert
Ambatoroa
Tsirakatanana
Ifotatra
Anivorano
Ambohidena Forest
Pte Larée
Ankirihiry
Antsara
Sahasifotra
La Crique
Voania
Kalalao Forest
Lonkintsy
Paradis
Atafana
d'Ampanihy
Maromandia
Anafiafy
Bambou
Chez Famindra
Ampanihy Forest
Marofilao
Bety Plage
Lagon Bleu
Drakkar
Lohatrozona
Zinnia
Marosoroka
Bungalows Orchidée

Ambodifotatra

Îlot Madame
Baie des Forbans
Betona
Pirates'
Cemetery
Mahavelo
La Baleine
Ambodiforaha
Lakana
Ankoatamare
Soanambo
Ambondrona

Stany's
Bungalows
Vohilava
Aniribe
Chez Vavate
Ankarenar
Chez Napoleon
Île aux
Nattes
Lighthouse
(Nosy Nato)

INDIAN

OCEAN

N

0   5km
0   5 miles

Ile Sainte Marie (Nosy Boraha)

OVERVIEW

Ile Sainte Marie is 50km long and 7km at its widest point. The only real town is Ambodifotatra (pronounced 'Amboodif<u>oo</u>tatr'). Other small villages comprise bamboo and palm huts. The island is almost universally known as Sainte Marie – few people use its Malagasy name. Here is a cliché of a tropical island with endless deserted beaches overhung by coconut palms, bays protected from sharks by coral reefs, hills covered with luxuriant vegetation, and a relative absence of unsightly tourist development. Most travellers love it: 'Nosy Be is for people who want A Good Time, Sainte Marie is for those looking for tranquillity and beauty.'

Sainte Marie unfortunately – or perhaps fortunately, given the dangers of overdevelopment – has a far less settled weather pattern than its island rival, Nosy Be. Cyclones strike regularly and you can expect several days of rain and wind all year round, but interspersed with calm sunny weather. The best months for a visit seem to be June and mid-August to November, although a reader tells me she twice had perfect weather in January, and another reports that in July most days were sunny and hot, but with frequent light rain overnight or in the morning, and fairly strong winds from the south.

One reader gives this warning about the endemic (?) fauna: 'If you carry food, or virtually anything else remotely edible, keep it in heavy-gauge plastic zip-up bags inside your backpack. Sainte Marie cockroaches are enormous, have gargantuan appetites and always come out after dark. They can easily chew through a plastic bag overnight. My lasting memory of the island is eating a meal in a restaurant while viewing a giant cockroach slowly crossing the floor towards the restaurant dog which obligingly got up to let it pass!' (G D Twigger)

For an all-inclusive package to Sainte Marie, with various options for excursions and transport by boat from Soanierana-Ivongo, contact Sainte-Marie Loisirs, BP 3650, Isoraka, Antananarivo; tel/fax: 22 611 40; email: corossol@malagasy.com.

The telephone area code is 57.

History

The origin of the Malagasy name is obscure. It means either 'Island of Abraham' or 'Island of Ibrahim', with probable reference to an early Semitic culture. It was named Ile Sainte Marie by European sailors when the island became the major hide-out of pirates in the Indian Ocean. From the 1680s to around 1720 these pirates dominated the seas around Africa. There was a Welshman (David Williams), Englishmen (Thomas White, John Every and William Kidd) and an American (Thomas Tew) among a Madagascar pirate population which in its heyday numbered nearly one thousand.

Later a Frenchman, Jean-Onésime Filet ('La Bigorne'), was shipwrecked on Sainte Marie while escaping the wrath of a jealous husband in Réunion. La Bigorne turned his amorous attentions with remarkable success to Princess Bety, the daughter of King Ratsimilaho. On their marriage the happy couple received Nosy Boraha as a gift from the king, and the island was in turn presented to the mother country by La Bigorne (or rather, put under the protection of France by Princess Bety). Thus France gained its first piece of Madagascar in 1750.

GETTING THERE AND AWAY
By air
Air Madagascar flies to Sainte Marie on Mondays, Wednesdays, Fridays and Saturdays from Tana and Toamasina. All flights are heavily booked, especially in July and August, and you should try to make your reservations well in advance. Reconfirm your return flight at the Air Mad office in the north part of Ambodifotatra. The office may be closed when the personnel are needed at the airport because a flight is coming in, but there is a café next door in which you can wait. However adamant the Air Mad people are that the flight is full, it is worth going stand-by.

By motor launch
A boat service runs between Soanierana-Ivongo, at the end of the surfaced road north of Toamasina, and Ambodifotatra. The *Samsonette* runs every day except Sunday, leaving Ambodifotatra (Ilot Madame) at 08.00 and S-Ivongo at about 10.30. The trip takes 2½ hours and costs 30,000Fmg per person one way.

By basic boat
Le Dugong may still be running from Soanierana-Ivongo. Enquire at the restaurant Le Barachois in Ambodifotatra, Sainte Marie, or in S-Ivongo. This boat waits to fill up with passengers, so the schedule is erratic.

If you are a committed masochist you can take the *Rapiko*, which leaves Toamasina on Wednesdays at 20.00 and takes at least ten murderous hours. Tickets are available from SCAC in Toamasina (see map) or in Sainte Marie from Roso's, next to Le Barachois.

A number of boats run regularly from Manompana, but this town is not always accessible from Toamasina – it depends on the state of bridges and ferries crossing the several rivers up the east coast. The *Monia* costs around 30,000Fmg per head and takes four hours. 'It's a dirty old motor cruiser, leaks constantly and has no safety equipment, but it somehow always makes it over and back. The *Maria II* is a lovely, well-built 1956 sailing schooner with no motor, four sails, and two grinning crew. The trip costs 20,000Fmg, but for 40,000Fmg it will take you across, wait for 24 hours and bring you back. Sailing time each way is about seven hours. If you're in a hurry, you can use *Ming*, a 9-metre outboard-powered sailing boat. It's clean, quick and expensive – 60,000Fmg, but this changes according to how much of a hurry you're in.' (Paul and Sarah McBride – 1995 information)

By pirogue
Rick Partridge sent this report: 'We took a taxi-brousse from Tamatave to Soanierana-Ivongo. Next morning we negotiated a fee to travel by dug-out canoe along the inland waters for about 15km to a small ferry-point village where there are bungalows. Then next morning we had to walk at least 15km to the headland (*pointe*), where there is a village called Andragazana, from where we took a larger dug-out sailing boat to Ile Sainte Marie. The crossing took 1½ hours. An unmissable

experience! Arriving at Bon Coin on Sainte Marie made us feel like Christopher Columbus.' There may now be a 4WD vehicle to take passengers to Andragazana. Check with the tour operator Nord-Est Nature in Soanierana-Ivongo.

Jeremy and Lindie Buirski made a similar crossing. 'The sailing pirogue cost 50,000Fmg for the two of us. It looked incredibly unseaworthy, full of water and with the sails held together with string. The crew rowed us along various river paths and out of the mouth of a small river well northwest of the *pointe*, where they hoisted the three sails and sat back. Going to Sainte Marie this way is a must, and I recommend it to anyone who is even remotely adventurous. For most of the trip over the wind was 10–12 knots, later increasing to 15–20 knots. The only water that came inboard was the occasional splash from the paddles as the crew rowed to stop the keel-less pirogue being blown too far northward. We saw lots of tuna jumping, and many fishermen. We reached Sainte Marie about 1km north of La Crique then stowed the sails and rowed up the coast to Loukintsy.'

These two reports were from five years ago. I have had no recent reports of adventurers taking to the seas in a pirogue, but no doubt it is still possible.

Getting around the island

There is now a taxi-brousse service, at least up the west coast. Prices are high but they run all day. Look out for the cheaper *taxi asaka*, yellow taxi-brousse, which charges only 5,000Fmg from the airport to Lonkintsy. Once or twice a week it goes as far as Cocoterie Robert (120,000Fmg). It's worth flagging down any vehicle. Most will stop and charge the standard rate.

Most hotels have bikes for rent (the French for mountain bike is VTT). You'll pay around 35,000Fmg per day. Bikes are cheaper at Ambodifotatra. You can see quite a lot of the island by bike, but don't reckon on covering much ground – the roads are very rough and most bikes in poor condition (check the brakes!).

You can hire motorbikes opposite the Hotel Soanambo and mopeds are also available in Ambodifotatra.

WHERE TO STAY AND EAT

Almost all Ile Sainte Marie's hotels are ranged along the west coast of the island, with only a few in the east or on Ile aux Nattes in the south.

Note: Most hotels have their own vehicles and meet the incoming planes. You will need to make a quick decision: once the vehicles have departed you may be stuck at the airport. But check with the driver that there is room at their hotel before climbing aboard.

If you are on a tight budget beware of staying at one of the distant hotels. You will be obliged to buy their (often pricey) meals and transport will be expensive.

West coast hotels

These hotels are listed in geographical order, from south to north. Their price/quality category is given in brackets.

Chez Vavate (*Category C*) Six rooms/bungalows. On first appearance an unprepossessing collection of local huts built on a ridge overlooking the airstrip. Don't be taken in by first impressions, the food here is wonderful (the *punch coco* also ensures that you spend your evenings in a convivial haze) and the relaxed family atmosphere makes this a very popular place with young travellers. The only catch is you must walk 1½km from the airport. There is no road, and the 'courtesy vehicle' is a man with a wheelbarrow! If you miss him take the wide grassy track which runs parallel to the airstrip then veers to the left up a steep hill, but be warned – if Chez Vavate is full you will have missed the vehicles going to the other places.

Bungalows Vohilava (Self-catering) Bungalows about 3km from the airport. From about 200Ff (two people) to 700Ff (eight people) per day. Fully-equipped kitchens; suppliers come daily to sell fresh food. For bookings contact: Sainte-Marie Loisirs in Tana.

Stany's Bungalows/Bungalows Mayer (*Category C*). About 10km south of Ambodifotatra, 20 minutes up the road from the airport. Adequate bungalows. Nice view looking out to sea. Bush showers and toilet. Very helpful and friendly owner.

Soanambo (*Category A*) BP 20; tel: 40. Manageress: Agnes Fayd'Herbe. 3km from airport, 10km from Ambodifotatra. The most expensive hotel on the island. 380Ff per bungalow (high season), 275Ff (low season). Very comfortable with a lovely garden with *Angraecum* orchids. Bicycles available for hire. Credit cards accepted.

Lakana (*Category B*) BP 2; 5km from the airport. Six simple but very comfortable wooden bungalows, including four perched along the jetty; 100,000–135,000Fmg; breakfast 12,000Fmg. Mountain bikes for hire. Visa cards accepted.

Hotel La Baleine (*Category C*) Owned by Albert Lanton, this set of bungalows receives rave reviews (consequently it is usually full). It is one of the few hotels on the island that is Malagasy-owned. With the proceeds of the hotel, Albert sponsors a youth football club and other local projects. There are eight rustic bungalows with mosquito nets and the minimum of furniture, about 7km from the airport. Communal bathroom with cold water. Very good food. The only negative point is that the beach is not particularly nice here... but who cares?

Bungalows Orchidée (*Category A*) Tel: 54. Located 3km south of Ambodifotatra, and trying, unsuccessfully, to outsmart Soanambo. David Sayers writes: 'the cabins badly need decorating, food is unimaginative and very expensive, and I do not like chickens feeding off the breakfast tables.' Single 250Ff; double 300Ff. Ten bungalows, four double rooms. Hot water, air conditioning, water sports, excursions. Bookings may be made in Tana, tel: 237 62/270 15; fax: 269 86. Also in Tamatave: tel: 333 51/337 66. Credit cards accepted.

Hotel Zinnia (*Category C*) Right by the harbour wall at Ambodifotatra. Six bungalows at 25,000Fmg for a double, with hot water, fans and outside flushing toilet. Good, neat and pleasant restaurant with excellent food and 'the best coffee on Sainte Marie'. Mountain bikes for hire at 25,000Fmg a day.

La Falafa (*Category C*) This restaurant in Ambodifotatra (good food) also has a few inexpensive rooms. 'The walls were paper thin and I heard everything within a one block radius, including the disco across the street. Additionally, I heard rats scurrying around all night.' (Anne Axel)

Hotel Drakkar (*Category C*) 1km north of Ambodifotatra. Simple bamboo bungalows with cold shower. Rooms from 25,000Fmg. The main building is an old colonial house with lovely decor and a sitting/dining room on the water's edge. Convenient for an early morning boat departure.

Hotel Bety Plage (*Category A*) 6km north of Ambodifotatra. Beautifully landscaped, and very well run. From 95,000Fmg; breakfast 17,000Fmg.

Hotel Bambou (*Category C*) Between Ambodifotatra and Loukintsy. Inexpensive beach huts, with a superb view of the sunset over a pristine sandy bay – and friendly. Recommended.

Atafana (*Category C*) BP 14. There are now two sets of bungalows, about 15 minutes from each other, about 4km south of La Crique, run by the Noel family. Described by some as having the best location, on a private bay, with good food and very friendly. Rooms with cold-water shower and wash basin are 50,000Fmg. Camping is permitted for 10,000Fmg. Communal flushing toilets. Power comes from a generator until about 21.00. Excellent swimming at the northern beach. Residents can rent two mountain bikes and a rowing pirogue.

Hotel Voania (*Category C*) Roughly 200m from the Atafana. On a clean beach, raked every morning to get rid of rocks and flotsam. 18,000Fmg for a basic double bungalow; more for those with a cold shower. Next to the local village, but the newest part is private and secluded. No electricity, but equipped with powerful pressure lanterns. The restaurant is slightly cheaper than Atafana's. The delicious large *crevettes* are recommended, but must be ordered in advance.

Hotel Bon Coin (*Category C*) This hotel at Loukintsy, with rooms at about 15,000Fmg, is described as 'OK' by Rick Partridge. It's 1km before La Crique, and the last place easily reached by road going north. The only minus point is 'an unhygienic beach'.

La Crique (*Category B*) BP 1. Deservedly the most popular of all hotels, in one of the prettiest locations, 1km north of Loukintsy, with a wonderful ambience and good food (but expensive: 90,000Fmg set meal). In September you can watch humpbacked whales cavorting offshore. Bungalows with shared facilities 127Ff/120,000Fmg; bungalows with en-suite bathrooms about 145Ff/110,000Fmg. Breakfast 16,500Fmg, dinner about 50,000Fmg (fixed menu). Often full, so try to book ahead. Electricity from 18.00 to 20.00 only. Transport to/from the airport costs 40,000Fmg, and there is a regular minibus to town. Mountain bikes available for 35,000Fmg per day.

Hotel Antsara (*Category B*) 300m north of La Crique. Five beach bungalows, plus eight more on a slope further from the sea. Rooms from about 15,000Fmg, with or without WC or bathroom. Excellent Réunionnaise-French hosts. Snorkelling gear available. Has a noisy disco, but only at weekends.

La Cocoteraie Robert (*Category A*) BP 29. In the extreme north of the island, described by one who knows as 'the most beautiful beach in the world', and has recently added 40 more bungalows. Transport from the airport is expensive, but a boat goes there from Soanambo (it's run by the same French family). It even has its own airstrip. 380Ff (high season), 275Ff (low season). Breakfast 25,000Fmg, dinner about 50,000Fmg.

East Sainte Marie

Hotel Boraba (*Category A*) A new upmarket hotel (bungalows) on the southeast coast. Bookings through Transcontinents in Tana (see page 90).

Restaurant Bungalows Paradis d'Ampanihy (*Category B*) On the river close to Anafiafy, opposite the Forêt d'Ampanihy. Run by Helène, a Malagasy woman, and her family. A basic bungalow with mosquito net is 30,000Fmg, more for those with shower. Four-course meals in a beautiful dining room with outside tables and several tame lemurs. A pirogue trip across the river to the Forêt d'Ampanihy and back is only about 4,000Fmg per person. Ten minutes' walk to the sea. Recommended by several readers.

Chez Famindra (*Category C*) This is not really a hotel (I've made up the name) but a family enterprise run by a friend of Madophile Rick Partridge. 'Clébert Famindra is a tourist guide (he speaks only French) who lives near Anafiafy on the other side of Sainte Marie in a really peaceful location by the Bay of Ampanihy. I would suggest staying with him and his family for a few days; it's an excellent way to get to know Malagasy people. His prices are inexpensive and negotiable. M Famindra has extra accommodation in the form of two beach-hut type houses a few hundred metres from the sea and river. Conditions are hygienic but not developed (eg: earth privy). He is gradually developing a hotel/restaurant business in addition to his tourist guide activities.

Hotel Lagon Bleu (*Category C*) On the east coast, near Marofilao, 7km from Anafiafy. A smallish cosy site, but clean and peaceful. Complimentary daily *punch coco*.

Ile Aux Nattes

There are several places to stay here – see page 263.

Where to eat
Ambodifotatra

Restaurant La Jardine serves good, inexpensive food and is recommended for breakfast. Home-made hot croissants with hot chocolate, and friendly people. The

Hotel Antsara is recommended for its inexpensive set dinner. **Bar-Restaurant Le Barachois** is across the road from the harbour, next to the ferry booking office, and has 'the most comprehensive menu encountered anywhere'. Quite inexpensive, and the tables on the porch are fine for people-watching.

Anafiafy
Restaurant Bar Bleu gets rave reviews!

Ile Aux Nattes
A tradition is a day trip to this little island for lunch at Chez Napoléon (now known as **Hotel Orchidée**), see page 000.

AMBODIFOTATRA
The town is growing and has several boutiques and a patisserie which runs out of bread in the late morning. The market is on Tuesdays and Thursdays. There's a bank which sometimes changes travellers' cheques.

Sightseeing
There are some interesting sights around Ambodifotatra and the Baie des Forbans which are an easy cycle ride from most of the hotels. In the town itself there is a **Catholic church** built in 1837, which serves as a reminder that Ile Sainte Marie had been owned by France since 1750. As a further reminder of French domination there is a **war monument** to a French-British skirmish in 1845.

The **Pirates' Cemetery** is just before the bay bridge to the town (when coming from the south). A signposted track, not usable at high tide, leads to the cemetery. It takes 20 minutes and you don't need a guide (though it may be hard to shake off the pestering kids). This is quite an impressive place, with gravestones dating from the 1830s, one with a classic skull and crossbones carved on it, but not many graves. There is now a 1,000Fmg charge to visit the cemetery.

The town cemetery is worth a visit, though it lacks the story-book drama of the pirates' final resting place. The graveyard is about 6km north of Ambodifotatra, at Bety Plage on the right side of the road.

EXPLORING THE ISLAND
The best way to explore Ile Sainte Marie is by bike (hard work), motorbike, or on foot. In the low season, if you are fit and energetic, you could walk or cycle around most of the island and take your chance on places to stay. During peak seasons most of the hotels would be full.

Crossing from west to east
Although possible to do on your own, it's easy to get lost so many young men have made a lucrative business of guiding visitors to the Indian Ocean side of the island. Many overcharge and have no information except for the route.

Anne Axel recommends two guides from the village of Maromandia: Lapace and Augustine (who runs a restaurant on the east side so eating there is part of the arrangement). Both are polite, knowledgeable, and charge a reasonable amount for their services – about 25,000Fmg. Lapace speaks good English and knows many of the plants and birds – and some folk stories. He can also arrange a pirogue ride to Anafiafy. The walk across the island takes about 2½ hours.

Another starting point for the walk across the island is Antsara. Bjørn Donnis describes his experience: 'It was steep at first, then relatively easy. All kinds of interesting plants, pepper, vanilla etc growing in semi-wild conditions. Gave as many handshakes during the 1hr 40mins crossing as during an average reception. Saw a primitive sugar press and a big hognosed snake.' The downside was that Bjørn forgot to fix the price with his guide first and was overcharged.

It is well worth taking a pirogue trip to explore the coast around the peninsula. 'The beach was the most beautiful I have ever seen. The colour of the water was a mixture of deep blue and emerald green. There weren't any other tourists – in fact I saw only three other people, fishermen, the whole time I was there. I ate a leisurely lunch then walked along the beach for miles. I would hate to see this place spoiled by tourism – it's so pristine!' (Anne Axel)

The far north
About one hour's walk from La Cocoteraie Robert is a beautiful and impressive *piscine naturelle*, with a waterfall, a big pool and enormous basalt rocks.

The Forêt d'Ampanihy, in the northwest, was visited by Jeremy and Lindie Buirski: 'A quite dramatic pirogue trip along the river, as the trees met overhead to form a tunnel. The pirogue will take you to an inlet where the peninsula is at its narrowest, and it's a five-minute walk to the sea on the other side. The coral reef is several hundred metres offshore, so you need another pirogue to dive there – diving from the shore is too dangerous because of the tidal flow. Absolutely deserted, with huge trees on the shore and here and there a lone fisherman.'

Ile Aux Nattes (Nosy Nato)
In recent years this island, off the southern tip of Sainte Marie, has been taken over by the tourist industry. I don't know how the local people feel, but it's hard to complain: it is a wonderful place. 'Our idea of what a tropical island should look like. Lovely bungalows, some with verandas, on lawns under palm trees next to a shiny white beach. The water was clear as glass all the way back to Sainte Marie.' (Jeremy and Lindie Buirski)

It is well worth taking a tour around this little island. There is much to see during a short walking tour, including the island's unique – and amazing – orchid *Eulophiella roempleriana*, known popularly as l'orchidée rose. It is two metres high with deep pink flowers. Don't try to walk right round the island at high tide – there are some tricky bits to negotiate past often rough seas.

A pirogue transfer here from near the airport on Sainte Marie costs 10,000Fmg.

Where to stay/eat
Hotel Orchidée (Chez Napoléon) (*Category B*) Napoléon, who died in 1986, was a charismatic character who 'ruled' – in various guises – this little island and enjoyed entertaining *vazahas*. Bungalows here (with hot water) are 80,000Fmg to 150,000Fmg. There are no fans, but mosquito nets are provided. There's a restaurant, where Napoléon's famous *poulet au coco* is still served to appreciative diners, even if taped pop music has replaced the sound of wind in the palm trees.

Hotel Pandanus (*Category B*) A double bungalow is 50,000Fmg. The communal toilets have soft paper and are very clean. Food prices are reasonable.

Les Bungalows Vohilava (*Category C*) Five bungalows, 28 beds, fans and showers.

WATER ACTIVITIES
Snorkelling and diving
The shallows around Sainte Marie are ideal for snorkelling and diving, although the island's inshore waters are horrendously overfished by local Malagasy, who set fine-mesh gill nets everywhere – watch out for them. These nets catch small, inedible fish as well as larger ones, and this must have an adverse effect on stocks,

which can only prove disastrous in the long term. Lobsters (crayfish) are very much in evidence in and around the reefs, of which there are many, six to ten metres down in clear water and close to Atafana and La Crique. There are also several huge coral 'tables', some nearly two metres wide, but unfortunately a number have been broken off by fish traps.

Balenottero Dive Centre Tel/fax: 57 400 36 (Ambodifotatra) or tel: 22 450 17 (Tana). Italian owned. Very good equipment, organised dive trips to wrecks off Sainte Marie as well as the coral reefs. Whale-watching, and swimming with the whales! 4WD vehicles for overland trips too.

Whale-watching

July to September seems to be the best time to see humpbacked whales; you can watch them from the beach at La Crique or Atafana, or take a boat excursion (offered by some of the hotels or the Centre Nautique). Several hotels offer whale-watching trips, with or without a beach barbecue. The cost ranges from 200Ff to 400Ff.

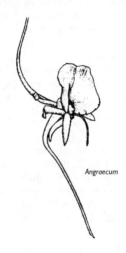

Angraecum

CoL_ourS of the INDIAN OCE_AN

Individually tailored journeys to Madagascar,
Seychelles, Comores, Maldives,
Mauritius, Réunion, Mozambique, Tanzania
& Zanzibar.

Tel (+44)181 343 3446   **Fax(+44)181 349 3439**

PARTNERSHIP TRAVEL LTD   Marlborough House, 298 Regents Park Road,
London, N3 2TJ
info@partnershiptravel.co.uk www.partnershiptravel.co.uk

ATOL

South and West of Toamasina

OVERVIEW

This chapter incorporates the increasingly visited Pangalanes lake resorts to the south of Toamasina and the most popular reserve in Madagascar, Analamazoatra (still known by most people as Périnet). Also included is Lake Alaotra, shunned by tour groups but quite popular with independent travellers.

The coastal area around Manakara and Mananjary is also included, as is the road south to Taolagnaro (Fort Dauphin) which is for the seriously adventurous only.

PANGALANES

This series of lakes was linked by artificial canals in French colonial times for commercial use, a quiet inland water being preferable to an often stormy sea. Over the years the canals became choked with vegetation and no longer passable, but plans are now supposedly being made to rehabilitate them and re-establish the unbroken waterway which stretched from Toamasina to Vangaindrano.

The quiet waters of the canal and lakes are much used by local fishermen for transporting their goods in pirogues and for fishing. With only 100 metres or so of land separating the canal from the ocean, sea and lakeside villages are in easy reach of each other.

In recent years Pangalanes has been developed for tourism, with lakeside bungalows and private nature reserves competing with the traditional ocean resorts for custom. There's even a shallow-draught canal cruiser, the *M/V Mpanjakamena*, which has six double cabins, sundeck, dining saloon and cocktail bar. The cruiser is operated by Softline, 25 Boulevard Joffre, BP 532 Toamasina (tel: 329 75). They have a contact in Tana, too (tel: 341 75). Although Softline's brochure implies that all 420km of the Pangalanes are navigable, this shouldn't be accepted as fact.

The centre for Pangalanes tourism is **Lake Ampitabe**, which has broad beaches of dazzlingly white sand, clean water for swimming (and only a few crocs which prefer dogs to people!), and a private nature reserve with several introduced species of lemur. The three hotels are in a small village called Ankanin'ny Nofy, which means 'House of Dreams'. Lake Ampitabe is 25km by boat from the village of Manambato on RN2, or there is a 35km track (negotiable by 4WD vehicles) linking the lake and RN2.

Getting there and away

Each hotel provides its own transport for booked-in guests. Reaching the lodges on Lake Ampitabe (Akanin'ny Nofy) from RN2 involves a drive to Manambato, at the edge of Lake Rasoabe, 7km south of Vohibinany, followed by a 45-minute boat journey along Pangalanes. You can also take a motor launch from Port Fluvial (Toamasina harbour). The ride takes 1½ hours and is most enjoyable, giving a

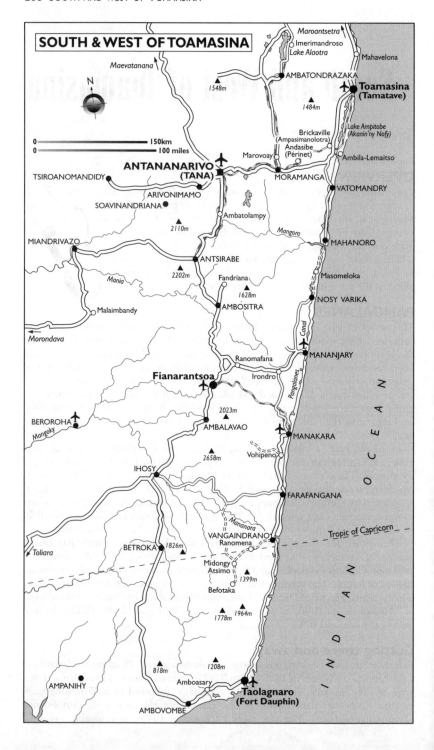

SOUTH & WEST OF TOAMASINA

good flavour of the lakes and connecting canal, and the activities of the local people. It's nice to see the speed boats slow down to a crawl when they pass the laden pirogues, to avoid capsizing them in the wash.

Independent travellers can take a taxi-brousse to Manambato where there is a hotel, and the possibility of hiring a boat or pirogue to take them further. Alternatively, take a taxi-brousse to Brickaville – 8,000Fmg, three hours – and walk along the railway track for three hours to Ambila-Lemaitso, which is 60km south of Toamasina and the nearest seaside resort for Tana bourgeoisie. If the train is running, take it.

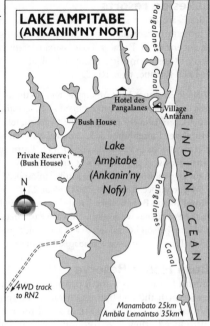

Brickaville and Ambila-Lemaitso
Brickaville

Brickaville is one those Malagasy towns which has resisted changing its name, despite the efforts of mapmakers. Rupert Parker offers this clarification: 'Brickaville is the last and only major town before you hit the coast on the way from Tana to Tamatave. You know you've past it when you go over a large iron bridge over the Rongaronga river. It's also got a railway station, which is the last station before Ambila Lemaitso. Everyone, Malagasy included, knows it as Brickaville, but I see from my map that the name is Ampasimanolotra, 134km south of Tamatave'. No one would stay in Brickaville out of choice, but you may get stuck there.

Where to stay
Hotel des Amis 'You wouldn't put your worst enemies there...' For Rupert Parker's description of the fine points of this hotel see page 115. 15,000Fmg.
Hotel Florida 'Near the railway station; at least half-decent but often full.' Bungalows for 30,000Fmg.

Ambilo-Lemaitso
This is a seaside/canalside resort town, where you can happily get stuck for a day or so. But now the trains are not running it is harder to reach by public transport.

Where to stay/eat
Hotel Relais Malaky Good situation close to the station and overlooking the ocean. Reasonable food. 70,000Fmg, shared facilities, 120,000Fmg en suite.
Ambila Beach About 3km from the station, overlooking the Pangalanes. Nice bungalows, some with cooking facilities. Good value restaurant, friendly staff. 30,000Fmg upwards.
Hotel les Cocotiers About 65,000Fmg for self-contained bungalows. Good, but about 3km from the station so a bit isolated.
L'Orchidaire On the Brickaville side of the Pangalanes canal; scheduled to open late 1999 and to cost around 90,000Fmg.

Lakeside resorts

There are three sets of beach bungalows at Ankanin'ny Nofy (Lake Ampitabe). Quoted prices usually include a double bungalow, plus transfers and meals. Phone the agencies in Tana or Toamasina (details below) for latest prices and availability.

For those wanting a cheaper look at the Pangalanes, there is an additional lodge at Lake Raoabe, near RN2.

Village Atafana Lake Ampitabe; two- to three-person bungalows on a lovely stretch of beach; excellent meals and excursions. Reservations in Tana through the agency MTB, 20 Rue Ratsimilaho (Isoraka, near the Colbert); tel: 223 64; postal address: BP 121.

Hotel des Pangalanes Lake Ampitabe. Seven two-person bungalows for 225Ff. Meals and excursions extra. Bookings: BP 112, Toamasina; tel: 334 03 or 321 77.

Bush House Lake Ampitabe. German-run, very comfortable, and in a beautiful situation. Only five rooms so a pleasant family atmosphere. Book through Boogie Pilgrim, 40 Av de L'Indépendance, Tana; tel: 22 331 85 or 22 204 54; email bopi@bow.dts.mg.

Hotel Rasoa Beach Lake Raoabe, near Manambato. A friendly hotel offering a good taste of the Pangalanes without the expensive transfers. Accommodation varies from two-person and four-person bungalows to a 'Tarzan' hut on stilts. Good food. For bookings phone 252 35 in Tana; website: www.madagascar-contacts.com/bushhouse.

Bush House Reserve

Bush House owns a small private reserve an hour's walk along the beach. This is well worth the 25,000Fmg entrance fee (plus 15,000Fmg for the guide, Sylvain). Although it's more a zoo than a real reserve in that most of the lemurs have been introduced, they are free-ranging but tame enough to make photographing normally rare species easy and rewarding. There are crowned lemurs, red-bellied lemurs (and a fascinating hybrid of the two), ring-tailed lemurs, black-and-white ruffed lemurs, and Coquerel's sifaka. There is also a rather desperately affectionate red-fronted brown lemur.

In a separate area you'll see chameleons and radiated tortoises, and there is a well-tended garden of succulents.

Lac aux Nepenthes

A few kilometres from Bush House. Here there are literally thousands of pitcher plants – a terrific sight!

Independent travel down the Pangalanes waterways

Difficult! There would be no problem having a tour operator put together an expensive package for you, but for shoestring travellers there are not enough cargo boats to make hitching an easy option. There are pirogues, however, so my hunch is that you should either do it in short hops by pirogue, taking pot luck in finding a place to stay each night (bring your own mozzie net), or make an expedition of it with your own boat. I'd love to hear from anyone who tries either of these two options.

ANDASIBE (PERINET)

This famous reserve is currently undergoing something of an identity crisis. Formerly known as Périnet (and formally as Special Reserve Périnet-Analamazoatra) the latest brochure calls it Andasibe National Park. This incorporates two protected areas: Mantadia National Park and Special Reserve Analamazoatra, still called Périnet by most people. Then there's an additional area of (mainly) primary forest, Maromizaha, which receives no formal

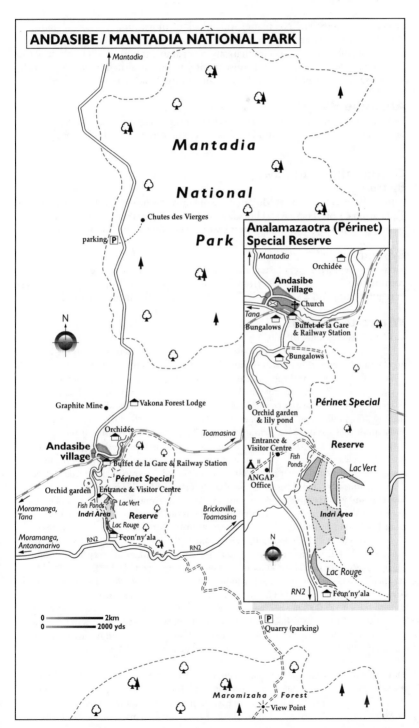

ANDASIBE / MANTADIA NATIONAL PARK

Mantadia

Mantadia National Park

Chutes des Vierges

parking P

N

Graphite Mine

Vakona Forest Lodge

Orchidée

Andasibe village

Buffet de la Gare & Railway Station

Périnet Special

Orchid garden | Entrance & Visitor Centre

Moramanga, Tana

Fish Ponds | Lac Vert

Indri Area

Reserve

Lac Rouge

Moramanga, Antananarivo

RN2

Feon'ny'ala

RN2

Toamasina

Brickaville, Toamasina

Analamazaotra (Périnet) Special Reserve

Mantadia

Orchidée

Andasibe village

Church

Tana

Bungalows

Buffet de la Gare & Railway Station

Bungalows

Périnet Special

Orchid garden & lily pond

Entrance & Visitor Centre

ANGAP Office

Fish Ponds

Reserve

Lac Vert

Indri Area

N

Lac Rouge

RN2

Feon'ny'ala

0 ——— 2km
0 ——— 2000 yds

P
Quarry (parking)

Maromizaha Forest

View Point

protection. Confused? No matter, this block of moist montane forest (altitude: 930–1,049m) is extremely rich in fauna and flora, including – some experts say – a higher number of frog species than any comparable rainforest on earth. It is also the reserve closest to Tana and consequently the most visited in Madagascar. In the winter months of June and July it can be quite cold here – be warned!

Andasibe Village
Few visitors bother to cross the river to look at the village. It's a shame that so little of the tourist revenue has found its way here; you can do your bit by shopping for fruit etc there.

Getting there and away
By train
This now runs only as far as Moramanga, and only spasmodically. In theory it leaves Tana at 06.45 on Tuesdays, Thursdays and Saturdays, taking about six hours. In reality it is unlikely to go at all. But it's worth checking at the station just in case!

By road
Taxi-brousses are much faster and those used on this route tend to be quite comfortable. You will pay less from Tana if you take a taxi-brousse to Moramanga (a regular stop) and a local taxi-be 25km to the Andasibe turn-off from RN2.

Where to stay/eat
Vakôna Forest Lodge BP 750, Antananarivo; tel: 213 94; fax: 230 70; email: izouard@bow.dts.mg; website: www.madagascar-contacts.com/vakona. This is the luxury hotel upmarket visitors have been wishing for (and as such is only accessible with your own vehicle). Its location near the graphite mine (same ownership) is not idyllic, but it now has its own small reserve and the hotel itself works to perfection. The main building has been thoughtfully designed as an octagonal reception area, bar and lounge-dining room with a huge log-fire in the middle. The upper storey houses a shop. The 14 bungalows are quiet and comfortable and there is a swimming pool. The management is efficient and courteous, and the food delicious. It really is quite something, and deserves longer than the normal couple of days so you can relax and enjoy some horse-riding, as well as the usual lemur-viewing. The price per room 200–300Ff full board. To reach Vakôna from Andasibe, cross the bridge into the village, and take the left fork. The hotel is signposted.

Hotel Feon' Ny Ala (18 bungalows, camping area) The name means 'Window of the Forest' or 'Voice of the Forest'. This popular place is on the right side of the road that runs from RN2 to Andasibe and is favoured by serious naturalists since it's right by the reserve – close enough to hear the indri call (hence its name). There is a beautiful orchid garden on the riverbank. The Chinese owners, M and Mme Sum Chuk Lan, are very helpful and eager to please. Some find the Voice of the Forest a bit too loud: 'Light sleepers should not stay here: neighbours snoring, 3.30am confused indri calling, and Hotel Dog which does a very passable imitation of an indri except the dog goes yelp when someone throws something at it.' 77,000Fmg per bungalow with en-suite facilities; meals 25,000Fmg. The Feon' ny Ala is the farthest hotel from the town of Andasibe (a 40-minute walk), so you should plan to eat your meals in the restaurant, or bring food with you from Tana if you're camping at the hotel (10,000Fmg for tent space). The hotel has no phone so booking a room in advance is difficult.

Hotel Buffet de la Gare Next to the station. Until 1993 this was the only place to stay in Andasibe, and its list of distinguished guests includes Prince Philip, Gerald Durrell and David Attenborough. Built in 1938 it must once have been appropriate for its role of housing the Great and the Good who wished to visit Périnet, but not within my memory. For the last two decades it has been a typical *Category C* hotel, with saggy beds, a non-functioning loo, and a certain amount of non-endemic wildlife in the bedrooms (one distinguished guest suffered a rat bite). A great social leveller. I am very fond of this place and of its courteous owner, Monsieur Joseph. The dining room is truly elegant – fresh flowers on the tables and a marvellous rosewood bar. Good food, too. A nice little feature of the dining room is the *phelsuma* gecko which stuck to the new paintwork near the door; the enthusiastic workman simply applied another coat of paint over the little body and there it remains. There is now a quieter and more comfortable option: five bungalows in a lovely meadow close to the forest about 75m towards the reserve. Each has three to four beds and hot water. Less luxurious but perfectly adequate are the seven chalet-type bungalows opposite the Buffet.

Maison des Orchidées A wooden hotel right in the village of Andasibe, so noisy. Inexpensive, comfortable, Malagasy-run, hot water.

La Forestière A new snack bar at the entrance of the reserve. There is also a campsite here and a long-drop toilet.

Permits and guides

You can get your permit from ANGAP in Tana, or at the park entrance (50,000Fmg). The Périnet guides are the best in Madagascar and an example to the rest of the country for knowledge, enthusiasm, and an awareness of what tourists want. The Association des Guides Andasibe (AGA) ensures that standards are maintained. All the guides know where to find indri and other lemurs. Those who I can particularly recommend are Maurice and his brothers Luke and Patrice, and sister Marie, along with Lala, Désiré, Eugene, Nirinha, Zac and Jean; but there are other rising stars. The fee is 20,000Fmg for two hours during the day; 40,000Fmg for an night walk. Some of the specialist guides such as Patrice (birds) charge a daily rate of 250Ff, for up to three people (so 500Ff if there are, say, five of you).

Information and souvenirs

At the entrance to the reserve is a shelter with some information and maps, and good souvenirs such as T-shirts. There is also a snack bar here and a rather splendid toilet, built by the Japanese – too splendid: it has been out of order for over a year.

Périnet (Analamazoatra) Special Reserve

This 810ha reserve protects the largest of the lemur family, *Indri indri*. Standing about a metre high, with a barely visible tail, black-and-white markings and a surprised teddy-bear face, the indri looks more like a gone-wrong panda than a lemur. The long back legs are immensely powerful, and an indri can propel itself 10 metres (30 feet), executing a turn in mid-air, to hug a new tree and gaze down benevolently at its observers. And you will be an observer: everyone now sees indris in Périnet, and most also hear them. For it is the voice that makes this lemur extra special: whilst other lemurs grunt or swear, the indri sings. It is an eerie, wailing sound somewhere between the song of a whale and a police-siren, and it carries for up to three kilometres as troops call to each other across the forest. The indris are fairly punctual with their song: if you are in the reserve between one and two hours after daybreak and shortly before dusk you should hear them. They call periodically throughout the morning before settling down to their noontime siesta in the tops of trees.

Indri are monogomous, living in small family groups of up to five animals, and give birth in June. Births usually occur every two years. At the last count there were 280 indris in Périnet.

In Malagasy the indri is called Babakoto which means 'Father of Koto'. It is *fady* to kill an indri, the legend being that the boy Koto climbed a tree in the forest to collect wild honey, and was severely stung by the bees. Losing his hold, he fell, but was caught by a indri which carried him on its back to safety.

There are nine species of lemur altogether in Périnet (including aye-aye), although you will not see them all. You may find the troop of grey bamboo lemurs which are diurnal and sometimes feed on the bamboo near the warden's house (though I have not seen them recently), brown lemurs, and perhaps a sleeping avahi (woolly lemur) curled up in the fork of a tree. It is worth going on a nocturnal lemur hunt (the guides are experts at this) to look for mouse lemurs and the greater dwarf lemur which hibernates during the cold season.

Lemurs are only a few of the creatures to be found in Périnet. There are tenrecs, beautiful and varied insects and spiders, as well as lots of reptiles. One of Madagascar's biggest chameleons lives here: Parson's chameleon, which is bright green and half a metre long. The male has twin horns at the end of its snout. Here also is the smallest chameleon, *Calumma nasutus*. The guides keep a selection of chameleons near the entrance for tourists to photograph. Tree boas are common here and quite placid.

This is also a great place for bird-watching (keen birders should ask for Patrice or Maurice to be their guide). Specials to look out for include the velvet asity and pitta-like ground-roller.

Botanists will not be disappointed. In French-colonial days an orchid garden was started by the lily pond to the right of the road to the reserve, and a variety of species flourishes here although most flower in the warm wet season.

Leeches can be an unpleasant aspect of Périnet if you've pushed through vegetation and it's been raining recently. Tuck your trousers into your socks and apply insect repellent.

Maromizaha

This 10,000ha area of mainly primary forest offers a great day's hiking for enthusiastic and fit visitors. An 18km trail runs from a stone quarry area to the village of Anevoka, on the road to Tamatave. It is slippery when wet and requires a full day (bring a picnic) but gives hikers the chance to see some additional species such as – if you are really lucky – the diademed sifaka, and black-and-white ruffed lemur. It is also the best place I know for finding some of Madagascar's thousand or so bizarre and colourful weevils! If you have only a half day available, it is still worth walking along the trail to the main viewpoint.

Maromizaha (pronouned Maroomeeza) is about 7km from Andasibe in the direction of Toamasina, off RN2. The track leading to Maromizaha (closed by a barrier) is on the right, about 4km from the Andasibe turning. Walk – or get permission to drive – up the track to the stone quarry. The trail starts to the left of the flat area above the workers' houses (as you face back to the road). Since this is not a protected area you can camp here. And since it is not a protected area, visit it soon. 'The whole area is being actively felled... Walking through this forest with eerie call of the indri accompanied by the chop-chopping of wood was one of the most enduring memories of the trip.' (Clare Hermans)

Mantadia (Mantady) National Park

This recently created national park is 25km to the north of Périnet. It lies at a higher altitude than the more popular reserve and consequently harbours different species. Now that it is officially open to tourists (it only formally became a national park in October 1999) it is a wonderful addition to Périnet for fit and energetic visitors.

What is so special about Mantadia is that, in contrast to Périnet, it is untouched primary forest. There are only a few constructed trails – visitors must be prepared to work for their wildlife – but this is a naturalist's goldmine, with many seldom-seen species of mammals, reptiles and birds. The forest is bisected by the road. On the left is the area for black-and-white ruffed lemurs (*very* hard scrambling) and to the right, if you are really lucky, you may see the beautiful golden-coloured diademed sifaka or *simpona* and almost certainly some indri (curiously much darker in colour than in Périnet). This section of Mantadia has some good, if steep, trails with gorgeous views across the forest and super birdwatching possibilities, particularly for ground-rollers, vangas and asitys. It really is a terrific place, but you must be in good shape.

There are gentler parts of Mantadia. An easy, two-hour trail leads up through the forest to a waterfall and lake (*Cascade* and *Lac Sacré*). Bring your swimsuit for a cooling dip in the pool beneath the waterfall.

To do justice to Mantadia you should spend the whole day there, bringing a picnic, and leave the hotel at dawn. You will need your own transport and, of course, a guide.

Torotorofotsy and Ampasipotsy

Torotorofotsy Marsh is being added to the itineraries of birding groups, for the rare endemics such as Meller's duck, Madagascar snipe, Madagascar rail, Madagascar crested ibis, Madagascar flufftail, grey emutail and even the very rare slender-billed flufftail. This is also the only known habitat for the golden mantella frog.

An excursion to Torotorofotsy takes all day – it involves a three-hour walk down the railway track from Périnet. A shorter option, where you will see most of the above birds, is Ampasipotsy, which is only 45 minutes' walk from the main road.

OTHER PLACES OF INTEREST ON RN2

Antsampanana

If you are driving up RN2 from Toamasina this is a popular place to stop to buy fruit. The little town is bursting with stalls offering all sorts of goodies. Nice for photography, too. If you want to dally longer there is the basic **Hotel Espérance** and some restaurants. From here it is about 1½ hours' drive to Andasibe.

Moramanga

This formerly sleepy town is about a half-hour drive from Andasibe. It gained a new lease of life with the completion of the Chinese road (there is a memorial here to the Chinese workers) and, during the 1980s and early '90s, from the absence of comfortable hotels in Andasibe. Moramanga is a lively town and still a popular lunch stop when driving to Andasibe from Tana. There's quite a bit of Moramanga beyond the main road.

Try to make a visit to the Museum of Gendarmerie. 'Surely the most comprehensive collection in Madagascar, not only police, but cultural, with excellent original exhibits. A must!' (K & L Gillespie)

The telephone area code is 56.

Where to stay/eat

Grand Hotel Tel: 620 16. Helpful, friendly; hot water. About 40,000Fmg.
Emeraude Tel: 621 57. Hot showers. Good value.
Mirasoa A newish hotel on RN2 about 1km from the centre on the Tana side of town. Basic but clean.

Other basic hotels include the **Restau-Hotel Maitso an'Ala**, the **Hotel Fivami**, and **Hotel au Poisson**.

The Chinese restaurant, **Guangzou** (tel: 62 089), serves good food and is popular with groups so reservations may be necessary in the high season. Almost as popular is the **Au Coq d'Or**; tel: 62 045.

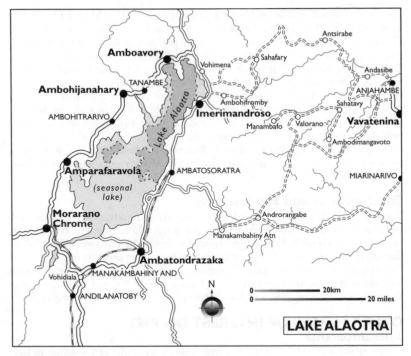

Map labels: Antsirabe, Amboavory, Vohimena, Sahafary, Andasibe, TANAMBE, Ambohijanahary, ANJAHAMBE, Ambohifromby, Sahatavy, AMBOHITRARIVO, Imerimandroso, Vavatenina, Manambafo, Valorano, Ambodimangavoto, Amparafaravola, AMBATOSORATRA, MIARINARIVO, (seasonal lake), Morarano Chrome, Androrangabe, Manakambahiny Atn, Ambatondrazaka, Vohidiala, MANAKAMBAHINY AND, N, 0 20km, 0 20 miles, ANDILANATOBY, **LAKE ALAOTRA**

Mandraka (Madagascar Exotic)
Described on page 162.

Marovoay
This is the first stop on the railway line north towards Lake Alaotra, and the name means 'Many Crocodiles'. Appropriately, there is a commercial crocodile farm which is open to visitors. There are over a thousand *Crocodylus niloticus*, some over two and a half metres in length, living in semi-wild conditions. The best season to visit is January, when the eggs are hatching. For a visit contact: Reptel Madagascar, 50 Av Grandidier, BP 563, Isoraka, Antananarivo; tel: 348 86, fax: 206 48.

LAKE ALAOTRA
This is the largest lake in Madagascar and looks wonderful on the map: one imagines it surrounded by overhanging forest. Sadly, forest has made way for rice, and this is one of the most abused and degraded areas in Madagascar. Half a million people now live around the lake, and deforestation has silted it up so that its maximum dry-season depth is only 60cm. Introduction of exotic fish has done further damage. However, all is not lost. The area has been designated a Site of Special Biological Interest by the WWF because of its endemic waterfowl, though it is too late to save Delacour's grebe (Alaotra little grebe) which is now extinct, and the Madagascar pochard may have gone the same way. Work done by the Durrell Wildlife Conservation Trust has ensured that the Alaotran grey bamboo lemur has a future. Not only are these animals breeding happily at Jersey Zoo (see box page 70) but the human inhabitants of the area have cooperated fully with the WWF and DWCT's programmes to introduce

conservation measures – another example of how sensitively organised projects can benefit both the local people and the wildlife. The authorities are now hoping that the region will be accepted by the Ramsar Convention, a globally signed treaty to protect wetlands.

Getting there and away
By rail
This is now the only place in Madagascar where rail travel is still preferable to road. A spur of the railway runs from Moramanga, with trains leaving Tana early in the morning, and ends at Ambatondrazaka near the southeast side of the lake. It takes 12 hours (to go 300km!) and costs 26,000Fmg.

By road
The dirt road (RN44) from Moramanga is being improved, bridges are being built, and it may soon be the easiest way to reach the lake. In 1998, however, it was still very muddy and hazardous after rain.

Bishop Brock, who cycled this route in 1996, writes: 'It's a good dirt road, nice scenery, sparsely populated. If you happen to be going that way I can recommend a stop at the Hotely Mahandry in Amboasary-Gara, about 60km north of Moramanga. This may be the prettiest *hotely* in Madagascar. The owner grows orchids, is very friendly, and rents a single room for 15,000Fmg.'

Ambatondrazaka
The main town of the area, and a good centre for excursions, with a couple of Category B/C hotels.

Where to stay/eat
Hotel Voahirana BP 65, Côte Postale 503. Most rooms have mosquito nets; no en-suite facilities but hot water available; 42,000Fmg. Good restaurant. Quite a walk from the station. Next door is the restaurant **Cantonnais**; very good value.

Hotel Max Near the station. 14 rooms. The restaurant Fanantenana is next door.

Excursions
Probably the best reason to come to Lake Alaotra is to meet the guide Jean-Baptiste Randrianomanana and join him for one of his excursions. 'He speaks excellent English, studied sociology and philosophy and is extremely knowledgeable about all aspects of Madagascar. His wife is a geographer. He will take you on a tour of the lake which involves a taxi drive to a traditional village on the shores of the lake, a night with a local family at Imerimandroso, a pirogue crossing on the lake to another village called Vohitsara to meet the medicine man and the school teacher etc, and a taxi-ride back to Ambatondrazaka.' (J and R McFarlaine)

Jean-Baptiste may be able to invite you to a *famadihana* and can give you detailed information for hiking the Smugglers' Path to the coast – a four- or five-day hike (see below). He usually meets the train and keeps an eye out for *vazahas* or he can be contacted through the Hotel Voahirana.

Imerimandroso
A small town near the lake; half an hour's walk to the south is a village from where you can take a pirogue.

There is one basic hotel, the **Bellevue**.

The Smugglers' Path

John Kupiec – an exceptionally adventurous and independent traveller – decided to do this trail on his own. In 1996 he wrote: 'From the following story you will see what happens when an out-of-the-way path in Madagascar gets touristed.' It is quite a long story. The core of it is that John's contact with the local people was almost entirely negative (in sharp contrast to his experiences elsewhere), he was cheated out of money at almost every stage (despite speaking some Malagasy), and the uncertainty of what would happen each day spoiled the walk anyway.

John's conclusion is that even with the FTM map it is not possible to follow this path without a guide, and that it would be better to seek out the services of Jean-Baptiste. In the three years that have elapsed since that letter I have had no feedback about this trail. In my view there are other, nicer, areas to hike in.

For the record, John's journey took him from the train station at Vohidiala then by taxi-brousse to Tanambe where there is a basic hotel. Next day he walked to Vohitsara and took a pirogue across the lake to Andromba where the Smugglers' Path begins. In Ambohitromby he picked up one of a series of guides to take him to Manambato. Three days and several villages later he reached the end of the trail at Anjahambe. From there it was a short taxi-brousse ride to Vavatenina, where he stayed in some hotel-bungalows, and thence to the east coast road.

COMMERSON

Joseph Philibert Commerson has provided the best-known quote on Madagascar:

'C'est à Madagascar que je puis annoncer aux naturalistes qu'est la véritable terre promise pour eux. C'est là que la nature semble s'être retirée dans un sanctuaire particulier pour y travailler sur d'autres modèles que ceux auxquels elle s'est asservie ailleurs. Les formes les plus insolites et les plus merveilleuses s'y rencontrent à chaque pas.'

'Of Madagascar I can say to naturalists that it is truly their promised land. There nature seems to have retreated into a private sanctuary to work on models other than those she has created elsewhere. At every step one encounters the most strange and marvellous forms.'

Commerson was a doctor who travelled with Bougainville on a world expedition in 1766, arriving at Mauritius in 1768. He studied the natural history of that island, then in 1770 journeyed on to Madagascar where he stayed for three or four months in the Fort Dauphin region. His famous description of 'nature's sanctuary' was in a 1771 letter to his old tutor in Paris.

'There are some birds the size of a large turkeycock which have the head made like a cat and the rest of the body like a griffin; these birds hide themselves in the thick woods, and when anyone passes under the tree where they are they let themselves fall so heavily on the head of the passengers that they stun them, and in the moment they pierce their heads with their talons, then they eat them.'
Sieur de Bois, 1669

THE SOUTHEAST COAST

For most people this begins with Mananjary, which is linked to the Highlands by both air and road. Adventurous souls, however, can slowly make their way south, leaving RN2 after Brickaville.

The route south from Toamasina to Mananjary

The following report is from Helena Drysdale. The journey she describes formed the basis of her book *Dancing with the Dead* (see *Appendix 4, Further Information*).

'We travelled from Tamatave [Toamasina] to Mananjary over two weeks. Generally people assured us it was impossible, that there were no roads, that all the bridges were down in the cyclone, and the ferries were *en panne* (that familiar phrase). But with luck and ingenuity we made it. One taxi-brousse per week from Tamatave to Mahanoro (two days), otherwise river boats available at Tamatave's river port for hitching (we went on boats travelling south to a graphite mine in Vatomandry – a very uncomfortable three days).

'In Vatomandry we stayed in the Hotel Fotsy; thatched bungalows. Good food here and some Chinese restaurants in town. From there to Mahanoro, one day by taxi-brousse, two by boat. Hotel Pangalanes, full of ladies of the night and noisy revellers but a nice atmosphere. Boat from Mahanoro to Masomelika one day; very simple hotel but friendly people (I asked for the toilet and was pointed to a bucket. This was the shower – the toilet was in the bushes). From Masomelika to Nosy Varika took half a day hitchhiking. There's a relatively expensive Chinese hotel here. Then on to Mananjary, one night by boat.'

The Chinese-owned hotel described by Helena is **Hotel Petite Oasis**, which 'serves excellent food, is clean and light and has rooms as well as little bungalows at the back' (Maggie Rush). Another nearby is the **Hotel de la Saraleona**.

MANANJARY AND MANAKARA

These two pleasant seaside towns have good communications with the rest of Madagascar and are gaining in popularity among discerning travellers.

Telephone area codes: 212 02 (Manakara); 213 80 (Mananjary).

Getting there and away

Mananjary is usually reached by road from Ranomafana, and Manakara is the end (or beginning) of the railway journey from Fianarantsoa (see page 178). The road between the two towns is surfaced, but badly potholed. Even so, the journey by taxi-brousse takes only four hours. Mananjary and Manakara are linked by air with Tana and Taolagnaro several times a week (HS 748 and Twin Otter). The Air Mad office in Manakara is in the Hotel Sidi.

Mananjary

A very nice small town accessible by good road and taxi-brousse (lovely scenery) from Ranomafana, and famous for its circumcision ceremony which takes place every seven years (see box). The next one will be in the year 2000.

There is a long beach with terrific breakers (dangerous swimming – and there are sharks) and the Pangalanes Canal, and all the attractions of people-watching. 'The men go out early (4am) in a tremendous surf and row or sail back into the river. Shrimps are sold to wholesalers. Other fish (some very pretty ones) are eaten. Some fishermen *fady*: Wives are not allowed to look at another man until

SAMBATRA (CIRCUMCISION) IN MANANJARY
Sally Crook

Sambatra means 'blessed' or 'happy' in Malagasy, and it is the word used for the circumcision ceremonies which are performed in much of Madagascar. The Antambahoaka, probably the smallest tribe in Madagascar, live around Mananjary on the east coast, and young boys and their families from the surrounding villages congregate every seven years for a communal circumcision ceremony there. They become 'blessed', though the actual deed of removal of the penis foreskin is now performed at a different time., usually in the hygienic conditions of a hospital.

When I was there, in October 1986, the week-long celebrations commenced at a leisurely pace and culminated (after a Thursday of inactivity, due to the *fady* nature of this day) on a Friday. Women collected reeds and wove mats in preparation for the big day, and later men carved and painted wooden birds, three of which were fixed on the roof of each *trano be* (literally 'big house'), facing east. This in itself caused much excitement and some unwished-for precipitous descents from the sloped, thatched roofs, while the men continued to beat their oval wooden or hide shields with sticks wielded like swords. Similar activity, drumming and chanting continued below, and the women chanted as they stepped from side to side in their dance. A boy standing astride a barrel on a wheeled cart, brandishing shield and stick, gave the most fiery display, encouraging the crowds around.

The fathers of boys to be circumcised wore long colourful robes, gathered at the neck. The *trano be* in which the people drink and talk for days should not be entered by foreign females, and even the Malagasy women must wear their hair in the traditional style - the many plaits on each side of the centre parting being drawn to a cluster at each side of the neck.

In the afternoon of the Wednesday, women shuffled around the *trano be* in an anti-clockwise direction, chanting and holding aloft the white braided and tasselled red ceremonial caps of their young sons. At the front and back of the procession, the rolled mats woven especially for the occasion were held aloft. After several circuits of the house, the crowds proceeded to the beach where, apparently spontaneously, the women's cries were periodically renewed.

12pm or something will happen to the husband at sea; a man who eats pork cannot go to sea.' (C and J Hermans).

Where to stay/eat

Jardin de la Mer A very pleasant set of beach bungalows; hot showers and WC en suite. Good restaurant. 90,000Fmg per bungalow (two beds).

Solimotel Bd Maritime. The second best hotel. Good, but rather expensive food.

Hotel aux Bons Amis Proprietor friendly and accommodating.

Snack Central Near the market, has a modest menu with modest prices, good food, and is willing to serve meals mid-afternoon.

Manakara

Compares unfavourably with Mananara because there are no beach hotels or restaurants. However, the old part of town is recommended by Andrea Jarman. 'The Allée des Filaos running between ex-colonial buildings and the ocean makes the waterfront a very attractive part of town. The new town and station are across the river bridge and of no interest. Pousse-pousses provide the best local transport.'

The excitement spilt over into a kind of fighting between men with green pointed sticks cut from the mid-ribs of palm fronds, and soon the fathers of the circumcision candidates were being routed and chased back into town as the green sticks were hurled at their retreating backs. The apparent terror with which men fled from these harmless weapons indicates a far greater symbolic significance than their physical power.

As Thursday became Friday at midnight, sacred water was collected from the wide River Mananjary where it enters the sea. In the morning gloom nine zebu were sacrificed – one for each clan – by the cutting of the jugular vein after prayers. Some escapees caused excitement before the animals could be bound and lain on their sides with a piece of wood between the teeth. At the first sight of blood, little boys rushed forward to collect it in buckets or in bamboo pipes, just as their 'cousins' in Toraja, Sulawesi, do to this day.

Dancing, music and the women's chant of 'Eeee-ay' changed to processions and a chorus of 'Aaa-ooh' as crowds converged once again on the beach. The young boys, in red and white smocks and wearing their tasselled caps, were carried on their fathers' shoulders. The mind-dulling chant continued as the separate clans were herded along like sheep by men with sticks, following the man with the sacred water held in a small pot on his head, protected by a movable 'hedge' of four poles carried by other robed men.

That night, the boys, bearing white marks on their faces to indicate their clan, were carried on the shoulders of adults around the *trano be*. Each was passed through the west door of the house and, wearing a string around the waist, was sat upon the severed head of a fine male zebu for a while in the presence of the clan leader, adorned with colourful striped cloth and a fez. The virility of the animal was thus conferred on the boy and, as he was passed through the east door, he became a man.

These tiny men were almost dropping with exhaustion as they were paraded once again near the house, whose outside northern end had been cordoned off and guarded from trespass throughout the ceremonial days. The joy of their mothers was vocal and infectious as if they were relieved to have their sons now accepted as adults.

The taxi-brousse station is some way from the centre of town; take a pousse-pousse if your bags are heavy.

You should not swim in Manakara because of dangerous currents and sharks.

The telephone area code is 73.

Where to stay/eat

Hotel Sidi The best hotel, though a bit dingy. Hot showers en suite. 38,000Fmg. Very good restaurant.

Parthenay Club Tel: 211 60. This used to be a posh tennis club for the locals, with a swimming pool, with some tourist bungalows on the side. It was severely damaged in the 1997 cyclone and I've had no reports of its current condition.

Hotel Manakara A friendly, once-pretty hotel popular with travellers (and ants), in town but near the ocean.

Le Chalet Suisse BP 31 Manakara; tel: 213 89. An excellent place to eat *grillades*, Swiss specialities including raclette and macaroni à la crème, and a variety of other well-prepared dishes. It is easy to spot its large red and white sign on the right side of the road to the airport, on the edge of town a short distance after you pass the railway station.

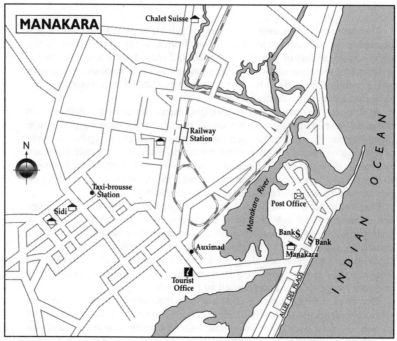

La Gourmandise This restaurant and cake shop is a few minutes walk from Hotel Sidi, opposite the taxi-brousse stop. 'Good value, yummy food and quite a lot of imported products to buy.'

Manakara to Fianar by train

With the Tana–Toamasina line in disrepair, this now offers the most interesting – and beautiful – train ride in Madagascar. The track is cyclone-damaged and the locomotives ancient, so it is an exciting ride. Mark Hughes took it in 1995: 'We

THE MAGIC SHOW

Chris Ballance

We saw a poster in Manakara for a Magic Show so bought tickets. The magician was quite good in a relaxed way. The audience were brilliant. About 120 people in a dingy youth centre hall without lights. He began with a couple of simple disappearing tricks that drew rounds of applause. It was the lesser tricks that were applauded; the better ones left the audience too spell-bound to think of clapping. His magic wand was a flute-sized rod which he empowered by touching a plastic skull with a red robe hanging from it. He used few other props – two or three magic boxes, a few packs of cards and a glass. He filled this with flour, wrapped it in a 'magicked' newspaper and turned it into a glass of bon-bons which he threw into the audience. From this moment the audience were his, body and soul. There was no 'willing suspension of disbelief'. These people had eaten the proof of his powers.

He repeated the trick later, turning coffee powder into cigarettes. He put one of the cigarettes into a guillotine and cut it. Then he put a volunteer boy's finger into the guillotine. Another boy had to hold a hat to catch the finger. Down came

couldn't book seats but were told to board the parked train with a porter and point out which ones we wanted. The following morning the porter took our luggage as soon as we arrived, and when we eventually boarded our luggage and the porter were waiting at our selected seats! The train ride is a story in itself. The views were great and the stops were interesting. Each station seemed to have a speciality – all the vendors sold bananas, or eggs, or fried things. Things got exciting as the train went uphill. It became a real *"Little Train that Could"* ("I think I can, I think I can..."). The engine was really straining and we weren't going anywhere. Three times the train started rolling backwards despite the squealing brakes and the engine's best efforts.'

The train is running on an erratic schedule. You will have to check at the station and see when it is likely to feel strong enough to make the journey. Without breakdowns it takes about seven hours to reach Fianar from Manakara, but 20 hours is not unknown. For the best views sit on the right-hand side.

CONTINUING SOUTH
Vohipeno
Situated some 45km south of Manakara, this small town is the centre of the Antaimoro tribe who came from Arabia about 600 years ago, bringing the first script to Madagascar. Their Islamic history is shown by their clothing (turban and fez, as well as Arab-style robes). They are the inheritors of the 'great writings', *sorabe*, written in Malagasy but in Arabic script. *Sorabe* continue to be written, still in Arabic, still on 'Antaimoro paper'. The scribes who practise this art are known as *katibo* and the writing and their knowledge of it give them a special power. The writing itself ranges from accounts of historical events to astrology, and the books are considered sacred.

The **Hotel du Sud** is basic but adequate.

Farafangana
Accessible by taxi-brousse from Manakara, this is a pleasant and comfortable town in which to spend some time.

Where to stay/eat
Hotel Les Cocotiers An upmarket hotel near the post office. Good restaurant. Cheapest rooms are 60,000Fmg.

---

the guillotine, the hand was hidden in the hat and then magicked better. As the boy left the stage he was mobbed. All we could see was a heap of every child in the audience. Suddenly a finger shot up from the centre of the heap, triumphantly showing everyone it was attached to its hand. And when the conjurer got a girl in the audience to lay an egg, everyone – but *everyone* – had to see it, touch it, and marvel at it.

The show ended with a draw in which names were put into a hat (we prayed we wouldn't win). There were prizes of 1,000, 5,000 and 10,000Fmg notes. Each winner was given the note to put into an envelope which was put into a magic box, magicked, and then given back. We suspected they got a message to the effect of 'You've been had'. The girl next to me goggled – that's the only word – at the sight of the money. '*Cinq mille francs!*' she kept repeating over and over in an ecstasy of hope. The sight of the 10,000Fmg note shut her up entirely.

Next day we changed £40 to last us for three days. We received 138,000Fmg. The obscenity of international finance, beside that girl, shamed us.

Hotel Les Tulipes Rouges The rooms are all called after different shades of red! Clean, good food and safe parking. 25,000–30,000Fmg.

Tsaravatsy Hotel Popular with Malagasy; good restaurant (Malagasy and Chinese specialities). Cold water, shared facilities. 30,000Fmg.

Le Croustillant bakery Good selection of breads and croissants across the road from Les Cocotiers.

Les Mimosas Salon de Thé Opposite Les Cocotiers. Lots of imported goodies available (at a price).

A couple of new hotels are being constructed on the west side of town.

To the south or west

The road from Farafangana to Ihosy has long been infamous for bandits, but has reportedly been improved, allowing a Highlands/East Coast circuit of great interest. You should check locally, however, about conditions and safety.

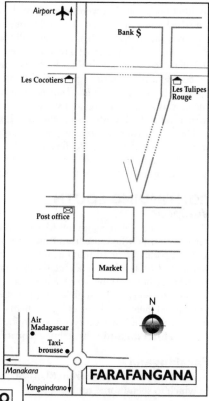

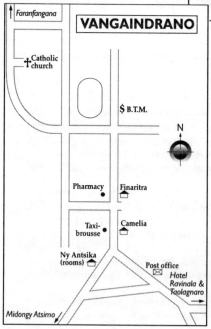

Those with time, a 4WD vehicle or mountain bike, or a light backpack and lots of energy, can continue south.

Vangaindrano

This has the feel of a frontier town, but there are several basic hotels, including the **Ny Antsika**, **Finaritra**, **Camelia** and **Ravinala**. Frances Kerridge stayed at the Ny Antsika in 1998: 'Cockroaches and ants, sagging squeaky beds. 25,000Fmg.' The others may be better. Or not.

To the far south

Vangaindrano is the end of the road for most people, but you can continue further: 'There is a road southwest to Midongy Atsimo (no regular taxi-brousse service, occasional bashie) which is maintained reasonably well because of a new coffee project. Muddy in places. 4WD advisable but not essential. 95km, 5–6 hours, with one excellent ferry. Food on the road in La Rose du Sud in Ranomena, oodles of *couleur locale*. No hotel in Midongy, but we rented a nice house with three beds, outside toilet, and tub of water for 4,000Fmg. All this, plus meals, was obtained from the *Epicerie* on the Befotaka road (south end of town). The road to Befotaka (40km) was impassable most of the time, very skiddy, but has some very good forest at 20–25km south of Midongy.'

'Maps show that you can follow the gloriously named RN12 to Fort Dauphin. Only those prepared to suffer some privations should attempt to do this. Transport in the area is erratic and unpredictable, the roads are very bad. Be prepared to travel over rickety bridges in overladen lorries, walk long distances, and cross rivers in what may appear to be very unstable dug-out canoes (without a counter-balance). Of the latter the secret is to get your centre of gravity as low as possible, so for *vazaha* this invariably means kneeling down in the bottom of the canoe and remaining still. It is also advisable to remove footwear for a crossing. You may only fear losing your luggage if the canoe capsizes, but remember that most people here cannot swim well and that luggage is not what they fear losing, but their lives.'

BOOGIE PILGRIM
TOUR OPERATOR

- BUSH HOUSE / Pangalanes Canal
- TSARA CAMP / Tsaranoro / Andringitra
- Fly-in SAFARI
- Special Interest Tours
- Ecotourism

Address : Villa Michelet Lot A11 - Faravohitra
ANTANANARIVO 101 - MADAGASCAR
Phone : 261 20 22 258 78 Fax : 261 20 22 625 56
e-mail : bopi@bow.dts.mg
web site : www.madagascar-contacts.com/boogie

HAINTENY

Reflect on regrets, Andriamatoa.
They do not look in at the door to be told 'enter!'
They do not sit to be told 'May I pass?'
They do not advise beforehand,
but they reproach afterward.
They are not driven along like sheep,
but they come following like dogs;
they swing behind like a sheep's tail.

MADAGASCAR
WILDLIFE & PHOTO TOURS

Join experienced guide, writer/photographer, and reptile expert **Bill Love** on a lifetime adventure in exotic Madagascar! We'll visit and explore all the best places to find and photograph the maximum number of odd chameleons, leaping lemurs, tortoises, boas, day geckos, weird insects, bizarre plants and more. I personally plan all trips to include areas in which I've found the most animals and taken my most spectacular slides. My tours emphasize hands-on fun and interaction as we travel to all regions of the island in our quests.

Come to this tropical mini-continent where few folks will ever venture in their lives. The fauna and flora are truly unique, and the people are ultra-friendly. Several tour plans offer a variety of amenity levels from semi-luxury to true adventure.

I work hard to make my tours the most memorable vacations you'll ever experience! Please request tour descriptions of the next scheduled trips, or call for more details.

 BLUE CHAMELEON VENTURES

P.O. Box 643
Alva, Florida · 33920 U.S.A.
TELEPHONE: 941-728-2390
FAX: 941-728-3276
E-MAIL: blove @ cyberstreet.com
INTERNET: www.cyberstreet.com/loveherp/

 STANFORDS MAPS CHARTS BOOKS

World Travel starts at Stanfords

Over 30000 Maps and Guides for all corners of the world.
Atlases. Travel Writing. Mountaineering Maps & Books. Globes.
Instruments. Travel Accessories.

Call us today for your *free* Africa catalogue
quoting reference *Bradt*
STANFORDS MAIL ORDER SERVICE
Tel: 0171 836 1321 Fax: 0171 836 0189
email sales@stanfords.co.uk

or visit one of our shops:

Stanfords, 12-14 Long Acre, London WC2
Stanfords, 52 Grosvenor Gardens, London SW1
Stanfords, 156 Regent Street, London W1
Stanfords, 29 Corn Street, Bristol BS1

Part Five

The North and West

Giant jumpinglrat
Rat and baobab tree

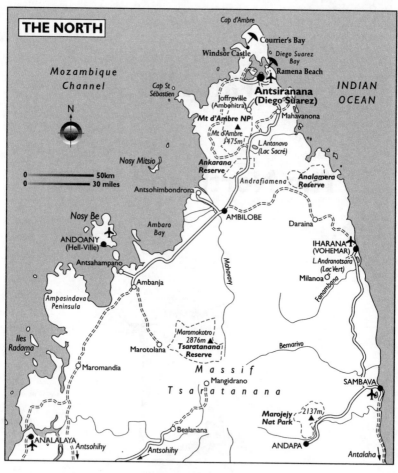

THE NORTH

Cap d'Ambre

Courrier's Bay

Windsor Castle

Diego Suarez
Bay

Ramena Beach

*Mozambique
Channel*

Cap St
Sébastien

**Antsiranana
(Diego Suarez)**

INDIAN
OCEAN

Joffreville
(Ambohitra)

Mahavanona

Mt d'Ambre NP

N

*Mt d'Ambre
1475m*

L. Antanavo
(Lac Sacré)

Nosy Mitsio

**Ankarana
Reserve**

Andrafiamena

**Analamera
Reserve**

0 — 50km
0 — 30 miles

Antsohimbondrona

AMBILOBE

Daraina

IHARANA
(VOHEMAR)

Nosy Be

*Ambaro
Bay*

L. Andranotsara
(Lac Vert)

**ANDOANY
(Hell-Ville)**

Milanoa

Antsahampano

Mahavavy

Fanambana

Ambanja

*Ampasindava
Peninsula*

*Iles
Radama*

*Maromokotro
2876m*
**Tsaratanana
Reserve**

Bemarivo

Marotolana

M a s s i f

SAMBAVA

Maromandia

T s a r a t a n a n a

Mangidrano

2137m
**Marojejy
Nat Park**

Bealanana

ANALALAYA

Antsohihy

Antsohihy

ANDAPA

Antalaha

Pachypodium

The North

OVERVIEW

The north of Madagascar is characterised by its variety. With the Tsaratanana massif (which includes Madagascar's highest peak, Maromokotro, 2,876m) bringing more rain to the Nosy Be area than is normal on the west coast, and the pocket of dry climate around Antsiranana (Diego Suarez) which has seven months of dry weather with 90% of the 900mm of rain falling between December and April, the weather can alter dramatically within short distances. With changes of weather go changes of vegetation and its accompanying fauna, making this region particularly interesting for botanists and other naturalists.

This is the domain of the Antankarana people. Cut off by rugged mountains, the Antankarana were left to their own devices until the mid-1700s when they were conquered by the Sakalava; they in turn submitted to the Merina King Radama I, aided by his military adviser James Hastie, in 1823.

Getting around

Roads in the area are being improved and Antsiranana is losing its isolation. Distances are long, however, so most people prefer to fly between the major towns.

ANTSIRANANA (DIEGO SUAREZ)
History

Forgivingly named after a Portuguese captain, Diego Suarez, who arrived in 1543 and proceeded to murder and rape the inhabitants or sell them into slavery, this large town has had an eventful history with truth blending into fiction. An often-told story, originated by Daniel Defoe, is that pirates in the 17th century founded the Republic of Libertalia here. Not true, say modern historians.

Most people still call the town Diego. The Malagasy name simply means 'Port' and its strategic importance as a deep-water harbour has long been recognised. The French installed a military base here in 1885, and the town played an important role in World War II when Madagascar was under the control of the Vichy French (see box). To prevent Japanese warships and submarines making use of the magnificent harbour and thus threatening vital sea routes, Britain and the allies captured and occupied Diego Suarez in 1942. There is a British cemetery in the town honouring those killed at this time.

Antsiranana today

This is Madagascar's fifth largest town (population about 80,000) and of increasing interest to visitors for its diverse attractions. Traditionally rated second in beauty after Rio de Janeiro the harbour is encircled by hills, with a conical 'sugar loaf' plonked in one of the bays to the east of the town. From the air or the top of

MADAGASCAR OPERATIONS IN WORLD WAR II
Peter La Niece (who was there)

After the fall of Singapore in 1942 a Japanese Strike Force bombed Colombo and sank three major British warships in the vicinity. At the time Madagascar was in the hands of the Vichy French sympathetic to the Axis Powers. Churchill and the War Cabinet feared that if Japan or Germany were afforded facilities in Madagascar the vital supply routes round the Cape through the Mozambique Channel to Egypt and India could be threatened and cut off. The capture of the strategic harbour of Diego Suarez was ordered.

The assault took place on May 5, 1942 on three beaches on the northwest corner of Madagascar. There was some opposition but the advance towards Diego Suarez proceeded satisfactorily until it reached the outskirts of the town where it was halted with fairly heavy casualties at a fixed defence line. It was decided to break the stalemate by despatching the ship's detachment of 50 Royal Marines from the battleship *Ramillies* to take the French defences from the rear. They were embarked in the destroyer *Anthony* which proceeded at 30 knots through the night round the northern tip of Madagascar and succeeded in entering Diego Suarez harbour undetected, landing the very seasick Royal Marines. All they had in the way of maps was a page torn from a 15-year-old tourist guide. They set off in the dark and soon came to a large barracks building. Inside they found all the French soldiers asleep and their firearms piled neatly in the entrance to their dormitories. The French were called upon to surrender which they did. The Royal Marines then set off again towards their objective. Very soon they arrived at the telephone exchange where an enterprising French-speaking Royal Marine officer phoned the commander of the French defences, informed him that his colleagues in the barracks had surrendered and requested him to do the same. He complied and Diego Suarez was in British hands.

The following month a Japanese submarine dropped two human torpedoes off the entrance to Diego Suarez and succeeded in sinking a tanker and heavily damaging the *Ramillies*. There were also indications that the town of Majunga on the west coast of Madagascar was being used as a base by Vichy French and probably German U-boats. It was therefore decided to launch two further operations and occupy Madagascar completely.

The second assault took place at Majunga on September 10, 1942 which, after incurring some casualties, was successful. Elements of an East African brigade started their march on the capital. The assault force was re-embarked and all ships went round and anchored in Diego Suarez Bay to finalise plans for the third operation.

On September 18 the whole force appeared off the east coast town of Tamatave. An ultimatum was signalled to the French commander to the effect that unless he surrendered, his positions would be bombarded by the *Warspite* and her escorting cruisers as well as air strikes from the carrier *Illustrious*. He capitulated and the landings were unopposed. Troops of the East African brigade set off immediately for Tananarive which fell on September 23. The Governor-General escaped southwards with 700 troops but was overtaken later in October which ended the campaign.

Montagne des Français, Antsiranana's superb position can be appreciated but the city itself is in the usual state of decay, though with a particular charm. The port's isolation behind its mountain barrier and its long association with non-Malagasy races have given it an unusually cosmopolitan population and lots of colour: there are Arabs, Creoles (descendants of Europeans), Indians, Chinese and Comorans.

The name 'Joffre' seems to be everywhere in and around the town. General Joseph Joffre was the military commander of the town in 1897 and later became Maréchal de France. In 1911 he took over the supreme command of the French armies, and was the victor of the Battle of the Marne in 1914.

In the past, Antsiranana suffered from its lack of a first-class hotel, but now everyone, whatever their budget, can enjoy the colour and sunshine, not to mention the splendid Montagne d'Ambre National Park. This is a pleasant town for wandering; take a look at the market, poke around the harbour, and investigate a few souvenir shops. If you want to relax on a beach for a few days stay at Ramena.

There's a standard taxi tariff for journeys within the town – around 3,000Fmg.
The telephone area code is 82.

Getting there and away
By air
There are flights from Tana (returning the same day) via Mahajanga on most days, also regular flights from/to Nosy Be. Twin Otters link Antsiranana with the east coast towns of Vohemar, Sambava and Toamasina.

A taxi from the airport, 6km from the town centre, will cost 10,000Fmg. A cheaper alternative is to walk to the main road and wait for a taxi-brousse.

By road
The overland route between Ambanja (nearest town to Nosy Be) and Antsiranana is popular. Tougher, less interesting, but possible is the road to Vohemar. Both routes are described later in this chapter.

Changing money
Bjørn Donnis recommend the bank at Richelieu in the north part of the city: 'the fastest service in Madagascar!'

Where to stay
Category A
King's Lodge Well designed, set on a gentle slope backed by a hill, with a shaded terrace and sea view. Good restaurant. 200–250Ff, depending on the season; meals 35Ff. Book through Le King de la Piste (see page 293); tel: 225 99; fax: 235 60.
Hotel Colbert 51 Rue Colbert; tel: 232 89; 232 90; email: hicdiego@dts.mg. A new, four-star hotel. 'Wonderful... an absolute bargain. Can't recommend it highly enough!' Rooms with en-suite bathrooms 135–205Ff.

Category B
Hotel Escale On the road to the airport; tel: 223 82. From about 100,000–115,000Fmg for a double bungalow. I have no reports on its quality but it's worth checking out.
Hotel Paradis du Nord Rue Villaret Joyeuse, across from the market; tel: 214 05. Good value since everything works – air-conditioning, hot water... The rooms themselves are cell-like except for No 1 which is marvellously spacious and overlooks the colourful market. There is a pleasant balcony dining room (with good food), a laundry service, and a secure garage if you are driving (you can rent cars from here, including 4WD).

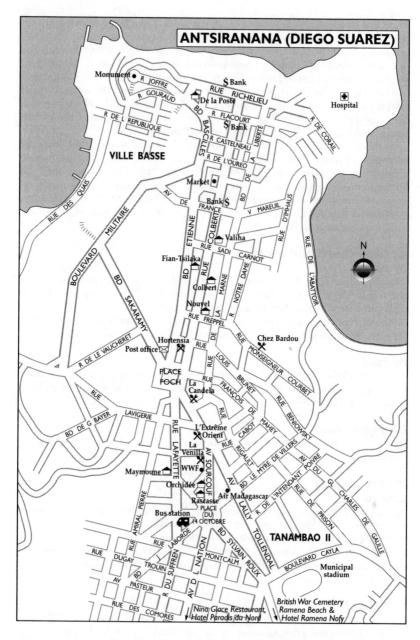

ANTSIRANANA (DIEGO SUAREZ)

Hotel de la Poste BP 121; tel: 214 53. Near Clémenceau Sq, overlooking the bay. A superb location but few other redeeming features. The food is quite good.

Hotel Maymoune 7 Rue Bougainville. Recent reports indicate that this formerly recommended hotel has doubled its price and halved its value. 'Decidedly seedy, with music from the nightclub opposite thumping through the walls until 3am.' 140,000Fmg. However, a big plus for some people is that it has CNN on television!

Hotel Valiha 41 Rue Colbert (BP 270); tel: 215 31. Popular, with helpful staff. About 70,000Fmg for rooms with air conditioning and hot water.

Hotel Orchidée Rue Surcouf; tel: 210 65. Friendly, helpful, Chinese-run hotel with a small restaurant and a few rooms for around 50,000Fmg.

Hotel la Rascasse Rue Surcouf, opposite Air Mad; tel: 223 64. Rooms from about 60,000Fmg. 'The restaurant and the terrace are mostly occupied by lonely men and easy-going girls.' (Clare Hermans)

Category C

Chez Layac 35, Rue François de Mahy; tel: 210 21. The best-value place in 1998: 'the cleanest I've ever stayed in, very friendly and quiet. Jacques and his family were very welcoming...astonishing breakfasts.' (Ania Dudziec) Highly recommended. 45,000Fmg.

Hotel Royale Rue Suffren, around the corner from the Paradis du Nord. 'Friendly, some English spoken, hand laundry, closet with lock in each room. I think this was my best find in Diego.' (John Kupiec)

Hotel Fian-tsilaka 13 Bd Etienne; tel: 223 48. Good restaurant.

Hotel Diamant Rue Mozambique, around the corner from the Royale.

Nouvel Hotel 75, Rue Colbert; tel: 222 62. Reportedly a bit tatty, with an all-night disco. Good restaurant.

Where to eat

Balafomanga A French-run, expensive restaurant, with very good food but French-sized (*nouvelle cuisine*) portions.

La Venilla Up the road from the Hotel La Rascasse and opposite the WWF office. Arguably the best restaurant in town, yet still keeps its prices reasonable. Especially recommended for breakfast, when little else is open.

La Candela North of La Venilla (next to the Alliance Française). Once popular with travellers but has now limited its menu to pizzas only.

Halmah Resto Rue Roi Tsimiaro. This is where the locals eat, and is always busy. Fish costs 5,000Fmg a plate and an omelette 3,000Fmg.

Restaurant Libertalia Next to La Candela. Offers a few good, low-priced meals on the first floor. 'Generally good but avoid the duck – tastes like dog!' (J Vive)

L'Extrème Orient A popular restaurant near Air Mad; inexpensive, good food.

Snacks and fast food are easy to find. The **Hortensia**, near the post office, does fast food at all times of the day. If your hotel does not serve breakfast, go to the **Boulangerie Amicale**, between La Rascasse and the cinema. Excellent hot rolls and *pain au chocolat*. **Glace Gourmande**, opposite Hotel Valiha, probably serves the best ice-cream in town, and is recommended for breakfast.

Nightlife

Vahinée Bar Rue Colbert, opposite BNI-CL bank. Great for people-watching.

Beaches

Ramena

This is a nice, uncrowded sandy beach about 18km from the town centre, 45 minutes from the airport. Get there by taxi-brousse or by private taxi. It's a beautiful drive around the curve of the bay, with some fine baobabs en route. The road down to the beach is just after the Fihary Hotel.

Where to stay/eat

Fihary Hotel (formerly Hotel Ramena Nofy) Tel: 228 62/294 15; fax: 294 13. 15 chalets with modern bathrooms, hot water, mosquito nets, a large restaurant (super food) with a terrace.

Badamera (Ramena) 'A stone's throw from the beach. The laidback approach to guests includes late-night guitar sessions. The bed and concrete floor offer the same degree of comfort and there is a cold shower. Wonderful food.' (Lorna and Ken Gillespie)

There's a beach-side restaurant, the **Oasis**, about 50m to the right from the 'pier'.

Sakalava
This is a beautiful and isolated beach, best reached by taxi (about 50,000Fmg if you hire it for the day).

Sightseeing and half-day excursions
British Cemetery
On the outskirts of town on the road that leads to the airport, the British cemetery is on a side road opposite the main Malagasy cemetery. It is well signposted. Here is a sad insight into Anglo-Malagasy history: rows of graves of the British troops killed in the battle for Diego in 1942, and the larger numbers, mainly East African and Indian soldiers serving in the British army, who died from disease during the occupation of the port. Impeccably maintained by the Commonwealth War Graves Commission, this is a peaceful and moving place.

Montagne des Français (French Mountain)
The mountain gets its name from the memorial to the French and Malagasy killed during the allied invasion in 1942. Another sad reminder of a war about which the locals can have had little understanding. There are several crosses but the main one was laboriously carried up in 1956 to emulate Jesus's journey to Calvary.

It is a hot but rewarding climb up to this high point with splendid views and some nearby caves. Take a taxi 8km along the coast road towards Ramena beach, to the start of the old road up the mountain. The track winds upwards, with obvious short cuts; the big cross is reached in about an hour. It's best to go very early in the morning (good birdwatching) or in the evening. The mountain supports unusual vegetation: baobabs, aloes, and until recently pachypodium, but these have evidently all been dug up.

The cross is not the highest point. Sven Oudgenoeg (from the Netherlands) writes: 'After the seventh cross there is a small path running up to the top of the mountain. Here there are ruins, with at least three buildings and a long, ruined, circular wall. These ruins are well preserved and very interesting. For instance, one can still distinguish what used to be a toilet and there is a small staircase betraying that there used to be a second floor.

'From this height you have an even better view of Diego Suarez and its bay. You can get on this path the following way: after the seventh cross take a path across an open field and then into the forest where the path becomes more distinct. Follow it until a junction with a smaller path off to the right. Follow this little path into dense bushes. After about five minutes you go through a tunnel and then come to a junction. A good path goes to the left. Do not take it! The path you want continues straight on and after about three minutes there is a path to the right which leads to the ruins and the top. Leave the first set of ruins (two buildings) on your right and continue higher to more ruins, the circular wall, and the splendid view.'

EXCURSIONS FROM ANTSIRANANA
Getting organised
Tour operators
Nature et Océan 5 Rue Cabot, BP 436, Antsiranana. They run 4WD vehicles to places of interest such as Montagne d'Ambre, Ankarana, Antanavo, Windsor Castle, Courriers Bay,

and Ambilobe. They also run sea trips and fishing expeditions. Madagascar Airtours also has an office here.

Le King de la Piste Bd Bazeilles (near Hotel de la Poste), Antsiranana; tel/fax: 225 99. This agency, run by Jorge Pareik (German), is recommended as the best in town for trips by 4WD (minimum two people) to hard-to-reach places such as Windsor Castle, Cap d'Ambre and Analamera. Jorge and his Malagasy wife also organise excursions by motorbike or mountain bike. Prices are quite high (and you must pay in cash – credit cards are not accepted) but worth it: this tour operator continues to receive top marks from readers. Highly recommended.

Many of Diego's hotels can organise tours so if your budget is limited it is worth shopping around.

Car and bike hire
The most economical place to hire a car is probably the Hotel Paradis du Nord. Bikes are available from The Blue Marine, 67 Colbert (near the Nouvel Hotel).

Windsor Castle and Courriers Bay
A half-day drive (4WD) or full-day bike excursion takes you to the fantastic rock known as Windsor Castle. This monolith (visible from Antsiranana and – better – if you arrive by ship) is steep-sided and flat-topped, so made a perfect lookout point during times of war. The views from there are superb. It was fortified by the French, occupied by the Vichy forces, and liberated by the British. A ruined staircase still runs to the top (if you can find it). There is some *tsingy* here, and many endemic water-retaining plants including a local species of pachypodium.

To get there take the road that runs west towards Ampasindava, where you turn right (north) along a rocky road, then left towards Windsor Castle. The road continuing north is the very rough one to Cap d'Ambre.

The stone staircase to the top of Windsor Castle is not easy to find, and alternative routes sometimes bring you to dense forest or an impassable rock face. Sven Oudgenoeg, who also initially failed to find the staircase, enlisted the help of a local fisherman who acted as a guide and showed him the path. He gives these precise instructions: 'Drive exactly 28.2km from Diego Suarez towards Cap d'Ambre; here you come to a fork in the road. The 'main' road (once metalled, now potholed) continues towards Cap d'Ambre, the left branch goes to Windsor Castle. After 4.2km the road passes through a clump of mango trees where it divides into two paths. Take the one to the left which leads along a steep ridge to the foot of the ruined staircase. The way up the staircase is not always clear, so you have to apply a little logic, but it can be done, and takes about an hour to the top.'

This is a hot, dry climb. Take plenty of water and allow yourself enough time.

Courriers Bay, half an hour beyond Windsor Castle, is an exceptionally fine beach.

Cap d'Ambre
To reach the northernmost tip of Madagascar you need a 4WD vehicle or motorbike and nerves of steel. Or a mountain bike and plenty of time. If you can carry enough water this area merits exploration; it is seldom visited and is particularly interesting for its flora. I have yet to hear of a traveller who has reached the Cape, however. This is a very difficult and potentially dangerous trip and should not be undertaken lightly.

Lac Antanavo (Lac Sacré)
The sacred lake is about 75km south of Antsiranana, near the small town of Anivorano. It attracts visitors more for its legends than for the reality of a not

particularly scenic lake and the possibility of seeing a crocodile. The story is that once upon a time Anivorano was situated amid semi-desert and a thirsty traveller arrived at the village and asked for a drink. When his request was refused he warned the villagers that they would soon have more water than they could cope with. No sooner had he left than the earth opened, water gushed out, and the mean-minded villagers and their houses were inundated. The crocodiles which now inhabit the lake are considered to be ancestors (and to wear jewellery belonging to their previous selves. So they say).

The crocodiles are sometimes fed by the villagers, so you may do best to book a tour in Diego; the tour operator should know when croc feeding day is.

There are two smaller lakes nearby which the locals fish cautiously – often from the branches of a tree to avoid a surprise crocodile attack.

THE NORTHERN RESERVES
Montagne d'Ambre (Amber Mountain) National Park
This 18,500ha national park was created in 1958, the French colonial government recognising the unique nature of the volcanic massif and its forest. The park is now part of the Montagne d'Ambre Reserves Complex which also includes the Special Reserves of Ankarana, Analamera, and Forêt d'Ambre. The project, initiated in 1989, is funded by USAID, the Malagasy government and the WWF; and was the first to involve local people in all stages of planning and management. The aims were conservation, rural development, and education. These have largely been achieved. Ecotourism has been encouraged successfully with good information and facilities now available.

Montagne d'Ambre National Park is a splendid example of upland moist forest, or montane rainforest. The massif ranges in altitude from 850m to 1,475m and has its own micro-climate with rainfall equal to the eastern region. It is arguably the most visitor-friendly of all the protected areas of Madagascar, with broad trails, fascinating flora and fauna, a comfortable climate, and readily available information. In the dry season vehicles can drive right up to the main picnic area, giving a unique opportunity (in Madagascar) for elderly or disabled visitors to see the rainforest and its inhabitants.

The name comes not from deposits of precious amber, but from the amber-coloured resin which oozes from some of its trees and is used medicinally by the local people.

Warning
Antsiranana is now firmly on the itinerary of cruise ships, with Montagne d'Ambre the focus of the day's excursion. This means that upward of 100 passengers will pour into the park. Independent travellers may wish to visit the port to check if a ship is due before planning their visit.

Permits and information
Permits (50,000Fmg) and a very good information booklet are available in Antsiranana from the WWF office on Rue Surcouf, opposite Air Mad (the entrance is on a side street). Permits and information leaflets are also available at the park entrance.

The ANGAP office is on the outskirts of town towards the airport. Permits are available here.

Getting there
The entrance to the park is 27km south of Antsiranana, 4km from the town of Ambohitra, or Joffreville as almost everyone still calls it. Taxi-brousses leave Antsiranana at 07.00 for Joffreville, and return at 14.00. The journey takes about an

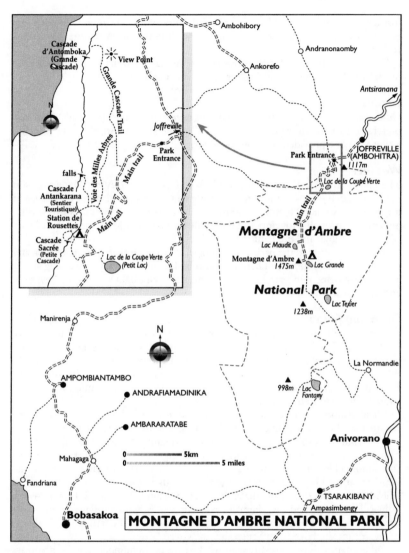

hour (the road is tarred). A private taxi costs around 100,000Fmg for the day – cheaper than organising the trip through a tour operator.

Where to stay

There are shelters and bunk beds in the park for visitors equipped with their own sleeping bags. From the wildlife point of view, staying in the park is far preferable to making a day trip, so if you have a tent bring this in case the shelters are occupied by a group. If you have no tent, there is accommodation at Joffreville.

Joffreville

Joffreville, once a decaying colonial town, has been given a face-lift, flowers have been planted, and the place may soon be restored to something near its former splendour. It would be a worthwhile endeavour. Meanwhile, it has a few new shops and a small restaurant and a newish hotel, the **Auberge Maréchal Joffre**.

There is a campsite (often crowded) at the car park/picnic area (known as Station de Rousettes) where a visitor centre is being built.

Guides

Guides are now compulsory (although not necessary on the clear trails), and it is preferable to have an experienced ANGAP guide such as Angeluc and Angelin, rather than one provided by a tour operator.

Weather

The rainy season (and cyclone season) is from December to April. The dry season is May through August, but there is a strong wind, *varatraza*, almost every day, and it can feel very cold. The most rewarding time to visit is during the warm season: September through November. There will be some rain, but most animals are active and visible, and the lemurs have babies.

The temperature in the park is, on average, 10°F cooler than in Antsiranana, and it is often wet and muddy. There may also be leeches. Be wary of wearing shorts and sandals. Bring rain gear, insect repellent, and even a light sweater, however hot and dry you are at sea-level.

Flora and fauna

Montagne d'Ambre is as exciting for its plants as for its animals. A very informative booklet available from the WWF or ANGAP offices gives details and illustrations of the species most commonly seen. All visitors are impressed by the tree ferns and the huge, epiphytic bird's-nest ferns which grow on trees. The distinctive Pandanus is also common, and you can see Madagascar's endemic cycad. Huge strangler figs add to the spectacle.

Most visitors want to see lemurs and, as the two diurnal species become habituated, this is becoming easier. The park is home to a subspecies of brown lemur, Sanford's brown lemur and the crowned lemur. Sanford's lemur is mainly brown, the males having splendid white/beige ear-tufts and side-whiskers surrounding black faces, whilst the females are of a more uniform colour with no whiskers and a grey face. Crowned lemurs get their names from the triangle of black between the ears of the male; the rest of the animal is reddish brown, with a light-coloured face and ears. Females are mainly grey, with a little red tiara across the forehead. Both sexes have a lighter-coloured belly; in the female this is almost white. Young are born from September to November.

Other mammals occasionally seen are the ring-tailed mongoose and – if you are really lucky – the fosa. And there are five species of nocturnal lemur.

Take time to look carefully at the forest floor; this is the place to find the leaf-mimic chameleon, little more than 2cm long, pill millipedes rolled into a perfect ball, frogs, lizards, butterflies, mysterious fungi and a whole host of other living things. At eye-level you may spot chameleons – although the drive up from Antsiranana is a better hunting ground for these reptiles.

Even non-birders will be fascinated by the numerous species here: the Madagascar crested ibis is striking enough to impress anybody, as is the paradise flycatcher with its long, trailing tail feathers. The forest rock thrush is tame and ubiquitous, and the black-and-white magpie robin is often seen. The jackpot, however, is one of Madagascar's most beautiful birds: the pitta-like ground-roller.

Trails, waterfalls and lakes

The park has, in theory, 30km of paths, but many of these are overgrown although they are gradually being cleared and renamed. The best, and most heavily used, trails lead to the Petit Lac, the Jardin Botanique, and two waterfalls, Cascade d'Antomboka (Grande Cascade) and Cascade Sacrée (Petite Cascade). There is also a Sentier Touristique with another lovely waterfall at the end.

The three waterfalls provide the focal points for day visitors. If time is short and you want to watch wildlife rather than walk far, go to the **Cascade Sacrée**. This is only about 100m along the track beyond the picnic area (Station de Rousettes) and on the way you should see lemurs, orchids and birds galore. Take a small path on your left to the river for a possible glimpse of the white-throated rail and the malachite kingfisher. The Cascade Sacrée is an idyllic fern-fringed grotto with waterfalls splashing into a pool. In the hot season there is a colony of little bats (I don't know the species) twittering in the overhang to the right of the pool.

The **Sentier Touristique** is also easy and starts near the Station de Rousettes (walk back towards the entrance, cross the bridge and turn left). The path terminates at a viewpoint above Cascade Antankarana: a highly photogenic spot and a good place to find the forest rock thrush and other birds.

The walk to the **Cascade d'Antomboka** is tougher, with some up and down stretches, and a steep descent to the waterfall. There is some excellent birdwatching here, some lovely tree ferns, and a good chance of seeing lemurs – especially if you bring a picnic which includes bananas... On your way back you'll pass a path on the right (left as you go towards the waterfall) marked **Voie des Mille Arbres** (formerly Jardin Botanique); don't be misled into thinking this will lead you to the rose-garden. It's a tough roller-coaster of a walk, but very rewarding, and eventually joins the main track.

Another easy walk from Station de Rousettes is the viewpoint above the crater lake, **Lac de la Coupe Verte**.

A full day's walk beyond Station de Rousettes takes you to a crater lake known as **Lac Maudit**, or Matsabory Fantany, then on for another hour to **Lac Grand**. Beyond that is the highest point in the park, **Montagne d'Ambre** (1,475m) itself. Unless you are a fit, fast walker it would be best to take two days on this trek and camp by Lac Grand. That way you can wait for weather conditions to allow the spectacular view.

Analamera Special Reserve

This 34,700ha reserve is in remote and virtually unexplored deciduous forest some 20km southeast of Montagne d'Ambre, and is the last refuge of the very rare Perrier's black sifaka which very few people have been fortunate enough to see. The reserve is now open to visitors and, for the enthusiast, easily merits between two and four nights' camping. There are no facilities of any kind, so visitors must be totally self-sufficient.

To reach the reserve from Diego you drive 50km south on a good road, and are then faced with a further 11km on a dreadful stretch which is impassable in the rainy season. Guides and porters can be organised in the nearby village of Menagisy, but it is more sensible to arrange the visit through an operator in Antsiranana. In addition to the black sifaka, you may also see the white-breasted mesite and Van Dam's vanga, which are also seriously threatened species. Nick Garbutt sent this report after his visit in December 1996: 'I hired a 4WD from Le King de la Piste and along with my driver-guide, Ali Baba (fortunately the 40 thieves had the day off), we set off on our four-day trip. After Menagisy, where we picked up a local guide, the track became almost non-existent. On the edge of Analamera we set up base camp, then walked for around 12km south, following the dry riverbed of the

Bobakindro river. The two main blocks of dry deciduous forest are on the hills either side of the river, but thin corridors follow the river like green ribbons. In November the mango trees are in fruit and the sifaka sometimes come down to these areas to feed. At first we found only crowned and Sanford's lemurs gorging themselves on the fruit. We walked up and down the dry riverbed several times. No sifakas. Next morning we were up before dawn and almost immediately heard agitated "tsisk tsisk tsisk" alarm calls from the trees. And there they were! A group of four black sifaka gazing down indignantly through piercing ruby red eyes.'

Ankarana Special Reserve

About 108km south of Antsiranana is a small limestone massif, Ankarana. An 'island' of *tsingy* (limestone karst pinnacles) and forest, the massif is penetrated by numerous caves and canyons. Some of the largest caves have collapsed, forming isolated pockets of river-fed forest with their own perfectly protected flora and fauna. Dry deciduous forest grows around the periphery and into the wider canyons. The caves and their rivers are also home to crocodiles, some reportedly six metres long. The reserve is known for its many lemur species, including crowned and Sanford's brown lemur, but it is marvellous for birds, reptiles and insects as well. Indeed, the 'Wow!' factor is as high here as anywhere I have visited.

After a preliminary look in 1981, an expedition led by Dr Jane Wilson (Bradt's very own medical consultant) spent several months in 1986 exploring and studying the area. Their findings excited considerable scientific interest, a TV film and a book (see *Further Information*).

Ankarana is a Special Reserve (18,220ha) which is included in the WWF's Montagne d'Ambre Reserves Complex. It is rightly becoming the western reserve most people want to visit, although at present it is a hiking and camping trip only.

Permits and guides

A permit for Ankarana should be purchased from the WWF (or ANGAP) in Antsiranana or from ANGAP in Tana.

A guide is compulsory and anyway it would be dangerous to go in to the reserve without one. Not only do they know the paths and the most interesting areas, but they know where the campsites are located and where scarce water is to be found. Most guides live in Matsaborimanga, but are available at the ANGAP office at Mahamasina. Recommended guides include Christo, Angelin and Felix. We had Angélique, who was superb: very knowledgeable and courteous.

Getting there and away

With a 4WD vehicle you can drive all the way to the main campsite, Campement Anilotra (Camp des Anglais), in the dry season. Most drivers approach from the north, turning off at Anivorano and heading for the village of Matsaborimanga. Allow five hours for this drive from Antsiranana.

By far the best way to get there, however, is to hike in from RN6, a good tarred road which runs between Ambanja and Antsiranana. The journey to the village of Mahamasina takes about three hours from Ambanja or 2½ hours from Antsiranana and is easily made by taxi-brousse or ordinary taxi. There is an ANGAP office near the trailhead at the 108km sign on the road. It's a super walk of about 11km in to the reserve; allow 2½ to 3 hours. The first part is down a wide track, then, after about 20 minutes, you turn right down a gully and cross a river. Shortly after that the trail levels out, enters some beautiful forest (you are now in one of the wide canyons). A huge ficus marks the halfway point and a steep gully indicates that you are arriving at Campement Anilotra.

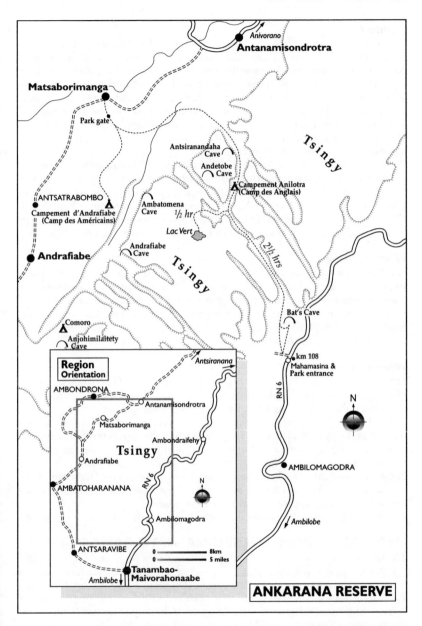

On the way back, if you use the same route, your guide will take you along an alternative trail to visit the bat caves – a tough scramble, but well worth it.

Organised tours

The easiest way of doing Ankarana is through a local tour operator. Recommended in Antsiranana is Le King de la Piste; it is worth paying a little more for their superb organisation.

Campsites

The main campsite, formerly known as Camp des Anglais (following the Crocodile Caves Expedition), has recently been renamed **Campement Anilotra** and equipped with long-drop toilets and picnic tables. There are three separate areas, so although it tends to get crowded you can usually escape from other travellers. Note that the camp offers considerably more shade than Campement d'Andrafiabe, as well as a chance to bathe in the river running through the cave. However, as the reserve becomes more popular, so does the likelihood of finding this campsite fully occupied. The water supply is a good ten minutes' walk away down a slippery slope.

The usual alternative campsite is **Campement d'Andrafiabe** (Camp des Américains), which is particularly good for birding and has a lovely setting. It now has a water supply and flush toilets. Other camps are **Camp des Africains** and **Camp de Fleur**. Camp des Africains is near the caves, some four hours' walk from Campement Anilotra. Camp de Fleur is about two hours from Campement Anilotra and is a good base for visiting Lac Vert and some of the best *tsingy*.

What to bring

You'll need strong shoes or boots, a rucksack, food for the duration of your stay and food for your guide (rice can be bought in Matsaborimanga), a two-litre water bottle, insect repellent, torch (flashlight) for the caves plus batteries. Plus, of course, a tent unless you are on a package tour. A light sleeping bag or sheet plus blanket is enough for the hot season. Oh, and bring earplugs. The lepilemurs and cicadas of Ankarana are highly vocal!

What to see

Ankarana reminds me of J-P Commerson's famous quote: 'There one meets the most strange and marvellous forms at every step!' Everything is strange and marvellous: the animals, the birds, the plants, the landscape.

The best *tsingy* is about two hours away, over very rugged terrain, just beyond the beautiful crater lake, Lac Vert. This is a very hot, all-day trip (bring a picnic and plenty of water) and is absolutely magnificent. Board walks have been constructed to allow safe passage over the *tsingy*, protecting the fragile rock while you admire the strange succulents such as *Pachypodium* which seem to grow right out of the limestone. Lac Vert is as green as its name, and if you are crazy enough you can hike down a steep, slippery slope to the water's edge.

Don't miss the wonderful bat caves, usually seen on the hike back to the road.

OVERLAND FROM ANTSIRANANA TO SAMBAVA

The first section of road is poor, transport erratic, and breakdowns frequent. Once you reach Iharana, however, it is plain sailing down one of the best roads in Madagascar. A taxi-brousse from Antsiranana (Diego) to Ambilobe (on RN6) takes about three hours. Then you head east, on a poor road, to the coastal town of Iharana (still usually known by its old name, Vohemar). The whole trip, from Antsiranana to Sambava, should be accomplished in one long day.

Ambilobe
Where to stay/eat

The following hotels are no doubt still open and others will have joined them: **Hotel Golden Night**, **Hotel Mahavavy**, and (bungalows) **Rève d'Or**. Then, near the excellent market, there's the **Hotel Bagdad**, the **Hazar** and the **Amical** which is near the taxi-brousse station.

Sirama

'I took a TB to Sirama where there is a sugarcane factory. I was given a complete one-hour tour (they seldom get tourists) seeing – and tasting – the whole process of making cane into sugar. There is also a distillery there and I had a couple of different tastes of rum. Wonderful!' (J Kupiec)

Iharana (Vohemar)

I'm convinced by Peace Corps volunteer Bronwen Eastman that this pleasant beach resort town is *the* place to recover from some rough travelling. It has all the right ingredients: a comfortable (but not expensive) hotel and some wonderful food. And a beach. There are enjoyable walks to be taken in the area too: 'I hiked to Lac Vert/Andranotsara, taking the road/path, and walked back along the coast.' (John Kupiec)

Getting there and away

Vohemar (most people, including Air Mad, use its old name) is accessible by Twin Otter from Antsiranana and Nosy Be, making a convenient link to marvellous northeast coast. Flights currently (1999) go on Wednesdays and Fridays. The Air Mad office is hard to find; it's tucked away in the Star Breweries yard!

The taxi-brousse journey to/from Antsiranana can be done in about 12 hours, and to Sambava in five or six.

Where to stay

Sol y Mar Excellent bungalows in a beautiful setting by the shore with shower and WC. Prices range from 30,000Fmg for a basic bungalow to 120,000Fmg for one facing the ocean, with hot water. 'Just a few paces from my room into the sea for a splendid swim. Also had good food.' (Philip Jones). 'The punch coco is out of this world, and the lychee punch isn't bad either. The meals, when the French co-owner is cooking, are really superb!' (BE)
Poisson d'Or Basic, with a good restaurant.
Railouvy Across from the Poisson.

Where to eat

In addition to the hotels, Vohemar has some great eateries.

Hotely Kanto A terrific place for meals, run by Madame Elizabeth, who as well as being very friendly is a tremendous cook. Her speciality is ravitoto with coconut. Meals cost 4,000Fmg. She also serves the best 500Fmg coffee in town.
La Florida You can order almost anything in this restaurant: calamari, shrimp coco, soupe Chinoise, etc. And it'll only cost around 10,000Fmg a plate! The atmosphere is equally good.

OVERLAND FROM ANTSIRANANA TO AMBANJA AND NOSY BE

RN6 has recently been improved, and this route is popular with travellers heading for Nosy Be but there is plenty to see in the area so it is a shame to rush through. The journey from Antsiranana to Ambanja at present takes about five hours.

The first place to break your journey is Ambilobe (see page 300). Then on to Ambanja (two hours), which merits a stay of a few days.

Ambanja

This is a pleasant little town set amid lush scenery. 'I took a nice walk along the river Sambirano. The path goes up and down/to and from the river, and at one high point there's a good view of the bridge in Ambanja. I saw lemurs high up in bamboo trees.' (J Kupiec)

Getting there and away

Most people stopping at Ambanja are on their way to or from Nosy Be. Josephine Andrews offers these hints for the trip to Antsiranana. 'There are some fixed-time taxi-brousses which leave at 11.00 and 13.00 (those big nine-place Peugeots) which cost only about 30,000fmg per place to Diego. There is a little office near to the main market in the north of the town. Otherwise there are always vehicles of every description heading north from the same market, or south from the little market at the far south of town.'

Where to stay/eat

Hotel Patricia The best hotel in Ambanja, and a perennial *vazaha* favourite. Run by M Yvon and his wife (Chinese/Malagasy) who go out of their way to be helpful. Rooms vary in quality and price, so there is something to suit everyone. Usually shut in the afternoon (for siesta) so be prepared to wait. There is an excellent Malagasy cookbook for sale here, written by M Yvon's sister.

Hotel Riviera Rooms have a shower and WC.

Ankify

With a beautiful beach and good hotel, this is the preferred place to break a journey between Antsiranana and Nosy Be (it is the departure point for ferries to the island). Taxi-brousses run here from Ambanja, taking about an hour. It's a rough but interesting road running through mangrove (rapidly being reclaimed for land) and rather nice timber plantations underplanted with cocoa (look out for the pods growing directly from the trunks) and coffee.

Where to stay

Le Baobab BP 85, Ambanja; tel: 65. Located about 2km northwest of the dock area, nestled between rocky cliffs and a beach that overlooks Nosy Komba. Very pleasant bungalows with separate bathrooms, hot water, table fans, mosquito nets. About 150Ff. Bill Love, who stays here regularly, writes: 'The grounds are beautifully planted in bougainvillea, palms, ylang-ylang, etc, with paved paths between cottages. The restaurant/bar is located on top of another hill, is open-air under a huge thatched roof, and is very comfy and with a great view of the bay... Crowned lemurs pass over the trees over the road nearby, and lower lifeforms abound on evening flashlight walks down the road outside the hotel.' Bill adds: 'The panther chameleons residing locally are among the most beautiful of all – greenish bodies with brilliant blue bands.'

Tsaratanana

Adventurous travellers look at a map of Madagascar and long to climb its highest mountain. However, Tsaratanana is not open to tourists and those who have tried to penetrate it for scientific research have had a rough time. In a nutshell, this mountain is largely deforested, waterless, trailless and hot.

BAYS AND INLETS ACCESSIBLE TO YACHTS

The bays below could be reached by adventurous hikers or cyclists (many are near villages) but are visited mainly by yachties (lucky devils!).

Russian Bay (Helondranon Ambavatoby)

This is a beautiful and remote place opposite the Nosy Be archipelago. It provides excellent anchorages, all-round shelter and is a traditional 'hurricane hole'. The marine life in the bay itself is terrific, offering wonderful snorkelling and diving, especially in the reefs outside the entrance. There is excellent fishing too. In the right season (October to December), whales are commonly sighted in the bay. This is one of the best spots in which to seek the very rare whale shark. The beaches are known turtle-nesting sites. The sambirano and moist tropical deciduous woods there harbour abundant birdlife, reptiles and lemurs, and there is a choice of trails for day hikes.

The bay's name dates back to an incident in 1905, during the Russo-Japanese war, when a Russian warship, the *Vlötny*, anchored there. The order was to attack any passing Japanese ship, but the crew took one look at life in Madagascar to realise that they did not wish to wage war nor to return to Russia. They had barely organised a mutiny before their officers gave in, having taken one look at the lovely Malagasy women. The ship was hidden in the reaches of Russian Bay and twice emerged to trade with pirate vessels in the Mozambique channel before they ran out of fuel for the boilers. The Russians were decimated by malaria, but the survivors quickly adapted to their new home, living by fishing. The last one died in 1936. The Russians sold anything they could remove from the ship, but the remains can still be seen at low tide.

Baramahamay Bay (Maroaka)
The Baramahamay river is navigable for about 3km inland and provides a beautiful, well-sheltered anchorage with verdant hills behind sunny, white beaches. The wide bay is conspicuous as a large gap in the coastline. Yachties should approach on the north side of the bay and anchor near the villages in 8m over sand and mud. These villages are known also for their blacksmiths, who make large knives and *pangas*. One of the small villages here is known for its wild honey, and there is a pool with good drinking water.

Your chances of seeing the (very rare) resident Madagascar fish eagles here are good.

Berangomaina Point
The bay inside this headland is an attractive, well-sheltered anchorage. Good visibility is needed to access the bay, however, as there are many scattered reef patches. The channel is at its deepest on the north side, where the depth exceeds 15m right up to the reef. Anchor off the beach before the village, in 10m over a mud bottom. This place is for self-sufficient travellers only, no provisions are available.

"... in the far north of the 'red island' there is a place that even by the heady standards of Madagascar is remarkable. A lost world within a lost world ... Wilson's nicely written and highly entertaining account is published as LEMURS OF THE LOST WORLD."
New Scientist

LEMURS OF THE LOST WORLD: exploring the forests and crocodile cards of Madagascar.
Illustrated paperback by Jane Wilson (Impact)

£5.00 post free or $10 from 22 Glen Dale, Rowlands Castle, Hants PO9 6EP

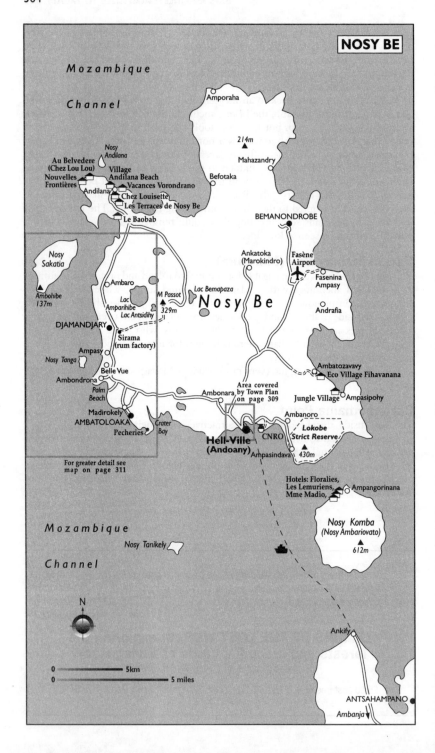

NOSY BE

Mozambique

Channel

Amporaha

214m

Mahazandry

Nosy Andilana

Au Belvedere
(Chez Lou Lou)
Nouvelles
Frontières

Village
Andilana Beach
Vacances Vorondrano

Befotaka

Andilana

Chez Louisette

Les Terraces de Nosy Be

Le Baobab

BEMANONDROBE

Nosy Sakatia

Ankatoka
(Marokindro)

Fasène
Airport

Ambaro

Lac Bemapaza

Fasenina
Ampasy

Ambohibe
137m

Lac Amparihibe

M Passot

Nosy Be

Lac Antsidihy

329m

Andrafia

DJAMANDJARY

Sirama
(rum factory)

Ampasy

Nosy Tanga

Belle Vue

Ambatozavavy
Eco Village Fihavanana

Ambondrona

Palm Beach

Area covered
by Town Plan
on page 309

Ambonara

Jungle Village

Ampasipohy

Madirokely

AMBATOLOAKA

Crater Bay

Ambanoro

Pecheries

*Lokobe
Strict Reserve*

Hell-Ville
(Andoany)

CNRO

430m

Ampasindava

For greater detail see
map on page 311

Hotels: Floralies,
Les Lemuriens,
Mme Madio,

Ampangorinana

Mozambique

Nosy Tanikely

*Nosy Komba
(Nosy Ambariovato)*

612m

Channel

N

Ankify

0 — 5km

0 — 5 miles

ANTSAHAMPANO

Ambanja

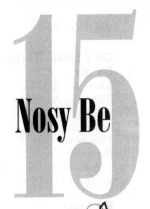

Nosy Be

OVERVIEW

The name means 'Big Island' and is usually pronounced 'Nossy Bay' although 'Noos Bay' is nearer the Malagasy pronunciation. Blessed with an almost perfect climate (sunshine with brief showers), fertile and prosperous, with sugar, pepper and vanilla grown for export, and the heady scent of ylang-ylang blossoms giving it the tourist-brochure name of 'Perfumed Isle', this is the place to come for a rest – providing you can afford it. Compared with the rest of Madagascar Nosy Be is quite expensive. However, you can cut costs by staying in Hell-Ville and hiring a bicycle.

Nosy Be developed tourism long before mainland Madagascar, so inevitably the island seems touristy or 'commercialised' to adventurous travellers. However, Nosy Be provides a taste of everything that is special to Madagascar, from wonderful seafood to beaches, from chameleons to lemurs, so for this reason is ideal for those with very limited time, who are looking for a hassle-free holiday.

Most of the easily accessible beaches on Nosy Be have been taken over by hotels, and it is becoming increasingly hard to find a completely unspoilt place. The FTM map of Nosy Be (scale 1:80,000), which is readily available in Tana and Hell-Ville, is worth studying; it is very detailed and marks beaches.

The telephone area code is 86.

History

Nosy Be's charms were recognised as long ago as 1649 when the English colonel, Robert Hunt, wrote: 'I do believe, by God's blessing, that not any part of the world is more advantageous for a plantation, being every way as well for pleasure as well as profit, in my estimation.' Hunt was attempting to set up an English colony on the island, at that time known as Assada, but failed because of hostile natives and disease.

Future immigrants, both accidental and intentional, contributed to Nosy Be's racial variety. Shipwrecked Indians built a magnificent settlement several centuries ago in the southeast of the island, where the ruins can still be seen. The crew of a Russian ship that arrived during the Russo-Japanese war of 1904–5 (see *Russian Bay* page 302), are buried in the Hell-Ville cemetery. Other arrivals were Arabs, Comorans, and – more recently – Europeans flocking to Madagascar's foremost holiday resort.

When King Radama I was completing his wars of conquest, the Boina kings took refuge in Nosy Be. First they sought protection from the Sultan of Zanzibar, who sent a warship in 1838, then two years later they requested help from Commander Passot, who had docked his ship at Nosy Be. The Frenchman was only too happy to oblige, and asked Admiral de Hell, the governor of Bourbon Island (now Réunion), to place Nosy Be under the protection of France. The island was formally annexed in 1841.

GETTING THERE AND AWAY
By air

There are regular flights from Tana, Mahajanga and Antsiranana. The airlines TAM and Austral operate between Réunion, Comoros and Nosy Be, providing an international link. All three airlines have offices in Hell-Ville. TAM flies between Nosy Be and Réunion on Mondays and Fridays (via Antsaranina on Mondays). They also serve domestic airports. Air Austral flies to Mayotte and Réunion.

A taxi from the airport to Hell-Ville should cost 25,000Fmg, but *vazahas* may pay from 40,000Fmg to 100,000Fmg.

By boat
From Mahajanga

If you're determined to go to Nosy Be the uncomfortable way, there are occasional cargo boats from Mahajanga. The company, Ramzana Aly, has an office on Armement Tawakal, around the corner from the Sampan d'Or restaurant. Boats leave once a week (currently Tuesdays) and in theory take 48 hours. Bring your own food and water and be prepared for a miserable trip of three days or more.

From Ankify or Antasahampano

Nosy Be's nearest mainland town of any size is Ambanja, where times of boats to Nosy Be are often posted on a board in the Hotel Patricia. Taxis leave from outside the Hotel de Ville for Ankify or Antsahampano, the departure points for the ferry. There are two ferries a day; the sailing times (and port) depend on the tide, and the trip takes 2½ to 3 hours and costs only 5,000Fmg. You have the alternative of going by steam boat (*vedette*). Being smaller, these are less tied to the tides, and often call first at Nosy Komba. Avoid the afternoon, when the sea tends to be rough.

A further alternative is using the fast, but often dangerously overcrowded, speedboats. The maximum number of passengers for safety is eight, including two crew. The best ones provide life jackets. Expect to pay around 25,000Fmg for the half-hour journey.

If you are taking the ferry back from Nosy Be to Ankify, check the board outside the ferry office in Hell-Ville (*A M Hassanaly et fils*) a few doors up from Air Madagascar.

Josephine Andrews (who lives in Nosy Be so is in the know) recommends that 'if you have hired a boat for yourselves it is worth going to Antsahampano (from Hell-Ville) because the last bit of the journey involves weaving through a wonderful mangrove area (recommended early in the morning).

'Occasionally it is possible to get transport direct towards Ambilobe or Diego from either of these ports, but otherwise go to Ambanja first and arrange transport from there.'

GETTING AROUND THE ISLAND

The roads are good and transport around the island is by taxi-be or private taxi (of which there are plenty).

Taxi

Shared taxis cost 1,000Fmg for anywhere in town; to Ambataloaka 2,500Fmg. Private taxis should charge a fixed rate: 17,500Fmg day-time or 35,000Fmg after 20.00. A reader recommends Tombu as a very reliable taxi driver.

Car, bike, motorcycle and plane hire

Many of the hotels rent out mountain bikes and mopeds/motorbikes. If you hire a motorbike, check your insurance policy: many companies will not insure you against motorbike accidents! Prices vary according to power: about 75,000Fmg for a 125cc (half day) to 150,000 for a 350cc.

Nos Autos Car Hire (Hell-Ville) BP 48; tel: 611 24/ 61 151. Five minibuses, 12 cars, two 4WD vehicles.

Location Jeunesse (Ambatoloaka) Nine Mobylettes, two 125cc motorbikes, two scooters. Also mountain bikes.

La Caravane Malagasy (Madirokely) BP 69; tel: 614 11/616 35; fax: 614 11. Cars, motorbikes, boats, ultra-light planes. Contact Michel in Madirokely.

Société Aeromarine (Hell-Ville); tel/fax: 611 25 or (mobile) 0331 144444. Cessna 206 and 207. Tours of the island by plane.

Air Hotel Operate a small plane to shuttle passengers to their hotel in Tsarabajina, Nosy Mitsio, but are planning to do air tours around all the islands. Contact them in Tana; tel: 285 41; fax: 22 285; email: Groupe.Hotel@simicro.mg.

Boat trips and charter yachts

Most hotels can arrange conventional excursions, but there are some specialist companies:

Madavoile (sailing trips) BP 110, Ambatoloaka; tel: 614 31

Nosy Be Croisière (sailing trips) BP 52, Hell-Ville; tel: 613 51. Two sloops (13.4m and 12.2m).

Alefa (round-island luxury pirogue trip) BP 89, Madirokely; tel/fax: 615 89. Trips last from two to 22 days, camping with cooks, tents etc provided. 350Ff per person per day.

Soconet (Daniel) Camp Vert, Hell-Ville; tel: 610 79; fax: 615 92. Still the leader in cheap and cheerful day-trips to Nosy Komba and Nosy Tanikely.

Blue Dolphin Tafitsaka Tel: 611 30. Hire the boat (7m fibreglass boat with 55hp motor) and English-speaking Malagasy guide for around 250,000Fmg (half day); 500,000Fmg (full day). Explore the islands at your own pace. Meals (beach grills and picnics) can be arranged.

Other similar boats can be hired on the spot at the main port.

WATERSPORTS
Diving

Nosy Be is Madagascar's main centre for diving – an activity which has become very popular around the pristine little islands of the region. May to October are the recommended months. The average cost, including all equipment, ranges from 190Ff for one dive to 1,520Ff for ten dives.

Blue Fish Tel: 613 94. In Hell-Ville, near the harbour. Diving, sea excursions.

Madagascar Dive Club Tel: 614 18. Behind the Marlin Club Hotel. Member of PADI International Resort Association. First-class equipment.

Oceane's Dream BP 173; tel: 614 26 (Ambataloaka). Organises diving trips to many of the outlying islands and even to the Comoros. Run by Laurent Duriez.

Tropical Diving (Centre International de Plongée) Annexe Coco Plage, Ambataloaka; BP 212; tel: 614 02; fax: 610 91; email: tropical.diving@simicro.mg. Specialise in night-diving (210Ff per dive) and underwater photography. Swiss owned.

Sakatia Dive Inn BP 186, Hell-Ville; tel: 610 91; fax: 613 97. See Nosy Sakatia (page 321).

Deep-sea fishing

Increasingly popular in Nosy Be. The recommended centre is at the **Hotel Espadon**, in Ambataloaka. Jean-Charles Tanfin takes clients fishing for marlin, swordfish, wahoo, barracuda, etc. He has several world-class boats. **Blue Fish** (see above) also does sport fishing.

SOUVENIR SHOPPING

The large number of tourists visiting Nosy Be has made this one of Madagascar's main centres for souvenir production, and provides a unique chance to buy direct from the makers and benefit the local people. Anyone interested in helping Madagascar overcome its environmental problems should visit the Community Centre of Ambanoro, where quality souvenirs made by local women are sold (see page 317) or buy the varied handicrafts for sale on Nosy Komba or Ampasipohy (see page 319).

If you are short of time, handicraft sellers frequent the road to the port and there are some high quality goods in Hell-Ville's many boutiques. The best shops in town are Chez Abud, which has the widest variety of goods, along with Maison L'Artisanat, at the north end of town (near the airport junction), Pok Pok next door, and Arts Madagascar – each shop has its own speciality. Also take a look at Parfum do Mangues, near the Oasis snack bar.

HELL-VILLE (ANDOANY)

The name comes from Admiral de Hell rather than an evocation of the state of the town. Hell-Ville is quite a smart little place, its main street lined with boutiques and tourist shops. There is a market selling fresh fruit and vegetables (which may also be purchased from roadside stalls), and an interesting cemetery neatly arranged according to nationality.

Where to stay in Hell-Ville

There is a good choice of budget hotels in Hell-Ville; staying here will save money while you firm up your plans for making the most of the island.

Category A

Blue Fish Lodge Tel 613 94. By the harbour. The hotel was closed at the time of writing but looked as if it would reopen soon; it is recommended. Six clean rooms, good food. If you stay two nights you get a free trip to Nosy Komba and Tanikely. Deep-sea fishing trips.

Category B

Hotel Abud Tel: 610 55. A five-storey building centrally located above Chez Abdul souvenir shop. Comfortable small rooms, with or without en-suite toilet. Some rooms have balconies overlooking the street. Restaurant. 82,000Fmg to 102,000Fmg.
Hotel Diamant 10 La Batterie (near Hotel de la Mer); tel: 614 48. Sixteen comfortable rooms, most with air conditioning; 86,000–131,000Fmg, depending on facilities.
Hotel/Restaurant Ambonara BP 151; tel/fax: 613 67. Near to Air Mad office on way out of town. Six comfortable thatched bungalows with shower/toilet. Closed in June. 85,000fmg plus 2,000fmg tax. Nice high-ceilinged thatched restaurant area and bar overlooking garden of coffee and banana plants.

Category C

Hotel de la Mer Bd du Docteur Manceau; tel: 613 53. The once infamous 'Hotel de Merde' is now a respectable and pleasant place to stay in town. 24 rooms; 32,500–80,000Fmg. There's a great view from the restaurant.

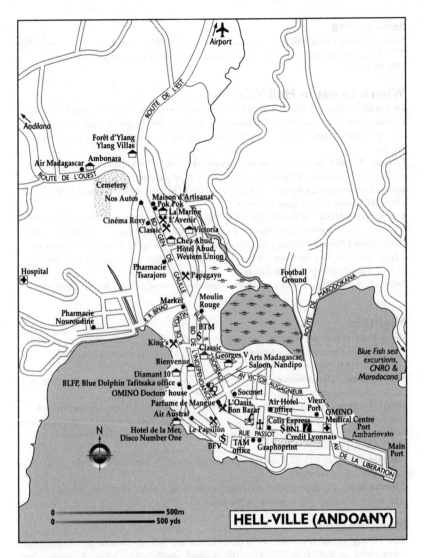

HELL-VILLE (ANDOANY)

Hotel Classic Rue Reine Tsiomeko; tel: 611 36/613 11. Same ownership as Restaurant Classic. Four rooms in one building; fans, shower and WC. 65,000–75,000Fmg; breakfast 15,000fmg.

Hotel de la Marine Off the main street near Hotel Abud; tel: 615 73/617 22. Eight rooms with shared WC/shower; 60,000–80,000Fmg; breakfast 14,000Fmg.

Hotel Georges V La Poudrière; tel: 615 61. Eight rooms with fans. 60,000Fmg double with shower.

Hotel Bienvenue Main street south of market. Eight simple rooms and a Chinese restaurant.

Hotel Victoria Tel: 613 25; fax: 615 64. Behind Chez Abud, on first floor of ONE office. Eight airy rooms with fans and shared bathrooms. Around 60,000Fmg double. Recommended for budget travellers.

Self-catering

Forêt d'Ylang Ylang Villas Maroankatsaka; tel: 615 85/610 83; in Tana: 22 228 54/22 352 37. Three self-catering villas at the edge of town on the road to the airport. Operated by Villa Blanche.

Where to eat in Hell-Ville

Le Papillon Tel: 615 82. On the right (as you walk towards the harbour) just before the Catholic church, where Bd de L'Indépendance becomes Rue Passot. Recommended. 'Excellent three-course dinner with wine, coffee etc for two people came to 136,000Fmg.' (1998)

L'Oasis Tel: 615 75. An excellent and low-priced snack bar on main road, opposite BFV bank. Fresh croissants and *pain au chocolat* daily. A good place to buy picnic supplies.

King's Restaurant La Batterie (not far from Hotel Diamant 10). Medium-priced, offering Chinese and international cuisine.

Restaurant Classic Bd Poincaré; tel: 611 36/613 11. Medium-priced open-air restaurant specialising in all types of grilled foods: brochettes, grilled chicken and seafood, steaks, etc.

Restaurant l'Avenir Malagasy-run small restaurant opposite the Roxy Cinema near to Classic Restaurant on the main street. Cheaper than the other restaurants but can still provide a good shrimp sauce and chips!

Saloon On main street. 'Very casual bar/restaurant with some rather awful but cheap rooms.'

Nightlife

Vieux Port A very popular place at the old port. 'Wild nights, usually gets going around 22.00, with live music. Great *salegy* and reggae music. 5,000Fmg to get in but drinks expensive.' (JA)

Moulin Rouge Discotheque Not far from the market; tel: 610 36. Serves pizzas during the day and disco every night from 21.30 until dawn.

Disco Number One In a basement beneath the Hotel de Mer. Thursdays and Saturdays.

Bar/Restaurant Papagayo New place near the main taxi rank close to the market, geared to the tourist market. Terrace-style bar/restaurant with potted palms. Has live music on Wednesdays. Popular.

Bar Nandipo Tel: 613 52. French-run bar in the centre of Hell-Ville, popular with expats. Pool table and darts.

Cinema Roxy On main road. 'Usual fare: commando, action, Indian love stories, or occasionally big hits such as Titanic in French.'

Music festival

The Donia music festival is held each Pentecost (May). A four-day celebration takes place in the Hell-Ville football ground southeast of town. Groups come here from Mauritius, Réunion and Seychelles as well as all parts of Madagascar. Lots of events and lots of fun, all for 5,000Fmg. Hotels get very booked up at this time.

BEACH HOTELS

Most visitors prefer to stay in beach hotels located along the sandy western coast. Hoteliers separate these into seven zones, including Hell-Ville and Nosy Komba. For simplification I have used the same divisions, but note there is beach accommodation in other areas such as Lokobe and some of the outlying islands. These are listed under the appropriate headings.

The prices are for high season (mid-July to mid-September, and over the Christmas holiday). Low-season rates are cheaper.

Andilana

Northern Nosy Be is the most beautiful part of the island, but will soon be the most developed. Two enormous luxury hotels are being built here. Andilana is 45 minutes' drive from Hell-Ville.

Category A

Hotel Village Andilana Beach Tel: 615 23/33. A huge new Club Med hotel complex (800 rooms) with shops, swimming pool, and other 'no-need-to-leave-the-hotel' facilities. Italian-owned.
Nouvelles Frontières Opening 2002 or 2003; 150 rooms planned.
Le Baobab BP 45, Hell-ville; tel: 614 37; fax: 612 93. An excellent French-owned hotel (seven bungalows) set in a fine garden, complete with baobab, by a beautiful beach with an outstanding restaurant. Air conditioning. High season 660Ff inc breakfast; low season 480Ff. Swimming pool. Fishing trips.

Category B

Au Belvedere (Chez Lou Lou) BP 301 Andilana, Nosy Be 207; tel: 611 22. Malagasy owned. Four rooms, four bungalows with shower and fan for 200Ff/200,000Fmg (double) including breakfast. Half board 350Ff per person. Lovely situation, good restaurant; Sunday all-you-can-eat buffet for 75,000Fmg, children free.

NOSY BE WEST

(Map labels:)
Andilana
N
Nosy Sakatia
Sakatia Passions
Lac Maintimaso
Sakatia Dive Inn
Ambaro
Chanty Beach
Lac Amparihibe
Lac Antsidihy
0 — 1km
0 — 1 mile
DJAMANDJARY
L'Ampasy Village
M Passot
Sirama (rum factory)
Ampasy
Nosy Be Hotel, Les Cocotiers & Nautilus Diving
Belle Vue
Nosy Tanga
Villa Blanche, Les Jolis Coins, Tsara Loky & Au Rendezvous des Amis
Ambondrona
Hell-Ville
Palm Beach
Madirokely
Marlin Club, Le Grand Large, Madiro Hotel, Mme Senga & Alefa Tours
AMBATOLOAKA
Robinson, Caravel, La Sirene, L'Espadon, Karibou, Ylang Ylang, La Résidence, La Saladerie, Le Glacier, Chez Angeline, Soleil et Découverte, Tropical, Coco Plage, Chez Gerard et Francine, Coucher du Soleil, Dauphin Blanc
Pecheries

Vacances Vorondrano BP 241, Andovokojabiaka, Andilana. Off the main road, in a nice secluded location. French owned. Three comfortable bungalows and one room. Good restaurant.

Category C

Chez Louisette Andilana; tel: 610 85; fax: 612 85. Four primitive rooms (no fans, no air conditioning, communal facilities) in gorgeous beach location. Good restaurant.

Self catering

Les Terraces de Nosy Be BP 3, Route d'Andilana; tel: 614 63. French owned. Five villas of two to three rooms for 300Ff per day. Price includes chambermaid who will prepare meals on request.

Belle Vue (Djamandjary area)

Djamandjary is an ugly small town with some strange igloo-shaped cement structures which, long ago, were provided by a relief organisation as cyclone-proof housing. They are, indeed, indestructible, and have mostly been abandoned by the villagers who have tired of waiting for them to fall down in the time-honoured Malagasy way. Opposite the town is a sugarcane and rum processing factory. Worth a visit. Bring your own bottle!

Although the beach here is uninspiring (it shelves too gradually for good swimming) it is shaded by coconut palms, and a chain of hotels stretches down the coast. Each hotel rakes away the dead seaweed that the high tide deposits daily on the beach.

Category A

Les Cocotiers BP 191; tel/fax: 613 14; email: cocotier@dts.mg; website: http://lescocotier.nemo.it. Italian/Malagasy owned. 26 pleasant bungalows, and very good Italian food. High season: 1,150Ff per person (double) half board. Or – wait for it! – 120 Euros. Less than half those prices low season. Airport transfers 60,000Fmg.

Nosy Be Hotel Tel: 614 30; fax: 614 06. Italian/French owned. The most popular mid-range hotel in the area; five bungalows, 22 rooms, some with air conditioning, others with fans. Swimming pool. Prices range from 365Ff to 750Ff, depending on the room and season. Some visitors have complained that the food is overpriced and monotonous and transfers from the airport cost a whopping 100Ff per person.

Category B

L'Ampasy Village (formerly Belle Plage Hotel) BP 19, Djamandjary; tel: 614 77; fax: 611 58. Sixteen bungalows with air conditioning and WC. Restaurant. 300Ff per two-person bungalow per day including breakfast. Fixed menu meals: 60,000Fmg.

Category C

Nautilus Diving BP 139, Plage Belle Vue; tel: 613 43. Four simple bungalows with fans and shared WC. 100,000Fmg to 120,000Fmg. Meal: 45,000Fmg. Diving, sea excursions.

Self-catering

Chanty Beach Ambaro BP 172; Tel: 614 73; fax: 614 74. Luxury two-person apartments with spacious veranda, equipped with air conditioning/fans and telephones, situated in a colonial mansion set in gardens next to a very quiet beach. Prices range from 500Ff per day/3,000Ff per week to 300Ff/1,800Ff. Includes breakfast.

Ambondrona

South of Djamandjary; some prefer it to the busier, noisier Ambataloaka. If you don't want to eat at your hotel it's close enough to walk to Ambataloaka through the sugarcane fields and get a taxi back.

Category A

Villa Blanche BP 79; tel: 610 85/611 85; fax: 612 85. 38 comfortable bungalows, including two family ones sleeping up to five. Single with breakfast 240Ff, double 360Ff. Fixed menu: 60,000Fmg. Airport transfer, 50Ff.

Category B

Les Jolis Coins BP 220, Ambondrona Avaratra. Eight bungalows, 11 rooms. Comfortable; varied menu in restaurant.

Category C

Tsara Loky BP 160; tel: 610 22. Malagasy run. Six simple bungalows with fans, showers and WC. 166,000Fmg. Six rooms with shared bathroom: 70,000Fmg double. Open-air restaurant.

Au Rendezvous des Amis Five simple bungalows by the sea. Reasonably-priced restaurant.

Madirokely
Just north of Ambatoloaka; quieter, but becoming quite developed.

Category A
Marlin Club BP 205; tel: 610 70; fax: 614 45; email: marlin.club@simcro.mg. 16 rooms. Very comfortable, price includes breakfast. From 680Ff (low season) to 780Ff (high season).

Category B
Madira Hotel BP 218, Madirokely; tel/fax: 614 18; email: madiro@simicro.mg. 15 very comfortable rooms, seven singles, eight doubles, with fans and fridges. 480Ff high season, 350Ff low season. Swimming pool. Tours offered include camping trips to other islands, water-skiing, parasailing. Also a scuba-diving centre.
Le Grand Large BP 89 Madirokely; tel: 615 84. 14 rooms with air conditioning and hot water. Double room from 290Ff (low season) to 350Ff (high season). Restaurant with patisserie. Water scooters; three boats for excursions.

Category C
Chez Madame Senga Three simple bungalows with WC, shower and fan; very good value at 80,000Fmg; breakfast 10,000Fmg; other meals 30,000Fmg to 80,000Fmg.

Ambatoloaka
This is a fast-growing but still charming fishing village with the best options for inexpensive places to stay as well as luxury accommodation. It is the liveliest centre on the island so if you're looking for nightlife, this is the place to be.

Where to stay
Category A
Hotel l'Espadon Tel: 614 28; fax: 614 27. Swiss-owned. 12 bungalows, ten rooms. Very comfortable with air conditioning, TV etc. Excellent restaurant. 300–550Ff, depending on location of room. Breakfast 25,000Fmg. Specialise in deep-sea fishing.

Category B
Hotel Ylang Ylang Tel: 614 01; fax: 614 02. Nine rooms. The best hotel in this category; British owned and very good value at 250Ff double including breakfast. Good restaurant.
La Résidence Ambatoloaka BP 130; tel: 613 68. This popular place is inconsistent in its service and food, but at its best is very good, with 12 pleasant air-conditioned en-suite rooms and a good terrace/lounge. 220Ff double (high season).
Chez Gérard et Francine BP 193; tel: 614 09. Comfortable family house, at a good, quiet location at the southern end of Ambatoloaka; nine rooms, some with en-suite shower. Deservedly popular so usually full. 185–240Ff including breakfast.

Category C
Hotel Soleil et Découverte BP3; tel: 614 24. (Four rooms) A lively place run by Daniel and Antoine in a central location. 100,000Fmg; breakfast 18,000Fmg.
Hotel Tropical BP 198; tel: 614 16. Seven newish bungalows with shower and WC; 96,000Fmg with breakfast.
Coucher du Soleil Hotel & Restaurant BP 134; tel/fax: 616 20. Seven very clean and comfortable bungalows with en-suite bathroom (basic showers, new toilets). Not on the beach, but sea view; 80,000Fmg with breakfast.

Hotel Caraval Route d'Ambataloaka; tel: 614 05 or 612 26. Ten new bungalows with en-suite bathrooms; hot water; fans. 110,000Fmg with breakfast.

Hotel Coco Plage BP159; tel: 616 14. 16 nice beach bungalows with bathrooms, about 1km south of the village. Those facing the beach cost more than the rear ones; 95,000–115,000Fmg per person with breakfast (but otherwise no meals).

Hotel Robinson Tel: 614 36. On the junction of the road to Madirokely. Six bungalows with shower, WC and fan. 95,000Fmg including breakfast (low season), 120,000Fmg (high season).

Where to eat in Ambataloaka

Most of the main hotels have good restaurants, with Ylang Ylang particularly recommended, but Ambataloaka has always been renowned for its little restaurants serving delicious food. Look out for the food stalls and snackeries not listed here, where you can often eat a marvellous meal very cheaply.

Chez Angeline Tel: 616 21. Nosy Be's most popular little restaurant, famous for its seafood and *poulet au coco*.

Karibou Tel: 616 47. Excellent Italian food. Live band on Thursdays.

Dauphin Blanc Tel: 616 23. Vietnamese and French bar/restaurant.

La Saladerie Tel: 614 52. Salads and sandwiches.

Le Glacier Drinks, snacks and ice-cream.

Nightlife in Ambataloaka

La Sirene Nightclub next to Hotel Caraval. Live music on Wednesday nights.

Karibou Restaurant Dinner dancing with local band every Thursday. Free if you have a meal, 5,000Fmg for the band only.

Glacier Snack Bar Live music on Friday nights.

Casino Just opened (1999) offering roulette, blackjack, etc.

PRACTICALITIES
Medical care

Josephine Andrews writes: 'There is always a doctor on call at the main Nosy Be hospital in Hell-Ville and people to patch you up in an emergency. However, if you can avoid the hospital, do. There is a very good clean hospital/clinic in Ambanja which has better facilities. In case of serious emergency you should plan to be flown out to Réunion or home. For minor problems go to one of Nosy Be's GPs, and pay 10,000Fmg for a consultation including prescription. Two efficient doctors who work for OMINO (the health service provided by Pécheries) live in the same building at La Batterie and give consultations at home when they are not at OMINO. They are very friendly and speak some English.'

Pharmacies

The two pharmacies in Hell-Ville stock most modern drugs. One of them is always open as a *Pharmacie de Garde* for emergencies (this changes each week but the taxi drivers usually know as there are announcements on the radio). Pharmacie Tsarajoro is on the main street north of the market, almost opposite Chez Abud; tel: 613 82. Pharmacie Nouroudine, in Andavakatoko not far from the small market to the west of town down the road from the main market; tel: 610 38.

Money

Very few hotels take credit cards. Banks are open 07.30–11.00; 14.30–16.30 weekdays only. Banks usually only work a half day before a holiday.

Banks

BNI (Credit Lyonnais) On the road down to the port, it often has the best exchange rates.
BTM Closest bank to the market, also on the main drag. Gives cash advances on MasterCard. Expect to wait at least an hour.
BFV Close to Oasis, almost opposite the post office. Gives cash advances on Visa but beware limit of 2,000FF/week; need to wait about an hour for them to get the OK on your card.

Western Union

Of great interest to people needing cash sent in a hurry! An office for Western Union has opened in the foyer of Chez Abud Hotel: you get a friend to deposit the money at a Western Union office in the UK (tel: 0800 833 833) or another country (eg: USA tel: 800 325 6000), they then get a code number which they fax, email or phone to you, you take this and some ID to the office, and collect your money in Fmg within minutes!

Photo shop

Graphoprint in Hell-Ville (opposite the Catholic church) do next-day service for developing prints, and sell film and camera batteries. Also photocopying service.

EXCURSIONS
Mont Passot

A popular excursion is the trip to the island's highest point, Mont Passot. There are marvellous views of a series of deep-blue crater lakes, which are said to contain crocodiles (though I have never seen one) and to be sacred as the home of the spirits of the Sakalava and Antakarana princes. It is *fady* to fish there, or to smoke, wear trousers or any garment put on over the feet, or a hat, while on the lakes' shores. It is, in any case, difficult to get down to the water since the crater sides are very steep.

The road to the peak runs from Djamandjary, and can be hiked or cycled. Tour groups come to Mont Passot to see the sunset, but in the clear air of Nosy Be this is generally less than spectacular, so it is better to make a day excursion of it and take a picnic. Souvenir sellers have discovered the joys of having captive *vazahas* waiting for the sun to dip, and have set up tables for their wares. This is not a hill of solitude.

Lokobe

Nosy Be's only protected area, Lokobe, is a Strict Reserve and as such is not currently open to visitors (although there are plans for it to become a National Park). However, it is possible to visit the buffer zone on the northeast side of the peninsula where permits are not required. The two little villages here, Ambatozavavy and Ampasypohy, now have simple hotels which allow visitors a chance to get a proper look at this lovely, unspoiled area. Ambatozavavy means 'Woman stone', a reference to the nearby sacred rock which is said to represent women's genitalia, and to bestow fertility on those who visit it.

For years an excursion to Lokobe was the preserve of Jean-Robert who runs day-trips from the main Nosy Be hotels to Ampasipohy, 45 minutes by pirogue from Ambatozavavy. This trip is still a good option for those who cannot spend the night (see *Where to stay*). During the course of the day you are served a traditional lunch and taken on a tour of the forest where Jean-Robert, who speaks excellent English and is a natural showman, explains the traditional uses of various plants and points out a variety of animals. You are bound to see a lepilemur which, unlike the species in Berenty, spends its day dozing in the fork of a favourite tree rather than in a hole (Jean-Robert likes to 'please' tourists by shaking the tree to make the animal jump:

THE BLACK LEMUR FOREST PROJECT

The black lemur, *Eulemur macaco macaco*, is restricted to a small area of forest in northwest Madagascar and, as with almost all of the lemurs, is threatened with extinction due to loss of its habitat.

The Black Lemur Forest Project (BLFP) understands that there can be no future for black lemurs or their forest habitat without integrated conservation measures that combine scientific research with practical environmental education and development projects. This work was recognised in 1995 when the BLFP received the Whitley Award for Conservation.

The BLFP was founded in 1991 by Josephine Andrews, a British anthropologist and conservationist. The strengths of the project lie in the fact that it is long-term and works both with and within the local Malagasy community. BLFP brings together the following: scientific research (on the ecology of black lemurs and their forest habitat, and on the development and impacts of tourism on local environment and culture); environmental education (directed particularly towards local schoolchildren and adults, and also towards visiting tourists); local community development (including specific development projects in two villages close to Lokobe Reserve, Nosy Be, and the introduction locally of simple solar-cooking technology); and the training of Malagasy students in all aspects of conservation.

In the late 1990s BLFP initiated a community scheme designed to allow local people to gain some income from tourism and so take the pressure off the local forest. A community centre in Ambanoro houses an exhibition describing local natural history and culture, and a group of villagers has been taught to make attractive souvenirs to sell to visitors. Young people have been trained as guides. All the proceeds from the sale of souvenirs and guided tours go to cover

visitors should say a firm 'no' to this cruelty.) You should see black lemurs (shyer, but in better condition than those on Nosy Komba) and with luck a boa and chameleons. The chameleons here are the panther (*pardalis*) species and in the breeding season (November to May) the male is bright green and the female a pinkish colour. The villagers grow vanilla and peppers, so you will observe the non-destructive combination of crops and forest, and a wide range of handicrafts can be bought direct from the maker.

Jean-Robert meets most planes, but if you miss him your hotel will know where he is. His 1999 price was 120,000Fmg.

Lokobe is the centre for the Black Lemur Forest Project (see above), a not-to-be-missed example of community-based conservation.

Where to stay

Eco-village Fihavanana BP 203, Ambatozavavy; tel/fax: 614 75. Designed for ecotourists rather than beach fanatics; Swiss-managed. Nine very comfortable, spacious palm-thatched bungalows with hot showers and solar-powered. 60Ff/195,000Fmg (high season). Transfer from Hell-Ville costs 25,000Fmg for two people. The manager can organise trips with local fisherman, but they also have their own Zodiac. An excellent feature is the Lokobe Nature Trail, which can be walked at night so is of particular interest to those devoted to reptiles and nocturnal fauna of all kinds.

Jungle village BP 208, Hell-Ville. Six lovely basic bungalows in Ampasypohy, run by Marc Dehlinger. Beautifully located, and excellent value at around 90,000Fmg per bungalow, or 500,000Fmg for the main house (5–6 people). Dinner 35,000Fmg.

the running costs of the centre and ultimately towards community needs such as school materials, medicines and rice.

The BLFP aims to help guide local tourism development so that it is responsible and sustainable.

How you can help:

1. With funding – for supporting any aspect of this work;

2. With materials – particularly clothing and materials for our students and guides, educational materials, and field equipment (if you are on your way home from a camping trip in Madagascar and pass through Nosy Be);

3. With the BLFP education project – contact us if you work in a zoo which holds lemurs or if you work in a school and would like to participate in our project;

4. Visit the Ambanoro community project and buy a souvenir or take a guided village tour.

5. In Nosy Be contact the BLFP to arrange for a slide show about Nosy Be wildlife and its conservation or for a guided tour to see wild black lemurs with the BLFP team (special trips can be arranged with the *Blue Dolphin* boat). Special arrangements can also be made to visit the BLFP base in Ampasindava, close to Lokobe Reserve.

Contact details Josephine Andrews, BP 235, Nosy Be 207, Madagascar; tel: Nosy Be (20) 86 611 30 (office hours); email (Madagascar): BLFP@simicro.mg; email (UK): c/o Isobel Andrews, Friends of BLFP: ISOPRYBLFP@ compuserve.com.

Ambanoro and the CNRO Museum

A visit to the Black Lemur Forest Project at Ambanoro is a must for anyone interested in conservation involving local communities. Ambanoro (Marodokana) lies 5km southeast of Hell-Ville – a pleasant walk or short taxi ride. The Ambanoro Community Centre (Projet Communautaire d'Ambanoro) houses a permanent exhibition about local natural history and culture. Entry to the centre is free, but you are encouraged to take a short guided tour of the village with one of the community project guides (around 15,000Fmg). The area was once an important Indian community, and there are the ruins of an ancient mosque, half-hidden by enormous sacred fig trees, and the elaborate Indian cemetery. Ambanoro was once the capital of Nosy Be (its other name, Marodokana, means 'many shops') and was a thriving port and trading centre up until the rise of Hell-Ville in the early 1800s. You may even be lucky enough to see wild black lemurs and chameleons if you opt for a slightly longer tour through coffee and vanilla fields and into forest at the edge of Lokobe Reserve.

There are special souvenirs for sale at the centre, such as soft-toy chameleons, frogs and turtles (see page 129), small embroideries with an environmental theme (eg: chameleon napkins), purses and baskets, and rag dolls in local dress. Also postcards. Refreshments include cake made in solar ovens! The project is entirely run by the villagers themselves with guidance and training provided by BLFP; all proceeds go towards running the project, and ultimately to a fund for community needs, such as rice, medicines and school materials. Do support them!

You can reach Ambanoro by taxi (20,000Fmg one way) or, at high tide, by boat (about ten minutes). Try combining a trip to Ambanoro with a visit to the CNRO

(Oceanographic Research Institute) museum (about 2km from town on the road to Ambanoro). Here you can see amazing examples of preserved fish (including a baby hammerhead shark) and a very good local seashell collection (weekday mornings only).

NOSY KOMBA AND NOSY TANIKELY

No visit to Nosy Be is complete without an excursion to these two islands. Nosy Komba's main attraction is the black lemurs, and the marine national park of Nosy Tanikely lures snorkellers and bird enthusiasts.

Getting there and away

All the Nosy Be hotels do excursions to Nosy Komba which is usually combined with Nosy Tanikely. Most will let you do the sensible thing of taking an overnight break in Nosy Komba, then rejoining the boat the following day for Nosy Tanikely. For Nosy Komba alone it is much cheaper to go by pirogue. Go to the small pirogue port (Port Ambariovato, to the east of the main port in Hell-Ville). The pirogues leave at around 11.00 each day after the morning's shopping in Hell-Ville. The trip should cost from 5,000 to 15,000Fmg. If you are a group of six or more, you can find a fast boat from the main port for around 25,000per person to Nosy Komba.

Yachties approaching from Nosy Be should wait until Nosy Verona (the island with the old lighthouse) then bear 020 degrees. Good anchorage in 3–7m over sand and mud.

Nosy Komba (Nosy Ambariovato)

Once upon a time Nosy Komba was an isolated island with an occasional boat service, a tiny, self-sufficient village (Ampangorinana), and a troop of semi-tame black lemurs which were held to be sacred so never hunted. Now all that has changed. Tourists arrive in boat-loads from Nosy Be and from passing cruise ships which can land over 100 people.

Komba means 'lemur' (interestingly it is the Swahili word for bushbaby which of course is the African relative of the lemur) and it is the lemurs that bring in the visitors. During the 1980s the villagers made nothing out of these visits apart from the sale of clay animals which they glazed with the acid of spent batteries. Then they instigated a modest fee for seeing the animals and increased the variety of handicrafts. Now that Nosy Komba is on some cruise-ship itineraries they have taken on the works: 'tribal dancing', face decoration, escorted walks... anything that will earn a dollar or two.

With all the demands on your purse, it sometimes takes a bit of mental effort to see the underlying charm of Ampangorinana, but it is nevertheless a typical Malagasy community living largely on fishing and *tavy* farming (witness the horrendous deforestation of their little island; when I first visited in 1976, it was completely covered with luxuriant trees) but it is the black lemurs that provide the financial support (and probably prevent further degradation of their environment). The ancestor who initiated the hunting *fady* must be pleased with himself. If you want the lemurs-on-your-shoulders experience and the chance to see these engaging animals at close quarters you should definitely come here. Only the male *Eulemur macaco* is black; the females, which give birth in September, are chestnut brown with white ear-tufts.

Nosy Komba also provides an excellent opportunity for observing lemur behaviour. Note the bossiness of the females, who make sure that they get the bananas first, and the way the males rub their bottoms on branches to scent-mark

MORE THAN JUST WORDS
Janice Booth

At Nosy Komba I was the first off the boat when it hit shore; and was still in the water when a girl – about eight years old – waded up and started trying to sell me little clay birds. She was expressionless, running through obviously familiar 'patter' in very basic French. I bought one.

After I'd been on the island for a few hours she came back, not recognising me from the first sale, and tried again. I explained slowly, in a mixture of simple French and sign language, that I'd already bought a bird, that I liked it, and that I didn't need another. She listened intently, her eyes locked on mine, absorbing every word and gesture. I could see the effort she was making to understand – she really wanted to. When I'd finished, just to make sure she'd got it right, she pointed a small finger questioningly at herself, as if to ask 'and was it really my bird that you bought?' When I nodded she broke into a most radiant smile, eyes still holding mine, as if we had become conspirators in some shared pleasure. She was so happy to have understood, and skipped away, still smiling.

On our way back from seeing the lemurs, girls were emerging from every alley with tablecloths, pestering us to buy. One spoke reasonable French and we were a little apart from the crowd, so I asked if she could tell me something – on my walk I'd heard some creature cry, but I couldn't identify it. I made the sound; and she unfolded one tablecloth and pointed to an embroidered bird. Trees and fruit were also embroidered on the cloth, and she pointed them out and named them for me one by one. I said the island was beautiful, and she glowed. I explained that I really didn't want a tablecloth but was so pleased to have the information and felt it was lucky that I'd asked someone knowledgeable. She looked so much happier with this than if I'd been 'just another tourist' buying goods.

them and gain some authority. Take a look at a lemur's hands: you will see the four flat primate fingernails (such wonderfully human hands!) and the single claw which is used for grooming. Be careful when feeding the lemurs: an accidental nip with their razor-sharp canines can give a nasty wound.

The BLFP (see page 316) is studying the lemurs of Nosy Komba and working towards improving the Nosy Komba experience (which, as the island becomes more commercialised, inevitably disappoints those who hate 'touristy' places). A management plan is being drawn up to benefit lemurs, villagers and tourists. It urgently needs funds to continue this work. It is easy to observe the detrimental effect that the loss of natural habitat and an unvaried diet of bananas is having on the lemurs' health: many have skin diseases, and scruffy-looking fur. Compare them with their sleek-looking counterparts on Lokobe.

A small fee (2,500Fmg) is charged to see the lemurs, and en route to Lemur Park everyone in the village will try to sell you something. Since you are buying direct from the grower/maker, this is the best place to get vanilla and handicrafts (carved pirogues, clay animals, and unusual and attractive 'lace' tablecloths, curtains and bedspreads). The handicrafts here are unlike any found on the mainland, so it is worth bringing plenty of cash (small change). If you intend to buy a bedspread (and this is the best place to do so) you will need around 200,000Fmg for a double-bed size.

One of the former glories of Nosy Komba, its coral, has sadly almost completely disappeared so snorkelling is no longer rewarding. The sea and beach near the village are polluted with human waste, but there is a good swimming beach round to the left (as you face the sea).

The best way to visit Nosy Komba is by yourself, or in a small group, and avoid the 'rush hour' (9.30–10.30). When there are few other tourists, Nosy Komba is a tranquil place, so consider an overnight stay or a stay of a few days. The available accommodation is comfortable enough and cheaper than beach options on Nosy Be. Given time to explore, it is possible to find and watch lemur groups away from 'Lemur Park' or to take a hike up the hill for spectacular views of the whole of Nosy Be (the top of Nosy Komba, at 630m, is higher than any point on Nosy Be) but start early before it gets too hot and bear in mind that there is little left of the primary forest; just secondary growth with lots of bamboo.

If you really want to learn about the black lemurs and get off the mass-tourist track, the BLFP organises special tailor-made trips to Nosy Komba with lemur expert and project founder, Josephine Andrews, as your guide (tel 86 611 30) or hire the boat *The Blue Dolphin* (same tel no, or see in port) as part of the fare goes to help BLFP activities.

Where to stay

Chez Bernie Mrs Bernie and Remo, who run Albatros (see *Cruising*), have four luxury bungalows. 450Ff full board (which includes unlimited boat hire). They also organise hiking trips across Nosy Komba and can provide camping equipment. Recommended.

Les Floralies BP 107, Nosy Be, fax: 613 67. Seven French-run bungalows and one beach house beautifully situated at the end of the quietest beach, with en-suite shower and toilet. Bar and restaurant. 130,000Fmg per person half board.

Hotel Lémuriens BP 185, Nosy Be. Good bungalows run by Martin (German) and Henriette (Malagasy), 100,000Fmg per bungalow (with shower and WC), 35,000Fmg shared facilities. This hotel deserves your support. Martin was responsible for the construction of water reservoirs, the school and a clinic for the islands' inhabitants. Can be prebooked by fax: 613 71 (Hell-Ville).

Hotel Karibu Run by an Italian and his Malagasy wife. Reasonably priced.

Hotel Madame Madio BP 207; Eight simple bungalows for only 25,000Fmg (shared facilities); three bungalows with en-suite bathrooms: 40,000Fmg. Breakfast 12,500Fmg. Order other meals in advance. Mme Madio shares some of her guests with her neighbouring cousin Mme Yvonne, an excellent cook.

Chez Alexandre Simple bungalows near the Buvette des Vahinys; 20,000Fmg.

Potable water is available from a number of public taps along the front of the village (best to purify it to be on the safe side).

Nosy Tanikely

Although now much visited, this is still pretty close to Paradise. Nosy Tanikely is a tiny island with a lighthouse and... a rumour of planning permission to build a hotel there. I'm supposing it's only a rumour! The island is a marine reserve and it is for the snorkelling that most people visit it. And the snorkelling is excellent (even if too many ships dropping too many anchors are beginning to take their toll on the coral). In clear water you can see an amazing variety of marine life – coral, starfish, anemones, every colour and shape of fish, turtles, lobsters...

With this new world beneath your gaze there is a real danger of forgetting the passing of time and becoming seriously sunburnt. Even the most carefully applied sunblock tends to miss some areas, so wear a T-shirt and shorts.

Don't think you have finished with Nosy Tanikely when you come out of the water; at low tide it is possible to walk right round the island. During your circumambulation you will see (if you go anticlockwise): a broad beach of white sand covered in shells and bleached pieces of coral, a couple of trees full of flying foxes and – in the spring – graceful white tropic birds flying in and out of their nests in the high cliffs. At your feet will be rock pools and some scrambling, but nothing too challenging.

Then there is the climb up to the lighthouse at the top of the island for the view.

Sadly, Nosy Tanikely has a problem with years of rubbish left by visitors, though the local Platform for the Environment, Nosy Be (a group of environmental organisations and interested individuals), is trying to get this removed through a series of volunteer clean-up days. The best time to visit is out of the main tourist season. If you can afford it, hire your own boat and take a picnic or arrange for the boat crew to grill a fish on the beach. Boats running trips to Nosy Tanikely may provide snorkelling gear, but it's safer to bring your own.

OTHER ISLANDS IN THE NOSY BE ARCHIPELAGO
With thanks to Josephine Andrews, Willem and Elize Strauss, and Christina Raimondo

Nosy Sakatia
This rather bare island lies off the west side of Nosy Be. Sakatia means orchid island, but a more remarkable aspect of its flora are the baobabs. This is the best island for keen divers and game fishermen. There are two well-run hotels catering for divers.

Where to stay
Sakatia Passions BP 295; tel: 61 462; fax: 61 435. 12 bungalows run by fishing specialists Jacques Toussaint and Jean-Claude Clement who own six boats fully equipped for deep-sea fishing. Also windsurfing, and kayaking.
Sakatia Dive Inn BP 186, Helle-Ville; tel: 61 514; fax 613 67. Six rustic bungalows with mosquito nets, basins and WC, 200Ff per day; five *huttes Canadiennes* (A-frame tents), 60,000Fmg. Communal facilities. Family-style dining. As the name implies, this place offers diving courses and excursions.
Delphino Villa Bungalows Tel: 61 668. Charming, rustic traditional Malagasy bungalows. 30,000Fmg per night, with refreshingly inexpensive drinks.

These places welcome visitors from boats. The channel between Nosy Be and Nosy Sakatia provides safe anchoring some 150m off the beach at 5m over a sandy bottom, if you don't wish to anchor off Hell-Ville. There are strong tidal currents in the channel.

Nosy Mitsio
The archipelago of Nosy Mitsio lies some 60–70km from Nosy Be and about the same distance from the mainland. This is the Maldives of Madagascar, with two exclusive (and expensive) fly-in resorts on stunningly beautiful small islands.

La Grande Mitsio
The largest island is populated by local Malagasy – Antakarana and Sakalava, who survive on their denuded island through farming, cattle and goats. 'Main mode of transport: pirogues, some very big – able to do shopping/selling trips to mainland (Port St Louis) and Nosy Be, even with the odd cow in the boat!' (JA). Overgrazing has devastated the island but some forest remains in the southern part. Huge basalt columns are a prominent feature on the northwest tip, used as an adventure playground by enterprising goats.

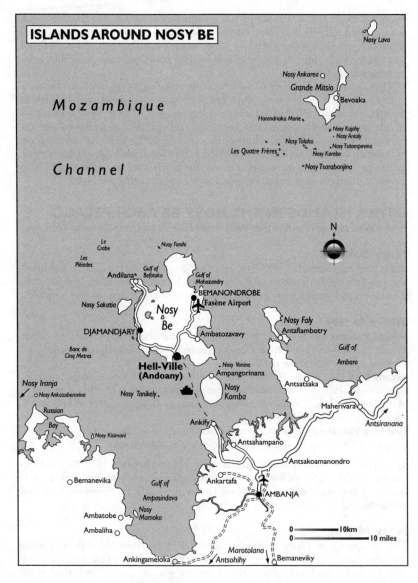

ISLANDS AROUND NOSY BE

Mozambique

Nosy Lava

Nosy Ankarea
Grande Mitsio
Bevoaka

Harandriaka Marie

Nosy Kajohy
Nosy Antaly
Nosy Toloho
Nosy Tsitampevina
Les Quatre Frères
Nosy Karabo

Nosy Tsarabanjina

Channel

N

Le Crabe

Nosy Fanihi

Les Pléiades

Andilana

Gulf of Befotaka

Gulf of Mahazandry

BEMANONDROBE
Fasène Airport

Nosy Sakatia

Nosy Be

Nosy Faly
Antafiambotry

DJAMANDJARY

Ambatozavavy

Gulf of Ambaro

Banc de Cinq Metres

Hell-Ville (Andoany)

Nosy Vorona
Ampangorinana

Nosy Iranja

Nosy Ankazoberovina

Nosy Komba

Antsatsaka

Maherivara

Nosy Tanikely

Antsiranana

Russian Bay

Nosy Kisimani

Ankify

Antsahampano

Antsakoamanondro

Bemanevika

Gulf of Ampasindava

Ankartafa

AMBANJA

Ambatobe

Nosy Mamoko

Ambaliha

Marotolana
Antsohihy

Bemaneviky

Ankingameloka

0 ——— 10km
0 ——— 10 miles

The island attracts yachties to its coral reefs and good anchorages. Maribe Bay provides good anchorage, protected between two hills. This is a good area for seeing manta rays.

Tsara Banjina

The name means 'good beaches' and this is a small but incredibly beautiful island, made famous by British actress Joanna Lumley who was 'cast away' here. The red, grey and black volcanic rocks, rising quite high at its centre, have a mass of lush, green vegetation clinging to them, from baobabs and other large trees to pachypodium and tiny rockery plants. But its real glory are the pure white beaches of coarse sand, along which lap a crystal-clear green/indigo sea. Turtles and rays rest near the beaches. Divers can be kept busy for a couple of days, and there are walking trails.

Yachties can anchor off the southwest, at 6m over a sandy bottom.

L'Hotel Tsarabajina has recently opened on the island. Built by an ex-South African, Richard Walker, and his partners, it is beautifully designed, constructed predominantly of natural materials and accommodating just a few people at a time. The building containing the bar/restaurant is separate from the 20 A-frame chalets which have en-suite bathrooms. Rates: high season 1,200Ff double; 750Ff single; low season: 960Ff double, 600Ff single. There is an additional tax of 3,000Fmg per day. Transfers by seaplane (400Ff per person for group of five) or speedboat (200Ff per person each way). Contact details: Main office (Tana); tel: (261) 285 14; fax: 285 15; email: Groupe.Hotel@simicro.mg.

There is a world-class scuba-diving centre, and a wide range of watersports such as windsurfing.

Nosy Ankarea

Another beautiful place to spend a few luxurious days. There are some gorgeous, sun-drenched beaches and the low hills make for pleasant walking excursions. 'The island is superb. Fabulous pachypodiums, flamboyants, etc. Surrounded by coral reefs in an azure sea. The forest on the island is relatively undisturbed, due to numerous *fadys* and the fact that no one lives there except Marlin Club tourists. It is possible to climb up the highest hill (219m – quite steep but well worth it) to reach a plateau covered with pachypodiums and lots of wierd and wonderful other succulents. From here you can see all of Nosy Mitsio and the surrounding reefs.' (Josephine Andrews)

Here is the **Marlin Club Ecohotel Annex** with six luxury tents, with beach parasols, showers and toilets. 900Ff per day inclusive. First-class meals in a thatched restaurant built around a huge baobab tree. Contact Marlin Club Hotel (page 313) for details.

Les Quatre Frères (The Four Brothers)

These are four imposing lumps of silver basalt, two of which are home to hundreds of nesting seabirds, including brown boobies, frigate birds and white-tailed tropic birds. A pair of Madagascar fish eagles nest on one of the rocks. The sides drop vertically to about 20–30m, and divers come here because three of the boulders can be circumnavigated during one vigorous dive. Yachties can anchor to the southeast of Nosy Beangovo, roughly 100m from the mouth of a cave, at a depth of about 10m. Currents reach up to one knot. The best marine life is in the lee. There are huge caves, spectacular overhangs and rockfalls in the area.

Nosy Iranja

The classic palm-fringed island (actually two islands, Iranja Be and Iranja Hely, connected by a sandbar exposed at low tide) with clear water for swimming and coral reefs off the east side providing excellent snorkelling. There is a small village of fisherfolk on Iranja Be; visitors are often taken to see the lighthouse, the village and its school. This is a breeding area for hawksbill turtles. 'Often we see large turtles lolling around the boat near Iranja, especially at night. And if you switch the spotlight on, you can see squid' (Willem Strauss). The turtle nesting beach on Iranja Hely was given special protection under a decree in 1923 – which seems to have been conveniently forgotten: a hotel is being built which may spell the end of the turtles which are extremely sensitive to light and noise.

To be worthwhile you need to make this a three-day excursion (with tents) from Nosy Be. This could cost up to 1,000,000Fmg.

Anchorage for yachts is best south or west of the smaller island, in 4–6m over sand.

Nosy Kivinjy

Otherwise known as Sugarloaf Rock, this is a great basalt boulder with 'organ pipes' formations on one side. Not recommended for diving (poor) or anchorage (very insecure). There are strong northeast-flowing currents around the islet.

Nosy Mamoko

This little island is at the southwest end of Ampasindava Bay. Known among the yachting fraternity for its exceptional shelter in all weather, it is a lovely, tranquil spot for a few days' relaxation. Nosy Mamoko is on the itineraries of two or three operators, based in Nosy Be, who organise lengthy trips into the region. There is good fishing here and whale-watching from October to December. Good anchorage is found in the channel between the island and the mainland, in 15m over a sandy bottom.

Nosy Radama

The Radama islands, which lie to the far south of Nosy Be and thus are only really accessible to yachties, compete with the Mitsios for the best diving sites in the northeast of Madagascar. They are set in a breathtaking coastline of bays backed by high mountains. Most of these high sandstone islands are steep-sided above and below water and covered with scrub, grass and trees. Sharp eroded rock formations, however, render the remaining forest rather difficult to explore.

Nosy Kalakajoro

The northernmost island, featuring dense, impenetrable forest on the south side. There are good beaches on the southern side and snorkelling is worthwhile off the southeast. Yachts should anchor 100m off the southeast side in 10–12m over good holding sand and mud, to get protection from the north-to-west winds.

Nosy Ovy (Potato Island)

This is the largest of the group, but the environmental degradation is terrible. Nearly all the trees have been cut and goats have completed the destruction of its flora. Red soil weeps from gaping scars into the surrounding water. If you still want to visit, boats can anchor off the east side, near a protected rocky outcrop.

Nosy Valiha

A small island, the southern and eastern shores of which drop steeply. Boats can anchor off the southeast, near the attractive beach over a sandy ledge, at 6–15m. A 100m deep channel runs just south of this island.

'The mercies of God [be bestowed on] this people, whose simplicity hath herein made them more happy than our too dear-bought knowledge hath advantaged us'.
Walter Hamond

Blue Dolphin Tafitsaka

Nosy Komba, Tanikely, Nosy Faly, Nosy Iranja...

Visit the islands at your own pace: hire the "Blue Dolphin"

Also: passage to mainland; dolphin watching; camping; snorkelling trips arranged

**Blue Dolphin Tafitsaka   Boat Hire and Excursions
Office at La Batterie, Nosy Be
Reservations: 86 61130 or see the boat in port**

British owned
hotel in village
centre, with nine
ensuite rooms,
restaurant and bar.

"beside the sea offering
the best cuisine on
the island."
Le Monde newspaper,
November 98

Hotel L'Ylang Ylang, Ambatoloaka, BP110, Nosy Be 207
Tel 00.261.20.86.614.01   Fax 00.261.20.86.614.02

Scott Dunn **World** ⊕ *The tailormade specialist to Madagascar*

✦ Personally Tailored Holidays for individuals or small groups
✦ Exotic flora and fauna in Isalo, Perenet, Berenty and Pangalanes
✦ Beaches and culture in Nosy Mitsio, Isle St. Marie, Nosy Be plus Tsingy and Baobabs
✦ Combinations with South Africa, Kenya, Mauritius, Reunion and Seychelles.
✦ Diving, Sailing, Deep Sea Fishing, Walking Safaris and Luxury Tented Camps.

For a brochure or to discuss your holiday please contact us on **0181 672 1234** or world@scottdunn.com

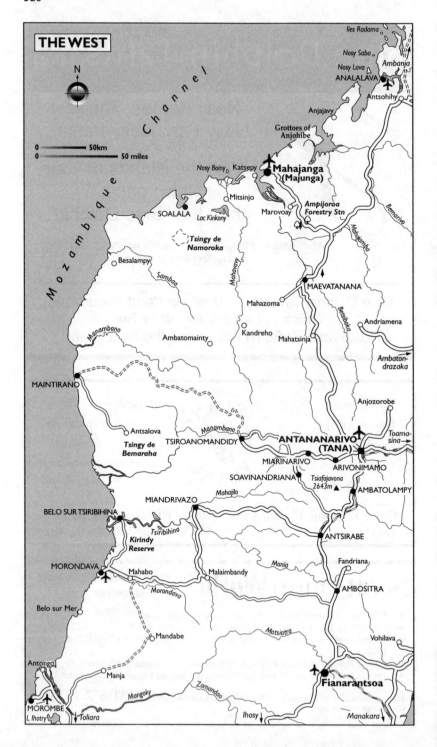

THE WEST

N

Iles Radama

Nosy Saba

Nosy Lava

Ambanja

ANALALAVA

Antsohihy

Anjajavy

Mozambique Channel

0 ——— 50km
0 ——— 50 miles

Grottoes of
Anjohibe

Nosy Boiny   Katsepy

**Mahajanga
(Majunga)**

Mitsinjo

SOALALA

Lac Kinkony

Marovoay

*Ampijoroa
Forestry Stn*

Bemarivo

*Tsingy de
Namoroka*

Besalampy

Sambao

Mahavavy

MAEVATANANA

Mahazoma

Mahagamba

Manambano

Mahazoma

Andriamena

Ambatomainty

Kandreho

Mahatsinja

Besiboka

*Ambaton-
drazaka*

MAINTIRANO

Antsalova

Manambano

TSIROANOMANDIDY

Anjozorobe

**ANTANANARIVO
(TANA)**

Toama-
sina

*Tsingy de
Bemaraha*

MIARINARIVO

ARIVONIMAMO

SOAVINANDRIANA

*Tsiafajavona
2643m* ▲

AMBATOLAMPY

MIANDRIVAZO

Mahajilo

BELO SUR TSIRIBIHINA

Tsiribihina

ANTSIRABE

*Kirindy
Reserve*

Mania

Fandriana

MORONDAVA

Mahabo

Malaimbandy

Morondava

AMBOSITRA

Belo sur Mer

Vohilava

Mandabe

Matsiatra

Antongo

Manja

Mangoky

Zomandao

FIANARANTSOA

MOROMBE

L Ihotry   ↓ Toliara

Ihosy ↓

Manakara

The West

OVERVIEW

The west of Madagascar offers a dry climate, deciduous forest (with two excellent reserves to protect it), endless sandy beaches with little danger from sharks – although the sea can be very rough – and fewer tourists than many parts of the country. The lack of roads is one of its attractions; this is the ideal area for mountain bikers or walkers. Adventurous travellers will have no trouble finding a warm welcome in untouristed villages, their own deserted beach and some spectacular landscapes.

This is the region to see one of Madagascar's extraordinary natural wonders: the *tsingy*. Pronounced 'zing' this is exactly the sound made when one of the limestone pinnacles is struck by a small stone (they can be played like a xylophone!). Limestone karst is not unique to Madagascar, but it is rare to see such dramatic forms, such an impenetrable forest of spikes and spires. The endemic succulents that struggle for a foothold in this waterless environment add to the unworldly feeling of a *tsingy* landscape.

Opposite major rivers the sea water along the west coast is a brick red colour: 'like swimming in soup', as one traveller put it. This is the laterite washed into the rivers from the eroded hillsides of the highlands and discharged into the sea: Madagascar's bleeding wounds.

History

The west is the home of the Sakalava people. For a while in Malagasy history this was the largest and most powerful tribe, ruled by their own kings and queens. The Sakalava kingdom was founded by the Volamena branch of the Maroserana dynasty which emerged in the southwest during the 16th century. Early in the 17th century a Volamena prince, Andriamisara, reached the Sakalava river and gave its name to his new kingdom. His son, Andriandahifotsy (which means 'white man'), succeeded him around 1650 and, with the aid of firearms acquired from European traders, conquered the southwestern area between the two rivers, Onilahy and Manambolo. This region became known as the Menabe. Later kings conquered first the Boina, the area from the Manambolo to north of present-day Mahajanga, and then the northwest coast as far as Antsiranana.

By the 18th century the Sakalava empire occupied a huge area in the west, but was divided into the Menabe in the south and the Boina in the north. The two rulers fell out, unity was abandoned, and in the 19th century the area came under the control of the Merina. The Sakalava did not take kindly to domination and sporadic guerrilla warfare continued in the Menabe area until French colonial times.

The Sakalava kingdom bore the brunt of the first serious efforts by the French to colonise the island. For some years France had laid claims (based on treaties made with local princes) on parts of the north and northwest, and in 1883 two fortresses in this region were bombarded. An attack on Mahajanga followed. This was the beginning of the end of Madagascar as an independent kingdom.

The Sakalava people today

The modern Sakalava have relatively dark skins. The west of Madagascar received a number of African immigrants from across the Mozambique Channel and their influence shows not only in the racial characteristics of the people, but also in their language and customs. There are a number of Bantu words in their dialect, and their belief in *tromba* (possession by spirits) and *dady* (royal relics cult) is of African origin.

The Sakalava do not practise second burial. The quality of their funerary art (in one small area) rivals that of the Mahafaly: birds and naked figures are a feature of Sakalava tombs, the latter frequently in erotic positions. Concepts of sexuality and rebirth are implied here. The female figures are often disproportionately large, perhaps recognising the importance of women in the Sakalava culture.

Sakalava royalty do not require an elaborate tomb since kings are considered to continue their spiritual existence through a medium with healing powers, and in royal relics.

Getting around

Roads are being improved, but driving from town to town in the west can still be challenging and in much of the area the roads simply aren't there. There are regular flights to the large towns and a Twin Otter serves many of the smaller ones.

MAHAJANGA (MAJUNGA)
History

Ideally located for trade with East Africa, Arabia and western Asia, Mahajanga has been a major commercial port since 1745, when the Boina capital was moved here from Marovoay. One ruler of the Boina was Queen Ravahiny, a very able monarch who maintained the unity of the Boina which was threatened by rebellions in both the north and the south. It was Mahajanga which provided her with her imported riches and caught the admiration of visiting foreigners. Madagascar was at that time a major supplier of slaves to Arab traders and in return received jewels and rich fabrics. Indian merchants were active then, as today, with a variety of exotic goods. Some of these traders from the east stayed on, the Indians remaining a separate community and running small businesses. More Indians arrived during colonial times.

In the 1883–85 war Mahajanga was occupied by the French. In 1895 it served as the base for the military expedition to Antananarivo which established a French Protectorate. Shortly thereafter the French set about enlarging Mahajanga and reclaiming swampland from the Bombetoka river delta. Much of today's extensive town is on reclaimed land.

Mahajanga today

A hot but breezy town with a large Indian population and enough interesting excursions to make a visit of a few days well worthwhile. 'I loved this town. Very different from the east coast. Nothing is open before 07.00 and people save their energy for strolling around town until late.' (F Kerridge)

The town has two 'centres', the town hall (Hotel de Ville) and statue of Tsiranana (the commercial centre), and the streets near the famous baobab tree. Some offices, including Air Madagascar, are here. It is quite a long walk between the two – take a pousse-pousse, of which there are many. There are also some smart new buses, and taxis which operate on a fixed tariff.

KING RADAMA II

The son of the 'Wicked Queen' Ranavalona, King Radama II was a gentle ruler who abhorred bloodshed. He was pro-European, interested in Christianity (although never formally a Christian) and a friend of William Ellis, missionary and chronicler of 19th-century Madagascar. After Radama's death, Ellis wrote: 'I have never said that Radama was an able ruler, or a man of large views, for these he was not; but a more humane ruler never wore a crown.' With missionaries of all denominations invited back into Madagascar, intense rivalry sprang up between the Protestants sent by Britain, and the Jesuits who arrived from France. Resentment at the influence of these foreigners over the young king and disgust at the often rash changes he instigated boiled over in 1863, and only eight months after his coronation he was assassinated, strangled with a silken sash so that the *fady* against shedding royal blood was not infringed.

The French-British rivalry was fuelled by the violent death of the king, even to the extent that Ellis was accused of being party to the assassination. But was Radama really dead? Both Ellis and Jean Laborde believed that he had survived the strangling and had been allowed to escape by the courtiers bearing him to the countryside for burial. Uprisings, supposedly organised by the 'dead' king, supported this rumour. In a biography of King Radama II, the French historian Raymond Delval makes a strong case that the ex-monarch eventually retreated to the area of Lake Kinkony and lived out the rest of his life in this Sakalava region.

A wide boulevard follows the sea along the west part of town, terminating by a lighthouse. At its elbow is the **Mahajanga baobab**, said to be at least 700 years old with a circumference of 14 metres.

The telephone area code is 62.

Getting there and away
By air
There is a service from Tana to Mahajanga on Tuesdays, Wednesdays, Fridays and Saturdays, with back-up flights by Twin Otter.

The airport is near the village of Amborovy; 6km northeast of the town. A taxi should cost 15,000Fmg but taxi-brousses pass close to the airport.

By road
Mahajanga is 560km from Tana by fairly good road. Taxi-brousses leave the Gare du Nord in Tana in the early afternoon, arriving in Mahajanga the following morning – a 15 to 18-hour journey. MAMI is recommended: 40,000Fmg for a comfortable minibus. It's a lovely trip (at least until it gets dark) taking you through typical Hauts Plateaux landscape of craggy, grassy hills, rice paddies, and characteristic Merina houses with steep eaves supported by thin brick or wood pillars. 'Try to be awake for crossing the Betsiboka: a huge red river with big rocks tossed about. Concentrate on the scenery, not the strength of the bridge supports.' (F Kerridge).

The taxi-brousse station in Mahajanga is on Avenue Philbert Tsiranana.

By sea
The *M/S Sam-Son* is a motor vessel belonging to the JAG Group, which owns several hotels in this part of Madagascar, running from Mahajanga to the Comoro

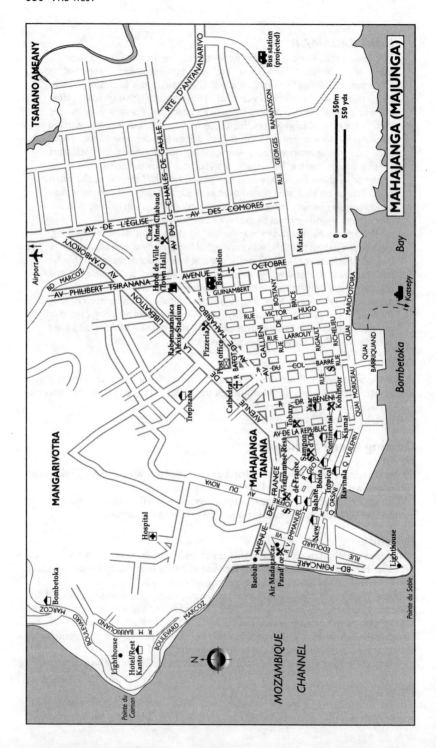

MAHAJANGA (MAJUNGA)

Islands. Prices: Mahajanga–Mayotte 450Ff per person (economy), 640Ff (first class). Mahajanga–Anjouan–Moroni 515Ff (economy), 700Ff (first class). Rates include all meals and non-alcoholic drinks.

A very different sea experience is provided by the cargo boat to Nosy Be (see page 306).

Where to stay
Category A
Le Tropicana This incorporates the Hotel Gatinière and the Restaurant Oasis; tel: 220 69. This fine hotel-restaurant is up the hill from the Don Bosco school behind the cathedral, in a 1930s French colonial house. Ten rooms, hot water, swimming pool, excursions to the Anjohibe caves etc. French and Malagasy cuisine. 'The dining is superb. Even on an oppressively hot day you can escape from the dust of urban Mahajanga and sit on the terrace with friends over lunch... telling stories of exotic places and pretending you are Joseph Conrad.' (Mark Ward)

Kanto Hotel Tel: 229 78. Overlooking the sea about 2km north of the town. A variety of rooms are available at a range of prices. Good food. There's an annexe near the central market: corner of Av de la République and Rue Henri Palu. Good value.

New Hotel Rue Henri Palu; tel: 221 10; fax: 293 91. For a while this was the best hotel in town, but recent reports suggest that it may have deteriorated. At its best it has clean, air-conditioned rooms with bathrooms en suite, hot and cold running water, and a very good restaurant.

Hotel de France Rue Maréchal Joffre. BP 45; tel: 237 81. Newly renovated with swimming pool.

Zaha Motel Tel: 223 24. At Amborovy beach (not far from the airport, and 8km from Mahajanga). A cool alternative to staying in Mahajanga. Rooms 78,000–138,000Fmg, depending on the season, and bungalows 143,000–253,000Fmg. Nice beach with blue, not red, sea.

Category B
Hotel Bomhetoka (Les Roches Rouges) Bd Marcoz; tel: 238 71. Near the beach 2km from the town. A rather sterile big hotel, with air conditioning. Rooms 75,000–100,000Fmg. Tours organised.

Hotel de la Plage Chez Karon BP 149 tel: 226 94. A beach hotel 2km from the town centre, with some air-conditioned rooms. Organises tours for hunting groups (Mahajanga is Madagascar's centre for duck shooting).

Boina Beach Bd La Corniche, opposite Les Roches Rouges; tel: 238 09. Nine air-conditioned rooms but said to be badly built and noisy.

New Continental Av de la République; tel: 225 70. Town centre hotel, with 15 air-conditioned rooms priced up to 100,000Fmg. Indian-owned, well run.

Hotel Kizmat Av de la République. Air-conditioned rooms at about 90,000Fmg. The restaurant is recommended for its good curry and samosas. It is Muslim, so no alcohol. Take-away food is sold here, too.

Hotel Voanio Tel: 238 78. In a quiet part of town; clean and friendly.

Hotel Ravinala Quai Orsini; tel: 229 68. About 85,000Fmg with shared bathroom. 'No atmosphere but a reasonable restaurant.'

Patel Hotel On the road to the airport. 50,000–75,000Fmg.

Category C
Hotel Tropic 22 Rue Flacourt (near the port); tel: 236 10. Eight rooms, the most basic have en-suite cold shower and shared WC. Clean and comfortable; 35,000–75,000Fmg.

Hotel Boina Tel: 224 69. About 60,000Fmg with shower.

Yaar Hotel Tel: 230 12. Near the New Hotel. About 35,000Fmg.
Hotel des Voyageurs Tel: 231 90. A basic hotel near the market.
Chez Chabaud (see Katsepy – *Where to stay and eat*) Tel: 233 27. Mme Chabaud's daughter runs a basic hotel near the Hotel de Ville. Rooms 30,000–50,000Fmg. The restaurant opposite is run by another daughter, Christiane. All the family speak English.

Where to eat

'Specialities include chapatis (*pakopako*), coconut sweetmeats, and *khimo* (minced meat in gravy with chili, lime and bread (not rice) as well as delicious yoghurt, milkshakes, ice-cream and fruit juice. There are milkshake bars everywhere!' (F Kerridge)

Vietnamese restaurant Name unknown (but possibly Chez Thilan Doan Van Bien, on Av P Tsiranana); near the post office, with very good food and friendly staff.
Kohinoor Restaurant Indian restaurant with good food and kitsch decor. One of the few places to do a vegetarian dish of the day.
Pizza restaurant On Av de Mahabibo. 'Strange, but good pizzas...'
Pakiza Av de la République, near the New Continental. Name may be missing but easy to recognise: 'Zebu heads and horns sticking out everywhere.' A great variety of ice-creams and milk shakes, also good for breakfast. Terrific tamarind juice.
Bar Tabany A popular meeting place in the west part of town, near the market.
Salon de Thé Saify Near the post office and cathedral. A perennial favourite for breakfast and snacks.
Parad'Ice Next to the Air Madagascar office off Bd Poincaré. 'The best ice-cream in Madagascar – The passionfruit ice-cream is out of this world!'

Maps

The Librairie de Madagascar (on Avenues de Mahabido and Gallieni) reportedly has a good selection of maps including the FTM one of the Mahajanga region.

Sightseeing and excursions
Recommended driver

Ibrahim Soumalla; tel: 230 12 (home); 220 35 (office). 1999 rates: Ampijoroa 200,000Fmg; Cirque Rouge 20,000Fmg; Marovoay 50,000Fmg.

Tour operator

The most reliable tour operator is probably the **Hotel Bomhetoka** (formerly Hotel les Roches Rouges).

Sightseeing in and around town
Museum

Mozea Akiba is situated about 2km from the centre of town, near the Plage Touristique (take a pousse-pousse or taxi). The rewarding result of cooperation between the universities of Mahajanga and Gotland, Sweden, it has a display showing the history of the region, as well as an exhibition of paleontology and ethnology, and photos and descriptions of some of Mahajanga's tourist sights such as the Cirque Rouge and Grottes d'Anjohibe. Signs are in English and French. Hours: 09.00–11.00, 15.00–17.00.

Fort Rova

This impressive fort was built on the highest point in Mahajanga in 1824 by King Radama I. The entrance has now been restored, and it is worth a visit for the views and sense of history. The fort is reached via Rue du Maréchal Joffre.

Day excursions
Cirque Rouge
About 12km from Mahajanga and 2km from the airport (as the crow flies). This is a canyon ending in an amphitheatre of red, beige and lilac-coloured rock eroded into strange shapes – peaks, spires and castles. The canyon has a broad, sandy bottom decorated with chunks of lilac-coloured clay. It is a beautiful and dramatic spot and, with its stream of fresh water running to the nearby beach, makes an idyllic camping place.

As a day trip a taxi will take you from Mahajanga and back, but make sure the driver knows the way: there are no signposts. A cheaper alternative is to take a taxi-brousse from the street west of Chez Chabaud (opposite the BTM bank). This will take you to the intersection of the Zaha Motel and airport, from where you can walk the final 6km. Give yourself at least one hour to look around. Late afternoon is best, when the sun sets the reds and mauves alight.

Katsepy
Katsepy (pronounced 'Katsep') is a tiny fishing village across the bay from Mahajanga which is reached in 45 minutes by ferry. The *Bac Baobab* runs twice a day: 07.30 (08.30 Sundays and holidays) and 15.30, returning an hour later (so the last ferry back is 16.30). The trip takes just under an hour.

Where to stay/eat
Until recently there was only one reason to go to Katsepy: to dine **Chez Chabaud**. Madame Chabaud trained as a cook in Nice and has been practising her craft for longer, I guess, than any other hotelier in Madagascar. I still go weak at the knees remembering my meal there in 1984 and until this year had not had a bad report of the place. Most visitors still praise the food and service.

Chez Chabaud is signposted. There are ten simple bungalows, with mosquito nets, shower and WC, and three meals a day. It's best to make a reservation in advance through Madame Chabaud's daughter in Mahajanga.

If you visit for the day and don't want to splash out on a major meal, there are a few *hotelys* near the landing stage which serve good meals using coconut as a main ingredient.

What to do
The animal highlight of Katsepy used to be the troop of extremely rare crowned sifaka in the garden of Madame Chabaud, but they have disappeared: reportedly killed and eaten by the local people. From every point of view this is a major tragedy, and a wasted opportunity for profitable ecotourism. However, you can still see Decken's sifaka in Katsepy. 'They hang around a white house, a couple of kilometres walk along the beach, past the boat builders. Keep asking for "*trano fotsy*" (white house). The guardian will show you the lemurs but it's best to stay the night so you can visit early morning or evening (the sifaka retreat into the forest during the hot hours and the guardian heads for Mahajanga).'

Don't try to sleep on the beach – robberies are common.

FURTHER AFIELD
Nosy Boiny (Nosy Antsoheribory)
This is a small island, about a kilometre long, in Boina Bay, with some fascinating ruins of an Arab settlement established around 1580 after a Portuguese raid on the mainland. The settlement thrived until 1750, when the Sakalava conquered the area. In its heyday the town, known as Masselage, probably supported a population of

about 7,000. The ruins include several cemeteries, houses and mosques. 'The surface of the island is scattered with pottery. There are also many baobabs.' (Dan Carlsson)

To reach the island start from Katsepy and continue by road to the village of Boeny-Ampasy on the west side of the bay. There are some bungalows here. A 1½-hour boat journey brings you to Nosy Boiny. Patrice Kerloc, tel: 236 62 (address: BP 376, Mahajanga), can arrange trips here and to the Grottes de Anjohibe.

Anjohibe caves

The Grottes de Anjohibe are 82km northeast of Mahajanga and accessible only by 4WD vehicle, and then only in the dry season. There are two places to visit, the caves themselves and a natural swimming pool above a waterfall. The caves are full of stalactites and stalagmites (and bats), and have 2km of passages.

To reach the caves turn left at the village of Antanamarina, from where it is another 5km. Then, to cool off, return to the village and take the road straight ahead to the waterfall and pools. There is a troop of sifaka here, and natural pools both above and below the waterfall. To add to the excitement there may be crocodiles in the lower pool.

Dan Carlsson of Project Madagascar (Sweden) excavated these caves in 1996. 'It seems as though the caves have been used for normal living but also as a place of sacrifice. We found...pottery with ash, charcoal and animal bones... also several hippopotamus bones believed to be some million years old.'

The best person to organise a tour here is probably Patrice Kerloc (see above). He can also arrange trips to Nosy Boiny.

Anjajavy

About 140km north of Mahajanga are some of the most impressive mangrove forests to be found in Madagascar. There are also a number of peculiar rock formations set among the trees. Although not true *tsingy*, they are nevertheless quite spectacular, the remarkably eroded rocks towering above the forest canopy.

The Anjajavy beach itself is exquisite, with coconut palms, white sand and incredibly blue water – surely one of the most attractive places along the Malagasy coastline. Perhaps the strangest thing about this beautiful place is that the beach has not only palm trees but also baobabs and very dense deciduous forest, as well as several more very odd rock outcrops.

Anjajavy also has its own airstrip, which can handle aircraft carrying between six and ten people.

A new lodge is being built at Anjajavy. For details contact the owners, Groupe l'Hôtel in Tana; tel: (22) 285 14; fax: (22) 285 15; email: Groupe.Hotel@ simicro.mg. This consortium specialises in luxury fly-in island lodges, so their Anjajavy hotel is likely to be pricey but wonderful. Formerly this was Jackie's Lodge, but in 1998 Jackie sold out and moved his hotel, piece by piece, to a new site 40km to the south. To check on his progress contact Jackie Cauvin, Villa Talio, La Corniche, Mahajanga; tel: (261) 20 62 23 279; fax: (261) 20 62 29 365.

AMPIJOROA FORESTRY STATION

This is part of the Réserve Naturelle Intégrale d'Ankarafantsika. Ampijoroa (pronounced Ampijeroo) is one of the few areas of protected western vegetation. Its administration is shared by ANGAP, Conservation International and the Direction des Eaux et Forêts, with funding from the German organisation KfW.

This is a super reserve. It is easy to get to, thrilling to visit with an abundance of wildlife of all kinds, and with many clear, level paths which make hiking a pleasure.

Ampijoroa straddles RN4 from Mahajanga. The main part of the reserve is on the southern side of the road (on your right coming from Mahajanga), with Lac Ravelobe to the north.

Getting there/staying there

The reserve is 120km from Mahajanga; it takes a little over two hours to make the journey by car. There is no accommodation in Ampijoroa, so if you don't want to camp you will need to make this a day trip and organise private transport, leaving before dawn to catch the best wildlife viewing (remember that all animals are less active in the heat of the day). If you are in a private car it is worth stopping at Lac Amboromalandy, a reservoir on the way from Mahajanga, which is an excellent place to see waterfowl.

Taxi-brousses also leave town early in the morning heading for Tana, so this is a much cheaper option.

Coming from Tana it is easy to miss Ampijoroa, so look out for Andranofasika. This little town lies on a T-junction; you will recognise it by the triangle of grass with blue-painted concrete benches and map of Madagascar. Ampijoroa is 4km further on.

If at all possible you should camp at the reserve (with your own tent). It costs 20,000Fmg per night for basic facilities: a well for drinking water and a pit latrine. To be on the safe side bring your own food, but usually Rabe, the warden, or his wife will cook a very good and inexpensive meal for you. There is also a tiny 'shop' with a freezer, so you can buy cold beers and other basic necessities.

In the local village you can buy pickled mango but that's about all (in 1999). You must walk to Andranofasika to replenish your supplies.

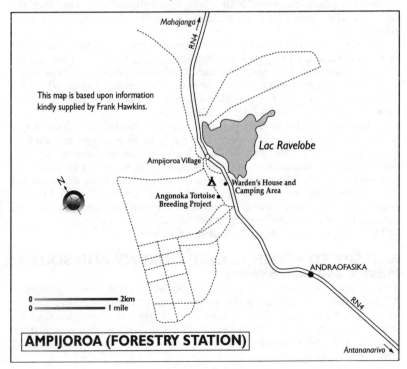

This map is based upon information kindly supplied by Frank Hawkins.

Mahajanga

Lac Ravelobe

Ampijoroa Village

Warden's House and Camping Area

Angonoka Tortoise Breeding Project

ANDRAOFASIKA

0 —— 2km
0 —— 1 mile

AMPIJOROA (FORESTRY STATION)

Antananarivo

Permits and guides

Unlike other reserves, permits for Ampijoroa (20,000Fmg) must be obtained from the Direction des Eaux et Forêts in Mahajanga (near the Ravinala Hotel) or in Tana, though you should also be able to get them at the reserve.

The four guides employed by Conservation International are all enthusiastic and very knowledgable. Their names are Jacky, Charles, Olivier, and Izo. When you arrive a guide 'bags' you and remains with you for your stay. You are not allowed into the forest unaccompanied, but the lake circuit can be done without a guide. There is a standard charge: day walk: 25,000Fmg; night walk 40,000Fmg.

Flora and fauna of Ampijoroa

This is typical dry, deciduous forest with sparse understorey and lots of lianas. In the dry winter season many of the trees have shed their leaves, but in the wet months the forest is a sea of bright greens.

Wildlife viewing in Ampijoroa starts as soon as you arrive. Right beside the warden's house is a tree that Coquerel's sifaka use as a dormitory. They are extremely handsome animals with the usual silky white fur but with chestnut-brown arms and thighs. You should also be greeted ecstatically by a brown lemur which was formerly a pet and hasn't integrated into a troop. It clearly prefers humans and loves a bit of mutual grooming.

On your walks you may also see mongoose lemur, woolly lemur and the sportive lemur if the guide shows you its tree. This is the only place in in the world where you might see the recently discovered (1998) golden-brown mouse lemur, *Microcebus ravelobensis*, named after Ampijoroa's Lake Ravelobe. There are always lots of reptiles, and this is a birder's paradise. 'Within minutes we found sicklebill, Chabert's and hook-billed vangas all nesting round the campsite... and then the highlight: white-breasted mesites which walk just like clockwork toys.' (Derek Schuurman).

After seeing the main reserve you should cross the road to the lake. A path runs right round the lake (7¹/₂km) providing excellent birding; lots of waterfowl and the very rare Madagascar fish eagle. 'The lake, Ravelobe, is sacred. Each New Year's day a zebu is slaughtered at the rudimentary wooden "shrine" you can see on the left side of the lake in the forest, and its blood poured into the water for the crocs, themselves considered sacred.' (Derek Schuurman)

Ampijoroa is also home to the Angonoka Tortoise Programme. This is one of Madagascar's most successful projects: Don Reid, the herpetologist employed by the Durrell Wildlife Conservation Trust, has been able to return to England, confident that the conservation work he initiated will be continued by Mamy, the Jersey-trained head of the project. After many years of research and much trial and error, the ploughshare tortoise – the world's rarest tortoise – is now breeding readily and trials are under way to reintroduce it to its original habitat. Equally rare, the attractive little flat-tailed tortoise (*kapidolo*) is also being bred here.

The latest project is to breed the freshwater terrapin.

KATSEPY TO MITSINJO, LAKE KINKONY AND SOUTH

Mitsinjo and Lake Kinkony

Taxi-brousses sometimes meet the ferry at Katsepy for the onward journey to **Mitsinjo** (and vehicles taking the ferry are almost certainly bound for that town). The journey takes about three hours. 'Mitsinjo is a lovely town with a wide main street, trees with semi-tame Decken's sifakas, a general store that has a few rooms available, and Hotely Salama which serves wonderful food and cold beer!' (Petra Jenkins)

Not far from Mitsinjo is **Lac Kinkony** (a protected area). Petra reports: 'About once a week in the dry season the fishermen of Lac Kinkony do a supply run to Mitsinjo and you may be able to get a lift. The lake is wonderful. It boasts fish eagles, flamingoes, sacred ibis ... need I say more? It is free from bilharzia but the northeast end is a bit silty for swimming. Cadge a lift by pirogue and you've got paradise! Crocodiles are friendly and don't bother swimmers (!).'

John Kupiec enjoyed a pirogue and walking trip with Patrick, the English-speaking son of the owner of Hotely Salama. They stayed away for five days and saw plenty of wildlife as well as the lovely lakeside scenery. On the southern part of the lake is the little village of **Antseza** which has a Thursday market where you may be able to reprovision if you are camping. In the lake is a small island, Mandrave. The legend is that this island rose up in the lake after the boats of the invading Merina had been sunk by the Sakalava. It is a sacred island with many *fady*:

MAHAVAVY RIVER RAFTING
Conrad Hirsh
In May/June 1998, I organised and led a first-time rafting trip down the Mahavavy du Sud, from Kandreho to Mitsinjo, an area that turned out to be extremely rich in both lemurs and birds, with large expanses of beautiful forest. Although the trip was not a scientific expedition, our team did include four experienced observers of wildlife: naturalist guide Gerard Ravoajanahary of Madagascar Airtours, the well-known rhino conservationist Anna Merz, and keen birdwatcher Joe Allie. Here is a brief summary of our observations, plus some remarks on the logistics of doing the Mahavavy.

Lemurs In general, the lemur-viewing on this trip was far superior to what I have experienced on the other rivers I know in western Madagascar (Manambolo, Tsiribihina, Mangoky) or in the protected areas I have visited (Périnet, Montagne d'Ambre, Ranomafana, Berenty, Ankarana, Kirindy, Beroboka, Isalo). Yes, you can find more different species in an area like Ranomafana, but for sheer numbers, proximity, and ease of viewing, the Mahavavy was superb, mainly for the two subspecies of Verreaux's sifaka (*deckeni* and *coronatus*) and *Eulemur fulvus rufus*. The outstanding areas for these species were around the Kasijy forest and the riverine tamarind gallery forest between Bekipay and Ambinany.

To give some ideas of densities in both the Kasijy area and also the forest between Bekipay and Ambinany, I can say that a short foray into the forest, moving maybe 2–300 metres, staying one hour, would produce five to six families of sifaka, which were remarkably unconcerned by our presence.

Red-fronted brown lemurs were very numerous, especially in Kasijy.

Birds The Mahavavy is very rich in birds, compared with the other rivers I know in western Madagascar. The most exciting sightings of the trip were of Madagascar fish eagles (a total of six).

Many herons and egrets were seen and Humbolt's and grey herons were seen together in an extensive heronry – tall trees on both sides of the river. For more information write to Conrad Hirsh, Remote River Expeditions, Box 59622, Nairobi, Kenya; fax: 254 2 891 307; email: conrad@swiftkenya.com.

you may not wear gold jewellery on the lake and if you have gold teeth you must not speak while on the lake! No-one can live on the island, nor urinate there, nor approach too close to the sacred tamarind tree that grows there (although prayers may be offered to it). A Sakalava king is buried beneath the tree.

An alternative 'hard way' of getting to Mitsinjo is via the River Mahavavy with the specialist river-runner, Conrad Hirsh. See box, page 337.

Soalala and beyond

From Mitsinjo you may be able to make your way to Soalala although there is no longer any road transport there. You may be able to catch a motor vedette from Mahajanga. These go (irregularly) to Soalala to collect prawns, crabs and fish. There is no hotel in Soalala, but you can camp on the beach and the local *hotely* serves nice meals.

There is an air service (Twin Otter, once a week) out of Soalala, or you can go on to Besalampy (which is no longer served by Air Mad). Then you can continue to make your way down the coast, taking cars, pirogues or whatever transport presents itself. This route is only practical in the dry season and for rugged and self-sufficient travellers. You can fly out of Tambohorano and Maintirano (and other towns – check the Air Mad timetable). Good luck!

THE ROUTE SOUTH FROM MAHAJANGA
Marovoay

This is the first town of any importance after Mahajanga on RN4 (8,000Fmg by taxi-brousse). Formerly the residence of the Boina kings, the town's name means 'many crocodiles'. When the French attacked the Malagasy forces assembled in Marovoay in 1895, in their successful drive to conquer Madagascar, it is reported that hundreds of crocodiles emerged from the river to devour the dead and dying. Malagasy hunters have since got their revenge, and you would be lucky to see a croc these days. Or a tourist. I've never heard of anyone stopping here... which gives the place a certain appeal!

From Marovoay to Antsohihy

After Marovoay you pass through the reserve of **Ampijoroa** (see page 334) to meet RN6, the road to Antsiranana. Heading north you can spend the night at **Mampikony**. The Hotel Les Cocotiers is adequate. **Port Bergé** (Boriziny) is a pleasant town with at least two hotels, the Zinnia and Le Monde.

The road improves after Port Bergé and is quite good to Antsohihy.

Antsohihy

Pronounced 'Antsooee', this town is a good centre for exploration; there is a Solima petrol station here so you can be sure of finding transport. Like many towns in Madagascar it is built on two levels. 'Warm, friendly people, music playing around every corner. Visit the market, the port, and just wander about!' (A Stockton)

Where to stay/eat

Hotel Blaina (Air Mad office) New, thatched bungalows with en-suite bathrooms, 30,000Fmg. Good restaurant. Recommended.

There are several other hotels: **Hotel Tsara Talio**, near the port, basic but very cheap; **Hotel de France**, **Hotel Diego**, near the taxi-brousse station, **Hotel La Plaisance** and **Hotel Central** in the Upper Town.

Getting there and away

A taxi-brousse to/from Mahajanga takes about 15 hours. You can reach Ambanja in ten hours. There are also Twin Otter flights between Antsohihy and Ambanja.

Excursions from Antsohihy

Antsohihy is situated on a fjord-like arm of the sea which becomes the River Loza. There is a regular boat service to Ananalava, an isolated village accessible in the dry season by taxi-brousse but otherwise only by boat or plane (Twin Otter). The Paradise Hotel is inexpensive, and the owner of the *épicerie* across the road from the Paradise has a few rooms to let.

'I loved the maze of paths on both sides of the village. There is a *fady* in effect on one stretch of the river. At one time this area was ruled by a queen and many trees may not be cut down and there are other taboos. In the boat everyone removed their hats when we passed. There is still a powerful queen in the area who occasionally grants an audience. In her presence you must ask your question to the guard who repeats it to the queen. Her answer is made the same way.' (J Kupiec)

Nosy Saba

From Ananalava you may be lucky enough to find a sturdy boat to take you to this almost perfect island for a few days. I have been here twice and doubt if any island comes closer to paradise. There is fresh water, a few fishermen's huts (abandoned in the rainy season), coconut palms, curving coves of yellow sand, a densely forested section with clouds of fruit-bats, coral, chameleons...

If arriving by yacht, the anchorage south of the eastern tip gives good shelter from the north to northwest winds. Anchor 100m off the beach over a sand shelf 1.5–4m deep over sand and tough seaweeds. The edge of the shelf drops off steeply. Close to the shore are shallow coral patches. But further out, watch the strong tidal currents, the northwest-flowing ebb making a rolling swell. The water is very clear and a remarkable number of large game fish can be seen even when snorkelling along the island's edge southwest of the anchorage. The coral is excellent, and rewarding scuba-diving can be had along the drop-off.

Nosy Lava

The large island of Nosy Lava (Long Island) lies temptingly off Ananalava. *Don't go there!* Why not? It's Madagascar's Devil's Island, a maximum security prison housing the country's most vicious murderers. By all accounts the prisoners lead pretty enjoyable lives: women from nearby Ananalava are said to cross over by pirogue to fraternise with the prisoners. They've also been provided with electricity and other mod cons not available to ordinary folk. One Malagasy informant commented that 'Nosy Lava is more like a holiday camp than a prison'. Nosy Lava had a brief moment in the international spotlight in 1993 when two notorious convicts boarded the yacht *Magic Carpet* and murdered its South African/German occupants.

From Antsohihy into the interior

Two roads run from Antsohihy in an easterly direction into the lush and mountainous interior: a lovely area for the adventurous to explore.

A tarred road runs southeast to Mandritsara, a small town set in beautiful mountainous scenery. Taxi-brousses leave every morning, passing through Befandriana Nord where there is a hotel, the **Rose de Chine**.

Mandritsara

The name means 'peaceful' (literally 'lies down well'), and was reportedly bestowed on it by King Radama I during his campaigns. There are several hotels here including **Hotel Pattes**, a nice little place with excellent food.

Mandritsara is linked with the outside world by Twin Otter.

Bealanana

An alternative (paved) road from Antsohihy runs northeast to Bealanana, 'a muddy, scruffy highland town with friendly people'. The town is quite high, and the temperate climate with ample rainfall allows the cultivation of potatoes and a great variety of fruit.

Hotel Ramagasy is family-run and friendly; basic rooms 20,000Fmg. **Hotel La Crête** has double rooms with basin and shower (but probably cold water). Good food.

The hotels will arrange for a taxi-brousse to pick you up for the return trip (four hours) to Antsohihy or Abatoriha. The road is good; the vehicles are not.

MAINTIRANO AND REGION

Maintirano, a small port due west of Tana, has been somewhat out on a limb, with very few foreign visitors. Bishop Brock, the indefatigable cyclist, provided most of the following information in 1996.

The road from Tsiroanomandidy to Maintirano

'I cycled from Tana to Maintirano, thence to Morondava, a distance of about 1,100km, of which only about 250km were tarred. The ride from Tsiroanomandidy to Maintirano is a difficult trek through a rugged, arid wilderness, that requires a large degree of self-sufficiency. Although there is ample water, it's not always conveniently located and at times I carried up to eight litres. There is no formal accommodation, and only one shop and *hotely* in Ambaravaranala, Beravina and Morafenobe. I camped in the bush, stayed in villages and with a family in Morafenobe. Crossing the Bangolava between Ambaravaranala and Beravina was difficult, and crossing the northern tip of the Plateau du Bemaraha east of Maintirano was brutal riding. The scenery was magnificent and varied, however, at times being so wide open that the sense of isolation was almost overwhelming. It took me eight days to cover this 438km.'

This road is also travelled by camions and 4WD taxi-brousses. Bishop recommends that you look for a vehicle in Tsiroanomandidy, rather than Tana. The journey should take two to three days. 'It is a potentially dangerous trip. Crossing the Bemaraha Plateau I came upon a Land Rover which had overturned, spilling all the fuel, and that was before the really difficult part!'

Maintirano

This small western port is attractive for people who want to get off the beaten track. Nothing much happens here. Bishop points out that although it appears to be a seaside town on the map, 'it's as though the town has turned its back on the sea: virtually nothing in Maintirano overlooks the ocean.' However, he found it one of the friendliest towns in Madagascar (no doubt its isolation has something to do with this). 'I was constantly entertained by local families (and the Catholic missionaries) and one man insisted that I take all my meals with his family during my stay there.'

The best hotel is the **Laizama**, which has rooms for 25,000Fmg.

Maintirano is one of the places served by Air Mad (Twin Otter) on its Tana–Mahajanga run, so there is an alternative to the overland journey. You can also float down the Mambolo River (see page 342).

The telephone area code is 69.

FROM MAINTIRANO TO MORONDAVA

Continuing by bicycle, Bishop Brock writes: 'This is somewhat easier than the Tsiroanomandidy to Maintirano stretch, and there are major towns/villages every day or two. Some self-sufficiency is still required, though, and water was a problem south of Bekopaka (all the rivers were dry; I had to get water from village wells). Although this route gives free access to the Tsingy de Bemaraha, in my opinion it is not a very interesting bike ride.'

Again, there is an alternative to cycling this route: 'The road is currently being served by a 6WD taxi-brousse that passes each way about once a week.'

Tsingy de Bemaraha National Park

Formerly the Réserve Naturelle Intégrale du Tsingy de Bemaraha, the reserve was regazetted as a national park in October 1998. It lies south of Maintirano, just to the north of the River Manambolo, and is one of Madagascar's largest protected areas at 152,000ha.

The main point of access is at Bekopaka on the north bank of the Manambolo river. Here is the main park entrance and from it lead a network of newly constructed paths and walkways through the best areas at the reserve's southern extremity. Some of the paths take you through and up on to the *tsingy*, where boardwalks have been constructed for safer access. However, some of the terrain is still tough going and is really only suitable for those who are reasonably fit (and thin – there are some tight squeezes through gaps in rocks!) This is an excellent place to see Decken's sifaka and also red-fronted brown lemurs. There are also unusual succulent plants growing in the *tsingy*.

Nick Garbutt, who visited the park in October 1998, reported a few teething problems: 'As with the majority of the reserves on the island, the new park is being administered by ANGAP. Unfortunately, this new set-up has caused a certain amount of antagonism with the local community. It seems clear that some of the basic park rules have been made by bureaucrats stuck in offices in Tana with no first-hand experience of national parks and their needs. For instance, during my visit there was no access to the park before 8.00am (by which time it was already murderously hot and the best time for bird and wildlife watching had long since gone). In the afternoon, walks in the park had to begin at 2.00pm (when it was still far too hot) or not at all. If you wanted to begin at 3.30pm for instance it was tough – the guides had all gone home and entry was refused. The guides seem to have been "trained" by numbers and a manual, and adhere to set routes and pre-rehearsed patter. Flexibility is an alien concept. At present their knowledge is rather scant, although they do appear to be very keen so this will undoubtedly improve with experience. In October nocturnal walks were not allowed, because the "guides had not been trained". This again was a real pity as the forest areas of Bemaraha are potentially excellent places for night walks. Hopefully, as this new park finds its feet and the needs and requirements of ecotourists are realised, the situation at Bemaraha will improve.'

Getting there

Without a 4WD vehicle access is very difficult, even in the dry season. From the north, the park can be accessed from Antsalova (see below). Most people, however, approach from the south, where the nearest town accessible by taxi-brousse from Belo Tsiribihina is Ankilizato (not to be confused with the town of the same name east of Morondava) which is 57km north of Belo. From there you must either walk (porters can be hired) or take an ox-cart the 24km to Bekopaka.

Organised tours
Baobab Tours (see Baobab Café, Morondava) organises tours to the Bemaraha. This seems to be the easiest and most reliable option.

Guides
The man to see in Antsalova (to the north) is Mr Christoph Randriamananjara, who lives in Antsalovabe, 2km from Antsalova. 'He took me to see the Grotte Christophe and some *tsingy mai* (burnt tsingy), about a 2½-hour walk east of Antsalova. The *tsingy* near Bekopaka is more spectacular, but the Grotte Christophe is a nice cave. It is a large, above-ground cavern composed of a number of tall, oval chambers, some lit by natural skylights... like being in a cathedral. There were lots of bats, and also many butterflies in this area, particularly at a permanent waterhole at the *tsingy mai*. We also saw lots of sifaka and red-fronted brown lemurs. This trip could be done in a day from Antsalova, but we spent two nights camping by the Antranompasazy River. The campsite is very near the river's source: it springs to life beneath a massive limestone boulder in the middle of the forest. Staying with Christoph and his wonderful family before and after our visit to the *tsingy* was the personal highlight of my trip.'

Where to stay in Bekopaka
Hotel Ibrahim Inexpensive bungalows, good food. Tours are organised by the hotel.
'Tsingy Hotel' These new bungalows for 50,000–70,000Fmg have no official name as yet. Good meals for 35,000Fmg. 'Owners, Michel Tertipis and Marcel 'Jacky' Kwan, are passionate about western Madagascar; we spent riotous nights drinking lychees in aviation fuel!' (Ken & Lorna Gillespie) Bookings: Sarariom; tel 22 (Tana) 276 60; fax: 277 76.

The Manambolo River
The descent of the Manambolo can be arranged through the tour operator Mad'Cameleon (see page 90). The trip takes three days (though five allows for some rest and sightseeing), beginning at Ankavandra. This is a spectacular trip, through the untouched homeland of the Sakalava. On the third day you pass through the dramatic Manambolo gorge between towering limestone cliffs, and through the Tsingy de Bemaraha reserve. The chances of seeing the area's special wildlife, such as Decken's sifaka lemur and the Madagascar fish eagle are high.

Belo sur Tsiribihina
Apart from being the town at the end of the river Tsiribihina (see *River trips*, page 349), this place has little to offer. The famous Avenue of Baobabs is nearer Morondava and an easy excursion from there. Likewise Kirindy, though travellers coming from the north can visit both attractions on their way to Morondava. Tsiribihina means 'where one must not dive', supposedly because of the crocodiles. Be warned!

Arriving from the north you have to cross the river by ferry to get to the taxi-brousse station for Morondava. There is no timetable and the journey takes half an hour.

Where to stay/eat
Grande Lumière Opposite the Menabe. Eight bright, clean rooms with cold shower, 30,000Fmg.
Restaurant Pacifique Near the market. Good food, especially the crevettes.

MORONDAVA
The Morondava area was the centre of the Sakalava kingdom and their tombs – sadly now desecrated by souvenir hunters – bear witness of their power and creativity.

This was evidently a popular stopping place for sailors in the past and they seem to have treated the natives generously. In 1833, Captain W F W Owen wrote of Morondava: 'Five boats came alongside and stunned us by vociferating for presents and beseeching us to anchor.'

Today Morondava is the centre of a prosperous, rice-growing area (and has successfully introduced ostrich farming to Madagascar!). For tourists it is best known as a seaside resort, with a laidback (almost too laidback) atmosphere. This will change: the airport is being enlarged to take direct flights from South Africa.

This is the centre for visiting the western deciduous forest, the famous baobabs, and the newly gazetted Tsingy de Bemaraha National Park.

There is not much in the way of sightseeing in the town, but the market is worth a visit: to the left of the main street as you leave town. Also, if you are not going to the south, there is a chance to see a didierea tree here: it's on the outskirts of the town, on the right as you drive in from the north.

The telephone area code is 95.

Getting there and away
By road
Morondava is 700km from Tana and served by a once-good road. A minibus leaves the Anosibe depot in Tana at 14.00, arriving at 07.00 the following day. The cost (1998) is 40,000Fmg. See also *Travelling between Morondava and Toliara*, page 347.

If you are driving, note that there is no diesel between Antsirabe and Morondava.

By air
There is a regular service from Tana or Toliara, and the Twin Otter calls here after visiting small west-coast towns. Once the airport expansion is finished there will be direct flights from South Africa.

By sea
There is a weekly boat from Morondava to Morombe, from where you can get a taxi-brousse to Toliara (see *Travelling between Morondava and Toliara*, page 347).

Where to stay
Category A
Baobab Café BP 77, Nosy Kely, Morondava; tel: 95 52 012; fax: 95 52 186; email: baobab@dts.mg. (12 rooms) A new hotel run by a very friendly French couple, Noel and Muriel Perrier. It backs on to the river opposite Chez Cuccu. En-suite facilities, hot water, 95–290Ff per room. Nick Garbutt writes: 'The fresh fish and other seafood here are sensational – the best I've had in Madagascar. And the chocolate mousse is better than sex (if you can force yourself to eat it slowly, it also lasts a lot longer!)' [Gosh!]
Royal Toera Hotel Up the beach from Chez Maggie and Chez Cuccu. New (1999) beautifully built A-frames by the sea, with a large, clean swimming pool. 380Ff single, 450Ff double. Meals 55,000Fmg; breakfast 35,000Fmg.

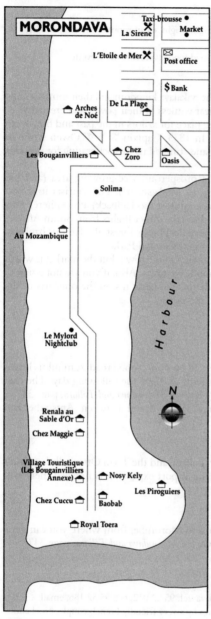

Chez Maggie BP 73; tel: 523 47. British-owned, by Maggie MacDonald, with comfortable two-storey chalets in a wonderful location on the beach. Swimming pool. 200,000Fmg.

Chez Cuccu BP 22; tel: 523 19. Bungalows 140Ff. Next to Les Bougainvilliers, Italian-owned, good food. Visa cards accepted (but with a surcharge).

Renala au Sable d'Or BP 163; tel: 520 89. One of the few hotels in town, rather than on the beach. Large, solid wooden bungalows surrounded by landscaped gardens and grass. Prices around 240–345Ff, depending on accommodation and beach frontage.

Category B

Les Bougainvilliers BP 78; tel: 521 63. Beach houses, from 40,000Fmg to 65,000Fmg, but with various levels of comfort; good food (though the restaurant/bar closes at 21.30), poor service. About 42,000Fmg per room. Visa cards accepted. The hotel can organise a variety of excursions.

Arche de Noé A new hotel on the waterfront. 'The bungalow was the most beautiful, and of the finest workmanship, that we saw in Madagascar.' 75,000Fmg (Anne Axel)

Nosy Kely BP 22; tel: 523 19. On the other side of the fence from the Bougainvilliers Annexe are several beach bungalows of varying prices.

Hotel les Piroguiers BP 73; tel: 526 19. French-owned (Pierre Boisard) bungalows in Betania (the beach area) past Nosy Kely. Horse-riding and water sports.

Au Mozambique Beach bungalows near Les Bougainvilliers. 90,000Fmg.

Les Paletuviers de Matanito Beach bungalows near the village of Avaradrova, 1km south of Morondava. Quiet and comfortable. 70,000Fmg.

Category C

Chez Zoro Four new beach bungalows plus tent site (16,000Fmg) behind Hotel Bougainvilliers. 45,000Fmg for shared facilities; one en suite for 70,000Fmg. Quiet, friendly, clean and cheerful.

Hotel Central BP 50; tel: 523 78. On the main street, newish and recently renovated. Hot shower and WC. No restaurant but breakfast served.

Hotel de la Plage Tel: 520 31. Not on the plage (100m away). Seven rooms, each with basin and communal WC. Pleasant and clean, with a balcony. Run by Moslems so no alcohol. Indian food (set menu).

Hotel Oasis Route de Batellage, Morondava; BP 232; tel: 522 22; email: vazahabe@dts.mad. A near-beach hotel (100m from the shore); family-run and very friendly. Bungalows 40,000Fmg, 50,000Fmg with air conditioning. Good restaurant and bar and often live music performed by the owner and local musicians. A friendly, popular place; shame about the illegally-kept pet lemur. Mountain bikes available here.

Hotel Menabe 23 spacious, inexpensive rooms, but a church bell next door tolls all night.

Where to eat
Renala On the seafront and specialising in seafood.
L'Etoile de Mer An open-air restaurant by the beach serving very good seafood.
La Serene Standard menu.

Tour operator and guides
Baobab Tours Run by Noel and Muriel Perrier of the Baobab Café. A large selection of vehicle and boat trips, plus flights over the *tsingy*.
Michael Golfier Recommended as an English-speaker guide/fixer. BP279, Morondava; tel: 52 140.
Jean le Rasta (Rasta Jean) Recommended by several travellers as being 'efficient, reliable and charismatic'. Speaks some English. Contact through the Hotel Oasis.
Joachim Theophile (Theo) He can usually be contacted through the main hotels. Give him a day's warning and he'll arrange everything.

Excursions from Morondava
Baobabs
This is the region of the splendid Grandidier's baobab, *Adansonia grandidieri*, best seen at the Avenue of the Baobabs. Also popular are Les Baobabs Amoureux (two entwined baobabs), and there's a Sacred Baobab as well.

Mountain bikes are available at some of the hotels and are an excellent way to see the baobabs. Beware of the heat, flies, and thorns on the road.

By car, the **Avenue of the Baobabs** is 45 minutes from Morondava. A taxi will cost around 80,000Fmg. Try to get there shortly before sunset (or – better – sunrise) for the best photos. **Les Baobabs Amoureux** are another half hour or so away. Nearby is a lake which is very good for birdwatching. There are two **Baobabs Sacrés** (sacred baobabs), one near the Swiss Forest and one near the turn-off from the main road to Belo. Both are the chunky *Adansonia rubrostipa* not the stately *A. grandidieri*. The former has signs of offerings nearby and *lambas* tied to the branches. The one near the main road also shows signs of offerings. This is its story: a woman medium or healer was unable to pass her powers on to an heir since her only child, a son, was a Christian and had rejected the traditional beliefs. So the woman was buried under the baobab with her amulets, and the tree became her heir, taking on her powers. So now the people come to the baobab to ask for good crops, a son, or healing – just as they would have come to the woman during her lifetime.

Marché de Zebus (Zebu market)
Recommended by Adela Stockton as an interesting local event, held on Fridays at the first village out of Morondava (on the main road to Tana).

Sakalava tombs: a warning

Although the Menabe region is famous for its tombs, some things of obvious interest to tourists should be left alone. This applies particularly to the famous erotic carvings on tombs in the area around Morondava.

These carvings are fertility symbols, and often depict figures engaged in sexual activities which the Sakalava consider *fady* to practise. One example is oral sex. Erotic carvings of this kind can nowadays be seen in cultural museums in larger towns such as Tana or Toliara, and small replicas are often carved and sold as souvenirs – erotica always has a ready market. In the early 1970s unscrupulous art dealers pillaged the tombs around Morondava, removing nearly all the erotic carvings. As a result, the Sakalava now keep secret the location of those tombs which still have carvings. As one guide reported: 'Some of the graveyards are for the tourists, but most are secret – for the people.'

Derek Schuurman recalls an unsettling experience while visiting a graveyard in the Menabe. Although he was accompanied by a reputable guide, they still had to collect a member of the Council of Elders from the village closest to the graveyard. When they arrived at the secret location, the elder led the way, sprinkling rum on the graves as Derek and the guide followed. Derek could tell from the tone of the elder's voice that he was very unhappy and pleading with the Ancestors for forgiveness at having brought a *vazaha* to the sacred place. There was clear evidence that the tombs had recently been desecrated. Fresh woodchips still lay scattered around where the carvings had been removed... This is why visitors who insist on seeing Sakalava graveyards must be accompanied by an elder from a nearby village. Many will be disappointed, though, because most of the carvings have already been stolen from the sites tourists have managed to locate.

RESERVES NORTH OF MORONDAVA

The dry deciduous forests between the rivers Morondava and Tsiribihina are of great biological importance. Many endemic species of flora and fauna are found here; the area is particularly rich in reptiles such as turtles, snakes and a variety of lizards. The fosa is common in these forests and seven species of lemur are found, including white sifaka and the rare pale fork-marked lemur and pygmy mouse lemur, the world's smallest primate. The giant jumping rat, Madagascar's most charming rodent, is unique to this small area.

There are three protected areas between the two rivers: Andranomena, Analabe, and Kirindy (The Swiss Forest). Heading north from Morondava, the first one you come to is **Andranomena**, a Special Reserve. As such it may be visited by tourists but there are no facilities or information.

Analabe has the same problem, although reports suggest that it could soon be welcoming visitors. It is a private nature reserve owned by M Jean de Heaulme, of Berenty fame. There are, as yet, no facilities for tourists. Analabe lies 60km north of Morondava, to the west of Kirindy by the village of Beraboka. In addition to forest it contains some mangrove areas as well as marshes and lakes typical of coastal plain.

Kirindy (The CFPF or Swiss Forest)

This is one of the most rewarding natural areas in Madagascar, but it is not a reserve. Until recently its sole purpose was the sustainable 'harvesting' of trees, but the Swiss managers have, in the last few years, turned to ecotourism as a way of conserving their forest and its inhabitants. Despite the selective logging that still takes place, the wildlife here is abundant. Indeed, it is probably the best western reserve for seeing Madagascar's endemic dry-forest species such as the giant jumping rat, which is found only in this area. This is also the best place to see the narrow-striped mongoose and perhaps a fosa.

Kirindy is a terrific place for wildlife, but there are two warnings for giant jumping rat enthusiasts: these mammals are seldom seen during the coldest months and keep out of sight when there is a full moon. Likewise tenrecs and tortoises will be less active (or in aestivation) in the winter. So try to visit between October and April (when you will be much too hot – or wet!) and on dark nights.

Getting there/staying there

Kirindy is about 65km northeast of Morondava – about 1½ hours by good road (in a private vehicle) or three tedious hours by taxi-brousse.

Facilities are very basic: there is no electricity and just one smelly long-drop toilet. There are four 2-person bungalows (with mosquito nets, but bring your own sleeping bag) for 15,000Fmg, or you can camp for 5,000Fmg. There is also a small restaurant (cold beer!); simple meals cost 5,000Fmg. Even if you normally dislike roughing it, you should stay the night here. Day visitors see far less than those able to observe wildlife at the optimum time of dawn and dusk, and a night-time stroll to look for the giant jumping rat is part of the Kirindy experience.

Information, permits and guides

Permits and some excellent information booklets are available from the CFPF (Coopération Suisse) headquarters in Morondava. The office is on the outskirts of town, on the right as you drive north. There are leaflets covering all aspects of the forest. Probably the most useful over all is *The Menabe Forest: highlights for the visitor*. Leaflets may also be available in Kirindy itself.

Entry to Kirindy is 20,000Fmg per person. Since this is not an official reserve a guide is not mandatory, but of course you will see much more with a guide's help, especially at night. He will cost you 5,000Fmg per hour (day) or 10,000Fmg per hour (night).

TRAVELLING BETWEEN MORONDAVA AND TOLIARA

There are two slow routes, road and road-and-sea. Or you can fly between the two main cities via Morombe, but this is not a journey to hurry: there are many attractions and places to relax in on the way.

By road

In the dry season, from April to the end of November, the venerable *Bon Bon Caramel*, a 28-year-old green Mercedes truck, makes the journey between Morondava and Toliara. It leaves Morondava on Monday at 06.00, arriving Tuesday at about 17.00. The return from Toliara is Thursday at 06.00, arriving Friday evening. The night is spent in Manja (where there are bungalows and good food), or at the river some 80km from there (where you can sleep on the beach). 'It is reasonably well organised. The staff are trained on being stuck. Once *Bon Bon Caramel* was with one wheel at least one metre stuck in mud; they fixed it in 20 minutes!' (Luc Selleslagh)

By road and sea

A weekly boat runs between Morondava and Morombe, from where you can get a taxi-brousse. Failing this you can find road transport between Morondava and Belo Sur Mer, and between Morombe and the Ifaty road-head north of Toliara. The sea stretch in the middle can be done (adventurously!) by pirogue.

Belo Sur Mer

Not to be confused with Belo Sur Tsiribihina, this little town south of Morondava is the base for visiting a cluster of nine very interesting offshore islands. The main island is Nosy Andravano, but there are numerous islets. Derek Schuurman reports: 'The islands themselves are little more than sandbanks. A tour here can be arranged in Morondava because you need to sail here. It takes about eight hours to sail to Belo. The village has an interesting collection of small houses and huts; each family keeps a pig which is allowed to forage at night – Belo's mobile garbage disposals. There are huge vessels among the coconut palms at the Belo lagoon, and these are still built using exactly the same designs as the pirates used centuries back.

'On the islands are temporary Vezo settlements; the people on these barren islands, which are surrounded by magnificent coral reefs, seem to make a living from exporting sea cucumbers to the Far East. These are left to dry in the sun, as are shark carcasses and turtle shells. The local bakery is quite something: a Vezo woman sits cross-legged in front of a small fire and flips a batter-like mixture into black iron pots. In a few minutes she produces delicious pancakes called *mokara*.'

Where to stay

Marina de Belo Sur Mer A French-owned, upmarket hotel; the high season full-board rate is 229Ff. This hotel runs some excellent tours. A traveller reports: They take you by speedboat from Belo, 40 minutes to the south where the boat stops off in a little bay. You then walk to the top of a huge sand dune from where the view is very reminiscent of Kenya: there are baobabs galore and on the lake were so many flamingoes that the whole place was pink. Then you return to the boat and they take you to the islands off the coast – another 40 minutes by speedboat. Here the diving was incredible: the most fantastic corals and marine life you could imagine. They can take you diving, fishing or snorkelling. All this for only about US$50 for the day trip.'

Morombe

Chris Ballance writes 'Morombe clearly died when the French left, but 9,000 souls remain and they spend their time walking up and down the only street, very slowly, shaking hands with each other and discussing the possibility that someone might build a proper road to them someday.'

Despite this, the town seems to be bursting with (inevitably empty) hotels, as well as having a smart BTM bank so you can pay for them (if it agrees to change money).

If you have your own vehicle, Ken and Lorna Gillespie report that the baobabs between Morondava and Morombe are better (for photographers) than the famous ones north of Morondava.

Where to stay/eat

Hotel La Croix du Sud BP 33 tel: 56. Eight spacious rooms with bathrooms and hot water; restaurant.

Hotel Baobab Fourteen concrete bungalows with Legoland-style red, green and blue tiled roofs, on the shore on the south side of the town. Air conditioning, restaurant. Same management as Hotel La Croix du Sud.

Hotel Le Dattier Inexpensive reed huts, five concrete and airless rooms. No restaurant.

Hotel Mozambic To the right of La Croix du Sud. Six double rooms with shower.

Hotel Brillant 'Mangrove poles under the mattress, but not too bad. Food OK. Good ambience.'

Hotel Kuweit City Very comfortable reed huts; in 1994 it was recommended as the best value in town, but I have had no recent feedback.

Andavadoaka

'The best beach in Madagascar' is 45km to the south of Morombe and has some very comfortable bungalows, **Coco Beach**, under the same management as Hotels Baobab and Croix du Sud in Morombe. Diving/snorkelling available.

An enterprising man who calls himself Monsieur Coco has inexpensive rooms in the village for 10,000Fmg.

The town has two motor vehicles, both owned by the Catholic Mission. It is sometimes possible to hitch a ride. Alternatively you can take a pirogue from Morombe, which takes about five hours.

Miandrivazo

Said to be the hottest place in Madagascar; and to have lots of manioc! The town lies on the banks of the Mahajilo, a tributary of the Tsiribihina, and is the starting point for the descent of that river. 'The name comes from when Radama was waiting for his messenger to return with Rasalimo, the Sakalava princess of Malaimbandy with whom he had fallen in love. He fell into a pensive mood and when asked if he was well replied *"Miandry vazo aho"*– I am waiting for a wife.' (Raniero Leto)

It's a ten-hour journey from Morondava by car or taxi-brousse, with one very bad stretch of road. 'It took five hours to do the 122km between Miandrivazo and Malaimbandy. Continuous potholes of huge dimensions.' (Lorna Gillespie)

Where to stay/eat

Hotel Chez la Reine Rasalimo Tel: 255 32. Concrete bungalows on a hill overlooking the river. Good restaurant. About 45,000Fmg.

Le Relais de Miandrivazo BP 22. On the main square. Comfortable rooms with mosquito nets, 27,000Fmg (1995). Reasonable food, good atmosphere. Intermittent water.

Hotel Laizama 'A simple but homely hotel – we often found ducks in the shower – with very helpful management. We ate at the Buvette Espoir in town. Meals must be booked in advance; great value.' (R Harris and G Jackson)

Descending the Tsiribihina River

This is a popular trip (see below) and can easily be set up from Miandrivazo.

David Rasolofoarijaona, who can be found at Le Relais de Miandrivazo, can organise this plus a variety of other tours.

José Rakotomamonjy and his wife Soul are warmly recommended by Thomas Feichtinger of Austria, not only for the canoe trip down the Tsiribihina but for other excursions. José is knowledgable about wildlife and speaks good French and some English. Soul comes along as the cook. José can be found at the Bar Amical in Miandrivazo.

RIVER TRIPS

Trips down the lazy western rivers of Madagascar are becoming increasingly popular, with many tour operators now offering them. Tour operators use fast (but noisy) motor boats, local people use canoes.

The most popular is down (or up) the Mahajilo and Tsiribihina rivers. 'The trip took us almost four days but was one of the highlights of our stay. The birdlife is phenomenal on this stretch and we saw many lemurs in the trees on the banks as well as chameleons and snakes. We camped on the beach at night, where it was too hot to use the tent – I simply arranged my mosquito net over my sleeping bag. A mosquito net is absolutely essential for this trip, and you need to bring fresh food and plenty of drinking water from Miandrivazo although of course you can purify or boil the river water. At the end of the wet season the trip changes dramatically: camping on the beach is impossible due to the high river so you walk to the nearest village. The trips are much shorter due to the faster-flowing river. Our guide said he had completed a trip in 2½ days.' (Leone Badenhorst)

Readers who have done this trip offer the following advice:

- Find out the language of your paddler. Ours did not speak much French.
- Look at the pirogue before agreeing to anything, and go for a test run. We didn't. Three minutes into our trip and we were back on shore – the pirogue was so unstable we would certainly have gone over. The paddlers found another one which worked out fine.
- Don't assume the paddlers are guides and know about the wildlife.
- Do your own food shopping or tell your paddlers exactly what you want. You should also pay for the food for your paddlers.
- A mosquito net is essential; a tent advisable.

Tour operators running river trips

All the main ground operators listed in *Chapter 4* organise river trips on comfortable vessels with good food and camping equipment, and experienced guides.

There are some specialist operators such as Mad'Cameleon (BP 4336, Antananarivo 101; tel: 630 86; fax: 344 20). They run canoe trips on the Manambolo river, allowing you to see the *tsingy*.

An expert on the rivers of Madagascar is Conrad Hirsh of Nairobi. For many years Conrad has been taking small, informal groups down the rivers Manambolo (between Ankavandra – west of Tana – and Bekopaka) and Mangoky (between Beroroha – west of Fianar – to Lake Ihotry, which is east of Morombe). He has recently added the Mahavavy (see page 337) and the Betsiboka.

REMOTE RIVER EXPEDITIONS

Exceptional calm-water rafting trips to wild and scenic parts of Western Madagascar: April – June

Conrad Hirsh, PO Box 59622, Nairobi, Kenya
Fax: (254 2) 891307

Appendix 1

HISTORICAL CHRONOLOGY
Adapted from Madagascar, Island of the Ancestors *with kind permission of the author, John Mack*

AD 500	Approximate date for the first significant settlement of the island.
800–900	Dates of the first identifiable village sites in the north of the island. Penetration of the interior begins in the south.
1200	Establishment of Arab settlements. First mosques built.
1500	'Discovery' of Madagascar by the Portuguese Diego Dias. Unsuccessful attempts to establish permanent European bases on the island followed.
1650s	Emergence of Sakalava kingdoms.
Early 1700s	Eastern Madagascar is increasingly used as a base by pirates.
1716	Fénérive captured by Ratsimilaho. The beginnings of the Betsimisaraka confederacy.
1750	Death of Ratsimilaho.
1787	The future Andrianampoinimerina declared King of Ambohimanga.
1795/6	Andrianampoinimerina established his capital at Antananarivo.
1810–28	Reign of Radama I, Merina king.
1818	First mission school opened in Tamatave.
1820	First mission school opened in Antananarivo.
1828–61	Reign of Ranavalona I, Merina queen.
1835	Publication of the Bible in Malagasy, but profession of the Christian faith declared illegal.
1836	Most Europeans and missionaries leave the island.
1861–1863	Reign of Radama II, Merina king.
1861	Missionaries re-admitted. Freedom of religion proclaimed.
1863–8	Queen Rasoherina succeeds after Radama II assassinated.
1868–83	Reign of Queen Ranavalona II.
1883	Coronation of Queen Ranavalona III.
1883–1885	Franco-Malagasy War.
1895	Establishment of full French protectorate: Madagascar became a full colony the following year.
1897	Ranavalona III exiled first to Réunion and later to Algiers. Merina monarchy abolished.
1917	Death of Ranavalona III in exile.
1942	British troops occupy Madagascar.
1947	Nationalist rebellion suppressed with many dead.
1958	Autonomy achieved within the French community.
1960	Madagascar achieves full independence.
1972	General Ramanantsoa assumes power.
1975	Didier Ratsiraka first elected president.
1991	Demonstrations and strikes. Ratsiraka steps down.
1991	Albert Zafy elected president.
1993	The birth of the Third Republic.
1996	Albert Zafy impeached.
1997	Didier Ratsiraka re-elected president.

Appendix 2

THE MALAGASY LANGUAGE
Some basic rules
Pronunciation

The Malagasy alphabet is made up of 21 letters. C, Q, U, W, and X are omitted.
Individual letters are pronounced as follows:

a	as in Father
e	as in the a in Late
g	as in Get
h	almost silent
i	as ee in Seen
j	pronounced dz
o	oo as in Too
s	usually midway between sh and s but varies according to region
z	as in Zoo.

Combinations of letters needing different pronunciations are:

ai	like y in My
ao	like ow in Cow
eo	pronounced ay-oo

When k or g is preceded by i or y this vowel is also sounded after the consonant.
For example *alika* (dog) is pronounced Aleekya, and *ary koa* (and also) is
pronounced Ahreekewa.

Stressed syllables

Some syllables are stressed, others almost eliminated. This causes great problems
for visitors trying to pronounce place names, and unfortunately – like in English –
the basic rules are frequently broken. Generally, the stress is on the penultimate
syllable except in words ending in na, ka, and tra when it is generally on the last
syllable but two. Words ending in e stress that vowel. Occasionally a word with the
same spelling changes its meaning according to the stressed syllable, but in this case
it is written with an accent. For example, *tanana* means 'hand', and *tanána* means
'town'.

When a word ends in a vowel, this final syllable is pronounced so lightly it is
often just a stressed last consonant. For instance the Sifaka lemur is pronounced
'She-fak'. Words derived from English, like *hotely* and *banky*, are pronounced much
the same as in English.

Getting started

The easiest way to begin to get a grip on Malagasy is to build on your knowledge
of place names (you have to learn how to pronounce these in order to get around)

and to this end I have given the phonetic pronunciation in the text. As noted in the text, most place names mean something so you have only to learn these meanings and – hey presto! – you have the elements of the language! Here are some bits of place names:

An-, Am-, I-	at, the place where	Manga	blue or good
Arivo	thousand	Maro	many
Be	big, plenty of	Nosy	Island
Fotsy, -potsy	white	Rano, -drano	water
Kely	small	Tany, tani–	land
Kily	tamarind	Tsara	good
Mafana	hot	Tsy, Tsi	(negative)
Maha	which causes	Vato, -bato	stone
Mainti	black	Vohitra, vohi-,	hill
Maintso	green	bohi–	

In Malagasy the plural form of a noun is the same as the singular form.

Vocabulary
Social phrases
Stressed letters or phrases are underlined.

English	Malagasy	Phonetic Pronunciation
Hello	Manao ahoana	Mano own
Hello	Salama	Salaam
(north & east coast)	Mbola tsara	M'boola tsara
What news?	Inona no vaovao?	Inan vowvow?
No news	Tsy misy	Tsimees

These three easy-to-learn phrases of ritualised greetings establish contact with people you pass on the road or meet in their village. For extra courtesy (important in Madagascar) add tompoko (pronounced 'toomp'k') at the end of each phrase.

Simple phrases for 'conversation'

English	Malagasy	Phonetic Pronunciation
What's your name?	Iza no anaranao?	Eeza nanaranow?
My name is	Ny anarako	Ny anarakoo
Goodbye	Veloma	Veloom
See you again	Mandra pihaona	Mandra pioon
I don't understand	Tsy azoko	Tsi azook
Very good	Tsara tokoa	Tsara t'koo
Bad	Ratsy	Rats
Please/Excuse me	Aza fady	Azafad
Thank you	Misaotra	Misowtr
Pardon me		
(ie may I pass)	Ombay lalana	m'buy lalan
Let's go	Andao andeha	Andow anday
Crazy	Adaladala	Adaladal
Long life! (Cheers!)	Ho ela velona!	Wellavell!

If you are pestered by beggars try:

I have nothing (there is none)	*Tsy misy*	*tsimeess*
Go away!	*Mandehana!*	*Man day han*

Note: The words for yes (*eny*) and no (*tsia*) are hardly ever used in conversation. The Malagasy tend to say '*yoh*' for yes and '*ah*' for no, along with appropriate gestures.

Market phrases

How much?	*Ohatrinona?*	*Ohtreen?*
Too expensive!	*Lafo be!*	*Laff be!*
No way!	*Tsy lasa!*	*Tsee lass!*

Basic needs

Where is...?	*Aiza...?*	*Ize...?*
Is it far?	*Lavitra ve izany?*	*Lavtra vayzan?*
Is there any...?	*Misy ve...?*	*Mees vay...?*
I want...	*Mila ... aho*	*Meel ... a*
I'm looking for...	*Mitady ... aho*	*M'tadi ... a*
Is there a place to sleep?	*Misy toerana hatoriana ve?*	*Mees too ayran atureen vay?*
Is it ready?	*Vita ve?*	*Veeta vay?*
I would like to buy some food	*Te hividy sakafo aho*	*Tayveed sakaff wah*
I'm hungry	*Noana aho*	*Noonah*
I'm thirsty	*Mangetaheta aho*	*Mangataytah*
I'm tired	*Vizaka aho*	*Veesacar*
Please help me!	*Mba ampio aho!*	*Bampeewha!*

Useful words

village	*Vohitra*	*Voo-itra*
house	*Trano*	*Tran*
food/meal	*Hanina/sakafo*	*An/sakaff*
water	*Rano*	*Rahn*
rice	*Vary*	*Var*
eggs	*Atody*	*Atood*
chicken	*Akoho*	*Akoo*
bread	*Mofo*	*Moof*
milk	*Ronono*	*Roonoon*
road	*Lalana*	*Lalan*
town	*Tanana*	*Tanan*
river (large)	*Ony*	*Oon*
river (small)	*Riaka*	*Reek*
ox/cow	*Omby/omby vavy*	*Oomby/omb varve*
child/baby	*Ankizy/zaza kely*	*Ankeeze/zaza kail*
man/woman	*Lehilahy/vehivavy*	*Layla/vayvarve*

Appendix 3

MADAGASCAR'S MAMMALS AND WHERE TO SEE THEM
Nick Garbutt

Although there are relatively few species (compared with mainland Africa), Madagascar is an exceptional place to watch mammals. Of course, everyone wants to see lemurs but for those with time, patience and a little luck, there is far more to see. Listed below are the best places to try and see Madagascar's mammals. Species marked with an asterisk (★) are nocturnal.

Lemurs

Common name	Scientific name	Distribution/Where to see
Grey mouse lemur	*Microcebus murinus*★	The dry forests of the west and spiny forests of the south. Best sites Ampijoroa Forestry Station, Kirindy Forest and Berenty Reserve.
Brown mouse lemur	*Microcebus rufus*★	Throughout the eastern rainforest belt. Analamazaotra Reserve and Ranomafana National Park.
Pygmy mouse lemur	*Microcebus myoxinus*★	Currently known only from the Kirindy Forests area.
Golden-brown mouse lemur	*Microcebus ravelobensis*★	Currently known only from the forests of Ampijoroa. Ampijoroa Forestry Station.
Hairy-eared dwarf lemur	*Allocebus trichotis*★	Central and northeastern lowland rainforests. Analamazaotra Reserve.
Greater dwarf lemur	*Cheirogaleus major*★	Eastern rainforests. Ranomafana National Park and Analamazaotra Reserve.
Fat-tailed dwarf lemur	*Cheirogaleus medius*★	Dry forests of the south and west. Ampijoroa Forestry Station and Kirindy Forests.
Coquerel's dwarf lemur	*Mirza coquereli*★	Dry forests of the west and moist forests of the Sambirano region. Kirindy Forest and secondary forests near Ambanja in the northwest.
Eastern fork-marked lemur	*Phaner furcifer furcifer*★	Rainforest centred around the Masoala Peninsula. Ambanizana and Andranobe on the Masoala Peninsula.

Pariente's fork-marked lemur	*Phaner furcifer parienti*★	Sambirano region in the northwest. Ampasindava Peninsula and the forests around the village of Beraty.
Pale fork-marked lemur	*Phaner furcifer pallescens*★	Dry forests of the west. Kirindy Forest.
Amber Mountain fork-marked lemur	*Phaner furcifer electromontis*★	Montagne d'Ambre, Ankarana and Analamera region of northern Madagascar. Montagne d'Ambre National Park and Ankarana Reserve.
Weasel sportive lemur	*Lepilemur mustelinus*★	Northern half of the eastern rainforest belt. Marojejy National Park, Anjanaharibe-Sud Reserve and Masoala National Park.
Small-toothed sportive lemur	*Lepilemur microdon*★	The southern half of the eastern rainforest belt. Analamazaotra Reserve, Mantadia National Park and Ranomafana National Park
Northern sportive lemur	*Lepilemur septentrionalis*★	Forests of the extreme north. Ankarana Reserve and Montagne d'Ambre National Park.
Grey-backed sportive lemur	*Lepilemur dorsalis*★	Sambirano region and offshore islands in the northwest. Lokobe Reserve on Nosy Be.
Milne-Edwards sportive lemur	*Lepilemur edwardsi*★	Dry forests of the west, north of the Manambolo river. Ampijoroa Forestry Station.
Red-tailed sportive lemur	*Lepilemur ruficaudatus*★	Dry forests of the west, south of the Manambolo river. Kirindy Forest.
White-footed sportive lemur	*Lepilemur leucopus*★	Spiny and gallery forests of the south and southwest. Berenty Reserve, Hazafotsy and Beza-Mahafaly Reserve.
Eastern grey bamboo lemur	*Hapalemur griseus griseus*	Eastern rainforest belt. Analamazaotra Reserve, Mantadia National Park and Ranomafana National Park.
Western grey bamboo lemur	*Hapalemur griseus occidentalis*	Sambirano region in the northwest, Namoroka, Soalala and Tsingy de Bemaraha regions in the west. Sambirano river valley near the village of Benavony.
Lake Alaotra reed lemur	*Hapalemur griseus alaotrensis*	Reed and papyrus beds and surrounding marshes of Lake Alaotra. Southwest shore of Lake Alaotra.
Golden bamboo lemur	*Hapalemur aureus*	Rainforests of Ranomafana and Andringitra in the southeast. Ranomafana National Park.
Greater bamboo lemur	*Hapalemur simus*	Rainforests of the southeast. Ranomafana National Park.

Ring-tailed lemur	*Lemur catta*	Spiny forests and gallery forests of the south and southwest and the Andringitra Massif. Berenty Reserve, Beza-Mahafaly Reserve and Isalo National Park.
Mongoose lemur	*Eulemur mongoz*	Dry forests of the northwest. Tsiombikibo forest near Mitsinjo and Ampijoroa Forest Station.
Crowned lemur	*Eulemur coronatus*	Forest of the extreme north. Ankarana Reserve, Montagne d'Ambre National Park and Analamera Reserve.
Red-bellied lemur	*Eulemur rubriventer*	The eastern rainforest belt (mid to high elevations). Ranomafana and Marojejy National Parks.
Common brown lemur	*Eulemur fulvus fulvus*	Dry forests of the northwest and central eastern rainforests. Ampijoroa Forest Station and Analamazaotra Reserve.
Sanford's brown lemur	*Eulemur fulvus sandfordi*	Forests of the far north. Montagne d'Ambre National Park and Ankarana Reserve.
White-fronted brown lemur	*Eulemur fulvus albifrons*	Rainforests of the northeast. Nosy Mangabe and Anjanaharibe-Sud Reserves, Marojejy and Masoala National Parks.
Red-fronted brown lemur	*Eulemur fulvus rufus*	Dry forests of the west and rainforests of the southeast. Kirindy Forest and Ranomafana National Park.
White-collared brown lemur	*Eulemur fulvus albocollaris*	Rainforest between the Manampatra and Mananara rivers in the southeast. Manombo Reserve and the forests to the west of Vondrozo.
Collared brown lemur	*Eulemur fulvus collaris*	Rainforests of the extreme southeast. Andohahela National Park and St Luce Private Reserve.
Black lemur	*Eulemur macaco macaco*	Sambirano region and offshore islands in the northeast. Lokobe Reserve on Nosy Be and the neighbouring island of Nosy Komba.
Blue-eyed black lemur	*Eulemur macaco flavifrons*	Forests just south of the Sambirano region in the northwest. Forests to the southwest of Maromandia and the vicinity of Marovato-Sud.
Black-and-white ruffed lemur	*Varecia variegata variegata*	Eastern rainforests. Nosy Mangabe Reserve, Ranomafana and Mantadia National Parks.
Red ruffed lemur	*Varecia variegata rubra*	Rainforests of the Masoala Peninsula. Andranobe and Ambanizana in Masoala National Park.

Eastern avahi	*Avahi laniger*	Throughout the eastern rainforest belt. Analamazaotra Reserve and Ranomafana National Park.
Western avahi	*Avahi occidentalis*	Western and northwestern Madagascar. Ampijoroa Forest Station.
Diademed sifaka	*Propithecus diadema diadema*	Central and northeastern rainforests. Mantadia National Park.
Milne-Edward's sifaka	*Propithecus diadema edwardsi*	Southeastern rainforests. Ranomafana National Park.
Silky sifaka	*Propithecus diadema candidus*	Northeastern rainforests (at higher elevations). Marojejy National Park.
Perrier's sifaka	*Propithecus diadema perrieri*	Dry forests in the extreme north between the Lokia and Irodo rivers. Analamera Reserve.
Verreaux's sifaka	*Propithecus verreauxi verreauxi*	Dry forests of the west, south of the Tsiribihina river and spiny forests of the south and southwest. Berenty Reserve, Beza-Mahafaly Reserve, Hazafotsy and Kirindy Forest.
Coquerel's sifaka	*Propithecus verreauxi coquereli*	Dry forests of the northwest. Ampijoroa Forestry Station.
Decken's sifaka	*Propithecus verreauxi deckeni*	Western Madagascar, between the Manambolo and Mahavavy rivers. Tsiombikibo forest near Mitsinjo and Tsingy de Bemaraha National Park near Bekopaka.
Crowned sifaka	*Propithecus verreauxi coronatus*	Dry forests between the Mahavavy and Betsiboka rivers. The Bongolava Massif and areas south of the Manambolo river. Near the lighthouse north of Katsepy and the forest around Anjamena on the banks of the Mahavavy river.
Golden-crowned sifaka	*Propithecus tattersalli*	Between the Manambato and Loky rivers in northeast Madagascar. Forests close to the village of Antsahampano, 10km east of Daraina.
Indri	*Indri indri*	Central eastern and northeastern rainforests. Analamazaotra Reserve, Mantadia National Park and Anjanaharibe-Sud Reserve.
Aye-aye	*Daubentonia madagascariensis*★	Eastern rainforests and western dry forests. Nosy Mangabe Reserve and Ile mon Désir (Aye-aye Island) near Mananara.

Other mammals
Carnivores

Fanaloka or striped civet	*Fossa fossana*★	Rainforest of the east and north, the Sambirano in the northwest and the dry forests of the extreme north. Ranomafana National Park and

		Ankarana Reserve.
Falanouc	*Eupleres goudotii*★	Eastern rainforests and dry forests of the northwest and extreme north. Montagne d'Ambre and Ranomafana National Parks.
Fosa	*Cryptoprocta ferox*	All native forests. Kirindy Forest and Ankarana Reserve.
Ring-tailed mongoose	*Galidia elegans*	Native forests of the east, north and west. Ankarana Reserve and Ranomafana National Park.
Narrow-striped mongoose	*Mungotictis decemlineata*	Dry forests of the west, south of the Tsiribihina river. Kirindy Forest.

Tenrecs

Common tenrec	*Tenrec ecaudatus*★	All native forest areas. Analamazaotra Reserve, Ranomafana National Park, Kirindy Forest and Ampijoroa Forestry Station.
Greater hedgehog tenrec	*Setifer setosus*★	All native forest types. Analamazaotra and Nosy Mangabe Reserves and Ranomafana National Park.
Lesser hedgehog tenrec	*Echinops telfairi*★	Dry forest of the west and spiny forest and gallery forests of the south. Hazafotsy, Ifaty and Beza Mahafaly Reserve.
Lowland streaked tenrec	*Hemicentetes semispinosus*	Eastern rainforests. Analamazaotra Reserve and Ranomafana National Park.
Large-eared tenrec	*Geogale aurita*★	Dry forests of the west and the spiny forest and gallery forest areas of the south and southwest. Kirindy Forest and Beza Mahafaly Reserve.

Rodents

Giant jumping rat	*Hypogeomys antimena*★	Western dry forest between the Andranomena and Tsiribihina rivers. Kirindy Forest.
Red forest rat	*Nesomys rufus*	Eastern rainforests. Ranomafana National Park.
Lowland red forest rat	*Nesomys audeberti*	Lowland eastern rainforests. Ranomafana National Park.

Bats

Madagascar flying fox	*Pteropus rufus*★	Eastern rainforests, western dry forests and southern gallery forests. Berenty Reserve, Nosy Tanikely off Nosy Be.

Appendix 4

FURTHER INFORMATION
Books

Madagascar's historical links with Britain and the current interest in its natural history and culture have produced a century of excellent books written in English. This bibliography is a selection of my favourites in each category.

General – history, the country, the people

Bradt, H *Madagascar* (World Bibliographical Series), Clio (UK); ABC (US) 1992. An annotated selection of nearly 400 titles on Madagascar, from the classic early works to those published in the 1990s.

Brown, M *A History of Madagascar* D Tunnacliffe, UK 1996. The most accurate, comprehensive and readable of the histories, brought completely up to date by Britain's foremost expert on the subject.

Covell, M *Madagascar: Politics, Economics and Society* Frances Pinter, UK (Marxist Regimes series) 1987. An interesting look at Madagascar's Marxist past.

Crook, S *Distant Shores: by Traditional Canoe from Asia to Madagascar* Impact Books, UK 1990. The story of the 4,000-mile Sarimanok Expedition by outrigger canoe across the Indian Ocean from Bali to Madagascar. An interesting account of an eventful and historically important journey.

Dodwell, C *Madagascar Travels* Hodder & Stoughton, UK 1995. An account of a journey through Madagascar's most remote regions by one of Britain's leading travel writers.

Drysdale, H *Dancing with the Dead: a Journey through Zanzibar and Madagascar* Hamish Hamilton, UK 1991. An account of Helena's journeys in search of her trading ancestor. Informative, entertaining and well-written.

Ellis, W *Madagascar Revisited* John Murray, UK 1867. The Rev William Ellis of the LMS was one of the most observant and sympathetic of the missionary writers. His books are well worth the search for second-hand copies.

Fox, L *Hainteny: the Traditional Poetry of Madagascar* Associated University Presses, UK and Canada 1990. Over 400 beautifully translated *hainteny* with an excellent introduction to the history and spiritual life of the Merina.

Kabana, J *Torina's World: the villages of Madagascar* 1997 A beautiful book of black-and-white photos aimed at giving American children a wider understanding of their counterparts in Madagascar. Available for $15.95 (including postage) from the author, Joni Kabana, 4855 Summit St, West Linn, OR 97068, USA.

Lanting, F *Madagascar, a World out of Time* Robert Hale, UK 1991. A book of stunning, and somewhat surreal, photos of the landscape, people and wildlife.

Murphy, D *Muddling through in Madagascar* John Murray, UK 1985. An entertaining account of a journey (by foot and truck) through the highlands and south.

Sibree, J *Madagascar Before the Conquest: the Island, the Country, and the People* T Fisher Unwin, UK 1896. With William Ellis, Sibree was the main documenter of Madagascar during the days of the London Missionary Society. He wrote many books on the island, all of which are perceptive, informative, and a pleasure to read.

Ethnology

Bloch, M *From Blessing to Violence* Cambridge University Press, UK 1986. History and ideology of the circumcision ritual of the Merina people.

Mack, J *Madagascar: Island of the Ancestors* British Museum, London 1986. A scholarly and informative account of the ethnography of Madagascar.

Mack, J *Malagasy Textiles* Shire Publications, UK 1989.

Powe, E L *Lore of Madagascar* Dan Aiki Publications (530 W Johnson St, Apt 210, Madison, WI 53703) USA 1994. An immense work – over 700 pages and 260 colour photos – with a price to match: $300. This is the only book to describe in detail, and in a readable form, all 39 ethnic groups in Madagascar.

Rund, J *Taboo: a study of Malagasy customs and beliefs* Oslo University Press/George Allan & Unwin, UK 1960. Written by a Norwegian Lutheran missionary who worked for 20 years in Madagascar. A detailed study of *fady, vintana,* and other Malagasy beliefs.

Sharp, L A *The Possessed and the Dispossessed: spirits, identity and power in a Madagascar migrant town* University of California Press, USA 1993. Describes the daily life and the phenomenon of possession (*tromba*) in the town of Ambanja.

Wilson, P J *Freedom by a Hair's Breadth* University of Michigan, USA 1993. An anthropological study of the Tsimihety people, written in a clear style and accessible to the general reader.

Natural history

Literature

Attenborough, D *Zoo Quest to Madagascar* Lutterworth, UK 1961. Still one of the best travel books ever written about Madagascar, with, of course, plenty of original wildlife observations. Out of print, but copies can be found.

Durrell, G *The Aye-aye and I* Harper Collins, UK 1992.The focal point is the collecting of aye-aye for Jersey Zoo, written in the inimitable Durrell style with plenty of humour and travellers' tales.

Jolly, A *A World Like Our Own: Man and Nature in Madagascar* Yale University Press 1980. The first and still the best look at the relationship between the natural history and people of the island. Highly readable.

Preston-Mafham, K *Madagascar: A Natural History* Facts on File, UK and US 1991. The most enjoyable and useful book on the subject. Illustrated with superb colour photos (coffee-table format), it is as good at identifying strange invertebrates and unusual plants as in describing animal behaviour.

Quammen, D *The Song of the Dodo* Hutchinson, UK 1996. An interesting account of island biogeography and its implications for nature reserves.

Wilson, J *Lemurs of the Lost World: Exploring the Forests and Crocodile Caves of Madagascar* Revised 1995 and available from the author (see page 284). An interesting and informative account of the Ankarana expedition and subsequent travels in Madagascar.

Specialist literature and guides

Bradt, H; Schuurman, D; Garbutt, N *Madagascar Wildlife: a visitor's guide* Bradt Publications (UK); Globe Pequot Press (USA) 1996. A photographic guide to the island's most interesting and appealing wildlife, and where best to see it.

Dransfield, J & Beentje, H *The Palms of Madagascar* Royal Botanic Gardens, Kew, UK 1996. A beautiful and much-needed book describing the many palm species of Madagascar.

Du Puy, D; Cribb P; Bosser J; Hermans J & C *The Orchids of Madagascar* Royal Botanic Gardens, Kew, UK 1999. A checklist of all known Malagasy orchid species, along with a complete bibliography, superby illustrated with colour photos. Pricey (£49.50) but orchid enthusiasts will not care.

Garbutt, N *Mammals of Madagascar* Pica Press (UK) 1999. The book we've been waiting for. Comprehensive, with wonderful photos and black-and-white illustrations, as well as authoritative text. My only complaint is it's too heavy to be used as a field guide.

Glaw, F; Vences, M *A Field Guide to the Amphibians and Reptiles of Madagascar* 1994. A thorough guide to the herpetofauna of Madagascar. In Britain this is available through the NHBS.

Hillerman, F E; Holst, A W *An Introduction to the Cultivated Angraecoid Orchids of Madagascar* Timber Press, USA. Includes a good section on climate and other plant life.

Inventaire Ecologique Forestier National Published in 1996 by the Direction des Eaux et Forêts. A brave and welcome attempt to make the island's botany more accessible.

Jenkins, M D, editor (1987) *Madagascar: An Environmental Profile* IUCN, Gland, Switzerland and Cambridge, UK. Descriptions of the nature reserves, with checklists of flora and fauna.

Jolly, A; Oberle, P; Albignac, R, editors (1994) *Madagascar* Pergamon Press, UK and Canada. This book in the 'Key Environments' series is mainly a translation of the French *Madagascar: Un Sanctuaire de la Nature*. Now a little dated, but nevertheless one of the best overviews of the natural history.

Martin, J (1992) *Chameleons* Facts on File, USA; Blandford, UK. Beautifully illustrated with photos by Art Wolfe; everything a chameleon aficionado could hope for.

Mittermeier, M et al (1994) *Lemurs of Madagascar* Conservation International. A detailed field guide to all Madagascar's lemurs.

Morris, P; Hawkins, F *Birds of Madagascar: a photographic guide* Pica Press (UK) 1999. One of two new bird guides; not suitable for use in the field (too heavy, no distribution maps) but the authoritative text and photos provide serious birders with the details they need for reliable identification.

Nicholl, M E & Langrand, O (1989) *Madagascar: Revue de la Conservation et des Aires Protégées* WWF, Switzerland. Currently available only in French, but an English edition is in preparation. A detailed survey of the reserves studied by the WWF, lists of species, and excellent maps.

Rauh, W *Succulent and Xerophytic Plants of Madagascar* Strawberry Press, Mill Valley, CA, USA 1995 & 1998. Two of the five intended volumes on the subject. Detailed and comprehensive; lavishly illustrated with photos.

Richard-Vindard, G & Battistini, R (editors) *Biogeography and Ecology of Madagascar* W Junk, Netherlands 1972. Largely in English including chapters on geology, climate, flora, erosion, rodents and lemurs. Each chapter includes an extensive bibliography.

Sinclair, I; Langrand, O *Birds of the Indian Ocean Islands* Struik, South Africa 1999. The most user-friendly of the two new field guides to Madagascar's birds. Clear layout with good illustrations and distribution maps allow for quick reference on the trail.

Tattersall, I *The Primates of Madagascar* Columbia UP, USA 1981. A comprehensive description of the biology of Madagascar's lemurs.

Where to buy books on Madagascar

Discover Madagascar (Seraphine Tierney) 7 Hazledene Rd, Chiswick, London W4 3JB; tel: 020 8995 3529; fax: 020 8742 0212. Seraphine puts out a catalogue of books on Madagascar which are in print but may be hard to find in conventional outlets. She also sells Malagasy music cassettes and CDs.

Mad Books (Rupert Parker) 151 Wilberforce Rd, London N4 2SX; tel: 020 7226 4490; email: 100572.2434@compuserve.com; website: http://ourworld. compuserve.com:80/homepages/Rupert_Parker/. Rupert specialises in old and rare (out-of-print) books on Madagascar, and will send out his catalogue on request. He will also search for books.

Eastern Books of London 81 Replingham Rd, London SW18 5LU; tel/fax: 020 8871 0880; email: info@easternbooks.com; website: www.easternbooks.com. An antiquarian bookseller (shop, catalogue and website) specialising in rare and out-of-print books on Madagascar and the Indian Ocean.

Editions Karthala (France) 22–24 Bd Arago, 75013 Paris. This French publisher specialises in Madagascar, both for new titles and reprints.

Natural History Book Service (NHBS) 2 Wills Rd, Totnes, Devon TQ9 5XN; tel: 01803 865913; fax: 01803 865280; website: www.nhbs.com.

Websites
General
www.madagascar-contacts.com – information on hotels, tour operators, etc.
www.air-mad.com – information from Air Madagascar.
www.madonline.com – chat and general information.
www.fco.gov.uk – British Foreign Office advice on safety.
www.unusualdestination.com – tour specialists based in South Africa.

Music
www.madagascan.net/music/justinvali.
www.froots.deon.co.uk/madaged.html

Natural history
www.wwf.panda.org (international) – World Wide Fund for Nature
www.wwf.org (USA)
www.wemc.org.uk – World Conservation Monitoring Centre
www.duke.edu/web/primate – Duke University Primate Center
www.conservation.org – Conservation International

Bradt Travel Guides

September 1999

Dear Readers,

This book is a group effort. If it wasn't for all the wonderful letters I receive correcting, augmenting and updating the guide, I could never bring out new editions with so much fresh information and so many different viewpoints. Apart from the practical aspect, I love hearing from you and travelling vicariously in my favourite country through your descriptions.

I do hope you will write. The guide is updated every two years, so the best time to send your letters is during the first six months of 2001; but it is never too early to send opinions, discoveries and stories.

Letters are welcome in any form (but please use capital letters for place names – and your name and address – in handwritten ones) and give the dates that you were in Madagascar. If you want to be really helpful you could indicate on the maps the location of hotels and other recommended places as well as giving contact details. Please put your name at the top of each page in case they become separated.

Best wishes,

Hilary Bradt

PS: The next total eclipse of the sun will cross southern Madagascar on June 21 2001. Isalo National Park will probably be the best viewing site. See you there?

41 Nortoft Road, Chalfont St Peter, Bucks, SL9 0LA, England
Fax/Telephone: 01494 873478; Email: bradtpublications@compuserve.com
Web: www.bradt-travelguides.com

BRADT TRAVEL GUIDES

Albania: Guide and Illustrated Journal
  Peter Dawson/Andrea Dawson/
  Linda White
Amazon, The Roger Harris/
  Peter Hutchison
Antarctica: A Guide to the Wildlife
  Tony Soper/Dafila Scott
Australia and New Zealand by Rail
  Colin Taylor
Belize Alex Bradbury
Brazil Alex Bradbury
Burma Nicholas Greenwood
Cape Verde Islands Aisling Irwin/
  Colum Wilson
*Chile and Argentina: Backpacking and
  Hiking* Tim Burford
Cuba Stephen Fallon
*East and Southern Africa: The
  Backpacker's Manual* Philip Briggs
Ecuador, Climbing and Hiking in
  Rob Rachowiecki/
  Mark Thurber
*Ecuador, Peru and Bolivia: The
  Backpacker's Manual* Kathy Jarvis
Eritrea Edward Paice
Estonia Neil Taylor
Ethiopia Philip Briggs
Galápagos Wildlife David Horwell/
  Pete Oxford
Georgia Tim Burford
Ghana Philip Briggs
Greece by Rail Zane Katsikis
Haiti and the Dominican Republic
  Ross Velton
India by Rail Royston Ellis
Laos and Cambodia John R Jones
Latvia Stephen Baister/Chris Patrick
Lithuania Gordon McLachlan
Madagascar Hilary Bradt

Madagascar Wildlife Hilary Bradt/
  Derek Schuurman/Nick Garbutt
Malawi Philip Briggs
Maldives Royston Ellis
Mali Ross Velton
Mauritius, Rodrigues and Réunion
  Royston Ellis/Derek Schuurman
Mexico, Backpacking in
  Tim Burford
Mozambique Philip Briggs
Namibia Chris McIntyre
North Cyprus Diana Darke
Palestine, with Jerusalem
  Henry Stedman
Peru and Bolivia: Backpacking and Trekking
  Hilary Bradt
Philippines Stephen Mansfield
Poland and Ukraine, Hiking Guide to
  Tim Burford
Romania, Hiking Guide to
  Tim Burford
Russia and Central Asia by Road
  Hazel Barker
Russia by Rail, with Belarus and Ukraine
  Athol Yates
South Africa Philip Briggs
Southern Africa by Rail Paul Ash
Spitsbergen Andreas Umbreit
Switzerland by Rail Anthony Lambert
Tanzania Philip Briggs
Uganda Philip Briggs
USA by Rail John Pitt
Venezuela Hilary Dunsterville Branch
Vietnam John R Jones
Your Child's Health Abroad
  Dr Jane Wilson-Howarth/
  Dr Matthew Ellis
Zambia Chris McIntyre
Zanzibar David Else

Bradt guides are available from bookshops or by mail order from:

Bradt Travel Guides
41 Nortoft Road, Chalfont St Peter, Bucks SL9 0LA, England
Tel/fax: 01494 873478 Email: bradtpublications@compuserve.com

MEASUREMENTS AND CONVERSIONS

To convert	Multiply by
Inches to centimetres	2.54
Centimetres to inches	0.3937
Feet to metres	0.3048
Metres to feet	3.281
Yards to metres	0.9144
Metres to yards	1.094
Miles to kilometres	1.609
Kilometres to miles	0.6214
Acres to hectares	0.4047
Hectares to acres	2.471
Imperial gallons to litres	4.546
Litres to imperial gallons	0.22
US gallons to litres	3.785
Litres to US gallons	0.264
Ounces to grams	28.35
Grams to ounces	0.03527
Pounds to grams	453.6
Grams to pounds	0.002205
Pounds to kilograms	0.4536
Kilograms to pounds	2.205
British tons to kilograms	1016.0
Kilograms to British tons	0.0009812
US tons to kilograms	907.0
Kilograms to US tons	0.000907

5 imperial gallons are equal to 6 US gallons
A British ton is 2,240 lbs. A US ton is 2,000 lbs.

Temperature conversion table
The bold figures in the central columns can be read as either centigrade or fahrenheit.

Centigrade		Fahrenheit	Centigrade		Fahrenheit
–18	0	32	10	50	122
–15	5	41	13	55	131
–12	10	50	16	60	140
–9	15	59	18	65	149
–7	20	68	21	70	158
–4	25	77	24	75	167
–1	30	86	27	80	176
2	35	95	32	90	194
4	40	104	38	100	212
7	45	113	40	104	

Index

Pic Boby 185
poetry see hainteny
population 4
present giving 84, 125–8
public holidays 121

Radama I, King 7, 9
Radama II, King 7, 329
railways 114, 169, 178, 231, 270, 275, 280
rainforest 58–9
Rainilaiarivony, Prime Minister 7, 151
Ranavalona, Queen 7, 9
Ranohira 191
Ranomafana 178–82
Ratsiraka, Didier 8
religion 5, 14
reptiles 45–7, 162–3, 221–2
responsible tourism 123–31
rice 174
Rio Tinto see mining
river trips 247, 337, 342, 349–50
robbery 104–5, 143
Russian Bay 302–3

safety 103–6, 233
sailing 81,199, 302–3, 307, 323–4, 339
Sakaraha 195
Sambava 244–5
Sandrandahy 175
Sarodrano 204
scientific classification 35, 56
sharks 233
silk 185
sisal 223
slash and burn see tavy
Smugglers' Path 276
snorkelling 84, 86, 91, 199, 263
Soalala 338
Soanierana-Ivongo 235, 258
spiny forest 64, 196, 201, 218
St Augustine's Bay 189, 204
stamps 155
Swiss Forest see Kirindy

Tamatave see Toamasina
Taolagnaro 210–17
tavy 37
taxi-brousse 109–11
telephone 120
thermal baths 164, 171, 182
Toamasina 230–3, 258

Toliara 195–201, 347
tombs 92, 93, 159, 168, 189–90, 195, 199
Torotorofotsy 273
tour operators 89–90
transport 108–14
tribes see ethnic groups
Tritriva, Lake 172
Tsaratanana (massif) 2, 11, 287, 302
Tsimanampetsotsa 205
tsingy 63–4
Tsingy de Bemaraha NP 341–2
Tsinjoarivo 167
Tsiribihina, River 349
Tsiroanomandidy 164, 340
Tuléar see Toliara

vanilla 246
Vatomandry 277
Vavatenina 235
vazimba 27
village life 20–1
vintana 15
visas 77–8
Vohemar see Iharana
Vohilengo 235
Vohipeno 281
voltage 5, 119

watersports see diving or snorkelling
whale-watching 210, 264
Windsor Castle 293
wine, 117, 178
working in Madagascar 72, 88, 93–4
World War I 8
World War II 8, 288, 292

yachts see sailing

Zafy, Albert 9
zebu 216
Zombitse NP 200–1
zoos 151, 235